THE AGRARIAN
HISTORY OF ENGLAND
AND WALES

THE AGRARIAN
HISTORY OF ENGLAND
AND WALES

GENERAL EDITOR
JOAN THIRSK

M.A., PH.D., F.B.A., F.R.HIST.S.
Sometime Reader in Economic History in the
University of Oxford

V. I

1640–1750: Regional Farming Systems

THE AGRARIAN HISTORY OF
ENGLAND AND WALES

* Already published

THE AGRARIAN
HISTORY OF ENGLAND
AND WALES

VOLUME V   1640–1750

I. REGIONAL FARMING SYSTEMS

EDITED BY
JOAN THIRSK

Sometime Reader in Economic History,
University of Oxford

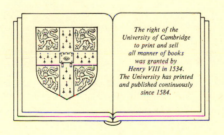

The right of the
University of Cambridge
to print and sell
all manner of books
was granted by
Henry VIII in 1534.
The University has printed
and published continuously
since 1584.

CAMBRIDGE UNIVERSITY PRESS

CAMBRIDGE

LONDON   NEW YORK   NEW ROCHELLE
MELBOURNE   SYDNEY

1984

Published by the Press Syndicate of the University of Cambridge
The Pitt Building, Trumpington Street, Cambridge CB1 2RP
32 East 57th Street, New York, NY 10022, USA
296 Beaconsfield Parade, Middle Park, Melbourne 3206, Australia

First published 1984

Printed in Great Britain by the
University Press, Cambridge

Library of Congress catalogue card number: 66-19763

British Library cataloguing in publication data

The Agrarian history of England and Wales.
Vol. 5: 1640–1750
1. Agriculture – Economic aspects – England – History
I. Thirsk, Joan
338.1'0942   HD1930.E5
ISBN 0 521 26257 7 the set of two parts
ISBN 0 521 20076 8 part 1
ISBN 0 521 25775 1 part 2

CONTENTS

By JOAN THIRSK, M.A., PH.D., F.B.A., F.R.HIST.S.,
Sometime Reader in Economic History, University of Oxford

PART I. REGIONAL FARMING SYSTEMS

NORTHERN ENGLAND

CHAPTER I

By ERIC J. EVANS, M.A., PH.D., F.R.HIST.S.,
Senior Lecturer in History, University of Lancaster
and J. V. BECKETT, B.A., PH.D., F.R.HIST.S.,
Lecturer in History, University of Nottingham

CHAPTER 2

By PAUL BRASSLEY, B.SC., B.LITT.,
Senior Lecturer in Agricultural Economics,
Seale-Hayne College, Newton Abbot

CHAPTER 8

By R. C. RICHARDSON, B.A., PH.D., F.R.HIST.S.,
Head of the Department of History and Archaeology,
King Alfred's College, Winchester

CHAPTER 9

By BRIAN M. SHORT, B.A., PH.D.,
Lecturer in Human Geography, University of Sussex

THE SOUTH AND SOUTH-WEST

CHAPTER 10

By J. R. WORDIE, M.A., PH.D.,
Lecturer in Economic History, University of Reading

CHAPTER 11

By GILES V. HARRISON, B.SC., M.SC., A.L.A.

WALES

CHAPTER 12

By FRANK EMERY, M.LITT., M.A.,
Vice-Master, Fellow, and Tutor, St Peter's College, Oxford;
University Lecturer in Historical Geography

TEXT FIGURES

TABLE

PREFACE

This work has been ten years in the making, but it appears at a moment when the experiences of seventeenth-century agriculture are likely to arouse more sympathy and understanding than at any other time in the twentieth century. A long depression in agricultural prices, coming after an equally long period of buoyant growth, sapped confidence, and yet also stimulated ingenuity and diversification. Agriculture was led along new paths which opened out into the agricultural revolution. Its history deserves to be better known.

Much new evidence for this study has accumulated in local archive offices throughout England and Wales in the last forty years. To see and transcribe it would have been impossible without the generous assistance of the Social Science Research Council. It financed the travels of research assistants, first to collect manuscript evidence on prices, wages, and rents, then to transcribe other relevant documents on general agrarian matters. No itinerary of this kind could include every available archive, but the authors hope that the sampling that was achieved will be deemed generous; the immense regional variety of English farming systems has been more fully explored here than in Volume IV (1967) of the *Agrarian History*, though it is obviously capable of still further refinement. Warm thanks are, therefore, extended to the SSRC for the invaluable support of its Economic and Social History Committee, and to Mr Bernard Eccleston, Mr Giles Harrison, and Mr Stephen Porter, who made the journeys and carried out the research in local archive offices.

All keepers of archives have been generous in their help and interest, and it is hoped that they will recognize these volumes as the fruits of their selfless labours. Appreciation is also expressed to the owners of private archives who have deposited them in accessible places, and given permission for them to be consulted and cited. In this connection, we wish to acknowledge the generosity of Lord Delamere, whose Hartlib manuscripts are in Sheffield University Library; of Mrs Turnbull, whose husband's transcripts of these documents were also made available to us in the Sheffield University Library; and of the Trustees of the Fitzwilliam (Wentworth) Estate and the Director of Sheffield City Libraries for the use of the Wentworth Woodhouse muniments. We also wish to thank Mr J. More-Molyneux of Loseley Park for access to the Loseley Manuscripts in the Guildford Muniment Room and

Mr J. L. Jervoise for permission to consult and cite the Sherfield Papers in the Herriard Collection, deposited in the Hampshire Record Office.

All authors, moreover, owe gratitude to the writers of unpublished theses who generously allowed their findings to be cited in these pages, and to the many scholars, too numerous to be named individually, who volunteered information arising from their own researches, or read and improved these chapters in draft.

Finally, the Editor wishes to express her own sincere thanks to all her fellow contributors to these volumes, who co-operated at every stage in bringing them to completion; to Mr William Davies at the Cambridge University Press, who offered continuous encouragement and never grew impatient; and to Mrs Jane Van Tassel, who was our scrupulous sub-editor at the Press. Our friends and helpers have saved us from many errors, but we know that mistakes and gaps remain. We can only hope that even the mistakes will promote our chief purpose, by stimulating others to take an active interest in the rich agricultural history of England and Wales.

JOAN THIRSK

Oxford
April 1983

ABBREVIATIONS

Agric. Hist.	*Agricultural History*
AHEW	*Agrarian History of England and Wales*, Cambridge, 1967–
AHR	*Agricultural History Review*
Amer. Hist. Rev.	*American Historical Review*
AO	Archives Office
APC	*Acts of the Privy Council*, N.S., London, 1890–
Arch. Aeliana	*Archaeologia Aeliana*
Arch. Camb.	*Archaeologia Cambrensis*
Arch. Cant.	*Archaeologia Cantiana*
Arch. J.	*Archaeological Journal*
B. Acad.	British Academy
BCS	*Bulletin of the Board of Celtic Studies*
BE	N. Pevsner, *The Buildings of England*, London, 1951–74
BL	British Library
Borthwick IHR	*Borthwick Institute of Historical Research*
BPP	British Parliamentary Paper
Bull. BCS	*Bulletin of the Board of Celtic Studies*
Bull. IHR	*Bulletin of the Institute of Historical Research*
Bull. JRL	*Bulletin of the John Rylands Library*
CCC	M. A. E. Green, *Calendar of the Proceedings of the Committee for Compounding, &c., 1653–1660*, 5 vols., London, 1889–92
Ch.	Proceedings in the Court of Chancery
CJ	Commons Journals
CRO	Cumbria Record Office, Carlisle
CSPD	*Calendar of State Papers Domestic*
CW2	*Cumb. & Westmor. Antiq. & Arch. Soc.*, 2nd series
E	Exchequer Records in PRO
EcHR	*Economic History Review*
EFC	M. W. Barley, *The English Farmhouse and Cottage*, London, 1961
EHR	*English Historical Review*
EPNS	English Place-Name Society

EVH	Eric Mercer, *English Vernacular Houses: A Study of Traditional Farmhouses and Cottages*, RCHM (England), London, 1975
GLCRO	Greater London Council Record Office
GMR	Guildford Muniment Room
HMC	Historical Manuscripts Commission
J.	Journal
JCH	*Journal of Comparative History*
JFHS	*Journal of the Friends' Historical Society*
JMH	*Journal of Modern History*
KRO	Cumbria Record Office, Kendal
LAO	Lincolnshire Archives Office
LJ	Lords Journals
LJRO	Lichfield Joint Record Office
LP	*Letters and Papers of Henry VIII*
LPL	Lambeth Palace Library
LUS	Land Utilization Survey
NLW	National Library of Wales, Aberystwyth
NQ	*Notes and Queries*
PP	Parliamentary Papers
PP	*Past and Present*
PRO	Public Record Office, Chancery Lane and Kew, London
PS	*Population Studies*
RASE	Royal Agricultural Society of England
RCHM	Royal Commission on Historical Monuments
Req.	Proceedings in the Court of Requests
RHS	*Royal Historical Society*
RO	Record Office
Roy. Inst. Cornwall	*Royal Institution of Cornwall*
UCNWL	University College of North Wales Library, Bangor
SP	State Papers
T & C	*Seventeenth-Century Economic Documents*, ed. J. Thirsk and J. P. Cooper, Oxford, 1972
VCH (name of county in italics)	*Victoria County History*
Yorks. Bull.	*Yorkshire Bulletin of Economic and Social Research*

INTRODUCTION

Circumstances do not often allow nineteen scholars to work together on one subject and one century. This volume is therefore unusual in its concentration of effort on one theme. It is also a fresh exploration of the available archives in public and private hands, and not a summary of existing knowledge. It both opens up new views of the period and offers the satisfaction of seeing scholars surveying different aspects of one subject and arriving separately at similar general conclusions. Because their authors have travelled by different routes to reach the same goal, these carry the more conviction. In the end, this period of 110 years, from 1640 to 1750, takes on a clearly defined shape, marking it off from two different experiences in the century before and the century after.

Before the present investigation was begun, the mid seventeenth century to the mid eighteenth could not unreasonably have been called a dark age in English agricultural history. It had not been entirely neglected, but it had not attracted research on the same scale as the thirteenth, the sixteenth, or the later eighteenth and nineteenth centuries. The reason is not difficult to find. Periods of spectacular economic growth tell a more dramatic story, and also yield more documents. A period of depression, or of only sluggish movement, lacks the same colour and excitement; those who live through it seem to be suspended in time, learning nothing and offering nothing to the future.

Yet in this instance, such a verdict on the years 1640–1750 has proved to be superficial. The documentary sources of information are plentiful enough. And, while they confirm the reality of the agricultural depression, they also bring to light the remarkable ingenuity of men battling against adversity. In that struggle farmers found means of survival which opened to their successors after 1750 the road to still more dramatic increases in agricultural production. Necessity was, indeed, the mother of invention.

The changed circumstances of the years after 1640 are succinctly described by Dr Bowden.[1] The general level of agricultural prices increased sixfold between 1500 and 1640, whereas between 1640 and 1750 it rose by only two percentage points. The worst-hit commodities were grain, which fell in price by 12 per cent, and wool, by 33 per cent; on the other hand, some other

---

[1] References in support of the statements in this introduction will be found in the chapters that follow.

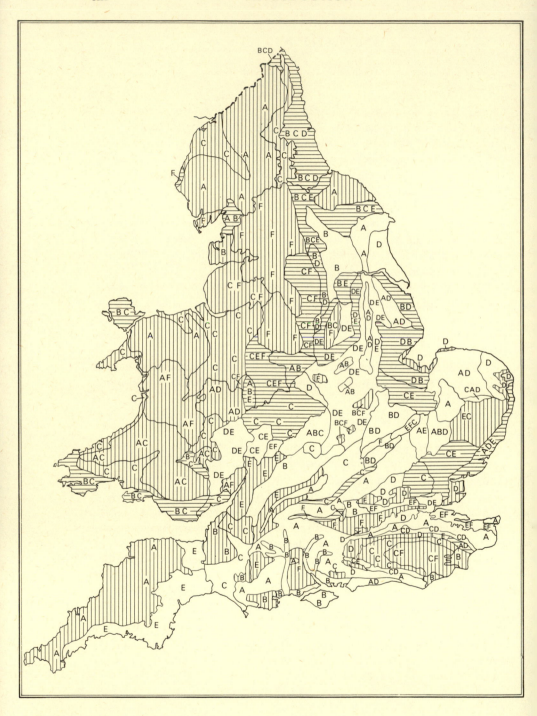

Key to farming types

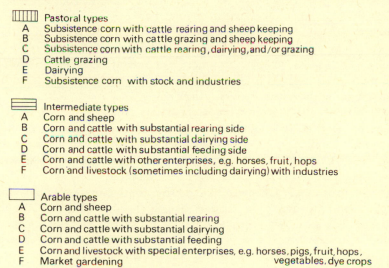

Pastoral types
A   Subsistence corn with cattle rearing and sheep keeping
B   Subsistence corn with cattle grazing and sheep keeping
C   Subsistence corn with cattle rearing, dairying, and/or grazing
D   Cattle grazing
E   Dairying
F   Subsistence corn with stock and industries

Intermediate types
A   Corn and sheep
B   Corn and cattle with substantial rearing side
C   Corn and cattle with substantial dairying side
D   Corn and cattle with substantial feeding side
E   Corn and cattle with other enterprises, e.g. horses, fruit, hops
F   Corn and livestock (sometimes including dairying) with industries

Arable types
A   Corn and sheep
B   Corn and cattle with substantial rearing
C   Corn and cattle with substantial dairying
D   Corn and cattle with substantial feeding
E   Corn and livestock with special enterprises, e.g. horses, pigs, fruit, hops,
F   Market gardening   vegetables, dye crops

Fig. 0.1. Farming regions of England and Wales, 1640–1750.

This map of farming regions adopts a different system of classification from that used in Volume IV, *1500–1640*. In Volume IV two separate groups of pastoral economies were identified, one being characteristic of wood pasture country, the other of open pastoral landscapes. The third main group represented mixed farming economies, which were characteristic of areas where much grain was grown for the market.

In this map, depicting farming systems in 1640–1750, three groups are again differentiated, but the two pastoral types of Volume IV have been treated as one, i.e. wood pasture and open pasture are amalgamated under the heading 'Pastoral types'. Economies in which grain was a major commercial objective are described as 'Arable types'. An 'Intermediate type' has been introduced to identify regions which were growing grain for the market, though not on the scale that characterized the arable regions. Within these three main groups, a more refined description of individual specialities, or groups of specialities, of smaller regions is indicated by capital letters (see key).

With the available data, it is not easy to differentiate farming specialities with great accuracy, especially since the systems of large and small farmers in the same region could vary considerably. The texts of the regional chapters give warning of this diversity, and of the problem of devising any simple classification. So also does the map, since some boundaries which separate farming types are also the boundaries between chapters. In other words, authors on either side of a county frontier have not always agreed in their identification of the dominant local farming type.

enterprises received marked encouragement: cattle prices rose by almost 13 per cent and pig prices by 71 per cent. Certain years, of course, diverged markedly from the general trend. Those between 1640 and 1663, and between 1692 and 1713, were marked by relatively high grain prices. But, in general, they persisted low, and in the years between 1664 and 1691, and between 1725 and 1750, they were more than usually depressed. In some of the worst, it is likely that farmers who concentrated on conventional agricultural produce barely covered their costs.

The roots of the agricultural problem lay, in Dr Clay's words, in over-production and underconsumption. Productivity improved, but fewer mouths consumed. Population growth slackened off, and contemporaries were convinced that deaths in the Civil War and the migrations of people across the Atlantic made matters worse. Demand was thus damped down by a conjuncture of factors. It has proved impossible for the authors of this volume to pay proper attention to population changes. The book by E. A. Wrigley and R. S. Schofield, *The Population History of England, 1541–1871* (London, 1981), which appeared after this volume was written, shows the scale of the task when it is the central theme of study.[2] The uncovering of national population trends, which was its main concern, must now be matched by an analysis of trends in individual regions. It is a challenging task for the future.

Some authors in this volume indicate the general direction of population change in particular regions. But the greater contribution of the regional chapters lies in uncovering more precisely the agricultural changes, which cannot but be associated with a redistribution of population. The expansion of meat and dairy production in Durham and Northumberland is a notable example. It can be shown to reflect a demand from increasing numbers of coal miners on Tyneside, who were no longer self-sufficient in food. Connections effected in a reverse direction are seen in alterations of land use which set people on the move. Enclosure and the conversion of arable land to pasture are most often given as a first example of such change. But it also occurred when the fens of eastern England were drained and turned from pasture into arable in the 1650s. Acute labour shortages resulted which were satisfied at first only by bringing in Scots and Frenchmen. Yet again, when some new crops were widely adopted in the seventeenth century, they called for meticulous weeding and laborious harvesting by armies of men and women who had to be found somewhere. Not surprisingly, the changing face of a general problem of labour supply is reflected in pamphlet literature in the later seventeenth century debating the merits of high or low wages. It is also mirrored in experiments in the early eighteenth century in southern England and lowland Scotland: seed drills were used in the fields in order

[2] Pp. 175, 185–7.

to reduce the wages bill. Yet the labour problem cannot everywhere have been the same. Like underconsumption, it almost certainly has a local history that is as rewarding to investigate as the national generalization. Regional agricultural history must one day be married with regional population history.

Overproduction seems at first sight a surprising phenomenon in a period that was preceded by long decades of anxiety over food shortages, and then starts with a civil war. Yet so serious did the problem become by the mid 1650s that the government was obliged, first to intervene to encourage all food exports, then to pay bounties to farmers on grain exported, and later to allow drawbacks of tax on exported malt. A stimulus to produce more food had been administered in the sixteenth century which evidently did not slacken in the seventeenth century; and the Civil War positively stimulated some branches of agricultural production. Large quantities of cheese and butter were needed to feed the army, and this demand undoubtedly invigorated the dairying business. Losses suffered by the gentry in the Civil War obliged them to turn more of their attention to the management of their estates, and these also then yielded more food than before.

That the gentry were influential pioneers of new crops and new systems of farming is made abundantly clear in this volume; experience through travel (often abroad), together with the reading of books, promoted agricultural improvement in widely scattered regions of the kingdom. The density of innovations was highest in the counties of the south-east and East Anglia, where foreign influences were strong, and where London offered a discriminating but appreciative market near at hand. But downland areas in southern England, where the gentry were socially powerful, were also advanced in their use of new agricultural techniques and new crops; and in some outlying areas of the kingdom, in, for example, Wales and Cumberland, an absentee landlord in London who was alert to the latest farming methods, and who had a steward in charge of his estate who was regularly primed with this information, could create an oasis of improved farming in a desert. This might have far-reaching consequences, for one gentleman could soon influence a wider circle of local gentry around him. That the means of influence were many and various is shown by Paul Brassley in a lively illustration from Northumberland: turnips for cattle fodder were said to have been introduced into the parish of Rock (north of Alnwick) in the 1720s by a landowner who purposely imported a gardener to launch the crop; the same gardener plainly made an impression, for he was then employed for many years afterwards "to sow turnips for all the neighbourhood". Thus the furthest counties of the kingdom were slowly drawn into the vortex of agricultural improvement.

Dr Bowden describes a parting of the ways in this period between the more efficient and the less efficient farmers. The parting was inflicted by the ending of a long and steady rise of agricultural prices from the previous century. A comfortable cushion was then removed, and all classes of farmers were driven to seek new expedients if they were to survive. Many farmers on good land raised productivity by applying more fertilizers (lime was especially valuable on grassland), and by interpolating artificial grasses in their arable rotations, whereby they fed more stock which better manured their crops. But adjustments to farming systems were more varied and complex than this simple statement suggests. Volume IV of the *Agrarian History of England and Wales* (1500–1640) identified the individuality of farming regions at a time when the list of possible agricultural products was comparatively short. It lengthened greatly with the wider adoption of new plants from Europe and America. After 1640 a profusion of sub-regions was being created, each with its own distinctive regime. Dr Short, writing on Kent, Surrey, and Sussex, distinguishes a regime for the North and South Downs, but within each of these hill formations he separates the relatively wooded from the relatively open arable. Dr Wordie distinguishes the north-east Chilterns from the south-west Chilterns. In East Anglia, one of the most progressive regions of all, Dr Holderness finds little uniformity anywhere in its arable systems. 'Sheep–corn husbandry', moreover, which served in the earlier period as an adequate, shorthand description of one farming routine in a number of regions of light soils, no longer suffices when the two main interests were changing in relative importance. And a shift from barley to wheat, or from wheat to barley, might also be effected within the same general framework. Even farmers who maintained their basic routine could, and did, embark on supplementary, or complementary, enterprises, choosing from a miscellany of other possibilities. In this way they prudently protected themselves against an undue reliance on corn and livestock. The growing of weld (for its yellow dye) in arable rotations made the sheep–corn husbandry of the North Downs of Kent distinctive; timber, and hop fields alongside grain and livestock, distinguished a corner of the Hampshire Downs and parts of the Weald.

As a result, the delineation of farming regions is considerably more detailed in this volume than in Volume IV, and doubtless it could be still further refined. In general, the greatest variety occurred near large towns, and most of all around London. It received most encouragement in the highly commercial south and east, not in the north and west. Hence the county of Bedfordshire alone is divided into three different zones, growing fine wheat in the north, cultivating vegetables on the central sandy ridge, and fattening stock in the south. More numerous still were the concentric belts of land which can be discerned in Middlesex, each devoted to different uses. Elsewhere, teasels around Cheddar in Somerset, canary seed in Thanet, 'greenweed' (that is, dyer's broom) at Chigwell in Essex, and hemp in innumerable places varied the colour of the fields and the routines of the farmer.[3] Diversification, whether modest or dramatic, was proceeding almost everywhere.

Urban demand was only one factor in introducing such variety into local farming systems. When once new crops were introduced, they wrought further differentiation between regions because they were usually better suited to one kind of soil than to another. Hence their spread was confined by these constraints: for example, clover spread rapidly in north Worcestershire and the Warwickshire Arden, but made little progress in adjoining regions. Turnips were successful on light, but not heavy, clay soils. Still more highly differentiated farming systems were made possible by the spread of other plants, apart from the fodder crops already mentioned. They included those which varied diet, like vegetables, fruit, and herbs, and industrial crops like dye plants, hops, coleseed, hemp, flax, and timber.

Good-quality samples of all the novelties in agriculture fetched high prices, and could bring more profit for outlay than conventional agricultural produce. If the demands which they made upon soils, labour, and capital suited the class of farmers concerned, they were warmly welcomed as alternatives to traditional agriculture; they offered a valued supplement to a farmer's basic income. The significance of this 'alternative agriculture' in its initial phase was not fully recognized in Volume IV. Hence the necessity here to review such developments, especially in market gardening, before 1640. And the eventual consequences of these enterprises holds further surprises. At first vegetable eating was an upper-class fashion; only when it began to spread through the middle classes in the seventeenth century was its full significance made clear. It did more than introduce variety into diet. It afforded much-needed work *and* taught important lessons about productivity when land was dug with the spade, when seed was carefully spaced, and plants in rows were thoroughly weeded. By the 1720s enterprising individuals were determined to adapt the same techniques for use in the field. Spurred on at first by the cost of seed, then by the rising cost of labour, they were to be galvanized afresh after 1750 by the renewed upward trend of grain prices. The rise of mass demand, when once population began to rise again, then set the agricultural revolution firmly in motion. Farmers in the later eighteenth and nineteenth centuries built their new system of production upon the lessons that had been taught by the gardeners and more resourceful farmers in the very different economic climate of the seventeenth century.

Horticultural and other special crops were of such importance as a supplementary source of income to mainstream agriculture that their costs and their profits plainly call for more investigation in farm accounts. The fact that not all continued to have the same economic importance after 1750

[3] For greenweed, see Essex RO, Quarter Sessions Roll, 402/131, Mich. 1664.

does not diminish their significance in our period. During a depression that lasted over a century, they could be veritable life-savers to at least three generations of farmers. So although the interest in special crops and other agricultural products faded when grain and livestock farming returned to prosperity after 1750, it would return again in the agricultural depression of the later nineteenth century, just as it returns today. Unfortunately, the statistical appendix of this volume does not contain price tables for liquorice, cider apples, coleseed, tobacco, etc. This omission reveals the difficulty of not knowing the end of the story at the beginning. But it is to be hoped that the role accorded these crops in this survey will encourage others to search for more exact information of prices and costs, of the kind offered here only for hops. When the inhabitants of the north Somerset parish of Winscombe are found in 1700 devoting 155 acres to the growing of teasels, we must assume that they expected satisfactory profits. Others put their views in explicit words. George Collett from Portbury in Somerset claimed c. 1712 that one acre of potatoes which "hit right" could be worth as much as three acres of wheat. This is only one of many similar statements relating to garden and industrial crops. Malcolm Thick demonstrates, moreover, an eighteenfold difference that could sometimes occur between the lowest and highest prices for vegetables at different seasons.

Special crops usually involved a gamble. Yet the gambling was not in practice as great a risk to one individual as it might at first seem. Partnerships in the growing of novel crops were not uncommon; the costs and the profits were shared, sometimes among landlords, tenants, and cultivators, sometimes between tenants and cultivators alone. Through partnerships, farmers and labourers with small means could become involved in the cultivation of new crops and other forms of agricultural improvement. Although the best evidence presented in this volume on the diffusion of new ways in farming concerns the pioneering efforts of the gentry, the spread of certain plants like clover, coleseed, and tobacco shows what could be achieved by yeomen, husbandmen, and even cottagers when once they were convinced of the benefits. Farmers of all classes were not slow to spot the successes that suited their situation; hence caution is needed when passing judgment on farmers, who, to the very end of the period, would not stir from their familiar routine. Common gossip described many ventures that failed, debts that overwhelmed, and good causes that were lost by ruse and conspiracy. Considering the general economic circumstances of the time, and the careful dovetailing of tasks needed to make an efficient farming system, the optimists and the adventurers were surprisingly numerous. Some brave souls took up new ideas and changed course with remarkable rapidity.

Many mistakes were made in the early trials with new crops, not the least of these arising from the notion that new crops would be the miraculous panacea, instantly turning barren land to good account. But slowly the requirements for the successful cultivation of every novelty were made clearer, the best soils were identified, and crops were selected by the appropriate class of farmers who could offer the best conditions. Thus vegetables and tobacco were chosen by poor men; hops, fruit, and coleseed by husbandmen and yeomen; woad by well-to-do yeomen and gentry. Since the gentry had more land at their disposal, they also selected from a range of further alternatives that were not available to others: they cultivated the taste for more fancy foods, and had more time and money to spend on recreation. They developed activities alternative to grain and conventional livestock production, planning and stocking deer parks, rabbit warrens, fishponds, duck decoys, dovecotes, and vineyards. Some of these pursuits provided food for the table and were justified as prudent household management; some yielded cash at the market. The breeding of fine horses was also undertaken, not always for pleasure alone, but sometimes for profit. And in Chapters 20 and 21, Professor Barley and Peter Smith show how these ventures are reflected in a changed layout of houses, farm buildings, and landscapes. In a gentleman's house, gardens, and fields, domestic comfort, food supply, and aesthetic display might all be conveniently served when a supply of water was procured for the house which also filled the fish pond and replenished a cascading waterfall or fountain.

Gentlemen were hard pressed in this period, both as landlords and farmers, as Dr Clay demonstrates. It was not easy to make estates pay in a century of generally depressed rents and prices and of rising taxation. Their policies on many counts differed from those in the sixteenth century. They were less flamboyant spenders, and more attentive to *Observations and Advices Oeconomical*, the significant title given by Dudley, Lord North, to a publication in 1669 arguing that "never was there more need of good menagery than now, at a time when revenues of the gentry are fallen beyond what could have been imagined of late years".[4] The gentry drew in their horns. They did not generally purchase extensive new tracts of territory, but rounded out and consolidated their ancestral estates with small purchases, sometimes paid for by the sale of other fragmented pieces. Since land values did not rise, capital charges could not be paid out of rising rents. Economies were imperative, unless marriages brought windfalls in the form of marriage portions.

In these circumstances the improvement of an existing property was more attractive than the purchase of more, for loans were not difficult to raise in the advanced agricultural counties, land tax was not reassessed after improvements, and improvements themselves were not generally costly. Yet they could yield a return of 12 to 20 per cent gross. Hence the gentry

[4] Dudley, Lord North, *Observations and Advices Oeconomical*, London, 1669, p. 2.

remained in the lead as agricultural improvers, setting an example on their home farms, and encouraging their more responsive tenants. They were the leaders in improved arable husbandry.

The various branches of livestock farming held up better than grain in this century, and some, indeed, made great strides forward. The demand for meat was maintained, the demand for dairy produce proved almost insatiable, and prices generally encouraged stock breeders. All the price series for livestock remained more stable than grain, and pig prices actually surged ahead. Government policy, through the Irish cattle acts, assisted cattle breeders, though the complaints of sheep farmers went unheard. The condition of grassland received more careful attention from improvers than hitherto, and all over England and Wales, even in arable East Anglia, a move to grow more grass and less grain was under way between 1660 and 1750.

Floated water meadows improved the fodder supply by making more good grass available earlier in spring. And although this was a costly capital improvement, the regional chapters show its popularity in certain areas. Elsewhere, clover, rye-grass, lucerne, sainfoin, and turnips facilitated the keeping of more livestock, while the more deliberate selection of fertilizers like lime and marl, ashes and seaweed gave the new grasses an even better chance of success. The pace at which these crops advanced across the country was far from uniform, but some regions showed a notable surge of interest in the grasses in the 1660s, 1670s, and 1680s. Turnips spread more slowly. They won favour in East Anglia from around 1650, and emerged into prominence elsewhere, for example in Somerset, from 1670 onwards. But for a long time in southern England turnips were only planted on odd bits of ground, and not until the period 1730 to 1750 did they spread more widely, becoming settled in an arable rotation by 1760.

The shape of the livestock business changed in subtle ways from region to region, as did arable systems. Breeders of livestock in the south-west even began to drive some of their beasts fat to London and some places experienced a positive shortage of pasture and meadow as a result. Some arable areas in the south-west turned to convertible husbandry, which gave more scope for livestock keeping, while some areas of convertible husbandry, like the south Midlands, turned back to permanent pasture.

Among the branches of livestock keeping which expanded markedly, we have found little beyond generalities to illustrate the rising fortunes of pig keepers. But the evidence of a much-enlarged dairying industry is impressive. Existing dairying areas expanded geographically, and became more specialized, and some individual dairymen launched into highly commercial businesses. The north Shropshire plain and the Vale of Gloucester are but two of the dairying areas yielding examples of farmers with milking herds of sixty and more cows. In north-eastern England, where miners on Tyneside consumed much of the local dairy produce, Mr Brassley even describes an uncomfortable surplus of production by 1735. Dairying was an ideal occupation for small farmers, and hence, as Dr Chartres shows, the marketing of dairy produce posed new practical problems, partly because of the many sellers, partly because the scale of production placed too many strains on a system designed in earlier, simpler days.

Sheep farmers came off worst of all stock producers because of the continually falling prices of wool. But their difficulties effectively concentrated their minds on better meat production, and such a goal came within firmer reach when better fodder was produced by the new grasses. Farmers seized the chance to change their breeds in order to improve the quantity and quality of their mutton, and though they continued to be interested in profits from wool, its quality and weight changed, usually producing a heavier, coarser fleece. While low wool prices constrained sheep farmers, the use of clover and turnips enlarged their horizons and promoted fresh thinking on new ways in livestock breeding.

The careful study of estate accounts and correspondence has yielded scant evidence of the selective breeding of animals, except in relation to horses and possibly dogs. But some improvements were occurring accidentally, and, in theory, more could have been deliberately planned at any time after 1650 when an experimental attitude towards the natural sciences became a firmly established feature of the rural scene. Yet it was evidently not until mainstream grain and livestock production was reinvigorated by the stimulus of rising prices — a state of affairs that can be perceived in some places in the 1730s and 1740s, although it was not generally recognized until after 1750 — that circumstances were ripe for another innovative leap forward. Dr Russell has recently uncovered the best-documented evidence of a publicized success in selective breeding, whether accidentally or deliberately contrived, in the dairying country of the west Lancashire plain.[5] Unusually young yearling bulls were being used in the late seventeenth century, which, he suggests, may have built up early-maturity genes, and genes for size, which later caused these animals to attract the notice of the breeders of the Midland plain like Robert Bakewell. Dr Howell, writing here on Welsh landowners, shows George Shakerly, at Gwenilt, corresponding with his cousin Sir William Williams, baronet, at Llanvorda (Oswestry), in 1728, announcing the purchase on his behalf of a bull calf and a heifer. "There are much larger to be had", he wrote, "in the further part of Lancashire, and I have made such enquiry that whenever you have occasion, I can give you full directions where to be fitted with the finest and largest kinds." Here are faint traces of a path towards selective breeding that was to be more confidently trodden by livestock farmers in the second half of the eighteenth century.

Commercial agriculture in the period 1640 to 1750 was greatly diversified,

[5] N. C. Russell, 'Animal Breeding in England, c. 1500–1700', unpub. London Univ. Ph.D. thesis, 1981, pp. 86ff. I wish to thank Dr Russell for permission to cite his recent thesis.

partly under the constraints of low prices for traditional produce, partly by changing fashions in food. Thus two forces were at work in the market pushing from different directions. The distinctive characteristics of regional economies multiplied. Yet farmers' and merchants' efforts to get the best prices at the market would ultimately lead to an integrated national price structure. That this last process was under way is demonstrated by Dr Chartres, but it was far from complete by 1750. Judged by prices, the market for wheat could be described as integrated by the 1690s, but not the market for other cereals. In newer items of trade, merchants were still experimenting, and many themes for further investigation come to light in Dr Chartres's account of partnerships, the new tyranny of factors like the London cheese dealers, and the competition between the old hop-production centre of Kent and its upstart rival in the south-west Midlands, centred on Worcester.

In the search for a marketing system which met the new challenges, some old-established markets and fairs fell into decline, and individual merchants bought increasingly at the farm gate or, in the Home Counties, by sample. But specialization in trading roles did not yet separate all producers from all consumers, certainly not in the dairying, meat, fruit, and cider businesses. Meanwhile, the government clung to the tradition of supervising marketing. But most of its actions were confined to the revision and amendment of old statutes; it rarely embarked on anything new. In emergencies, the law was strictly enforced in the early eighteenth century, but in general regulation was gradually allowed to lapse. From 1680 onwards, merchants operated in an atmosphere of increasing *laissez-faire*.

An agricultural economy in depression taxes the ingenuity of all. Some farmers did not weather the storm. It may be possible in the future to show more precisely which size of farm in which regions was hardest hit. In general, average-to-small farmers on less-than-ideal soils, and at a distance from water transport to market, seem to have suffered most. But alternative activities that could supplement declining incomes made a long list, and did not exclude anyone with resource. They extended to enterprises such as the trapping of wheatears on the Sussex coast to be sold as delicacies in Tunbridge Wells, the production of asses' milk for the delicate stomachs of Canterbury and London citizens, the collecting of osiers and reeds for the making of barrel hoops and baskets in the Somerset fens, the production of fish in old hammer ponds in Sussex, and the fattening of pigs on distillers' and starch makers' waste grain in town suburbs. To these agricultural pursuits were added a multitude of industrial employments that could be satisfactorily pursued in the sheds and parlours of country cottages and farms. In many such cases, in the handicraft industries, in metalworking, and in potting, women and children were needed as well as men. Still more work was offered to the women and children when the new crops of this period received careful weeding, on a scale not generally given to conventional arable crops. Family incomes, rather than men's wages, now became a fairer measure of rural prosperity.

Landlords were similarly ingenious in devising expedients for survival. They accommodated their tenants in many different ways in order to retain them on the land. They revised rents, took grain in payment, shifted some of the burden of taxation, and helped with the cost of repairs and the manuring of land. The decline of the small farmer would have been a more catastrophic phenomenon without the realistic adjustments of policy by landlords, particularly by those who were resident on their estates and perceived the problems at first hand. Cold calculation from a landlord's point of view confirmed that large farms made better sense than small. Yet many gentlemen were content to uphold conservative farming practices, while some who were concerned to raise standards of efficiency nevertheless found expedients that did not require them to drive all small farmers off the land. The rate of return on land was not their only consideration. Gentry valued the political influence that land conferred on them, and in depression, when grand ambitions faltered, intellectual arguments about the long-term husbanding of estates and tenants carried weight. The final sum of self-interest, as Dr Clay explains, could reinforce ancient traditions of paternalism rather than subvert them.

The depressed condition of conventional agriculture slowed down some changes in landownership, tenancy, and land management, and staved off the ruin of many a small subsistence farmer. At the same time, it stimulated inventiveness among farmers in all ranks of society. When different circumstances supervened after 1750 and rising numbers presented once again, as in the sixteenth century, an insistent, mass demand for basic foodstuffs, the full harvest of men's ingenuity in the period 1640–1750 was reaped.

NORTHERN ENGLAND

CHAPTER 1

CUMBERLAND, WESTMORLAND, AND FURNESS

The present (post-1974) administrative county of Cumbria forms an identifiable region which may conveniently be used for the study of agricultural developments in the late seventeenth and early eighteenth centuries. It comprises the historic counties of Cumberland and Westmorland together with the Furness and Cartmel districts of Lancashire, to the north of Morecambe Bay. Far from the softer plains of the south and Midlands, largely mountainous and difficult of access, the region seemed to its few visitors uniquely poor, barren, and inhospitable. Celia Fiennes wrote in 1698 of "those inaccessible high rocky barren hills which hangs [sic] over ones head in some places and appear very terrible". She at first mistook dwellings "made up of drye walls piled together" for "a sort of houses or barns to fodder cattle in".[1] Some twenty years later, Daniel Defoe, only a passing traveller, considered Westmorland "a country eminent only for being the wildest, most barren and frightful of any that I have passed over in England, or even in Wales it self". Cumberland stood but little higher in his estimation.[2]

It is not surprising that southern visitors should dwell on the spectacular bleakness of the landscape, but the region was both more diverse and more productive than their notes suggest. Cumbria may be divided into five distinct topographical sub-regions. The central mass of mountains, the Borrowdale volcanic series, form the highest range in England, with three peaks of over 3,000 feet. Immediately to the north and south are the Skiddaw slates of the Ordovician age and the Silurian slates, on which stand Coniston, Windermere, and Kendal. For the most part, soil quality is poor and acid, calcium and other mineral elements having been leached by heavy rainfall. The lakes of the Lake District radiate from the central mountain mass something like the spokes of a wheel. In the valleys among the rivers and lakes, soil fertility is naturally rather higher; 'brown earth' is found up to

The authors wish to acknowledge a large debt to Dr J. D. Marshall and the late Professor G. P. Jones, whose pioneer work has done so much to make the economic and social history of the most remote English region as accessible as any. We wish to express our gratitude to Dr Marshall also for his helpful comments on an earlier draft of this chapter.

[1] *The Journeys of Celia Fiennes*, ed. C. Morris, rev. edn, London, 1949, p. 196.
[2] *A Tour through the Whole Island of Great Britain*, ed. G. D. H. Cole and D. C. Browning, 2 vols., 1962, *II*, pp. 269–70.

about 1,000 feet, containing oxidized iron, and permitting in the late seventeenth century that modest cultivation in small closes consonant with subsistence agriculture and capable of limited further development.[3] This was not in general true of the second mountainous area – the western slopes of the north Pennine range, which rise from the Eden valley to the borders of Northumberland and Durham. Here, frequently above the tree line and rising to 2,000 feet, only rough summer sheep pasture was possible. The most fertile land lay in the third region, the Eden valley, running south-east from Carlisle towards Appleby. Here sandstones and magnesian limestone predominate. The area is mostly protected from harsh winds, and, since rainfall at 35–40 inches per annum is less than half the levels recorded on exposed Lakeland fells, mixed farming was perfectly feasible. West and south-west from Carlisle stretch the plains of the Solway, and west Cumberland, mostly on sandstone, both of which provided good-quality pasture land, also susceptible of some arable cultivation. The fifth area, essentially the lowland part of the Furness peninsula, lies partly on sandstone and partly on carboniferous limestone. It was in parts densely afforested and exposed to wet westerly winds bringing rainfall of between 45 and 60 inches per annum. The area was amenable to stock rearing but largely unsuited to intensive arable cultivation. Natural features determined farming patterns, more obviously in Cumbria than elsewhere, but they neither imposed an absolute straitjacket nor consigned the seventeenth-century farming community to utter dependence on the hardier breeds of sheep. Sir Daniel Fleming of Rydal conceded in 1671 that a great part of the soil was barren, but drew attention to the "fruitfull valleys" of Westmorland "abounding with good arable, meadow, and pasture grounds, and commended for plenty of corne and cattle".[4]

At the end of the seventeenth century the combined populations of Cumberland and Westmorland probably totalled about 95,000. The estimate of Thomas Denton, recorder of Carlisle, for the population of Cumberland in 1688 was 67,185. As this assumes an average of five persons to the family, an estimate considered by demographers to be rather high, it is probably safe to reduce his estimate to about 65,000 – rather above the estimate for the county in 1701 achieved by the use of Rickman's multiplier. A round figure of 30,000 for Westmorland is obtained by multiplying Gregory King's estimate of the number of houses in the county (6,691) by four and a half. The 1801 census figures indicate that the population of Cumberland at that date was 117,230, an increase of approximately 80 per cent over 1688; that of Westmorland was 36 per cent higher than the estimate for the 1690s.[5]

---

[3] For the ecology and physical geography of the Lake District, see W. H. Pearsall and W. Pennington, *The Lake District: A Landscape History*, London, 1973, pp. 17–42, 121–32.

[4] E. Hughes, ed., 'Fleming Senhouse Papers: Sir Daniel Fleming's Description of Cumberland, Westmorland and Furness, 1671', *Carlisle Rec. Ser.*, II, 1971, p. 3.

[5] These figures derive from G. P. Jones, 'Population Problems relating to Cumberland and Westmorland in the 18th Century', *CW2*, LVIII, 1958, pp. 123–9.

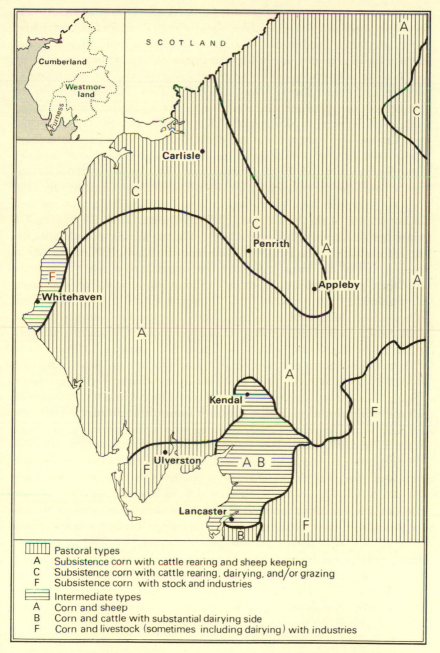

Fig. 1.1. Farming regions of Cumberland, Westmorland, and Furness.

The greatest population increases seem to have taken place in areas where cultivable plainland was extensive, where minerals abounded, and where there was access to the sea. In this context it is not surprising that Cumberland's growth was greater than that of Westmorland.

It is more germane to our purposes, however, to discover whether these increases over more than a century mask stagnation or even decline in the first half of the eighteenth century. Deane and Cole argue, on the basis of calculations by Farr, Brownlie, and Talbot Griffith, that the populations of both Cumberland and Westmorland declined by approximately 10 per cent between 1701 and 1751, the former county from 90,182 to 81,060, the latter from 40,134 to 35,951.[6] These calculations are based on too-generous compensation for the assumed underestimates in Rickman's estimates for 1701 from parish register data. The figures for 1701 seem much too high and they do not accord with the findings of Denton's empirical survey. Such a population decline is anyway intrinsically unlikely in view of industrial and commercial developments in west Cumberland and south Westmorland in the first half of the century. While economic growth in south Lancashire undoubtedly exercised a pull even at this time, Deane and Cole's estimates of migration of 10 per cent from Cumberland and 7.6 per cent from Westmorland during this period are clearly exaggerated.[7] As will be seen, some rural areas were indeed drained of population by migration but more to growing urban centres within the region than outside it.

A more realistic picture is obtained by using a survey of families made in 1747 by John Waugh. The calculation by the chancellor of the ancient diocese of Carlisle covers only the seventy-one Cumberland and twenty-four Westmorland parishes located in that diocese and thus excludes Whitehaven and Kendal, the two most rapidly growing areas in the region, as these were in the diocese of Chester. This important caveat notwithstanding, Waugh's survey suggests an overall increase of about 24 per cent between the Denton survey of 1688 and 1747 (39,093 to 48,501).[8] Thus, although there was stagnation and even decline in some rural areas, overall population growth between 1700 and 1750 seems to have been running at approximately half the pace of the post-1750 increase. This is broadly in line with national trends.

In all but two of the sixteen parishes studied in Professor Jones's demographic essay baptism rates exceeded burial rates between 1701 and 1750; in all sixteen, however, the excess was considerably greater in the subsequent half-century. A similar picture emerges from Furness. The ratio of baptisms to burials in nine Furness parishes between 1701 and 1750 was 1.21:1; between 1751 and 1800 it rose to an average of 1.63:1.[9] In these

[6] P. Deane and W. A. Cole, *British Economic Growth*, 2nd edn, Cambridge, 1969, p. 103.

[7] *Ibid.*, p. 115.

[8] Jones, *op. cit.*, pp. 129–31. The adjustment involves reducing Denton's estimate of 5 persons per household to one of 4.5.

[9] Calculations from figures in J. D. Marshall, *Furness and the Industrial Revolution*, Barrow-in-Furness, 1958, p. 98.

gains, after a period of equilibrium in the late seventeenth century, it is particularly noticeable that birth rates are rising. There is no Cumbrian evidence after 1650 to suggest that epidemics or famine were checking population as they had, for example, in 1597, 1623, and as late as 1649, when a general famine throughout the north of England was stated to be particularly severe in Cumberland and Westmorland.[10] Plague was much less of a scourge, though epidemics in 1645–7 in Carlisle, Cockermouth, Crosthwaite, and Keswick are well-documented. The most significant epidemic occurred in Furness and west Cumberland in 1728–9. Influenza was very possibly the cause, afflicting a population debilitated by harvest shortages. Six per cent of the entire population of the Furness township of Broughton are known to have been buried there in 1729. In neighbouring areas – Millom, Colton, Bootle, Lamplugh, and Whicham – burial rates were approximately twice the annual average.[11] The epidemic, however, did not check the overall rise in population. Broughton numbered some 500 souls in 1700; it reached 520 in 1720, 576 in 1730, and 637 in 1750, an increase of 27 per cent over the half-century.

Estimates of regional population growth conceal important variations. The established urban centres – Carlisle, Penrith, and Kendal – showed substantial increases. The population of the town and suburbs of Carlisle increased from between 2,000 and 3,000 at the turn of the eighteenth century to more than 4,000 by 1763, with a much sharper rise to just over 10,000 in 1801; Kendal grew from about 2,000 in 1700 to nearly 8,000 in 1801, while Penrith increased from 1,350 to 3,800 during the century. Rates of increase in the new commercial and industrial communities of west Cumberland, however, were much larger. Workington developed from an estimated population of 945 in 1688 to 6,440 in 1801. The population of Whitehaven, the great Lowther creation, stood at 1,089 in 1685; by 1762 this had swollen to over 9,000, making it already comfortably the largest town in the region. The growth rate slowed thereafter and by 1801 the population had not reached 11,000.[12]

Whitehaven, Workington, and Kendal in particular seem to have drawn much of their increased population from the rural hinterland. Parish register evidence indicates that many rural parishes suffered a steady decline in

[10] For which see A. B. Appleby, *Famine in Tudor and Stuart England*, Liverpool, 1978, pp. 109–54, and T & C, pp. 51–2.

[11] G. P. Jones, 'The Population of Broughton in Furness in the Eighteenth Century', *CW2*, LIII, 1953, pp. 140–3. No clear diagnosis of the cause of the 1728–9 population crisis is likely to emerge. Contemporaries spoke only of "the great fever" or "the fever", which would seem to rule out smallpox, superficially the likeliest cause. It has been argued that the crisis affected a population debilitated by a run of poor harvests – A. Gooder, 'The Population Crisis of 1727–30 in Warwickshire', *Midland Hist.*, I, 1972, pp. 1–22.

[12] Figures for Carlisle, Penrith, and Workington from C. M. L. Bouch and G. P. Jones, *The Lake Counties, 1500–1830*, Manchester, 1961, p. 217. There is a census of Whitehaven for 1762 in CRO; there is an obviously inflated estimate of 16,400 for Whitehaven in 1785 in W. Hutchinson, *History of the County of Cumberland and Some Places Adjacent*, 2 vols., Carlisle, 1794, II, p. 49.

population between 1688 and 1750. Thirty-six of the seventy-one parishes in the Denton survey, indeed, had not regained their 1688 values even by 1801. Professor Jones's detailed calculations for three west Cumberland parishes – Whicham, Whitbeck, and Lamplugh – reveal declines in population of 30 per cent, 11 per cent, and 13 per cent respectively between 1700 and 1750. In Westmorland, the parish of Crosby Garrett is estimated to have declined from 251 to 135 between 1690 and 1747.[13] Since the ratio of baptisms to burials is fairly consistently in favour of the former, the likeliest explanation of these population patterns is short-distance migration from countryside to town. Naturally, the fastest-growing towns gained most from this movement, but there was modest movement also into the slower-growing towns of the region. By 1750 the extreme north-west possessed the necessary demographic springboard for both urban and industrial expansion.

Progressive agriculture, informed by new techniques, is hard to find in the region. This is explained by three factors. First, landscape and climate in a predominantly mountainous area were inimical alike to investment and experiment. Secondly, farms remained small throughout the period; even in 1750 those realizing a rent of £100 per annum were rare. It is unwise to be dogmatic about farm sizes in this period, however. Upland farms, containing large tracts of rough pasture, were naturally larger than lowland holdings while letting for correspondingly lower rents; they were also less susceptible of improvement. More important, in Cumbria as elsewhere, there are problems in identifying the precise size of customary acres, which are rather larger than their modern equivalents. While the statute acre is based on a rod of $16\frac{1}{2}$ feet, most Cumbrian acres were based on rods of 18, 20, or 21 feet, though this by no means exhausts the variations.[14] It is therefore almost impossible to be certain that like is compared with like, whether statute acres or the various genera of Cumbrian or customary acres, although the imperfect evidence clearly suggests the smallness of most lowland farms.

Thirdly, and related to the size of farms, patterns of tenure had an inhibiting effect. Landowners found it difficult to consolidate their property and encourage the use of new techniques because of the prevalence of customary tenure. Sir James Lowther of Whitehaven, writing in the middle of the eighteenth century, believed that "one of the principal things that makes our country so miserable is the great number of little tenancy estates".[15] Bailey and Culley, the Board of Agriculture reporters, observed in the 1790s that "there are probably few countries where *property in land*

---

[13] It must be admitted that in the case of Crosby Garrett, where the decline in population was abnormally steep, the ratio of baptisms to burials was 0.9:1 between 1700 and 1750. In both Whicham and Lamplugh, by contrast, it was 1.3:1 – G. P. Jones, 'Population Problems', p. 136.

[14] R. S. Dilley, 'Some Words Used in the Agrarian History of Cumberland', *CW2*, LXX, 1970, p. 195.

[15] CRO, D/Lons/W, Sir J. Lowther to J. Spedding, 1 Jan. 1751.

is divided into such small parcels as in Cumberland; and those small properties so universally occupied by the owners; by far the greatest part of which are held under lords of the manors, by that species of vassalage, called customary tenure". Nicolson and Burn made much the same point in the first true history of Cumberland and Westmorland: "Every man lives upon his own small tenement, and the practice of accumulating farms hath not yet here made any considerable progress."[16]

The tenacity of what amounted to a series of feudal tenures is largely explained by the history of border hostilities and Scottish raids. Tenants on most manors in the early seventeenth century had to perform military service at the behest of the Warden of the Marches. 'Tenantright' and other similar tenures proved almost impossible to break down, and some estates could even be sold or mortgaged without permission of the lord. Vigorous attempts by the crown, and spasmodically enthusiastic efforts by local gentry families, to break tenantright and substitute economic rents met with little success even after 1603. Legal decisions only confirmed tenants' rights, and the resultant situation remained a hindrance to would-be improving landlords throughout the period and into the nineteenth century.[17]

The importance of customary tenures in hampering enclosure and in delaying the development of leases aimed at improvement, therefore, can hardly be overstated. Average holdings seem to have been very small. A survey of lands in the manor of Witherslack, stretching north from the estuary of the river Kent in south Westmorland, in 1736 reveals that 42.9 per cent of tenants held less than ten acres. The same percentage held between ten and fifty acres, and only 14.3 per cent held more than this. Land worth between £5 and £20 a year was farmed by 54.3 per cent of tenants, and 17.1 per cent held land worth more than this.[18] Common rights were still being protected early in the eighteenth century by the manor court, though much piecemeal enclosure had taken place during the previous century. Though holdings in general remained small, they did not remain always in the same hands. In fact there was considerable vitality in the land market for customary tenures and smaller freehold properties, but usually they passed to other small proprietors rather than to the gentry or peerage. Not until the second half of the eighteenth century did the peerage and upper gentry

---

[16] J. Bailey and G. Culley, *General View of the Agriculture of Cumberland*, London, 1794, p. 11; J. Nicolson and R. Burn, *The History and Antiquities of the Counties of Cumberland and Westmorland*, 2 vols., London, 1777, *I*, p. 9.

[17] On the legal complexities of tenure in this area see C. B. Phillips, 'The Gentry in Cumberland and Westmorland, 1600–1665', unpub. Univ. of Lancaster Ph.D. thesis, 1973, pp. 127–39; S. J. Watts, 'Tenant-Right in Early Seventeenth-Century Northumberland', *Northern Hist.*, VI, 1971, pp. 64–87; Bouch and Jones, *op. cit.*, pp. 74–6; J. Rawlinson Ford, 'The Customary Tenant-Right of the Manors of Yealand', *CW2*, IX, 1909, pp. 147–60; M. Campbell, *The English Yeoman*, New Haven, 1942, pp. 149–55.

[18] G. P. Jones, 'The Witherslack Survey, 1736', *CW2*, LXIX, 1969, pp. 214–15.

begin to make significant inroads into the market for customary property.[19] Some gentry attempted to improve the situation either by enfranchising their tenants or by buying up numbers of customary tenancies. Between 1659 and 1665 Henry Curwen of Camerton reduced the rents and fines on his manors of Greysouthen, Redmain, and part of Blindcrake to nominal sums in return for cash calculated at twenty-six years' rent. George Denton of Cardew reduced his tenants' rents to 1d. on the manor of Parton in 1676. Fines were also abolished.[20] Tenants at Natland (1675) and at Middleton and Little Langdale (1685) were enfranchised, as were twenty-six tenants of the earl of Thanet in 1722–3.[21] Even if they could afford it, however, many customary tenants clearly felt that enfranchisement was a poor bargain, given their already privileged status. Robert Scott of Brampton, for example, paid the earl of Carlisle £110 in the 1730s for land he had previously rented for a mere 4s. 6¾d. a year.[22] Many tenants found themselves embarrassed by calls on their estates in the form of fines and were forced to sell up.[23] Much of the land thus released passed to men of similar status since the major gentry families of the region, the Flemings of Rydal, the Musgraves of Edenhall, and the Stricklands of Sizergh, showed little interest in it. One or two gentry families only were in the market. In particular, the Wilsons of Dallam Tower embarked on an expensive programme of consolidation, and during the early part of the eighteenth century lords of the manor were ever more willing to extinguish tenantright rather than regrant any property which fell to them.[24]

Landed society in Cumberland and Westmorland can be very roughly divided into peerage, gentry, and 'yeomanry' – the latter an ill-defined agglomeration of small freeholders and some tenant farmers. The continuing vitality of this group, coupled with the small numbers of upper gentry, ensured that the distinction between yeomanry and gentry was a hazy one.[25] Many of those who called themselves gentlemen would not have been accorded that status elsewhere. Of seventy-three gentry families in Cumber-

[19] On Cumbrian landownership in general, see J. V. Beckett, 'English Landownership in the Later Seventeenth and Eighteenth Centuries: The Debate and the Problems', EcHR, 2nd ser., xxx, 1977, pp. 567–81.

[20] PRO, C 5/31/62, C 78/597 no. 13 and C 5/502/24; Phillips, op. cit., pp. 138–9.

[21] J. M. Ewbank, ed., Antiquary on Horseback, Kendal, 1963, pp. 10, 36, 140; CRO, D/Lons/L Addnl Accts., 16 Mar. 1722 – 20 Apr. 1723.

[22] Durham Univ., Howard of Naworth MSS, C/170/60, C/181a/21.

[23] For amplification of this point, see G. P. Jones, 'The Decline of the Yeomanry in the Lake Counties', CW2, LXII, 1962, pp. 201–9.

[24] J. V. Beckett, 'Landownership in Cumbria, c. 1680 – c. 1750', unpub. Univ. of Lancaster Ph.D. thesis, 1975, p. 147.

[25] For a wider discussion of the usage of the term 'yeoman' and the position of that group vis-à-vis the gentry, see Beckett, thesis, pp. 95–8, 139–41, 400–17. See also J. V. Beckett, 'The Decline of the Small Landowner in Eighteenth- and Nineteenth-Century England: Some Regional Considerations', AHR, xxx, 1982, pp. 97–111.

land and Westmorland in 1642 whose incomes can be estimated with any accuracy, only a quarter had an annual income of more than £200, and forty-one (56 per cent) survived on less than £100. It is clear that Defoe's computation eighty years later of £100 per annum as a minimum for gentry status did not apply in Cumbria; many families with incomes well short of this figure were locally recognized as gentry. Such as they were, the upper gentry were on the decline. In 1642 six baronets and eleven knights resided in Cumberland and Westmorland, a small enough total. Yet by 1700 only eight and five respectively were resident, and by 1747, seven and nil.[26] The two counties provided fewer than 1 per cent of the nation's baronets, knights, esquires, and gentlemen, according to Gregory King's calculations in 1688. Robert Price, a baron of the Exchequer, noted during a summer circuit in 1710 that Westmorland was "a county depopulated of gentry", a view endorsed by Sir Christopher Musgrave, himself a member of a prominent local gentry family.[27]

Nor were the paucity and poverty of the Cumbrian gentry offset by the influence of the peerage. Cumberland and Westmorland emerged as the two poorest counties in England judged by most of Charles Davenant's criteria in 1695, and, not surprisingly, the peerage chose to reside elsewhere.[28] Only two peerage families, the earls of Carlisle and Derby, retained a continuous landed interest with direct descent between 1661 and 1751, and neither was resident. The pre-eminent family was the Lowthers of Lowther. Sir John Lowther was created first viscount Lonsdale in 1696 and the line survived until 1751. The Lowthers were anxious to consolidate their land by purchase in the two counties and in Yorkshire. Though active also in sales, these were mostly of enfranchisements until the aftermath of the South Sea Bubble enforced more substantial selling in the 1720s. The dukes of Somerset and earls of Carlisle also made purchases, but the dukes of Norfolk and Wharton and the earl of Sussex sold all their estates in the region. Overall, sales exceeded purchases; the aristocracy's interest in its Cumbrian estates was less than consuming, although good care was taken to safeguard burgage and other electoral interests. As a consequence, the natural leaders of society were a gentry group less favourably circumstanced than elsewhere.

The tenacity of subsistence farming necessitated systems based on mixed husbandry. Arable cultivation was both for fodder and for domestic consumption, though only the coarser grains could be grown. Arable was,

---

[26] Phillips, op. cit., p. 18–20; Beckett, thesis, pp. 97, 412, 414; Daniel Defoe, *The Complete English Tradesman*, 2 vols., London, 1745, I, p. 245.

[27] HMC, 15th Report, Appendix pt IV, *Portland MSS*, IV, p. 578, R. Price to R. Harley, 29 Aug. 1710; Levens Hall MSS (at Levens Hall, near Kendal) box D, Sir Christopher Musgrave to J. Grahme, n.d. For a cautionary note on Gregory King's categories and methods, see G. S. Holmes, 'Gregory King and the Social Structure of Pre-Industrial England', RHS, XXVII, 1977, pp. 41–65.

[28] Davenant's calculations are reprinted in T & C, pp. 802–3.

of course, subordinate to dairy and pasture throughout this upland region and throughout the period. Also, cattle rather than sheep were the linchpins of the Cumbrian agricultural economy. During this period there were considerable developments both in rearing and fattening; winter, as well as summer, fattening was widely practised. Holdings of sheep were neither so large nor relatively so profitable as has usually been assumed. In an area usually, if correctly, stigmatized as the most backward farming region in England, the primacy of the cow merits special attention at the outset of a discussion on farming systems.

Cattle rearing was the surest source of income in the region. The Lonsdale estate made a profit of over £100 a year from cattle sales in the 1690s, rising to more than £250 in 1708. Agistment of cattle, bought from Scotland, wintered, and resold for the journey south in the spring, was also profitable. Humphrey Senhouse's day books, kept for his aunt Bridget Hudleston of Millom Castle, reveal good profits from the buying and selling of cattle at Dalton and Ravenglass fairs around 1700. Breeding and rearing was a major occupation at Levens in the 1690s; the accent was on rearing alone on the estate of the Lowthers of Holker.[29] The evidence of cattle farming among the yeomen is striking. The value of cattle recorded in inventories is consistently higher than that of sheep; somewhat surprisingly, also, a larger proportion of fell farmers seem to have kept cattle than sheep. Marshall's sample of three hundred inventories reveals that 87 per cent of 'hill yeomen' (those farming predominantly above 400 feet) kept cattle and 70 per cent kept sheep.[30] Small yeomen and customary tenants kept a cow or two for milk and perhaps butter. For the small man, in fact, the emphasis was on dairying rather than wintering or fattening. Nevertheless, the inventories do not support the view that a wholesale autumnal slaughter of animals took place to provide food stocks through the winter.[31]

Prosperous yeomen might deal in cattle at local fairs. Benjamin Browne of Troutbeck (1664–1748), a member of a long-established Lakeland yeoman family, rose in status to become high constable of the Kendal ward and, from

[29] CRO, D/Lons/L Check List 16/25, A2/15, ff. 1, 2, 15, 16, 23, and A1/16; Lancs. RO, DDCa 22/2 and 1/30; Levens Hall MSS, box 18 I, Banks's Accounts; G. P. Jones, 'Two Hudleston and Senhouse Account Books', *CW2*, LXVI, 1966, pp. 328–9. The Flemings of Rydal were also very active in the cattle trade. In 1683, 77 beasts were bought by Daniel Fleming at cattle fairs in Hawkeshead, Ravenglass, and Lancaster. The average cost was £3 13s. In 1685, about £146 was spent on purchases of cattle – W. F. Rawnsley, ed., *Rydal by the Late Miss Armitt*, Kendal, 1916, pp. 249–50.

[30] J. D. Marshall, 'The Domestic Economy of the Lakeland Yeoman, 1660–1749', *CW2*, LXXIII, 1973, pp. 197–9. For further evidence of cattle and sheep farming, see C. Moor, 'The Old Statesman Families of Irton', *CW2*, x, 1910, pp. 151–5. Since this chapter was written, J. D. Marshall has further developed his analysis of the Cumbria yeoman in 'Agrarian Wealth and Social Structure in Pre-Industrial Cumbria', *ECHR*, 2nd ser., XXXIII, 1980, pp. 503–21.

[31] For a statement of the old view, see T. H. Bainbridge, 'Eighteenth-Century Agriculture in Cumbria', *CW2*, XLII, 1942, pp. 56–66.

1729 to 1737, steward of Lord Lonsdale's property in the barony of Kendal. He traded in cattle on his own account, buying both Scottish drove cattle and Lakeland beasts, and keeping them over the winter. In November 1729, for example, "eight Scotts kine" were purchased for £1 8s. each at Penrith. In the following year, between January and June, he disposed of five Scottish calves for £1 17s. 6d. and sold seven Scottish cows between August and October for £18 0s. 11d. Browne's activities, though essentially small scale, ranged widely. He traded not only at Penrith, but also at fairs in Hawkshead, Ambleside, and Rosley. In the 1720s his cows were sold for between £3 and £3 10s. and calves for 5s. to 8s. Good-quality wethers, by contrast, rarely fetched more than 5s. and ewes 3s. to 4s. In addition, Browne sold small surpluses of wool, rarely more than five stones, for about 4s. a stone. His trading account regularly showed greater profit from cattle than from sheep. In 1723 cattle were sold to a total value of £11 18s. 6d.; sheep for £4 2s. In 1724–5, similarly, cattle realized 87 per cent of livestock sales; sheep only 13 per cent.[32] Browne's flock of sheep rarely exceeded one hundred and was kept largely for domestic purposes, while wintered cattle made a regular cash profit.

Inventory evidence, which remains reliable in this area until the end of the period, suggests that activity in the cattle trade was increasing from the end of the seventeenth century onwards and was beginning to attract even the less prosperous freeholders and customary tenants.[33] Reference was increasingly made to "black cattle" (usually Scots) purchased from drovers. Scottish cattle arrived in the region from June to December. Many were sold for wintering in the lowlands on hay and straw, and were resold by Cumbrian farmers to graziers further south the following spring. Some were kept throughout the summer on upland pastures before eventual sale to Lancashire and Yorkshire graziers or to London dealers at spring fairs. By 1730 John Ireland, a London butcher, was buying both cattle and sheep direct from Humphrey Senhouse at Netherhall, near Maryport.[34] The extent of sales of fat cattle to the Whitehaven butcher Thomas Lucas suggests that here meat was being salted for use in ships' stores.

In the early eighteenth century cattle markets were being held not only in the substantial towns like Carlisle, Penrith, Alston, Brough, Cockermouth, Kendal, and Kirkby Lonsdale, but in smaller places such as Orton and Shap.[35] The vitality of the trade is evident. As early as 1662–3 imports of 18,364 Scottish cattle were recorded at Carlisle. By the end of the eighteenth century

[32] KRO, D/TE, Benjamin Browne's Memoranda Books, LE and OB.

[33] On inventory evidence, see n. 70 below.

[34] E. Hughes, *North Country Life in the Eighteenth Century*, Vol. II, *Cumberland & Westmorland, 1700–1830*, Oxford, 1965, p. 12.

[35] J. D. Marshall, *Old Lakeland*, Newton Abbot, 1971, pp. 76–96. On drovers, see K. J. Bonser, *The Drovers*, London, 1970, esp. pp. 132–5, 148–59.

10,000 Scottish cattle were sold annually at the September Brough Hill fair alone.[36]

The importance of the cattle trade is also shown by the institution of 'border service' in 1662. By an 'Act for preventing of Theft and Rapine upon the Northern Borders of England', justices of the peace were empowered to raise £2,000 annually with which to employ an official, known as the country-keeper, to catch "thieves and robbers, who were commonly called Moss-Troopers", engaged in horse and cattle stealing. The act, amended in 1678 to make the country-keeper responsible for losses sustained from border predators, remained in operation until 1757. It was designed to deal with the last vestiges of border feuding. Cattle stealing was especially attractive because of the separate legal systems of England and Scotland, whereby offences committed in one country could not normally be punished in the other. There is little to suggest that border raids were a major problem, or that they seriously interrupted the cattle trade even during the 1715 and 1745 rebellions, but border landowners considered it worth while to support this policing-cum-insurance system from their own pockets until the middle of the eighteenth century.[37]

As the trade developed, wintering of Scottish cattle began to provide small surpluses even for quite modest yeomen. The surprisingly extensive credit network enabled larger numbers to participate.[38] Cash on credit could be used to buy cattle for wintering and to take advantage of the extensive drove roads which operated on both easterly and westerly routes through the two counties.[39]

The strength of the cattle trade was in part due to the impact of the Irish Cattle Act of 1667. The import of beasts from Ireland was prohibited and the price of English and Scottish livestock thereby raised, benefiting the cattle counties of north and west. The extent of this bonus may be gauged by the fact that between 8,000 and 9,000 Irish cattle had been arriving in Carlisle annually in the early 1660s through the Cumberland ports, particularly Workington. This represented between one-quarter and one-third of all imports to England.[40] By 1695, Charles Davenant was arguing that the north-west was underassessed for taxation purposes because "The prohibition

[36] PRO, S.P. Dom., Charles II, vol. 79, no. 3; A. Pringle, *General View of the Agriculture of Westmorland*, Edinburgh, 1794, p. 22.

[37] The act establishing border service is 13 & 14 Car. II, c. 22. J. Kirby, 'Border Service, 1662–1757', *CW2*, XLVIII, 1948, pp. 125–9.

[38] G. P. Jones, 'Sources of Loans and Credits in Cumbria before the Rise of Banks', *CW2*, LXXV, 1975, pp. 275–92. This picture is reinforced, largely from Lincolnshire evidence, by B. A. Holderness, 'Credit in English Rural Society before the Nineteenth Century', *AHR*, XXIV, 1976, pp. 97–109.

[39] J. D. Marshall provides maps of known and assumed routes in *Old Lakeland*, pp. 82, 84.

[40] 18 & 19 Car. II, c. 2. The act is reprinted in part in T & C, pp. 155–60. D. Woodward, 'The Anglo-Irish Livestock Trade of the Seventeenth Century', *Irish Hist. Stud.*, XVIII, 1972–3, p. 497. See also pt II, ch. 16 below, pp. 453–4.

of Irish cattle is wholly beneficial to the northern and western counties, and is hurtful to the rest of England."[41]

The act did not erect an impenetrable barrier, however. A report on Whitehaven to the Committee of Customs in 1704 remarked "that the country here is in a great measure supplied with beef and other provisions from Ireland which happens by their going thither for victualling their ships to Virginia before they take in their cargo here. Upon their return they sell what they can to the country, which is a very great prejudice to the market of this place." The reporters were also given to understand that Irish clothing was in regular use in the area.[42]

The only significant check to the trade was the cattle plague of the late 1740s. It reached the Pennington area of Furness in May 1749 and watches were placed on the Lancashire–Cumberland border to prevent the movement of cattle. With such restrictions in force in southern Lakeland some landlords could not let good grazing ground, and tenants were unable to fill stints which previously had been precious. One writer has suggested that the plague was serious enough to encourage tenants to plough up their pastures and seek better arable cultivation through enclosure. This is an extreme view. More likely the plague was a temporary setback and the enclosures of the later eighteenth century, particularly in west Cumberland, were facilitated rather by the pressures of human population.[43]

Estate records further emphasize the primacy of cattle in the agricultural economy of Cumbria. Sheep rearing took second place on the estates of the Lowthers of Lowther. Though wool valued at £250 was disposed of in 1719, no regular income came from this source. Similarly, the Lowthers of Maulds Meaburn, though they sometimes held flocks in excess of 500, sold wool only spasmodically, as in 1732 and 1743 when £117 and £168 respectively were realized. Sales of sheep themselves averaged less than £10 a year between 1738 and 1745. The 2,000 sheep on the Muncaster farm of the Pennington family were valued in 1730 at £435, considerably more than the value of their cattle. The estate was leased out at this time, and when the home farm was worked again in the 1730s, cattle rearing resumed pride of place.[44]

Butter and cheese production in the region was largely domestic in scale.

---

[41] *An Essay upon Ways and Means*, repr. in T & C, pp. 806–7.

[42] CRO, D/Lons/W Misc. Harbour Papers. Irish beef was still being supplied to west Cumberland in 1730, as the Lowther accounts make clear – *ibid.*, Housekeeping Accounts, 1729–39, entry Nov. 1730.

[43] CRO, D/Pen, Agents' Correspondence, Herbert to Pennington, 4 Dec. 1750; C. F. Mullett, 'The Cattle Distemper in Mid-Eighteenth-Century England', *Agric. Hist.*, xx, 1946, pp. 144–65; G. Elliott, 'Field Systems of Northwest England', in A. R. H. Baker and R. A. Butlin, eds., *Studies of Field Systems in the British Isles*, Cambridge, 1973, p. 80; J. F. Curwen, *The Later Records of North Westmorland*, Cumb. & Westmor. Antiq. & Arch. Soc. Report Ser., VIII, Kendal, 1932, p. 225. See also below, pt II, ch. 16, pp. 359–61.

[44] CRO, D/Lons/L box Acc. 5, A2/78, AM66, AM74, AM11; D/Pen 97 and 219.

More substantial yeoman families, such as the Fells of Swarthmoor Hall, had a small regular income from butter sales at local markets; some cheese was also sold, realizing not quite £2 in 1674, for example, but cheese production was on a much smaller scale in Furness than in the remainder of Lancashire. Cheese presses are rarely encountered in Cumbrian inventories.[45]

The size of Cumbrian sheep flocks has been overestimated. Inventories suggest that yeoman flocks rarely exceeded 200, with a late-seventeenth-century average around 50 for both highland and lowland farmers.[46] If Hutchinson's calculations of seven fleeces to the stone weight be accepted, wool at 4s. 6d. to 5s. a stone in the late seventeenth century offered no prospect of riches; in some years it hardly offered a surplus.[47] Some yeomen, of course, operated on a larger scale. In 1672, William Sawrey of Coniston Waterhead possessed cattle, sheep, and horses worth together £87 10s.; his wool was valued at £12 10s., which represented clippings in excess of sixty stones. John Braithwaite's 150 sheep in 1672 produced wool worth only £3 6s. 8d., despite the fact that his flock was well above the average size.[48] The larger flocks seem to have been concentrated in southern Lakeland, particularly in the vicinity of Kendal. The reason is clear. Kendal was the main woollen town of the region and was from the late seventeenth century growing both in size and prosperity. Though increasingly importing long-stapled wool from the Midlands for use in the stocking trade, Kendal still made use of the coarse, short-stapled wool of the Cumbrian fell sheep in traditional woollen manufactures, in the so-called Kendal cottons and in linsey-wolsey.[49] Such branches of the textile trade relied to a greater extent on domestic outwork. Local wool was spun by yeoman families, and Furness

[45] J. D. Marshall, 'Domestic Economy', p. 204; N. Penney, ed., *The Household Account Book of Sarah Fell*, Cambridge, 1920, pp. 26–166.

[46] 'Domestic Economy', p. 193. The inventories do not support E. Kerridge's contention that "sheep farming was supreme" in the Lake District – *The Agricultural Revolution*, London, 1967, p. 165.

[47] Hutchinson, *History of Cumberland, I*, pp. 532, 570. In the first half of the eighteenth century, wool prices only rarely exceeded 5s. a stone. In 1707, 1709, and 1736, prices were as low as 2s. 6d. – KRO, Browne MSS, vii, p. 149, B. Browne to Lady Elizabeth Otway, 25 Oct. 1707; *ibid.*, vii, p. 151, 23 Jan. 1709; CRO, D/Lons/W, Spedding to Lowther, 26 Oct. 1736. In 1713, 1723, and 1751 prices were between 4s. 6d. and 5s. – Levens Hall MSS, box D, Thomas Pierson to James Grahame, 22 June 1713; KRO, Browne MSS, vii, p. 172, Browne to Otway, 24 Dec. 1714; CRO, D/Lec/170, John Walker to Thomas Elder, 28 Feb. 1723; *ibid.*, D/Pen, Agents' Correspondence, Herbert to Pennington, 11 Oct. 1751. Only in 1746 and 1748 is there clear evidence of wool prices reaching 5s. 9d. to 6s. – CRO, D/Pen, Agents' Correspondence, L. Herbert to Sir John Pennington, 25 June 1746; *ibid.*, D/Pen/114, Herbert to Pennington, 15 June 1748.

[48] J. D. Marshall, 'Domestic Economy', p. 194.

[49] *Ibid.*, pp. 194–6, and J. D. Marshall, *Kendal 1661–1801: The Growth of a Modern Town*, Kendal, 1975, pp. 23–6. On the unsatisfactory evidence regarding breeds of Cumbrian sheep, see Bouch and Jones, *The Lake Counties*, pp. 102–3, 347–8.

inventories between 1663 and 1681 indicate that spinning-wheels were kept in about one-third of their cottages. The extent of domestic outwork servicing the Kendal trade should not be overestimated. It was restricted both geographically and in range and should be seen as part of an essentially subsistence economy, except in the immediate vicinity of Kendal.[50]

Most subsistence farmers kept a few pigs and chickens. John Grigg of Milnthorpe was quite exceptional in possessing as many as fifteen pigs in 1673. Very few yeomen brought bacon to market. Eggs were probably more common, though prices were low and it is more realistic to see hens and chickens supplying the needs of the family. The small farmer did not have the resources to keep hens and chickens secure from the depredations of foxes.

Arable crops were mostly oats and bigg for animal and domestic consumption. The first was a fodder crop and also the basis of the oat bread – or 'clap-bread' – which so impressed Celia Fiennes and which was the staple diet of the farming community. Bigg, a coarse variety of barley, was also much grown both on lowland and fell; it too was a fodder crop but used also in the home for malting and brewing. These two crops dominate inventory lists. Wheat and rye are seldom mentioned, though on the coastal plain peas and beans seem to have been grown in increasing quantities both for animal and domestic consumption.[51]

Most cereal production took place in the lowlands of Furness, in the Solway plain, and in the Eden and Kent valleys. Around Kendal, the Reverend Thomas Machell found "a good store of arable ground" in 1692. Almost eighty years later Arthur Young was surprised to find rotations of turnips, barley, wheat, and oats near Penrith. He was also told that "much land, even within two or three miles of *Penrith* hath been sown every year with either barley, oats, or pease for these seventy years". On his southward journey after the "dreary prospect" of uncultivated Shap Fells "melancholy to behold", he descended into "one of the finest landscapes in the world; a noble range of fertile inclosures" just north of Kendal.[52]

Subsistence farming dictated that more land should be under the plough, permanently or temporarily, in this period than later. Marshall has calculated that two-thirds of yeoman farmers in the southern part of the region had

[50] J. D. Marshall, 'Domestic Economy', p. 195. Marshall notes that inventories probably understate involvement in the trade, since some wheels were considered wives' property and not included in their husbands' effects.

[51] Fiennes, *op. cit.*, pp. 193–4; J. D. Marshall, 'Domestic Economy', pp. 200–1. Sarah Fell's account books make occasional reference to small sales of wheat. One peck was sold for 3s. 1d. in Sept. 1676 – Penney, *op. cit.*, p. 306. Inventories usually list crop values collectively, thus preventing systematic analysis of particular grains from this source. Wheat is mentioned in only 2 of the 80 sample inventories of the deaneries of Coupland and Kendal in the 1660s in the Lancs. RO.

[52] Ewbank, *op. cit.*, p. 4; Arthur Young, *A Six Months Tour through the North of England*, 4 vols., London, 1770, *III*, pp. 125–6, 169.

between four and eight modern acres of land devoted to oats or bigg. In good years arable production was sufficient, even on the small, shifting arable closes owned by fell farmers or on intakes from the waste, to feed a yeoman family and permit sales of surplus at local markets. With difficulty it was possible to clear small portions of upland of heather, moss, and stones, and sow oats, bigg, or even beans in temporary cultivation. Even in good years, however, sales rarely realized more than £2 or £3; in bad years soaring market prices bore heavily on stocks of available cash.

The smallest proprietors in remote dales needed to be self-sufficient, as their cash reserves were usually slender. George Dawson of Grasmere, who died in 1660 owning only three heifers and twenty-eight sheep, had small quantities of hay and corn valued at 16s. His livestock was valued at £7 16s. 8d. out of total assets of £9 15s. 3d. Robert Dixon of Langdale had total assets of £19 2s. 10d. in 1662, £15 of which represented cattle and sheep; £1 12s. of the remainder derived from hay and corn. Inventory appraisers often failed to separate hay and corn in their valuations, and this was an almost invariable practice in dealing with small freeholders and customary tenants worth £30 or less. It is thus impossible to speak with precision, but such examples as these indicate something of the delicate calculations necessary for mixed farming to succeed in the Cumbrian uplands.[53]

Common arable fields in Cumbria varied greatly in size, but arable farming here too was practised essentially within the context of a pastoral economy. 'Townfields', as the common fields were often called, were divided into strips known as 'furlongs', 'doles', or 'rivings' of variable size; they were often spring-sown with oats. Arable fields were frequently used for summer grazing, tethered stock being introduced into parts of the field divided by 'merestones', ring dykes or 'reans'. Trespass of cattle on growing crops remained a problem, as manor court evidence indicates.[54] Some portions of the common fields were also regarded as meadow, and hay crops were taken. In Aspatria 119 of 270 acres of infield were so regarded; documents frequently refer to 'arable meadow and pasture'.

Individual holdings within townfields seem to have been dispersed, as elsewhere, but fields were subject to far less regulated cultivation.[55] In Furness, townfields were generally small. The Askam field comprised only thirty-four acres of arable and meadow doles. Dendron had two townfields

[53] J. D. Marshall, 'Domestic Economy', p. 200; Lancs. RO, Inventories of the archdeaconry of Richmond – deaneries of Coupland and Kendal.

[54] KRO, Musgrave D.P. Court Rolls, 1704, 1706; CRO, D/Lons, Kirkandrews Court Roll, 1703. For evidence of the variable size of holdings, see Baker and Butlin, *op. cit.*, pp. 45–6, and T. H. B. Graham, 'The Common Fields of Hayton', *CW2*, VIII, 1908, p. 344. See also evidence of regulation at Torver, Muchland Manor, 1738, in J. D. Marshall, *Furness*, p. 13.

[55] Recent investigation goes against the view of H. L. Gray, *English Field Systems*, Cambridge, Mass., 1915, pp. 234–5, that holdings in the north-west were generally consolidated – Baker and Butlin, *op. cit.*, pp. 50–2.

with intermixed strips early in the eighteenth century. One was laid to pasture for three years while the other was ploughed or mown for hay. In High Furness, as in Church Coniston and Broughton, common fields were mostly farmed for hay to feed stock. Visitors to the area were scathing. Thomas Pennant asserted in 1772 (though he exaggerates) that "within these twenty miles even the use of dung was scarcely known to them". Thomas West criticized the system of "mixed lands and township fields" in 1773: "domestic economy calls for improvement of every acre; this can never be done where there is a common of pasture, by which every man has it in his power to prevent his neighbour's industry".[56]

As has already been indicated, the region had few large farms, and most arable cultivation took place on small landholdings. New husbandry techniques were rare and introduced very slowly. In Cumberland, primitive methods resulted in overcropping on small estates; white crops were sown year after year, the stubble to be grazed by cattle. As late as 1800, Housman castigated Cumberland farmers who "injudiciously exhaust their land by long continued cropping". "The most general rule is to sow from two to five or six white crops in succession; and there are some instances where land has been ploughed and sown with corn from time immemorial." His working notes on Greystoke show that arable land was of poor quality, as meadow and pasture "are the husbandman's chief objects...On the banks of Ullswater, one parcel of arable land has been cropped yearly for above a century, barley or bigg one year, and oats the next and so alternately."[57] The copyholders of Holme Cultram in the middle of the seventeenth century ploughed up most of Colt Park three years in succession, then left it as a stinted common for the next six. The 344 acres of 'Acre-dales' were divided into four 'rivings' and similarly sown for three years, then left to common pasture for nine. On Rydal demesne, too, shifting cultivation was practised, oats alternating with bigg. In the third year the land fell back to grass and another part of the fields was cultivated. Ploughing began in February with oats sown in mid March. Barley for malting was bought in to supplement the small quantities sown. In 1698, for example, seven bushels were sown and fifty-two bushels obtained for brewing purposes.[58]

Given the importance of winter feed, much attention was paid to the hay crop. Most of the lowest valley closes in the highland zone were meadow and permanent grass. In the moorlands, shifting long-ley cultivation, mostly of oats and bigg, was in operation and in small closes near farmsteads up-and-down husbandry was practised. In Westmorland, which has much

[56] Thomas Pennant, *Tour in Scotland*, Chester, 1774, p. 26; Thomas West, *Antiquities of Furness*, London, 1774, p. xxiii, quoted in J. D. Marshall, *Furness*, p. 13.

[57] J. Housman, *A Topographical Description of Cumberland, Westmorland and Lancashire*, Carlisle, 1800, p. 59. See also W. Dickinson, 'On the Farming of Cumberland', *J. Roy. Agric. Soc.*, XIII, 1852, p. 226, and Hutchinson, *op. cit.*, I, p. 406. See also Housman's comments on repeated cropping – *op. cit.*, p. 678.

[58] Kerridge, *op. cit.*, p. 172; Rawnsley, *Rydal*, pp. 251–3.

less lowland than Cumberland, Pringle estimated in the 1790s that only 20,000 acres were under corn crops in any one year. "The remaining 115,000 acres [of cultivation] are cut for hay, or depastured with fattening beasts and rising stock, or with cows applied to the purposes of the dairy." The most common course was to plough the grass when overrun with moss and spring-sow oats for harvest in September. Bigg was sown the following year and oats again in the third. Animal grazing over the autumn stubble provided enough manure to permit a three-year arable cycle. Spring-sowing was, therefore, a prerequisite. After three years "The land is then left to itself, and in the first year it produces a light crop of hay of bad quality...In seven or ten years it is again mossed over, and is again ploughed up to undergo a similar treatment."[59] Minor variations are found, but on yeoman estates there was little significant deviation from this unimaginative course. It answered the basic purposes of a largely subsistence fell-country economy which survived almost intact throughout the period.

Important developments in agriculture took place between 1640 and 1750, nevertheless. Cumberland saw much piecemeal enclosure. In the Pennine foothills, Melmerby was enclosed some time between 1677 and 1704. On the Solway, the commons of Burgh barony, which the first viscount Lonsdale acquired from the duke of Norfolk in 1685, were enclosed in 1699. Almost 1,500 acres of common land had been enclosed in Hayton, probably early in the seventeenth century. The Musgraves of Edenhall, substantial purchasers in the buoyant land market at the end of the seventeenth century, generally followed such activity by consolidation. When they leased Carlisle Field from the cathedral dean and chapter between 1674 and 1702, they introduced systematic liming and considerably raised the value of the corn crop. Sir John Clerk noted the "rich pasturage and fine corns just a reaping" on view at Sir Christopher Musgrave's estate in 1731. The Musgraves extended and consolidated their lands east of Penrith and near Kirkby Stephen, with a net expenditure in excess of £10,000 between 1705 and 1750.

In Aspatria land was reallocated among tenants of both the east and west outfields, which ensured the consolidation of a number of previously scattered riggs into two or three compact holdings well before formal enclosure in 1758–9. In Westmorland, too, enclosure proceeded piecemeal, though not extensively by 1750, except around Kendal. Here Celia Fiennes, approaching the town from the south-west, noted "very good land enclosed, little round green hills flourishing with corn and grass...green and fresh".[60]

Not all the families in a position to enclose did so; the Lowthers of

[59] Pringle, *op. cit.*, pp. 18–21; Baker and Butlin, *op. cit.*, pp. 63–7.

[60] Baker and Butlin, *op. cit.*, pp. 76–84; CRO, D/Lons/L S.L. Barony of Burgh 14; Beckett, thesis, pp. 99–100; G. Elliott, 'The Enclosure of Aspatria', *CW2*, LX, 1960, pp. 100–1. See also evidence for similar consolidation of strips into three fields at Brigham in 1640 – Fiennes, *op. cit.*, p. 190.

Whitehaven provide a prime example of one which did not. Sir John Lowther (1642–1706) and his second son, Sir James (1673–1755), bought massively in an attempt to acquire a monopoly of coal-bearing ground and make Whitehaven a commercial and industrial centre of the first rank. Sir John is known to have spent over £11,000 on fifty-seven separate purchases of property between 1661 and 1705, mostly within a five-mile radius of Whitehaven. His son extended the enterprise. Between 1706 and 1754 over £47,000 was expended on property in seventy-nine purchases extending the Lowther interest in the north to Holme Cultram and southwards to Calder Abbey, a few miles south-east of Egremont. Such activity naturally raised land prices in an area where property was already changing hands at a rate considerably greater than the national average. The Lowthers' interest, however, was in the coal beneath the land, and for various reasons associated with colliery production they would lease land near Whitehaven only in small parcels. Even so, they paid little attention to properties further afield, and farm sizes were allowed to remain much as they always had been.

The basic lack of concern over farms is reflected in antiquated leases. A tenant of Sir John Lowther at St Bees in 1689 was enjoined to "well and orderly husband and till the said demised ground; and the same when ploughed shall lime or manure according to the need thereof". A standard clause in leases from the 1740s was more precise but by no means indicative of the spread of new techniques. The tenant was "not to plough above one-third in any one year and no part above three years together and then to lie fallow six years, to manure what is ploughed, to keep down the whins, to spread the vestures and leave the manure at the end of the term".[61] Similarly, the Lowthers of Lowther did little to influence their tenantry. Leases changed little from a standard covenant to follow the usual course of husbandry. In the 1730s, however, the maximum number of acres to be ploughed was stipulated and penalties laid down for those who exceeded the quota. On the Holker estate, likewise, none of the leases made any stipulation about the cultivation of crops. Tenants were not to plough for more than three years, then leave in ley, generally for six. The Grahmes of Levens were also unadventurous. The stipulation in a lease from 1681 that the Heversham demesne was to be manured once every three years if put to crops was unchanged by the 1740s. When the Penningtons of Muncaster offered Langley Park for lease in 1730 the covenants enjoined not to plough more than 20 of the 227 acres in any one year, nor any parcel of ground more than three years together.[62]

The only sustained evidence of progressive leases in the region comes from

[61] Beckett, thesis, pp. 211–15, 229–31; CRO, D/Lons/W, box Estate memoranda books, estate ledger, 1738–57, f. 110.

[62] CRO, D/Lons/L S.L. Cardew 8; Lancs. RO, DDCa 10/72–4, 84; 2/4–5; Levens Hall MSS, boxes 6/3, 2/18, 14/29; CRO, D/Pen 203 f. 109.

the estates of the earl of Carlisle in the 1730s and 1740s. The number of acres which might be converted to tillage and to the use of lime were both precisely stipulated. In 1750 the farmers of Brampton Townfoot were to fallow 40 of the 401 acres on the farm, planting 20 with rye and 20 with turnips. Significantly, some of the largest farms in the region were on the Carlisle estate; Askerton, leased in 1741 for £265 per annum, may have been the biggest of all, and large farms resulted from positive enclosure policies between c. 1690 and 1740.[63]

Such experiments as there were in new husbandry took place largely on the home farms of the upper gentry and peerage, and most spectacularly on that of the earl of Carlisle. Here John Nowell, steward to the earl's estates centred on Naworth Castle in north-east Cumberland, developed improved stocks by new husbandry techniques in the 1730s and 1740s; stock value in 1739 was £1,200. Turnips and clover were extensively used and some of the oxen sold in 1739 were specifically advertised as having been fed on turnips. The same programme was in use at Naworth Park in the 1740s after Brampton Townfoot was leased out. Such developments indicate that previous claims for the introduction of new crops to Cumbria by Philip Howard of Corby Castle in the 1750s are in need of substantial revision.[64] The improvements did not spread very far, however, the heavy clay soils of north-east Cumberland hardly inviting extensive turnip cultivation.

Dutch white clover was grown on the home farm of Sir James Lowther of Whitehaven in the 1750s, and considerable experimentation was carried out on Lord Lonsdale's Lowther estate between 1720 and 1751. The third viscount had sainfoin and clover sent from London in 1724 for planting on Thrimby Moor. In 1732 horses were bought specifically for "marling the Hare park". Clover seed was sent to Lowther in 1749 and in 1751 instructions were printed "for the management of the ground and the sowing of turnips etc."[65] In Westmorland a half-hearted attempt seems to have been made to introduce asparagus at Levens in 1695; ten bushels of sainfoin and two of ryegrass were purchased for the estate of Robert Lowther at Crosby Fell in 1734, but these seem to be the only references to improved husbandry in the county, and there is no evidence to suggest that either venture was successful or continued during this period.[66]

[63] Durham Univ., Howard of Naworth Papers C/117, C 129a/14, C 170/53, C 172/52, C 629/63, 65.

[64] *Ibid.*, C/627, C 173/55. The old view on improvement is found in T. Bainbridge, 'Eighteenth-Century Agriculture in Cumbria', *CW2*, XLII, 1942, pp. 56–66. Bainbridge concentrates on the second half of the century and relies on Arthur Young's northern tour and the evidence of the Board of Agriculture reporters.

[65] CRO, D/Lons/W Housekeeping Accounts, 1750–5; D/Lons/L A2/52, ff. 32, 34, A2/76 f. 47, A2/78 f. 15; box D/Lons VII stray letters, Lonsdale to R. Wordsworth, 9 Mar. 1732.

[66] Levens Hall MSS, box C, H. James to J. Grahme, 12 Mar. 1695; CRO, D/Lons/L AM 58, entry, 16 Mar. 1734.

Liming and marling were not unknown in the extreme north-west during the period. Lime was introduced early in the seventeenth century and used on many estates, particularly on the limestone areas of Furness and west Cumberland. Sir John Lowther recommended to his Whitehaven tenants that they lime their land in the 1680s, and Sir William Lowther and Sir William Pennington introduced systematic liming of their estates at Holker and Muncaster respectively at the end of the seventeenth century. Inventory references to lime are infrequent, but there are just enough to suggest that its use was not confined to a few substantial gentry families on their home farms. Henry Caddy of Muncaster, for example, had "corn, hay, hemp and lime" to the value of £13 in a total estate valued at £33. Benjamin Browne of Troutbeck limed arable ground in the 1720s on which he grew oats, bigg, and peas. As the ports of Whitehaven and Workington developed, lime was regularly burned in west Cumberland coastal parishes such as Cleator and Distington before being shipped to Scotland. Housman remarked at the end of the eighteenth century that farmyard dung and lime were still the only effective improvers in use in Cumberland. Despite the discovery of extensive deposits of marl on the estate of the Lowthers of Whitehaven in 1729, this fertilizer was not much used by 1750.[67] Housman, in explaining its absence, indicated that "it would be difficult, perhaps, to persuade the farmers to make experiment so averse are they, in general, to the adopting of any new mode, however well recommended". In Westmorland, "great attention is paid to the making of *compost*...One hundred cart loads of earth, raking of roads, mud, or rotten leaves, and fifty of dung, carefully mixed with three hundred Winchester bushels of lime, are laid upon three acres with great advantage." Housman's attack on Cumberland farmers was equally relevant to those of Westmorland and was typical of the blanket condemnation of the late-eighteenth-century improvers: "the greatest bar in the way of improvement, is, *the unconquerable prejudice* of the farmers in favour of old-established systems and their aversion to experiments and to the calculation of the advantages of the different modes of management".[68]

The region may claim some kind of primacy in the cultivation of one crop. The inventory of Christopher Gaitskell of Ponsonby, north of Gosforth, dated 7 March 1664, lists "Beans, pease, hempseed and potateis" to the value of 8s. This is one of the first pieces of evidence of potato cultivation in

[67] Lancs. RO, DDCa10/40; CRO, D/Lons/L Survey List 2, correspondence bundle 19, Lowther to Lady Lonsdale, 21 Oct. 1700; D/Pen 203 f. 43; Lancs. RO, Misc. Probate Inventories, Deanery of Richmond; KRO, D/TE Benjamin Browne's Account Books; Hutchinson, *op. cit.* II, pp. 29, 99. James Lowther's agent, John Spedding, informed his master in Feb. 1729 that gentlemen had employed "a Lancashire man to try their grounds for marl, of which he had found good veins in Mr. Brisco's, Mr. Appleby's and some other grounds" – CRO, D/Lons/W, Spedding to Lowther, 26 Feb. 1729. These experiments seem to have had little immediate result.

[68] Housman, *Topographical Description*, pp. 63, 65, 98–9.

England, though it is not entirely clear whether it predates the introduction of the tuber to west Lancashire. At all events, potatoes were being grown in Furness by the 1670s. Sarah Fell of Swarthmoor paid 8d. for one peck in October 1673 and 1s. for three "hoopes of setting potaties" in April 1674. William Gilpin wrote from Whitehaven to Sir John Lowther in 1697: 'Wee have the Lancashire potato (esteemed better than the Irish) but ye ground here either is not proper or wee have not arrived at skill sufficient to raise them to ye perfection they are in elsewhere. The markett is however comonly plentifully supply'd with them." Humphrey Senhouse was buying seed potatoes at 4d. a peck in Millom in 1701; potatoes were sold in Drigg by 1707 and over 650 bushels were sold from there in 1727. It seems reasonable to infer that potatoes were firmly established in south-west Cumbria by the first decade of the eighteenth century. From there they spread out slowly north and east, and are listed in the occasional east Cumberland inventory in the 1730s and 1740s,[69] but remain an essentially plainland phenomenon. On the Lancashire mosses potatoes rapidly established themselves as a cash crop, but cultivation remained on a fairly small scale in Cumbria. They were grown mostly in gardens. Sarah Fell used them as such and grew potatoes alongside cabbages and onions for domestic consumption. No doubt they were used also as an animal feed, though on a smaller scale than in Lancashire south of Morecambe Bay.

There seems to have been a general if moderate increase in prosperity during the period. A sample of 400 inventories for the periods 1661–90 and 1721–50 from Kendal deanery (admittedly one of the wealthiest parts of the region) analysed by Marshall indicates that whereas 39 per cent of yeomen had property valued at less than £40 in the latter seventeenth century, only 25 per cent were so circumstanced in the second quarter of the eighteenth. The percentage of those owning property worth more than £100 had increased from 24 to 45. Total gross values increased from £18,055 to £29,073 (61 per cent). The income of fell farmers – those from districts more than 400 feet above sea level – rose by 52 per cent; that of lowlanders by 68 per cent.[70] The inventories record a total increase in value of all farm goods of 30 per cent, but the more significant increase is in the amount of credit in bills and bonds. These totalled £7,767 in the earlier period and £14,170 in the later, an increase of 82 per cent. Since total moneys owing listed in inventories rose from £3,663 to £8,918 (143 per cent), it seems clear that a significant debt and credit network was developing and was available

[69] J. D. Marshall, 'Domestic Economy', p. 203; CRO, D/Pen 90; Penney, op. cit., pp. 5, 57; CRO, D/Lons/W, W. Gilpin to Sir John Lowther, 29 Dec. 1697; Hughes, op. cit., p. 14; CRO, Misc. Probate Inventories.

[70] The full table is printed in J. D. Marshall, Kendal, p. 17. Marshall recognizes that in general fewer people submitted detailed inventories in the later period, but challenges the view that this increased the likelihood of fatally biased samples which exaggerate the average wealth of Cumbrian yeomen. As befits a remote area, detailed inventories remained rather more common in the Lake District in the 1730s and 1740s than elsewhere.

to quite humble farmers in the region. The property listed by Marshall in his analysis of 775 inventories throughout the region in bills and bonds averaged 37.7 per cent of the total in 1661–90 and 47.9 per cent in 1721–50. Almost a quarter of the sample 400 yeomen from Kendal deanery who died between 1660 and 1689 were credited with bonds or mortgages of £25 or more.

The account books of Sarah Fell are full of examples of small loans made to servants, local craftsmen, and traders in the 1670s which lubricated day-to-day commerce; some debts and loans, though, were for considerable sums. In 1674, for example, £200 was borrowed at $5\frac{1}{2}$ per cent from Hugh Tickell of Portinscale. By the end of the period we know of one large-scale moneylender in south Lakeland. Margaret Lancaster of Lyth was regularly lending sums of between £200 and £300. She was the widow of Richard Lancaster, who in 1737 left property worth £2,659, of which no less than £2,606 was in credits. The Lancaster family was obviously exceptional, and Richard's inventory was almost four times as valuable as any other in Marshall's survey.[71] Nevertheless, it seems clear that the extent of medium- and long-term credit for commercial and possibly agricultural enterprise has been seriously underestimated.

Various impressive industrial developments in this period partially or totally liberated increasing numbers from dependence on the land as a source of income. Most spectacular among these was the development of Whitehaven as a coal-producing and commercial centre. The existence of plentiful and relatively accessible coal seams persuaded Sir John Lowther to develop a purpose-built community in west Cumberland for its production and marketing. His 'new town' of Whitehaven became one of the most celebrated and busy ports in Britain during the first half of the eighteenth century. Employment opportunities multiplied as the Lowthers opened new pits, while the rapidly expanding coal trade to Ireland provided further jobs. For a few years in the 1740s, also, Whitehaven had a considerable re-export trade in tobacco to France. Sir James Lowther failed to obtain the monopoly of coal-bearing land which he sought in the 1720s, but his efforts spurred others with the result that the Curwens, in the fight against Lowther expansionism, developed Workington as an industrial rival in west Cumberland. A few miles further north, Maryport was in the early stages of development by 1750.[72]

---

[71] G. P. Jones, 'Sources of Loans', pp. 275–92. It is a serious defect of our present knowledge that we have so little evidence of the uses to which such loans were put. We are grateful to Dr Marshall for information about Richard Lancaster.

[72] J. V. Beckett, *Coal and Tobacco: The Lowthers and the Industrial Development of West Cumberland, 1660–1760*, Cambridge, 1981. See also D. Hay, *Whitehaven*, Whitehaven, 1979; R. Millward, 'The Cumbrian Town between 1600 and 1800', in C. W. Chalklin and M. A. Havinden, eds., *Rural Growth and Urban Development, 1500–1800*, London, 1974, pp. 204–28; and see J. E. Williams, 'Whitehaven in the Eighteenth Century', EcHR, 2nd ser., VIII, 1956, pp. 393–404.

Whitehaven stimulated various kinds of by-employment. Coal 'leaders', moving coal from pit-head to harbour in carts pulled by their own horses, were often yeoman farmers adding to their farming income. Sir John Lowther recognized the need for other occupations in the town. He observed perceptively in 1686 that "the country is already in the practice of making linen, sacking, coarse woollen stockings, hats etc. If wool, flax, hemp or other materials were but laid in as a stock and distributed to such as would employ themselves therein I doubt not that workmen might more easily be had to make them up."[73] Lowther in fact attempted to establish a domestic knitting industry around Whitehaven in 1697 while imports of raw Irish wool were permitted. When the trade embargo was reimposed in 1699, however, the enterprise had to be abandoned, as indigenous Cumbrian wool was too coarse for the industry.

Developments in coal stimulated other activities. For a while in the early eighteenth century something akin to mining mania gripped the gentry. Some had temporary success, but too many overstretched their resources in inflated expectation of massive profits from coal, copper, iron, or lead. It may be significant that six of the gentry families forced to sell up during this period are known to have been heavily committed to mining investment but without the extensive capital resources necessary for success.[74] In west Cumberland coal mining stimulated the iron industry. Iron ore was mined here throughout the seventeenth century and a furnace was built at Clifton, near Workington, in 1723. Here Isaac Wilkinson, father of the ironmaster John Wilkinson, began his career before moving south to Furness c. 1730.[75] The large quantities of coppice wood in Furness which could be used in charcoal burning gave that area a natural advantage in iron production, a benefit accentuated by the availability of haematite ore in Dalton. 'Bloomsmithies' had been used to make iron, largely for domestic use, from the sixteenth century. Bloomery forges developed during the seventeenth century. They were in existence at Cunsey in 1623, Ulpha by 1625, and Colwith by 1652. The Backbarrow forge is known to have been in operation by 1685.[76]

Blast furnaces, revolutionizing the technology of the iron industry, did not come to Furness until 1711, when the Backbarrow Company was

---

[73] CRO, D/Lons/W, Letter Books, Sir J. Lowther to T. Addison, 25 Sept. 1686.

[74] The financial troubles of Thomas Lamplugh and the Blennherhasset family can probably be ascribed to mining adventures. The Lowthers apart, only Eldred Curwen in Workington can have been entirely happy with the financial return. In 1742 and 1743 his mining profits, after resisting a Lowther attempt to buy him out, totalled more than £2,000 – Beckett, *Coal and Tobacco*, p. 81.

[75] W. H. Chaloner, 'Isaac Wilkinson, Potfounder', in L. S. Pressnell, ed., *Studies in the Industrial Revolution*, London, 1969, pp. 24–5.

[76] A. Fell, *The Early Iron Industry in Furness and District*, Ulverston, 1908, pp. 105–21; Bouch and Jones, *The Lake Counties*, pp. 127–30.

founded by four local ironmasters anxious to meet the challenge of a smelting furnace built by two Cheshire entrepreneurs at Cunsey Beck, near the western shores of Lake Windermere. This company built a second blast furnace at Leighton, near Arnside, in 1713. The shrewdness of local masters in establishing a cartel to regulate both price and availability of precious charcoal, combined with a sharp rise in prices after the suspension of trade with Sweden in 1717, effected a considerable iron boom in Furness. Between November 1717 and October 1718 the Leighton furnace made a book profit of £1,965, about £2 13s. 6d. on every ton of iron produced. Production costs barely exceeded £4 a ton. By 1749 the total capital of the Backbarrow Company was set at £16,000.[77]

The boom hardly swept all before it. Probably a maximum of six furnaces were operational at any one time before 1750; the furnaces themselves were worked by about a dozen men each. Their presence, however, gave rise to considerable by-employment for yeomen, labourers, and rural craftsmen, in carting, tanning, and carpentry. Skilled forgemen could command wages of more than £1 a week at the height of the boom, but they were usually brought in from elsewhere. Ancillary labourers, including carpenters, had to be content with between 5s. and 7s.[78] The situation permitted some increase in prosperity; many yeomen, particularly in the south and west of the region, were able to supplement their normal income. Rights of cutting and coaling in charcoal woods were frequently leased out by ironmasters or other landowners to yeomen and husbandmen for intakes from the Furness fells, secure from the roamings of sheep, to be planted with oak saplings. Oak bark was an important ingredient for the local tanning industry, which was therefore also stimulated by developments in iron, and which provided an additional source of by-employment for yeoman farmers.

Though it had its roots in the southern hinterland, tanning was a growth industry in Kendal. Arthur Young considered it the fourth industry of the town after knitting, linsey-wolsey, and 'cottons'. The main stimulus to tanning was the cattle trade, particularly droving. The market for leather was further enhanced by transport developments in the middle of the eighteenth century. Sporadic references are made to tanners in High Furness, and iron smelting in lowland Furness incidentally stimulated the trade, as has been indicated. Iron forges required bellows, usually made from hides, and leather harnesses were in great demand for the transport of iron to the coast prior to shipment south or to Scotland.

Mention should also be made of the important lead mines in east Cumberland, particularly on the Derwentwater estates near Alston. Nicolson and Burn referred to no fewer than 103 mines on Alston Moor in the 1770s, though this probably represented a resurgence from the position in mid

<hr/>

[77] J. D. Marshall, *Furness*, pp. 19–29; T. S. Ashton, *Iron and Steel in the Industrial Revolution*, Manchester, 1963, p. 198.   [78] Marshall, *Furness*, pp. 39–40.

century after a grandiose project for intensive workings had come to grief. In the 1770s, iron workings in the area provided employment for upwards of a thousand persons.[79]

Along the west Cumberland coast salt panning provided a source of additional income. Some of the gentry dabbled; Sir John Lowther took a lease of the duke of Somerset's pans in the 1680s, but the experience induced him to sublet rapidly. His son James was involved during the 1730s, when he had two pans built at Saltom. It is not clear whether the enterprise was successful. Yeomen were to some extent involved in salt manufacture near the Cumberland coast, and in addition to their activities in curing and preserving, yeomen have been identified as part owners of fishing vessels and even as miners in addition to their smallholdings; some miners even traded in black cattle early in the century.[80]

As in all regions, the most important by-employment was textiles. It should be borne in mind, however, that domestic spinning, still less weaving, was far from a universal occupation. The emphasis was on woollen spinning in south Westmorland and Furness. Domestic outworkers were involved in spinning the long-established 'Kendal cottons', rough wool used in the manufacture of uniforms and linsey-wolsey. This last was a combination of rough wool and lowland flax. It is perhaps surprising to discover from an admittedly small sample of inventories in Kendal and Furness deaneries that hemp manufacture was almost as prevalent as woollen spinning in the dales.[81] Hemp was used not only for rope but also to make shirts and sacks. Flax was also grown on a few lowland homesteads, particularly in west Cumberland. In Westmorland the third viscount Lonsdale ran a small linen manufactory during the 1740s, partly supplied with local flax.[82] Inventories suggest that wool, hemp, and flax were not held in sufficient quantities to provide a major source of cash. More often they fitted into a quasi-subsistence pattern which the provisions of winter work did little to distort.

The growing prosperity of Kendal in the early eighteenth century was to a large extent due to the development of the knitting industry. Arthur Young, in his *Six Months Tour through the North of England* in 1770, stated

---

[79] Nicolson and Burn, *Cumberland and Westmorland, II*, p. 440; Hutchinson, *op. cit., I*, pp. 213–15; Bouch and Jones, *op. cit.* p. 256; Beckett, thesis, p. 83; F. J. Monkhouse, 'An Eighteenth-Century Company Promoter', *CW2*, XL, 1940, pp. 141–53.

[80] J. D. Marshall, 'Domestic Economy', p. 207; Beckett, thesis, p. 215; W. H. Makey, 'The Place of Whitehaven in the Irish Coal Trade', unpub. Univ. of London M.A. thesis, 1952, pp. 205–6.

[81] A sample of 89 inventories by Marshall revealed 35 instances of clear involvement in spinning or weaving. Wool or woollen yarn was mentioned on 18 occasions, and hemp also on 18. A sample of 36 inventories from Kendal deanery by Evans between 1660 and 1689 revealed 9 references to woollen yarn and 7 to hemp and linen.

[82] J. V. Beckett, 'The Eighteenth-Century Origins of the Factory System: A Case Study from the 1740s', *Business Hist.*, XIX, 1977, pp. 55–67.

that the stocking trade was the chief industry of the town, employing between 3,000 and 4,000 people, 2,400 of whom were knitters.[83] It was claimed that 3,000 stockings per week were being made in Kendal, most of which were transported to London for sale. Young wrote while the textile boom, generated by the demands of the Seven Years' War, was still in full swing, but the primacy of stockings was certainly established by 1750. It employed a small number of skilled woolcombers and a small army of domestic knitters. Labour for these duties was drawn not from the traditional textile areas of southern Lakeland but from eastern Westmorland, around Dent and Kirkby Stephen. Textile production, albeit on a small scale, was found elsewhere in the region, notably around Penrith and Cockermouth.[84]

Overall, therefore, Cumbria sustained a considerable amount of by-employment; despite its remoteness it was far from industrially backward. Dr Marshall's sample of inventories shows irrefragable evidence of industrial by-employment in only 8 per cent of cases, but this certainly underestimates the total involvement. By-employment is not always detectable in this way. His sample does, however, reveal clear evidence of greater ancillary employment in west Cumberland and Furness than elsewhere in the region.[85]

Parts of Cumbria underwent dramatic change during the period. It would be fair to conclude that Furness and west Cumberland experienced a form of industrial revolution in the first half of the eighteenth century. Developments in and around Whitehaven drew population from the rural hinterland, transport improvements were made, and one historian has described the west Cumbrian industrial and commercial complex in 1755 as "the most valuable industrial plant in England".[86] Here the subsistence economy had been entirely superseded. Elsewhere material advancement may be traced as the development of the cattle trade and a range of by-employments helped to spread the flow of cash. No serious inroads were made into customary tenures during this period and the majority of the region's farmers remained in 1750 as in 1640 small owner-occupiers or secure customary tenants following a deeply traditional way of life. It is not surprising, therefore, that the region was so little affected by the new husbandry. Cumbria in the middle of the eighteenth century showed at once rapid industrial development and antique agricultural practice. For many, indeed, in the extensive fell country the elements of a subsistence economy remained largely untouched; others in the region were amongst the first to experience the impact of an industrial revolution.

[83] Young, *A Six Months Tour*, III, pp. 170–4; Bouch and Jones, *op. cit.*, p. 264; J. D. Marshall, *Kendal*, pp. 23–4.

[84] Fiennes, *op. cit.*, p. 198; Edward Chamberlayne, *Angliae Notitia*, 18th edn, 1694, p. 12.

[85] J. D. Marshall, 'Domestic Economy', p. 12.

[86] J. U. Nef, *The Rise of the British Coal Industry*, 2 vols., London, 1966, II, p. 7. See also *ibid.*, I, pp. 69–72, 229–30; L. A. Williams, *Road Transport in Cumbria in the Nineteenth Century*, London, 1975, pp. 20–5.

CHAPTER 2

NORTHUMBERLAND AND DURHAM

Northumberland and Durham contained some of the least productive farmland in the country and, potentially, some of the most productive. It is generally agreed that the region can be divided into three major farming zones, from the highlands in the west through the foothills to the coastal lowlands in the east. From the lavas and granites of the Cheviot massif in the north the carboniferous rocks of the Border fells and the north Pennines form a virtually continuous range of hills constituting the highland zone. This is dissected by the rivers which drain the 'border dales' of Northumberland, namely Upper Coquetdale, Redesdale, and North Tynedale, and the 'lead dales' of south Northumberland and Durham, Allendale, upper Weardale, and upper Teesdale. In these bleak, wet hills the growing season is short and the predominant soil, except for the alluvial loam in the valleys, is an acid peat. The foothills are an intermediate zone, where relief and climate are less harsh. They consist of the plateaux and scarp and vale lands of Northumberland, and the Pennine spurs and sandstone plateau in Durham. Here much of the lower land is covered by glacial material, forming soils of variable texture. Soils in the eastern lowlands of the region are also largely derived from glacial material, but tend to be heavier, although there is much variation, from the clays of south-east Northumberland and south-west Durham to the free-draining, easily worked loamy sands of the Tweed, Till, and Breamish valleys, described in 1733 as "the finest plain in Northumberland".[1]

In the highlands climate, soil, and topography combined to ensure that animals and animal products formed the mainstay of the agricultural economy. Only one-quarter of the strips in the townfield at Newbiggin, in Teesdale, were in arable crops in the early seventeenth century, and a survey of the township of Barresford in North Tynedale in 1755 showed only 172 acres of arable in a total area of 1,231 acres.[2] The probate inventories tell

---

[1] G. Hickling, 'Structure and Topography of Northumberland and Durham', *Proc. Geologists' Assoc.*, XLII, 3, 1931, pp. 224–7; A. E. Smailes, *North England*, London, 1960, pp. 50–5; R. A. Butlin, 'Field Systems of Northumberland and Durham', in A. R. H. Baker and R. A. Butlin, eds., *Studies of Field Systems in the British Isles*, Cambridge, 1973, p. 94; R. M. Gard and C. Shrimpton, eds., *A Revolution in Agriculture*, Univ. of Newcastle upon Tyne School of Education, Archive Teaching Unit, no. 8, 1972, Handbook, p. 9.

[2] J. M. Britton, 'Farm, Field, and Fell in Upper Teesdale, 1600–1900, unpub. Durham Univ. M.A. thesis, 1974, p. 85; Alnwick Castle MSS, (A) A i 6.

Value of livestock as a percentage of the value of live and deadstock in highland inventories

	Northumberland	Durham
1630–40	75.5	86.1
1680–90	77.0	91.9
1710–20	81.8	80.9

the same story: at least three-quarters of the total value of the stock on the farm was accounted for by animals (see table).

It can be seen that conditions were broadly similar in the highland areas of both counties, although arable farming was even less important in Durham than in Northumberland. Later, between 1724 and 1740, corn (mainly rye) was regularly bought in Newcastle to be sold to lead miners in Weardale employed by the Blackett family. It is also apparent from this table that the bulk of the highland farmer's wealth was in the form of cattle, sheep, corn, and hay. Few farms had more than five horses, most had two or three, but some had none. Those that were kept were riding or pack animals rather than plough horses, and many bulk commodities, such as corn, coal, and lead ore were carried on horseback rather than in carts. In Allendale hay was brought in from the fields on sleds; and carts, wains, and other farm implements such as ploughs, harrows, and hand tools formed only a small part of the wealth of highland farmers.[3]

The most important animals on the highland farms were the cows. They themselves provided dairy products for home consumption, and their offspring provided traction, meat, and ready cash when sold as stots and stirks to lowland farmers for fattening. Cattle altogether usually accounted for about half the value of all the farmer's possessions, but few farmers had more than twenty animals, and many had fewer than ten. There is unfortunately little reliable information on the type of breed of these animals: although Bailey and Culley, writing in 1805, stated that "the *short horned* kind have long been established over the whole country", they admitted that they lacked hardiness, and it is reasonable to suppose that there was much Scottish, rather than shorthorn, blood in the highland cattle. Clearly, the activities of the drovers in the seventeenth century and later gave rise to the passage of many West Highland cattle (kyloes) through the highland areas of both counties, and kyloes and kyloe crosses were popular in Northumberland in the later eighteenth century.[4] All farms kept some cattle, but not all kept

[3] P. W. Brassley, 'The Agricultural Economy of Northumberland and Durham in the Period 1640–1750', unpub. Oxford Univ. B.Litt. thesis, 1974, pp. 135–40.

[4] J. Bailey and G. Culley, *General View of the Agriculture of Northumberland*, 3rd edn, London, 1805, p. 139; K. J. Bonser, *The Drovers*, London, 1970, p. 51; S. Macdonald, 'The Development of Agriculture and the Diffusion of Agricultural Innovation in Northumberland 1750–1850', unpub. Univ. of Newcastle upon Tyne Ph.D. thesis, 1974, p. 264.

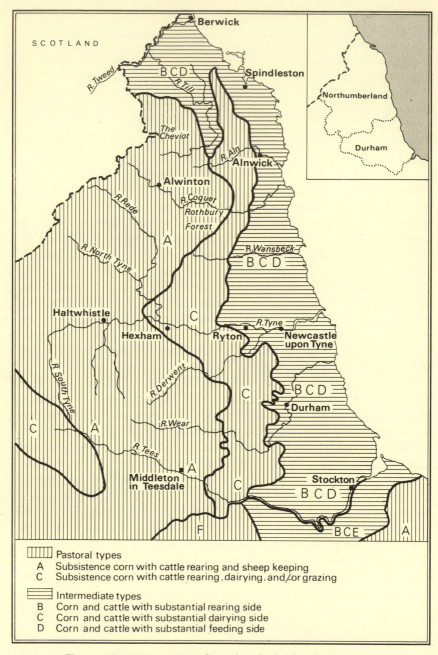

Fig. 2.1. Farming regions of Northumberland and Durham.

sheep, and the size of sheep flocks varied much more than that of cattle herds, flocks of more than one hundred being as common as those of fewer than fifty. The Cheviot Hills "produce the best and soundest mutton, and the country...is almost wholly laid out in sheep walks", wrote Bishop Pococke in 1760, and the farms in Kirknewton parish, on the edge of the Cheviots, often had large sheep flocks. Robert Reed, a gentleman who died there during lambing time in April 1683, had 300 "lambed and unlambed" ewes, 180 gimmers and dinments, 95 hoggs, 20 barren ewes, and 20 tups, worth in all £165, in addition to £100 worth of cattle, horses worth £13, and corn worth £118. Thomas Aymers, a yeoman who died in 1677, had 616 ewes, 294 lambs, 80 dinments, and 154 wethers, worth in all £269 14s. as well as £138 worth of cattle, 11 horses worth £31, and corn worth £135. Alexander Davidson, also of Kirknewton, was a much poorer man than Reed or Aymers, having a total estate worth less than £50, yet he still possessed 99 ewes and 52 younger sheep, worth in all £26 in 1685. The white-faced, hornless Cheviot sheep were bred only in this district, as far south as Redesdale, the moorlands from North Tynedale south to Teesdale being given over to the horned, black-faced heath sheep, an ancestor of the Scottish blackface. Each type was particularly suited to the district in which it was found, for the hardier heath sheep could be kept profitably on their heather-covered hills, while the Cheviots needed the coarse grass of the Cheviot pastures. Many highland farmers kept one or two riding or pack horses, and a few had pigs and poultry, although the numbers of these were so small that they clearly formed part of the domestic, rather than the agricultural, economy.[5]

Bigg, rye, wheat, and peas were grown in the highlands, but the most widely sown crop, and the one best suited to the short, wet summers, was oats. In 1638 Gavin Aynsley had oats worth £18, and rye and wheat worth £12 sown at Harbottle, and in the same year John Gibson of Middleton in Teesdale harvested 20 thraves (i.e. 480 sheaves) of bigg worth £4 4s, and 40 thraves (960 sheaves) of oats worth £1 10s. Information on yields is scarce, but if the evidence from Robert Reed's farm at Kirknewton may be applied generally, they do not seem to have been high. Reed died in April 1683, having sown rye, oats, and bigg, and the inventory assessors estimated that 20 bolls of bigg seed would produce a harvest of 60 bolls, 28 bolls of rye would produce 80 bolls, and 60 bolls of oats 160 bolls. Reed's farm was clearly typical in its emphasis on oats, although he may have had a larger farm than was common.[6]

[5] J. C. Hodgson, ed., 'The Northern Journeys of Bishop Richard Pococke', in *North Country Diaries*, *II*, Surtees Soc., LXXIV, 1915, p. 220; Bailey and Culley, *op. cit.*, pp. 144–8; Brassley, thesis, p. 136.

[6] Durham Univ. Dept of Palaeography and Diplomatic, Probate Inventories. In fact it is virtually impossible to specify a useful average farm size, since what little evidence is available shows acreages ranging from under 20 to over 1,000, together with common grazing rights – Brassley, thesis, pp. 120, 136.

The arable land in the highlands lay either in closes or in small common fields around the hamlets and small villages. Single farms with no subdivided fields were found only at the upper limits of settlement, such as the Forest of Teesdale above Newbiggin. In Newbiggin township itself most men held one parcel of meadow and one of arable, although some had meadow closes also, for by 1640 a gradual process of enclosure had been going on for at least thirty years. The same basic pattern was apparent in Northumberland, with the small settlements towards the heads of the dales having small common fields, while larger settlements further down the dale had larger areas of arable laid out rather more rigidly in two or three larger fields.[7] The many references to "infields and outfields" or "ingrounds and outgrounds" which are found in both counties are not necessarily indicative of an infield–outfield or runrig type of field system, for references to them also occur in lowland townships which can be shown to have had three common fields. It seems more likely that the terms arose as a result of the vast area of many highland townships and the large proportion of waste, or poor pasture, contained in them, so that the term 'outfield' seems in many cases to be synonymous with 'common waste'. Nevertheless it is clear that the outgrounds might be cropped occasionally: at Broomhope, near the confluence of the Rede and the North Tyne, a dispute arose in 1745 over the amount of tithe that should be paid on corn ground on the outgrounds. That this was no new development was shown by the fact that parts of the outgrounds had been in tillage when the defendant's father had the farm, and there were "several antient furrows or ridges both in the ingrounds and outgrounds that this deponent never saw in tillage".[8]

The main function of the common waste in the highlands, however, was to provide grazing land. The way in which this was organized changed in this period, for the system of transhumance, in which flocks and herds were taken to the shieling grounds between seed time and harvest in North Tyndale and Redesdale, disappeared by the end of the seventeenth century.[9] Thus the moorland grazing was allocated to the farmers of one township, rather than to men of one surname, as had previously sometimes been the case. It may be argued, however, that this made little immediate difference. The farms in North Tyndale, wrote the surveyors of the duke of Northumberland's estate in 1755, "are in a hilly barren country, undivided and only proper for breeding sheep and keeping some young beast...as little or no improvements can be made by enclosing, these farms must be let to stock masters".[10]

[7] Britton, thesis, pp. 36–7; Butlin, op. cit., p. 125.

[8] Butlin, op. cit., p. 137; PRO, E 134, 17 Geo. II, Trin. 2 (Northumb.). This point is confirmed by Macdonald, thesis, pp. 203–4.

[9] P. Dixon, 'Shielings and Bastles: A Reconsideration of Some Problems', Archaeologia Aeliana, 4th ser., L, 1972, p. 250. For a description of the shieling system, see J. Thirsk, ed., AHEW, IV, pp. 22–4.   [10] Alnwick MSS, (A)A i 6.

	Eldon 1715 (%)	Hartburn 1715 (%)	Eslington 1715 (%)	Kirkwhelpington 1755 (%)
Arable	33.9	23.8	27.7	12.3
Meadow	13.8	10.6	14.5	5.4
Pasture	25.0	54.0	44.7	32.2
Arable and pasture	—	—	4.1	—
Arable and meadow	4.1	7.1	2.1	1.8
Pasture and meadow	3.8	—	5.5	1.6
Waste	19.4	4.5	1.4	46.7
Total acreage	1,056	434	1,445	1,924

Sources: PRO, F.E.C. 2/82 and 2/83; Alnwick Castle MSS, (A)A i 6.

The Pennine foothills of Northumberland and Durham were, for most agricultural purposes, an intermediate zone. This was demonstrated particularly by the pattern of land use and the size of farm business. Whereas the average highland farmer had between £40 and £60 worth of goods, the average farmer in the foothills had between £80 and £100 worth, a figure which remained static over the whole period, although again some farms were considerably larger than this: Henry Ogle of Edlingham and Thomas Scott of West Whelpington both owned crops and stock worth about £350.[11] Surveys made in 1715 and 1755 show that the bulk of the land was devoted to the production of fodder, although the proportion of arable land was perhaps greater than that found in the highlands. Until enclosure the pattern of cultivation was based on three or four large common arable fields, although in some townships (East Brandon in Durham, for example) considerable areas of meadow were found among the arable lands of the open fields.[12]

A sample of probate inventories for the period 1630–1710 shows that whereas crops formed about 14 per cent of the value of the live and deadstock of the average farm in the highlands, the comparable figure in the foothills was 22 per cent. Farmers in the foothills also had more farm implements, in the form of ploughs, harrows, and carts to the value of about £3 to £4. With this rather greater emphasis on arable farming it is not surprising to find that the number of draught animals on the farm was greater than in the highlands. Most farmers kept oxen, four being the usual number, and

[11] Probate Inventories.   [12] Butlin, *op. cit.*, pp. 120, 129.

a few were keeping plough horses by the early eighteenth century: in 1712 Andrew Oliver of Fourstones in Warden parish had draught horses and fillies worth £19 1s. 6d. in addition to his four oxen, and in 1711 Henry Ogle of Eglingham had seven horses, which were specifically noted as "work horses" and valued at £2 each. The major crop in the foothills was barley, or its hardier relatives bear and bigg, but oats, peas, and rye and wheat were also sown, the last two often being sown together as maslin. When Edward Keenley's farm at Eglingham was valued in April 1637 he was found to have sown 4½ bolls of rye worth £9 6s. 8d., 5 bolls of bear worth £6, and 8 bolls of oats worth £6. In June 1682 George Shawter of Ingleton near Staindrop had corn crops worth £45, consisting of 8 acres of wheat and rye, 10 acres of barley and bigg, 4 acres of oats, and 3 acres of peas, while in 1711 Zachariah Whittingham of Lanchester had 5 acres of wheat, 3½ acres of bigg, 4 acres of oats, and 1½ acres of peas. The inventories provide little information on yields in the foothills, although when Thomas Fforster of Chatton died in December 1637 the assessors estimated that the 10 bolls of winter corn he had sown would amount to no more than 30 bolls at harvest. It seems probable that by 1750 yields had risen: Arthur Young, visiting the Blackett family estate around Cambo in the late 1760s, reported local estimates of yield ratios at about double this level.[13]

For reasons of climate and topography, therefore, the foothills of Northumberland and Durham were not well suited to corn growing, and it was the cattle and sheep that formed the mainstay of the agricultural economy. Many farmers had more than ten cattle of all types, and the importance of cows in the inventories suggests that dairy production and stock rearing were more important than stock fattening. Some farmers had herds of a considerable size: in 1635, for example, Randall Fenwick of Kirkwhelpington had 20 oxen, 30 cows, and 41 younger beasts. The size of sheep flocks was much more variable, flocks of 200 or more being as common as those of 20 or fewer, and some farmers concentrated on fattening sheep rather than on breeding and rearing. John Mare of St Helen Auckland was probably one of these, fattening sheep brought down by the Scots drovers, for in 1716 he had a number of two-shear and three-shear "scots" sheep. Pigs and poultry were more a part of the domestic than of the agricultural economy: most farmers had a few pigs and some hens, and some kept geese to run on the commons, and Timothy Whittingham of Lanchester who owned live and deadstock worth £254 in 1682 (in addition to cash and household goods to the value of £290) even kept some turkeys.

The size of the farm business in the lowland zone tended to be larger than in the foothills or the highlands, the total value of crops and stock listed in the inventories of local farmers often exceeding £100. The largest farms were found in the Tweed valley and in the northern part of the coastal plain of

[13] Brassley, thesis, pp. 140–2; A. Young, *A Six Months Tour through the North of England*, 2nd edn, London 1771, *III*, p. 77.

Northumberland: Henry Orde, who farmed the demesne land at Norham, had £413 worth of stock and £251 worth of corn when he died in 1638, and in March 1712 Robert Edmeston, who also farmed at Norham, had livestock worth £279 and corn worth £196. Some farms in the south-western lowlands of county Durham were also large, but in general farms there tended to be of small to medium size: in the 1750s there were seventy-six farmers in Hurworth parish holding, on average, 32 acres each, and seventy-three in the township of Great Aycliffe farming an average of 30 acres each. This explains why the wealth of farmers in this area was often lower than that of men farming similar land, but in larger units, in Northumberland. Many of the farms in the mining areas were also quite small. There were thirteen tenants on the 316-acre Ravensworth estate of the Liddell family in 1712, and the largest farm comprised only 74 acres. At Farnacres and Whickham the average farm size was 28 acres, and only four farmers out of twenty-four had more than 50 acres. However, such men were often able to supplement their incomes by hiring their carts and their labour for the transport of coal; and in some cases the diversification of their businesses went even further: in 1684 John Rawling of Whickham owned, in addition to his three "cole" carts, a set of boring rods, and Robert Procter of Ryton built up a business which involved corn growing, trading in timber, and bark- and ship-owning. Procter died in possession of goods worth £1,500 and yet was illiterate.[14]

Not surprisingly, arable farming was more important in the lowlands than on the higher lands, and a sample of inventories from the period 1630–1710 shows that crops accounted for about one-third of the wealth of lowland farmers. This is reflected in the relatively high proportion of land described as "arable", "arable and meadow", or "arable and pasture" in a survey of four townships on the coastal plain of Northumberland, carried out in 1755. The same pattern prevailed at Ravensworth in north Durham, where farms had up to one-third of their acreage in arable or arable and meadow, and the greater scarcity of pasture and waste land gave rise to the practice of 'gaiting' (i.e. stinting) pastures in many of the lowland townships.[15] In most of the townships for which evidence is available the arable land was laid out in extensive common and open fields until enclosure. The usual number of common fields in a lowland township was three, although some townships had only two fields, and some had four or more, and tenant holdings were distributed among fields in direct proportion to their size.[16]

[14] Probate Inventories; Durham RO, Land Tax Vouchers 1759; R. I. Hodgson, 'Agricultural Improvement and Changing Regional Economies in the Eighteenth Century', in A. R. H. Baker and J. B. Harley, eds., *Man Made the Land*, Newton Abbot, 1973, p. 152; E. Hughes, *North Country Life in the Eighteenth Century: The North-East 1700–1750*, London, 1952, p. 134.

[15] Hughes, *op. cit.*, p. 134; Butlin, *op. cit.*, p. 135.

[16] This description of north-eastern field systems follows Butlin, *op. cit.*, pp. 111–20. Butlin shows that H. L. Gray (in *English Field Systems*, Cambridge, Mass., 1915, p. 225) was wrong in asserting that the three-field system reached only as far north as Durham and that the Northumberland field system was a hybrid between the Midland and Scottish systems.

	Loughoughton (%)	Acklington (%)	Birling (%)	Guyzance (%)
Arable	38.3	45.1	57.3	57.8
Meadow	2.2	4.2	5.4	4.1
Pasture	25.6	40.8	31.1	22.8
Arable and pasture	7.2	—	—	4.6
Arable and meadow	6.7	6.4	3.9	2.3
Unclassified	20.0	3.5	2.3	8.4
Total acreage	1,665	1,965	739	346

Source: Alnwick MSS, (A)A i 6.

Oats were the most important crop being eaten by both people and animals. A soldier passing through Felton Bridge in 1745 noted that the usual breakfast was "hasty pudding, made of oatmeal and water boiled together, till it comes to the consistence of paste, which some eat with beer, nutmeg and sugar; others with milk; then 'tis tolerable...Oatcakes are here also in fashion." In 1769 Arthur Young found that oats were often grown for two years in succession in a four-year rotation on the coastal plain of Northumberland, and the evidence of the probate inventories shows that they may have been even more important earlier. In the spring of 1680 John Gray, a husbandman at Stannington, had sown $3\frac{1}{2}$ bolls of wheat, 9 bolls of bigg, 6 bolls of rye, and 60 bolls of oats. It must be remembered that the seed rate used for oats was twice that of other cereals; nevertheless, the accounts of crops harvested or in store present the same picture: 162 bolls of oats were harvested at Spindleston on the north Northumberland coast in 1677, together with 26 bolls of wheat, 33 bolls of bigg, and 17 bolls of peas. In Durham oats were perhaps somewhat less dominant, but still Christopher Sheraton had 30 acres of oats, worth £45, as well as 36 acres of wheat and bigg, worth £70, sown on his farm at Elwick in south-east Durham in April 1712.[17] The winter corn was wheat or rye, although sometimes both were sown together as maslin for breadmaking, a practice which was thought to benefit the yields of both grains. The cultivation of bigg or bear, a four-rowed variety of barley, seems to have declined after the beginning of the eighteenth century: Young in his *Northern Tour* made no mention of bigg, and in 1805 Bailey and Culley in their *General View* of Northumberland reported that although bigg used to be the only type of barley to be cultivated in the county,

[17] Macdonald, thesis, p. 181; Young, *op. cit.*, III, pp. 19–26; Probate Inventories; Northumb. RO, Simpson MSS, ZSI 2.

it was by then rarely grown, and then only on the poorer soils. Exports of bigg from Berwick amounted to between 2,000 and 3,000 quarters per year in the period 1710–20, but in the 1730s this figure had fallen to about 250 quarters per year, whereas over 25,000 quarters of barley were being exported every year from Berwick and Alnmouth, in contrast to the 182 quarters which formed the total export in the period 1714–17.[18] The yields of cereal crops appear to have risen between the mid seventeenth and the mid eighteenth centuries. On William Gray's farm at Fenwick in north Northumberland in 1638 it was estimated that for every boll of wheat and rye sown, two and a half would be harvested, for every boll of oats three, for every boll of bear, three, and for every boll of peas sown only one and a half bolls would be harvested. Forty years later at Spindleston, a few miles to the south, the yield ratio of the oat crop was similar to this, but for every boll of bigg sown, six were harvested, and for every boll of peas, four. In 1760, however, when Sir John Delaval's bailiff set out to calculate the prospective return from Flodden North farm, he assumed rather better yields than these. He planned to sow 3 bushels of wheat to the acre, 2 bushels of barley per acre, and 6 bushels of oats per acre, and to reap 24 bushels of wheat, 30 bushels of barley, and 30 bushels of oats per acre. These yield ratios are in fairly good agreement with those reported by Arthur Young at several places along the Northumberland coast in 1769. Yields, therefore, appear to have improved, particularly in the latter half of this period. Clearly the figures for bear and bigg and barley cannot be compared directly, but as barley replaced bigg, in the lowlands at least, by the 1730s the comparison is useful. The reasons for these increases in yields, and their effects upon the farm economy, are discussed below.[19]

In the lowlands, as in the rest of the region, animal production formed the basis of the rural economy, and livestock accounted for the greater part of the wealth of the farmers. Nevertheless, as a result of the importance of arable farming, draught animals, both oxen and horses, often accounted for nearly one-half of the total value of livestock on the average farm. A soldier marching from Alnwick to Belford in 1745 reported that "we frequently saw country-men ploughing with four couple of oxen, and one of horses; the ground being so hard and strong does commonly require ten and twelve cattle". Therefore the larger farmers of Northumberland in particular kept large numbers of oxen: in the 1630s Thomas Forster of Bamburgh had 42, and in 1712 Robert Edmeston of Norham had 6 plough horses and 24 oxen. In Durham and south-east Northumberland, where farms were not so large, most farmers had fewer than 10 oxen. Most farmers also had fewer than 10 cows, the usual number being about 5 or 6. They also possessed younger

[18] Bailey and Culley, General View of Northumberland, pp. 80, 81; PRO, Berwick Port Books, E 190, 168/10, 12; 169/3, 4, 5, 6; 173/12, 13; 174/1, 2, 6, 9.

[19] Northumb. RO, Delaval MSS, ZDE 19/4; Young, op. cit., III, pp. 13, 20.

animals, stirks, stots, quies (heifers), and steers, some of which were sold off as stores at a relatively early age, while others were kept on to join the milking herd or the plough term. Thus some steers achieved relative old age before slaughter: on the early of Derwentwater's farm at Spindleston in 1677 there were 30 five-year-old stotts and 30 four-year-old steers and heifers.[20] By the middle of the seventeenth century tanning had become the most important trade in Alnwick, 22 tanneries being listed there in 1646, and hides were regularly shipped from Berwick to London in the first half of the eighteenth century.

The liquid milk trade was restricted to the immediate vicinity of the larger towns, particularly Newcastle, and could be very profitable. In the early 1730s tenants on the Park and Shipcote estates at Gateshead were able to pay rents of almost £2 per acre by selling their milk in Newcastle. By 1735, however, supply was beginning to exceed demand, and the steward notes that the milk trade "is now much worse than formerley by means of so maney following that way of liveing that the demand is less and larger pennyworths given than were formerley". Further away from centres of population milk was converted into butter and cheese. Many inventories record the possession of cheese presses and "cheesefats" (i.e. cheese vats), and from time to time cheese entered the coasting trade, 22 hundredweight being sent from Berwick to London in 1715. The greater emphasis, however, was placed on butter production. North-eastern gentlemen in temporary exile in the south wrote of their unaccustomed difficulty in buying butter, and of the high prices they had to pay "for butter that you would not eat in the north", and the prices quoted by Young show that in 1769 butter was often twopence and sometimes threepence per pound cheaper in the north-east than in the Midlands or in London. In the seventeenth century it was reported that the Dutch exported the best of their own butter, and replaced it with cheap butter bought from Ireland and the north of England, and by the middle of the seventeenth century a significant trade in butter was being carried on from north-east coast ports from Stockton to Berwick. By 1730 over 15,000 firkins of butter, each containing 56 pounds, were sent annually to London from Newcastle alone, a quantity which represented about 5 per cent of London's total butter supply. Even larger quantities were sent from Stockton, and the smaller ports also contributed to the trade.[21]

Before the introduction of Bakewell's Dishley breed in the 1760s, the long-wool sheep of the lowlands were called mugs and were, according to

[20] Macdonald, thesis, p. 261; Northumb. RO, Simpson MSS, ZSI 1; Brassley, thesis, pp. 147–8.

[21] G. Tate, *The History of the Borough, Castle and Barony of Alnwick*, I, Newcastle upon Tyne, 1866, p. 311; Hughes, *op. cit.*, pp. 140, 142; T. S. Willan, *The English Coasting Trade, 1600–1750*, Manchester, 1938, pp. 84, 116; Young, *op. cit.*, pp. 27, 325; Sir William Temple, *Observations on Trade between England and the Netherlands*, London, p. 208; G. E. Fussell, *The English Dairy Farmer, 1500–1900*, London, 1966, pp. 266, 269, 271.

Bailey and Culley, "a slow feeding tribe". Most farmers had sheep, but the size of sheep flocks was much more variable than that of cattle herds. The usual median flock comprised between 40 and 80 animals, but some of the large farmers of north Northumberland possessed several hundred sheep, and in the 1670s the flock of Sir Thomas Haggerston of Haggerston fluctuated in number between 2,000 and 3,000, divided into six flocks, each with its own shepherd. On the other hand, the flock at Spindleston, just as big as Haggerston's, was kept together. Of a total of about 2,250 sheep, taking one year with another, between 800 and 900 were ewes; 300 and 400, wethers; 350 and 450, gimmers and dinments; and 500 and 700, lambs. About 20 tups were kept. The fertility of the ewes varied: in a good year they might average one lamb each, but when the flock was afflicted by adverse weather conditions at lambing the losses of both ewes and lambs could be high: after the hard winter of 1694–5 the level of mortality rose from its customary 10 per cent of the flock to 15 per cent, and the bailiff notes that 235 hoggs "dyed by reason of the badd spring". In a normal year the average fleece sold off the farm weighed just over two pounds, but this figure included fleeces of young sheep. The average weight of 11,629 fleeces shipped from Berwick in 1715 was 2.96 lbs. The fleeces of Northumberland sheep were not thought to be of high quality, having too much kemp and being spoilt by the practice of salving with butter and tar to protect the sheep from the effects of rain: nevertheless this trade developed to significant proportions by the middle of the eighteenth century, when nearly 200,000 pounds of wool were dispatched annually from Berwick and Alnmouth to Hull. In some areas sheep were also kept for their milk, which was probably used for cheesemaking. By the middle of the eighteenth century, however, many farmers were of the opinion that prolonged milking weakened the ewes, and the practice had almost died out.[22]

This rather static picture of the agrarian economy in the three parts of the region neglects the changes that came about during this period. Yet it is clear that this was a time of considerable change, and it can be shown that many of the developments occurred as a reaction to changing patterns of demand for food. Between 1640 and 1680 the output of coal in Northumberland and Durham doubled, and by the latter date the north-eastern coalfield was producing 40 per cent of national output. By 1750 output had doubled again, although the proportion of national output declined, and as the coal industry expanded so did the trades which served it, such as shipping, shipbuilding, river navigation and transport, and the trades which used its products, such as saltmaking; glass, lime, and copper works; and the ironworking trades. On the western side of the region lead mining in the Pennine dales of Durham and south Northumberland developed steadily from the beginning of the eighteenth century.[23] The result of all this activity was a dramatic change in the population of the areas affected, as the demand for coal, lead, and manufactured products led in turn to a demand for the labour to produce the goods. During the period between 1666 and 1736 the total population of the whole region rose by about 50 per cent, but the population of the industrial areas rose much more: at Chester le Street the 469 families of 1666 had increased to 1,875 by 1736, and at Washington, where 97 families were living in 1666, Bishop Chandler in his visitation of 1736 found 150 families, "Many of y^m Colliers new come in". Between 1676 and 1716 a number of men were fined in the manorial court for bringing strangers to live at Byshottles near Durham and for erecting cottages without the lord's consent. Many of the new industrial workers migrated from agricultural areas, esppecially the less fertile districts like the border dales, where overpopulation had been such a problem in the sixteenth century. The result was a growth in the number of people who consumed food without producing it, and therefore the demand for food in the market-place rose by more than the simple increase in population.[24]

In contrast, the other factors affecting the demand for food, wages, and prices apparently remained remarkably stable. In the long term miners' wages increased slightly, but the wage rates of rural day labourers hardly changed at all. There were changes during the year, of course, since the amount of work to be done in August was three times as great as during any of the winter months (on the Cotesworth estates in Gateshead at least). A mower could earn 1s. 2d. per day during the hay and corn harvests, but he had to be content with 6d. or 8d. per day for the rest of the year, if he could get work at all. Those who were employed for the whole year as herds and hinds were in a more fortunate position, but they had little impact on the food market, as much of their pay was in kind.[25] However, if there was no rise in wages, neither does there seem to have been any long-term rise in prices in the region. The only available long-term price series is restricted

[23] J. U. Nef, *The Rise of the British Coal Industry in the Sixteenth and Seventeenth Centuries*, 2 vols., London, 1932, I, pp. 19–23, 34–42; Smailes, *North England*, pp. 129, 132, 136, 143; *VCH Durham*, II, pp. 296–309; C. J. Hunt, *The Lead Miners of the North Pennines*, Manchester, 1970, p. 5; S. Middlebrook, *Newcastle upon Tyne: Its Growth and Achievement*, Newcastle, 1950, p. 86.

[24] Brassley, thesis, pp. 12–15, 16–22, 186–97; PRO, Hearth Tax Returns, E 179, 158/110 (Northumb.) and 106/28 (Durham); Newcastle upon Tyne Central Library, 'Bishop Chandler's Visitation' (1736), L253, no. 21,245; S. Ingleson, 'Settlement Agrarian Systems and Field Patterns in Central Durham 1600–1800: A Study in Historical Geography', unpub. Durham Univ. M.A. thesis, 1972, p. 48; Hughes, *op. cit.*, p. 252.

[25] Nef, *op. cit.*, I, pp. 180–8; T. S. Ashton and J. Sykes, *The Coal Industry of the Eighteenth Century*, Manchester, 1929, p. 84; Northumb. RO, Simpson MSS, ZSI 1, 2, 3, 4; Swinburne MSS, ZSW 220/1; Trevelyan MSS, ZTR 15; Durham Univ. Dept of Pal. and Dip., Baker Baker MSS, 72/251–2; Gateshead Central Library, Cotesworth MSS, CN/2/132–234; J. Campbell, 'The Northumbrian Agricultural Labourer', North-East Group for the Study of Labour History, *Bull.*, no. 2, 1968, p. 29.

to the first half of the eighteenth century and shows that the Michaelmas price of wheat was normally beteen 2s. 6d. and 3s. 6d. per Winchester bushel, while the Michaelmas price of rye was normally between 2s. and 2s. 6d. per Winchester bushel. The price of oats at Michaelmas varied even less, normally remaining within the range 1s. to 1s. 4d. per Winchester bushel. So far as it is possible to determine from the limited evidence available, livestock prices also showed no discernible upward or downward trend in the long run. But if the demand for food increased, the only way in which this price stability could have been brought about was through an increase in the supply of food.[26]

Most of the region's food supply was home-produced, but the area of most concentrated consumption, Tyneside, had a well-established grain trade by the middle of the seventeenth century. The main source of corn entering the port of Newcastle was East Anglia, although shipments were received from most of the east-coast ports from Scotland to Sandwich at some time between 1650 and 1750. Barley and rye accounted for much of the trade, and the quantities imported rose rapidly in the last quarter of the seventeenth century. However, the vast quantities of rye (over 100,000 quarters) which had to be brought in from Danzig and the Dutch ports in 1728, when the harvest failed all over eastern England, shows that interregional trade, amounting to about 20,000 quarters of grain per year, accounted for only the minor part of total cereal requirements. Clearly, therefore, the amount of food produced within the region itself must have risen rapidly enough to cater for the increased demands of the growing urban and rural populations.[27]

One of the most significant factors affecting the supply of food from the farms of the north-east in this period was the change in the fortunes of landowners in the region. It has been argued that the entry of merchants and professional men into the landowning classes, so typical of the late sixteenth and early seventeenth centuries over much of England, was delayed until the 1670–1750 period in the north-east, when a new gentry class, owing their original rise and continued prosperity to the industrial and commercial activity associated with the coal trade, took over. There were certainly several instances which support this thesis. William Cotesworth, the son of a Teesdale yeoman, rose through the coal and salt trades to possession of agricultural estates near Haltwhistle in south Northumberland. While Cotesworth rose further and faster than most, others moved in the same direction. The White

[26] Brassley, thesis, pp. 47–50, 198–209; Northumb. RO, Northumb. Quarter Sessions Order Books, vols. 8–86; Durham RO, Durham Sessions Order Books, Apr. 1686 – July 1700, Oct. 1700 – Jan. 1732.

[27] R. Welford, 'The Walls of Newcastle in 1638', Archaeologia Aeliana, NS XII, 1887, p. 233; W. H. D. Longstaffe, 'The Importation of Grain on the Tyne in the Seventeenth Century', Newcastle Central Library, Local Tracts, LO42; PRO, Newcastle Port Books, E 190, 192/9, 198/3, 209/1, 211/2, 220/4, 220/6, 227/4, 229/4, 233/9, 234/2, 235/5, 237/3, 238/7, 247/5, 249/10; Brassley, thesis, pp. 44–7.

and Ridley families used the profits of their commercial activities on Tyneside to buy, respectively, the Blagdon and Heaton estates which the Fenwick family had owned since the fourteenth century. Sir Edward Blackett, a lead merchant, acquired the Wallington estate, forfeited for treason in 1697 by another branch of the Fenwick family. John Douglas, a Newcastle lawyer, bought the Matfen estate from the Carnaby family between 1680 and 1702, and another lawyer, John Ord, bought the Fenham estate from the Riddells in 1695. In 1662 George Allgood, a lawyer in Hexham, began the buildup of the extensive Allgood family estates when he bought the Lambley estate in the Tyne valley from Sir John Lowther, and other lawyers and merchants followed his example.[28] But the new men were not the only ones who were successful in trade, and neither were they the only buyers of land. The Liddells took a predominant part in the coal trade, and bought the forfeited Eslington estate in north Northumberland in 1719, but the bulk of their property, at Ravensworth in Durham, had been acquired at the beginning of the seventeenth century. The Bowes, Lambton, and Lumley families, prominent in the Wear valley coal trade, were landowners of long standing, and the Delavals, who did much to develop the coalfield and the coal-using industries of south-east Northumberland, had held large estates in the area since the twelfth century. Moreover, many of the old-established families in the region managed to retain their land, despite the random forces of marriage and the death or absence of heirs and other stresses, often more significant in this period, resulting from the political events of the time.[29]

Clearly the events of the Civil War period imposed extra financial burdens on most landlords, and very heavy ones on some. The Scottish army effectively occupied Northumberland and Durham for periods totalling over three years between 1638 and 1647, and the costs of their maintenance fell upon the local population. As a result of their depredations, and of the English armies which succeeded them, tenants "suffered very much", having their meadows destroyed, and hay, horses, cattle, and servants "taken away for service, to the great dammage of their husbandry". The damage done to the parliamentarian earl of Northumberland's estate in the summer of 1648 was estimated at £3,000, and tenants on many estates were unable to pay their rents. Some landlords faced even greater problems, for 60 gentry families were affected by the acts providing "For the sale of Lands and Estates forfeited to the Commonwealth for treason" passed in 1651 and 1652. As in other areas, this did not necessarily mean that the landowners concerned

---

[28] Hughes, op. cit., pp. xviii, 5; J. Hodgson, A History of Northumberland in Three Parts, Newcastle upon Tyne, 1820–58, II, pt 1, pp. 254–64; pt 2, p. 333; pt 3, pp. 107, 443; R. Welford, Men of Mark twixt Tyne and Tweed, Newcastle upon Tyne, 1895, III, p. 235; Northumb. Co. History Cttee, A History of Northumberland, Newcastle upon Tyne, 1893–1940, IX, p. 295; X, pp. 400–10; XIII, p. 174.

[29] R. Surtees, A History of Durham, Durham, 1820, II, pp. 160–74, 209, 253; Welford, op. cit., III, p. 42.

lost their land: it is possible to follow the fortunes of 31 of the families involved, and of these 14 compounded, 6 recovered their estates through the services of an agent, 1 assigned his estate to his son so that only his life interest could be sold, and 9 recovered their estates fairly quickly, although the precise means by which they did so is not known. Only the Ridleys of Willimondswick lost their land permanently.[30] However, the repurchase of estates and the payment of composition fines often involved the acquisition of much larger sums of money than many landowners had available; it is therefore common to find north-eastern landowners borrowing money by use of mortgages in the period after the Civil War. In some cases the estates were in debt for much longer. The Thornton family of Netherwitton in Northumberland took nearly fifty years to reduce their debts, which had amounted to over £5,000 in 1666, to £1,000, during which time they borrowed from neighbours, Newcastle merchants, and London goldsmiths. Then in 1715 John Thornton was one of a number of the Northumberland gentry who took part in the Jacobite rising, so that by 1720 his son was faced with the task of finding £13,520 to buy the estate back from the men who purchased it from the Forfeited Estates Commission. This again was accomplished with the aid of a number of mortgages. However, some of the men in a position similar to Thornton's were not so successful in managing their debts, and then the mortgage was equally useful to those who bought their land from them. By 1752, for example, the Allgood family had mortgaged debts for over £33,000, the interest on which accounted for nearly half the rental of their estate.[31]

The judicious use of the mortgage therefore helped some men in their efforts to rise in the world, and prevented others from declining. Such a policy could only be successful, however, if incomes increased, and a large mortgage debt therefore provided one reason for increasing rent levels on estates in the north-east. It was not the only reason, however. In the last quarter of the seventeenth century and in the first half of the eighteenth century a number of the gentry and the resident nobility began to build new houses, or to rebuild and extend their existing houses, a movement which culminated in Vanbrugh's work at Seaton Delaval. At the same time increased rents demanded increased investment upon the farms which were to provide them, so that a spiral of development came into being.[32]

It is clear that many landlords, and probably most of the successful ones,

[30] Alnwick MSS, QII 153, 155; *Records of the Committees for Compounding, etc., with Delinquent Royalists in Northumberland and Durham during the Civil War, 1643–1660*, ed. R. Welford, Surtees Soc., III, 1905, p. XI; Brassley, thesis, pp. 55–60.

[31] Northumb. RO, Trevelyan MSS, ZTR 1–63; Mark Hughes, 'Lead, Land and Coal as Sources of Landlord Income in Northumberland, 1700–1850', unpub. Durham Univ. Ph.D. thesis, 1963, II, p. 122. A full account of the sources and use of mortgages by the Thornton and Allgood families is given in Brassley, thesis, pp. 60–7.

[32] J. Hodgson, *History of Northumberland*, II, pt 1, pp. 218–19; Northumb. Co. History Cttee, *op. cit.*, IX, p. 84; XII, pp. 54–5; XIII, pp. 286–7; E. Hughes, *The North-East*, pp. 25–6.

succeeded in increasing their rents in the 1680–1750 period. On the Netherwitton estate the Thorntons increased their rent income from £352 in 1663 to £1,348 in 1715, and by 1724 it had risen by another £400. Nearby at Wallington rents were increased by 68 per cent at May Day 1722, and by 1754 had increased a further 27 per cent. On similar land, rents doubled between 1702, when John Douglas gained control of the Matfen estate, and 1738, and trebled on the Swinburne estate around Capheaton between 1670 and 1750. In the highlands increases were not so large, being of the order of 60 per cent on the Allgood estate between 1705 and 1751, but in the lowlands they were considerable: on the Howard family estate around Morpeth rents more than quadrupled between 1670 and 1750. This vast increase should be set in context, however, for even after it rent levels per acre on the Howard estate were only a little higher than those for land of comparable quality in other parts of the region. Nevertheless, the overall picture of a generally prosperous economy, in which landlords were able to let farms at increased rents, and so service their debts, is clear. This development gave tenant farmers a strong incentive to increase their cash incomes, and, in a period of stable prices, this could only be done by producing more or (which probably amounted to the same thing) selling more from their farms. Both landlord and tenant were thus given a direct interest in agricultural improvements.[33]

One of the landlord's main contributions to agricultural improvement consisted of the provision of capital, for, if higher rents were to be paid, substantial tenants had to be attracted and provided with suitable farms and farm buildings. Those who failed to appreciate this suffered the consequences: in the mid eighteenth century farms on the Whitfield family estate at Whitfield in south Northumberland were said to be "very small – seldom above £20 a year – and the dwelling houses and farm offices upon them all of the most wretched description". The family were forced to sell the estate in 1750 and attributed their downfall to the fact that they embarked upon improvements to the family seat without carrying out any improvements to the estate to provide money for the venture. Other landlords, however, were not so improvident, and many used their woods and quarries to provide building materials. At Double Dykes farm in Haltwhistle parish, on the Allgood estate, the landlord provided all the timber and stone necessary to build a new stable adjoining the new dwelling house in 1730, and paid

[33] PRO, Forfeited Estates Commissioners' MSS (henceforth FEC), 2/82, 83; Northumberland RO, Trevelyan MSS, ZTR 13/1, 2a; Wallington MSS, ZWN D3/1, 4; Blackett (Matfen) MSS, ZBL 85/2; Swinburne MSS, ZSW 220/1; Durham Univ. Dept Pal. and Dip., Howard MSS, N75, N111–17, N119. The Alnwick estate rentals, which were collected on a rent-and-fine basis until at least the early eighteenth century, are more difficult to analyse, but indicate the same rising trend. They are discussed in detail, together with rent movements on other estates, in Brassley, thesis, pp. 69–85.

William Elliot, a "joyner" of Haydon Bridge, £10 to carry out the work. The cost of building could thus be kept to a minimum. A number of new farmhouses were built on the Howard estate around Morpeth between 1700 and 1750 at a cost of about £60 each; older houses were repaired; barns, byres, and boundary walls were built; and land on the estate was set aside as a nursery in which quicks could be raised for new hedges. This expenditure was noted in the estate building account, which often amounted to more than £1,000 per year, and over a fifty-year period must have wrought great changes. Towards the end of this period landlords also began to look outside their estates, and were the major force in the development of the road system, particularly in Northumberland, where in 1752 an act was obtained enabling a road to be built from Hexham through Rothbury to Alnwick and Alnmouth, so that corn could be sent down to the coast without having to pay the high port dues charged at Newcastle. This 'Corn Road', as it became known, was apparently the brainchild of Sir Lancelot Allgood, but most of the larger landowners in the county contributed to the cost entailed.[34]

The most significant improvement, however, was enclosure. The process of enclosure in north-east England occurred in two stages: in the first the emphasis was placed on the enclosure of the open townfields, the arable and meadow lands of the township, and the better areas of common pasture; the second stage involved the enclosure of the common waste, which even in the lowlands often formed a considerable part of the township. Nevertheless the first stage was most important in the lowlands to the east of the region, while the second had its greatest effect in the highland west. In both counties the first stage was virtually complete by 1750, predating the main period of parliamentary enclosure, and the second stage was mainly brought about by act of parliament after 1750. Beginning in the late sixteenth century in Northumberland, enclosures by agreement continued fairly regularly throughout the seventeenth and early eighteenth centuries. The records of twenty-five enclosures by agreement concluded in the 1640–99 period and of a further thirty from the period 1700–50 have been found, most of which relate to townships owned by the earls of Northumberland and their successors. The majority of these enclosures involved the common fields; in only a few cases was the whole township or part of the waste enclosed. Although many enclosure agreements may have failed to survive, it seems clear that this method was the most widely used in the enclosure of Northumberland, for by the middle of the eighteenth century only 15 per cent of the area of the county remained to be enclosed by private or general acts.[35] In Durham much of the better land in the south and east of the county

[34] J. Hodgson, *History of Northumberland, II*, pt 3, p. 101; Northumb. RO, Allgood MSS, ZAL 60/2, 84/19; Durham Univ. Pal. and Dip., Howard MSS, N75, N111–19; W. G. Dodds, 'The Turnpike Trusts of Northumberland', unpub. Durham Univ. M.A. thesis, 1965, p. 23.

[35] W. E. Tate, 'Handlist of Northumberland Enclosure Acts and Awards', *Proc. Soc. of*

was enclosed in the 1630–80 period, although it is significant that the coal-mining areas of the Tyne and Wear valleys were also affected. Twenty-eight enclosure awards were confirmed by a decree of the Bishop's Court of Chancery, and a further twenty-two enclosures were made, but not confirmed, between 1640 and 1750. However, the land affected by parliamentary enclosure, local decrees, and unenrolled agreements accounts for only about half the area of the county. The other half must therefore be accounted for by other means.[36]

Clearly there would have been some land which was never enclosed or held in common, and other areas for which written agreements existed once but no longer survive. But this was also a period in which a great deal of piecemeal enclosure or encroaching on common land was carried on. In 1677, for example, William Taylor was fined 5s. in the manorial court at Brancepeth for "incroaching one acre on the lord's common", and two other men who had encroached three acres were fined 15s. Thereafter these men and others guilty of the same offence were presented regularly to the court, and regularly fined, and it becomes plain that the fines were intended to serve as a rent for the improved land, since they were singularly ineffective as a deterrent: the number of presentments increased from 10 in 1696 to 40 in 1709 and to 50 in 1716. The process continued through the first half of the eighteenth century; in 1754, for example, a map of Lanchester parish was prepared to show the extent of encroachment upon common land by the Clavering family of Greencroft and Weston. Piecemeal encroachment was not confined to Durham. It affected parts of south-west Northumberland, and, on the Alnwick estate, land in Rothbury Forest, a large area of acid moorland, it occurred so extensively that the estate administrators evolved a standard procedure for dealing with new encroachments. For eighteen or twenty-one years they were let at a low rent, usually 6d. or 1s. per acre, and no fine was paid. They were subsequently deemed to be improved, and although the rent remained the same, a fine of three or four times its value was imposed at the beginning of succeeding leases. By 1702 thirty-seven tenants shared 1,354 acres of this improved land, some holding only a few

Antiquaries of Newcastle upon Tyne, 4th ser., x, 1, 1942, p. 43; R. A. Butlin, 'The Evolution of the Agrarian Landscape of Northumberland 1500–1900', unpub. Liverpool Univ. M.A. thesis, 1961, pp. 100, 106; Butlin, 'Field Systems', p. 99; Butlin, 'The Enclosure of Open Fields and Extinction of Common Rights in England, *circa* 1600–1750: A Review', in H. S. A. Fox and R. A. Butlin, *Change in the Countryside: Essays on Rural England, 1500–1900*, Inst. British Geographers, Special Publication no. 10, 1979, pp. 74–5.

[36] J. Grainger, *General View of the Agriculture of Co. Durham*, London, 1794, p. 43; W. E. Tate, 'Handlist of Durham Enclosure Acts and Awards', *Proc. Soc. of Antiquaries of Newcastle upon Tyne*, 4th ser., x, 3, 1943, pp. 128, 136, 138; R. I. Hodgson, 'The Progress of Enclosure in County Durham, 1550–1870', discussion paper presented to the Agrarian Landscape Research group of the Inst. of British Geographers, 1970; R. I. Hodgson, in Baker and Harley, *Man Made the Land*, p. 148; *id.*, 'The Progress of Enclosure in County Durham, 1550–1870', in Fox and Butlin, *op. cit.*

acres while others had as many as 75 or 100. In total they yielded a rent of £65 7s., although they were said to be worth twice as much. At Lordens-hawshead, for example, in 1727 Francis Anderson paid only 1s. per acre for "a certain pcel of wast very barren ground improved there where he has erected a good ffarme house, barne, byer, and granery, cont by estimacon xxxv ac to his great expence and charges of impr^{mt}". In the highlands, the foothills, and the lowland, surveyors maintained that the solution to the problem of poor tenants and low rents lay in enclosure, and the tenants agreed with them. Though the expense might be great (the poorer tenants at Middridge in Durham in 1636 thought that the cost of hedging "would beggar them"), the benefit was undoubted by men who predicted that one acre enclosed would "yield more proffitt than twoe acres antientlie plowed".[37]

The enclosure of the whole or part of a township thus brought about great changes in the structure of agriculture. But often the individual farm was not only part of a township but also part of an estate, and the estates of the nobility and gentry, which sometimes included whole townships, formed another level of organization which underwent substantial changes in this period. Since the estates were the decision-making units, controlling factors as basic as farm size, capital investment, and sometimes farming practice over a large area of the two counties, their reorganization was of great significance from the point of view of agricultural production and productivity. The reorganization of many of the estates in the highlands began in the early seventeenth century, when a number of court cases concerning the tenure of land on the border had to be settled. Forms of land tenure long outmoded further south had been maintained by the crown, which owned many of the border manors, in order to retain a sufficient supply of fighting men. After the Union the crown lands on the border were granted to royal favourites, who tried to improve the commercial potential of their estates, which were let to customary tenants. Customary tenure was very secure, and in the large manors of Wark and Harbottle descent was by partible inheritance, so that potential fighting men were virtually guaranteed enough land for subsistence, but no more. The resultant overpopulation had deleterious effects upon the commercial viability of the area, so that when fighting men were no longer needed landlords began to argue that customary tenants were in fact tenants at the will of the lord. Therefore, they argued, they could legally convert customary tenants into leasehold tenants. This policy met with much legal opposition, but despite this it seems to have achieved its objective of gradually reducing the population. Certainly by the Civil War period the officers and

[37] Durham RO, Brancepeth MSS, E 6; R. I. Hodgson, in *Man Made the Land*, p. 149; E. Hughes, *op. cit.*, pp. 124–5; Alnwick MSS, (A)A i 6, (A)A vi 1; Northumb. RO, Allgood MSS, ZAL box 57/20; Durham Univ. Pal. and Dip., Chancery Decrees (copies), nos. 254,593½, 244,381, 244,385, 244,386, 244,155, 244,390, 244,392.

troopers of the Northumberland Horse felt the need to petition the leaders of the parliamentary army, claiming that the "ancient tenures" of the county had been destroyed to the detriment of the common people, forcing them to become "hinds, half hinds, quarter hinds, shepherds and herdsmen". The change was by no means instantaneous, and many of the old border gentry such as the Herons of Chipchase were reluctant to eject their tenants. However, when the Herons finally succumbed to their debts the Allgoods, who took over their estate, soon began to reduce the number of tenants.[38] By 1720, therefore, an agricultural structure was established in the highlands which was to last until the parliamentary enclosure of the wastes: a few manors in the upper valley of the South Tyne remained in customary tenure, but most of the larger estates were engrossed into substantial farms let by lease. The small freeholders were able to withstand this process until the enclosure of the wastes in the later eighteenth century, and highland parishes such as Alwinton and Simonburn were mostly farmed by men who owned land worth less than £5 per annum.[39]

The process of engrossing also occurred on a number of estates in the foothills. At Brancepeth in Durham the Belasyse family estate was reorganized in the 1730s into a number of compact farms. Eleven tenants held land owned by the Swinburne family at Hamsterley in Durham in 1668, but by 1715 this number had declined to four farmers and two smallholders. By 1747 the Swinburnes had only two tenants in the township, one paying a rent of £145 and the other only £20 for the mill and some land. The same process occurred on their Northumberland estates, the nineteen tenants at Heugh in 1668 having been reduced to six in 1745; and the Thornton estate at Netherwitton, which had been farmed by nine tenants in 1702, was divided among only five in 1715. These changes were sometimes associated with enclosure by agreement, as when William Craster took over all the 544 acres allotted to Sir John Swinburne after the enclosure of Lowick in 1724, but more often the farms were reorganized independently of enclosure. The enclosure of Clarewood and Halton Shields near Corbridge was carried out between 1680 and 1705, but it was not until 1715 that the six farms at Clarewood were reduced to two, while the takeover of the two smaller farms at Halton Shields by the tenants of the two larger farms did not occur until 1727.[40]

[38] PRO, Exchequer Bills and Answers, E 112/112/170; E 134 (Depositions), 18 Jas. I, Mich. 20 (Northumb.); S. J. Watts, 'Tenant-Right in Early Seventeenth-Century Northumberland', *Northern Hist.*, VI, 1971, p. 67; H. N. Brailsford, *The Levellers and the English Revolution*, London, 1961, pp. 447–8; Northumb. RO, Allgood MSS, ZAL 23/4.

[39] E. Hughes, *op. cit.*, p. 119; Bailey and Culley, *General View of Northumberland*, pp. 25, 205; J. Hodgson, *History of Northumberland*, III, pt 1, pp. 271–3, 302–9.

[40] Ingleson, thesis, p. 77; Northumberland RO, Swinburne MSS, ZSW 214–18; Trevelyan MSS, ZTR 11/34, 12/1; PRO, FEC 2/82–3. It is important to note that these changes were seldom brought about overnight, but often occurred in several stages, spread over a number of years – Brassley, thesis, pp. 111–17.

It therefore appears that enclosure and engrossing were not inevitably linked, but were both stages in the reorganization of the structure of agriculture; and, indeed, on estates in the lowlands enclosure took place without any great degree of engrossing, although the size of farms increased. Using surveys of the earl of Northumberland's estate, Tawney pointed out the economic equality of tenants in the north-east in the sixteenth century, showing how each had roughly the same amount of land as others in the township, and that most farms were between twenty and sixty acres in extent. The reason for this he attributed to the military importance of tenants, but subsequent surveys of the same estate show that the land remained evenly divided for a long time after 1603. Even in 1727 the surveyors were able to give the value of holdings in a township as, for example, "between £9 and £10 per farm". Nevertheless the estate did change, for whereas in the mid sixteenth century only one-quarter of its farms were of more than forty acres, by 1755 only one-quarter of its farms were of under forty acres. At the same time, however, the number of tenants on the estate fell by less than 10 per cent between 1685 and 1755, and in any one township the number of farmers usually declined by only one or two between 1620 and 1755, sons often succeeding their fathers for generation after generation. Clearly the process of enclosure of the old arable land of a township, and the extension of arable cultivation to land formerly held as common waste, affected all farmers equally.[41] The same thing happened on the earl of Carlisle's estate around Morpeth: again the number of tenants remained virtually constant, while the size of their farms increased. This is not to say that the earl's steward was against the amalgamation of farms; indeed, in the early eighteenth century he repeatedly urged amalgamation as a method of increasing both fertility and rent. However, if tenants were able to pay increased rents, landlords seem to have been loath to go to the trouble and expense of enclosing and engrossing. At Newburn in 1685 it was said that "the tenants are the better enabled to pay their rents by reason of their carrying coales from his Graces severall collieryes", and many small farms, of twenty-five acres or less, remained in the township in 1755. On large estates in the lowlands the landlord often owned the whole township, and it was therefore comparatively simple to add former waste land which was of reasonable quality to existing farms. On smaller estates in the highlands and the foothills the waste was not so potentially productive, so engrossing was also necessary.[42]

In a pastoral region like the north-east enclosure had an immediate effect upon the profitability of farming, since the greater regularity of defoliation

[41] R. H. Tawney, *The Agrarian Problem in the Sixteenth Century*, London, 1912, pp. 63–6; Alnwick MSS, A. vi 7, 8, (A)A vi 1, (A)B i 3, (A)A i 4, (A)A i 6; Brassley, thesis, pp. 120–3.

[42] Durham Univ. Pal. and Dip., Howard MSS, Niii; Alnwick MSS, (A)B i 3, (A)A vi 1, (A)A i 4.

and dunging must have brought about a significant improvement in the quality of pastures, and where the farmer was aware of the benefits of manuring and alternate husbandry the improvement would have been considerable. It is therefore impossible to discuss the management of grassland and arable separately, for the two were intimately linked. In many townships, in fact, grassland was probably ploughed, cropped, and allowed to revert to pasture long before enclosure occurred, as parts of the outfields, which many townships possessed, were cultivated from time to time. George Liddell, reporting to his father in Gateshead on the condition of the newly purchased Eslington estate in 1719, described how the tenants would "grow corne till it will do no more and then lay it down", as a result of which they were "as poor as charity". This was hardly alternate husbandry, however, since the outfield arable formed only a small part of the total arable acreage, and the exhausted arable was not sown with grass seeds but allowed to grow anything that would germinate. Real improvements were seen when the old arable lands of a township, "waisted and worne with continuall ploweing and thereby made bare barren and unfruitful", were enclosed and yields increased "by reason of the ploughing up of fresh grounds and converting them into tillage which heretofore were used in pasture". This was the change which the proponents of enclosure at Middridge in Durham in the 1630s promised. Later in the seventeenth century the newly enclosed land was managed even more explicitly according to the tenets of alternate husbandry. When John Douglas took over the management of Clarewood and Halton Shields in 1686 he enclosed common pastures and meadows and brought them into cultivation and decreed that one of the old common arable fields should be laid to "lee". In addition, another small field was to be a "lee close".[43]

The improvements brought about by the development of alternate husbandry were reinforced by the use of lime, manure, and new crop species. Early in the seventeenth century farmers near Newcastle carted ashes and dung from the town to spread on their land, but by the beginning of the eighteenth century landlords were prescribing in some detail the way in which farms should be managed. This did not always meet with the approval of their tenants: Thomas Tinlin of Broomhouse farm near Haltwhistle saw no reason why his landlord should interfere with his farming so long as he paid his rent, whereas the landlord wanted Tinlin to increase his use of manure and improve his grassland management. The dispute began in 1736 and lasted until 1740, and in the end the two parties compromised, Tinlin making the required improvements and the landlord granting a twenty-one-year lease instead of the short lease he would have preferred for an awkward tenant.[44]

[43] Mark Hughes, thesis, I, p. 177; Durham Univ. Pal. and Dip., Chancery Decrees (copies), no. 29; Northumb. RO, Blackett MSS, ZBL 14, 85/2.

[44] PRO, E 134 20 Jas. I, E18; Gateshead Central Library, Ellison MSS, A52/12–17, A27/46, A28/30, 37, 43; Cotesworth MSS CN/7/129, 53.

In general, however, the terms of the lease and the husbandry clauses it contained admitted no argument. In late-seventeenth-century leases on the earl of Carlisle's estate clauses were inserted which prevented the ploughing up of pasture and meadow, "except such as were before in tillage during the said tenure". When Isabel Cleugh took the lease of a farm at Hepscott for twenty-one years in 1716 the management of two meadow closes was specified in even more detail: after four years from the beginning of the lease she was to

Sumer fallow all the arable ground in two meadow closes above mentioned and then lay twenty ffothers of limstons burnt into lime and thirty ffothers of muck upon each acre of the same when ffaughed as aforesaid after taking one crop or two at the most of and from the same shall and will lay down and convert to meadow and pasture.

Later leases were more specific still, and when her son took over the farm even the number of cultivations of the fallow, together with the time at which they should be done (the first "stearing" by midsummer, the second before August 10th, and so on), were laid down.[45]

Lime was applied to land on the coastal plain of Northumberland by the 1670s, if not before. The cheapness of coal from small local pits must have contributed to its popularity, and by the 1720s, according to John Laurence, its use was widespread in Northumberland and Durham. Laurence gave 150 bushels per acre as the average dressing of the summer fallows and stressed the importance of lime in the reclamation of wastes, which might be "turned into arable land; and so far improved by lime and inclosures, that what was not worth above one shilling an acre, is now become worth twenty". Dung, home-produced and laid on fallow land in large quantities, was the most common manure, but Laurence also described how in "near all the populous places along the sea coast" vast quantities of coal ash were also used, a treatment which was "observed to have a strange property of making the soil run much to clover grass or trefoil, which of all others is the sweetest and richest feed for cattle".[46]

When Laurence published his *New System of Agriculture* in 1726, clover had only recently been introduced into the north-east. It first appeared as a cultivated crop on Tyneside, and in 1722 was undersown in a barley crop on William Cotesworth's estate at Gateshead. In 1723 two sacks of clover

---

[45] Durham Univ. Pal. and Dip., Howard MSS, N11/9, 14, N115. Similar conditions were found in leases of farms in Northumberland, e.g. Northumb. RO, Swinburne MSS, ZSW 12/3 and Trevelyan MSS, ZTR 1/75.

[46] John Laurence, *A New System of Agriculture*, London, 1726, pp. 78–9, 80–1. In 1769 John Wallis, in *The Natural History and Antiquities of Northumberland*, London, 1769, I, pp. 36–7, reported that on the land around Newcastle much manure was used, "some native, and vast quantities extraneous, brought at an easy expense from *London*, by way of ballast in the coal ships".

seed were unloaded at Berwick, and trefoil and sainfoin seed as well as clover were often sent by sea from London, mainly for landowners with contacts in the capital who would select a reliable sample of seed. Ryegrass was introduced at about the same time as clover, and at Gateshead in 1733 the two were sown together. By 1737 ryegrass was "so common everywhere" in the region that it was possible to dispense with the importation of seed from London. Nevertheless the new fodder crops were not always accepted without question. In 1748 Robert Swinburne, the rector of Hebburn, mentioned hearing "objections to sowing clover etc" which he thought proved "nothing but ye great want of experience in ye objectors", and in the 1750s a lease of land on the earl of Carlisle's estate near Morpeth stipulated that only the sweepings of the barn floor should be used to seed pastures, and that no bought-in seed should be used.[47] These exceptions notwithstanding, it is clear that by the middle of the eighteenth century a combination of better management, better manuring, and better strains of forage crops had significantly increased the productive potential of much land in the north-east.

Improvements in farm and pasture management seem to have been the main reason for the increase in the numbers and weight of fatstock in the first half of the eighteenth century. In the middle of the eighteenth century John Wallis wrote fulsomely of "the largest and fattest oxen, commonly sold to the butchers of North Shields, for the ships in the coal trade, and to the contractors of the navy", and he carefully attributed the quality of the oxen to the quality of the grass, "a short sweet and lovely sort, mixed with daisies and yellow, crimson and white perennial clovers, eat up to the very roots by the sheep and cattle". Some improvements were bred into the shorthorn, which had been the dominant breed in the region since the early seventeenth century at least, when Mr Michael Dobison imported Dutch bulls in the early eighteenth century, but the most notable developments in cattle breeding had to wait until the second half of the eighteenth century. The same was true of sheep, although by 1750 farmers were beginning the practice which was later to become so popular, of feeding sheep to great weights. As the *Newcastle Courant* reported on 15 January 1749, "Last Xmas was exposed to sale at Barnard Castle...a sheep...weighing near 20 stone; the quarters of which, one with another, weighed 45 lb each." More significant than this, however, was the increase in the value of lamb and wool tithes in the parish of Norham; these were worth £30 per year in 1666 and £94 per year in 1736. The magnitude of this change may not have been repeated everywhere, but its direction at least was common.[48]

[47] E. Hughes, *op. cit.*, p. 143; Gateshead Central Library, Cotesworth MSS, CN3/13; Ellison MSS, A27/46; *Newcastle Courant*, Feb. 1729; Durham Univ. Pal. and Dip., Howard MSS, N52/55.

[48] Wallis, *op. cit.*, I, p. 31; G. Culley, *Observations on Livestock*, London, 1786, p. 28; Brassley, thesis, pp. 165–7.

Considering the importance that they were to attain in the later eighteenth century, turnips, as a field crop, were introduced relatively late into the north-east. Inventories, which become sparse by the 1720s, do not mention them, and this reinforces the evidence of Bailey and Culley, who put the date of their introduction at some time between 1710 and 1730. It was then that Mr Procter, the proprietor of Rock, near Alnwick, brought Andrew Willey, a gardener, to his estate to cultivate turnips for cattle fodder. Willey subsequently took up residence at Lesbury, a short distance away, and built up a business as a cultivator of the crop for neighbouring farmers. It seems possible that there was an additional source of innovation, for in 1721 eight acres of turnips were broadcast at Reaveley Greens near Brandon in the Cheviot foothills and in the following year more were sown at West Chevington.[49] Introduction was no earlier in Durham. John Laurence, in his *A New System of Agriculture* (published in 1726), criticized the late introduction of turnips as "a piece of great neglect in the farmers of the north, that they are not easily to be brought into this piece of good husbandry".[50]

Once introduced, however, the crop soon became popular, on the lighter land at least. By 1740 turnips were being grown on Sir John Swinburne's home farm at Capheaton, and in 1743 the steward there indicated the impact of the crop in Northumberland in complaining that "turnip mutton keeps our marketts soe low for ffat". On the heavier land around Hexham the introduction of the turnip had to wait until the latter part of the eighteenth century, but by the middle of the eighteenth century the crop had become popular enough to be attacked in print: John Wallis, writing in the 1760s, was surprised

that turnip husbandry should be so much in fasion, which spoils the dairy, and the shambles, sends such gross flavoured milk, cream and butter, beef and mutton to our tables. It is well enough for a *succedaneum* in the cold winter months, or in unfavourable summers for grass, but to give it so much of our care and attention, to the neglect of other cultures, and the cherishing of natural herbage, can be nothing but the effect of avarice and sloth.

Wallis was voicing the former attachment of the north-eastern farmer to grass. There was, in this period, usually no shortage of grazing land in most villages, and the late introduction of the turnip is probably nothing more than a reflection of this.[51]

[49] As Willey hoed his crop, it may have been sown in drills, which suggests that it was not he who introduced turnips at Brandon – Bailey and Culley, *op. cit.*, p. 92; Macdonald, thesis, p. 315.

[50] Laurence, *op. cit.*, p. 111. Before being appointed to the rectory of Bishopwearmouth in 1721 Laurence had lived in Northamptonshire, where he had written several books on gardening and had travelled extensively in the Midlands – G. O. Bellewes, 'Notes on the Life and Works of John Laurence, Rector of Bishopwearmouth, 1721–32', *Antiquities of Sunderland*, IV, n.d., pp. 35–57.

[51] Northumberland RO, Swinburne MSS, ZSW 212/3, 5; Macdonald, thesis, p. 315; Wallis, *op. cit.*, p. 410.

Rape was grown in county Durham by 1680. When John Marsh, rector of Haughton le Skerne, died in November 1680 he had nine and a half acres of rapeseed, worth £27. As an educated man (his library was valued at £50) farming a large area of fertile land it would not be surprising if he was one of the early adopters of the crop. The fact that the crop was described as "rapeseed" suggests that Bailey in his *General View* of Durham was correct in ascribing the first use of rape as a fodder crop for sheep to the 1740s, and it is clear that the rape grown on the Allgood estate in North Tynedale in 1709 was grown for seed (which was crushed for its oil) rather than for fodder, since several men were paid to thresh it. It is unlikely, however, that local production did more than supplement imported supplies: rapeseed and rape oil were included in a number of general cargoes arriving by sea at Newcastle and Berwick from Hull and London in 1729.[52] Mustard was also grown in Durham by the 1740s, if not earlier, The product was "proverbial for its excellence" and in 1742 New College, Oxford began buying Durham mustard seed regularly at 2s. per pound. By 1769 Young found much mustard cultivated in the villages around Durham city, and although it could be sown on pared and burnt land its distribution seems to have remained confined to that area.[53]

Potatoes were more widely grown, both in Durham and Northumberland, by the eighteenth century, although landlords were often hostile to them as a consequence of their high nutrient requirement. In 1755 a tenant at Elemore Hall near Durham was forbidden to sow potatoes except for his own consumption, and near Morpeth tenants were fined £3 for every acre planted with potatoes; since some men were prepared to pay £4 10s. per acre for potato land, this may not have been a very effective deterrent.[54]

In many of the pasture farming areas of England in the seventeenth and early eighteenth centuries agriculture was combined with manufacturing activities, but in the north-east there is little evidence for the existence of handicraft trades in the countryside itself. This is not to say that such trades were entirely absent from the region, or that agriculture was the only occupation. Manufacturing trades were found in many of the small towns, such as Berwick, which in 1684 was exporting worsted stockings, "the manufacture of this place", and Wooler and Rothbury, where hats were made. Stockings were also knitted in the district around Barnard Castle, and many were sent by ship from Newcastle, while Darlington produced worsted

[52] Brassley, thesis, p. 168; J. Bailey, *A General View of the Agriculture of Durham*, London, 1810, p. 146; Northumb. RO, Allgood MSS, ZAL 44/1; PRO, Newcastle and Berwick Port Books, E 190, 173/2, 234/9.

[53] J. E. T. Rogers, *A History of Agriculture and Prices in England*, VII, pt 1, Oxford, 1902, pp. 245–9; Young, *Northern Tour*, III, p. 1.

[54] Bailey, *op. cit.*, p. 165; Bailey and Culley, *op. cit.*, p. 90; Durham Univ. Pal. and Dip., Baker Baker MSS 40/14; Howard MSS, N52/1, 2, N11/14, N41/28.

and linen, and Durham produced carpets by the end of the seventeenth century. Compared to the primary industries of mining and the trades related to mining, however, the textile trades were of little importance. As a report of 1605 concluded,"in the countyes of Durham and Northumberland there be no great trades as clothing and suchlike used, by which the poorer sort are sett on worke and relieved from begery saving only the trades of colyery and salting". Clearly an industry as closely related to one small area as was the main coal-mining industry cannot be termed a rural industry. Yet it must be discussed at this point, first because the importance of coal mining perhaps accounts for the insignificance of other rural industries, and secondly because the winning of coal for export by sea was not the only type of mining in the region. The demand for labour resulting from the expansion of the coal industry in this period meant that even in a pastoral area such as this there was seldom any great pool of unemployed or underemployed male labour. Many of the workers in the Tyneside and Wearside coal trades came from the farming areas, particularly the poorer farming areas such as the border dales, and in some cases the migration was seasonal, the men returning to their families in the winter. In addition to pits in the Tyne and Wear valleys (known as 'sea-sale' pits) large numbers of small pits were scattered all over the two counties, catering for the local demand for coal, and these too provided full- or part-time work. In 1687, for example, John Hasty took the lease of a small farm at Lyardean near Durham, but he also worked for his landlord from time to time and in a neighbouring coal mine. The men who worked in the lead mines which were developed in the northern Pennine dales from the beginning of the eighteenth century were also usually small farmers, although in this case it seems that their holdings were so small that farming was very much a subsidiary to their main occupation of mining. Ironstone was also mined in Weardale, and in addition to the mining industries a number of trades used the products of the mines: swords were made at Shotley Bridge in the Derwent valley, and further downstream at Winlaton the Crowley ironworks employed large numbers, while at the mouth of the Tyne coal was used to fire large numbers of salt pans.[55]

As far as the farming areas were concerned, a shortage of male labour was more likely than a surplus, and this, as George Culley explained to Arthur Young in 1790, meant that "our girls are all employed in agriculture. Hoing, haymaking, and reaping, etc. etc." At Spindleston in north Northumberland in the 1680s and on the Shipcote and Park estates at Gateshead in the 1730s the hay and corn harvests were largely dependent upon female labour, and some female day labourers were employed for most of the year. The concentration of labour in the primary industries therefore explains why manufacturing trades had little, if any, significance in the rural area. The

[55] *VCH Durham*, II, pp. 288, 315, 355; PRO, E 190, 192/4; Brassley, thesis, p. 34; Durham Univ. Pal. and Dip., Baker Baker MSS, 72/251–2; Hunt, *Lead Miners*, p. 151.

north-east produced a wide range of primary commodities, but only a few manufactured products. The list of exports from ports in the region confirms this picture. While ships leaving the Tyne usually carried coal, those sailing from smaller ports such as Berwick, Alnmouth, and Stockton carried, in addition to their main cargoes of corn and dairy products, a wide range of agricultural products, such as eggs, packs of wool, heather, and raw hides, and an even wider range of non-agricultural products. In the seventeenth century large quantities of fish (especially salmon) were sent from Berwick to London, and in the eighteenth century Berwick exported sealskins; rabbit, hare, and other skins; juniper berries; grindstones; and beeswax. With the exception of products such as these the rural population of the north-east concentrated upon agriculture, and even the borderers' practice of stealing from their neighbours (perhaps the most talked-about by-employment in the sixteenth century) was by the end of the seventeenth century "vary much laid aside".[56]

It is apparent that the years between 1640 and 1750 saw a great transformation in north-eastern England. A region which in the sixteenth century had been mainly remarkable for lawlessness and poverty began its association with industry and trade, and as a result its agriculture began the rise to the pre-eminence which it attained in the nineteenth century. In 1750 many of the necessary improvements in cattle and sheep breeding, cultivation methods, and grassland management were still unknown; but enclosure and estate reorganization had changed a system reminiscent (in Tawney's phrase) of "a medieval survey" into one in which the later innovators could flourish.[57]

[56] Macdonald, *thesis*, p. 188; Northumb. RO, Simpson MSS, ZSI 1–4; Gateshead Central Library, Cotesworth MSS CN/2; PRO, E 190, 162–77; E. Gibson, ed., *Camden's Britannia*, London, 1695, p. 874.
[57] Tawney, *The Agrarian Problem*, p. 66.

CHAPTER 3

YORKSHIRE AND LANCASHIRE

Yorkshire and Lancashire contained a great variety of natural scenery and agrarian systems. Here were rich pastures on the plains and in the marshlands and fens, fertile arable lands on the magnesian limestone belt in the Vale of York, places that specialized in producing such things as butter, potatoes, or liquorice, and a great number of villages, hamlets, and isolated farmsteads on the coalfield and the edge of the Pennines where peasant-craftsmen were laying the foundations of the Industrial Revolution. But elsewhere in the region, much of the High Wolds was fit only for sheepwalks and rabbit warrens, and vast acres of moorland were of hardly any agricultural value at all: "The north Lancashire hills", wrote Daniel Defoe, "had a kind of inhospitable terror in them, all barren and wild, of no use or advantage either to man or beast."[1]

North of the river Lune the soils that overlay the carboniferous limestone were thin and poor and difficult to till. John Lucas wrote that the greatest impediment of the early-eighteenth-century farmers of his native Warton was "the great quantity of stones that are found therein, some whereof are very large...the most mischievous are those which are covered with soil, but yet are not out of the way of the plow". In his time, gunpowder had been used to dislodge "vast numbers of these stones", which were removed on sledges by "the diligent husbandman".[2] In 1649 the manor of Warton contained five hundred acres of unstinted common pasture and turbary in a coastal marsh, which was "much wasted and more likely to bee by reason of the sea daily overflowing and washing away the same".[3] The farming was geared towards the rearing of cattle and of small flocks of sheep, "whose flesh is much commended and esteemed". Yet even in this unpromising area enough corn was produced for local needs in normal times. Barley, oats, rye, and grey wheat were grown on the better soils, small quantities of hemp and flax were nourished on the alluvial lands near the marshes, and though "there are some fields in this parish that appear to be nothing else but a gathering of pebbles, insomuch that earth cannot well be discover'd among them; yet

[1] D. Defoe, *A Tour through the Whole Island of Great Britain* (1724–6), 2 vols., London, 1962, II, p. 269.
[2] *John Lucas's History of Warton Parish* (1710–40), ed. J. R. Ford and J. A. Fuller-Maitland, Kendal, 1931, p. 3.
[3] PRO, E 317/Lancs. 30.

do they yield abundance of good corn, especially oates, barley and pease, yea more than some contiguous lands that are not so stony".[4]

A small part of the parish of Warton was farmed under a common-field system. Some lands were tilled continuously, but the rest followed a course of three years' corn and six years' pasture. The farmers preferred oxen when ploughing their stony lands, and Lucas had often seen a plough team of six oxen without even a horse to lead them. Harrows were used, but there were "no such instruments as either a roller or clodding mell. They weed their corn about the latter end of May or beginning of June, with an instrument like a pair of smith's tongs, which they call a pair of gripes, jagged like a rasp on the inner sides, to take the firmest hold; with which they pluck up the weeds by the roots." At harvest time, "they shear it all, except the bands which they pull up by the roots...and mow none".[5]

South of the Lune the concern of the coastal farmers was with the spread of the sand. The Church Mere at Formby was marked on maps drawn between 1588 and 1610, but it had been covered with sand by 1750. The normal solution was to plant star grass on the dunes, and this communal obligation was written into lease covenants and enforced by the manorial courts. Thus, in 1730, Peter Jump was fined 2s. by the court leet of Formby "for not setting starr on two days", and watchers were appointed by the court to prevent the rushes being stolen by the makers of mats and brushes. Stable dunes, or 'hawes', could be used as sheep pastures and for growing rye.[6]

Beyond the dunes lay the Lancashire plain. Extensive glacial deposits meant that sands, gravels, loams, clays, and peats, well-drained and poorly-drained soils, podzols, and rich warps could all be found within a few miles' radius of each other, and farming practices differed accordingly.[7] Most of the plain was held in severalty in farms of under fifty acres, and by the second half of the period there were numerous smallholders with under ten acres who were dependent upon their common rights.[8] Much of the land was freehold,

[4] Lucas, op. cit., pp. 55, 4. Hemp was recorded in 26 of 224 Lancashire inventories dated between 1640 and 1750, and was grown particularly in the north-western part of the Lancashire plain.

[5] Ibid., pp. 134–5, 4.

[6] E. Kelly, ed., Viking Village: The Story of Formby, Formby, 1973, pp. 23–4. The Formby sandhills were divided by agreement in 1669. F. A. Bailey, History of Southport, Southport, 1955, pp. 11, 12, 24; E. Salisbury, Downs and Dunes, London, 1952, pp. 211, 213, 293.

[7] E. Crompton, The Soils of the Preston District of Lancashire, Soil Survey of Great Britain, Harpenden, 1966.

[8] In 1731 George Farington's lands in Leyland, Penwortham, and Ulnes Walton were leased to 220 tenants, of whom 56 had under 1 acre and 122 between 1 and 10 acres (Lancs. RO, DDF/85), though it is not clear whether these are statute or customary acres (651 Lancs. acres = 1,210 statute acres). At Fox Denton in 1727 10 people held fewer than 5 acres, 9 people had between 5 and 9 acres, 12 people had between 10 and 19 acres, 5 people had between 20 and 29 acres, 11 people had between 30 and 56 acres, and there were just under 100 acres attached to the Hall farm (Lancs. RO, DDX/275/1). A similar pattern of holdings can be observed at Charnock Richard in 1665

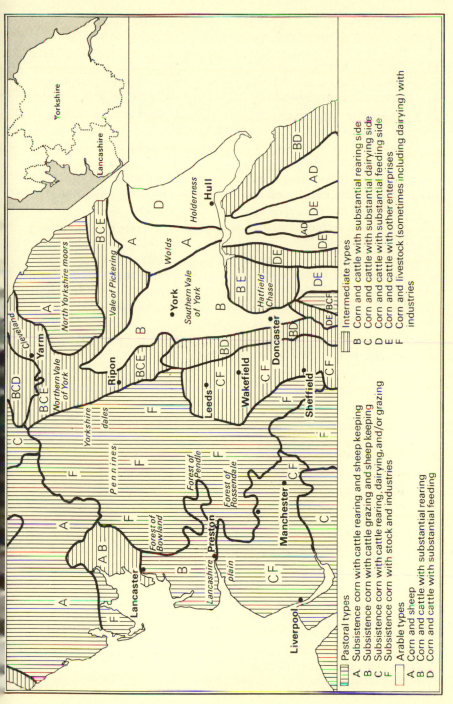

Pastoral types
A Subsistence corn with cattle rearing and sheep keeping
B Subsistence corn with cattle grazing and sheep keeping
C Subsistence corn with cattle rearing, dairying, and/or grazing
F Subsistence corn with stock and industries

Arable types
A Corn and sheep
B Corn and cattle with substantial rearing
D Corn and cattle with substantial feeding

Intermediate types
B Corn and cattle with substantial rearing side
C Corn and cattle with substantial dairying side
D Corn and cattle with substantial feeding side
E Corn and cattle with other enterprises
F Corn and livestock (sometimes including dairying) with industries

Fig. 3.1. Farming regions of Yorkshire and Lancashire.

and the tenants of the great landlords normally held for three lives or for twenty-one years at competitive entry fines but easy rents.[9] Where common fields existed they rarely covered more than 150 acres or a tenth of a township. Many townfields had been enclosed quietly and by agreement long before the Civil War and few remained to be rearranged by parliamentary enclosure. Most of the surviving strips had been adapted to convertible husbandry; and in the late seventeenth century the fields of Little Crosby were unusual in being "very much bared by reasons of long tillage".[10] The great variety of soils makes it difficult to generalize about the husbandry of the Lancashire plain. Probate inventories show that some farmers had many acres under tillage, yet others had no crops at all. In parts of the plain at least half, and usually more, of the former arable was put down to grass, and in times of harvest crisis corn had to be imported into the region. Oats and barley (with a few acres of the northern varieties, groats and bigg) were the chief crops, and oats was the general bread corn.[11] However, wheat was grown more extensively than has often been supposed.[12] Wealthy farmers such as Nicholas Blundell of Little Crosby could afford to experiment with clover, trefoil, ryegrass, coleseed, and turnips, but they were exceptional. Most soils were unsuitable for turnips, and as late as 1795 Holt acknowledged that they were cultivated only "on a very contracted scale".[13]

Whatever the size of their holdings, Lancashire people of all classes seem to have placed most emphasis upon the rearing of beef and the keeping of small dairies. The famous black longhorns were all-purpose cattle, valued for

(DDA1/127), Clayton le Woods in 1681 (DDM/14/1), Kirby in 1696 (DDM/14/3), Samlesbury in 1719 (DDPt/39/11), and Eccleston in 1720 (DDSc/25/9). See also Manchester Univ., John Rylands Library, Tatton 17 and Clowes 544. The Kirby tenants were local people almost to a man, and at this period the surnames of all classes of Lancashire and West Riding families contained a remarkably high proportion that were derived from local place names.

[9] Lancs. RO, DDA1/127, DDB/1/54/8, DDF/85, DDM/14/1, DDPt/39/11; PRO, E 317/Lancs. 18. However, boon labour was still enforced on some estates, and during the Civil War "oppressive landlords" were able to evict those tenants who supported parliament – *The Great Diurnall of Nicholas Blundell of Little Crosby*, 3 vols., Manchester, 1968–72, I, p. 136; T & C, p. 142.

[10] G. Youd, 'The Common Fields of Lancashire', *Historic Soc. of Lancs. & Cheshire*, CXIII, 1961, pp. 1–42; R. Cunliffe Shaw, 'The Townfields of Lancashire', *ibid.*, CXIV, 1962, pp. 23–36; G. Elliott, 'Field Systems of Northwest England', in A. R. H. Baker and R. A. Butlin, eds., *Studies of Field Systems in the British Isles*, Cambridge, 1973, pp. 41–92.

[11] Lancs. RO, probate inventories and EDC/5; J. Bankes and E. Kerridge, *The Early Records of the Bankes Family at Winstanley*, Manchester, 1973, p. 6; *The Autobiography of William Stout of Lancaster, 1665–1752*, ed. J. D. Marshall, Manchester, 1967, p. 204: "1729...There was some flower imported here from America, and about six hundred loads of wheat and oats from Hamburg... corn was continually brought into Liverpool till harvest, and it was compuited that there was imported into this country and Chester this year, corn to the value of one hundred thousand pounds."

[12] Wheat is recorded in the 1640s in inventories from Adlington, Aughton, Great Harwood, Kirby, Leigh, Parbold, Scarisbrick, Wigan Woodhouses, Winwick, etc.

[13] Blundell, *op. cit.*, I, p. 297, and II, pp. 14–18; J. Holt, *General View of the Agriculture of the County of Lancaster*, London, 1795, p. 64.

their beef, milk, tallow, hides, and horn, and for their strength in draught. The calves were mostly bred in the plain, but others were brought from the Pennines, Scotland, Ireland, and the Isle of Man. Some were sold later to the graziers of central and southern England.[14] A sample of 124 Lancashire inventories that recorded cattle between 1640 and 1699 had a median average of nine head per holding, which is not very large when compared with neighbouring counties. Most farms were small and their tenants were dependent upon by-employments, but some yeomen, of course, had much larger herds than this; Robert Walthew of Pemberton (1676), for instance, had 9 stirks, 6 heifers, 1 fat cow, 7 milch cows, 9 young calves, and a sucking calf, worth in all £87, and John Kay of Worsley (1719) had 5 stirks, 2 bulls, 17 cows, "young cattle upon the moors", and a cow at hire, valued together at £97. 5s. A list of the cattle belonging to William Molyneux at Sefton, Newpark, and Aintree (1691) comprised 6 oxen for drawing, 7 oxen for beef, 6 steers, 9 three-year-old bullocks, 7 two-year-old bullocks, 1 young bullock for beef, 3 Manx bullocks for beef, 3 bull segs for beef, 10 cows for beef, 7 cows for milk, 20 northern cows, 18 head of cattle in tenants' hands, and 13 heifers, 2 bulls, and 11 weaning calves for sale.[15] A sample of 84 inventories taken between 1700 and 1709 and during the 1740s reveals a decline in the number of large herds and a median average of only 7 head per holding. There is no evidence in the inventories that the Fylde had already acquired its late-eighteenth-century reputation as the prime breeding ground. Indeed, the largest herds of cattle were generally to be found in the eastern part of the plain, well away from the mosslands. Most farmers had a few milkers amongst their cattle, and 99 of the sample of 224 Lancashire inventories refer either to cheese or to cheese presses. 'Cheshire' cheese was made in the Vale of Warrington, but everywhere the scale of production was small, and 'Lancashire' cheese did not become a speciality until the late eighteenth century.[16]

The farmers' dependency upon cattle proved dangerous and even disastrous when a severe winter followed a poor hay harvest or when cattle plague infected the area. William Stout of Lancaster records that in the winter of 1682–3 "people were very much straitned to keep their cattel alive, and many starved"; in 1733 cattle were "very low and few sold. This went hard with

---

[14] Holt, op. cit., pp. 143–5; T & C, p. 157; E. Kerridge, The Agricultural Revolution, London, 1967, p. 146; D. Woodward, 'The Anglo-Irish Livestock Trade of the Seventeenth Century', Irish Hist. Stud., XVIII, 172, 1973, pp. 489–523; O. Ashmore, 'Inventories as a Source of Local History, II – Farmers', Amateur Historian, IV, 5, 1959, pp. 186–95; Lancs. RO, probate inventories and DDCa/23/1.

[15] Lancs. RO, probate inventories and DDM/11/32. A seg is a bull that is castrated when fully grown.

[16] Kerridge, op. cit., pp. 129–31; Lancs. RO, probate inventories (these rarely list rooms, but Thomas Rutter of Wightington had a cheese loft in 1741, and John Shaw of Nether Wyersdale had £8 worth of cheese in a shop at Lancaster in 1746); Stout, op. cit., pp. 95, 106–7.

poor farmers, and broke many". In 1741 many horses died "for want of fodder, and cattall so weake that the seeding was got in with much difficulty". The justices of the peace were continually concerned in 1747–9 with the spread of the "pestilential distemper", as were all regions where cattle were the mainstay. In the parish of Tunstall alone, 591 head of cattle were killed.[17]

Lancashire and Cumbria led the way with the cultivation of the potato. By tradition this tuber was introduced from Ireland towards the middle of the seventeenth century at North Meols, at Formby Point, or at the mouth of the Ribble. The soils of the reclaimed mosslands and the mild climate were ideal, and although probate inventories show that only a minority of farmers planted potatoes, by the end of the seventeenth century small plots were a common sight throughout the western parts of the plain especially in the mosslands south of the Ribble. James Cowper, a Burscough butcher, had £1 worth of potatoes recorded in his inventory in 1664, and sufficient quantities were being grown by 1680 for a specialized potato market to have been established as far inland as Wigan. In 1684 the rector of Croston successfully sued thirteen Mawdesley men for a tithe of potatoes grown in 1683–4, and it has been said that by this time the cultivation of potatoes was as far advanced in the mosslands as it was a hundred years later anywhere else in England. The people who grew them in the earliest years were mostly yeomen or gentry like Nicholas Blundell or Robert Hesketh, the squire of Rufford. By the first half of the eighteenth century their cultivation had spread to east Lancashire to such places as Pendlebury (1715), Dumplington (1716), Pilsworth (1719), Sharples (1744), and Urmston (1747). Here they were grown in the fallows before wheat and as the first crop on converted grassland. They provided excellent fodder for young cattle and were welcomed in the homes not only of the poor but of the ordinary farmers. In 1727 Stout noted that "Potatoes was plenty and cheap, from 2s. 6d. to 3s. a load, which was releife to the poor", and a lease of land granted to an Orrel husbandman in 1729 stipulated that he should not "digg or set any potatoes except for his own household use".[18]

Marling was the traditional improvement available to the farmers of the Lancashire plain, and Holt spoke truly in 1795 when he wrote, "Marle is the great article of fertilization, and the foundation of the improvements in

---

[17] Stout, op. cit., pp. 79, 213, 231; 'Tunstall Registers, 1625–1812', Lancs. Parish Register Soc., XL, 1911, pp. 204–6; West Yorks. RO, Quarter Sessions records; Nottm Univ. Library, G12,209/21; Notts. RO, PR6,468: "The rageing distemper broke out in this town of Misson in Aprill in the yeare of our Lord 1748 and in three mounth time there died of the rageing distemper 700 horned cattle and upward."

[18] R. N. Salaman, The History and Social Influence of the Potato, Cambridge, 1949, pp. 451–3; Lancs. RO, probate inventories and DDBa/D/10/B8, DRL/3/1; Manchester Central Library, 942/72/H43; Kerridge, op. cit., p. 227; Stout, op. cit., p. 201.

the agriculture of this county." Nicholas Blundell recorded the customary festivities that were held on his estate in July 1712 when fourteen marlers completed their work. The marl pit was dressed with garlands, eight sword dancers performed to music in his barn, and the occasion was celebrated with feasting, dancing, and bull baiting. Marling improved sandy land, whether it was arable or grass, and prevented the reclaimed peat mosses from shrinking, but it was less useful on clay, and so ancient and widespread was the practice that by this period parts of the plain had reached saturation point and the effects of overmarling had to be counteracted by liming. Nevertheless, marl carts are recorded in inventories from Elton (1663), Mawdesley (1668), Maines in Singleton (1717), and Worsley (1719), and the reclaimed mosslands and the newly enclosed commons were always marled in preparation for a first crop of oats.[19] As for lime, the expense of importing it from Wales or of carting it a distance of up to twenty miles from the kilns in Clitheroe was soon recouped by the purchaser.[20] It was also a widespread practice to use a manure consisting of cow dung mixed with turf ashes; the inventory of Robert Heyes of Brindle (1742) recorded thirteen loads of ashes worth £20, and Blundell referred to leading dung and turf ashes and to the use of "skilling dust" (the husk of winnowed grain) as a fertilizer.[21]

The most spectacular improvements in the Lancashire husbandry of this period centred on the draining and reclamation of some of the glacial meres and mosses that formed such a barrier to communications between the coastal villages and the mainland. A petition drawn up in 1655 claimed that the regular flooding of Marton Mere not only ruined the meadows and "utterlie spoileth and decayeth all our mosses for digging and getting of turfe", but meant that the local inhabitants were "many times in the winter debarred from the benefitt of the marquett at Preston". This mere was successfully drained into the river Wyre in 1731, and thousands of other acres at Bootle, Kirkham, Meols, Pilling, Tarleton, and elsewhere were drained during this period. The construction of sod drains, banks, walls, sluices, and floodgates was an expensive business that could be undertaken only by wealthy and enterprising men. The most ambitious project was that planned and financed by Thomas Fleetwood, the squire of Bank Hall, who in 1692 employed two

[19] Lancs. RO, probate inventories and DDM/14/3; Holt, op. cit., p. 111; Blundell, op. cit., I, pp. 22–7; C. Leigh, The Natural History of Lancashire, Cheshire and the Peak of Derbyshire, Oxford, 1700, p. 55; Surrey RO, LM/778/28/78 (Robert Hindley of West Houghton to Sir Thomas Molyneux, 1726: "Our commons are never broke up without improvement wich is alwaies made by marling"); Manchester Central Library, 942/72/H43 (4 June 1719: "Dumplington Green Field was marled for 6 days. Every cart was so large as would carry 1 qt. coals; 15 men had 3s. 6d. per day").

[20] Crompton, op. cit., p. 35; W. S. Weeks, Clitheroe in the Seventeenth Century, Clitheroe, n.d., pp. 55–7; Lancs. RO, DDKe/14/37; J. J. Cartwright, ed., The Travels through England of Dr. Richard Pococke (1750–1), 2 vols., London, 1888–9, I, p. 200.

[21] Blundell, op. cit., I, p. 289, and II, p. 2.

thousand men to cut a 1½-mile channel from Marton Mere to the sea. In 1755, five years after the lease expired, the mere was neglected and allowed to revert to its former state, and it was not until 1849 that a drainage scheme was completely successful. Even so, both here and elsewhere, much improvement took place long before steam engines drained the land satisfactorily. There were also numerous minor projects, local agreements, and detailed regulations issued by manorial courts concerning the scouring of ditches and the prevention of flooding.[22]

The undrained marshes and mosses provided summer grazing and extensive commons of turbary.[23] The turves were dug in spring and collected in autumn for fuel, on a considerable scale. In a sample of 224 Lancashire inventories dated between 1640 and 1750, 66 people had a store of turf and 13 of them had special turf carts; 29 of the same people also had coals, and another 11 had coal but no turf. William Stout noted that in 1742, "The season being fair, there was great quantetys of turf dug up, and coles got at nine shillings a tune."[24]

Some townships on the plain were dependent almost entirely upon agriculture and the crafts that were intimately associated with farming, but in the more populous townships the range and number of craftsmen with more diverse skills were considerable. In Walton-le-Dale, two miles south-east of Preston, the 76 weavers, 16 whitsters (i.e. bleachers), 1 "fustian man", and 48 other men employed in crafts and miscellaneous occupations outnumbered the 5 gentlemen, 11 yeomen, 25 husbandmen, and 10 labourers whose occupations were recorded in the baptism and burial registers between 1720 and 1724. The craftsmen who were recorded in the registers of the chapelry of St Helen's between 1727 and 1731 included such specialists as 10 linen weavers, 3 weavers, 1 coal master, 27 colliers, 11 nailers, 3 glassmakers, and 2 potters.[25] Industrial crafts were already of fundamental

---

[22] H. C. Collins, *Lancashire: Plain and Seaboard*, London, 1953, p. 88; R. Millward, *Lancashire: An Illustrated Essay on the History of the Landscape*, London, 1955, p. 52; Kerridge, *op. cit.*, p. 144; Blundell, *op. cit.*, II, pp. 1, 12.

[23] E.g. Kirby had 2,461 statute acres of common pasture and 800 acres in 3 mosses (Lancs. RO, DDM/14/3), and Little Crosby Marsh was 101½ acres (Blundell, *op. cit.*, II, pp. viii–ix). It was normal manorial policy to encourage or allow the enclosure of the commons, sometimes as a prelude to draining (Lancs. RO, DDM/52/38, 39, and DDM/36/69; *VCH Lancs.*, III, p. 21. When Swinton Moor and Hodge Common in Eccles were enclosed by agreement in 1684, it was resolved that "those parts of the said commons fit for turbary or moss roomes shall continue as before" (John Rylands Library, Crutchley 739).

[24] Stout, *op. cit.*, p. 233; Manchester Central Library, L1/10/106/3: "digging & tending turves" in Little Harwood, 1674.

[25] *Lancs. Parish Register Soc.*, XXXVII, 1910 (Walton), and CVII, 1968 (St Helen's), Even in non-industrial areas few parishes had many labourers during the years when baptism and burial registers record occupations, for this was a pastoral region with small family farms – *ibid.*, XXXIII, 1908 (Lytham, Bispham), XXXIX, 1910 (Blackley), XL, 1913 (Middleton), XCI, 1950 (Walton-on-the-Hill), CIII, 1964 (Woodplumpton), CVIII, 1969 (Melling).

importance in certain rural economies. In the metalworking districts there was a marked tendency for products to be confined to a few localities, with lock and hinge manufacturers in Ashton-in-Makerfield; watchmakers, pewterers, wire drawers, and pinmakers in the towns of the south-west; and colonies of nailmakers in the villages and hamlets near Wigan. Nailing had been established in these parts as a by-employment during the medieval period. Poor nailers like Oliver Withington of Winstanley (1610) had only "a nale smethe and som smale laind thereuntow" worth 40s. per annum, but others were farmer–craftsmen of moderate means, and the leading figures in the trade were men of some standing in their locality; in the 1630s John Smith of Atherton, Richard Hampson of Westleigh, Richard Battersby and Thomas Higginson of Shakerley, and John Withington of Westhoughton each left personal estate worth over £200, while Robert Smith of Little Hulton had goods and chattels valued at £542 and credits totalling £177 upon his death in 1628.[26]

The major craft in the Lancashire plain was linen weaving. Flax was grown in the marshlands and in parts of the coalfield during the seventeenth century, but most of the supply was imported from Ireland. Tithe disputes at Childwall (1728) and Sefton (1731) show that flax was still being introduced into new areas during the eighteenth century, but home production fell drastically during these years. Much of the heckling, spinning, and weaving were done by poor people who bought their raw materials on credit. "The poor of these parts", claimed a petition from Clitheroe in 1695, "mostly employ the winter in spinning flaxen yarn." But the craft was also a useful by-employment for farming families, and such organizers of the trade as William Mylls of Atherton or Richard Bullocke of Bartle were of yeoman rank.[27] During this period linen was produced throughout Lancashire, but was particularly important in the west and the south; the cotton trade was centred upon Manchester; the speciality of the central parts was the manufacture of fustians; coarse, narrow woollen cloths were produced in the Pennine villages, hamlets, and farmsteads in the vicinity of Rochdale; and the manufacture of worsteds became established during the early eighteenth century in and around Burnley and Colne.[28]

The Lancashire textile industry was basically agrarian in character, but was dependent upon the services provided in the towns. For example, the clothiers

[26] G. H. Tupling, 'The Early Metal Trades and the Beginnings of Engineering in Lancashire', *Lancs. & Cheshire Arch. Soc.*, LXI, 1951, pp. 1–34; *VCH Lancs.*, II, pp. 364–7; Bankes and Kerridge, *op. cit.*, p. 39; R. Sharpe France, 'Lancashire Nail Makers, 1579–1646', *Lancs. RO Report*, 1956, pp. 7–13.

[27] N. Lowe, *The Lancashire Textile Industry in the Sixteenth Century*, Manchester, 1972; *VCH Lancs.*, II, pp. 378–9; Weeks, *op. cit.*, pp. 37–8; Lancs. RO, probate inventories and DRL/3/2, DRL/3/12; Stout, *op. cit.*, p. 235; Defoe, *op. cit.*, II, p. 260.

[28] A. P. Wadsworth and J. De L. Mann, *The Cotton Trade and Industrial Lancashire, 1600–1780*, Manchester, 1931, pp. 23, 79.

of the Forest of Rossendale obtained their raw materials in Rochdale and took their cloths there to be fulled, dyed, finished, and sold. Most of the wool must have been imported into the county, for sheep are mentioned in only 53 of the sample of 224 inventories, and the median average value of the recorded flocks was as low as £3. James Hathornthwaite of Hathornthwaite near Lancaster (1663) was exceptional in having 110 sheep worth £27. 10s. Even in the forests of Pendle and Rossendale flocks were small and most farmers there had no sheep at all. People of all ranks were involved in the manufacture of cloth on the edge of the Pennines, and spinning-wheels were a normal household possession. The proportion of poor weavers with no more land than a cottage garden grew as the population increased during the eighteenth century, but farmer-craftsmen of moderate means and yeoman-clothiers who acted both as chapmen and sometimes as small employers long remained characteristic figures in the trade.[29] Thus, Edmund Jones of Hanging Chatter, husbandman (1696), had looms and warping instruments worth £2 and farm stock worth £57; William Halstead of Henhead, yeoman (1692), had yarn, wool, cloth, and looms worth over £21 and farm stock valued at £140; and Abraham Fish of Holden Hall, clothier (1698), had £78 invested in his farm. They were typical of many others. A fluid organization and much practical individualism marked a system which was dependent upon the availability of credit to all sections of the community.

The farmer-craftsmen of the western slopes of the Pennines had secure copyholds, which for all practical purposes were as negotiable as freeholds. In the extensive honour of Clitheroe the fines were certain, and the copyholders had taken advantage of the right to enclose their commons at 6d. per acre in proportion to their customary rents. In addition to these new intakes, many old tenements had been divided by partible inheritance, with the result that by 1662 there were half as many holdings again as there had been in 1608. Of the 654 householders recorded in part of the honour in the poll-tax returns of 1660, 406 held land worth less than £5 per annum, 145 had holdings valued between £5 and £10, 68 had tenements worth between £10 and £20, and only 30 held land valued at over £20.[30] Few large proprietors were to be found on the edge of the Pennines; most families were smallholders who were dependent upon a dual occupation and their common rights. A boy from Pendle told Dr Pococke c. 1750 that "oat-cake and butter-milk was their common food, that on a festival they had a piece of meat and a pye-pudding; that his father paid six pounds a year, kept a horse, three cows, and forty sheep; that his father and he wove woollen cloth both for their clothing and to sell".[31] The twelve Pendle men who were described

---

[29] *Ibid.*, *passim*; G. H. Tupling, *The Economic History of Rossendale*, Manchester, 1927.

[30] Tupling, *Rossendale*, p. 163; T. Woodcock, *Haslingden: A Topographical History*, Manchester, 1952, pp. 89–98; PRO, E 317/Lancs. 8. Cf. Wadsworth and Mann, *op. cit.*, p. 27.

[31] Cartwright, *Pococke*, p. 203. He described Whalley (p. 201) as "a village chiefly supported by farming and spinning woollen yarn".

as craftsmen in their probate inventories each had farm stock that accounted for 40 to 60 per cent of their personal estates, with five to ten head of cattle, and a pattern of husbandry similar to that of the yeomen and husbandmen. But many more people were involved in the woollen trade than is implied by the description of their occupations in the probate records. Cards, combs, and wheels are listed in 93 of the 123 Pendle inventories, and 45 people had at least one pair of hand looms.[32] Once again, all sections of the community were involved in the local industry, and the typical figures during this period were the people who combined the running of a smallholding of under twenty acres with regular employment as semi-independent manufacturers of cloth.

An emphasis on pastoral farming was dictated by the topography. The copyholders of Pendle had pleaded in 1607 that their lands were "extremely barren and unprofitable and as yet capable of no other corn but only oats – and that but only in dry years and not without continued charge of every third year's manuring". In the Forest of Rossendale cattle had been of prime importance since the Middle Ages; in Pendle the inventories show that whatever the size of the farm, about 60 per cent of the stock value was in cattle. Robert Bulcock of Whitough (1640), the wealthiest of the farmers whose inventories have survived, had 10 cows, 15 twinters, 7 stirks, 7 calves, 6 oxen, and 2 bulls, worth in all £118, and most families in this area bred beasts for rearing on the plain and kept a few cows for their milk, cheese, and butter.[33]

Across the county boundary, the farmers of the Yorkshire dales pursued a similar form of economy. Wensleydale inventories from 1670–1700 show that only one in seven farmers in the lower dale grew crops, and as few as one in twenty in the upper dale. Small meadows and pasture closes occupied the dale bottoms, and large stinted pastures covered the fell sides; common rights were vital for the smallholders. Many farmers kept sheep, but multi-purpose black longhorns were the mainstay, averaging eight per farm in the first quarter of the eighteenth century, when dairying was becoming more important. Most of the other dales had small areas of arable land with residual common fields.[34] In 1664 the farmers of Wharfedale and Airedale

---

[32] This analysis is taken from M. Brigg, 'The Forest of Pendle in the Seventeenth Century', *Historic Soc. of Lancs. & Cheshire*, CXIII, 1961, pp. 65–96. The valuations of 123 seventeenth-century Pendle inventories ranged from £5. 10s. to £603, with a mean between £70 and £90; 35 were valued between £5 and £50, 48 between £50 and £100, 18 between £100 and £150, 11 between £150 and £200, and 9 above £200.

[33] *Ibid.*; Tupling, *Rossendale*, p. 17.

[34] R. T. Fieldhouse, 'Agriculture in Wensleydale from 1600 to the Present Day', *Northern Hist.*, XVI, 1980, pp. 169–95; T. S. Willan and E. W. Crossley, 'Three Seventeenth-Century Yorkshire Surveys', *Yorks. Arch. Soc. Rec. Ser.*, CIV, 1941; J. Tuke, *General View of the Agriculture of the North Riding of Yorkshire*, London, 1800, p. 101; J. T. Cliffe, *The Yorkshire Gentry from the Reformation to the Civil War*, London, 1969, pp. 50–1; Bradford City Library, Cunliffe-Lister, box 27 (1704 agreement re the previous conversion of a town field called Marr Field, in Masham, to pasture).

told the Georgical committee that on the slopes they planted wheat or maslin in winter and black oats in spring; they limed their clay lands, and then followed a rotation of fallow, barley, beans or oats, and wheat; and on their lowest and most fertile grounds their course was wheat, barley, beans, and fallow. They improved their land with lime, dung, and marl and believed that the best preventive of smut was "to buy the purest wheat growing in the more champion country about 12 miles of [= off] neer Wetherby, as those who theyr have the best seed do yearly buy theyrs att like distance of about York". They said that their ploughs were "strong and plain with crooked beams...we cut all our corn with sickles, mow none with scythes".[35] In and around Harrogate turnips and rapeseed were grown in small quantities during the second half of the seventeenth century, and potatoes were cultivated in Nidderdale by 1713. The previous year, the vicar of Masham had demanded tithes of potatoes, turnips, carrots, hemp, flax, and rape from his parishioners. But the dales farmers were chiefly concerned with dairying and the rearing of young cattle and sheep. The lower and better parts of the moors were stinted pastures which provided summer grazing for cattle and year-round nourishment for sheep: the enclosed grounds were reserved for milk kine and for young beasts that were being fattened for the butcher. The commons at Stockplain in Bishopside were enclosed in 1689, but a contemporary scheme to enclose the Forest of Nidderdale was overcome by the opposition of both the freeholders and the customary tenants, who feared a great rise in the poor rates if the cottagers were deprived of facilities for grazing their cows. Ilton freeholders of only £3–4 per annum were said in 1717 to keep 200–300 sheep upon the wastes, even in winter. These wastes covered many thousand acres of unstinted pasture, and several freeholders and tenants often bought 300–400 sheep at north-country fairs, kept them on the wastes during summer, and then sold them at south-country fairs.[36]

Extra income was provided by rural industry. Lead was mined both by independent miners and by large companies, and other families combined their farming activities with the manufacture of wool or linen cloth, or coarse stockings. The system of partible inheritance meant that farms were small and that their occupants could survive only if they had a dual occupation and generous common rights. A yeoman from Dentdale claimed in 1634 that "the tenements are much divided and increased, so that the inhabitants have to live by knitting coarse stockings". Many farms were of only three or four acres, and few were larger than eight or nine acres. In Swaledale by the middle of the seventeenth century the fragmentation of holdings meant that farmers

[35] R. V. Lennard, 'English Agriculture under Charles II', EcHR, IV, 1932, pp. 23–45; Derbys. RO, D 258/47/14 (lime burning at Sedbergh, 1716).

[36] B. Jennings, ed., *A History of Nidderdale*, Huddersfield, 1967, pp. 133–50; *id.*, ed., *A History of Harrogate and Knaresborough*, Huddersfield, 1970, pp. 192–213; Bradford City Library, Cunliffe-Lister, boxes 27 and 45; Leeds City Archives, Ingilby 2,462 (Haverah "out pasture", 1727), Vyner 5,563 (1 acre of potatoes in Dallagill, 1735), Vyner 5,508 (10 Scots beasts at Studley, 1733).

had increasingly to turn to part-time mining; by the late eighteenth century it is more accurate to speak of miners who were part-time farmers. The scale of mining operations grew considerably from the late seventeenth century onwards, and many farming communities took on an industrial character with agriculture reduced to the role of subsidiary employment.[37] Since the reign of Elizabeth the stocking trade had provided work for many families within a twenty-mile radius of Richmond, and both men and women knitted during periods of leisure, or whilst they kept an eye on their livestock. And, as in other crafts, the middlemen of the trade were prosperous yeomen; the probate inventory of John Peacocke of Sealhouses in Arkengarthdale (1680), for example, recorded "38 dozen of stockins at 10s. y dozen, some mens, some boyes, some for children, £19, 40 dozen more of stockins at 8s. y dozen, £16, two stone & a halfe of wooll, 18s.... one press for stockins with boards thereto belonging".[38] The wealthiest hosiers were Richmond aldermen like William Wetwange, who had 490 dozen pairs of stockings valued at £253 upon his death in 1672. In Nidderdale and in the district around Harrogate and Knaresborough considerable local variation in the pattern of farming can be observed, but by the reign of Queen Anne it is clear that the size of farms had declined and that the relationship between farming and the textile crafts was less close than it had been. Many weaver-farmers on the old pattern survived, but increasing numbers of cottagers were almost entirely dependent upon their craft. The production of linen was now more important than the manufacture of wool cloth, and both the number of linen weavers and the number of looms per weaver had risen considerably. The linen industry provided employment for the squatters on the edges of the forests and commons, but it did not take hold where manorial control was strong and where regulations governing the use of stinted pastures prevented encroachments.[39]

Linen weavers also inhabited the northern Vale of York and the Vale of Pickering, particularly on the edges of the moors and in and around the former forests of Galtres and Pickering.[40] The glacial drifts that covered these vales had produced a great variety of soils, ranging from light sands to quite

[37] A. Raistrick and B. Jennings, *A History of Lead Mining in the Pennines*, London, 1965, pp. 310–13; J. Thirsk, 'Industries in the Countryside', in F. J. Fisher, ed., *Essays in the Economic and Social History of Tudor and Stuart England*, Cambridge, 1961, p. 70.

[38] R. Fieldhouse and B. Jennings, *A History of Richmond and Swaledale*, Chichester, 1978, pp. 178–83; M. Hartley and J. Ingilby, *The Old Hand-Knitters of the Dales*, Clapham, 1951, pp. 21–4. A survey of property in Mashamshire, *c.* 1660, records 50 tenants with holdings from 3 to 131 acres, with a median average of 20 acres – Bradford City Library, Cunliffe-Lister, box 1.

[39] Jennings, *Nidderdale*, pp. 163–74; Jennings, *Harrogate and Knaresborough*, pp. 205–17.

[40] *The Journeys of Celia Fiennes*, ed. C. Morris, London, 1947, p. 93; Cartwright, *Pococke*, p. 175; Tuke, *op. cit.*, p. 312; G. C. Cowling, *The History of Easingwold and the Forest of Galtres*, Huddersfield, 1966, p. 97; J. McDonnell, ed., *A History of Helmsley, Rievaulx and District*, York, 1963; H. Best, *Rural Economy in Yorkshire in 1641, Being the Farming and Account Books of Henry Best of Elmswell, East Riding of Yorkshire*, Surtees Soc., XXXIII, 1851, pp. 105–6; North Yorks. RO, PR/TOP/5/1.

heavy clays. Some townships still had a high proportion of arable land,[41] but many open fields had disappeared by 1650 and others were enclosed during the next few decades.[42] Pressure on the commons meant that grazings were stinted and that agreements to enclose were frequent.[43] The North Riding had a high proportion of resident nobles and gentlemen, but most of the land was held by farmers of under thirty acres; William Marshall wrote in 1788 that more than half of the Vale of Pickering was laid out in farms of under £20 a year, and that perhaps three-quarters lay in farms of less than £50 a year; by then, farms were normally held at will, but leases for lives were still the normal tenure on the archbishop of York's estates.[44] Both open and enclosed lands were farmed by a system of convertible husbandry within a strong manorial framework. The farmers of the liberty of Ripon told the Georgical committee in 1664 that "Many of late have pared, dryed, and burned their pasture and worser sorts of grounds – which doth yield three or ffour good cropps, the first sowne in Aprill or beginning of May with barley upon one tillage; the second of masline sown at Michaelmas following with one tillage; the third barley againe sowne in Aprill with two tillages or ploweings; the fourth, peas, beanes, or oates. And after these cropps the spreading thereon a small quantity of lime or dung, or marle and dung mixed, maketh good pasture grounds followe." On the other hand, when the steward at Bilbrough tried to persuade the tenants to change from corn to dairying in 1729, he found that they were "like old cart horses, one can't thrust 'em out of their old beaten track".[45]

The typical farms of the northern vales were varied in their interests, with a little more emphasis on corn on the wheat-and-bean lands of Cleveland than elsewhere. Records of new crops are not plentiful and most farmers placed more importance upon raising cattle for their milk, meat, and hides, and upon breeding horses for the coach and saddle.[46] "The ancient breed

[41] North Yorks. RO, ZAG/188; West Sussex RO, Petworth, 1,447.

[42] J. A. Sheppard, 'Field Systems of Yorkshire', in Baker and Butlin, eds., op. cit., p. 166; M. W. Beresford. 'Glebe Terriers and Open-Field Yorkshire', Yorks. Arch. J., xxxvii, 1951, pp. 325–68; Sir T. Lawson-Tancred, Records of a Yorkshire Manor, London, 1937, pp. 95, 100; W. Marshall, Rural Economy of Yorkshire, 2 vols., London, 1788, I, p. 17; Leeds City Archives, NH/2,187/A, He2; North Yorks. RO, ZAG/188, ZAL/8/16, ZON/1/1/1/47.

[43] North Yorks. RO, ZAG/184, ZAG/196, ZAG/247, ZAL/8/16, ZON/5/2, ZDV/IV (enclosure by agreement of 1,500 acres of Sutton-in-the-Forest, 1656); Leeds City Archives, Vyner 5,559, Milnes Coates 453, Ingilby 1,709, 2,570, He37(a); Marshall, op. cit., I, pp. 51–2.

[44] Marshall, op. cit., I, pp. 19, 20 (re partible inheritance in the Forest of Pickering), 21, 32, 42, 254; Tuke, op. cit., pp. 28, 32; North Yorks. RO, ZAG/184, ZDV/III, ZNK/v/3/3; Leeds City Archives, NH 2,115, Vavasour 238, He2; PRO, E 317/Yorks. 42.

[45] Lennard, op. cit.,; Kerridge, op. cit., pp. 23, 214–15; Marshall, op. cit., I, pp. 256, 296; Leeds City Archives, He 37(a).

[46] Borthwick IHR, probate inventories; W. H. Long, 'Regional Farming in Seventeenth-Century Yorkshire', AHR, viii, 2, 1960, pp. 103–14; Marshall, op. cit., pp. 271–2; Tuke, op. cit., pp. 247, 273, 308; crops included rape (North Yorks. RO, ZAG/247; Lawson-Tancred, op. cit.,

of Black Cattle...were the only breed of cattle" in the Vale of Pickering in the early years of the eighteenth century, according to Marshall, and "The old *common* stock of the Vale was a thin-carcased, ill-formed, white-faced hornless breed." He also observed that "In the uninclosed state of this Vale, the commons and cars were applied chiefly to the rearing of working oxen and a few dairy cows. In the West Marshes and other central parts of the Vale, which have been inclosed time immemorial, and which, until of late years, have always lain in a state of rough grass, great numbers of young cattle were reared for sale." The farmers reared most of their own stock, except for an annual intake of Scots cattle, which were used for clearing the rough pastures in winter and which were fattened on the secondary grazing grounds during the ensuing summer.[47] The chief product of these northern farmers, however, was butter, which was exported in large quantities to London and the Continent through the market town and inland port of Yarm, and from Stockton and Whitby. In 1675, at the peak of this trade, nearly 42,000 firkins were shipped from these ports. The frequent prosecutions of butter packers or 'firkeners' who sold rancid butter or gave short measures show that such people came to Yarm from distances of up to thirty miles. During the eighteenth century continental demand ceased and new outlets were found along the improved river navigation from York.[48]

The North York moors were described in a Queen Anne survey as "very barren grownde and covered with ling and bent throughout". Apart from the common rights of turbary and some rough grazing, they were of little value, and remain so today. But the enclosed lands in the dales and the

p. 163; Marshall, *op. cit.*, I, pp. 29, 30, 293), clover (Leeds City Archives, Harewood, survey 26, and Vavasour 1,031), and potatoes (Leeds, City Archives, NH/2,249/B). There were also large farmers like Jonathan Cotham of Marske, who in November 1694 had "12 draught oxen, £53, 4 stears 4 years old, £19, 4 stears 3 years old, £16, 4 steares 4 years old, £14, tenn steares 4 heifers 2 years old, £20, 12 kine & a bull £50, 10 yeareing calves, £10, 140 sheep, £32, 12 draught horses, £30, 5 young horses 4 years old, £40, 5 young horses 3 years old, £20, 5 young horses & mare 2 years old, £18, 6 foals & the ston'd horse, £30, 10 swine, £5, wheat in ye barne, £140, peas in ye stackgarth, £40, oats in ye Stackgarth, £4, hay in ye stackgarth, £14, corne on ye ground abt. 60 acres wheat, £120, for waynes coopes harrowes plowes & other husbandry geere, £30" – Borthwick IHR, Cleveland inventories.

[47] Marshall, *op. cit.*, II, pp. 180–1, 219; Leeds City Archives, NH/2,194/B (Scots cows at Dishforth, 1732), NH/2,320/A: cattle in the constabulary of Dishforth, 26 Dec. 1646: 89 oxen (14 owners), 105 kine or cows (34 owners), 43 beasts (13 owners), 505 sheep (21 owners), 38 horses (19 owners) – 37 owners in all: Ingilby 3,591 (an ox bred and fed at Newby was killed 14 Nov. 1692, aged 6½ years, weight 145 stone 6½ lb. A red ox was killed at Newby 22 Dec. 1707, weight 148 stone 11 lb. They were both of the Holderness or Dutch breed, with large bodies and limbs, and little horns turning inwards).

[48] D. Pearce, 'Yarm and the Butter Trade', *Cleveland & Teeside Loc. Hist. Soc. Bull.*, no. 9, 1970, pp. 8–12; North Yorks. RO, Quarter Sessions records; Borthwick IHR, inventories of Jane Postgate of Great Ayton (Aug. 1700), Henry Mason of Ingleby Greenhow (Sept. 1703), and William Taylor of Great Busby (Nov. 1703); Leeds City Archives, NH/2,649/B; Marshall, *op. cit.*, I, p. 293.

unstinted common pastures on the edges of the moors provided an adequate, if not an easy, living. In 1664 only one house in Goathland was assessed at more than one hearth, and that belonged to a gentleman with two hearths. The conservatism of the area was reflected in its buildings and in the fact that this was the only part of Yorkshire with more oxen than horses. Cattle and sheep were the farmers' mainstay, but, as today, greater emphasis was laid on arable farming in the lower and sheltered parts than in the Pennine dales. At harvest time "Moor folk" left the hills to seek employment in the vales and on the Wolds, and at other times they were dependent upon by-employments; in the western moorlands they knitted stockings, and in the east they manufactured coarse linens.[49] Well over one hundred labourers and craftsmen obtained employment at the alum works on the coastal cliffs, principally at Mulgrave, Asholme, and Sandsend. These had begun production in 1611 and were the only ones of their kind in Britain.[50]

In the early eighteenth century the Wolds township of Wetwang was described as being in open countryside with "scarce a bush or tree for several miles". This was sheep country, and, indeed, the cold, dry climate and the thin, porous soils made the High Wolds fit for little else. About two-thirds of these chalklands were laid down to grass or taken up with rabbit warrens, and rents were lower and farms were larger than in any other part of the East Riding. The townships that were sited on the northern and western slopes often had arable and meadow land in the vales, but elsewhere such land was scarce. Wetwang farmers leased meadows that lay seven miles away, and in 1693 the farmers of Bishop Wilton were still interchanging their doles every year so that all could share the best available hay.[51] The poor quality of much of the arable meant that many of the High Wolds townships worked an infield–outfield system, whereby the furlongs nearest the villages were cropped according to a two- or three-course rotation, but the more distant lay fallow for several years at a time. The furlong, rather than the field, was the normal unit of cropping.[52] The Georgical committee was told that the farmers "have in many townes 7 feilds and the swarth of one is every yeare broken for oates and lett ly fallow till itts turne att 7 yeares end, and these seven are outeffeilds". The usual winter corn was wheat, with a little rye,

[49]   R. B. Turton, ed., 'The Honor and Forest of Pickering', *N. Riding Rec. Ser.*, I, 1894, p. 112; A. Hollings, *Goathland: The Story of a Moorland Village*, Whitby, 1971, p. 86; PRO, E 317/Yorks. 50; Best, *op. cit.*, p. 106; Tuke, *op. cit.*, p. 312.

[50]   North Yorks. RO, ZNK/v/3/3/131, ZNK/v/3/8/1; Borthwick IHR, probate inventory of William Mann of Stokesley, 2 Jan. 1702/3, and R/vII/H/3,498; T & C, pp. 239–43; C. E. Whiting, ed., 'Ralph Ward's Journal', *Yorks. Arch. Soc. Rec. Ser.*, CXVII, 1951, pp. 180, 189; A. Raistrick, *Industrial Archaeology*, St Albans, 1972, pp. 62–4, 214–16.

[51]   A. Harris, 'The Agriculture of the East Riding before the Parliamentary Enclosures', *Yorks. Arch. J.*, XL, 1962, pp. 119–27; Borthwick IHR, R/vIII/G/3,020.

[52]   A. Harris, *The Open Fields of East Yorkshire*, York, 1959, pp. 4, 7–11, 14–15; *VCH East Riding*, II, pp. 88, 184, 212, 220, 267; East Yorks. RO, DDGR/15/1, DDWA/12/1/e.

sown after Michaelmas but as near Martinmas as possible, and the chief spring crop was barley, in a rotation of barley, fallow, barley, peas. Henry Best noted that "Many have alledged that White-wheate is the best to imingle and sow with rye, and that it will be soonest ripe; but wee finde experimentally that Kentish wheate is the best or that which (hereabouts) is called Dodde-reade". The Georgical committee heard of practices such as the steeping of barley seed in water before sowing, but it seems that the nature of the soil did not encourage advances in cropping techniques or the introduction of new crops.[53]

However, Henry Best's keen observations in his lengthy, practical treatise on sheep management show that men with capital and intelligence were capable of improving their livestock. At Elmswell he "kept constantly five plowes going and milked fourteene kine", and he regularly employed "Moor folk" to assist him at harvest time. But his wealth came chiefly from his sales of wool to the West Riding clothiers and of mutton in the market towns. The Wolds breed was small and compact, with fine, short wool. An average of one or two sheep per acre grazed the poorest soils in summer and were folded by night upon the arable. In a sample of 100 Wolds inventories that were appraised in the 1690s, 83 farmers kept sheep in flocks that ranged in size from 6 to nearly 1,000. The average flock numbered 27 on the Wolds but only 10 in the lowlands at either side.[54] The lack of an adequate water supply and the shortage of meadows meant that less emphasis was placed upon the rearing of cattle. Six out of every ten Wolds farmers in the 1690s had flocks of sheep that were at least equal in value to their herds of cattle. Hay was cut on the grass leys and headland balks of the common arable fields, but a critical farmer told the Georgical committee that "Those meadows and inclosures we have we use them so very slovenly as nothing can be said of them save that they are cultivated by the worst of husbands." The problem was not so acute on the Lower Wolds, where Scots cattle were fed on the pastures, but the median average 8 head of cattle for all the wolds inventories is much lower than the 12 head per farm in the Vale of York and the 15 head of Holderness. The shortage of adequate feeding meant that Best had to rent pastures for his beasts in other parishes, and that cow pastures on the commons were regulated by complex stinting.[55]

The Wolds was a region of small, nucleated villages, most of which were dominated by their squires, so hardly any rural industry took hold and very

---

[53] Lennard, op. cit.; Best, op. cit., p. 45; H. E. Strickland, General View of the Agriculture of the East Riding of Yorkshire, London, 1812, pp. 143–5.

[54] Best, op. cit., pp. 9–10, 26–7, 48, 52, 110, 115; Strickland, op. cit., p. 231; Harris, 'Agriculture', p. 127.

[55] Harris, 'Agriculture', p. 127; Lennard, op. cit.; Best, op. cit., pp. 118–20; Long, op. cit.; East Yorks. RO, DDGE/3/42, DDGR/13/8, DDHV/10/1(80), (78), DDLG/16/1, DDMC/202, DDWR/3/9.

little religious dissent. A significant amount of early enclosure had been carried out, both of common fields and of common pastures, and several townships converted some of their arable lands into grass leys. Thus, a survey of the manor of Thwing in March 1650 records "All those seventy two lands or ridges of areable & pasture ground lyinge dispersedly within the ffeilds of Thwinge", and agreements to divide fields and commons are plentiful in local deeds.[56] Even so, it was not until the second half of the eighteenth century that the greater part of the Wolds was enclosed and that isolated farmsteads were first built.

To the east of the Wolds lay the glacial-drift district known as Holderness. This was essentially boulder-clay land that was treated with lime brought down the rivers from Brotherton, Knottingley, and the district immediately west of Doncaster.[57] The arable land was farmed almost entirely on a two-field system, with a field on each side of the village on ground slightly higher than the pastures and meadows. When it was agreed to enclose Brandesburton in 1630, there were 1,174 acres in East Field and 1,321 acres in West Field, and "one of the said fields used to be sowed one year and the other field another year". At the end of the century thirty-six of the forty-four villages whose field systems are known had just two fields. The lands were unusually long, and had often been converted into grass leys; a plan of Skeffling in 1721, for instance, shows that almost every strip holding was at least partly under grass.[58] Some townships had already been completely enclosed for pasture during the sixteenth and early seventeenth centuries; in 1650 the "inclosed pasture ground" of the manor of Patrington included South Field (131 acres), North Field (50 acres), West Field (131 acres), and Hall Marsh (35 acres), "the four last mentioned closes being distinguished by their respective mounds...laid together and now used as cow pasture by the inhabitants". But early enclosure by agreement was frequently concerned with only part of the fields and commons, especially the heavier, well-watered soils, which produced fine meadows and pastures. Abut 250 acres of field land were enclosed at Sewerby c. 1650; some of the Settrington commons were divided in 1668; from 1672 onwards parts of the common fields at Hunmanby were laid down for pasture; and about 1680 parts of the common fields at Great Kelk were ploughed annually, but "other part being meadow is usually mowed by the respective owners thereof, and other part thereof is some years laid down and cast for pasture". Paul was enclosed between

[56] Harris, *Open Fields*, p. 3; *VCH East Riding*, II, pp. 85, 98, 106, 112–13, 205–6, 275; PRO, E 317/Yorks. 57, E 134/1650 Trin. 1; East Yorks. RO, DDHV/22/9, DDWA/12/2(a). For the effects of absentee landlords, see P. Roebuck, 'Absentee Landownership in the Late Seventeenth and Early Eighteenth Centuries: A Neglected Factor in English Agrarian History', AHR, XXI, 1, 1973, pp. 1–17.

[57] Strickland, *op. cit.*, p. 205.

[58] Harris, *Open Fields*, p. 4; East Yorks. RO, DDHV/1/8; PRO, E 317/Yorks. 28; Sheppard, *op. cit.*, pp. 149–53.

1662 and 1716, Routh between 1685 and 1716, Little Hatfield in 1718, and Catwick in 1731, but despite five agreements to enclose in Burton Agnes between 1702 and 1758 the process was not completed there until the nineteenth century. Elsewhere in Holderness much remained to be reallotted after 1750 by parliamentary enclosure.[59]

Wheat and beans (sometimes mixed with peas) were the principal Holderness crops and they were grown by nearly all the farmers. Fewer than one in five grew any oats or barley, and fewer still had any rye. Some of this corn was exported via Hull or Bridlington to Rotterdam, and along the same route went a considerable quantity of rapeseed. In 1692 John Hogg loaded fifteen lasts of rapeseed on keels at Howden, so that they could be taken to Holland by a Hull factor; twenty-five years later the probate inventory of Hugh Bethell of Rise recorded a similar quantity of rapeseed in a chamber at Hull, valued at £220. Bethell also had wheat, rye, and some oats valued at £193, and barley, malt, mead, and beer worth £120, together with bricks worth £48, and his livestock, which was valued at £801. The East Riding was famous for its coach and saddle horses, and Bethell's stock was appraised at £418. He also had sheep worth £55, 2 bulls, 15 cows, 10 beasts, 2 steers, and 16 calves worth £126, 17 oxen valued at £100, and (at Watton) 2 large oxen and 10 fat north-country oxen worth £102. Some Scots cattle were bred in Holderness in the early eighteenth century, but the great majority of farmers preferred the local breed, which was justly famed for its large size and its abundant supply of milk. The average head of fifteen cattle per farm was the highest in Yorkshire, and it was as a corn and cattle-rearing district that Holderness thrived.[60]

In the late 1690s Celia Fiennes wrote of her journey from Beverley to Hull, "The meadows are cloth'd with good grass", because of the overflowing of the waters. The shallow Holderness valleys and the 'ings' and 'carrs' along the river Hull were flooded regularly and could be used only for growing coarse hay or as summer pasture for working animals and young beasts. In a survey of Brandesburton in 1743, the Great Ox Carr (49 acres) was described as "coarse boggy land in which no cattle can go, it is in a dry year always mown and the sedge and flaggs serve for young or dry cattle in the winter but this is under water 9 months at least and sometimes all year". The Ing Carr (556 acres) was more suitable for pasture on the higher parts, but more than three-quarters was "nothing but boggs upon which no

[59] East Yorks. RO, DDCC/71/5; Harris, 'Agriculture', pp. 121–2; Beresford, op. cit., pp. 325–68; PRO, E 317/Yorks. 28, 41; K. J. Allison, The East Riding of Yorkshire Landscape, London, 1976, pp. 126–8.

[60] Harris, Open Fields, p. 9; Harris, 'Agriculture', pp. 125–7; Long, op. cit.; Strickland, op. cit., p. 220; East Yorks. RO, DDR/1/45/1, DDSY/101/90; PRO, E 134/7 Wm 3, Mich. 31, E 134/12 Wm 3, Mich. 28. Special 'Holderness scythes' were produced in the Derbyshire parish of Norton – D. Hey, The Rural Metalworkers of the Sheffield Region, Leicester, 1972, p. 24.

cattle ever goes and in a wett summer at least 9 parts in 10 lyes under water". On the other hand, many Hull valley farmers had boats, nets, and fowling-guns recorded in their inventories, together with small quantities of peat. These little extras were undoubtedly vital in the economy of the the poorer husbandmen and labourers. The steward of the manor of Anlaby and Hessle complained of "the ill management of their common and publique pastures", because they kept "what they will in the carre", including an estimated three hundred horses, but the locals feared that "if ever they came to terms & broke their ancient customs the Lord of the Manour would gett all their common". Such distrust prevented many drainage schemes from being put into operation. A marked improvement in the efficiency of the Court of Sewers took place after 1660, and wealthy local men such as Sir Joseph Ashe of Wawne (1675), Sir James Bradshaw of Routh (1693), and Lord Micklethwaite of Swine (1726) were able to put private schemes into operation, but the first major improvements did not come until after 1760.[61]

The southern Vale of York possesses a great variety of soils, and its husbandry varied accordingly. The ill-drained lands could be used only for grazing, and the manor of Drax was typical of the low-lying areas in having much more pasture, and perhaps more meadow, than arable land. Some of the townships on the heavy clay soils were fully enclosed before or during the period, and in others the open-field pattern was considerably altered in a piecemeal fashion. Examples of complete enclosure include Allerthorpe (1640), Dunnington (1707), Escrick (soon after 1713), West Fulford (early eighteenth century), Fangfoss (1723), and Stillingfleet (1740). Most townships followed a system of convertible husbandry, and the use of closes for pasture meant that some of the larger commons remained unstinted. In 1691 the common at Barnby Moor was said to cover 1,000 acres and to support 400 horses, and several hundred sheep and other "beasts" in the summer. On the other hand, there are several examples of partial or complete enclosure of stinted pastures.[62] Much thought was given to the choice of crops best suited to the different soils. The Georgical committee was told that on the better warps the farmers used small ploughs with four oxen led by two horses. One ploughing was sufficient for a first crop of barley, after which the soil was "fitt for barley againe, being thrice plowed, or otherwise after the first crope beinge but once plowed t'will bringe wheat, without any sort of manure alsoe, and soe will continue for nigh twenty yeares fallowing once

[61] Fiennes, op. cit., p. 87; Harris, Open Fields, p. 12; Harris, 'Agriculture', pp. 121–2; East Yorks. RO, DDHV/1/8, DDBL/4/4, DDBL/20/17, DDBL/3/6; PRO, E 317/Yorks. 41, E 134/7 Wm 3, Mich. 33; J. A. Sheppard, The Draining of the Hull Valley, York, 1958, pp. 2, 11, 13; Sheffield Central Library, WWM Br 182, re Flaxfleet and South Cave, 1657: "These lands are very improveable...much of the ground is over run with rushes...other meadows are overrun with sedge and coarse grass for want of scouring the drains."

[62] Beresford, op. cit.; Harris, 'Agriculture', p. 121n; East Yorks. RO, DDEV/32/11, DDFA/14/274, PR 2,005; VCH East Riding, III, pp. 8, 15, 24, 25, 33, 49, 71, 85, 101, 107, 116, 124–5, 137, 143, 153, 168, 181, 186, 194.

every seaventh yeare, beareinge good oates in any of the first yeares from
the first crope, but noe beanes untill after the first seaven years". The clayland
was treated very differently. After a fallow it was ploughed five times and
dressed with lime or dung; then it was either sown with wheat or left until
the spring and ploughed again for barley. The following year beans were
grown, then wheat or barley, followed by beans or oats, and a fallow every
fourth year. Smaller plough teams and wooden rather than iron harrows
were used on the sandy soils, and the usual cropping sequence was rye, barley,
and oats. Many farmers around Selby, Snaith, and Sykehouse had a few acres
of flax, and further east hemp was sown "upon land made very fat". Potatoes
were also grown in the Cowick area by the 1730s, and rape was grown as
a new crop in Stillingfleet in 1697, but everywhere more emphasis was laid
on cattle than on crops.[63]

Hatfield Chase had been partly drained by Vermuyden in the late 1620s,
and Dutch and Flemish settlers had improved much of the new land of the
Levels by warping.[64] Here they grew oats, some winter corn, and rapeseed,
and some were encouraged by the mild climate to cultivate hops.[65] Hatfield
Park was divided into parcels in the 1660s and put to tillage, and each
township also had a small area of commonfield. In the 1720s clover replaced
peas, and turnips partly replaced rye in the Hatfield townfields; and turnips
were grown as a field crop in Stainforth by 1749. Turnips and clover are
also recorded in probate inventories from the second decade of the eighteenth
century onwards.[66] Around the common fields were the closes and ings, and
beyond lay the extensive common pastures and turf moors.[67] The

[63] Lennard, *op. cit.*; Borthwick IHR, probate inventories, Doncaster deanery and Snaith
peculiar (flax), Snaith peculiar (potatoes: Thomas Woodhead, 1738, Benjamin Brunyee, 1747,
William France, 1751 – I am indebted to Mr D. Byford for these references and for comments
on this area); PRO, E 134/2 Jas 2, Mich. 19; *VCH East Riding, III*, pp. 32, 107, 143.

[64] J. Tomlinson, *The Level of Hatfield Chace and Parts Adjacent*, Doncaster, 1882. There were
also minor drainage schemes, e.g. of the carr between Austerfield and Misson (PRO, E 134/1658/9
Hil. 23). William Millman of Dikesmarsh, husbandman had a "dutch plough" recorded in his
probate inventory, 17 Aug. 1696.

[65] Leeds City Archives, TN/HC/C1 (rapeseed 1711); Notts. RO, PR 6,468 (tithe of rapeseed
at Misson, 1726); Borthwick IHR, probate inventories, e.g. Oct. 1719, Jacob Oxley of Hatfield
Levels, "rape seed, £22"; Dec. 1719, Samuel Dobson of Thorne Levels, husbandman, "rape seed,
£20"; June 1725, Abraham Morrillion of Hatfield Levels, "Hop yard – crop & poles, £5". In
the eighteenth century a hop market was held at Doncaster, and several minor place names in
the neighbouring villages mention hops; see also PRO, E 134/12 Geo. 2, East. 2.

[66] Borthwick IHR, glebe terriers, and R/vii/I/1,397, probate inventories, e.g. Edmund
Wright, Sykehouse, yeoman, 1718, Samuel Dobson, Thorne Levels, husbandman, 1719, William
Hudson, Hatfield, yeoman, 1719 (clover); PRO, E 134/2 Jas 2, Mich. 9; Sheffield City Library,
Cooke of Wheatley deeds, box viii.

[67] In his manuscript "History of Hatfield", written in the late 1690s (BL, Lansdowne 897),
Abraham de la Pryme described the village as standing "in the midst of an almost round field,
not disfigured by hills and dailes, perpetually green with corn in one part or other, and the pleasant
oaks, and woody pastures and closes which encompass this field and town round about, gives a
most delectable prospect to the eye".

importance of these commons is demonstrated by the inventories of Thomas
Pirkins, a Fishlake gentleman (1692), who had 8 oxen, 8 cows, 1 heifer, and
6 horses in his Bank Ing, 3 calves in the Green Garth, a sow and 9 pigs in
the fold, and 7 horses and 91 sheep on the commons, and of Richard Hawood
of Sykehouse, yeoman (1695), who had 8 kine, 1 bull, and 4 young calves
in a close, and 5 stirks, a bull, 4 mares and 2 followers, 2 foals, a horse, and
22 sheep on the commons. Probate inventories show that even before
Vermuyden's drainage more cereals were grown than was once supposed,
but throughout our period the district was noted principally for rearing and
fattening, together with some dairying and horse breeding. The 50 probate
inventories that were appraised between 1695 and 1699 record an average
thirteen head of cattle in the former chase. Thomas Dearman of Hatfield,
yeoman (1695), had 17 beasts and 5 cows; Thomas Hoyland of Thorne,
yeoman (1697), had 32 beasts and 5 spaning calves, together with a bull and
5 milk cows; and Robert Mallinson of Stainforth, yeoman (1693), had 13
beasts, 4 oxen, 5 cows, and 3 calves.[68] Only 30 per cent of the inventories
record sheep, but a few of the wealthier farmers kept large flocks. The horses
were sold at the fairs that were held at Doncaster, Howden, Snaith, and
Thorne.

The new farms on the Levels were larger than elsewhere in the chase, for
the ancient custom of partible inheritance meant that most old holdings were
small ones of under twenty acres. The generous common rights and such
little extras as turves, wood, thatch, and bricks were vital to this rural
economy. The inhabitants of Thorne often had "turves on the moors"
recorded in their inventories, both for their own use and for sale down the
river, and several were boatmen as well as part-time farmers. William
Middlebrooke, sailor (1726), was among the most prosperous, with farm
stock valued at £77 15s. 6d., "turves paid for, deliver'd & undeliverd, £10",
other personal estate worth over £110, money upon interest amounting to
£280, debts of £66 due to him, and a share in three keels. But perhaps more
typical was his neighbour, Thomas Sutton (1727), whose total personal estate
of £19 included "2 cows an old boat riggin, £8 10s. od., 2 small heffers,
£2, turves on the moores, £2 10s. od."[69]

The farmers on the sands and Keuper marls to the south-west of Hatfield
Chase placed equal emphasis upon arable and pasture, and kept more sheep
than in the marshlands. Arthur Young described the road from Bawtry to
Doncaster as leading "through a very light sandy country, greatly resembling
the western parts of Norfolk". Turnips were grown on these sandy soils by

    [68] Leeds City Archives, TN/HC/C1: letter written 6 Sept. 1693, "Thos. Haggard has 20 Scotch
steers – wants £56, offered £54, keeping them well & in good edish [i.e. aftermath] until Thorne
Fair".

    [69] Borthwick IHR, probate inventories; A. Young, *A Six Months Tour through the North of
England*, 4 vols., London, 1770, I, pp. 239–40; J. Hunter, *South Yorkshire*, I, London, 1828, p. 158;
PRO, LR/2/193. For the high proportion of dissenters in this area, see D. Hey, 'The Pattern of
Nonconformity in South Yorkshire, 1660–1851', *Northern Hist.*, VIII, 1973, pp. 86–118.

the 1720s and were included in the rotations noted by Young.[70] Immediately to the west of these sands, the calcareous, loamy and freely drained, red-brown soils that overlie the narrow band of magnesian limestone provided the best arable land in Yorkshire. Stretching as far north as the glacial deposits that lay beyond the river Wharfe, this region was characterized by small, nucleated villages, many of which had shrunk or decayed in earlier times. The manorial framework was strong, and the parishes were the smallest in the north of England; in most villages the squire and the parson had unshakable authority. Piecemeal enclosure continued throughout the period, but many townships retained their common fields and common pastures until they were divided by act of parliament.[71] This was a region of mixed husbandry, and a sample of 86 probate inventories taken between 1695 and 1739 shows that the farmers paid equal attention to livestock and crops. On most farms, both oxen and horses were used for draught, and an average head of 11 or 12 cattle were reared for beef or milk. Among the large farmers, Thomas Yarborough of Campsall, esquire (1698), had 20 beasts, 12 oxen, a bull, 10 cows, 9 geldings and mares, and 172 sheep; George Bladwin of Tickhill, gentleman (1692), had 15 beasts and calves, 6 steers, 2 horses, 3 mares, 2 foals, and 122 sheep; and John Sheppard of Braithwell (1699) had 16 oxen, 2 bullocks, a bull, 6 cows, a heifer, 13 horses, and 160 sheep. In general, fewer farmers kept sheep during the second half of the period than during the first. The main cereals were wheat, barley, oats, and peas, with some rye and beans, and the fertile soils encouraged early experiments with new crops; hops were grown in Wadworth in the 1630s and in Owston in 1717, turnips were cultivated in Laughton by 1693, rapeseed had been sown in Hooton Pagnell by 1698, clover is recorded at Hellaby and Owston between 1717 and 1719, and turnips, cabbages, hops, and sainfoin were planted on Viscount Molesworth's estate in Edlington during the first decade of the eighteenth century.[72]

Few rural industries gained a foothold on the magnesian limestone at this

[70] Young, *op. cit.*, *I*, pp. 102, 108; Borthwick IHR, probate inventories, e.g. George Winter, Barnby Dun, 1729 ("5 acres turnip land, £10"), Francis Newsam, Armthorpe, yeoman, 1738 ("7 acres turnips, £5").

[71] A. G. Ruston and D. Witney, *Hooton Pagnell, The Agricultural Evolution of a Yorkshire Village*, London, 1934; Cliffe, *op. cit.*, pp. 33–5; D. Holland, *Warmsworth in the Eighteenth Century*, Doncaster, 1965; Beresford, *op. cit.*; W. S. Rodgers, 'The Distribution of Parliamentary Enclosures in the West Riding of Yorkshire, 1729–1850', unpub. Leeds Univ. M.Com. thesis, 1952; K. J. Allison, 'Enclosure by Agreement at Healaugh (West Riding)', *Yorks. Arch. J.*, XL, 1962, pp. 382–91; F. S. Colman, *A History of the Parish of Barwick in Elmet in the County of York*, Thoresby Soc., XVII, 1908, p. 127; Sheffield Central Library, Bacon Frank Ms deeds, 178–870, Nicholson papers, 72–104, MD 5,778; *Yorkshire Diaries and Autobiographies in the Seventeenth and Eighteenth Centuries*, Surtees Soc., LXV, 1875, p. 211.

[72] Leeds City Archives, BW/R/13; Borthwick IHR, probate inventories, Doncaster deanery; Cliffe, *op. cit.*, p. 277, Clwyd RO, D/GW/Y/701; D. Holland, ed., *History in Laughton-en-le-Morthen*, Doncaster, 1969, p. 40; Hooton Pagnell parish registers; Nottm Univ., Galway MSS, G12,362.

time. In 1628 the manor of Campsall was said to contain "greate store of lymestone an excellent compost beinge burned to manure cold grounds", but quarrying and lime burning did not develop on a large scale until the rivers were made navigable.[73] Judging by the few parish registers that record occupations, the farm labourers accounted for between 22 and 38 per cent of the adult male population. A similar proportion of labourers lived further west in those townships which did not specialize in the production of metalware or cloth.[74] In 1697 Celia Fiennes described the land on the coal-measure sandstones between Leeds and Elland as "good grounds for feeding cattle and for corne", where the inhabitants "are so well provided that together with their industry they needs be very rich". In this region, although there were poor sandy soils on the hills and ill-drained clays on the flatter surfaces, many fertile sandy loams could be farmed. A mixed farming economy of dairying and arable production seems to have been as common by the late seventeenth century as it is today. An examination of 81 probate inventories for the southern half of this region, appraised between 1695 and 1699 (inclusive), shows that the average number of cattle was only eight head per farm, and that even where farming was combined with industry there was often a significant amount of arable as well as pasture.[75] Agreements to enclose were frequent, but many townships retained their common fields until the age of parliamentary enclosure.[76] Arthur Young found much to criticize in the arable farming of this region, but, on the other hand, several improvements are worthy of note. The Rotherham plough was patented by

[73] Corporation of London RO, R.C.E. Rental 6.16, f. 18. Doncaster people knitted woollen garments until the end of the period, when competition from the framework knitters of the Midlands caused the trade to decline rapidly, e.g. Borthwick IHR, probate inventory of Dorothy Wells, 29 Dec. 1700. Doncaster wool staplers provided the West Riding clothiers with wool from Lincolnshire, Leicestershire, Norfolk, etc. e.g. Borthwick IHR, probate of William Rowbotham, 7 Dec. 1702. Outcrops of reddle, a red ochre that was used for marking sheep and for colouring timber, were worked near Micklebring – Borthwick IHR, inventory of Thomas Sheppard, 4 Mar. 1728/9.

[74] *Yorks. Arch. Soc. Parish Register Ser.*, Cantley (1941), Hemsworth (1926), Maltby (1926), Wath-upon-Dearne (1902); Sheffield City Library, parish registers; Arksey (PR 14), Bolton-on-Dearne (PR 20), Royston (PR 20), Worsbrough (PR 3); Rev. C. Osborne Brown, *Thorpe Salvin Registers*, 1592–1726, Bingley, 1892.

[75] Fiennes, *op. cit.*, pp. 220–1; Hey, *Rural Metalworkers*, pp. 16–18; W. H. Long, *A Survey of the Agriculture of Yorkshire*, London, 1969, pp. 63–4. Farms varied greatly in size, but were generally under 50 acres – Sheffield Central Library, NBC 294, Sp. St. 60, 194/21, WhM7 and 71 (I am grateful to S. Fraser, Esq. and to the earl of Wharncliffe for permission to quote from these collections); Kirklees Library, Ramsden MSS, surveys of Almondbury and Huddersfield, 1716. For the purchases of Scots bullocks, oxen, and steers, see Leeds City Archives, TN/EA/13/57; Sheffield City Library, WWM Br. 164, WWM A 224, Sp. St. 60, 656/1.

[76] J. C. Harvey, 'Common Field and Enclosure in the Lower Dearne Valley: A Case Study', *Yorks. Arch. J.*, XLVI, 1974, pp. 110–27; Beresford, *op. cit.*; Sheffield Central Library, NBC 13, 289–93, PR 8 (Thurnscoe parish register), Sp. St. 64, 726, WWM Br. 194, 76/16, WWM C2; Nottm Univ. Library, Galway MSS, G12, 128; Borthwick IHR, R/VII/510; parliamentary enclosure awards.

Disney Stanyforth and Joseph Foljambe in 1730 and soon became popular over a wide area; great attention was paid to the spreading of lime, especially after the Aire and Calder Navigation Act of 1699 and the Don Navigation Acts of 1726–7 had facilitated its transport; and occasional experiments were made with new crops: sainfoin was grown at Birstall in 1689, clover at Kirkburton in 1696, and turnips at Badsworth, Felkirk, and Shelley in the early eighteenth century.[77] As early as 1652 Pontefract was noted for the liquorice which was grown in its garths and gardens, and Celia Fiennes commented that "Any body that has but a little ground improves it for the produce of Liquorish, of which there is vast quantetyes, and it returns severall 100 pounds yearly to the town." The local importance of the crop is well attested in wills, inventories, and tithe disputes.[78]

On the edge of the Pennines more emphasis was laid upon dairying than upon rearing. However, several farmers kept a few bullocks, and 75 per cent had some sheep.[79] Many of the small townfields of the Pennine hamlets survived into this period,[80] but, as Defoe said, "As for corn, they scarcely sow enough for their cocks and hens." Oats was the chief cereal, and as hay was essential in this economy, the meadows were eagerly sought after. In a famous passage Defoe described the Halifax hills as "spread with enclosures

[77] G. Marshall, 'The "Rotherham" Plough', *Tools & Tillage*, III, 3, 1978, pp. 150–67; Young, *op. cit.*, I, pp. 126, 272; G. B. Rennie, R. Brown, and J. Shirreff, *General View of the Agriculture of the West Riding*, London, 1794, p. 51; Kirklees Library, Thornhill collection: "23 loads of lime on old lands", 1727, DD/WBW/45/9; Borthwick IHR, probate inventory of Lewis Nawl, Sheffield Park, cutler, 1 Oct. 1697, "30 load lime, £15"; Halifax Central Library, SH 1/SHA/2; Nottm Univ. Library, EM74-13; Bradford City Library, Sp. St. 2, 639, Cunliffe-Lister, box 15 (which records further that in May 1725 the chimney sweepers of Holbeck were paid "for spreading about 4 qt soot upon the sown barleys in East Leys" in Farnley, and that ashes were spread in the rape close there in 1696); for sainfoin, Leeds City Archives, TN/BL/C5 and Borthwick IHR, probate inventory of Benjamin Barber of Cawthorne, yeoman, 1729; for clover, Borthwick IHR, probate inventory of John Couldwell of Kirkburton, yeoman, 1696; for turnips, Borthwick IHR, inventory of Robert Wharam of Wentworth, Dec. 1736, Sheffield City Library, WWM Br. 167, A. N. J. Royds, ed., *The Registers of the Parish Church of Felkirk*, Rochdale, n.d., p. 6, and PRO, C 5/626/10. The cultivation of rape was fairly widespread, as its oil was used in preparing wool for carding and combing – PRO, E 112/765/193.

[78] Fiennes, *op. cit.*, p. 95; Young, *op. cit.*, I, p. 382; W. Blith, *The English Improver Improved*, 3rd edn, London, 1652, pp. 246–8; Borthwick IHR, R/vii/H/4,560, R/vii/H/4,538, R/As/52/25, 26, and 28, will of Robert Sutton (proved Sept. 1694), inventories of William Knutton (proved July 1692) and John Addinall (proved Dec. 1689). HMC, *Portland MSS*, VI, 1901, p. 91 (re Pontefract, 1725): "Its chief commodity is liquorice...It is now all farmed by two persons who allow the planters a certain rate for so many years, provided they break up no more ground to be employed that way." Ralph Ward grew liquorice at Guisborough in 1756 (Whiting, *op. cit.*, p. 218).

[79] Hey, *Rural Metalworkers*, p. 16.

[80] C. F. Innocent, 'The Field System of Wightwizzle', *Hunter Arch. Soc.*, II, 1924, pp. 276–8; enclosure award for the Graveship of Holme, 1834; Sheffield City Library, LD835–5; J. Dransfield, *History of Penistone*, Barnsley, 1906, pp. 178–9 (enclosure of Thurlstone fields in 1696 by the agreement of 23 families); East Yorks. RO, DDBM/14/8, 9 (enclosure of Midhope fields in 1674).

from two acres to six or seven each, seldom more, and every three or four pieces of land had a house belonging to them". To have a dual occupation was the normal way of life, and men were described alternatively by their farming status and by their craft name. The 100 probate inventories that survive for the Graveship of Holme from 1690 to 1762 show that nearly all the husbandmen and yeomen were involved in the cloth trade and that all those who were described as clothiers had some farm stock. Defoe goes on to describe how streams were turned by gutters or pipes into the clothiers' workshops, and how they emerged to enrich the land with the oil, soap, tallow, and other ingredients which had been used in dressing and scouring.[81] The area had very few large proprietors, and the custom of providing for younger sons increased the tendency towards small farms of under twenty, or even ten, acres. Copyholds were secure, and manorial policy allowed the enclosing of new intakes from the extensive wastes and commons. But to obtain a living it was necessary to have a dual occupation and generous common rights. Humphrey Bray, a Hepworth copyholder of £10 per annum, claimed in 1676 that without the common pastures it would have been impossible to manure his farm and support his flock of sheep.[82]

Both on the Pennines and on the exposed coalfield, industry and agriculture were inseparable: the gentry and yeomen profited from their investment or from their organizational roles, while most of the clothiers, metalworkers, colliers, and potters, glassmakers, and other craftsmen combined their trade with farming. Some of these craftsmen were poor cottagers or smallholders, but others prospered modestly, and the yeoman-factors were often substantial men who acquired the capital and expertise to finance the early developments in the Industrial Revolution. In the south, the 'little-mesters' in the rural cutlery and nailing trades were still able to preserve their traditional independence and to combine their work in the smithy with spells on the farm, though as the century progressed the great increase in their numbers meant that fewer of them had a share in the land. Further north, by the end of the period, the West Riding woollen industry had grown to national pre-eminence, and the worsted industry, which had been introduced after the Restoration, was soon to achieve equality with the Norwich region. The worsted industry had been organized on a more capitalistic basis from

---

[81] Defoe, *Tour, II*, pp. 193–6; Borthwick IHR, probate inventories, Pontefract deanery. In 1741 "the lower sort of people" in Sheffield were said to eat oatbread, the price of oats being "wholly governed" by Rotherham market – John Rylands Library, Bagshawe, 5/4/1.

[82] J. Charlesworth, ed., 'Wakefield Manor Book, 1709', *Yorks. Arch. Soc. Rec. Ser.*, CI, 1939; M. Ellis, 'A Study in the Manorial History of Halifax Parish in the Sixteenth and Early Seventeenth Centuries, pt 1', *Yorks. Arch. J.*, CLVIII, 1960; PRO, C 5/448/19; Northants. RO, Brudenell F/iii/193. See also J. Radley, 'Holly as a Winter Feed', AHR, IX, 2, 1961, pp. 89–92. As early as 1648 Adam Eyre of Hazlehead, a captain in the parliamentary army, had planted turnips and mustard in his *garden* on the edge of the Pennine moors – *Yorkshire Diaries and Autobiographies*, p. 106.

the start, and in the woollen industry a few large-scale clothiers employing domestic weavers and spinners became increasingly important. Even so, the small-scale, independent clothier remained the typical figure in the woollen trade, and the agricultural side of his dual occupation continued to be significant. The West Riding was also a noted tanning centre, and this craft provides an example of one of the many subtle links between agriculture and industry in this region, for not only were extra hides imported from London when ships returned from carrying cloth and metalware, but a cheap and ready supply of bark was obtainable from the springwoods that the ironmasters felled for charcoal.[83]

The seeds of industrial change that transformed much of the West Riding and Lancashire during the next century were planted and nourished between the years 1640 and 1750. Well before the end of this period some rural parishes on the coalfields and on the edges of the Pennines had a pronounced industrial character. Manchester, Sheffield, and several other towns were already growing at a rapid rate, the major rivers had been made navigable, and steps had been taken to improve the pack-horse routes with guide stoops and better bridges and to turnpike some of the most important highways.[84] The growth of neither the rural nor the urban population has yet been analysed satisfactorily, but it is evident that this growth was checked and perhaps reversed for a time by the great mortality of 1723–9, the last of the series of fevers that swept the country in the wake of disastrous harvests. The vicar of a parish in the southern Vale of York described the events of 1729 as "the greatest mortality that ever can be remembered, or made out to be in the parish of Arksey". In Lancashire, the burial registers of Deane contain many marginal references to "fever", "ague fever", and "pluraisy", and William Stout reported at the close of 1728 "a very sickly summer, and great mortality in the plaine countrie, much more then in the towns; and the buryalls were double this year to what they were last year". His remarks are confirmed by a study of the parish registers of north-west Lancashire and

[83] M. J. Dickenson, 'The West Riding Woollen and Worsted Industries, 1689–1770: An Analysis of Probate Inventories and Insurance Policies', unpub. Nottm Univ. Ph.D. thesis, 1974; W. B. Crump and G. Ghorbal, *History of the Huddersfield Woollen Industry*, Huddersfield, 1935; H. Heaton, *The Yorkshire Woollen and Worsted Industries*, 2nd edn, Oxford, 1965; Hey, *Rural Metalworkers*; Borthwick IHR, probate inventory of William Naylor of Hoyland Moorside, "collyer and husbandman"; D. Hey, 'The Use of Probate Inventories for Industrial Archaeology', *Indust. Arch.*, X, 1973, pp. 201–13; L. A. Clarkson, 'The Leather Crafts in Tudor and Stuart England', AHR, XIV, 1, 1966, pp. 25–39; D. F. E. Sykes, *The History of Huddersfield and the Valleys of the Colne, the Holme, and the Dearne*, Huddersfield, n.d., pp. 169–70 re Thomas Pickles of Kirkheaton, tanner, who in the mid 1640s had "Eleven score hides bought at London, £220, 120 hides bought at London and not yet at Hull, £150".

[84] Wadsworth and Mann, *Cotton Trade*; Hey, *Rural Metalworkers*; Defoe, *op. cit.*, II, pp. 183, 261–2; T. S. Willan, *River Navigation in England, 1600–1750*, Oxford, 1936; W. B. Crump, *Huddersfield Highways Down the Ages*, Huddersfield, 1949; D. Hey, *Packmen, Carriers and Packhorse Roads*, Leicester, 1980.

of several other parts of the county; for example, 155 people were buried at Woodplumpton during 1728, "many more than ever was known before". As late as 14 April 1752 the *Manchester Mercury* advertised a cordial elixir which "did numbers of cures in the great sickness in 1725 and 1726". Different parishes were affected in different years, but it is noticeable that, as at Woodplumpton, few infants or children died of the fevers. Nicholas Blundell noted in December 1727, "Never so sickly a time known in Lancashire as from May till the end of this year, abundance died, but generally those over 50 years old, the distemper was an uncommon sort of fever, which eather took them off or ended in a violent ague which often lasted severall months". A similar tale could be told from Yorkshire.[85]

But, in general, agriculture and industry in Lancashire and Yorkshire provided a sufficient living for most people, even if this was not won easily. Men showed increasing concern with the poor as the population rose, but the problem did not become acute until the later years of the eighteenth century. Centuries of experience had shaped and reshaped the farming systems of the different regions, and although there was a great deal of conservatism and inefficiency, many improvements were put into effect between 1640 and 1750. In large parts of Yorkshire and Lancashire farmer–craftsmen profitably combined their husbandry with industry. Before 1750 this way of life had not been overwhelmed by the population explosion and the changes associated with the Industrial Revolution.

[85] A. Gooder, 'The Population Crisis of 1727–30 in Warwickshire', *Midland Hist.*, I, 4, 1972, pp. 1–22; Hey, *Rural Metalworkers*, pp. 54–7; E. L. Jones, *Seasons and Prices*, London, 1964, p. 137; *Lancs. Parish Register Soc.*, LIV, 1917, and CIII, 1964; Stout, *op. cit.*, pp. 201, 276n; Kelly, *Viking Village*, p. 46; *Yorkshire Diaries and Autobiographies*, pp. 292, 296; Nottm Univ. Library, Galway MSS, G12,207/1; Northants. RO, Brudenell F/iii/184; Surrey RO, LM/778/28/23 (Robert Hindley of West Houghton to Sir Thomas Molyneux, 12 July 1723: "It has been a bad year among us, our hay and corn has been very bad"); T. Gent, *History of Hull*, York, 1735, p. 196: (1727) "Even beans were sold, in the West Riding at 40 shillings a quarter, and corn would have been miserably dear, had not his Majesty, in commiseration to his poorer subjects been so gracious as to take off the duty of foreign grain: hereupon, in our distress, we were supply'd with ship loads, from Italy, Flanders, Poland, and other distant parts, to the unspeakable comfort of many house keepers"; C. E. Whiting, ed., 'The Diary of Arthur Jessop', *Yorks. Arch. Soc. Rec. Ser.*, CXVII, 1952: "December 31st, 1730:...conclusion of another year and many hath been taken away...reduced to great straits...forced to live upon coarse mean fare such as is not usual for man to eat but life was preserved to turn our scarcity into plenty and a plentiful crop the last year and...another plentiful crop this year".

THE MIDLANDS

CHAPTER 4

THE EAST MIDLANDS:
NORTHAMPTONSHIRE, LEICESTERSHIRE,
RUTLAND, NOTTINGHAMSHIRE, AND
LINCOLNSHIRE (EXCLUDING THE FENLAND)

The east Midlands region considered here consists of the five counties Northamptonshire, Leicestershire, Rutland, Nottinghamshire, and Lincolnshire excluding the fenland. In 1801 the five counties had together a total population of 627,000, or nearly 7 per cent of the total population of England and Wales at that date: Lincolnshire, as might be expected, boasted the largest population, at 209,000; Rutland had a mere 16,000; and the figures for Northamptonshire, Leicestershire, and Nottinghamshire were respectively 132,000, 130,000, and 140,000. In the hundred years before 1750 the population of the region was much less urbanized, and was much more evenly spread over the area, than it was to be later. Even the county towns were very limited in size. Nottingham was the largest city of the region, having an estimated population of 5,000–6,000 in 1674 and 10,720 in 1739. These figures represented rather less than 10 per cent of the population of the whole county (estimated at 90,000–95,000 in 1690). Leicester ran Nottingham fairly close, with an estimated 6,000 in 1700. Northampton had some 5,000 in the middle eighteenth century, a figure considerably below those for Nottingham and Leicester, while "antient, ragged, decay'd" Lincoln, as Defoe called it, probably had some 3,000 in 1705 and a little over 4,000 in 1721.[1]

As centres of consumption, therefore, the influence of the county towns was small. However, together with the numerous and even smaller market towns spread through the region, they were important as trading centres and as centres for craftsmen in the processing and service industries essential to a flourishing agriculture. They served, too, as collecting points for livestock and commodities intended to be sold in distant markets. Wool and corn, for instance, were sent from Lincolnshire into Yorkshire, and leather and skins were brought to nearby market towns to be sold in far-off destinations. Stock from north Leicestershire and the Forest area of Nottinghamshire went to

---

I am greatly indebted to Miss Margaret Roake, who kindly spent many hours in analysing the probate inventory material for this chapter.

[1] J. D. Chambers, *Nottinghamshire in the Eighteenth Century*, London, 1932, pp. 82–3; Sir Francis Hill, *Georgian Lincoln*, Cambridge, 1966, pp. 146–7; D. Defoe, *A Tour through England and Wales*, 2 vols., London, 1928, *II*, p. 91.

the Birmingham area, and some was driven to Rotherham for eventual sale in the manufacturing towns of Yorkshire and Lancashire.[2] A little "neat market town" like Uppingham had in Celia Fiennes's time an important Saturday market "affording great quantities of corn, leather, yarn and cattle", and such a concourse of people gathered there that Celia's landlord told her he often had as many as a hundred horses lodged in his inn.[3] But a great deal of the farm produce of the region came under the influence of the "grand vortex", as Marshall called it, and was sent to London and sold in the great metropolitan markets. Here the turnpiking of the main roads near the capital, which proceeded rapidly in the later years of our period, played a prominent part; it is significant that numbers of the early turnpikes were supported by local landowners.[4] In his celebrated *Tour* Defoe noted how turnpikes had eased the passage to London of livestock and produce from the Midland counties, a traffic which he described as "exceeding great", for "these are counties which drive a very great trade with the city of London, and with one another, perhaps the greatest of any counties in England". Because of the great volume of traffic, he went on, the roads to Bedfordshire and Hertfordshire were formerly much out of repair and inadequate for "the drifts of cattle, which come this way out of Lincolnshire and the fens of the Isle of Ely...the large heavy bullocks, of which the numbers that come this way are scarce to be reckon'd up".[5]

Besides turnpikes the region also had access to distant markets by means of the navigable rivers, such as the Soar and Welland in Leicestershire, the Witham and Ancholme in Lincolnshire, and above all the Trent, as well as by Hull and the Lincolnshire ports of Grimsby and Boston. Although the smaller rivers were subject to silting, the Trent was readily navigable to Gainsborough, Newark, and Nottingham, and "by the help of art", as Defoe said, as far upstream as Burton-on-Trent.[6] It is evident that the land routes to the capital were also much used, and that distance was not considered a great obstacle – Leicester was just under 100 miles from London, Nottingham 123 miles, and Lincoln 132 miles. There are numerous documentary references to the trade with London. A Lincolnshire farmer asked in October 1670 for four strikes of sainfoin seed to be sent him from London by the drovers who were taking up sheep to be sold in the capital.[7] In August 1699 John Day of Harrington, Lincolnshire, told Sir Thomas Hussey that he had

[2] Joan Thirsk, 'Agrarian History 1540–1950', in *VCH Leics.*, II, p. 220n.

[3] Celia Fiennes, *The Journeys of Celia Fiennes*, ed. C. Morris, London, 1947, pp. 161–2.

[4] William Marshall, *The Rural Economy of the Midland Counties*, 2 vols., London, 1790, I, p. 230; William Albert, *The Turnpike Road System in England and Wales, 1663–1840*, Cambridge, 1972, p. 98.

[5] Defoe, *op. cit.*, II, pp. 118, 123.

[6] *Ibid.*, pp. 140–1.

[7] LAO, MM vi/2/51. A 'strike' was usually equivalent to a bushel, but might in some areas mean only $\frac{1}{2}$ bushel, and sometimes as much as 2 or 4 bushels.

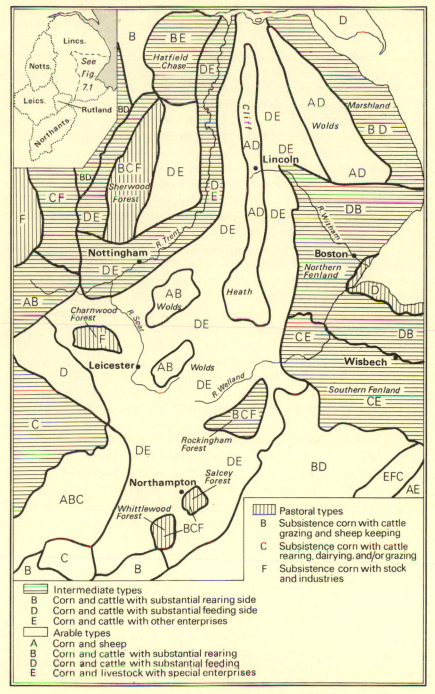

Fig. 4.1. Farming regions of the east Midlands.

recently sold two "parcels" of sheep in London, one of twenty sheep, the other of nineteen, and had just sent up twenty-eight more.[8] And in October 1702 George Woodcocke, a drover, delivered the sum of £25 15s. 2d. to Lord Fitzwilliam in London:[9] drovers, like the captains of coastal vessels, were frequently employed for delivering cash, and for carrying out transactions in London on behalf of farmers and country tradesmen.

As a farming region the east Midlands as a whole is well suited to both arable and pasture. The rainfall is adequate both for crops and for grass, but it is not excessive, and is well distributed through the year; temperatures also are rarely extreme. Leicestershire and Nottinghamshire, for instance, have a rainfall averaging about 24–8 inches, and mean temperatures ranging from 37 °F in January to 62 °F in July, ideal for the growth of crops and grass over a long period of the year. Rainfall is lowest in February, March, and April, allowing spring work on the farms to be started early and finished in good time.

The larger part of the region consists of an undulating plain, mainly underlain by rocks of Permo-Triassic age. Post-glacial erosion has not succeeded in removing all the thick and extensive deposits of boulder clay which cover much of the basin of the Soar and spreads over the higher ground in the north-west of Northamptonshire, the east and north of Leicestershire, and southern Nottinghamshire. The boulder clay gives rise to heavy soils, and the upland Wolds of this area have generally poor clays with extensive areas given over to woodlands on the hilltops. Large cultivated woodlands were also to be found in Rockingham Forest, lying to the south-east of the Welland between Market Harborough and Stamford, in Leighfield Forest in Rutland, a continuation of Rockingham Forest, and in Whittlewood and Salcey forests on the southern borders of Northamptonshire. Charnwood Forest, consisting largely of woodlands and waste, formed the only extensive district of its kind in Leicestershire, while in Nottinghamshire the much larger area of the ancient Forest of Sherwood stretched some twenty-five or thirty miles from near Nottingham to the northern boundary of the county.

But the soils of the region are very mixed, and in addition to the heavy clays and the poor soils of the woodlands and waste, there are tracts of fertile lighter soils, consisting of Keuper marls, whose red colouring imparts a dominant tinge to the ploughland, despite the intervening deposits of glacial drift. When Celia Fiennes entered Leicestershire she found it "a very rich country, red land, good corne of all sorts and grass both fields and inclosures; you see a great way upon their hills, the bottoms full of inclosures, woods and different sort of manureing and herbage, amongst which are placed many little towns, which gives great pleasure of the travellers to view".[10] In

---

[8] Bodleian Library, MS Top. Lincs. C3, f. 44.
[9] Notts. RO, F(M)C 1237.
[10] Fiennes, *op. cit.*, p. 161.

Charnwood Forest extremely ancient volcanic rocks protrude to create a series of ridges built up of pre-Cambrian quartzites and other hard rocks. Outcrops of younger rocks, such as the Bunter sands and pebble beds, may form coarse and 'hungry' soils, occupied mainly by woods and heathland, as in Sherwood Forest. The Dukeries, where the large Nottinghamshire landowners carved out extensive parks from the Forest, were established on these poor soils.

To the east of the Forest in Nottinghamshire are tracts of Keuper waterstones which give rise to good friable, arable soils, and the heavier clays are often found with an admixture of sand. The flat Vale of Trent has some rich alluvial soils near the river, and elsewhere in the vale the clays are lightened by sand and gravel. The vale and adjoining claylands run north-east towards Lincoln, where the level is abruptly terminated by a steep rise of 150 or 200 feet to the limestone ridge. This ridge is known as the Cliff north of Lincoln, and as the Heath to the south of the city. The Cliff section, stretching up to the bank of the Humber, is only a few miles in width, but the Heath south of Lincoln broadens out, and was described by Defoe as "a noble plain", a "most rich, pleasant and agreeable" country.[11] The Cliff and Heath are mainly underlain by oolitic limestone, covered by a reasonably fertile but chalky boulder clay. Towards the east the ridge falls away gently and is separated from the chalky Lincolnshire Wolds by the central vale of boulder and Oxford clays. In the northern section of the vale there are low-lying lands, called carrs, subject to flooding by the river Ancholme; there are also some barren, sandy stretches around Scunthorpe, Frodingham, and Flixborough. To the east of the clay vale rise the Lincolnshire Wolds, an extensive district averaging some eight miles in width and forty-five miles from north to south. The surface is generally thin and chalky, but to the south the hills are more broken and the soils more fertile: there the chalk has been washed off the hills to expose the underlying clay, and there are fenland areas along the river valleys. Finally, between the Wolds and the Lincolnshire coast runs the strip of Marshland, low-lying and covered with boulder clay, with patches of sand and gravel, and rich alluvial silts near the shore. The western boundary of the Marshland is clearly marked by the upward slope to the Wolds, while to the south the fenlands around the Wash are distinguished by their dark-coloured peats and silts, forming a separate natural region.

The east Midlands region, then, was one of mixed soils and varied relief, and consequently supported a wide range of farming activities. Generally speaking, most of the farming consisted of some combination of crops and livestock, with areas of specialized cultivation, and the differences between one district and another were largely of degree rather than of kind. However, the range of soils, relief, and climate did create varying opportunities and

[11] Defoe, op. cit., I, p. 94.

limitations, and we may distinguish four different types of land use. First in importance were the clayland vales and alluvial river valley bottoms, the home of the classical Midland mixed farming or arable-fattening systems. Second come the upland areas: the clay Wolds of south Nottinghamshire, eastern Leicestershire, and north-western Northamptonshire, leaned more to the grazing livestock, while the limestone ridge of Lincoln Cliff and Heath, and the chalk Wolds of Lincolnshire relied on a sheep–corn system. Third in order we take the less fertile but extensive Forest lands, those of Sherwood in Nottinghamshire, Charnwood in Leicestershire, Leighfield in Rutland, and Rockingham, Whittlewood, and Salcey in Northamptonshire. Last comes the distinctive Lincolnshire Marshland, lying between the Wolds and the sea, and largely devoted to the fattening of livestock.

The first of these areas, that of the lowland mixed arable and pasture, covered a great part of central Northamptonshire, much of Leicestershire, eastern Nottinghamshire, and Lincolnshire west of the Cliff and Heath together with the central vale lying between the Cliff and Heath and the Lincolnshire Wolds. Over much of this large area arable crops were still grown in common fields, though enclosures had increased the extent of land given over to various forms of convertible husbandry and to permanent pasture, especially around Northampton and to the east and south-west of Leicester. The most famous fattening pastures of Leicestershire were located in the valley of the Welland, centred on Market Harborough and extending northwards. Wheat was everywhere of some importance, but the pre-dominant use made of the arable was to produce fodder for the rearing and fattening of livestock. In Northamptonshire, and in the claylands of Nottinghamshire and Lincolnshire, the arable crops were mainly wheat, barley, and peas; in Leicestershire and Rutland, barley, oats, and peas and – especially – beans. Beans gave rise to the term "Bean-belly Leicestershire", and it was said that one had only to shake a Leicestershire yeoman by his collar to hear the beans rattle in his belly.[12]

In the majority of places the common-field arable system was a simple three-course: wheat or barley, beans and/or peas, and fallow. Nearly 80 per cent of open parishes in Leicestershire had their land in three fields in the seventeenth century.[13] Common-field farmers believed that beans and peas had the advantage of smothering weeds, though observers remarked their crops to be very foul, nevertheless. Although the value of farmers' livestock was often nearly equal to that of their crops, not all the farmers had flocks large enough to fold their lands effectively. They generally kept some cows, but more so on the riverside pastures where dairying was especially important. In common-field parishes the enclosed grass grounds were

[12] G. E. Fussell, 'Four Centuries of Leicestershire Farming', in W. G. Hoskins, ed., *Studies in Leicestershire Agrarian History*, Leicester, 1949, p. 154.

[13] M. W. Beresford, 'Glebe Terriers and Open Field Leicestershire', in Hoskins, *op. cit.*, p. 94.

generally shut up at Holy-day, some kept shut for hay, and some part opened at old May Day, and all commoned from old Lammas.[14] Oats and rye were sometimes grown, but usually only on the poorer patches of sandy or gravelly soil. Rye, once important as a field crop in Leicestershire, had declined considerably by the seventeenth century.

There is evidence that farmers diverged from this general pattern quite frequently. Common-field farming was never entirely rigid, and often allowed for innovation and for adjustment of the proportion of the acreage devoted respectively to arable and pasture. Sometimes the fields were divided to allow for a more complex pattern of cropping; sometimes land in the fields was laid down to a pasture ley, and beasts were tethered on it to fatten. Glebe terriers of the seventeenth century show many holdings of leys and 'grass-grounds' in the fields.[15] At Wigston Magna near Leicester grass leys took up an average of a fifth of the total area of the common fields in the seventeenth century and first half of the eighteenth, with the larger farmers having an even higher proportion of ley ground.[16] Numbers of villages saw over the years an increase in the size of farms, the gathering of 'lands' or strips into more compact holdings, and also a good deal of piecemeal enclosure, by which small areas of common-field land were divided off and used as additional closes for new fodder crops, or for dairying and fattening. At Laxton in Nottinghamshire, where the common fields survive today, a survey of 1691 shows that about half the acreage of the parish was in closes, and further surveys reveal that this proportion was increased by piecemeal enclosure in subsequent decades. At Eakring, nearby, thirty-five acres were taken out of the Grass Field between 1744 and 1746 and divided into pasture closes. And at Crowle in the Isle of Axholme three new enclosures were made in 1732.[17] Where the common pasture became inadequate and was being overgrazed, the farmers agreed to stint it, rationing its use between the various farmers and common-right cottagers according to the respective size of their common-field holdings. At Wigston Magna a new regulating of the common was necessitated by the growth of population and the extension of the arable land; the new stint agreed in 1707 was solemnized by enrolment in Chancery.[18] Sometimes, as at Barrowby in Lincolnshire, the farmers decided to improve the common pastures by ploughing them up, a third at a time, keeping each third part in tillage for a period of years in turn, and then putting it back to grass.[19] At Cotgrave in Nottinghamshire the

[14] R. Lowe, General View of the Agriculture of Nottinghamshire, London, 1798, pp. 37, 42.

[15] Beresford, op. cit., p. 92.

[16] W. G. Hoskins, The Midland Peasant: The Economic and Social History of a Leicestershire Village, London, 1957, p. 233.

[17] BL, Egerton MS 3,564; Nottm Univ. Archives, Manvers, Kingston surveys and estate accounts.   [18] Hoskins, Midland Peasant, pp. 238, 240.

[19] Joan Thirsk, English Peasant Farming: The Agrarian History of Lincolnshire from Tudor to Recent Times, London, 1957, p. 185.

farmers agreed in 1717 to enclose one of their four common fields in order to remedy a shortage of grass land, and rules were drawn up for sharing and maintaining the new pasture.[20]

Thus there is much evidence that the ancient common-field system was capable of improvement and in places was modified and adapted to accommodate new crops or meet changing needs. Nevertheless, there can be little doubt but that most of the best farming was to be found on enclosed land. Contemporary observers distinguished carefully between the practices of common fields and those of enclosures, and it was evidently in the latter that new departures, such as the cultivation of turnips or artificial grasses and legumes, like sainfoin, trefoil, and clovers, were most likely to be seen.

In the enclosed farms a system of convertible husbandry was practised. As described by Edward Lisle about the end of the seventeenth century, the method was to take four corn crops in succession, three of barley, and one of wheat, and then to sow grass seeds in the wheat field in the spring. The resulting grass ley was left in being for a period of years before it was ploughed up for a series of corn crops as before.[21] Almost a century later, in 1790, William Marshall described a similar form of convertible husbandry. He saw it as something characteristically Midland, though it is worth noting that his account was primarily concerned with a limited region consisting only of western Leicestershire (the part of the county lying to the west and south-west of Charnwood Forest) together with the neighbouring parts of Warwickshire, Staffordshire, and Derbyshire. In Marshall's account the ley was kept down for six or seven years before being broken up by a single ploughing for oats; in the following season the oat stubble was ploughed two or three times for wheat, and the wheat stubble subsequently ploughed two or three times for barley and grass seeds. There were complaints, he said, that under this system the limited amount of cultivation made it difficult to keep the land free of weeds, and it was becoming the practice, on the lighter soils at least, to have an additional turnip fallow to clean the soil in preparation for the barley and grass seeds to follow.[22]

Marshall's description differs in detail from that of Lisle, but it seems certain that both writers were discussing variants of a basically similar convertible system, one which doubtless differed in its elements from place to place and from time to time. Lisle noted in his day that already Leicestershire farmers were growing "great quantities" of turnips, and that experiments had been made with clover on ley ground. Pigeon dung was harrowed in on land sown with corn, and malt dust was spread on cold, wet grass grounds at the rate of four quarters to the acre, and also on barley ground. Other manures included lime and soot, the latter used as a top

---

[20] BL, Egerton MS 3,622, ff. 202–4.
[21] Fussell, *op. cit.*, p. 162.
[22] Marshall, *op. cit.*, I, p. 187.

dressing for wheat in February, and in such quantities that "the land is black with it". The common-field farmers went in for numerous ploughings in preparation for their corn crops. Five ploughings were given for barley, five also for oats, and four for wheat, though only one for peas and beans.[23] This heavy outlay of time and labour on cultivation was partly a reflection of the difficulty of controlling weeds, partly on the heavy nature of much of the land, which required much work in creating a fine tilth and good seed bed.

Convertible husbandry, based on rotations which included a pasture ley, was a well-established feature of the better farming of the region. Young related in his *Northern Tour* of 1770 that round Stamford a great many turnips were grown for feeding with sheep, and that quantities of sainfoin were sown with barley after turnips, at the rate of between four and five bushels of seed to the acre. Farmers could mow two loads of hay on each acre of their sainfoin for as long as a dozen years together. A two-year ley of mixed trefoil and clover was sown between a crop of wheat and a following one of barley.[24] Young's friend Thomas Ruggles made a tour into Lincolnshire in 1786 especially to obtain information about the cultivation of sainfoin, "as there are many fields of it in the country about Lincoln";[25] Lincolnshire farmers, as already noted, had been using sainfoin since at least 1670.[26] Farming accounts of the 1730s and 1740s also show frequent purchases of turnip seed and trefoil seed. In April 1737, for instance, Sir Humphrey Monoux's steward paid £1 9s. 2d. in Nottingham for 140 lb of trefoil seed at $2\frac{1}{4}$d. per lb.[27] And in May 1746 accounts of the Willoughby family of Wollaton, near Nottingham, show a payment for ryegrass, trefoil, and clover seed amounting to £4 17s. 6d.[28] Intelligent farmers understood that it was advantageous to plough up old, worn-out pastures and lay them down afresh. Andrew Love, steward of the Leigh estates near Oakham, argued in 1717 that if an old, thin-swarded pasture were to be ploughed and laid down again, the grass would be sweeter and more profitable for cattle, and the beasts would the more readily feed and grow fat on it. He could obtain, he said, the opinions of the best graziers in the district to support the view that the land would be greatly improved by ploughing.[29]

There is evidence, too, that some farmers were experimenting with areas of hops. By the mid eighteenth century, if not earlier, they were widely grown in villages where they are quite unknown today, their cultivation remembered only by the name "The Hop Pole" on an occasional inn sign. In Nottinghamshire the variety grown was known as the North Clay hops, stronger in flavour than the Kentish kind, and hop grounds were well

[23] Fussell, *op. cit.*, pp. 162–3.

[24] A. Young, *A Six Months Tour through the North of England*, 4 vols., London, 1770, I, pp. 76–7.

[25] A. Young, ed., *The Annals of Agriculture*, VIII, London, 1787, p. 168.

[26] See above, p. 90.   [27] Notts. RO, DDF 1/1.

[28] Nottm Univ. Archives, Middleton A 130.   [29] Hants. RO, 5M50 596, 600.

established around Retford and Southwell, while markets for the sale of the hops were provided at Retford and Tuxford on the Great North Road. In 1740 Sir Humphrey Monoux's steward paid £10 10s. for 1,460 "hop poles best" and £6 for 1,660 "worst hop poles". Three years earlier an Eakring farmer asked permission of his landlord, Sir George Savile, to drain and manure a close of seven acres which was excessively boggy, in order to see whether it would serve as hop land.[30]

Woad, hemp, and flax were also grown in parts of the region. According to Walter Blith, a farmer might expect to obtain three crops of woad a year, or even as many as five or six crops in an exceptionally good year. Apart from its value in the dyeing industry, a winter crop of woad was thought useful for feeding sheep. It was held to be "good against the rot", and though the sheep had to be pressed to eat it, once they had tried it "they will take to it most powerfully, and that with love, and it will continue them in good heart, and strength, till sowing time again".[31]

Although large areas of the lowland clays were devoted to arable, livestock played a key role in the farming systems. Cattle and sheep were valued for their manure as well as for their meat, milk, skins, tallow, and wool. In the autumn the sheep were folded on the fallows and wheat ground, but in the winter and early spring the land was too wet to take them, and the barley had to be dunged with manure carried out from the yard and fold. But though an essential adjunct of crop production, livestock were valuable in their own right. Farmers large and small maintained areas of permanent pasture, and specialized in breeding and fattening. Defoe remarked that in Leicestershire there were few sources of urban or industrial wealth: hence "most of the gentlemen are graziers, and in some places the graziers are so rich, that they grow gentlemen". The county, he said, boasted the largest sheep and horses to be found. The sheep bred there, and in Lincolnshire, "bear not only the greatest weight of flesh on their bones, but also the greatest fleeces of wool on their backs of any sheep of England...These are the funds of sheep which furnish the city of London with their large mutton in so remarkable a quantity...The horses produced here, or rather fed here, are the largest in England, being generally the black coach horses and dray horses, of which so great a number are continually brought up to London."[32] Horse breeding was, indeed, an important activity over a great part of the east Midlands. There were several noted horse fairs, such as those at Nottingham, Mansfield, Newark, and Horncastle, at Leicester, and at Rothwell in Northamptonshire, while Northampton itself, Defoe reported, was "counted the centre of all the horse-markets and horse-fairs in England, there being no less than four fairs in a year...Here they buy horses of all sorts, as well for the saddle as for the coach and cart, but chiefly for the two latter."[33]

[30] Notts. RO, DDF 1/1; DDSR 28/12/1737.
[31] W. Blith, *The English Improver Improved*, 4th edn, London, 1652, p. 226.
[32] Defoe, *op. cit.*, II, p. 89.   [33] *Ibid.*, pp. 86–7.

The feeding of cattle and pigs was also of great importance. The meadows along the Trent, Nene, Soar, Welland, Witham, and Ancholme were frequently utilized for dairying, especially in the vicinity of the larger towns. The meadows to the east of Nottingham produced the locally marketed Colwick cheese. The more famous Stilton was associated with rich pastures in the Vale of Belvoir and the district round Melton Mowbray. It was made from cream, and so regarded as a luxury cheese. Marshall stated that Stilton cheese was first made by a Mrs Paulet at Wymondham, a few miles east of Melton Mowbray. She was connected with the proprietor of the Bell inn at Stilton on the Great North Road, and her cheese was sold there, so becoming known as 'Stilton'.[34] Mrs Paulet was still living when Marshall was compiling his *Midland Counties* in the middle 1780s, and if the story was true she must then have been well advanced in years, for Stilton cheese was known to Defoe writing more than sixty years earlier. The real origins of the cheese are probably found in Kirby Bellars, a few miles from Melton Mowbray. There, in the second half of the seventeenth century, it is likely that Mary, Lady Beaumont, created the cheese solely for private family use. The recipe was passed on to the Ashby family at Quenby Hall, some miles to the south. "Lady Beaumont's cheese" was made there, again for family use. A Mrs Orton, former housekeeper to the Ashbys, took the secret of its making with her when she moved to Little Dalby, quite near to Kirby Bellars. She made the cheese from the milk of cows kept in a single pasture known as Orton's close. From these obscure origins this celebrated cheese spread slowly in the eighteenth century to the rich pastures of the neighbouring district.[35]

The hard-pressed Leicester Red was more of a commercial or 'family' cheese, made in quantity for distant markets. 'Factor's cheese' produced in the Midlands was marketed in London and in the manufacturing towns of the Midlands and north. Atherstone, just over the Leicestershire border in Warwickshire, was renowned for a great cheese fair held on the 8th of September. From its market cheese factors carried away "vast quantities" to Stourbridge Fair, there to be sold again for the benefit of consumers in East Anglia.[36]

The dairy cattle in use were of local Staffordshire and Derbyshire blood, not a particularly distinguished kind of cattle apparently, but one thought good for dairying purposes. The grazing cattle, also, were mainly of longhorn types, but in Leicestershire, in particular, they were improved by crossing with cattle from Lancashire, Westmorland, and Craven in Yorkshire. The evidence for this is not decisive until the later eighteenth century but it is possible that the crossing of Leicestershire with Lancashire longhorns was

---

[34] Marshall, *op. cit.*, I, pp. 355–6.
[35] W. G. Hoskins, *Midland England*, London, 1949, pp. 93–6.
[36] Defoe, *op. cit.*, II, p. 88.

occurring in the first half of the eighteenth century. Since at least the 1680s
and 1690s Lancashire dairymen had been breeding from unusually young
yearling bulls, and their longhorns may in consequence have built up
early-maturity genes, plus genes for size, which caught the notice of, and
were exploited by, Midland graziers.[37] Many of the cattle fattened in the
Midland pastures, however, were bought from drovers at markets or casually
on the road, and consisted of Welsh runts or the Scotch black cattle.

The sheep to be seen in the commons and in the common fields were
mostly shortwool ewes brought in principally from the hills of Shropshire,
though also from Staffordshire and Derbyshire. These 'field sheep', having
reared their lambs, were sold at the Walsall market or to colliery butchers
in the Birmingham area. Some were kept over winter for another flock of
lambs, and in autumn the lambs were driven into Worcestershire and
Shropshire to be fattened. By this system the Shropshire farmers had a market
for their surplus ewes, for which they had insufficient keep, and the
Worcestershire and Warwickshire farmers were supplied with lambs from
the surplus of the Leicestershire men. The longwool 'pasture sheep' was a
strong, large-boned animal, widely used throughout the enclosed pastures
of Northamptonshire, Leicestershire, Rutland, and Nottinghamshire. It was
known in Leicestershire as the 'Old Leicestershire' breed, and was probably
derived from the old Lincoln or Lindsey type.[38]

It is not surprising that breeders of this great sheep-producing area
involved themselves in the second half of the eighteenth century in strenuous
efforts to produce an improved breed. This achievement has long been linked
with the name of Robert Bakewell, though Marshall ascribed its origin to
Joseph Allom of Clifton (probably Clifton Campville, in Staffordshire).
Allom bought his breeding ewes from a Mr Stone of Goadby Marwood near
Melton Mowbray, and with these animals he laid the foundation of the more
compact, small-boned animals which Bakewell developed into his famous
Dishley or New Leicester breed. It is possible, though as yet unproven, that
this more deliberate policy of selective breeding had been started by one or
two Midland farmers just before the end of our period, perhaps in the 1740s.[39]

The old Lincolnshire, which until this time still dominated in its home
county, was a slightly larger sheep than the old Leicestershire, but was like
it in being hornless, white-faced, and white-legged. By the later eighteenth

[37] N. C. Russell, 'Animal Breeding in England, c. 1500–1750', Univ. of London Ph.D. thesis,
1981, pp. 86–94. I wish to thank Dr Russell for permission to quote from his as yet unpublished
thesis. See also N. C. Russell, 'Who Improved the 18th-Century Longhorn Cow?', in *Agricultural
Improvement: Medieval and Modern*, Exeter Papers in Economic History, no. 14, 1982, pp. 19–40.

[38] Robert Trow-Smith, *A History of British Livestock Husbandry, 1700–1900*, London, 1959, pp.
59–60.

[39] Marshall, *op. cit.*, I, pp. 381–2. For a general discussion on this question, see Russell, thesis,
pp. 116, 131–3.

century the mature Lincoln wether weighed about 25 lb the quarter, and bore a fleece of 8–14 lb – claimed to be the heaviest weight of wool of all British breeds. And if the fleeces of the ewes were excluded, the average was as high as 15 lb. Wool, rather than mutton, was the great product of the Lincolnshire longwools, and they supplied a great part of the combing wool used in the worsted industries of East Anglia and the West Riding. The Lincolns were slow feeders and better suited to the rich pastures of the Marsh than the short grass of the uplands where they were bred. So every spring numbers were sold to the Marshland graziers for fattening; the marshes with their dangerous, deep drainage ditches and lack of shelter were not well calculated for breeding purposes. Middlemen came every July to the farms to purchase the clips on credit, many of them forming a permanent association with particular graziers. The Lincoln longwool was not a good meat animal: it took a full four years to fatten, was coarser in its mutton than the Old Leicester, and had the further disadvantages of being larger in the head, narrower in the shoulder and body, higher in the leg and rump, and thicker in the bone. The upland graziers of Lincolnshire also kept flocks of 'heath' sheep for use on their own farms. These were small, hardy animals better adapted than the longwools for pasturing on cold, exposed hillsides, and also for moving from field to field for folding on the arable. The heath sheep produced a light fleece of short wool suitable for carding for the woollen industry. As the raising of new fodder crops spread on the uplands and it became more profitable for the graziers to think in terms of mutton rather than wool, the heath type were eventually replaced by improved Lincolns which could now be fattened on the local fodder supplies.[40]

The evidence of probate inventories shows that arable holdings in the common fields varied very considerably in size. In the seventeenth century the holdings rose from as little as $1\frac{1}{2}$ acres to about the 100-acre mark, but the average clayland farmer's arable was only between about 16 and 20 acres. On the Lincolnshire claylands barley occupied 41 per cent of the arable acreage in the 1690s, pulses took up 32 per cent, wheat 23 per cent, and rye and oats together occupied the remaining 4 per cent.[41] A few individual inventories may be drawn upon to illustrate the variations in the scale of the farming. Thus Ann Hoyle, widow of Greens Norton, Northamptonshire, had her 11 acres of cropland distributed as follows in June 1665: $5\frac{1}{4}$ acres under wheat, $2\frac{1}{2}$ acres barley, and $3\frac{1}{4}$ acres in peas. In store she had 5 strikes of barley, and a similar quantity of wheat and rye, and her farming equipment included a plough, 2 harrows, and an "old cart body".[42] In a bigger way of business was George Kane of Oakham, Rutland, who in April 1691 had

---

[40] Trow-Smith, *op. cit.*, pp. 60, 142; J. A. Perkins, *Sheep Farming in Eighteenth- and Nineteenth-Century Lincolnshire*, Sleaford, 1977, pp. 6–11, 35.

[41] Thirsk, *Peasant Farming*, pp. 98–100, 188.

[42] Northants. RO, Northampton Invs. 1665.

15 acres sown with corn and 17 acres with peas. He also had peas in store
worth £4 10s., and his equipment extended to 2 ploughs, 3 harrows, 2 carts,
and a waggon.[43] In December 1718 William Lewins of Ashley,
Northamptonshire, had 13 acres of corn, 11 acres of peas, and 14 acres in
"tilth and mucking". In store he had large quantities of hay, oats, and wheat,
and he boasted as many as 2 carts and 3 waggons.[44] The larger farmers, like
William Heans, yeoman of Raunds, Northamptonshire, had substantial
acreages of crops. In May 1713 Heans had as much as 50 acres in beans, peas,
and oats, as well as 30 acres of barley and 29 acres of wheat. He also had
£28 worth of wheat and barley in store, and could dispose of 4 ploughs,
4 harrows, a "rowle" or roller, and 2 carts and a waggon. The total value
of his goods came to £338 5s.[45]

Lincolnshire clayland farmers had in the seventeenth century an average
of 21 cattle, 50 sheep, and 5 horses, and these numbers represented a
considerable advance over those common in the previous century.[46] Over
the east Midland plain area as a whole the numbers of cattle seem to have
remained fairly steady between the 1660s and the 1740s. Cattle reared for
sale and kept for fattening averaged about 19, while dairying declined
somewhat, the average number of cows falling from between 6 and 7 to 4
over the period. Sheep flocks remained fairly stable in size, averaging a little
over 60 in the later seventeenth century, and rising to about 70 in the early
eighteenth century. Pig keeping was generally a minor activity, with an
average of only between 3 and 5 pigs per farmer, and horses varied in number
from 3 to 4, though some farmers were evidently specializing in horse
breeding. Not untypical of the medium-size farmers was John Christian the
elder of Cottesmore, Rutland, whose inventory was taken in April 1742. He
had then 6 cows, 2 calves, and 4 heifers, 71 sheep, a sow, and 8 pigs, together
with 7 horses and a foal. His cropland extended to 60 acres, including 9 acres
of wheat, 25 of barley, and 26 of peas. In store he had 2½ quarters of malt,
5 of wheat, 6 of barley, and 4 of maslin. His farm gear included ploughs
and harrows, a "rowle", and 3 carts and 2 waggons. The total value of his
goods was £285 16s.[47]

In the river valleys of the plain area certain differences might be noted.
Dairying, as is to be expected, was on a somewhat larger scale, although the
small increase in the average number of cows, from 6 to 7, tends to mask
the presence of specialist dairymen. Fattening was a prominent activity, so
that cattle and sheep were numerous; indeed, the flocks in the valleys were
considerably larger by the eighteenth century than elsewhere on the clayland
plain. George Heat, yeoman of Sutton upon Trent, may have been a fairly
common type of wealthier vale farmer. His inventory, taken in August 1717,

43 *Ibid.*, Peter Invs. 1692.
44 *Ibid.*, Peter Invs. 1718/19.
45 *Ibid.*, Northampton Invs. 1713/69.
46 Thirsk, *Peasant Farming*, pp. 187–9.
47 Northants. RO, Peter Invs. 1742.

totalled £437 6s. 9d., and he was much taken up by the dairying and fattening business, having 9 cows, 14 "feeding beasts", and 12 "young beasts", as well as 67 pasture sheep and 84 fallow sheep. His arable land amounted to 52 acres, but livestock occupied his main interest: his house included a "cheese chamber", he had quantities of cheese in store, and he was owed £4 12s. for a cow.[48] Another farmer of the Vale of Trent district was William Brett of Carcolston, Nottinghamshire. He specialized more in dairying, having 14 cows, 5 haystacks, and as many as 1,200 cheeses in store in 1748. These three items alone accounted for over half of the total value of his inventory, which was £205 18s.[49]

The uplands of the east Midlands consist of three detached districts. In Lincolnshire the limestone ridge of the Lincoln Cliff and Heath is separated by the broad central clay vale from the larger area of chalk Wolds to the east. Both of these upland formations lie in a generally north–south direction, though the eastern dip slope of the Wolds follows the south-easterly drift of the coastline at a distance of some four to eight miles from the shore. The narrow ridge of Cliff and Heath runs some fifty miles from the bank of the Humber to the vicinity of Sleaford, broadening out considerably to the south of Lincoln. The Wolds, again beginning very near the Humber, run some forty miles in a southerly direction. Their width varies from only four miles in the north to as much as twelve miles towards Louth and Market Rasen, and their total area is of the order of 300 square miles. In the south, near Spilsby, a number of rivers cut through the upland to provide sheltered valleys, and the villages are much more numerous there than on the more bleak northern Wolds. In the south, too, the chalk has been washed away from the hillsides to bring clay and sandstone to the surface.[50] The third upland area consists of the clay Wolds, a broken upland whose scattered portions begin to the south of the Trent, with the eastern edge abutting on the Vale of Belvoir, and with a large section situated south of the river Wreak below Melton Mowbray and running southwards to the east of Leicester; a further smaller portion lies in Northamptonshire south-west of Market Harborough. These clayland Wolds form detached areas of hilly, windswept upland where the settlements are small and somewhat sparse. The village names prepare the traveller for steep climbs and exposed table lands – Willoughby on the Wolds in Nottinghamshire, Cold Overton and Burrow on the Hill in Leicestershire, and Cold Ashby in Northamptonshire.

The clay Wolds had many common fields, cultivating what was generally a cold clay soil on the familiar basis of two crops and a fallow. There were some enclosures, but the soil did not encourage an early adoption of the new fodder crops such as turnips and clover. The hilltops were often given over to extensive woodlands, and the exposed hillsides to stinted pastures for young

[48] Notts. RO, PRNW 1718.   [49] Ibid., PRJW 8/76.
[50] Thirsk, Peasant Farming, p. 79.

beasts and horses. Sheep were generally quite numerous, and the evidence of the probate inventories suggests flocks ranging from between 60 and 70 strong in the 1660s to as large as 115 in the 1740s. Cattle numbers ran between 4 and 8 in the earlier part of the period to between 7 and 10 towards the end. There is little evidence about arable cultivation, though evidently the farmers of the Wold uplands grew some barley, peas, oats, and wheat. John Palmer of Willoughby on the Wolds, Nottinghamshire, had in 1698 crops on the ground valued at £35, while his livestock were worth £47 10s., making up nearly half of his total valuation of £105 10s. He kept 4 cows, 2 heifers, and 2 feeding cows, and a flock of 29 sheep, supplemented by 3 mares, 2 fillies, and a gelding, along with 4 store swine.[51] Richard Smith of nearby Wysall had 8 cows, 2 calves, and 3 heifers, a flock of 80 sheep, and 5 mares, a gelding, and 2 other horses. His arable crops were valued collectively at £50, and in store he had some barley, wheat, rye, and malt worth together £10 8s. The total value of his goods was £180 11s.[52] Much poorer than these men was William Clark of West Haddon in Northamptonshire. Of his total goods, worth £56 12s. 6d. in 1746, his 28 sheep and 15 lambs accounted for £13 5s., and his 2 horses for another £8 10s. His land, in grass and corn, was estimated at £10, and he had in store peas, hay, corn, and wool worth together £13.[53]

In Lincolnshire the limestone ridge and the chalk Wolds were farmed in broadly the same way. Except in the southern part of the Wolds, where the chalk had disappeared and left considerable areas of reasonably deep and fertile ground, the soils are generally thin and poor. However, the elongated shape of some parishes on the Cliff and Heath meant that they stretched into the neighbouring claylands and so contained some better soils, while parishes on the eastern border of the Wolds included sections of the Marsh, and in the south some fenny ground along the riversides.[54] But, generally, the predominance of poor soils made sheep the mainstay of Lincolnshire upland farming. Large areas were given over to sheepwalks, and at night the sheep were driven down from the hill pastures to be folded on the arable fields in the valleys and lower levels. The area devoted to arable was generally small, however, and it was wool which provided most upland farmers with the bulk of their profit. On the arable land barley was by far the most important crop, followed by oats, wheat, and rye, together with pulses and a very little lentils.[55] There is evidence that by the later seventeenth century parts of the Wold sheepwalks were being ploughed up for oats and sainfoin. Sir Drayner Massingberd, who had land about South Ormsby, six miles north of Spilsby in the southern Wolds, referred as early as 1682 to "that part of the north sheep walk in South Ormsby...which was plowed up last winter and sowne

[51] Notts. RO, PRNW 1698.   [52] Ibid., PRSM 1/112.

[53] Northants. RO, Northampton Invs. & Wills 1747.

[54] Thirsk, Peasant Farming, pp. 80–1.   [55] Ibid., pp. 84–9.

this last spring with oats and saintfoynes".[56] His successor, Burrell Massingberd, arranged for quantities of sainfoin seed and clover seed to be sent down from Ware in Hertfordshire. In 1706 he wrote to say he hoped to get 11 quarters of sainfoin seed and 50 more of clover. In 1714 he was informed that sainfoin seed was about 28s. per quarter.[57] An agreement with a farmer made in 1723 allowed him to plough up part of a sheepwalk and keep it ploughed as long as he laid all his manure upon it. "If he takes in any more he is to lay it down with St Foyn after the third crop."[58]

Turnips were introduced in the early eighteenth century to provide a third leg to the traditional dual basis of sheep and barley. The arable system, however, was a fairly primitive one in which one of the two common fields was fallowed in alternate years. Enclosed pastures were kept in being for long periods, and were ploughed up and reseeded only infrequently, when the grass had become thin and overgrown by weeds and moss.[59] The average herd of cattle was tending to increase in size in the later seventeenth century, when it reached 19 beasts; the average flock rose to about 48 by the same time. After wool, the chief marketable commodities were fat and draught cattle. Sir Drayner Massingberd sold as many as 361 fleeces in 1670, and 555 in 1672. Numbers of upland farmers rented pastures in the Marshland a few miles to the east. These were once widely used for the fattening of sheep, but when the growing of turnips came in, the practice of sending sheep to be fattened in the Marsh declined: they could now be fattened at home or sent into other districts where turnips were plentiful. Cattle then became the more usual occupants of the Marshland pastures, and the upland farmers replaced their stock sent there to fatten with droves of hardy Scotch cattle. For these cattle, it was said in 1726 by Thomas Lowe, steward of the Drake family of Croft, "having been bread up in so cold and poor a country (as Scotland is), even the would country of Lyncolnshire is so much better than what they come out of, that it is sufficiently rich and good enough to feed them". The changes were not all beneficial, however. Wool, said Lowe, had fallen in price, and in the absence of visiting chapmen and buyers the graziers were obliged to take their wool to Colchester, Bury, and Norwich, at considerable cost to themselves; similarly, they were obliged to drive their fat cattle to distant markets, such as St Ives or Smithfield.[60]

Inventory evidence suggests that sheep flocks on the Wolds came to average about 100 in the first half of the eighteenth century. Horse breeding was important on both Cliff and Heath and on the Wolds, though perhaps a little more so in the first of the two districts. Richard Hill of Great Sturton on the Cliff had in January 1712 cropland worth only £7, but livestock of a total value of £102 13s. 4d. out of the complete valuation of £160 19s. 8d.

[56] LAO, MM vi/2/29.
[57] Ibid., MM 4/1/8, 14.
[58] Ibid., MM vii/1A/130.
[59] Thirsk, Peasant Farming, pp. 171–3.
[60] Ibid., pp. 173–7; Lincs. RO, Tyr 2/2/21.

In addition to his flock of 79 sheep, he had 6 cows, 3 calves, 4 young cattle, 6 draught beasts, and 5 horses.[61] William West in 1718 evidently combined horse breeding with his 107 sheep and 29 cattle, for he had 5 mares, 3 horses, 2 foals, 2 colts, and a filly. His horses were worth £71, more than either his cattle or his sheep.[62] Martin Jayes, a Wolds farmer of Walesby, near Market Rasen, kept in 1747 only 3 mares, 4 cattle, and 2 oxen. His flock, however, was a large one of 144 sheep, and his arable included small areas of a variety of crops – 6½ acres of wheat, 4 acres each of oats and rye, 2½ acres of barley, 1 of peas, 4 of turnips, and 6½ of lentils. The total of his inventory came to £381 2s. 3d.[63]

The third region to be considered is distinguished principally by the predominance of poor, sandy, and infertile, 'hungry' soils, particularly in Sherwood and Charnwood. Because at one time the whole or greater part was occupied by woodland it was still known as forest land, and its livestock as forest cattle and forest sheep, though by our period the woodland was restricted in area, and much of the former forest area had been cleared for cultivation.

In Nottinghamshire the forest district was extensive, taking up a great sweep of country stretching northwards from Basford, north-east of Nottingham, as far as Tickhill and Bawtry on the Yorkshire border. The length from north to south was some twenty-five or thirty miles, and the breadth from seven to ten miles. Bordering the sandy Forest region to the west was a narrow strip of limestone, and beyond that a belt of cold blue or yellow clay lying over the coal measures on the extreme western edge of the county. A small detached area of poor land lay in a tongue projecting east of the Trent into Lincolnshire around Thorney and Harby. This last was a district of low, barren commons, very much drowned by the river in winter, and unimprovable without effective means of drainage. There were some areas of barren waste, too, within the bounds of Sherwood, and large parts of the Forest region were taken up by extensive rabbit warrens, especially at Clipston, Oxton, Blidworth, Calverton, and Newstead. Considerable sections of the Forest around Ollerton had been enclosed privately by royal grant or otherwise, and had been converted into private parks and plantations, as at Welbeck, Clumber, Thoresby, Rufford, Newstead, and Clipston. The noble proprietors of these intakes had experimented first with plantations of firs, and discovered in time that trees of all kinds could be made to succeed in the poor sandy soils, if properly planted and well protected.

The only area of poor land of consequence in Leicestershire consisted of Charnwood Forest. This was a tract of upland country, some of it useful land, marked by picturesque outcrops of ancient rocks. Its highest point is Bardon Hill, 912 ft. By our period the once "vast forest" had largely gone,

---

[61] LAO, 203/285.   [62] Ibid., 205/176.
[63] Ibid., 212/71.

and the remaining forest area covered a limited district of some fifty or sixty square miles. Sparsely populated, Charnwood was settled sporadically by squatters, both legal and illegal. They were largely engaged in woodland occupations and in the grazing of the common pastures.

Leighfield Forest in the south-west of Rutland was made up of the surviving remnants of the ancient Forest of Rutland. It had been disafforested about 1630, but detached areas of woods remained in Oakham hundred and in part of Martinsley hundred. Little is known about the management of the woods or the farming of the area, but it seems likely that they were much the same as in the neighbouring Forest of Rockingham, which lay on similar soils. There were probably, therefore, common grazing rights exercised by village landholders, private enclosures used for pasture, and woods cut systematically for fuel and for timber used in local woodland industries.

Northamptonshire had its three ancient forests, Rockingham, Salcey, and Whittlewood, noted for their grey loam soils and fine ash timber. Rockingham, the largest, stretched in a long curving arc eighteen miles long by eight miles at the greatest, from the south-east of Market Harborough in a north-easterly direction to within a few miles of Stamford; Salcey lay towards the south of Northampton, on the border with Buckinghamshire, and stretching into that county; Whittlewood lay further to the south-west, below Towcester, and again bordering and running into Buckinghamshire. Once very extensive, these royal forests had been much reduced by sales and leases, grants of timber, and disafforestation; Geddington Chase had been carved out of Rockingham Forest, and Yardley Chase out of Salcey; large outlying portions, cultivated as purlieu woods and still subject to the depasturage of deer, had been absorbed into the estates of neighbouring landowners. Reports made under an act of 1786 for inquiring into the condition of crown forests showed that the remaining crown woodlands in Salcey in 1790 covered an area only about two and a half miles long and one and a half miles broad, or perhaps some 2,400 acres; Whittlewood in 1792 consisted of 5,424 acres. The dukes of Grafton had acquired the title to the underwood of Salcey and to the major part – 3,476 acres – of the copsewood in Whittlewood; fifteen parishes enjoyed rights of pasture over 4,486 acres of Whittlewood. The woodlands in Rockingham consisted in 1792 of scattered areas making a total of 9,482 acres, mainly in private hands.[64]

By the later seventeenth century large areas of former forest land in both Nottinghamshire and Northamptonshire had been adapted for cultivation and grazing. Each forest village had a small amount of permanently enclosed land near the homesteads, while the rest lay open, common to the villagers' sheep and cattle as well as the king's deer. By permission of the lord of the manor, and subject to inspection by the forest verderers, the villagers were allowed to make forest breaks or temporary enclosures of the waste, and to

[64] *VCH Northants., II*, pp. 346–9.

keep them in tillage for periods of five or six years. After this period the
break was abandoned and allowed to revert to rough grazing, perhaps to
be cultivated again after a long interval when it was judged to have recovered
a degree of fertility. In Rockingham Forest the villages lay in the valleys where
tributaries of the Nene had washed away the surface soil and exposed
limestone, sands, and clays. Common fields were small, for arable farming
was subordinate to pasture. The villagers' cattle were supported by the closes
made from Forest assarts, by rented pastures in private enclosures in the forest,
and by common rights which were often extensive and little subject to strict
regulation. Those villages which had no resident lord became quite populous,
since immigrants found it easy to erect cottages and assume common rights.
The woodlands offered casual work in managing coppice, stripping bark for
the Northamptonshire leather industry, and cutting, sawing, and transporting
timber. Fuel was plentiful and cheap, and incomes could be supplemented
by growing and processing a little hemp, and by poaching game and nutting
in the woods.[65]

In the Forest district of Nottinghamshire the usual course of crops in the
breaks was oats or peas, followed by barley, then by rye, oats once again,
and lastly "skegs" (a form of oats). In the better parts the sandy soil was
capable of a degree of convertible husbandry, and towards the mid eighteenth
century turnips and clovers were sometimes introduced. The turnips were
fed off with sheep, and could then be followed by a good crop of barley.
By Robert Lowe's time (1798), well-managed forest breaks were cultivated
on the following system: the land was broken up for (a) turnips, laying on
ten quarters of lime per acre; (b) barley; (c) rye, or sometimes wheat; and
(d) oats undersown with clover and ryegrass, which was mown once for hay
and then thrown open as common grazing. The best farming of the area,
however, was to be found in the permanent enclosures made by the large
proprietors.[66]

Documentary sources show forest villagers introducing new crops. In
January 1751, for instance, the major part of the inhabitants of Kirton agreed
at a meeting to sow clover with their peas in the ensuing season; the clover,
they agreed, was to be a reserved pasture for their cattle and horses only,
and sheep were to be excluded.[67] Some farmers in the Forest went in for
unusual crops. Weld or dyers' weed, a plant used by the cloth manufacturers
for dyeing cloth yellow, was grown quite widely about Scrooby, Ranshill,
and Torworth. It was sown with the barley and clover, and pulled up from
among the clover, tied in bundles, and dried. As much as half a ton could
be obtained from each acre, and its value was considerable. Hops were also
grown around Rufford, Ollerton, and Elkesley, although the major hop-
growing area in Nottinghamshire lay further east on the clays. Liquorice was

---

[65] P. A. J. Pettit, *The Royal Forests of Northamptonshire: A Study in their Economy, 1558–1714*,
Northants. Rec. Soc., XXIII, 1968, pp. 5, 141–2, 148–9, 150.

[66] Lowe, *op. cit.*, pp. 21–2.   [67] Notts. RO, PR 6,237.

once a feature of the Worksop area, but was abandoned, perhaps because of a fall in demand or because of its precarious nature.[68]

Cattle numbers in Sherwood Forest were moderate, though tending to rise; and there were numerous sheep, described as being of the old Forest breed. They were small animals with grey faces and legs. Their wool was very fine and light, requiring from 13 to 18 fleeces to make up a tod of 28 lb. The carcase, when fat, weighed only 7–9 lb a quarter.[69] Forest wethers could be bought cheaply in Nottingham and the Forest markets at Mansfield and Worksop. Twenty-four bought in 1746 for the Willoughby family of Wollaton cost only about 7s. 3d. each.[70] Like sheep elsewhere in the east Midlands region, the Forest breed was improved by crossing with Lincoln-shires, and later with Bakewell's Dishleys, resulting in a much larger animal producing more meat and a heavier weight of fleece, but one of coarser wool.

The Brudenell family held land at Deene in Rockingham Forest, and the letters written in the middle and late 1720s by their land steward, Daniel Eaton, reveal the importance to the estate of the woodlands, and throw light on the farming practices and problems of the district. Much of the steward's time was spent in inspecting and measuring trees in the woods, and arranging for their sale. In June 1725, for example, he wrote: "I went likewise in to Corby and Stanion Woods; the roads in them & to them are so bad that the bark can hardly be carryed out, & it is a sad wet time for the tanners." And late in December 1726 he wrote:

We view'd Stanion Sale yesterday, which according to our valuation, comes to £80 3s. 0d., which I hope will be sold at the price. It is better than we expected, as Corby sale was worse, but it is most evident that if your Lordship does not take those woods while they are younger, they will be destroy'd as my Lord Rockinghams woods are. There is some old men remember the underwood in these woods as flourishing as ours, and by letting it stand to be old (for no other cause can be assign'd), it is now become not worth 30s. an acre at full growth.

Eaton had a good deal to say about bad tenants, men who ruined their fences by improper cutting, neglected to scour their ditches, and sold off their hay to pay the rent, so keeping no cattle. There were difficulties, too, with diseased cattle, rot among the sheep, bad weather, poor crops, and arrears of rent. He recommended trefoil, ryegrass, and cinquefoil for land that needed to be laid down after ploughing, and he pointed out that trefoil sown after barley and oats would "make the land worth 20s. an acre the first year, and the trefoil will continue till the natural grass kills it, which will be four years at least'.[71]

---

[68] Lowe, *op cit.*, pp. 27–8; John Holland, *History of Worksop*, Sheffield, 1826, p. 6.

[69] Lowe, *op. cit.*, pp. 124–5.

[70] Nottm Univ. Archives, Mi A 130.

[71] *The Letters of Daniel Eaton to the Third Earl of Cardigan, 1725–32*, ed. Joan Wake and Deborah Champion Webster, Northants. Record Soc., XXIV, 1971, pp. 4–5, 6–7, 23, 73, 86, 98.

Analysis of inventories made in the decades of the 1660s, 1690s, 1710s, and 1740s shows that the Forest regions contained wealthy farmers as well as numbers of poorer ones. The average number of cattle owned by each farmer remained quite stable in the Rockingham Forest area at between 14 and 15 beasts, but the inventories from Sherwood show a rising trend throughout the period: by the 1740s the average of 9 cattle to each farmer, found in the 1660s, had more than doubled. It is hardly surprising that, as a result, there is much evidence that cheese was a considerable Forest product, though more so in Rockingham than in Sherwood. While cattle numbers tended to rise in the Sherwood area, the sheep numbers there, though large, showed a considerable decline, the average flock falling from 90 in the 1660s to 68 in the 1740s. A contrary trend showed itself in the Rockingham area, where the average flock rose from 60 to a little over 100. Rockingham farmers kept throughout an average of 6 horses, while in Sherwood the number rose steadily from 3 in the 1660s to 6 by the 1740s. Pig keeping was on a fairly small scale in both areas, with the Sherwood farmers keeping only between 2 and 4 pigs, and the Rockingham ones an average of 6.

From the inventories it appears that wheat and rye were widely grown, with oats and peas as the chief fodder crops. Beans were everywhere uncommon. However, wheat, barley, and peas were all more widely grown on the Rockingham loams than in Sherwood, where the poor sandy soils were better suited to oats. Barley was evidently of importance for malting in Rockingham, and the district boasted a number of quite well-to-do maltsters. The inventories of the 1740s refer for the first time to the occasional growing of turnips, vetches, sainfoin, and coleseed in Rockingham, and by this time clovers had become fairly commonplace in Sherwood.

One of the smaller maltsters and cheesemakers in Leighfield Forest was Thomas Towel of Egleton, Rutland, whose inventory was taken in October 1698. He had then 18 cattle, 11 horses, 8 pigs, and a flock of 80 sheep. He had in store some hay, oats, and a little wheat, together with malt worth £8 4s. and as many as 80 cheeses worth £2 10s. The sum of £30 was owing to him.[72] John Goodham, a yeoman of Cuckney in Sherwood Forest, had in May 1663 farm stock and goods of almost the same total value as those of Thomas Towel. He kept 9 oxen, 4 bullocks, and 5 cows with 5 calves, together with 7 horses, 4 pigs, and 50 sheep. His cropland consisted of 17 acres of barley, 14 of rye, 3 acres lying fallow, and some peas and skegs. His implements included 3 ploughs, 4 harrows, and 4 wains, and he had a store of 50 loads of wood.[73]

As examples of the small cultivators we have Christopher Mold of Rothwell and John Goode of St Peter Aldwinkle, both in Northamptonshire. Both men were described as labourers. Mold's inventory of October 1696 totalled £21 15s. 4d. He had 3 cows, 2 calves, and a bullock, as well as 3

72 Northants. RO, Peter Invs. 1648.   73 Ibid., PRSM 1/196.

pigs, and 26 sheep with 8 lambs. In store he had some hay, malt, and cheese. His three-room cottage was furnished with bedsteads, blankets, pillows, tables, chairs, chests, boxes, cheeseboards, and a linen wheel.[74] John Goode's inventory of June 1712 totalled £52 1s. 8d., and his livestock included 3 cows and a calf, a horse, 2 hogs, and 22 sheep. He cultivated $3\frac{3}{4}$ acres of peas, 3 acres of barley, and $2\frac{1}{2}$ acres of wheat. His store of produce, kept in a chamber over his parlour, included bacon, malt, wheat, barley, and cheese.[75] A little more well-to-do was William Wright of Blidworth, in Sherwood, described in June 1717 as a yeoman, but evidently concerned also with stocking-frame knitting, for he possessed two frames in his workroom. His house was extensive, with a parlour, kitchen, dairy, and three chambers, and the parlour was furnished with a bed, table, six chairs, a chest of drawers, cushions, and a basket. His farming operations revolved round 2 cows and 2 calves, a mare, and 16 sheep, including a tup and 5 lambs. His corn on the ground was valued at £10.[76]

Some of the larger farmers were heavily involved in specialized crops. For example, Edward Sharpe of Elkesley, Nottinghamshire, had in January 1717 hop poles valued at £70, and hops in store worth £32.[77] By the 1740s new fodder crops were in evidence. Francis Baker of Barton Seagrave, Northamptonshire, had on the ground in July 1746 14 acres of turnips and 6 acres of coleseed, as well as 15 acres of barley, 8 of wheat, and 6 of peas. His sainfoin hay in store was valued at £9. He was a man in quite a big way of business, with 30 cattle, 9 horses, 20 pigs, and as many as 277 sheep.[78]

The Marshland of Lincolnshire forms the last of our natural areas. It forms a rather narrow strip of coastal plain which runs southwards from the Humber, following the line of the coast, until meeting the fenland of Lindsey where the Steeping river runs into the sea near Wainfleet. The coastline of the Marshland stretches over some seventy miles, and its whole area covers about 500 square miles. There are two distinct kinds of marshland: that nearest the sea is the saltmarsh, much of it reclaimed at some period from the sea, composed of clays and silts; south of Grimsby it stretches back from the shoreline about five miles, but north of that port its width is considerably more restricted. The inland strip of middle marsh, with soils consisting mainly of boulder clay, fringes the Wolds to the west and the saltmarsh to the east, except for a small area just south of Grimsby where the middle marsh expands all the way to the shore.

The saltmarsh was the richer and more valuable land, but was subject to risk of flooding and erosion by the sea, and involved the maintenance of sea walls. There were common fields, but the corn lands were very restricted by comparison with the large areas of pasture. The middle marsh, however,

[74] Ibid., Northampton Invs. & Bonds 1696/16.
[75] Ibid., Peter Invs. 1712.
[76] Ibid., PRSW 117/27B.
[77] Ibid., PRNW 1718 Retford.
[78] Ibid., Northampton Invs. & Wills 1746.

had a much higher proportion of arable, and the pasture of the middle-marsh
farmers was provided partly by leys in their common fields and partly by
the availability of rented pasture in the saltmarsh. Livestock constituted the
kingpin of the farming in both middle marsh and saltmarsh, although breeding
was more important inland and fattening more a feature of the coastal marsh;
the saltmarsh outside the sea wall was the empire of the shepherd and his
flock. According to Christopher Merret, writing near the end of the
seventeenth century, marshland fleeces averaged seven to ten pounds, and
every year several hundred loads of wool were sent to East Anglia, the north,
and the west country to be manufactured into cloth.[79] Another
knowledgeable writer, Thomas Lowe, stated about 1723 that the Marsh
farmers depended on their wool to pay their rents, "for the carcasses must
alwaies go to buying of stock againe for ye succeeding spring".[80]

By the mid seventeenth century an increasing number of farmers from
outside the Marshland were renting grazing land in the marsh for the purpose
of fattening sheep, probably sheep bred on their farms on the Wolds or even
further west in the central vale or on the Heath. In the 1660s, for instance,
Henry Pacey of West Keale had 140 sheep feeding in the Marsh as well as
a further 140 sheep at home. Another farmer who kept stock in the Marsh,
including cattle and horses, was Thomas Hornby of Raithby, near Spilsby,
on the Wolds; he had land on the Marsh at Ingoldmells, north of Skegness,
at a distance of ten or twelve miles from Raithby.[81] The keen demand for
Marsh pastures drove up the rents, and apparently was a factor in forcing
the smaller Marshland farmer to give way to the wealthier farmers and gentry
who could afford the high sums demanded, although in time the growing
of turnips on the Wolds came into vogue and provided the Wolds graziers
with an alternative to the expensive saltmarsh grazings.[82]

In our period the crops in the Marshland were principally pulses, such as
peas, beans, and lentils, with some barley, rather less wheat, and a very little
oats.[83] The limited acreage of arable was mainly concerned with producing
fodder rather than human food and drink. Quite often the arable was almost
insignificant. For example, a survey of Keelby, in the middle marsh, showed
in 1672 only 63 acres devoted to arable out of a total of 958 acres – a mere
6.6 per cent. The meadows and pastures of the village supported 75 cows
and 813 sheep.[84] In 1722, when a Robert Vyner of Uxbridge was
contemplating the purchase of an estate at Withern, he sent a number of
agents to view the place for him. Withern lies to the west of Mablethorpe,
and H. Stead, who came from Kirton in Lindsey to view the village, formed
the opinion that the highways leading there were "so intolerably bad that
the land and ground must certainly be very good". In summary, Robert

[79] Thirsk, *Peasant Farming*, pp. 69, 152.   [80] LAO, Tyr 2/2/21.
[81] Thirsk, *Peasant Farming*, pp. 149–50.   [82] LAO, Tyr 2/2/21.
[83] Thirsk, *Peasant Farming*, p. 157.   [84] LAO, Lind. Dep. 88/20/12.

Vyner's various inquiries established that the soil was indeed very rich and valuable, and the 200 acres of arable field land "extraordinarily good", low-rented, and well worth enclosing; there was a great deal of low-lying ground, but the water did not remain on it long, and the estate was little subject to sheep rot; there was, however, little wood of value except for fencing.[85]

Most of the farmers inhabiting the Marshland were small men. In the 1690s the median size of flock was only 36 sheep, the median number of cattle 9, and that of horses and of pigs 4 each. A study of probate inventories at Burgh le Marsh, a few miles north of Wainfleet, showed that between 1680 and 1714 the average number of cattle was 13, that of horses 5, and of pigs 3. In the whole of the Marshland the area of sown land on the median farm was also small, averaging only $13\frac{1}{2}$ acres between the 1630s and the 1690s.[86]

There were of course some wealthy inhabitants of the Marshland. A farmer of Marsh Chapel, in the saltmarsh some seven or eight miles south-east of Grimsby, left goods worth £654 8s. 4d. in October 1692. He had at that date a total of 592 sheep, and another 40 were on the road to be sold in London; his other stock included 12 cows, 14 calves, 8 steers, and 4 fat beasts, in addition to 18 horses and 18 swine. Corn and hay in store were valued at £70.[87] Another man in a large way of business was Fownson Mackinder of Welton le Marsh, in a middle-marsh breeding area to the north-west of Skegness. His flocks totalled 691 sheep, and included 323 ewes and 225 lambs, and the whole of his flocks were valued at £580 11s. 6d. in 1748. He also kept 20 cattle, 11 horses, and 6 swine, and was engaged in growing coleseed and turnips.[88] Ambrose Etherington, yeoman of Withern, was not so impressive a grazier, but in 1665 he had large sums lent out on bonds and bills, totalling £659 4s., with a further £60 in leases and in interest due to him.[89] Smaller men, with enterprises based firmly on some combination of breeding, fattening, and corn might still go in for some degree of specialization. Such a one was Cornelius Cloke, yeoman of Killingholme, on the Humber estuary north of Grimsby. When he died in September 1665 his 60 sheep, 6 cows, 3 calves, and 7 young cattle were combined with 13 horses and 4 foals and 34 acres of corn. Unusual was his keeping of numerous pigs for profit, as represented by an investment of £15 in 40 swine. The total value of his farming assets was here £122 13s. 4d.[90]

Most of the tenant farmers in the east Midlands held their farms at will or by annual agreements. This was particularly so with the small tenants of the large owners of the region such as the Pierreponts or the Saviles, and it appears that small men were rarely turned out of their holdings unless they exhibited gross neglect or were incapable of paying their rents. In some

[85] Leeds Archives Dept., NH 2,368.
[86] Thirsk, *Peasant Farming*, pp. 149, 153, 153n.
[87] LAO, 212/67.
[88] *Ibid.*, 212/124.
[89] *Ibid.*, 165/122.
[90] *Ibid.*, 165/111.

districts, especially in parts of Sherwood Forest, there were numbers of copyholders, but this type of tenure was not common in the region as a whole. Large farms, or those farms which required considerable outlays on the part of the tenants to bring them into good condition, were often let on leases for terms of years.

The length of such terms was evidently a matter of negotiation between landlord and prospective tenant. The evidence suggests that the tenant had as much say in the matter as had the landlord: indeed, it was not always easy to find tenants who were willing to commit themselves to any form of lease. Where a lease was negotiated, the term of years agreed on was influenced by the size of the farm, its condition, and the tenant's personal circumstances. The landlord was concerned to protect his farm from incompetent or neglectful occupiers and was likely therefore to contemplate granting a lengthy term only to a reputable man, while the tenant, for his part, was reluctant to assume a commitment for too long ahead. Thus in 1712 Andrew Love, steward of the Leigh estates near Oakham, made inquiries of the existing tenants there to see if they would take long leases of their farms. It was his view that this was the best means of improving the standard of the farming, but he found that few of them were interested in the idea of a long lease. A little later he wrote to report that two men had agreed to take twenty-one-year leases, but two others would accept only a shorter term of eleven years. Richard Russell wanted the shorter term because in the event of his death his lands would be divided among his wife and his children, and so large a quantity of land would be inconvenient for them. Robert Peake, similarly, argued that his wife and three daughters would be unable to manage the land in the case of his early demise.[91]

It is not surprising, therefore, that leases were arranged for varying periods of years. At Croft in Lincolnshire some farmers agreed in 1717 to terms of seven years, while in 1719 the prospective tenant of a farm near Grantham insisted on having a term of twenty-one years. This farmer was willing to repair the outhouses and fences if the landlord would put the farmhouse in order. He also proposed to plough up a close and sow it with turnips, and to follow this with corn and sainfoin.[92] The clear definition of the respective responsibility of landlord and tenant and the strict regulation of the husbandry were among the advantages of having a lease. In 1726, for example, the articles of agreement entered into between John Cook, yeoman of Whaplode, Lincolnshire, and the landlord, Montague Garrard Drake of Shardeloes, Buckinghamshire, included the provision that Cook was to erect a barn upon the land, though with the safeguard that if he and the landlord were unable to agree on its value then Cook was to be free to dismantle and remove it at the end of the term of thirteen years. The land covered by their agreement consisted of eighty acres of pasture in Holbeach Marsh,

91 Hants. RO, 5M50/528, 531, 743.   92 LAO, Tyr 4/3/7; Mon 7/12/168.

and it was specified that the land should be divided into two parts, one to be ploughed immediately and kept in tillage for five years, and then manured and laid down again, at the end of which period the other half was to be treated in the same way. The rent was to be £40 a year, with the landlord meeting parliamentary taxes and tithes.[93] Some leases still occasionally specified payments in kind as well as cash rent. In 1669 Sir Drayner Massingberd of South Ormsby, Lincolnshire, agreed to lease a farm of 191 acres to Robert Toppam for a term of thirty-one years, if he or his wife should so long live, at a rent of £94 per annum. Toppam was required to do two days' boon labour a year on request, and to give two fat capons at Christmas and two fat hens at Easter. He was not to carry off any compost or dung, nor to plough up any land not ploughed in the previous three years – at a penalty of 40s. per acre. One of the three fields allotted for tillage was always to be kept in a bare fallow each year.[94]

Evidence from the Kingston estates in the region indicates that in the second and third quarters of the eighteenth century there was a tendency for leases for lives and leases for terms of years not to be renewed when they fell in, probably because it proved difficult to find tenants willing to take farms on long-term agreements. At Sneinton, Nottinghamshire, in 1729, for instance, the end of a twenty-one years' lease was followed by division of the farm among three other tenants.[95] In Northamptonshire, it has been stated, it was common after 1710 for leases for lives to be converted into leases for terms of years at rack rents.[96] On the Kingston estates in Nottinghamshire, however, even leases for long terms of years tended to be replaced by leases for shorter terms or simply by tenancies-at-will. The changes may be connected with the problem of tenants' running a farm down when the end of their lease was approaching; the landlord may have wished to secure a stricter control over the property and to have greater freedom in the reassessment of rents. However, other circumstances, such as the accumulation of rent arrears and bankruptcies among farmers, indicate that tenancies-at-will may have been more a response to farmers' unwillingness to undertake long-term commitments at a time of low prices and uncertain conditions in agriculture.

At all events the small tenant-at-will was established as a common feature of the farming of the region, and of Nottinghamshire in particular. No doubt the large proportion of tenants-at-will in the county arose in part from the dominance of large estates: in 1881 two-fifths of the acreage belonged to fifteen proprietors, and as much as a quarter to only five owners.[97] Farms

[93] *Ibid.*, Tyr 4/3/14.
[94] *Ibid.*, MM U1/3/28.
[95] Nottm Univ. Archives, Manvers, Kingston estate rentals.
[96] H. J. Habakkuk, 'English Landownership, 1680–1740', EcHR, 2nd ser., x, 1940, p. 17.
[97] G. C. Brodrick, *English Land and English Landlords*, London, 1881, p. 167.

certainly varied very much in size. In enclosed districts it was quite common to find individual closes let as a unit, and probably such closes were used for dairying, market gardening, hops, or other forms of specialized production, as well as for accommodation land by village craftsmen, butchers and innkeepers. In open-field parishes, too, rentals and surveys show that units could be as small as an acre or two, and as large as 150 or 200 acres.

It is difficult, however, to obtain any very precise idea of farm sizes from the evidence of rentals and surveys. Most villages were divided between two or three large proprietors, as well as an often considerable number of small freeholders. Farmers often rented land from more than one proprietor, and numbers of the freeholders also rented additional acreage from one of the large estates. Thus a complicated pattern of landholding might prevail. At Eakring, Nottinghamshire, in 1737, for instance, there were, in addition to the duke of Kingston and Sir George Savile, thirty-seven freeholders owning together 633 acres. The largest of them owned 77 acres, and fifteen owned less than 2 acres. Thirteen of these thirty-seven freeholders rented land from the two big owners, and nine of them rented much more land than they owned themselves; three freeholders were tenants of both Sir George and the duke. Of the whole parish, the duke of Kingston owned 1,011 acres and had twenty-five tenants; Sir George Savile owned 753 acres with thirty tenants; and, as noted, the thirty-seven other freeholders owned the remaining 633 acres. Of the fifty-five tenants of the two large owners, thirteen were freeholders owning together 295 acres and renting another 527 acres, or nearly a third of the tenanted land. One of these thirteen freeholders rented his house and 12 acres of land from the duke, and owned himself only 1 acre; another rented a cottage and land amounting to 5 acres from the duke and a further 17 acres from Sir George, and owned himself 20 acres.[98]

This interweaving of ownership and tenancy was no doubt of some significance in the slow progress of large-scale enclosure in the arable claylands of central Nottinghamshire. Some villages, too, possessed a large number of independent freeholders who may have posed a considerable obstacle in the path of a would-be encloser. Laxton, for instance, boasted in 1732 as many as fifty-seven freeholders, owning among them 1,365 acres, well over half the parish.[99] Other difficulties arose from the fact that in numerous parishes the large owners held divided sway, and the essential preliminary to an enclosure was a clear agreement among themselves, something which it was often difficult to achieve. The nature of the soil, too, was sometimes discouraging, being perhaps a wet or "clarty" clay (as they called it at Laxton), which was expensive to cultivate and unsuited to convertible husbandry. Such land was not attractive to large, progressive farmers, and so landlords had little prospect of bringing about a technical

[98] Nottm Univ. Archives, Manvers, Kingston estate, Eakring Book of Tenures 1737.
[99] *Ibid.*, Manvers, Kingston estate, Laxton survey 1732.

revolution by enclosing their heavy soils and engrossing their small farms. In practice small tenants enjoyed great security of tenure, not only because the possibilities offered by their land were limited, but also because large proprietors like the duke of Kingston, Sir George Savile, or the duke of Newcastle were unwilling, as Edward Laurence remarked, to incur the odium of turning "poor families into the wide world by uniting farms all at once".[100] For reasons of conscience, family pride, popularity, and politics they accepted the necessity of keeping small tenants in being.

Landlords' interest in enclosure sprang mainly from the higher rents which enclosed farms could command. Lesser considerations were the probability that the occupiers of more efficient holdings might better withstand the effects of bad seasons or unprofitable prices; and the pride that might be taken in having an estate that was characterized by improved farming and satisfied tenants. There is considerable evidence that in our period much of the initiative for enclosure arose from the farmers themselves, from their desire to overcome the serious weaknesses in the prevailing system of common fields and common grazing. This motive lay behind the regulation of common pastures and partial enclosures that were a common feature of open villages at this time, and which aimed at remedying a shortage of pasture, improving the conditions of the livestock, or facilitating a greater degree of specialization. Thus an agreement at North Luffenham, Rutland, in 1653 was concerned with the enclosure of a cow pasture called Haverlands. Each freeholder in the village was permitted to enclose his portion of the pasture by dike or quickset and to lay it out in a number of closes; for the future no one in the village was to be allowed to keep more beasts in the fallow fields than he had acres, owned or rented, in the cow pasture.[101]

Changes of this fairly limited kind were readily adopted because they were less costly and caused less upheaval than would a complete general enclosure of the fields and commons. It was much simpler and more usual to stint a common than to enclose it, and stinted commons became a regular feature of the open-field villages of the region in the earlier eighteenth century. The trouble and cost of establishing new holdings and hedges were evidently factors which discouraged the early adoption of general enclosure in this period of generally low price levels. For example, when in 1759 the enclosure of Barrow upon Soar, Leicestershire, was mooted, some of the proprietors held back, thinking that a stint might be better, and that the costs of "making waterings, buildings, clearing and taking care of the young fences, ploughing the land and seeding it in proper order" would give rise to a great outlay.[102]

Even piecemeal enclosure, however, could give rise to disputes and ill feeling if not carried out with the knowledge and acceptance of the various interests involved. Some farmers arbitrarily took it into their own hands to

---

[100] Edward Laurence, *The Duty of a Steward to his Lord*, London, 1727, pp. 3, 35.
[101] LAO, 3 Anc 7/12.   [102] Leics. RO, DE 108/38.

make small enclosures which affected other farmers' rights of common grazing and might also reduce the value of the tithes. In 1755 it was reported that at Cotgrave in Nottinghamshire a Mr Scrimshire had taken the "pretty bold step" of enclosing part of the fields without regard to right of common or even giving notice of his intentions. It was true that some part of the fields had been enclosed some years previously, but that enclosure, it was said, had been taken by common consent and for the common good, and the land so enclosed proved so productive of manure as to almost double the amount of grain that could be grown in the lordship. Mr Scrimshire's enclosure, by contrast, was of some of the best corn land in the fields. The incumbent, like the other freeholders, had not been consulted; in a general enclosure his view would be respected, "but in these partial enclosures, which tend to a general one, he is seldom taken notice of. Therefore it behoves him to take care of himself."[103] In another instance not far away at Gedling, near Nottingham, in 1742, the rector, the Rev. Richard Chenevix, "in order to assert and preserve his own undoubted right of common", broke down the fences erected by John Dawson, and turned his horses into Dawson's new enclosure. Dawson's illicit fences affected land that had been open and subject to right of common "time out of mind", and he was obliged to acknowledge his trespass, pay £7 to the overseers of the poor, and undertake to pay £20 if the offence were repeated.[104]

The defects of the old farming system were frequently too deep-seated and too pervasive to be satisfactorily remedied by a reduced stint of the common or partial enclosure of the fields. The advantages arising from the enclosure of good land were reflected in the great increase in the rent which could be obtained – at Withern in the Lincolnshire Marshland, for instance, an increase in 1722 from 2s. 6d. per acre to as much as 12s. or 14s.[105] The farmers were not so blinded by conservatism or prejudice as to fail to see the advantages of a general enclosure, and like the freeholders of Slawston, Northamptonshire, might easily be persuaded to fall in with the plan.[106] Sometimes the initiative sprang directly from the farmers rather than the proprietors. At Gayton in the Marsh, in Lindsey, the inhabitants drew up in 1706 an agreement to enclose all the fields, meadows, commons, and wastes of the parish. Their reason for acting was that "the inhabitants of Gayton suffer considerable losses and inconveniences by reason of the scarcity of enclosure belonging to the said town of Gayton, wanting means and provisions for succouring and relieving their cattle in the winter season and also suffering very great casual losses and misfortunes in their stock going on the commons or wastes of Gayton".[107] Sometimes, as at Gayton, the

[103] Nottm Univ. Archives, Manvers M 4,135.
[104] *Ibid.*, Manvers M 4,129/3.   [105] Leeds Archives Dept., NH 2,368.
[106] Northants. RO, Brudenell Fiii 268 (1726).
[107] Leeds Archives Dept., NH 2,352.

agreement was to be confirmed by obtaining a decree in Chancery. In other cases the authority of a private act of Parliament was sought, and this gradually developed as the standard procedure. Early in the eighteenth century private acts were uncommon, though they were occasionally used to support a regulation of commons where the change was thought sufficiently important. At Castle Donnington, Leicestershire, for instance, the proprietors of the beast gates and sheep commons obtained in 1737 a private act to authorize a reduction in the existing stint of the Beast Pastures. Prior to this step the 490 acres of the pastures were subject to rights of grazing for 941 horses or cattle and 4,805 sheep, so it is not surprising that the owners of the common rights found the pastures "insufficient to support so numerous a stock, that they are eaten up early in the summer", and that as a result for the rest of the open season the stock were forced "to live chiefly upon water which leads to distempers in the cattle. Likewise many sheep die of starvation."[108]

The prevalence of partial enclosure, leaving little behind it in the way of records, makes it difficult to be precise about the extent of enclosure in our period. Many open-field parishes had substantial and growing areas in closes, and the general enclosure, when it came, was often more of a tidying-up operation on a rump of land still farmed in common than a major transformation. The vague references of contemporaries are often untrustworthy. In 1744 the author of "A Short Geographical Description" of Northamptonshire stated that "most of it is champion and lies so open to the eye in many places that 20 or 30 churches present themselves at one time to view".[109] By his time, in fact, much of the area around Northampton and in the more northerly part of the county was already enclosed. It has been calculated by W. E. Tate that before 1749 some seventy-two parishes in the county were enclosed by agreement, and a further four by private act. In total 41 per cent of the county was enclosed by agreement, leaving nearly 60 per cent to be enclosed by act – a very high proportion to be affected by parliamentary enclosure. At least one of the early-eighteenth-century enclosures later gave rise to local hostility, culminating in a riot. This occurred in 1810 when troops were marched from Oundle to Benefield, where Lord Powis had made some new enclosures, an innovation which many local gentry regarded as constituting a great injustice to the poor.[110]

Most of the early enclosures, as in neighbouring Leicestershire, were for pasture or for fattening, dairying, and horse breeding. In Leicestershire it was the rich pasture land in the east of the county, to the east and south of Melton Mowbray, and also in the south-west, around Market Bosworth, which was

[108] Leics. RO, DG 8/24.

[109] Bodleian Library, MS Top. Northants. a 2.

[110] W. E. Tate, 'Inclosure Movements in Northamptonshire', Northants. Past & Present, I, 2, 1949, pp. 29–31.

most affected by early enclosure.[111] The pace of enclosure picked up after the Civil War, and in the 1650s at least seven places were wholly enclosed, in addition to a considerable amount of partial enclosure. In the fifty years between 1660 and 1710 another forty-one places were entirely enclosed. Thirsk has estimated that 47 per cent of the county had been enclosed by 1710, and that by 1730, allowing for partial enclosure, it is likely that over half the county had been enclosed. Many of the seventeenth-century enclosures occurred in places already affected in some degree, and were directed towards completing the process. The first of Leicestershire's enclosure acts was passed in 1730 in order to complete, or more likely to confirm, the enclosure of Horninghold, and subsequent confirmatory acts were passed in 1734 in respect of Great and Little Claybrooke, and in 1748 for Norton-juxta-Twycross. The full flood of parliamentary enclosure in Leicestershire was felt only from the 1750s onwards.[112]

Nottinghamshire was also a county of extensive enclosure by private act; between 1759 and 1860 a third of the county was so enclosed. Estimates suggest that a great deal of enclosure occurred by agreement in the first half of the eighteenth century, and that by 1759 about 45 per cent of the county was already enclosed. Many of these early-enclosed parishes were in the pasture region along the Trent valley, and were in places marked by the domination of one or two great owners and a paucity of small proprietors, whose numbers had been diminished by the gradual buying-up of their lands in preceding years.[113] In the arable claylands of the county, however, the small freeholders often survived in strength, and their presence, together with the unfriendly nature of the soils, tended to delay the onset of large-scale enclosure. In the case of the second duke of Kingston's estates in the county, parliamentary enclosure was also delayed by the duke's indifference to the matter, and was taken up only after his death in 1773. Parts of the Forest area were subject to early enclosure, especially round the homes of the great magnates like the dukes of Kingston, Newcastle, and Portland, who carved great parks for themselves out of the Forest lands. At Thoresby in 1734–5 the duke of Kingston bought up the property of neighbouring copyholders in order to extend the bounds of his park, and it is interesting that he paid for these lands partly in cash, partly in other land, and partly in interest-bearing bonds, in which the duke agreed to hold the money until the copyholder died or his son came of age.[114]

Early enclosure in the claylands of Lincolnshire was especially vigorous in the southern portion of central Lindsey, where the soils were well suited to pasture and were liable to flooding from the river Witham. On the Cliff

[111] See N. Pye, ed., *Leicester and its Region*, Leicester, Br. Assoc., 1972, pp. 251–4.
[112] Thirsk, 'Agrarian History', pp. 218–19, 223–5.
[113] Chambers, *Nottinghamshire*, pp. 149, 168–70.
[114] BL, Egerton MS, 3,598, ff. 173–83, 186–8.

few villages were affected, and on the Heath it was the district south of
Grantham rather than that nearer Lincoln which most experienced the
encloser's hand. On the Wolds many scattered partial enclosures were made,
and, as we have seen, by the early eighteenth century farmers were nibbling
at the sheepwalks for land designed to provide additional fodder. Most of
the eastern Wolds, indeed, had been enclosed before 1750, and for a variety
of reasons. One was to restore old and exhausted arable land to renewed
vigour by putting it for a prolonged period under fallow or grass; another
was to enclose and lay down arable land in order to remedy a shortage of
pasture and meadow. And here, as elsewhere, enclosure was an opportunity
to undertake a redistribution of scattered holdings into more convenient and
efficient units. In the Marshland, already much devoted to pasture, enclosure
was largely concerned with the protection of saltmarsh holdings from the
ravages of the sea, and with the reclamation of new land by means of banks
and dikes.[115]

The reclamation of land for some form of systematic cultivation was one
of the major developments of the period. In the Lincolnshire Marshland, as
just noted, new pastures were gained from the sea; considerable effort, too,
was expended on constructing and maintaining sea walls to prevent the kind
of erosion which wore away the cliffs at Cleethorpes and made inroads on
the shores at Humberstone and North Cotes and between Mablethorpe and
Skegness. Christopher Merret, writing in 1696, stated: "The sea looseth and
gaineth considerable in this county, for about Holbeach, Sutton, and
Wainfleet, great marshes have been lately taken in but northward of
Ingoldmeals it hath lost much more...and at Mawplethrop they are often
in danger of being drowned, their defence being only banks or hills of a small
sand called meals, the former church having been devour'd by it."[116]

Reclamation of some better land in the Forest regions was also a feature
of the period, with landlords establishing large plantations and woodlands,
systematically cultivated for building timber, coppice wood, and other
purposes. As the landlords made their major incursions into the ancient extent
of forest, so the peasants developed their modest and temporary 'breaks' into
permanent arable and pasture. Landlords were also involved in the
maintenance of embankments along rivers in places where winter floods
periodically inundated the farmland. The Trent in the neighbourhood of
Nottingham was particularly prone to serious floods, and near Holme
Pierrepont, where the Pierrepont family kept an ancient residence, the
problem of containing the river continually exercised the Pierreponts and
other local owners. One of the more remarkable of the drainage schemes
was for improving the land on the banks of the river Ancholme in the central
lowlands of Lindsey. A scheme promoted by Sir John Monson, a local

[115] Thirsk, *Peasant Farming*, pp. 68, 163–7, 182.
[116] *Ibid.*, pp. 144–5.

proprietor, was begun before the Civil War. During the war, however, the works were neglected, and the commoners resumed occupation of the lands allotted to Monson as compensation for his expenditure. In 1661, when the Restoration had again brought stability, Monson procured an act to confirm him in his allotment of nearly 6,000 acres of Ancholme lands, but there were complaints from villagers that they no longer had any means of controlling the flow of water in the river, and that as a result their land was in worse condition than before. Monson's scheme was evidently only a partial success at best, and a subsequent report made in 1766 by three engineers (including the famous John Smeaton) showed that once again the Ancholme was badly silted up and its width much reduced.[117]

Landlords with property by the sea were not infrequently alarmed by reports from their tenants of damaged sea banks and inundated farm lands. In 1652 a farmer in Holbeach Marsh wrote to report that the bank had "blown up" and his land made incapable of producing a crop for two years. "Sir it is a common calamite fallen amongst all us Marsh men", he concluded sadly. Six years later another farmer at Holbeach wrote to say that salt water had got into the farmland and had destroyed all his corn, including six lasts of dressed wheat already sold and waiting to be shipped to market.[118] Complaints of this kind continued through the years. In January 1731, for instance, it was reported that the sea had broken the bank at Skegness and had partially destroyed a rabbit warren at Ingoldmells, as well as flooding the saltmarsh in the area. "What will be done there I do not know because it belongs to many lords."[119] Sometimes landlords failed to adjust their rents when lands were lost to the sea, and this was a further cause of tenants' complaints.[120]

Most of the agricultural improvements of the period, however, were unambitious and quite small in scale. They consisted of a series of local changes and modifications, such as the regulation of commons, partial enclosures, consolidation of scattered holdings, intakes of waste, and conversion of old arable land to grass and the breaking up and improvement of ancient pastures. These changes worked in the direction of greater flexibility, giving farmers greater scope for initiative and innovation. They were better able to use their land to the best advantage, and to practise greater specialization or variation of output in order to meet changing market trends. On suitable soils various forms of convertible husbandry were developed, which not only allowed the land to be kept in good heart without recourse to numerous bare fallows, but also enabled the farmers to achieve a better balance between stock and crops.

These improvements to the farming systems were accompanied by an advance in the standards of farmhouses, cottages, barns, and outbuildings.

[117] *Ibid.*, pp. 189–92.   [118] Norfolk RO, NRS 15,994.
[119] LAO, MM vii/1C/5.   [120] *Ibid.*, MM 8/167.

The evidence of estate accounts and of surviving farmsteads and cottages shows that there was a considerable amount of new building in the middle decades of the eighteenth century, and many of the old timber, mud and stud, and thatch constructions were replaced by more substantial buildings in brick, tile, and slate. In part the provision of improved buildings was connected with the effects of the low prices in the 1730s and 1740s, and with the ravages of the cattle plague in the years after 1745. A landlord beset by impoverished and failing tenants, such as the second duke of Kingston in Nottinghamshire, felt obliged to help them out by increasing his expenditure on repairs, as well as by other measures, such as rent abatements, payment of parish rates, gifts of seed, and payment for the clearing and liming of land. Sometimes it was necessary to rebuild a farmhouse or provide a new barn in order to attract a new tenant to a neglected holding.[121]

The greater flexibility of much of the farming and the advantages provided by improved buildings were not, however, any safeguard against the ravages of animal disease. Veterinary knowledge was primitive, and it was difficult or impossible to check the spread of outbreaks, especially where flocks and herds were grazed together on common pastures. In some years within living memory, a farmer once told Arthur Young, "rot has killed more sheep than the butchers have".[122] The sheep rot was connected with excessive wet, and a long spell of rainy weather caused great alarm because of the danger of heavy losses of both stock and corn. Thus on 1 May 1682 a Lincolnshire farmer wrote: "There has been a great deal of rain, not having had a fair day since Easter, which makes mighty floods and will endanger a general rot of sheep. Corn has been drowned in most places."[123] Since the breeding of horses was an important activity over large parts of the region, outbreaks of distemper among horses were also a serious threat. In April 1699 it was reported from Northamptonshire that "not one horse escapes".[124] The 1740s saw heavy losses caused by the cattle plague in the Midland counties. In 1748 gentlemen in Lincolnshire were said to have already given up two years' rents,[125] and the vicar of Misson in Nottinghamshire made the following entry in his parish register: "the rageing distemper broke out in this town of Misson in Aprill in the yeare of our Lord 1748 and in three months time there died of the rageing distemper 700 horned cattle and upward".[126] But disease and floods were not the only causes of livestock losses and crop failures. Severe winters, dry or late springs, and wet summers had complex effects, including lack of hay, a late growth of grass, an

---

[121] See G. E. Mingay, 'The Agricultural Depression, 1730–1750', EcHR, 2nd ser., VIII, 1956, pp. 328–30.

[122] A. Young, *General View of the Agriculture of Oxfordshire*, London, 1809, p. 102.

[123] LAO, Mon 7/12/35.

[124] Northants. RO, F(M)C 1,080.

[125] Leeds Archives Dept., NH 2,833/86.   [126] Notts. RO, PR 6,468.

insufficiency of fodder crops, a reduction in the sown acreage, and a thin harvest. In such circumstances sheep and cattle had to be sold off for whatever they would fetch because the farmers had no means of keeping them.[127]

In contrast to the conditions prevailing before 1640 and those found after 1750, the period was marked by a frequency of low prices and difficult markets for produce, which hit the east Midlands harder than regions having alternative routes of escape. Possibly conditions were generally better between about the middle 1690s and 1720, in a period which Chambers found to be one marked by demographic expansion and growth in both industrial activity and transport developments in the Vale of Trent region.[128] How far agriculture was influenced by this expansionary phase remains uncertain, however. Farmers have a reputation for never finding conditions quite to their liking, but there is no doubt that many of the years between 1640 and 1750 were unprofitable for them. William Spooner, writing from the Lincolnshire Marshland, complained in 1655 of "the hardness of the time by which grain is so cheap as has not been known in late days".[29] In 1670 another resident of that area reported that he had approached a prospective tenant who had said that "times and trading were now so bad that he would see further before he took any other land".[130] John Fleck of Stroxton found himself with several farms in hand in "this severe year", and, in addition to considerable losses of stock over the winter, he now expected that wheat would barely yield as much as the seed, and that his hay would amount to only ten loads where he had had a hundred the year before.[131] Sir John Newton was faced six years later with requests for rent abatements. Times were very hard, he was told, "and the best of your tenants make the heaviest complaints for indeed they find that unless stock quicken they cannot stand long".[132] In November 1690 a further report told Sir John that two farms had been given up and could not be relet without abatements

according to yᵉ extreme badness of the times...for what can a farmer do with barley at 10s. per qtr., beans 12s., wheat 20s., oats 7s., rye 12s. Best wool is at 16s. per tod and small wool 12s. and these are the best prices that are given. Horses cannot be sold at any rate and beasts and sheep are fallen to just over half of what they were a dozen years since. All men complain sadly and that man counts himself most happy that deals least.[133]

A Northamptonshire landlord, Lord Fitzwilliam, was informed by his steward in December 1688 that corn was so cheap that farmers could not find their rents. "All sorts of grayne are very cheape, to[o] Cheape for yᵉ poore farmers, wheat 2s. 6d. a strike, rie 2s., malt 2s., barley 18d. Beans and

[127] E. Sussex RO, FRE 8,973.
[128] J. D. Chambers, *The Vale of Trent, 1670–1800*, EcHR, suppl. no. 3, 1957, pp. 3, 6–15.
[129] Norfolk RO, NRS 15,994.   [130] E. Sussex RO, FRE 8,973.
[131] LAO, Mon 7/12/41.   [132] *Ibid.*, Mon 7/12/69.
[133] *Ibid.*, Mon 7/12/70.

pease 2s., oats 12d." One of the tenants had decided to give up his farm and requested it be taken in hand at Lady Day, "but where to gitt a tent yt will give ye rent I knowe not".[134] A few years later, in 1692, Lord Fitzwilliam's steward complained: "I never knew it [rent] so hard to git up in my life." He had still one farm in hand that he had not been able to relet, and "I should be loath to have any more but if these times hold I fear wee shall."[135] The difficulty of finding tenants continued in 1694. Rents would have to come down, the steward believed, or further farms would come into hand. One or two farmers had agreed to inspect a vacant farm but had not yet put in an appearance: "I have beene at all ye fayres and markitts about us to see for a tent but cannot light of one yett. Corne and stock sell well but yett for all ye tents are very hard to gitt. Yr Honr speakes of rayseing ye rents, but they will not heare of it, their are many farmes about us stand empty."[136]

Freak weather conditions were sometimes the cause of serious losses. In 1719, for instance, Lincolnshire farmers were badly hit by a 'great draft' which scorched the earth. As a result very little stock could be made fit for sale in the following season. Sir John Newton's steward reported that until the farmers had disposed of their wool rents could not be collected: "There is not a gentleman in Lincolnshire of such an estate has so great arrears upon it and if twenty pound would save a man from ye jayle its not to be had among all your tenants."[137] Wool production, the mainstay of the Lincolnshire graziers, became markedly less profitable for them after 1723. In that year an increase in the numbers of sheep sent to market coincided with a decline in the demand for wool, and prices fell. This fall gave another sharp thrust to the long-term decline in wool prices: a tod of long wool which averaged 20s. 7d. in 1718–22 fetched only 16s. 3d. in 1723–7, and generally less than 16s. over the next fifteen years. Some sheepwalks, in consequence, were stripped of their sheep and stocked with Scots cattle, while marginal pastures were converted to rabbit warrens.[138]

The 1730s and 1740s were remarkable for an almost unbroken succession of exceptionally good seasons, a run broken only by the extraordinarily severe winter of 1739–40 when seed was frozen in the ground and "many hens and ducks, even the cattle in the stalls, died of cold": the spring of 1740 was extremely cold, and the harvest was further held back by drought, and was not over until late in the autumn. But taking the two decades as a whole the long series of fine harvests led to an excess of supply, and this again meant very low prices. Wheat ruled at below 30s. a quarter, with the lowest prices occurring in 1731–3 and 1742–5. Barley, too, fell to 15s. a quarter in the 1730s, and was even lower in the middle 1740s. In consequence heavy arrears of rents were commonplace among the small arable farmers. The duke of

[134] Northants. RO, F(M)C 674, 685.
[135] Ibid., F(M)C 778.
[136] Ibid., F(M)C 835.
[137] LAO, Mon 7/14/225.
[138] Perkins, Sheep Farming, pp. 12–13, 16, 33.

Kingston's Nottinghamshire tenants fell seriously into debt, and numbers gave up their farms or "fled away". Similar difficulties were experienced by the tenants of Lincolnshire landlords, such as Lord Monson, the duke of Ancaster, and Richard Wynn. On Lord Monson's farms arrears of rent had accumulated by 1741 to the sum of £8,000, twice the annual rental of the properties.[139]

Nor were the difficulties confined to arable lands: between 1729 and 1736 the prices of beef, mutton, butter, cheese, and wool all fell seriously, and livestock had often to be disposed of at a loss. In June 1735, for example, Samuel Dakin, writing from Ormsby in Lincolnshire to Mrs Massingberd, had the following to report:

Stock has sold at such a low price that never was known in the memory of man in these parts. It is much worse since May Day than before. There hav been ewes and lambs sold in these markets for 7s. each that I gave 17s. a piece for when I took to farming. If they don't mend in price in a short time there will be many tenants broke of yours and everyone elses. There is many broke this spring in the marsh that were called very rich men within a few years. There was one, Stur at Addlethrope, upon Mrs Amcocks land, is broke, they say in arrears 3 years that was one of the soberest and best stock masters about the place. She was so kind to him as to take him into her own house and he died last week.[140]

In the Ormsby area conditions continued to be bad, and again in December 1747 Samuel Dakin was saying that he could not find any tenants with money at the present; at this time the losses caused by the cattle plague had added to the farmers' other difficulties.[141]

The dependence of farmers on grain and stock was reduced in many areas by the availability of by-employments. Farmers could use idle teams and carts in winter to transport coal, charcoal, malt, bricks, tiles, slates, timber, and building stone. Many farmers relied on the 'land carriage' business to eke out their farm earnings, particularly when they were within easy reach of major towns or navigable rivers and the coast. Northamptonshire was especially renowned for its fine building stone, quarried at ancient sites such as Barnack, Stanion, and Weldon, as well as at Raunds and elsewhere; also famous were the stone slates of Collyweston, Easton, and Kirby. Tobacco-pipe clay was raised in Northampton Fields and transported into Warwickshire and Leicestershire.[142] The burning of lime was carried on throughout the east Midlands, and there were some particularly well-known lime quarries at Barrow upon Soar.[143] The use of soot and other town materials as fertilizers also called for much carriage, and some farmers filled their carts on the return journey from market. The forest areas of Sherwood,

---

[139] See G. E. Mingay, 'Landownership and Agrarian Trends in the Eighteenth Century', unpub. Nottm Univ. Ph.D. thesis, 1958, pp. 39–43.

[140] Oxon. RO, MM II/7.   [141] LAO, MM VII/2/91.

[142] VCH Northants., II, pp. 296–7, 308.   [143] VCH Leics., III, p. 43.

Rockingham, Salcey, and Whittlewood produced large quantities of timber which had to be thinned, cut, stacked, and transported; and the forests gave rise to employment in charcoal burning and the making of hurdles, posts and rails, hop poles, besoms, and the like. Local husbandmen often combined their farming with some part-time occupation in the woods.

Some of the larger towns in the region developed manufacturing industries which called for supplies of raw materials from the countryside, and gave rise to rural employment in processing and transport. Nottingham, Leicester, and Northampton were pre-eminent in this respect, but not insignificant was the growth of industry in smaller centres such as Lincoln, Stamford, Newark, Mansfield, Hinckley, Loughborough, Melton Mowbray, Market Harborough, and Lutterworth. And the growth of leather manufacturing, especially boots and shoes, was of great importance in Northamptonshire. Already in the sixteenth century the town of Northampton had nearly a quarter of its workforce engaged in the leather trades.[144] Cattle from the rich pastures of the Nene valley and elsewhere provided abundant hides, and the forest districts supplied oak bark and fuel for the tanners and leather dressers. Apart from the great shoemaking industry of Northampton, a whipmaking industry was centred at Daventry, while glovemaking was important at Nottingham, Towcester, Daventry, and Kettering as well as Northampton.[145]

Though none of the east Midland counties was particularly renowned for its cloth, and most of the region's wool was carried away to be used elsewhere, there was, nevertheless, some local cloth manufacturing: Kettering, for instance, was known for its serges, tammies, and shalloons.[146] By far the most important textile activity, however, was hosiery. Framework knitting spread into the towns and villages of Leicestershire and Nottinghamshire in the course of the seventeenth and eighteenth centuries. In Leicestershire it was the western half of the country that was mainly affected, and in Nottinghamshire Nottingham itself and the coalfield district in the north-west of the county. Evidence for 1710–15 collected by D. G. Hey shows that the industry was concentrated in a few major towns: Nottingham had at least 69 master framework knitters, Leicester 58, Hinckley 56, and Wigston, a village nearly adjoining Leicester, 28. Despite this concentration, however, the industry was already widely spread at this time, with numerous villages having as many as half a dozen or more master framework knitters, and a large number of others having one or two.[147] Small farmers, as we have seen, sometimes operated a frame in their spare time, and a combination with framework knitting of a handful of acres and a few stock was quite

[144] L. A. Clarkson, *The Pre-Industrial Economy in England, 1500–1750*, London, 1971, pp. 88–9.

[145] *VCH Northants.*, II, pp. 209, 331.

[146] *Ibid.*, p. 333.

[147] Figures by private communication and kind permission of Dr D. G. Hey.

commonplace. When Daniel Vann, a framework knitter of Wigston Magna, died in 1680, his effects included three cows and a pig as well as four frames. A much humbler knitter, Thomas Fallows of Little Thorpe, had two cows and only one frame when he died in 1725, the three items together accounting for the larger part of his stock of worldly goods valued at £16.[148] Subsequently, as framework knitting in the villages declined, its place was taken by the making by hand of boots and shoes. Numbers of the village womenfolk had long been engaged in making cloth and in gloving, and many came to be employed in preparing yarn for the stocking frames. In Northamptonshire there was some pillow lace, especially in the neighbourhood of Wellingborough, and in the villages in the south-west of the county, largely an extension of the more widespread lacemaking of Buckinghamshire and Bedfordshire.[149]

There were many other local trades, both for men and for women – basketwork, rush-mat making, pottery, coastal and river fishing, metalworking and woodworking, to mention but a few. Altogether, these occupations supplemented considerably the incomes of small husbandmen and labourers, and helped to provide some kind of reserve against the uncertainties inherent in farming. But before the spread of hosiery transformed the character of many Leicestershire and Nottinghamshire villages, mainly after 1750, it was the various branches of farming, singly or in combination, which throughout the east Midland region remained the mainstay of the great bulk of the rural population.

[148] *VCH Leics., III*, p. 7.
[149] *VCH Northants., II*, p. 337.

CHAPTER 5

THE NORTH-WEST MIDLANDS: DERBYSHIRE, STAFFORDSHIRE, CHESHIRE, AND SHROPSHIRE

The north-west Midlands was essentially a pastoral region, where farmers concentrated upon dairying and the rearing of cattle and sheep. It is true that eastern and southern Derbyshire were areas of mixed husbandry and that pockets of fertile arable land could be found elsewhere, but in most parts so little attention was paid to growing cereals that the inhabitants were dependent upon the bread corn and malt that were imported through their markets. This was a matter of necessity for those who farmed the poor, thin soils and endured the harsh climate of the Peak District, but in the lowlands it was a matter of choice, for more profit could be obtained from cattle. The meadows and pastures along the Dove and the Trent and in the Cheshire plain provided some of the finest grazing in the country. Elsewhere, in the woodlands and on the Pennines, part-time involvement in industry ensured the survival of small family farms and attracted great numbers of cottagers. To have a dual occupation was the rule rather than the exception for the rural metalworkers, miners, potters, weavers, knitters, and numerous other craftsmen, whose activities did so much to lay the foundations of the Industrial Revolution, and for most of the period farming and industry remained inseparable.

In his "History of Derbyshire", written in 1712, William Woolley described "the east and south parts of the county" as "well cultivated and fruitfull yielding a very spacious and pleasant prospect". The best arable lands in the region lay in the east along the borders of Yorkshire and Nottinghamshire, where, for a short distance, the Derbyshire boundary crossed the magnesian limestone belt. Here, small estate villages surrounded by their common fields occupied an area fourteen miles long and never more than seven miles wide. The farmers of these fertile soils followed a system of mixed husbandry, where the cultivation of cereals was as important as the dairy or the rearing of livestock. A sample of 22 probate inventories had a median average of 11 head of cattle per farm, and nearly everyone kept a flock of sheep and a few pigs, and grew wheat, barley, oats, and peas. Godfrey Norburne of Barlborough (1664) was one of the better-off husbandmen, with 2 bulls, 6 kine, 3 calves, 8 young beasts, 4 steers, 6 oxen and 4 old oxen, 7 horses, 87 sheep, and 18 swine, valued together at £139, and crops of barley, wheat, oats, peas, and hay worth £108. Clover was grown at Barlborough by 1724, and was included in four of six inventories taken from the 1740s.[1]

Immediately west of the magnesian limestone lay the rolling hills and well-wooded vales that were described by Defoe as "a rich fruitfull part of the country, though surrounded with barren moors and mountains". In the north, alternating bands of sand and clay overlay the coal-measure sandstones, with grits and shales on the Pennine foothills, and two outliers of carboniferous limestone at Ashover and Crich. South of Alfreton the sandstones petered out and the soils were a mixture of clays and alluvium.[2] This was a region of mixed husbandry and of dual occupations. The farms were generally small ones of between ten and thirty acres or even less, with secure tenures that were normally held by leases for terms of years; cottages, such as the thirty-one recorded on the wastes of Eckington in 1650, were often held at will.[3] Here were several villages and market towns, but most of the farmers and craftsmen lived in hamlets or dispersed farmsteads, whose hill meadows and pasture closes were collectively far more extensive than the open arable fields that had once surrounded each village and hamlet. The open fields were gradually whittled away or divided by agreement until few remained to be enclosed by act of parliament; where they survived, as at Wadshelf, many of their strips were converted into grass leys. Open fields were of secondary importance to the hedged or walled enclosures that caught the eye of the travellers and the topographers. Duffield, for instance, was described by William Woolley as having "a great many enclosures, especially in the valleys, of large extent and value". Duffield Frith had been divided between the king and the freeholders in 1633, and, despite protests and

[1] William Woolley, MS vol. "History of Derbyshire", 1712, Derby Central Library, f. 3,343a; LJRO, probate inventories; Derbys. RO, D 505/bk 4. Twenty-two inventories produced 21 references to sheep, 18 to pigs, 20 to wheat and to barley or malt, 19 to oats, and 15 to peas; clover was recorded in 1748–9 at Barlborough, Clowne, Whaley Hall, and Whitwell. At Scarcliffe and Palterton 550 acres of open field and 420 acres of waste were enclosed by act of parliament in 1726; at Elmton the open fields and Markland common were enclosed by Sir John Rodes in 1732–5 – Derbys. RO, Rodes papers.

[2] D. Defoe, *A Tour through the Whole Island of Great Britain*, 2 vols., London, 1962, II, p. 180; J. Pilkington, *A View of the Present State of Derbyshire*, Derby, 1789, p. 296; J. Brown, *General View of the Agriculture of the County of Derby*, London, 1794, p. 15.

[3] Derby Central Library, deeds, 12,569 (Crich, 1655: 29 people held under 10 acres each, another 29 farmed between 10 and 30 acres, and a further 7 held between 31 and 128 acres), Brookhill 134 (Pinxton, 1699: 12 tenants held under 20 acres each, 12 held between 20 and 49 acres, and 5 held between 50 and 135 acres); G. G. Hopkinson, 'Stretton in the 17th and 18th Centuries', *Derbys. Arch. J.*, LXXI, 1951, pp. 51–65 (Stretton, 1656: 15 cottagers with less than an acre each, 13 tenants with under 10 acres, a further 13 with between 10 and 25 acres, 5 tenants with 50 to 100 acres, and the hall farm of 242 acres); Sussex RO, HI/ST/E/108/1 (Tibshelf, 1692: 14 tenants held under 20 acres each, 7 held between 20 and 49 acres, and 9 held between 50 and 124 acres); *VCH Derbys.*, II, pp. 305–20; T. W. Hall, *Court-Roll and Parliamentary Survey of the Manor of Eckington*, Sheffield, 1924.

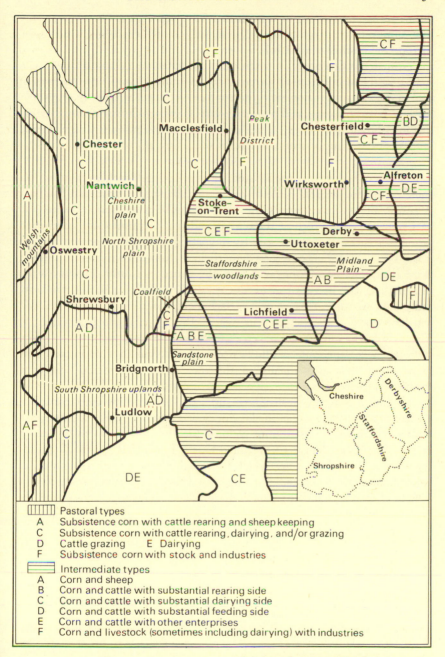

Fig. 5.1. Farming regions of the north-west Midlands.

disturbances, the agreement was ratified forty years later. Elsewhere, many townships retained large commons until the age of parliamentary enclosure. In 1692 the commons of Tibshelf were measured at 363 acres, and in 1650 the estimated 1,000 acres of commons and wastes in Eckington were said to be "for the most part very barren and yield little or no profitt to the present lord of the mannor, the tennants thereof having the herbage for their cattle". Titus Wheatcroft expressed another point of view in 1722 when he wrote that in Ashover there were "four rich and spacious commons well furnished with all sorts of moor game, besides foxes, hares, and the like", as well as "ten fair woods, and several very good springs of water for fish to breed".[4]

Celia Fiennes described the Saturday market at Chesterfield in 1697 as "like some little faire, a great deale of corne and all sorts of ware and fowles". A sample of 115 inventories shows that, throughout the period, wheat and oats were the chief crops of the region, and that a considerable number of farmers also grew barley and peas. By this period little rye was grown, though it had been a major crop in the Chesterfield region in the sixteenth century. A good example of a farmer with typically varied interests is Thomas Wade of Handley, who in 1715 had 3 cows, 3 calves, 4 heifers, 4 horses, 38 sheep, and 2 pigs, worth in all £56 9s. 2d., farm equipment priced at £4 13s. 4d., and hay worth £5, together with wheat, barley, oats, and peas valued at £30 6s. 8d. The importance of cereals in this region is attested by the 54 corn mills that were operating within Scarsdale hundred in 1652. However, new crops occur only occasionally in the records of this period; clover is mentioned in the Alfreton Park accounts for 1724 and in the inventory of Joseph Gill, a Staveley husbandman, in 1745, and turnips are recorded at Alfreton Park in 1741 and in the inventory of Thomas Pyinger, a framework knitter of Loscoe, in 1748. Improvement usually took the form of liming, and in 1722 Titus Wheatcroft claimed that Ashover was "especially noted for limestone and lime kilns, which furnisheth all the country round about us with lime for land and building". A limekiln was in production at Newbold in 1731, and loads of limestone are frequently recorded in the probate inventories.[5]

Longhorn cattle were the mainstay of the 115 farmers whose inventories

[4] W. E. Tate, 'Enclosure Acts and Awards relating to Derbyshire', Derbys. Arch. J., LXV, 1944–5, pp. 1–65; Sheffield Central Library, Barker 764; Woolley, op. cit.; G. E. Fussell, 'Four Centuries of Farming Systems in Derbyshire, 1500–1900', Derbys. Arch. J., XXIV, 1951, p. 12; Sussex RO, HI/ST/E/108/1; Hall, op. cit.; Rev. C. Kerry, ed., 'Ashover Memoranda by Titus Wheatcroft, A.D. 1722', Derbys. Arch. J., XIX, 1897, pp. 24–52; PRO, E 317 Derbys. 10.

[5] Celia Fiennes, The Journeys of Celia Fiennes, ed. C. Morris, London, 1947, p. 96; D. Hey, 'Introduction', in J. M. Bestall and D. V. Fowkes, eds., Chesterfield Wills and Inventories, 1521–1603, Matlock, 1977; Sheffield Central Library, Beauchief 80; Derby Central Library, Alfreton Park MSS; Kerry, op. cit., p. 25; Derbys. RO, D 803/M/E3; LJRO, inventories (lime), John Allsop, Somercotes, 1659, John Marshall, Woodthorpe, 1662, George Booth, West Handley, 1667, John Cowper, Ripley, 1692.

have been examined. The median average was 13 head per farm, and 7 holdings supported more than 30 cattle each; the largest farm in the sample was that of William Cock of Duffield (1748), who had 47 cattle appraised at £124. In the northern part of the region, in and around Chesterfield, tanning was an old and important industry, with men like Robert Outram of Unstone (1645), who had hides, leather, and bark worth £79, or Arthur Mower of Moorhall, on the edge of the Pennines (1665), who had similar goods worth £260. The farmers of the clays and alluviums in the south spent more time in dairying, and many were involved in the great cheese trade centred upon Uttoxeter. Cheese chambers were recorded in the inventories of Ruth Holmes, an Alfreton widow (1643), Samuel Hibbert of Morley, yeoman (1711), Thomas James of Morley, husbandman (1715), and John Kennion of Ilkeston, miller (1745), and by the eighteenth century nearly all the farmers south of Alfreton made various quantities of cheese. Ninety-four of the 115 farmers also kept a few pigs, and during the eighteenth century there were increasing numbers of young and mature horses; 120 horses of all kinds were recorded in 21 inventories from the 1740s, compared with only 39 horses in 30 inventories taken a hundred years previously. The largest herd was kept by Francis Ryle of Edingale (1743), who had 10 draught horses and mares, a hackney mare, 4 foals, 2 colts, and 2 fillies, priced together at £142.

Sheep were also important in this mixed economy; 99 of the 115 farmers had flocks of sheep, and about half these flocks numbered over 50. Richard Heath of Pleasley (1717) had 160 sheep valued at £48, Samuel Lowe of Crich, yeoman (1718), had 113 sheep and 38 lambs worth £51 10s., and a further 6 farmers had flocks of over 100. The manufacture of woollen cloth was an old, but declining, industry, with a few farmer-weavers still pursuing a dual occupation.[6] They were insignificant compared with the great number of people who were employed in the hosiery trade. Hand knitting, an occupation for women, children, the old, and those otherwise irregularly employed, provided additional earnings throughout the period, while south of Alfreton framework knitting became one of the country's most spectacular growth industries. Centred upon the county towns of Nottingham and Leicester, and owing much to an influx of capital and enterprise from London, it spread quickly over the Midlands countryside. Apprenticeship indentures for the period 1710–15 refer to masters living in fifteen different places near the Nottinghamshire border, and undoubtedly this region contained many other settlements with framework knitters by that time. Some masters had a considerable interest in agriculture; Thomas Pyinger of Loscoe (1748), for example, was a small employer with six frames in his shop, worth £40 5s.,

[6] LJRO, inventories of Edward Lowe, Plaistow, yeoman (1694), William Lomas, Duffield (1694), and William Bargh of Rumbling Street, weaver (1697). Very little flax or hemp was grown, though both were the subject of a tithe dispute in South Normanton in 1719 (Derby Central Library, Brookhill 134).

and farm stock valued at nearly £67. Others had a single frame and a smallholding, but during the eighteenth century men with little or no land became the characteristic figures in the trade. Framework knitting provided employment for the growing population, and supplied much of the capital, the techniques, and the labour force for the revolution which Derbyshire helped to pioneer in the textile industry.[7]

In north Derbyshire, men turned instead to the metal trades. In 1672 over 100 smithies were recorded in the parishes which lay immediately south of Sheffield. Nailers, cutlers, and sickle makers were to be found in the scattered settlements of Eckington parish, and the scythemakers were concentrated in the parish of Norton. Typical of these craftsmen were Henry Brownell of Jordanthorpe (1634), who had farm goods worth £29 and 256 scythes valued at £17 5s. 4d., and William Bate of Little Norton, cutler (1669), who had farm stock priced at £19 5s. Farming was of fundamental importance in this distinctive economy, and it remained so until the population explosion of the eighteenth and nineteenth centuries created a labour force that was far too large to be supported on the land as well as in industry. The local gentry owned furnaces, forges, slitting mills, and charcoal woods, and William Bullock of Norton, esquire (1667), was a gentleman-manufacturer on a considerable scale, with axes and hoes valued at £190. His neighbour, William Blythe, a yeoman whose timber-framed house still stands at Norton Lees, was a prosperous farmer and miller and, like his father, an organizer of the scythe trade. In 1666 his inventory listed over 2,000 scythes, including special Scottish and Holderness scythes, which he sold in the northern market towns, well away from the markets of the Belbroughton scythesmiths. The trade in agricultural edge tools was both extensive and profitable.[8]

The Derbyshire coalfield was of national importance by the seventeenth century. In 1692 John Houghton was informed that "the chiefest Cole-mines" were at Smalley, Heanor, and Denby, "through which abundance in summer are carried as far as Northampton-shire, from whence is brought back barly". At this time, colliers too were part-time farmers.[9] The region also benefited

---

[7] S. D. Chapman, 'The Genesis of the British Hosiery Industry, 1600–1750', *Textile Hist.*, III, 1972, pp. 7–50; PRO, IR/1/41, 42, 43 (of the 25 masters, 8 were from Horsley, 2 from Horsley Woodhouse, and 1 from Kilburn in the same parish; the tax on apprenticeship indentures was widely evaded, and the figures must be regarded as minimal).

[8] D. Hey, *The Rural Metalworkers of the Sheffield Region*, Leicester, 1972. Sixty-seven of the 209 fathers who had a child baptized at Norton in 1733–49 were metalworkers, including 35 scythesmiths, 4 scythe grinders, 6 sicklesmiths, and 14 cutlers – Kerry, *op. cit.*, p. 25 (Ashover noted for its scythe sand and grindstones).

[9] John Houghton, *A Collection for Improvement of Husbandry and Trade*, London, 1692, II, no. 38; Sheffield Central Library, Beauchief 80 (24 pits in 15 different townships within the hundred of Scarsdale, 1652); PRO, E 317 Derbys. 10; Derbys. RO, D 37M/RL 16; LJRO, inventories of Robert Linsey, Higham (1643), John Cowper, Ripley (1692), and Robert Mower, Grangewood (1714).

from the lead trade, for here were plentiful supplies of fuel for smelting, at a convenient point between the mines and the inland ports.[10] Throughout the coalfield, a great deal of extra wealth was provided by rural industry, and a wide cross-section of society profited by it.

At Chatsworth, wrote Daniel Defoe, "begins a vast extended moor or waste, which, for fifteen or sixteen miles together due north, presents you with neither hedge, house or tree, but a waste and houling wilderness". Beyond Chapel-en-le-Frith was "the most desolate, wild, and abandoned country in all England."[11] The farmers of this inhospitable region held their land by attractive tenures. On the duchy of Lancaster estates, land in the manors of Castleton and High Peak was mostly freehold, and in Wirksworth manor the copyholders of inheritance had the right to sublet land for lives or years by copy of court roll, and to make fines certain at one year's ancient chief rent. Elsewhere, probate inventories frequently gave a valuation for the remaining years of a lease. However, during the eighteenth century tenancy-at-will became common, and in 1794 Brown reported that "leases are wearing out of use".[12] At a more humble level, the opportunities for employment offered by lead mining encouraged a great number of poor people to erect cottages upon the wastes, for it was an ancient custom that miners could occupy such buildings as long as they were working upon their rake. By 1649 thirty cottages had encroached upon the wastes of Wirksworth, and their occupiers had acquired leases for terms of years; in 1650, numerous cottagers were recorded in the manors of Castleton and High Peak; and two years later, 76 cottages were listed in a survey of the Youlgreave area, namely 20 at Bradford, 28 at Caldwell End, 11 on Winster waste, 10 others in Winster tithing, and 7 on the waste of Stanton tithing.[13]

The commons and wastes were graded into the best, middle, and worst sorts. Castleton manor had 732 acres of the best grade, 150 acres of the middle sort, and so much of the worst kind that the size could not be estimated nor the bounds defined at all accurately. Wormhill had just over 1,000 acres of middle and best commons in the late 1630s, Bradwell had 1,352 acres of all grades in 1688, and the commons at Litton were said in 1741 to cover about 3,000 acres and to be walled in and stinted. Great tracts of moor, with up

---

[10] Sheffield Central Library, Beauchief 80 (21 smelting houses in Scarsdale hundred, 1652); Kerry, op. cit. p. 24; LJRO, inventory of Peter Calton of Prattenhall, yeoman (1640): "a pig of lead, £1".

[11] Defoe, op. cit., II, pp. 175-6.

[12] PRO, E 317 Derbys. 12 (Castleton, 1650), 20 (High Peak, 1650), 28 (Wirksworth, 1649); LJRO, inventories (e.g. Edward Booth of Bettenhill, Glossop (1640): "a lease for years, £50"; John Radcliffe of New Mills, yeoman (1694): "years in the farm, £80"); Derbys. RO, D 513/M/E375 (rack rents and holdings-at-will on Mr Shallcross's estate in Shallcross and Fernike, c. 1720, where the tenants had "large pieces of new improving land laid to their respective farms"); Brown, op. cit., p. 45.

[13] PRO, E 317 Derbys. 24, 28, 12, 20, 30.

to sixty inches of rainfall per annum, were suitable only for the rough grazing of sheep. The best pastures were reserved for cattle. Common rights were vital to the inhabitants of this region, and the copyholders of Wirksworth manor claimed by prescription not only common of pasture for all manner of cattle, but liberty to get turves, peats, clods, limestone, clay, marl, sand, gravel, slate, stone, heath, fern, furze, and gorse, and to fell or cut for reasonable estovers any hollies or underwoods growing on the wastes.[14] On the duchy of Lancaster estates, the enclosure agreements made during the reign of Charles I were ratified later in the century. The commons at Hayfield were divided equally between the king and the tenants in 1640, the commons and wastes of Hope and other parts of the High Peak were divided similarly in 1675, an agreement to divide the Castleton commons was reached by 1691, and the division of common pastures near Chapel-en-le-Frith, which had been agreed upon in 1640, was finally completed in 1714, when the freeholders were allowed to enjoy their moiety of 973 acres.[15] Numerous examples of enclosure by agreement may be cited from other parts of the Peak District. Some of the peaty pastures of Macclesfield Forest were enclosed upon the Restoration, by 1665 nearly half of the 900 acres of land at Fairfield, in the parish of Hope, had been enclosed and divided, the pastures at Beeley were enclosed by agreement in 1673, and fourteen years later about 2,000 acres of Morridge common were divided equally between the lord and the freeholders. Stinted pastures were divided at Kniveton (1697), Tissington (1726), Doveridge (1731), and Alsop (1758) according to the number of sheep gates or beast gates that were held. The lack of a stint was said to have led to injustices at Eyam, and a unanimous agreement to enclose 153 acres of pasture in 1702 made the freeholders "very well pleased contented and satisfied". Elsewhere, selfish enclosure by prominent local families met with fierce resistance; about 1650 forty-four inhabitants of Litton protested against enclosures by the Bradshaws, and in 1665 the Bagshawes were accused of the illegal enclosure of parts of the commons of Abney and Great Hucklow.[16]

[14] Derbys. County Library, M 35/2/42/8 (Castleton); PRO, MPC/18 (Wormhill), 52(1) (Bradwell), also 13 (Taddington and Priestcliffe), 20 (Mellor), 29 (Ollersett Moor), 39 (Hope), 40 (Monyash), 78 (Chelmorton); Univ. of Manchester, John Rylands Library, B13/3/434 (Litton); C. S. Davies, *The Agricultural History of Cheshire, 1750–1850*, Manchester, 1960, p. 137; C. E. B. Bowles, 'The Manor of Abney', *Derbys. Arch. J.*, XXIX, 1907, pp. 138, 140; PRO, E 317 Derbys. 12, 20, 28.

[15] PRO, MR/10; Derbys. County Library, M 35/2/42/6, and PRO, MPC/16 and 71; Derbys. RO, 267/Pashley, and Sheffield Central Library, Bagshawe 241; Derbys. RO, 743/2, 239/1, and C. E. B. Bowles, 'Concerning the Commons and Waste Lands in Various Townships in the High Peak', *Derbys. Arch. J.*, XXIV, 1902, pp. 32–41; John Rylands Library, B13/3/143.

[16] Davies, *op. cit.*, p. 112; Derbys. RO, D 258/31/59, D 258/58/7, D 231/M/E/5,030, 5,038, 5,045, D 239/A/282; V. S. Doe, 'The Common Fields of Beeley in the Seventeenth Century', *Derbys. Arch. J.*, XCIII, 1973, pp. 45–54; Derby Central Library, deeds, 10,349; C. E. B. Bowles, 'Agreement of the Freeholders in Eyam to the Award for Dividing Eyam Pasture, 12th November 1702', *Derbys. Arch. J.*, XX, 1898, pp. 1–11; Sheffield Central Library, Bagshawe Collection, Eyre MSS 1,644 and 2,094.

In 1794 Brown reported that in this region "About one-fifth of the enclosures may be arable, and this fifth part chiefly employed in growing oats; the remainder is in pasture, and the greatest part employed in dairying and breeding of stock." Though some townships along the major rivers had land fit for growing crops, most bread corn had to be imported by badgers. The open fields were of minor importance, and many disappeared by agreement during this period. For example, the open fields of Beeley were enclosed in the middle of the seventeenth century; in 1674 ten people agreed to enclose lands which were dispersed in the open fields, meadows, and pastures of Tissington; and in 1667 it was claimed that the tithes of Brassington had been greatly reduced in value "as the town (as all other thereabouts) is enclosed, yet formerly maintained tillage...Now by mowing the ground they get more profit with less labour and charge, by reason the poorer sort, who are numerous, employ their labour in lead grounds in lordships 4 or 5 miles around." This conversion of arable land to meadow also meant that fewer sheep were kept; "Brassington has 73 oxgangs of land whereof 35 have not one sheep belonging to them. All the fields of Brassington have been enclosed about 50 years, except part of a field enclosed 30 years ago."[17]

Lime was obtained readily and was frequently used to improve the land. In 1652 the freeholders of Carsington agreed on the temporary enclosure of the sixty-two acres of their lower, stinted pasture, which was to be ploughed and put to tillage for seven years and laid open after each harvest. Every man agreed to lay at least sixty horse loads of well-burned limestone per acre within the first four years, and at the last ploughing to ridge up his lands and "leave the same evenly harrowed whereby to be better grass in future". Fourteen limekilns were at work alongside the quarries at Dove Holes in 1650, and ten more at Bradwell town end, these "being sett upp ordinarily and taken downe again by the people att their pleasure without any licence".[18]

In a sample of 166 inventories from this region, the valuations given to cereals were small, and crops were normally listed simply as "corn"; where crops were distinguished, they were chiefly oats and barley.[19] A major concern of the Peak farmers was the rearing of cattle, and large herds were

[17] Brown, *op. cit.*, p. 15; Doe, *op. cit.*; Derbys. RO, D 239/A/21; Derby Central Library, Gale bequest, bdle 3.

[18] Derbys. RO, D 258/61/22a; PRO, E 317 Derbys. 12, 20; Sheffield Central Library, Oakes, 1,175 (in 1738 William Bagshaw of Ford Hall employed men to spread 20 loads of good lime, well burned, each working day from 7 May to 15 Aug.).

[19] T & C, pp. 35–6 (in 1631 the corn of the High Peak was reported to be "chiefly oats and oatmeal, little other grain growing in the said hundred"); R. Plot, *The Natural History of Staffordshire*, Oxford, 1686, p. 109 ("The black moorish and gouty grounds of the moorelands, with the best helps are fit indeed only for oates and barley"); Houghton, *op. cit.*, II, no. 44; Pilkington, *op. cit.*, p. 303; Woolley, *op. cit.*; Derbys. RO, quarter sessions, badger licences, 7 July 1746 to 7 July 1747 (170 badgers, mostly from the north and north-west of the county); LJRO and Cheshire RO, inventories.

kept in the closes and on the extensive common pastures. The 166 farmers
whose inventories have been examined kept a median average of 16 cattle
per farm, and by the 1740s this number had risen to 18 or 19 head. The
average for the 63 Derbyshire inventories was only 12 head per farm, but
that for the 90 Staffordshire inventories was 21; by the 1740s the Derbyshire
farmers were keeping 14 or 15 cattle on average, whereas the Staffordshire
men were averaging as many as 23 per farm. Plot claimed that in Staffordshire
"Both moorelands and woodlands [had] goodly cattle, large and fair spread,
as Lancashire itself, and such as the grasiers say will feed better." Twenty-three
of the 166 farmers kept herds of more than 30 cows and no doubt took full
advantage of their common rights. Richard Edge of Horton, gentleman
(1647), had 65 head of cattle, James Janney of Ipstones (1663) had 51 head,
William Allen of New Grange, Leek (1748), had 56 head and 156 cheeses
valued at £40, and Henry Bowman of Smerrill Grange, Youlgreave, farmer
(1747), had 2 bulls, 2 cows, 14 milch cows, 21 calves, a heifer, 3 bullocks,
10 twinters, 19 stirks, and 14 steers, worth £164, as well as 523 sheep valued
at £158, 16 mares and young horses worth £53, hay and corn valued at
£115, and other farm goods and equipment appraised at £27. Plot wrote
that "The warm limestone hills of the very moorelands...though in an open
cold country" produced "a fine sweet grass", which enabled the farmers
to keep milch cows for the dairy and to rear beef for the graziers of the
Midland plain. Half of the Derbyshire farmers made small quantities of
cheese, and in the Staffordshire uplands this product was recorded in two
out of every three inventories, often in large amounts. Cheese chambers were
listed among the rooms of Thomas Whiston of Cheadle Grange (1645),
William Ersworth of Kingsley (1692), and William Harvey of Colton (1748),
and inventories taken during the 1740s recorded stocks of cheese worth
between £20 and £40 at Alstonfield, Hanbury, and at Heath Grange and
New Grange in the parish of Leek. A third of the Staffordshire inventories
recorded oxen, though the numbers fell sharply in the eighteenth century;
very few were kept in Derbyshire. With so little arable land, few draught
animals were needed, and many farmers had only a riding mare; however,
by the 1740s each inventory recorded three or four horses on average.[20]

Two out of every three farmers kept a few pigs, and 136 of the 166
inventories recorded sheep; 24 farmers had flocks of more than 100, and 7
of these had more than 200. On the carboniferous limestone, George
Hambledon of Ballidon, husbandman (1668), had 200 sheep and 90 lambs
worth £90 10s. and wool valued at £20; John Goodale of Tissington,
yeoman (1692), had 184 sheep, 40 ewes, and 40 lambs worth £37; and Joshua
Barnsley of Aldwark Grange (1748) had 400 sheep and 85 lambs worth £145

---

[20] Plot, op. cit., pp. 107–8; H. Kirke, 'Dr. Clegg, Minister and Physician in the 17th and 18th
Centuries', Derbys. Arch. J., xxxv, 1913, p. 27: "Dec. 22nd 1729: The Scotch cow was killed,
and proved to be very fat."

and wool priced at £28. On the millstone grit, George Howe of Edale, yeoman (1691), had a flock valued at £50; William Allen of High Forest, Leek, husbandman (1698), had 110 sheep, 69 ewes, and 69 lambs worth £55; John Goodyear of Ladybooth, Edale, yeoman (1711), had 31 sheep, 183 old sheep, and 63 hoggs, valued at £54; and John Kinder of Hill House, Glossop, yeoman (1748), had 147 sheep worth £33, yarn and wool priced at £30, and woollen cloth valued at £39. A wool fair was held annually at Chapel-en-le-Frith and a great wether fair was held at Leek.[21] The manufacture of woollen cloth was a well-established industry in north-west Derbyshire and the adjoining parts of Cheshire, and inventories suggest a structure similar to that in the West Riding and Lancashire. Thus, John Radcliffe of New Mills (1694) was a yeoman who had two pairs of looms and a dyeing lead, Robert Fox of Bamford (1697) was a cardmaker whose farm stock was appraised at £61, and William Jackson, a Mottram clothier (1747), had 4 kine, hay, and corn valued at £16, cloth and wool worth £25, and looms and other equipment worth £5. Flax and hemp were grown only in small quantities, and linen weavers like William Moss of Ashton (1741) and Thomas Wylde of Hyde (1747) probably used imported Irish flax, as did the weavers of Lancashire. As for other branches of the textile trades, there were silk manufacturers in seventeenth-century Leek, and framework knitters by the second decade of the eighteenth century at Litton and some of the neighbouring settlements. Much of this latter development was due to the Baker and Gardom families, who made cotton, worsted, and silk stockings, and socks, gloves, and mitts for sale in Yorkshire and the American colonies. The connection with agriculture was again a strong one, and in 1743 Francis Baker of Tideswell, hosier, had 103 old sheep, 56 hoggs, 5 horses, 2 bullocks, and 11 stocking frames, as well as debts due to him of £517.[22]

Derbyshire millstones had long enjoyed a national reputation, and the task of transporting them across the moors to the inland port of Bawtry, though laborious, was nonetheless a profitable one. In 1692 John Houghton referred to the "rich quarries of mill-stones [that] serve most part of the kingdom, and they are worth 8, 9, or 10 pounds the pair", also "grindstones of all sorts, from 5 or 6 foot diameter and under, and scythe-stones in abundance, which serve all parts of the kingdom".[23] But of course it was the lead

[21] Plot, op. cit., p. 109 ("Nor comes this northern part of Staffordshire much behind the south in breeding of sheep", which were small, with black noses and coarse wool); Cheshire RO, DCH/II/39; D. W. Shimwell, 'Sheep Grazing Intensity in Edale, Derbyshire, 1692–1747, and its Effects on Blanket Peat Erosion', Derbys. Arch. J., XCIV, 1974, pp. 35–40.

[22] H. Holland, General View of the Agriculture of Cheshire, London, 1808, p. 326; Davies, op. cit., p. 138; VCH Staffs., II, p. 206; PRO, MPC/39 (map of Hope, 1635–40: "the tenters at Walkmill place"), IR/1/41, 42, 43; Chapman, op. cit.; Sheffield Central Library, Barker, 248, 277–8, 430, 510, 511, 518; Peak Forest parish records, probate inventories of peculiar jurisdiction.

[23] Houghton, op. cit., II, no. 44; Plot, op. cit., p. 110; D. Hey, Packmen, Carriers and Packhorse Roads, Leicester, 1980, pp. 140–7.

industry that was the chief source of wealth for all classes of society in the limestone part of the Peak District. The dukes of Devonshire and Rutland benefited from royalties and invested in plant; gentry families like the Gells of Hopton, the Eyres of Hassop, and the Bebingtons of Dethick were deeply involved in the trade; and families such as the Barkers rose to prosperity as lead merchants, responsible for exports via the Trent river ports. Anthony Wall of Wensley (1716) was a middleman, with £87 invested in farm stock and equipment, £180 in bonds and securities, and ore, lead, and offal valued at £340. By 1640 most of the larger lead veins had been worked down to the water table, and drainage soughs and, eventually, Newcomen pumping engines had to be installed. Companies with strong financial backing were necessary for such projects. Nevertheless, the typical miner remained an independent figure, working a small mine in a wild countryside, grazing a few animals, and cultivating a close of oats or barley. Bryan Melland, a Middleton-by-Youlgreave miner (1635), had corn upon the ground, haystacks, and 2 fields of hay, worth £15 15s., 3 kine, 2 bullocks, and 1 heifer worth £11 10s., and mining tools valued at £1 2s. A much poorer family was described vividly by Defoe as living in a cave on Brassington Moor. The father worked in the mines, and when the mother had time to spare, she washed the ore. They had a little close of barley, which was ready to be harvested, and a few pigs and a cow. Yet the five children looked "plump and fat, ruddy and wholesome", the cave was partitioned into three rooms, and there was nothing that "look'd like the dirt and nastiness of the miserable cottages of the poor" of other regions. Hundreds, if not thousands, of miners were poor, but not desperately so, at that time.[24]

At Wirksworth, Defoe found that "however rugged the hills were, the vales were everywhere fruitful, well inhabited, the markets well supplied, and the provisions extraordinary good; not forgetting the ale". The lowlands of south Derbyshire and east Staffordshire formed part of the great Midland plain. The Bunter sands and Keuper marls were overlain with soils which varied from deep, sandy loams to strong clays, and along the wide river valleys were rich alluviums, which provided some of the finest meadows in the country. Brown described this part of Derbyshire as the fertile region.[25] Farms were generally of small or medium size; at Burton-on-Trent in 1655

[24] T. D. Ford and J. H. Rieuwerts, eds., *Lead Mining in the Peak District*, Bakewell, 1968, p. 15; N. Kirkham, *Derbyshire Lead Mining through the Centuries*, Truro, 1968, pp. 24, 25, 85, 91, 112; Hey, *Packmen*, pp. 119–23; PRO, E 317 Derbys. 24, 28; Defoe, *op cit.*, II, pp. 161–5; Peak Forest parish records, inventory of Henry Hill, miner, of Peak Forest, 20 Apr. 1763 (includes "a two years old colt, £3. 10s. od., a stirk, £1. 10s. od., 17 sheep, £4. 5s. od., a cart and gares belonging, £1. 10s. od.").

[25] Defoe, *op. cit.*, II, p. 158; Brown, *op. cit.*, *passim*; W. Marshall, *The Rural Economy of the Midland Counties*, 2nd edn, 2 vols., London, 1796, I, p. 133 ("The four grand objects are mixed, in a singular manner; grain of almost every species; breeding in all its branches; dairying on a large scale; grazing, both cattle and sheep").

31 tenants had under 10 acres each, a further 8 tenants had under 20 acres, 76 families had between 20 and 50 acres, another 23 tenants had between 50 and 100 acres, and 5 families had farms of over 100 acres; and at Cubley in 1677, 30 tenants held 2,032 acres among them, and 19 cottagers held a further 46 acres. As the eighteenth century progressed, leases for years became less common, and by the 1790s farms were generally held at will.[26]

Chaddesden was typical of the region in being "a large district of good field land and excellent meadows reaching down to the Derwent". Convertible leys and multiple-field complexes enabled much of the district to remain in an open state throughout the period. The fields of Walton-upon-Trent were enclosed by agreement in 1652, and those of West Hallam about 1713; and the piecemeal enclosures at Weston-upon-Trent from 1660 onwards meant that by 1755 "What was arable before is now converted into pasture land." The process was completed by act of parliament in 1786, and ten years later Marshall reported that the region had been enclosed almost entirely.[27] According to Robert Plot, the Staffordshire claylands were generally allowed to lie fallow in ridges in the final year of a three-course rotation. Unless they were folded with sheep, the fallows were manured with cow or horse dung, and ploughed in mid June, and again at the end of August, in preparation for a crop of winter wheat. A sample of 169 probate inventories shows that throughout the period wheat and barley were the main cereals, followed by oats and peas. Woolley wrote that the principal trade of Derby was malting, "with which they supply a great part of Cheshire, Staffordshire and Lancashire", and travellers through the region were loud in their praise of its ales.[28]

Dung, lime, and marl, often mixed together, were the common manures,[29]

[26] Univ. Coll. North Wales, Lligwy coll. 846; Univ. of Reading, farm accounts, DER/2/1/1; Marshall, op. cit., I, pp. 13–14; Staffs. RO, D 1,721/3/261; Derby Central Library, deeds, 4,778; E. M. Yates, 'Aspects of Staffordshire Farming in the Seventeenth and Eighteenth Centuries', N. Staffs. J. of Field Studies, xv, 1975, pp. 26–40.

[27] Woolley, op. cit.; Tate, op. cit., p. 51; Derbys. RO, D 1,129/A/PZ1; Derby Central Library, Misc. Catton, box 16A (I wish to thank Mr D. W. H. Nielson for permission to quote from these records); Marshall, op. cit., I, p. 9; Brown, op. cit., p. 33; B. K. Roberts, 'Field Systems of the West Midlands', in A. R. H. Baker and R. A. Butlin, eds., Studies of Field Systems in the British Isles, Cambridge, 1973, p. 218.

[28] Woolley, op. cit.; Houghton, op. cit., II, no. 39 (Derby malt also exported down the Trent); Derbys. RO, D 179; Plot, op. cit., pp. 109 ("the arable lands about Marchington, Draycott in the Clay, Rolleston, Horninglow, and some other townes about Needwood, are of so rich a clay, that they produce as good hard-corne (i.e. wheat and rye), peas, beanes, etc. as any in the south, though not so much"), 340–1 (stiff lands were sown with red lammas or bearded white wheat; otherwise white lammas or a mixture was used); Marshall, op. cit., I, pp. 182, 189 (red lammas was the principal wheat, and long-eared barley was the old stock).

[29] Plot, op. cit., p. 341; Pilkington, op. cit., p. 286; Derby Central Library, deeds, 1,931 (inventory of Tobias Ireland, Marston Montgomery, gentleman, 1651: "8 loads of lime, £2"); Derbys. RO, D 410M/2a/62 (Vernon Sudbury estates: "1677. Paid Wright the lime man for 360 loads of lime, £18"), D 513M/E374 (Tunstead, c. 1700: a great quantity of ground newly limed).

but the rich meadows by the rivers, "esteemed by many, the best feeding land of England", required no treatment, for the seasonal floods "do feed them fat". At Tutbury in 1649, a meadow of fourteen acres "called the Trenches" was supplied by "the new stream of water which was latly cutt" from the Dove, and Plot noted a series of artificial channels leading from this river. The cheese producers considered that the natural grasses of the region were superior to the cultivated ones, and though clover was the subject of a tithe dispute at Lullington in 1726, it was not recorded in any of the 169 inventories; furthermore, only Robert Hawford of Yeldersley, yeoman (1741), had any turnips.[30] The average number of cattle was 16 per farm, and the number rose gradually from 13 head in the 1660s to 21 head in the 1740s. Only one of the 37 farmers in the 1660s had more than 30 cattle, but by the 1740s 10 of 33 farmers kept more than 30 head, and 4 of these men had between 45 and 60. Not only was farming becoming more specialized, small farms were obviously being engrossed into larger holdings.[31] North-country longhorns, suitable either for breeding, fattening, or the dairy, were brought into the region by the graziers. Inventories demonstrate the importance of beef cattle, but dairy products made these grazing grounds famous. The rich pastures and meadows, wrote Plot, "supply Uttoxater mercat with such vast quantities of good butter and cheese, that the cheesmongers of London have thought it worth their while to set up a factorage here, for these commodities, which are brought in from this, and the neighbouring county of Derby, in so great plenty, that the factors many mercat days (in the season) lay out no less than five hundred pounds a day, in these two commodities only". By no means all the farmers were involved in this trade, for only 96 of the 169 inventories from this region recorded cheese. As in the Cheshire cheese country, the trade expanded rapidly in the late seventeenth century in order to meet a far greater demand than before. Only Edward Bentley of Thurlanstone (1640) and Robert Hurd of Hilltop, Longford (1668) had cheese chambers in 56 inventories taken between 1640 and 1670, but during the 1690s similar rooms were listed in inventories from Aston-on-Trent, Kirk Hallam, Osmaston, Stretton-on-the-Field, Uttoxeter Woodlands, and Weston-on-Trent. In the 1740s 26 of the 33 inventories recorded cheese, with cheese chambers at Brailsford, Cubley, Ellastone, Hodnaston, and Sandiacre, and a great rise in the valuations given to dairy

---

[30] J. Norden, *The Surveyor's Dialogue*, London, 1607; PRO, E 317 Staffs. 44; Plot, *op. cit.*, p. 107; E. M. Yates, 'Enclosure and the Rise of Grassland Farming in Staffordshire', *N. Staffs. J. of Field Studies*, XIV, 1974, p. 57; Derby Central Library, deeds, 7,682.

[31] LJRO inventories (Robert Holland of Spath House, Longford, 1741, had a bull, 18 cows, 11 weanlings, 9 heifers, 16 stirks, and 5 steers, worth £140; James Osborne of Brailsford, 1744, had 21 cows, 17 calves, 8 heifers, 4 oxen, 2 bullocks, 2 bullock stirks, and 5 cow stirks, worth £193; Derby Central Library, deeds, 1,931 (inventory of Sir Francis Burdett of Foremark, 1646: 6 bulls, 24 cows, 8 calves, 19 heifers, 13 oxen, and 6 steers).

products. Cheese was also produced in neighbouring parts of the Staffordshire woodlands and on the clays and alluviums of east Derbyshire.[32]

Both oxen and horses were used for ploughing in the early years of the period, but oxen disappeared early as draught animals and were recorded in only 4 of the 46 inventories taken during the 1690s. Two horses per farm were normal in the 1640s, but a hundred years later the average number in the inventories had risen to 6½, and Ashbourne and Derby horse fairs had acquired wide reputations. Most farmers also kept a few pigs, and sheep were a major concern, for 135 of the 169 inventories recorded flocks. Two out of three flocks numbered under 50 sheep, but 11 farmers had more than 100, and Humphrey Harris of Compton, near Ashbourne, yeoman (1718), was a grazier with an exceptionally large flock of 72 shear sheep, 203 ewes, 85 wethers, and 129 lambs, together worth nearly £290, and 360 fleeces of wool, valued at £61. He also had cattle, horses, and pigs worth £133, cheese in a chamber valued at £14, and a store of hay priced at £60, but he grew no corn other than a crop of oats worth £16 3s. 4d.[33]

Few rural industries flourished in this region during the seventeenth century, though Ticknall pottery enjoyed a wide reputation,[34] and a few weavers were scattered around the countryside. A census of the small market town of Melbourne and the hamlet of King's Newton, taken in 1695, named 20 farmers or landowners, 44 labourers, and 54 men who were employed in 29 different trades or crafts. During the eighteenth century framework knitting became the chief source of employment for the region's landless poor. Masters had established themselves in many of the villages by 1715, and though Melbourne had no knitters in 1695, by 1789 it had 80 frames. As in Leicestershire and Nottinghamshire, a greatly increased population was supported by this humble craft.[35]

[32] J. J. Cartwright, ed., *The Travels through England of Dr. Richard Pococke* (1750–1), London, 1888, I, p. 220 ("They have a great trade at Burton in tanning and well frequented markets"); Pilkington, *op. cit.*, p. 313; Plot, *op. cit.*, p. 108; A. Henstock, 'Cheese Manufacture and Marketing in Derbyshire and North Staffordshire, 1670–1870', *Derbys. Arch. J.*, LXXXIX, 1969, pp. 32–46; J. C. Cox, *Three Centuries of Derbyshire Annals*, London, 1890, II, p. 292 (the cattle plague reached Derbyshire in 1747).

[33] Plot, *op. cit.*, p. 352 (fleeces were somewhat finer than in the north); Woolley, *op. cit.*; E. Kerridge, *The Agricultural Revolution*, London, 1967, p. 92; Marshall, *op. cit.*, I, p. 331. 'Fleaks' or hurdles for folding sheep are recorded in LJRO, inventories of William Blunstone, Sandiacre (1692), Paul Blunston, Kirk Hallam (1692), Joseph Crawshaw, Measham (1698), and John Bates, Measham (1747).

[34] Ticknall ware is recorded in LJRO, inventory of Henry Baddeley, Cannock, labourer (1690); Leics. RO, inventories of Richard Wilburne, Syston, matmaker (1664), Thomas Simpson, Syston, shoemaker (1667), William Fryer, Countesthorpe, miller (1674), Christopher Almey, Syston, labourer (1680), John Simpkin, Thurmaston, yeoman (1682); and Cheshire RO, inventory of Thomas Bancroft, Marple, yeoman (1694).

[35] PRO, IR/1/41, 42, 43, records framework knitters at Aston-upon-Trent, Breadsall, Chellaston, Derby, Dovefield, Ireton Wood, Kirk Ireton, Little Eaton, Melbourne, Mugginton, Sawley, Shardlow, and Smisby; W. G. Briggs, 'Records of an Apprenticeship Charity, 1685–1753',

Staffordshire was described by the justices of the peace in 1636 as "for the most part barren, one fourth being heath and waste, and another fourth being chases and parks". Fifty years later Plot concluded that "a third part at least, if not half this county, must be confest when all's done, to be barren heathy, and gorsy grounds, and woodland". Much of the Staffordshire woodland region consisted of strong clays or clay loams that were difficult to work, or of poor heathy soils, suitable only for grazing. Nevertheless, there were many fine pastures, and Celia Fiennes described the district beyond Uttoxeter as "well wooded and full of enclosures, good rich ground". For all practical purposes, Cannock Chase and Kinver Forest had lost their status as royal forests, though they retained their character as areas of wood pasture and large commons. Needwood Forest, on the other hand, survived intact until the early nineteenth century. In 1654 the Commonwealth tried to claim 4,610 acres and to divide a similar portion among the twenty-two townships claiming common rights there. The plan was resisted fiercely, and troops had to be brought in to control the many people who were outraged at the threatened loss of their privileges. A similar scheme in 1663 provoked further rioting, for without the common pastures the whole economy of the small family farms would have collapsed. The justices of the peace understood this economy better than did the government's advisers, and their further concern with maintaining the poor led them to support the protesters.[36]

As this was a woodland region, settlements were scattered, and the manorial and parochial boundaries were confused. The lords and the parsons did not have the authority of their counterparts in the champion districts. Freeholders were numerous, and it was common for individuals to hold separate parts of their estates by different tenures. At the beginning of the period, long leases at low rents but with large entry fines were widespread, and sometimes, as in the manor of Newcastle under Lyme, these fines were certain. However, the long process by which these tenures were replaced by annual leases and rack rents was soon under way. In his last treatise before his death in 1691, Richard Baxter pleaded eloquently for the poor husbandman, who was constantly worried by the insecurity of his position. On the Leveson-Gower estates, the number of family farms declined during the eighteenth century until there was a marked contrast between the large

Derbys. Arch. J., LXXIV, 1954, pp. 43–61, refers to framework knitters in Mickleover (1691), Brailsford, Breadsall, Chaddesden, Chellaston, Dalbury Lees, Duffield, Mugginton, Quarndon, and Derby, Horsley, Kilburn, and Nottingham.

[36] AHEW, *IV, 1500–1640*, p. 99; Plot, *op. cit.*, p. 110 (33 of the 50 parks that had been well stocked with deer in the Civil War were still in existence in 1686); PRO, E 317 Staffs. 44 (9 parks which covered 1,880 acres on the edge of Needwood Forest in 1649 were much decayed, having little timber other than saplings, but deer still roamed within their pales); J. Thirsk, 'Horn and Thorn in Staffordshire: The Economy of a Pastoral County', *N. Staffs. J. of Field Studies*, IX, 1969, pp. 1–16; Fiennes, *op. cit.*, p. 109; Staffs. RO, D 1,721/3/261.

tenant farmers with 200–400 acres and the great majority with under 20 acres.[37]

The hearth-tax levies of the reign of Charles II show that whereas half the Staffordshire townships had a mixture of all classes, in the other half the rich and poor were kept apart. The parish of West Bromwich was typical in that, until the eighteenth century, settlement consisted largely of small groups of cottages or 'ends' around the heaths. The opportunities for industrial employment and for keeping a few cows and sheep attracted a great influx of squatters and supported a natural increase in population. By 1723, 99 cottages had encroached upon the West Bromwich wastes. The freeholders made sporadic attempts to check these encroachments, but in the long run their efforts were to no avail. Nearby, in Walsall and Bloxwich, it was reported in 1763 that 42 acres had been taken in by 211 separate encroachments.[38] Occasionally, agreements were made to enclose parts of the commons, as at Kingswinford (1684), Mapleton Callow (1731), and Trentham (1731), but, in general, large tracts of heath and wood remained. Common rights were vital to both farmers and cottagers, and the provision contained in the lease acquired by Edward Lyddyatt of Himley in 1653, which gave him the right to graze 30 beasts and 200 sheep on the common, was both usual and necessary.[39]

The amount of arable land was kept to a minimum, and the small open fields of the ancient villages and hamlets varied greatly in size and in rate of survival.[40] In a sample of 197 inventories from the Staffordshire

[37] M. B. Rowlands, *Masters and Men in the West Midland Metalware Trades before the Industrial Revolution*, Manchester, 1975, p. 16; PRO, E 317 Staffs. 38; R. Baxter, *The Reverend Richard Baxter's Last Treatise*, ed. F. J. Powicke, London, 1926; J. R. Wordie, 'Social Change on the Leveson-Gower Estates, 1714–1832', EcHR, xxvii, 4, 1974, pp. 593–609; Staffs. RO, D 590/349, D 593/H/14/3/27 and 36, D 615/E/13/1, D 1,721/3/261, D 1,744/22.

[38] Thirsk, 'Horn and Thorn'; *VCH Staffs.*, xvii, pp. 3, 28, 183; LJRO, Inventories of Henry Baddeley of Cannock, labourer, 1690 (4 cows, 4 heifers, 3 yearlings, a calf, a colt, 42 sheep and lambs, cheese, an old cart and gears for a horse, a crop of hay, but no corn), and John Barnes of Shelton, workman, 1691 (2 kine, 1 heifer, 1 swine, 10 sheep and lambs, hay and corn).

[39] Dudley Central Library, box 1, bdle 15, and box 11, bdle 20; Derbys. RO, T 201 to 221; Staffs. RO, D 595/L/1/7/2; Cheshire RO, DWS/16/9/8.

[40] K. R. Thomas, 'The Enclosure of Open Fields and Commons in Staffordshire', *Staffs. Historical Collections*, 1931, pp. 60–9 (only 21 townships had open fields enclosed by act of parliament); Dudley Central Library, box 1, bdle 15 (Himley, 1653 lease of "a leasow or pasture being part of the upper field or clayfield, containing 18 acres"; in 1690, field lands were said to have been worth only 6s. an acre before enclosure, but to have sold afterwards at 10s.); Staffs. RO, D 593/B/1/17/10 (1685 agreement to enclose at Over Penn), D 1,788, pcel 17, bdle 1 (1714 consultations about enclosure at Meretown, "all the neighbouring fields being in a manner inclosed"), D 661/1/82 (1699 enclosure proposals at Lichfield met with opposition from "sheepmasters"), D 590/349, 369; Derbys. RO, T 201 to 221; Plot, *op. cit.*, pp. 107, 109, 340–5; Roberts, *op. cit.*, pp. 190, 210, 221; P. and M. Spufford, *History of Eccleshall*, Keele, 1964, pp. 30–5; R. Hebden, 'The Development of the Settlement Pattern and Farming in the Shenstone Area', *Lichfield & S. Staffs. Arch. & Hist. Soc.*, iii, 1961–2, pp. 27–39; Yates, 'Enclosure', p. 49.

woodlands, 110 listed cereals simply as corn or "corn and malt". The crops that were listed included oats, barley, wheat, rye, and a few beans and vetches.[41] Estate accounts and inventories show that a great deal of attention was paid to improving the grassland by sowing clover and ryegrass, and by marling and liming. Clover was recorded in inventories from Patshall (1697), Trysull (1698), Wombourne (1716), and Stapencells (1718), in the south-western part of the county, and during the 1740s at Bobbington, Bradley, Colton, Enfield, Gayton, Hamstall, and Lapley; it was also grown on several of the large estates from at least 1707 onwards and was the subject of tithe disputes at Sedgley (1714) and Leighford (1738).[42]

The farmers' main investment was in cattle. The 197 inventories had a median average of 17 head per farm, rising from 15 or 16 in the 1640s to 21 a hundred years later. But even at the beginning of the period there were some large herds; Edward Brett of Burslem, yeoman (1646), had 56 head of cattle, and John Lovatt of Shelton, yeoman (1665), had 53. Dairying was particularly important in those woodland townships that lay within convenient travelling distance of Uttoxeter or which adjoined the Cheshire plain. Thus, John Belcher of Field (1747) had 20 milch cows amongst his 55 cattle, and Benjamin Cotton of Bradley (1748) had 24 cows, 15 calves, 19 twinters, 13 stirks, 7 bullocks, and 4 feeding beasts. Cheese was recorded in 129 of the 197 inventories, and by the 1660s fairly large quantities were being produced. William Penn, a Dunsley scythesmith, had a cheese chamber in 1642, and similar rooms were recorded in the 1660s at Chelsey, Knulton, Oulton, and Stone, and between 1690 and 1750 at Bradley, Burslem, Colton, Hamstall Ridware, Ingestre, Lapley, Leigh, Longton, Meaford, and Seisdon. Elsewhere, more emphasis was placed on rearing. Lord Gower's steward reported in 1715 on his purchase at the fairs of 53 oxen and 43 barren cattle, but the smaller farmers bred most of their own replacements. Tanning was

---

[41] LJRO, inventories (wheat was more common in the 1740s, and Thomas Harding of Gayton (1746) had an exceptionally large store, valued at £115, compared with a valuation of £36 10s. for the rest of his crops. Joseph Hawksford of Handsworth, tanner (1748), had "three heifers and two calves in the turnips", and this root crop is recorded in estate papers between 1706 and 1754); Staffs. RO, D 603/C45/XVIC, D 661/18/1, D 661/21/4/1, D 661/21/5/3-5, D 1,788/V7; E. J. Evans, 'Tithing Customs and Disputes: The Evidence of Glebe Terriers, 1698–1850', AHR, XVIII, 1, 1970, pp. 17–35, refers to a dispute over tithes of turnips and carrots at Darlaston (1708), and of potatoes, parsnips, carrots, and turnips at Caverswall (1722); Staffs. RO, D 1,788, pcel 61, bdle 3, refers to hop ground and an apple mill at Aqualate, and apples are recorded in the inventories of Thomas How, Leigh (1713), Humphrey Parks, High Onn (1716), and John Wright, Bradley (1740: in an "apple chamber").

[42] Staffs. RO, D 593/F/2/16, D 661/21/4/1, D 661/21/5/3-5, D 798/2/4/2 and 3, D 1,788/V7; Dudley Central Library, box 5, bdle 5. For marl and lime, see Plot, op. cit., pp. 109, 119; Staffs. RO, D 593/F/1/35, D 798/2/4/2; PRO, E 317 Staffs. 38; LJRO, inventories of Thomas Fenton, Boothen (1639), Edward Brett, Burslem (1646), Katherine Machin, Seabridge (1664), and John Lovatt, Shelton (1665).

an important associated activity, and Walsall, in particular, became a centre for the leather trades and general saddler's ironmongery.[43]

The average number of horses per farm rose from just over 2 in the 1640s to $7\frac{1}{2}$ by the middle of the eighteenth century; none of the 40 inventories from the 1640s recorded more than 5 horses, but a hundred years later there were strings of 17, 20, and 24. Horse fairs were held at Brewood, Dudley, Tutbury, and Penkridge, where Defoe found "really incredible numbers of the finest and most beautiful horses that can any where be seen", including some from north Yorkshire and Durham.[44] Pigs are recorded in 179 of the 197 inventories, though never in large numbers, and 137 of the farmers kept flocks of sheep; more than two out of three flocks numbered less than 50, but 18 farmers kept more than 100. The largest flocks were in or near Kinver Forest, by the Shropshire ryelands. William Penn of Dunsley (1642) had 284 sheep, John Spencer of Stapencells (1718) had 273, and Hugh Moor of Penn (1745) had 253. At Kinver "the woollen manufacture" was "carried on pretty briskly in narrow cloths, both coarse and fine", and there were other centres of the cloth and felting trades at Burton, Newcastle under Lyme, and Tamworth. The rural workers in these trades were, as usual, part-time farmers. Hemp and flax were sown throughout the region in Plot's day, and the Staffordshire methods of cultivation were praised by Robert Sharrock. These crops were the subject of tithe disputes at Tixall (1698), Bulterton (1698), and Biddulph (1705), but inventories suggest that all the textile crafts were in decline by the late seventeenth century, and were soon to be of little importance.[45]

Staffordshire was rich in minerals, and by the seventeenth century its two coalfields were producing great amounts of cheap fuel. Colliers formed an important element in the rural population, and they still preserved their

[43] LJRO, inventories; Staffs. RO, D 593/F/2/16, D 593/F/3/2/18, D 1,788, pcel 69; D. G. Vaisey, ed., 'Probate Inventories of Lichfield and District, 1568–1680', Staffs. Rec. Soc., 4th ser., v, 1969; L. A. Clarkson, 'The Leather Crafts in Tudor and Stuart England', AHR, XIV, 1, 1966, pp. 25–39; W. H. B. Court, The Rise of the Midland Industries, 1600–1838, rev. edn, London, 1953, p. 31.

[44] Defoe, op. cit., II, p. 78; Dudley Central Library, box 24, bdle 5 (accounts of three horse fairs per annum, 1702ff); Staffs. RO, D 798/3/1/7, D 1,788, pcel 69; Cheshire RO, DCR/28/21; LJRO, inventories of John Belcher, Field (1747), Benjamin Cotton, Bradley (1748), and Thomas Harding, Gayton (1746).

[45] Staffs. RO, D 593/F/2/16, 25, D 1,788, pcels 61, 69; Plot, op. cit., p. 109; LJRO, inventories of Richard Stringer, Fenton Calvert, feltmaker, 1662 (felts and wool worth £65, and 17 cattle, with other livestock, corn, and equipment, worth £89) and Ralph Scragge, Milwich, webster, 1647 (farm stock accounted for 85 per cent of an inventory valued at £37 9s.); hemp was recorded in 33 inventories, and flax in 23; 21 of 40 inventories mentioned some textiles in the 1640s, but only 6 of the 35 inventories recorded similar items a century later; Dudley Central Library, box 5, bdle 5 (tithe of flax at Coseley, 1714); E. J. Evans, op. cit., pp. 21–7; R. Sharrock, An Improvement to the Art of Gardening, London, 1694, pp. 43–4.

attachment to the land.[46] The rural metalworkers of south Staffordshire were also part-time farmers until about 1720, when the shift to a predominantly industrial economy became pronounced, but a generation later there were still nailers like Joseph Whitehouse of Sedgley (1743), with four cows worth £17 and crops of wheat and oats valued at £5 5s., who clung to the older way of life. The area was characterized by a great diversity of occupations and by considerable localization of the different trades. The continuity of family names is striking in the scythemaking, lockmaking, and nailing trades in Sedgley, and no doubt elsewhere, for the family was the unit of production, and the workshops rarely contained more than one hearth. The scythesmiths, in particular, had an important stake in the land, and they tended to be concentrated in the better agricultural districts, near to the markets. The rural nailers practised husbandry on a much more modest scale, but yeomen like William Stringer of West Bromwich (1695) and John Gibbins of Sedgley (1698) also had smith's workshops and tools. Richard Baxter thought that the metalworkers were better off than husbandmen with only one string to their bow, for the work was less arduous and the earnings more certain. A recent writer concludes that this was not a poor district where families eked out a living through by-employments, but one rich in industrial resources with expanding opportunities for profit. So vigorous was the response to these opportunities that by the end of the period the craftsman-farmers were heavily outnumbered by those engaged solely in industrial employments.[47] North Staffordshire also had its metalworkers, and an iron market was held at Newcastle under Lyme, but the area was famous chiefly for its pottery. In the seventeenth century the scattered settlements of Burslem parish contained twenty to thirty farmer-potters, about half of whom were of yeoman rank. The proportion of personal estate invested in farming declined as the number of potters doubled between 1660 and 1710 and doubled again by 1760, and after about 1720 the industry could no longer be described as domestic in terms of size, specialization, and division of labour.[48] The connection with agriculture was gradually weakened, but for most of the period 1640–1750 Staffordshire provided outstanding examples of the way in which farming and industry could be combined with profit.

[46] Staffs. RO, D 593/F/1/35, D 593/K/1/1/4, D 593/P/13/13, D 593/P/16/1/16, D 1,788, pcel 61, bdle 5; PRO, E 317 Staffs. 38; LJRO, inventories of Humphrey Stringer, Longdon, collier (1657), and Edward Brett, Burslem, yeoman (1646).

[47] Rowlands, op. cit., upon which this section is based; Court, op. cit., pp. 65–8; Thirsk, 'Horn and Thorn'; LJRO, inventories, e.g. John Browne, Kingswinford, nailer (1661), Joseph Darby, Kingswinford, nailer (1698), William Penn, Dunsley, scythesmith, 1642 (farm stock £240, cheese chamber, wool chamber, 3 leases, etc.); Dudley Central Library, box 1, bdle 15 (lease of a blademill and land at Himley, 1653).

[48] L. Weatherill, The Pottery Trade and North Staffordshire, 1660–1760, Manchester, 1971; PRO, E 317 Staffs. 38 ("One messuage called Iron Markett Hall, lying in a street called Iron Markett Street").

In the seventeenth century families with ten to fifty acres and generous common rights formed the stable core of Cheshire and Shropshire's rural communities. The hearth-tax returns show that here were fewer of the very rich but also fewer paupers than in the corn-growing regions. The family farms were sometimes freehold, but more commonly they were held by leases for three lives, a system of tenure that had become normal in the region during the previous century. Leaseholders usually had the right to sell their leases, to sublet, and to add new lives as they saw fit. On the Bridgewater estates, the entry fines were increased fifteenfold on average between 1637 and 1641 (and in some cases up to thirtyfold), but the money was paid off over a short period of years without great difficulty. The yeomen and husbandmen of this pastoral region were obviously flourishing at the time. In line with national trends, entry fines were reduced considerably after the Restoration, but they still maintained a higher level than before the wars. However, by the end of the period great changes were under way, so that by the nineteenth century the farming communities of Cheshire and Shropshire were divided sharply between the rich and poor, with comparatively few of the middling peasants. The border region was one of the last places to attract immigrant squatters, but by the second half of the seventeenth century they were giving cause for concern. Whereas they had previously been absorbed into the existing communities, they now formed distinctive squatter settlements on the edges of the heaths, hills, woods, and commons. By 1700 labourers probably composed between a third and a half of the population. But the greater threat to the family farms came from above. The middle and late eighteenth century saw the end of the three-life lease system in favour of tenancy-at-will, the engrossing of tenements into farms of 300–400 acres, and in some places a change of emphasis to a more mixed form of husbandry. On the whole, however, the traditional pasture economy associated with family farms survived during the period 1640–1750.[49]

The Cheshire plain had been extensively glaciated and was overlain with a wide variety of soils, especially blends of boulder clays, sands, and gravels. The most productive were the brown-earths, which were easy to work and which had attracted early settlers. More common, however, were the gley soils, which were heavy to till, but excellent for grazing. There were also peat mosses near the Mersey, and patches of sandy heaths, especially in north

[49] D. Hey, *An English Rural Community: Myddle under the Tudors and Stuarts*, Leicester, 1974; E. Hopkins, 'The Re-leasing of the Ellesmere Estates, 1637–42', AHR, X, 1, 1962, pp. 14–28; Wordie, *op. cit.*; M. C. Hill, 'The Wealdmoors, 1560–1660', *Shrops. Arch. J.*, LIV, 1951–3, pp. 255–326; Davies, *Cheshire*, pp. 13–18, 33–5; Holland, *Cheshire*, pp. 93, 108; J. Plymley, *General View of the Agriculture of Shropshire*, London, 1803, p. 135; PRO, E 317 Cheshire 12, 19; Univ. Coll. N. Wales Library, Mostyn 6,090, 6,093; Derby Central Library, Brookhill 137; Cheshire RO, DCH/C/745; DCH/1/112, DCR/8c, DCR/59/6, DDX 267; Salop. RO, Attingham 112/2, 698 (1716: "Tenants at rack in this country will not be tied to any repairs, as for taking leases they do not at present seem forward thereto").

Shropshire. The pastoral economy had been developed during the century and a half prior to 1640. The small open fields were enclosed quietly and by agreement; only two parliamentary acts were needed to complete this process in Cheshire, and only seven acts were required in Shropshire.[50] The enclosure of commons and wastes by the agreement of lords and freeholders continued throughout the period. In north Shropshire, parts of Moston common, 200 acres of Weston common, and 500 acres of Moreton wood were enclosed on the Hill estates, 73 acres of Kingsall common and Ridge moor were enclosed on the Bridgewater estates, and agreements were made to enclose 253 acres of Espley-upon-Hine-Heath in 1693, Little Drayton heath in 1704, and 600 acres of the dry part of Whixall common in 1703, the residue being "wet moorish ground always used as common of turbary". In Cheshire, 277 acres of Soughall common had by 1650 recently been taken in, and an example of the numerous small enclosures of this period is provided by a lease to John Coppocke of Timperley (1648) of 4 Cheshire acres lying upon the moss, "stumped, holed, or meyred out too be inclosed".[51] Sufficient common grazing was normally preserved to enable the small farmers to gain a livelihood.[52] However, not all enclosures were carried through peaceably; in 1650 some Marbury tenants threw down the fences erected by a neighbour, and after the Restoration a protracted dispute began over proposals to enclose Delamere Forest. The protagonists argued that enclosure would increase tillage, furnish the markets, and bring increased revenue to the state, but those who lived in or near the forest understood the value of their common rights and knew that the poor were dependent upon the underwoods for fuel. The crown finally dropped its proposals in 1673. When the Little Drayton commons were enclosed in 1704 the poor were left an allotment, and his experience at Little Budworth and elsewhere caused Viscount Cholmondeley to reject further enclosures in 1713 on the grounds that such action would cause a great increase in the poor rates.[53]

[50] W. B. Mercer, *A Survey of the Agriculture of Cheshire*, London, 1963; D. Sylvester, *The Rural Landscape of the Welsh Borderland*, London, 1969; T. Rowley, *The Shropshire Landscape*, London, 1972, p. 138; G. Elliott, 'Field Systems of Northwest England', in Baker and Butlin, *op. cit.*, pp. 90–2; Hey, *Myddle*, pp. 31–9 (the draining of glacial meres and clearing of the woods had generally occurred prior to 1640).

[51] Salop. RO, Attingham 112/2,379, 2,443, 2,480, 2,703, 212/395, Acton Reynold 322, 427/1; PRO, E 317 Cheshire 22; Univ. Coll. Wales Library, Baron Hill 335. One Cheshire acre = 10,240 sq. yd.

[52] Cheshire RO, DDX 267 (Rudheath common covered 260 Cheshire acres in 1658), DBN/C/17B/1 (rights of turbary on Halton Moss); Staffs. RO, D 593/H/14/2/17 (882 acres of commons and waste in Albrightlee, 1666); Shrewsbury Public Library, deeds, 2,665 (568 acres on the Weald moors in Kinnersley, 1719); W. J. Slack, *The Lordship of Oswestry, 1393–1607*, Shrewsbury, 1951, pp. 19–20 (3,600 acres within the lordship of Oswestry remained unenclosed until 1786. This area formed a continuation of the Denbighshire hills and was Welsh in character).

[53] Holland, *op. cit.*, p. 208; Cheshire RO, DAR/A/14, 29, 47, 52, 74, DAR/H/10, DCH/L/33; Salop. RO, 327/box 49.

Cereals were grown only as subsistence crops, and in times of dearth corn had to be imported into the region. Fine crops of barley could be grown on the brown-earths, but most soils were unsuited to arable production. When Myddlewood common was "cutt and burnt and sowed with corne" during the Civil Wars, most of the barley had to be pulled up by the root because it was too short to be cut, and the experiment was not repeated. In a sample of 306 Cheshire inventories and 270 north Shropshire inventories, 266 refer only to corn or "corn and malt", and during the 1740s 23 of 65 Cheshire inventories listed no crops at all. Barley, oats, wheat, peas, rye, beans, and vetches were each recorded, but the valuations were small compared with those given to livestock.[54] Small plots of potatoes were cultivated near the Lancashire border; otherwise new crops were rarely tried.[55]

Lime was spread on some north Shropshire estates during the first half of the eighteenth century, but transport costs were usually prohibitive, and the Cheshire records of this period are silent about the practice.[56] The traditional improvement was marling, and though the claylands had by now taken as much as they could absorb profitably, marl was still valuable in preventing the reclaimed mosslands from shrinking and in providing a physical bond which enabled sandy land to retain water. Marl carts are recorded in inventories from Nether Alderley (1642), Sunderland (1716), Baguley (1743), and Over Peover (1745), and estate agents throughout the period stressed the value of spreading marl. Other experiments included the use of sea sludge and of small pieces of moss earth, called mullock, as manures; and it was claimed in 1749 that "the kinds of these enrichments are very numerous and some places abound with those kinds which are not known in other parts". Small-scale improvements put into effect between 1640 and 1750 were collectively of great importance. William Watkins was a

[54] Holland, op. cit., p. 125; W. Stout, The Autobiography of William Stout of Lancaster, 1665–1752, ed. J. D. Marshall, Manchester, 1967, p. 204; R. Gough, Antiquityes and Memoyres of the Parish of Myddle, London, 1875, p. 33; Cheshire RO, DAR 1/44, DEO/2/1, EDC/5/70 (vetches and 'frenchwheat' grown on new ground at Ribchester, 1670: I am indebted to Dr J. Addy for this reference); LJRO and Cheshire RO, inventories (during the eighteenth century less attention was paid to all crops, particularly to peas, beans, and rye).

[55] Turnips were grown as a garden crop on the Cholmondeley estates, 1697 – Cheshire RO, DCH/L/10. Hops are recorded in the inventories of Elizabeth Cotton, Cumbermere (1647), Humphrey Hayes, Hatherton (1716), Henry Tyrer, Poulton-cum-Seacombe (1742), and John Becket, Wrenbury (1744). For potatoes, see Davies, op. cit., pp. 112, 131; Cheshire RO, inventories of John Dunbebin, Over Walton (1696), Richard Irlam, Ashton-upon-Mersey (1716), John Richardson, Etchells (1741), George Barlow, Altrincham (1742), John Becket, Wrenbury (1744); Salop. RO, Attingham 112/box 20 (1747: "George Watson has a piece of ground called the paddock part of which is boggy, which he has a mind to improve. He thinks it could best be done by digging it for potatoes. He would only plant these provided the vicar were not to have the tithes").

[56] Shrewsbury Public Library, deeds, 18,219, 18,290; Salop. RO, Attingham 112/box 20, Willey 1,224/box 177; LJRO, inventory of David Powell, Hodnet (1740).

Shropshire gentleman, whose "chiefe delight was in good husbandry...He found [Shotton] farm much overgrowne with thornes, briars and rubish. He imployd many day labourers (to whom he was a good benefactor) in cleareing and ridding his land; and having the benefitt of good marle, he much improved his land." But Richard Gough, the author of these remarks, could tell also of many families who wasted their estates through excessive drinking, and of characters like Thomas Newnes who "was unskilled in husbandry, tho' hee would talke much of it".[57]

The spirit of improvement is also evident in a letter from John Witter, dated 1669, which accompanied a parcel of French sainfoin seed sent from London to his parents in Cheshire. "It loveth to groe upon such kind of warme sande barin ground as the windmill hill ground is", he wrote, and he gave detailed instructions as to its cultivation. Its use would have been restricted to the sandy pastures that were given over to sheep grazing. In 1808 Holland maintained that "the species of grass met with were generally such as nature offers, or arose from seed sown without any regard for selection". The natural grasses grew early in the spring and continued late in the year, for the climate was mild, the rainfall high, and numerous streams flowed through the heavy clays. In north Shropshire, clover was grown at Berwick (1694), Hodnet (1697), Quaking Bridge (1704), Smethcott (1711), Baschurch (1713), and on one out of every five farms in the 1740s. In Cheshire, however, although clover was grown at Weverham (1694), Altrincham (1697), Larton (1699), Eyton (1710), Ashley (1717), Utkinton (1720), Halton (1746), and Agden (1759), it was not recorded in any of the 65 inventories taken from the 1740s. On most of the Cheshire farms cattle could be fattened and milk yields maintained just as well without the aid of clover.[58]

Cattle were the chief source of wealth for all farmers, and detailed descriptions of the herds as weanlings, yearlings, twinters, heifers, bullocks, etc. are in marked contrast to the way in which cereals were described collectively as corn. Black longhorns were the common type, but they were mixed with Irish cattle, Welsh bullocks, and a few Scots cows. The north Shropshire inventories had a median average of 15 or 16 head during the seventeenth century and 23 head in the 1740s, when the farms were getting larger. The Cheshire inventories had a median average of 16 or 17 in the

[57] Cheshire RO, DAR/A/187, DAR/H/10, DAR/1/44, DBN/C/17B/1, 11, DCA/8B, DCH/C/175, DEO/133; Salop. RO, Attingham 112/2,698, 2,703, Acton Reynold 322; Davies, *op. cit.*, pp. 110–11, 119; Mercer, *op. cit.*, pp. 3–5; Holland, *op. cit.*, p. 221; C. Leigh, *The Natural History of Lancashire, Cheshire and the Peak of Derbyshire*, Oxford, 1700, pp. 55, 65; John Rylands Library, Clowes 1,566 (mullock); Univ. Coll. N. Wales Library, Mostyn 6,093 (sea sludge); Gough, *op. cit.*, pp. 64, 129; Hey, *Myddle*, pp. 227–8. For other examples of bad management, see Salop. RO, Attingham 112/2,388 and 2,400.

[58] Cheshire RO and LJRO inventories; Cheshire RO, DAR/A/30/1, DAR/1/57, DBN/C/17B/1, DCH/L/11, DEO/2/1, DVA/5; Salop. RO, 3,067/2/76, Willey, 1,224/box 177; Shrewsbury Public Library, deeds, 18,290–1, MS 5,287; Holland, *op. cit.*, pp. 156–83.

1640s, and greater numbers of milch cows raised the average to 22 head in the 1660s. Thomas Carden of Kinnerton (1648) had 23 milking kine amongst his 68 cattle, and John Ashbrooke of Great Stanney, yeoman (1660), had 47 kine in a herd of 85 cattle. By the 1690s, however, fewer stores were kept, and hardly any oxen, and the average head fell again to 16 per farm, at which number it remained during the 1740s. Celia Fiennes remarked that she "did not see more than 20 or 30 cowes in a troope feeding, but on enquiry find the custome of the country to joyn their milking together of a whole village and to make their great cheeses".[59]

Samuel Pearson had 23 heifers grazing at Monkmoor, near Quaking Bridge (1704), and about 14 oxen which were being driven towards London. Shropshire had eighteen markets during the seventeenth century, and the sale of beef cattle attracted buyers from many parts of the country, notably London and the Wealden vales. The Attingham estate agent wrote that good, lean oxen had sold very well at the Shrewsbury horn fair in March 1748, and that "many chapmen are still in the country and want more cattle before they return". He wrote further on 15 January 1750 about the sale of a fat cow, which weighed over fifteen cwt, "She is to be slaughtered for Saturday market. She was the wonder of the market...people came in crowds from all parts of the town to look at her." Thus, rearing and fattening continued to be important, and the plentiful supply of hides provided ample opportunity for tanners.[60] However, the Cheshire plain was chiefly famous for its dairy products. The salt that was necessary to preserve such produce was obtained locally, and the grass had "a peculiar richness in it, which disposes the creatures to give a great quantity of milk".[61] Throughout the period one-half, sometimes nearly two-thirds, of the north Shropshire inventories recorded cheese, and in Cheshire the proportion was as high as five out of six. During the 1640s, the quantities were usually small, and cheese was often valued with the butter,[62] but after the Restoration the trade expanded rapidly in response

[59] Cheshire RO, DEO/133 (Egerton of Oulton demesne stock, c. 1700: 87 head of cattle), DCH/L/1/15 (Welsh bullocks, 1716), EDC/5/6 (Doddleston: Irish cattle fattened for market on Kinnerton meadows; I am indebted to Dr J. Addy for this reference); D. Woodward, 'The Anglo-Irish Livestock Trade of the Seventeenth Century', *Irish Hist. Stud.*, XVIII, 1973, pp. 489–523; T & C, p. 68; Univ. Coll. N. Wales Library, Kinmel 1,675 (Scots cattle); Cheshire RO and LJRO inventories (no oxen in the sample of 131 Cheshire inventories, 1710–50); Fiennes, *op. cit.*, p. 177.

[60] Shrewsbury Public Library, MS 5,287; Salop. RO, Attingham 112/box 20; Gough, *op. cit.*, p. 74; Kerridge, *Agricultural Revolution*, p. 131; Holland, *op. cit.*, pp. 325–6; Davies, *op. cit.*, p. 12 (hides exported down the Dee and Weaver); Cartwright, *Pococke*, p. 6 (tan leather gloves made at Nantwich); LJRO and Cheshire RO, tanners' inventories, e.g. John Chettoe, Horton, 1659, Francis Lewis, Press, 1659, Thomas Gaskell, Bradbury, 1716.

[61] PRO, E 317 Cheshire 19, 20, 21A (salt); Defoe, *op. cit.*, II, p. 72.

[62] Nevertheless, Robert Hand of Ightfield (1640) and John Prichett of Brindley (1642) both had £30 worth of cheese, Thomas Carden of Kinnerton (1648) had cheese and butter priced at £30 10s., Ralph Meakin of Crewe (1649) had 24 cwt of cheese worth £38 8s., and Elizabeth Cotton of Cumbermere (1647) had a cheese chamber.

to demand. Forty-four of a sample of 63 Cheshire inventories taken during the 1660s recorded cheese, and a quarter of these had stocks valued at over £10; John Ashbrooke of Great Stanney, yeoman (1660), had a store worth £90, Thomas Ormston of Poulton (1665) had cheese and butter priced at £140, and Thomas Parker of Whatcroft, yeoman (1667) had cheese in his cheese chamber valued at £84. During the 1690s 21 of 66 Cheshire inventories had stocks worth more than £10, and a further 36 had smaller amounts. Large quantities were made throughout the county except on the poorer grasslands of the Wirrall. The expansion of the trade in north Shropshire came a little later; John Wilson of Hinton (1690) and Ralph Harrison of Wem (1698) were yeomen with stocks worth £58 and £40, respectively, and during the 1710s six cheese chambers were recorded in a sample of 61 inventories. It is possible that people with large stores, like George Moore of Dutton Hall, yeoman (1718), who had 2 tons 5 cwt of cheese worth £49 10s., and a further £42 18s. "due for cheese sold but not gone", were not only manufacturers but factors. The cheese was sent by sea to London and the naval ports, or overland to the markets and fairs. It was said of some Cheshire carriers heading south in 1707 that "a good part of their loading with cheese was bought of them in Northampton, Dunstable and other great towns on the road". By that time, cheese was "the principal commodity of this county, and the rents of almost all the estates in it depend thereon".[63]

Too much dependency upon cattle could be dangerous, and the cattle plague brought disaster in the spring of 1750; for example, Richard Fisher of Edgeheath lost 17 head, Thomas Morton of Duckington lost 14, and in another township twenty-one farmers lost 286 cattle between them.[64] The whey milk from the dairies encouraged nearly all farmers to keep a few pigs, and Shropshire hogs, in particular, were bought for the London market.[65] Horses were normally confined to the poorer pastures or the aftermaths, and the average head per farm never rose above 4 in Cheshire; in north Shropshire it rose from fewer than 3 in the seventeenth century to 6½ in the 1740s. By that time a number of young horses were being reared on local farms, and farmers were less dependent upon imports through the fairs.[66] The inventories show that only half the Cheshire farmers kept any sheep, but that

[63] Cheshire RO, DAR/A/65/2, DBN/C/17B/11, DCH/K/1/2, DCH/K/2/52, DEO/133, DTD/9/27; P. R. Edwards, 'The Development of Dairy Farming on the North Shropshire Plain in the Seventeenth Century', *Midland Hist.*, IV, 3–4, 1978, pp. 175–90.

[64] Cheshire RO, DTD/9/3, 5, 7, 26; Salop. RO, Attingham 112/box 20.

[65] Salop. RO, Attingham 112/box 20 (1748: "We had a great fair of fat hogs on Wednesday which were all sold and at a much better price than was expected and but very few bought for London"), Acton Reynold, 1,322; Cheshire RO, DEO/133.

[66] Salop. RO, Attingham 112/box 20 (1749: "There is a fair at Stourbridge on 17 March where there usually comes a good choice of black horses. Otherwise there is only Northampton or London"), Whilley 1,224/box 299.

flocks were reared on two out of every three north Shropshire farms, particularly upon the sandy heaths. Twenty-five of the 270 Shropshire farmers had flocks valued at more than £20, and during the 1740s only 6 of 52 farms there had none at all. Richard Gough wrote in 1700 that "There is a good stoare of sheep in [Myddle] Parish whose wool if washed white and well ordered is not much inferior to the wool of Baschurch and Nesse which bears the name of the best in this country." He stressed the value of the wool rather than the mutton.[67] Between a third and a half of both the Cheshire and the north Shropshire inventories recorded wool, cloth, yarn, tow, flax, or hemp. Some craftsmen were yeoman-weavers, like William Ellis of Ruyton (1645), but generally in this region the weavers were poor people of labouring rank. In Cheshire the woollen industry became concentrated in the north-eastern uplands, and the use of local flax and hemp was gradually abandoned. In north Shropshire, however, the proportion of people involved in the textile trades hardly varied throughout the period, and Arthur Young noted that "hemp is almost universal with farmers and cottagers". Nor are all the by-employments that sustained a local economy revealed by the inventories, for wood crafts were probably widespread, and Dr Pococke noted a great manufacture of knit stockings in Nantwich.[68]

The valleys and escarpments of the Shropshire coalfield extended a little over ten miles from north to south and not more than three miles from east to west. By the early eighteenth century this coalfield was the second most important nationally, and a major iron-making district. Much of the industry was highly capitalized, but the rural population included colliers, pipemakers, potters, weavers, and metalworkers such as locksmiths, nailers, and needle makers, most of whom were part-time pastoral farmers. There were weavers like William Cludd of Madeley (1726) with no farm at all, poor colliers such as Richard Wood of Little Wenlock (1666) with 3 kine, 1 young cow, 2 pigs, and some hay, straw, and muncorn worth about £10, craftsman-farmers like Jeremiah Smith of Garmston, weaver (1723), with farm stock valued at £27, and more prosperous figures such as William Viggars, the clerk of Leighton furnace (1732), whose agricultural interest was worth £87. In general, there was ample opportunity to supplement earnings with the profits from a smallholding, or to combine a trade with the running of a farm in such a way that it is necessary to describe such families as having pursued a dual

[67] Gough, *op. cit.*, p. 175; S. Bagshaw, *History, Gazetteer, and Directory of Shropshire*, Shrewsbury, 1851, p. 22 ("The old Shropshire sheep had a black mottled face and legs, and in size were comparable with Southdowns"); Welsh sheep are referred to in Cheshire RO, DAR/1/44, DCH/L/1/10, DEO/133.

[68] Hey, *Myddle*, pp. 153–62, 180–1; A. Young, *Tours in England and Wales (Selected from the Annals of Agriculture)*, London, 1932, p. 146; Cartwright, *Pococke*, p. 6; Salop. RO, Attingham 112/box 20; Cheshire RO and LJRO, inventories (hemp was recorded in 86 north Shropshire inventories and flax in 61. Hemp was grown on 23 out of 62 farms in the 1640s, but not at all by the 65 farmers whose inventories were sampled from the 1740s).

occupation. Farming practices were similar to those elsewhere in the
county.[69]

The sandstone plain to the east of the river Severn supported more sheep
and corn and fewer cattle than any other part of Shropshire. The region was
described in 1739 as having "a fine dry sandy soil, fit for rearing rye, barley,
etc., and is therefore commonly distinguished by the name of the rye land
from the other parts of the country that lie on the west of the river". The
common fields of Bridgnorth were said to "bear grain of all kinds, and one
of them being yearly appropriated for corn, nay, the very sides of the rock
on which the town stands, though the soil there be shallow, yet when well
manured produce great crops of peas, beans, cucumbers, asparagus and all
sorts of garden herbs in perfection". As in other areas of mixed husbandry,
the sheepfold was important for maintaining fertility. In a sample of 40
inventories, 33 farmers kept sheep, and several had large flocks. Elizabeth
Barsley of Aston (1649) had 120 sheep and lambs worth £20 and wool valued
at £34; John Brooke, a Worfield gentleman (1661), had 390 sheep worth
£68; Thomas Taylor of Shipley, yeoman (1698), kept a flock of 240 sheep
valued at £82 and a store of wool worth £55; and Edward Baker of Hilton
(1749) had 500 sheep priced at £140. The inventories reveal an average of
only 7 head of cattle per farm and demonstrate the importance and the variety
of the crops. Thomas Taylor, for example, had "all sorts of corn" worth
£126 and hemp valued at £7, John Brooke had rye, muncorn, barley, peas,
oats, malt, and hay worth £133, and Edward Baker's crops included flax
valued at £32 and hemp at £16 11s. During the period 1640–1750 many
agricultural improvements were made in the valleys of the Worfe and the
Severn. The Davenports and the Whitmores invested their capital in floated
meadows, and they and others experimented with new crops and grasses.
Clover was recorded at Worfield (1694), Quatt (1691), Chelmarsh (1694),
Eardington (1712), on the Davenport estates (1717), Walton (1729), and
Shifnal (1746); sainfoin and turnips were grown on Coton Hall farm (1745);
and potatoes were cultivated at Walton (1742) and Worfield (1750). The soils
and climate also favoured hops and cider apples.[70]

South Shropshire consisted of mountain and moorland pastures, gentle

[69] Rowley, *Shropshire*, pp. 22–3; B. S. Trinder, *The Industrial Revolution in Shropshire*, Chichester, 1973, pp. 5–19; I am indebted to Dr Trinder for the references to the inventories; Salop. RO,
Davenport House MSS, 2,713/box 29 (tithe of rape at Dawley Green, 1739). B. Trinder and J. Cox,
Yeomen and Colliers in Telford, Chichester, 1980, contains a detailed analysis of inventories for four
parishes between 1660 and 1750.

[70] Rev. Mr Richard Cornes, 'A Short Topographical Account of Bridgenorth in the County
of Salop, 1739', *Trans. Shrops. Arch. Soc.*, IX, 1886, pp. 193ff; NLW, inventories for Bridgnorth
peculiar; Shrewsbury Public Library, deeds, 9,602, 9,607, 13,777; Salop. RO, 330/12–13,
Davenport House MSS, 2,713/box 29, 30; Univ. of Reading, farm accounts, SAL/5/1/1 (Coton
Hall farm, 1745: including Scots cows, Dorsetshire ewes and lambs, use of muck from the Severn
as manure).

sandstone and limestone edges, and broad clay vales. Settlements were small and scattered, and labouring families in search of a living continually erected cottages on the fringes of the hills, woods, and wastes. In Ditton and Middleton forty-eight cottages had been erected on the Brown Clee hills and Netchwood common by 1728, and about the same time it was said at Bransom that the lord had enclosed 600 acres during the previous seventy years, and had built over sixty dwellings there; nevertheless, some 3,000 acres remained as rough common pasture, and though other instances of enclosure may be cited, sufficient common grazing was still available in most townships by the end of the period.[71] Crops were grown on a subsistence basis, and in a sample of 159 inventories, 103 referred only to corn or to "corn and malt". Hops and cider apples were grown along the Worcestershire and Herefordshire borders and in the valleys, though Walter Poole of Neen Sollars (1745) was probably exceptional in having 456 lb of hops worth £31, 12,000 hop poles valued at £30, and 12 hogsheads of cider, together with 4 hogsheads of windfall cider and perry worth £14. Turnips were grown at Brompton (1726) and Ludlow (1736), and clover was recorded at Kinlet (1692), Acton (1693), Lydbury (1714), Morville (1714), Brompton (1717), Sundorne (1721), Bitterley (1747), and Stotesdon (1748). The land was also improved by liming at Brompton (1724), Willey (1744), and Sundorne Castle (1745).[72]

The average head of cattle per farm rose steadily from 19 in the 1660s to 23 in the 1740s. Eight farmers in the 1660s had herds of more than 30 cattle, and John Hawkes of Stanton Lacy (1666) had 49. The stock on the Bromfield estate in December 1683 comprised 2 bulls, 22 milch cows, 4 fat cows, 16 yearlings, and 46 bullocks and heifers. Twelve of the 37 inventories taken from the 1740s recorded more than 30 head of cattle; Paul Bristoe of Worthen (1747) had 70 head, Edward Barter of Broughton, gentleman (1742), had 76, and Abigail Jones of Whitcot Evan (1746) had 78. Beasts were sold at the local fairs to be driven to the fattening grounds in southern or central England, and small 'Welsh' horses that roamed the moors were exported from the region as pit ponies and pack horses. Dairying was less important than in the northern lowlands, but cheese chambers were recorded at Neen Savage (1663), Greete (1694), Neen Sollars (1745), Hughley (1747), and Onibury (1749), and the accounts of a farm at Much Wenlock (1734–6) referred to "butter sent to London". Most farmers also kept a few pigs and used the wastes as sheep pastures; nearly half the 137 farmers who kept sheep

[71] Shrewsbury Public Library, deeds, 734; *VCH Shrops.*, *VIII*, pp. 30, 37, 125, 185, 253; Salop. RO, 260/1, 279/331–2, 837/56, Park Hall papers, 665/3/70, Eyton MSS 665/338.

[72] NLW, inventories; Shrewsbury Public Library deeds, 9,602, 9,607, 9,632, 18,219, 18,290–1; Salop. RO, Willey MSS, 1,224/box 177, Davenport House MSS 2,713/box 30, Marrington MSS, 631/2/1, Walcot 5/1/96 (Suffolk turnip seed sent to Ludlow, 1736); Meteorological Office Library, ED2/stock (1) ("Observations of Me, Thos. Like, 1691–1708").

had flocks of more than 50, and the median average rose steadily from 33 per farm in the 1660s to 60 per farm in the 1740s. By that time, a third of the farmers had flocks of over 100; Paul Bristoe had 360, and Abigail Jones kept 688. Thomas Like of Whitcott Keysett had noted the activities of sheepmasters earlier in the century, including the driving of ewes across the country to Essex. At a more humble level, extra income was earned from textile crafts; Arthur Young observed that almost all the cottages had a piece of hemp, and nearly half the inventories recorded either hemp, flax, wool, yarn, tow, or cloth.[73] Once again, an alternative employment and the chance to graze a few animals on the commons kept many families safely above the poverty line, while, as in the north-west Midlands at large, others prospered as pastoral farmers. Throughout the period, the ability to adapt husbandry practices to the natural resources of the various regions was evident amongst all classes.

[73] NLW, inventories (the number of oxen increased from 2½ per farm in the 1660s to 5 per farm in the 1740s. By the 1740s horses averaged 5 per farm, and Abigail Jones had 4 horses worth £18, and 18 wild horses valued at £27), Powis Castle 21,192; Salop. RO, Marrington MSS 631/2/1, Willey 1,224/box 299; Meteorological Office Library, "Thos. Like"; Young, op. cit., p. 144.

CHAPTER 6

THE SOUTH-WEST MIDLANDS: WARWICKSHIRE, WORCESTERSHIRE, GLOUCESTERSHIRE, AND HEREFORDSHIRE

By comparison with the counties of south-east and eastern England, the south-west Midlands were a backwater in 1600. Kent, Essex, and Norfolk were all much more advanced and diversified by agricultural innovation and industrial activity, dating from the early sixteenth century or much earlier. The south-west Midlands emerged later upon the same scene, but they telescoped a similar experience into a shorter space of time. The years 1640 to 1750 were crucial.

The economic transformation of the south-west Midlands did not, of course, affect all regions equally. In 1750 the Herefordshire border and Clun Forest were will remote outposts, far from the lively hub of industrial activity and agricultural improvement taking place in northern Worcestershire and Warwickshire. But most areas were affected in some degree by stronger tides of commerce and consumption surging between Bristol and Birmingham, while roads and drove routes regularly carried the influences of London through this territory into Wales, and brought back Welsh products for dispersal throughout the Midlands.

This phase of accelerated change in the seventeenth century was, of course, set in motion much earlier. The dissolution of some large monastic houses, as, for example, in the vales of Tewkesbury and Gloucester, and in the Arden Forest of Warwickshire, gave rise to a lively market in land in the years 1580 to 1620, and settled some vigorous gentlemen on estates that comprised much parkland and woodland.[1] This land was convertible to other uses, or capable of upgrading, and public discussion of land improvement in general tended increasingly in the seventeenth century to focus on the possibilities of such improvement.[2] Here then, were many opportunities to make different, and more profitable, use of the land and raise the value of estates.

Such enterprise was further encouraged by industrial and commercial

---

[1] Map of monastic Britain, South sheet, Ordnance Survey, Chessington, Surrey, 1950; J. Thirsk, 'Projects for Gentlemen, Jobs for the Poor: Mutual Aid in the Vale of Tewkesbury, 1600–1630', in P. McGrath and J. Cannon, eds., *Essays in Bristol and Gloucestershire History*, Bristol, 1976, pp. 150–1.

[2] See pt II below, ch. 19, pp. 540–1.

developments. Their scale is measured at the end of the period in the remarkable density of some populations, many of them once rural but now becoming urban, in Warwickshire, Worcestershire, and Gloucestershire (though not in Herefordshire), and in the extensive improvement of the road systems by turnpikes converging on Bristol. The turnpikes were mostly set up between 1720 and 1750, but before that the Severn was being better exploited as a waterway inland, and Bristol was well used as a port for carrying goods by sea to London and Wales. Moreover, foodstuffs and manufactures were readily shipped from Bristol to France and Spain, and were meeting a growing demand across the Atlantic. The industrial products seeking an outlet from the south-west Midlands multiplied rapidly in the later seventeenth century, and their makers, who came to rely more than hitherto on purchased foodstuffs, stimulated the demand for agricultural produce. Such was the need for industrial labour that it may sometimes have threatened shortages of manpower in farming. Certainly a restructuring of economic activity occurred in north Worcestershire, when the burgeoning metal-working industries enforced specialization, and separated more decisively than before the industrial from the agricultural parishes.[3]

Another thrust to new enterprise resulted from the damage wrought by the Civil War. The west Midlands was one of the most fought-over regions in the kingdom. All four counties suffered from prolonged warfare in the 1640s as control of different areas passed from the royalist to the parliamentarian side and back again. Many people were obliged to pay taxes and contributions to both.[4] But such losses, and the passage of armies, could also spur new developments, even if born of desperation. Among other things, they gave a push to the commercial production of cider, since soldiers camped in the south-west Midlands developed a taste for this drink and carried its fame further afield. Producers were encouraged to aim for a higher-quality brew.[5]

From the 1650s onwards small circles of energetic gentlemen in this region were striving to promote one or several bolder economic schemes. A web of associates in Herefordshire clustered around John Beale, the parson who promoted improved cider production both there and (from 1661 onwards) in Somerset. He inherited his interests from his grandfather, and more especially from his father, Thomas Beale, who had divided his energies between a legal career and a private hobby of improving fruit orchards. The

---

[3] C. M. Law, 'Some Notes on the Urban Population of England and Wales in the Eighteenth Century', *Local Historian*, x, 1, 1972, pp. 21–6; J. M. Martin, *The Rise in Population in 18th-Century Warwickshire*, Dugdale Soc. Occ. Paper 23, 1976, pp. 12ff; E. Pawson, *The Turnpike Trusts of the Eighteenth Century: A Study of Innovation and Diffusion*, School of Geog., Oxford Univ., Research Paper 14, pp. 20–1, 23; P. F. W. Large, 'Economic and Social Change in North Worcestershire during the Seventeenth Century', unpub. Oxford Univ. D.Phil. thesis, 1980, pp. 153–72.

[4] See pt II below, ch. 14, p. 121.   [5] See pt II below, ch. 19, pp. 550, 562.

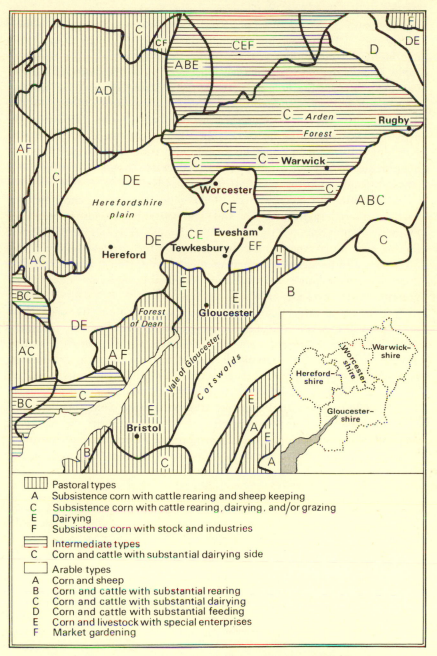

Fig. 6.1. Farming regions of the south-west Midlands.

Beale family had a close friendship with the Scudamores of Holme Lacy, among whom John, the first Lord Scudamore, was a great pioneer of new fruit varieties. He, or Thomas Beale, or both together, seem to have been responsible for establishing, or increasing, the popularity of the Redstreak apple, and in the activities of these ancestors of our seventeenth-century improvers we see the long pedigree of those achievements. By the mid seventeenth century, the devotees of fruit growing were no longer a few lonely pioneers; Beale's book *Herefordshire Orchards* cites by their initials the names of contemporaries in his neighbourhood who were all carrying on agricultural experiments, including some with fruit. They were a circle of like-minded people, not without political influence in London, who later used it to campaign for better transport facilities as well.[6]

In Worcestershire, another circle of energetic, improving gentry included Andrew Yarranton from Astley and Thomas, Lord Windsor, later Lord Plymouth. This group was promoting more industrial development, and paid for Yarranton's journey to Saxony to study the tinplate industry. But Yarranton also inspected river management on the Rhine, advised on river improvements at home, and wrote an influential book to encourage clover growing on the ryelands of Worcestershire.[7]

A select group of gentlemen and parsons were thus effective pioneers of innovation in the west Midlands, but their success in influencing others did not depend on their exerting a tight, authoritarian hold over rural society. Many parishes, indeed, entirely lacked a firm hierarchical framework, possessing multiple settlements that sometimes numbered as many as a dozen hamlets. In Gloucestershire, for example, Winchcomb had eleven hamlets, Bishop's Cleeve seven, and Minchinhampton twenty. Some hamlets grew in size at a faster rate than parent villages, so that authority did not reside unquestionably in one place. Furthermore, centuries of lax control by monastic and other ecclesiastical landlords had permitted the growth of large

[6] J. Beale, *Herefordshire Orchards*, London, 1657, *passim*, but esp. pp. 38, 56, 62; Mayling Stubbs, 'John Beale, Philosophical Gardener of Herefordshire, Part I, Prelude to the Royal Society (1608–1663)', *Annals of Science*, XXXIX, 1982, pp. 465–7. For attempts under the Commonwealth to improve the river Wye, to ease the traffic from Herefordshire in corn, fruit, and cider, and to Herefordshire from Bristol in coal and lime, see T. S. Willan, 'The River Navigation and Trade of the Severn Valley, 1600–1750', EcHR, VIII, 1937–8, *passim*, but esp. p. 75. Action did not follow till the Restoration.

[7] *DNB*, *sub nomine*; A. Yarranton, *The Improvement Improved, by a Second Edition of the Great Improvement of Lands by Clover*, London, 1663. Yarranton expressed deepest gratitude to Lord Windsor in the dedication of his *England's Improvement by Sea and Land*, London, 1671. For a circle of Warwickshire gentry with bookish, and probably also practical, interests in agricultural improvement, see J. Thirsk, 'Plough and Pen: Agricultural Writers in the Seventeenth Century', in T. H. Aston *et al.*, *Social Relations and Ideas*, Cambridge, 1983, pp. 312–13; V. Skipp, *Crisis and Development: An Ecological Case Study of the Forest of Arden, 1570–1674*, Cambridge, 1978, pp. 102–3. On Andrew Archer of Tanworth, see P. Styles, *Studies in Seventeenth-Century West Midlands History*, Kineton, 1978, pp. 8–9. I wish to thank Dr J. M. Martin for this reference.

communities of freeholders, or of copyholders who enjoyed the security of freeholders. They subdivided their land and their houses as they pleased, enclosed their land as and when they thought fit, and relied on self-help for survival. The scale of this subdivision and the remarkable persistence of small units of landholding are shown at the enclosure of Foleshill in Arden in 1775, which had 107 proprietors claiming a share in 794 acres of land.[8] When the chaplain to the Gloucester garrison, John Corbet, portrayed the society which he encountered during the Civil War in the Vale of Gloucester, he furnished a description that applied equally in other pastoral regions of the south-west Midlands and in some arable areas as well:

> There was no excessive number of powerful gentry…but the inhabitants consisted chiefly of yeomen, farmers, petty freeholders, and such as use manufactures that enrich the country, and pass through the hands of a multitude; a generation of men truly laborious, jealous of their properties, whose principal aim is liberty and plenty; and whilst in equal rank with their neighbours they desire only not to be oppressed, and account themselves extremely bound to the world if they may keep their own. Such, therefore, continually thwart the intentions of tyranny…The countryman had of his own, and did not live by the breath of his great landlord; neither were the poor and needy at the will of the gentry, but observed those men by whom those manufactures were maintained that kept them alive.[9]

A free tenantry enjoyed great freedom to exploit the agricultural (and industrial) innovations, demonstrated by the parish gentry, clergy, and substantial traders who lived modestly, rather than presiding authoritatively, in their midst.

The four counties of the south-west Midlands exhibit three main arable farming systems and two pastoral. An arable corn–cattle economy characterized those parts of the Midland plain that lie in south Warwickshire (in the region known as the Felden), on the rich clays and loams of south Worcestershire, and on the central plain of Herefordshire. A second variant, with far more special crops, especially vegetables and fruit, predominated in the Vale of Evesham, while a third system characterized the Cotswold Hills, where a sheep–corn economy dovetailed the use of the valleys for grain and the hills for fine pasture. Pastoral country was divided between dairying on the one hand, and breeding-with-feeding on the other. Dairying was the speciality of the Arden, north Worcestershire, and the Vale of Gloucester. The breeding-with-feeding areas lay in the Forest of Dean in Gloucestershire and along the western edge of Herefordshire. Breeding-with-feeding and

---

[8] J. Thirsk, 'New Crops and their Diffusion: Tobacco-Growing in Seventeenth-Century England', in C. W. Chalklin and M. A. Havinden, eds., *Rural Change and Urban Growth, 1500–1800*, London, 1974, pp. 88–93; Skipp, *op. cit.*, pp. 7, 103; J. M. Martin, 'Warwickshire and the Parliamentary Enclosure Movement', unpub. Birmingham Univ. Ph.D. thesis, 1965, p. 81.

[9] Thirsk, 'New Crops', p. 93, citing *Somers Tracts*, V, 1811, p. 303.

dairying shade into each other, however, and some parishes may have been changing their emphasis from one to the other between 1600 and 1750. Hence it is difficult to draw a precise boundary line between the two specialities, even though, of necessity, one is shown on the map. The Golden Valley in Herefordshire illustrates the problem: Rowland Vaughan's account of his farming *c.* 1600 suggests that he was engaged in much cattle rearing and feeding, as well as milking, while his neighbours were only dairymen.[10]

FELDEN WARWICKSHIRE

Typical of arable systems mixing corn with livestock enterprises was that practised in the vale lands of Felden Warwickshire. Common fields persisted, usually following a three-course rotation of wheat, barley and/or oats, and peas. Folded sheep were a principal agent for manuring the fields, and individual flocks were large and probably increasing – one or two hundred sheep were not unusual. Peas and oats mostly satisfied as fodder crops, for the inventories mention beans infrequently. Judging by the same source, though it is not a wholly reliable guide on this matter, clover and ryegrass did not become common until the eighteenth century.[11]

From the common-field parishes of Felden Warwickshire farmers supplied grain to those parts of the Midlands where land had already been enclosed and much of it put under grass. Old enclosure had facilitated the steady consolidation of holdings and the growth of more large farms, and so the economies of such parishes, even in the Felden, had often taken a divergent path. Enclosure had led to the steady extension of grassland, for prices between 1640 and 1750 did not encourage grain growers, other than those who were very efficient and farmed the best soils. And when parliamentary enclosure got under way in the 1730s, yet more Felden parishes reduced their arable acreages and turned over to grass.[12] Some, indeed, adopted the dairying speciality of their neighbours in the Arden; others simply increased the number of their sheep and beef animals. Either way, more ploughland was converted, either to temporary leys (under a system of alternate husbandry) or to permanent pasture. The revised edition of Camden's *Britannia*, published in 1727, summed up the trend: the tillage of the Felden was being reduced, and great parcels of ground made pasture for sheep.[13] Farmers who enclosed, but still maintained their traditional arable system,

[10] E. B. Wood, ed., *Rowland Vaughan, his Booke*, London, 1897, pp. 31, 76–8.

[11] Worcs. RO, Probate inventories, *passim.*

[12] M. Turner, *English Parliamentary Enclosure: Its Historical Geography and Economic History*, Folkestone, 1980, p. 74; I owe information on the conversion of arable to pasture in Hillmorton and Grandborough, after enclosure, to the kindness of Dr J. M. Martin.

[13] J. Yelling, 'The Combination and Rotation of Crops in East Worcestershire, 1540–1660', AHR, XVII, 1, 1969, pp. 29–30.

introduced clover or sainfoin into the rotation, sometimes interpolated woad, and very occasionally found room to add a fruit orchard (though not generally a hop garden) as a supplementary source of income.

The varying specialities of common field and enclosed parishes which adjoined each other geographically set up a pattern of interdependence which had a certain economic justification in terms of promoting a self-sufficient regional economy. It also enhanced social differentiation. Common-field communities sustained more small farmers, cottagers, and labourers, while enclosed parishes advanced fewer, but larger, farmers. The distinction between 'open' and 'closed' parishes became more pronounced as the two paths of development continued firmly to diverge: certain places like "Hungry Harbury", Tysoe, Napton, and Brailes in south-east Warwickshire were identified almost from the beginning of this period, if not before, as 'open' parishes, possessing a labour surplus. Parishes that had been enclosed, and sometimes depopulated, in the fifteenth and sixteenth centuries became 'closed' villages, only too willing to make use of the surplus labour of their neighbours. But the differences should not be described too sharply or explained too simply. A community of many smallholders did not necessarily mean many poor, seeking work in other parishes. They could be moderately prosperous, as in the Avon valley, an area of diverse soils and varied production.[14]

The diversity of economic goals and social structure in Felden Warwickshire, in fact, directs attention at the whole Midland plain's potential for flexible production. But changing economic circumstances and opportunities in this period were not as propitious as in the Arden, and so Felden farmers in general lacked the strong stimulus that galvanized their pastoral neighbours. On many of the clay soils they had to wait until after 1750 to see their brightest future.

SOUTH WORCESTERSHIRE

The rich clays and loams of south Worcestershire are an extension of Felden Warwickshire, and supported the same mixed arable systems. Many parishes followed a four-course, rather than a three-course, rotation of wheat, barley, pulses or vetches, and fallow in the common fields, and they retained those commonable fields to the end of the period. But alternative fodder crops like clover and turnips were introduced, to permit more extended rotations, and these probably made more rapid progress than in the Warwickshire Felden. Turnips along with clover and flax are singled out in a late-seventeenth-century document relating to tithes in Claines parish as a great advance in the last seventy years, the turnips having eliminated the fallow.[15]

[14] This paragraph is based on Martin, thesis, *passim*.
[15] Christ Church, Oxford, MSS, Estates 97, no. 182.

The importance in common-field townships of cereal production and, what is more, of wheat for the best bread is illustrated in farm inventories of Powick in the period 1676 to 1775, showing 67 per cent of its land growing wheat, only 6 per cent barley, and 27 per cent pulses.[16] These proportions imply, of course, that some of the land in Powick was already in closes. But elsewhere, under the influence of industrial expansion, more and more tillage land was being devoted to livestock feeding and dairying, and this tended to shift the emphasis from winter-sown to spring-sown grain and pulses. This generalization could be further refined, for Yelling has identified in east Worcestershire many smaller regions pursuing distinctive crop preferences between the mid sixteenth and mid seventeenth century; they represent many subtle variations, based on varied soil conditions, that cannot be elaborated here.[17] But in illustration of the general trend, the heavier emphasis on producing grain for livestock can be seen on some of the more specialized dairy farms. Francis Best's farm at Pershore, for example, supported a dairy herd of 26 cows and 12 calves in March 1747. He had in store £110 worth of hay, and, for additional fodder, 30 acres of clover and 53 acres of peas, compared with 45 acres of grain.[18] The increasing importance attached to fodder crops was ultimately reflected in the values of livestock, which by the mid eighteenth century generally much exceeded those of grain enterprises in farmers' inventories. In Powick, for example, 30 out of 64 inventories show livestock representing more than 60 per cent of all agricultural assets.[19]

Alongside the central core of its grain and livestock enterprises, south Worcestershire showed initiative in another direction: in developing alternative sources of farm income. The county had long been noted for its orchards, but in the period 1640–1750 fruit developed a reliable and sustained market, and whereas this item had frequently been omitted from inventories in the past, being regarded as the produce not of men's labour but of nature, now it was of sufficient monetary value to receive careful valuation. Gathered fruit, cider houses and cellars, cider mills, and hogsheads of the liquid were carefully enumerated. Similarly hops and hop poles: Worcester was plainly a noted hop market, judging by the sacks of hops awaiting sale there when their owners died; and considerable capital was laid up in hop poles. The rector of Stanford-on-Teme, Richard Taylor, whose main interests lay in lending money (£300) and studying his books and manuscripts (worth £50), also possessed at his death in 1718 a hop chamber in his house, and had £56 5s. laid up in 15,000 hop poles.[20] But perhaps the best illustration of new farming alternatives that supplemented the traditional system is given in the inventory

[16] J. A. Johnston, 'The Probate Inventories and Wills of a Worcestershire Parish, 1676–1775', Midland Hist., I, 1, 1971, pp. 26–7.   [17] Yelling, op. cit., passim.

[18] Worcs. RO, Worcs. invs., 008 – 7 – 505.   [19] Johnston, op. cit., p. 26.

[20] Herefs. RO, Hereford Wills, 72. See also pt II below, ch. 17, p. 492.

of Stephen Gwillam of Leigh in May 1747. His animals were valued at
£154 17s. and comprised a cattle herd of 33 animals (including 9 cows), 10
horses, 21 pigs, and 56 sheep, while his sown crops were valued at £67 17s.
Muck collected from Worcester was valued at £8, and this probably helped
his hop growing. (Nash in the later eighteenth century complained how a
few acres of hops could swallow up the manure of a whole farm.) At all
events, 8 bags of hops were valued at £42, 25 hogsheads of cider at
£34 10s. 10d., and 5 hogsheads of perry at £5.[21] Other special crops
featuring in south Worcestershire were woad (it was tithed at Hardwick in
1649/50),[22] vegetables, and hemp and flax. Tithes at Kempsey in 1649
included carrots, turnips, and hemp and flax, along with apples and pears.
Such variety in special crops may well explain in part why a dean and chapter
estate in Kempsey which was confiscated in 1649 yielded copyhold rents
worth only £3 15s., whereas the more realistic improved rent was thought
to be £44 6s. 8d. – fourteen times more.[23]

THE VALE OF EVESHAM

It is necessary to classify the Vale of Evesham separately from Worcestershire's
arable region, for it already had a distinctly more varied agricultural system.
It would be overstating the case to call it a market-gardening area in this
period, and yet it was plainly moving towards that speciality. Nor can the
area be precisely defined geographically. Some farmers in the Vale of
Evesham continued to cultivate their land under the conventional corn–
livestock system of southern Worcestershire,[24] while some Worcestershire
specialists in the gardening of vegetables, fruit, and flowers lived beyond the
strict confines of the Vale of Evesham, in and around Worcester or even
further north. Nevertheless, the Vale of Evesham can be recognized as the
centre of horticultural influences, and they extended into north-east
Gloucestershire as far as Winchcomb, Bishop's Cleeve, and Tewkesbury.
Soils in the area were ideal for gardeners. The liassic clay subsoils are lightened
by alluvial gravel and sand, ideal for those who worked with the spade.

Worcestershire was already a noted fruit-growing county in the Middle
Ages; and it seems likely that a tradition of vegetable gardening at the abbeys
of Evesham and Pershore survived, however weakly, from the Dissolution
onwards, to be revitalized when economic conditions and fashion again

[21] Worcs. RO, Worcs. invs., 008 – 7 – 504; T. Nash, *Collections for the History of Worcestershire*,
London, 1781, *I*, p. xi.

[22] T. Cave and R. A. Wilson, eds., *The Parliamentary Survey of the Lands and Possessions of the
Dean and Chapter of Worcester, Made in or about the Year 1649*, Worcs. Hist. Soc., 1924, p. 70.

[23] *Ibid.*, p. 226.

[24] See, for example, the inventory of Samuel Kyte of Ebrington in 1740 – Gloucester City
Library, Probate Invs., 1740 (50).

favoured it. That smallholders in south Worcestershire were affected by the growth of fashionable horticulture in its early stages is unlikely, but it is perhaps suggestive of growing demand from the common man that a new market site for the sale of garden produce was allocated in Worcester in 1595.[25] Even if this gave no new or stronger stimulus to commercial horticulture, it shows that the trade existed when another wave of powerful outside influences reinforced endeavour between 1640 and 1660.

The Civil War brought many newcomers into the area from south-east England, including gentlemen who took for granted the luxuries they had enjoyed at home of fine vegetables, fruit, and flowers. They had kitchen gardens next to their houses, and employed private gardeners, in whose work they took a personal interest. The fashion that had already been set around London now came into contact with a separate, but deep-rooted, local horticultural tradition whose persistence owed much to the fact that smallholders were numerically strong in this area. The population seized on every chance to use the spade rather than the plough. Villages in south-east Worcestershire and north-east Gloucestershire had already welcomed tobacco growing after it had been introduced into the parish of Winchcomb in 1619. Fourteen places in Worcestershire, including Evesham, Badsey, Wickhamford, Littleton, Charlton, and Conderton, were named for their illegal tobacco growing in a report to the Privy Council in 1627. Another thirty-nine places were named in Gloucestershire.[26] Plainly these were villages and townships that disposed of plentiful labour to undertake the many tasks needed to grow tobacco successfully – these entailed planting, replanting, transplanting, watering, snailing, suckering, topping, cropping, sweating, drying, making, and rolling – tasks that were carefully enumerated by Thomas Fuller after the Restoration because he was obviously impressed by the immense care and cost expended, yet knew that, despite all that, many great estates had been built upon the crop.[27]

Gardening skills among labouring men and gardening interests among the gentry were obviously widely diffused in the area by the mid seventeenth century, and spread thereafter. Tithes levied on vegetables and fruit are one indication; books on horticulture are another. John, Lord Somers, of Evesham received the dedication of John Evelyn's work on salads, finally printed in 1699. In north Worcestershire, at Kinlet, near Bewdley, lived John Rea, author and "exquisite florist", owner of the largest collection of tulips in England; his son-in-law, Samuel Gilbert, wrote *The Florist's Vade-Mecum* (1682), and dedicated it to the bishop of Worcester, "the greatest florist amongst the chiefest pillars of our church", whose palace garden was a

[25] A. D. Dyer, *The City of Worcester in the Sixteenth Century*, Leicester, 1973, p. 73; Worcester Guildhall, Chamber Order Book, I, f. 191, for which reference I wish to thank Dr Dyer.

[26] *APC*, Jan.–Aug. 1627, p. 409.

[27] T. Fuller, *The Worthies of England*, ed. J. Freeman, London, 1952, p. 186.

showplace for auriculas.[28] Finally, Worcestershire's eighteenth-century historian, Treadway Nash, traced the county's gardening tradition back to the Restoration, giving the credit to an Italian gentleman, Francis Bernardi, Resident in Britain for the Republic of Genoa, who decided to remain in England after his official appointment ended, and moved to Worcestershire in 1662. His son was born in Evesham, and later claimed for his father the greatest fame of all gentlemen of his time for his fine gardens. His work deserves more investigation.[29]

It is significant that, in this cluster of references, the horticultural interests of gentlemen, clergymen, and foreigners meet with an existing tradition of gardening among the local population. Such a conjuncture of circumstances is characteristic of the history of many agricultural innovations in their pioneering stages in the seventeenth century. It is matched again in a later period of rapid horticultural advance in the Vale of Evesham: in the nineteenth and twentieth centuries another wave of improvement owed much to the enterprise of gentry, foreigners, and other newcomers, galvanizing local producers to new effort and achievement.[30]

Because commercial horticulture developed among humble men, its progress is not well documented. But certain labour-intensive crops attracted notice for special reasons – tobacco, because it was banned by the government from 1619 onwards, and woad and tobacco, because they called for specialists at the curing stage and so depended on commercial partnerships. Poor tobacco growers disregarded the law for many decades, and it was not until 1654 that the government finally decided rigorously to enforce the statutes against the crop.[31] Eckington, Pershore, Upton Snodsbury, and Kempsey in Worcestershire were all reported for their illicit growers in 1659. The information reaching Quarter Sessions claimed large profits for landlords, and by implication for cultivators as well. Sir John Redding at Kempsey was alleged to have pocketed £400: he received 20s. for every rod of ground let to growers. Ralph Huntingdon was informed against for letting 400 rods at the same rent in Upton Snodsbury. The informant in all the cases brought in 1659 in Worcestershire was William Harrison, a gentleman of Pershore.[32] But usually local gentlemen were quietly in league with the tobacco growers, for they all benefited. Either they agreed to let their land for the purpose or they turned a blind eye. As a Privy Council searcher explained in 1667,

[28] N. 23 above; Blanche Henrey, *British Botanical and Horticultural Literature before 1800*, 3 vols., Oxford, 1975, I, pp. 191, 193–8.

[29] R. W. Sidwell, 'A Short History of Commercial Horticulture in the Vale of Evesham', *Vale of Evesham Hist. Soc.*, Research Papers, II, 1969, pp. 43–4.

[30] *Ibid.*, p. 50.

[31] Thirsk, 'New Crops', p. 94.

[32] J. Noake, *Notes and Queries for Worcestershire*, London, 1856, pp. 244–5; Worcs. RO, Quarter Sessions Papers, 110: 1659 (2) informations 10, BA 1; 11, BA 11; 12, BA 1; 13, BA 1; 15, BA 1; 16 BA 1.

he found tobacco growing "upon the High Sheriff's land, the bishop's land, and scarce one of the justices but on their land tobacco is planted, possibly without their privity. The tenants set [i.e. let] their ground to planters that are poor people who plant and give half the crop for the use of the ground. So, if destroyed, the planter loseth, the tenant loseth his half of the crop, and thereby is disabled to pay his rent."[33] Plainly, all classes in the community, not excluding landowners, had an interest in tobacco growing. Privy Council letters reminding justices of the peace of the ban on tobacco growing were sent regularly after the Restoration to all four counties in the south-west Midlands, and troops of horse annually trod down the crops of smallholders in the vales of Evesham and Tewkesbury. By the 1680s these annual forays were at last on the way to stamping out the crop entirely, helped by the fact that the price of Virginia tobacco was falling and the taste for the American leaf was growing. The last order from the Privy Council urging the destruction of the English crop reached Gloucestershire in 1690.[34] After that the government ceased to take an interest in the plant; yet in 1856 two local writers noted that it still grew in a half-naturalized state in north Worcestershire, near Bewdley.[35]

Tobacco growing reveals the tip of an iceberg — it gives an inkling of the efforts of smallholders in the Vale of Evesham to make a living from labour-intensive crops, mostly grown on small plots of land. Other such profitable plants included vegetables, both the commonplace and the luxury kind, hemp, flax, and woad (though woad also required a mill and a specialist to handle the leaves after picking). And an important clue to the way land, labour, and cash were mobilized is found in the existence of partnerships. In the first experiment with tobacco as a field crop in 1619 landlords were brought in as partners. Later partnerships were often confined to the lessees of land and the labouring cultivators. The virtue of partnerships was that they could be infinitely flexible; and an apparent partnership of two or three people could mask financial risks that were borne by any number of others, who contributed cash, kind, or labour to sub-partnerships entered into by the principals. Partnerships were also the means by which tobacco was grown in Holland in the seventeenth century and in Germany in the eighteenth.[36]

[33] PRO, SP 29/212, no. 108, cited in Thirsk, 'New Crops', p. 97.

[34] Thirsk, 'New Crops', p. 95; Glos. RO, QSO/2, Easter 1690.

[35] Noake, op. cit., p. 245.

[36] John Stratford's pioneering experiment in Winchcomb in 1619, ostensibly with two others, turned out to be a more subdivided partnership, Stratford alone dividing his share among 8 persons – PRO C 24/498/22. For partnerships in Holland, see K. Roessingh, 'Tobacco-Growing in Holland in the Seventeenth and Eighteenth Centuries: A Case Study of the Innovative Spirit of Dutch Peasants', Acta Historiae Neerlandicae, XI, 1978, pp. 25–7. On France, see M. R. Toujas, 'Notes sur la culture du tabac au XVIIe siècle...', Actes du dixième congrès d'études de la fédération des sociétés academiques et savantes, Languedoc–Pyrénées–Gascogne, Montauban, 1956, p. 198. I owe this reference to the kindness of Dr H. K. Roessingh. On partnerships in Germany, see A. D. Thaer, The Principles of Agriculture, tr. W. Shaw and Cuthbert Johnson, London, 1844, II, pp. 558–62.

Special crops other than tobacco may have been grown under similar arrangements, though such partnerships are hardly ever recorded in documents that have survived. A rare example is a lease of 1722 in which Joseph Sylvester, yeoman, of Welford, in Gloucestershire, took from a widow, Anne Harwood of Broad Marston, "The Little Woad Ground" to grow flax for a year at a rent of £4 an acre. Anne was to carry out the ploughing, harrowing, mounding, and trenching of the ground; Sylvester was to pay for all other work. If the crop failed, Anne promised to reduce the rent by 2s. 6d. an acre. It is significant that this unusual document has wandered some way from its original home, to lie at present in the Clwyd Record Office in Wales, a country with a much larger population of smallholders than England.[37]

Landlords could be persuaded to let their land for crops that were known to be exhausting to the soil, but this does not explain how cultivators managed to keep up continuous cultivation. They needed large quantities of cattle manure, which explains why contemporaries complained that the cornfields were deprived.[38] But they also used lime in large amounts, and this accounts for an otherwise seemingly strange association of ideas in John Aubrey's description of the history of liming in agriculture, written c. 1684. "Liming of ground", he wrote, "began about 1590s or some time after the bringing in of tobacco by Sir Walter Raleigh."[39] In other words, lime was heavily used to keep the land in a condition to grow tobacco year after year.

The smallholding economy of the Vale of Evesham was a flexible affair, capable of exploring a great many commercial possibilities, often at short notice. And the better-off kept their interest in corn and livestock alongside horticulture. One such was the gardener Walter Osborne of St Swithun's, Worcester, whose inventory was taken in November 1646, when one would not expect to find much in the ground. Though named as a gardener, he had £28 worth of unthreshed barley, a rick of pulses, rye in the granary, with threshed barley and beans, 1 old cow, 2 breeding sows, 4 little pigs; 5 store and 4 fat swine, and poultry. On 7 acres of ground he had turnips, cabbages, and other garden crops, plus onion and other garden seeds in store ready for the next season. Four little cabins on his land housed spades, pickaxes, and other implements; and he evidently reckoned to carry his produce to market, for he had 5 cart horses and carts.[40]

The whole region around Evesham displayed resourcefulness and a zest for making the most of many varied, and seemingly trivial, sources of income. The inhabitants of Tewkesbury even gathered mustard seed from plants growing wild in the hedges and made the mustard for which Tewkesbury was famous.[41] In view of all this, it is worth noticing the uncertain history – or

[37] Clwyd RO, Rhual MS, D/HE 134.
[38] Thirsk, 'New Crops', p. 89.   [39] T & C, p. 181.
[40] Worcs. RO, Wills, 008 – 7 – 3,585/244, no. 1647/135.
[41] Thirsk, 'New Crops', p. 91.

rather the undetermined chronology – of tenantright, which later evolved
as a valued system of compensation among Evesham market gardeners. It
enabled tenants leaving their holdings to receive full recompense for
improvement from an incoming tenant without the intervention of the
landlord. The custom was not formally recognized until about 1865, but a
writer extolling its virtues in 1939 believed that it had a much longer history,
going back over centuries of Evesham gardening experience.[42] We can only
speculate on its beginnings, but Walter Blith in his *English Improver Improved*
published in 1653 wrote in praise of a custom of tenantright that already
existed in Flanders.[43] The compensation for improvements which he
described was agreed between landlord and tenant, rather than between
tenants. But the sharing of risks in cultivating special crops was, as we have
seen, already thoroughly familiar in the vales of Evesham and Tewkesbury,
and it variously involved landlords, tenants, and cultivators. Co-operation
in paying compensation for improvement is only one step removed.
Moreover, we have noticed already how some horticultural practices – in the
growing of tobacco, for instance – marched in step with one another in the
Low Countries and in similarly congenial centres in England. Yet again, in
Part II, Chapter 15 (page 284) the testimony of the land agent of the Chirk
Castle estate in Wales in 1725 is cited as saying that allowances were used
now and then between tenant and tenant for such improvements as the
composting of ground. And certainly in other areas of the west Midlands,
notably south Staffordshire, where industrial development was causing
damage to agriculture, conflicts of interest were being resolved in this period
by the payment of compensation. It is not impossible that simple agreements
of a similar kind were also being arrived at by gardeners, though the
documentary evidence will be hard to find.

THE CENTRAL HEREFORDSHIRE PLAIN

Central Herefordshire is an extension of the Midland plain, and it followed
a corn–livestock system similar in outline to that of Felden Warwickshire
and south Worcestershire. But it placed a very different emphasis on the
components of that system. Its major cereal was, from the very beginning
of the period, and, indeed, long before 1640, wheat rather than barley. Almost
certainly its livestock fattening surpassed that of Worcestershire, while its
dairying was less ambitious. Fruit and hop growing were both important,
but pig keeping, linked with the fruit, featured far more prominently than
in Worcestershire. It should also be noted that it was generally the home
of smallholders. Even in the *Agricultural Returns* of 1866 the majority of

[42] C. H. Gardiner, 'Family Subsistence Farming: Example of the Evesham Vale', *Gloucestershire Countryside*, III, 4, 1938, p. 347; no. 6, 1939, p. 409.

[43] W. Blith, *The English Improver Improved*, 4th edn, London, 1653, Epistle Dedicatory.

holdings were shown to be under fifty acres, and this proportion was almost certainly higher, rather than lower, a century before.[44]

Documents of the period do not reveal all the refined differences among districts within the plain, which must have been known to contemporaries. The mostly heavy loams derived from the Old Red Sandstone were varied locally by drift: hence the ryelands of Ross and Archenfield in the south with their sandy, gravelly soils were one eccentric region; another encircled Bromyard and more closely resembled the farming of north Worcestershire. Nevertheless, the heavier loams were predominant, and it was they which made the best wheat land – so much so that Herefordshire claimed to rely on Gloucestershire for its malting barley, selling to it wheat in return.[45] Rye continued to be grown, though this crop was disappearing from other counties; Archenfield and Ross were a particularly congenial habitat. Nor was rye always found in a mixture with wheat. It was often grown on its own, and probably denotes a local taste for rye bread. Second in importance to wheat was barley (though it often ranked first on the ryelands), while oats ranked third. Peas were the commonest fodder crop, though pulses (which presumably included beans) were sometimes mentioned, but very rarely vetches.[46] A typical distribution of crops obtained on the farm of John Lewis of Doore in 1716: he had 64 acres of sown wheat, and in store the harvest of 75 acres, worth £158 17s., compared with 20 acres of barley, 34 acres of peas, and 45 acres of oats and pulse.[47] When John Duncumb in 1805 described wheat as the grand dependence of the farmer on the stiff clays, and marvelled at the plentifulness of the crop for export to Bristol and other places, he was describing a situation that already prevailed in this earlier period.[48]

The arable crops of central Herefordshire were not, for the most part, grown in common fields. Ploughland was largely enclosed by this period. Indeed, it has been estimated that in 1675 only about 8 per cent of the whole county was not already enclosed, and at most only 4 per cent was enclosed by later parliamentary acts; the first of these to concern arable fields was not passed until the late 1790s.[49] Herefordshire wheat was thus the product of enclosed land, highly cultivated in order to feed as well its many livestock.

[44] G. M. Robinson, 'Agricultural Depression, 1870–1900', *Woolhope Nat. Field Club*, XLII, 3, 1978, p. 261.

[45] BL, Add. MS 11,052, f. 117. Even in 1800, ⅔ of all land on the plain was arable – H. C. Prince, 'England *circa* 1800', in H. C. Darby, ed., *A New Historical Geography of England*, Cambridge, 1973, p. 405.

[46] Herefs. RO, Herefordshire Wills, *passim*.

[47] *Ibid.*, 72.

[48] J. Duncumb, *General View of the Agriculture of the County of Hereford*, London, 1805, pp. 40, 63.

[49] E. L. Jones, 'Agricultural Conditions and Changes in Herefordshire, 1600–1815', *Woolhope Nat. Field Club*, XXXVII, 1962, p. 37; M. Turner, *op. cit.*, p. 198.

Productivity was maintained by the use of lime, and this proved especially beneficial on the gravelly, sandy soils of Ross and Archenfield. It was lime which enabled farmers to grow more and more wheat here and reduce their acreage of barley. Then, by growing clover as well, they could support more livestock.[50]

The scale of the plain's livestock enterprises was impressive. Large cattle herds included many dairy cows, heifers, and calves, but much more numerous were the oxen, bullocks, and young beasts.[51] White-faced Herefordshire cattle are nowadays noted for their meat, not their milk, and this emphasis on feeding and fattening for the butcher, rather than on dairying, is clearly discernible in the inventories of Herefordshire farmers in this period. Only in the north-east, on the Bromyard upland towards the Worcestershire border, where the terrain is sharply broken by narrow valleys and the soils on the hillsides are lighter and poorer, was more dairying in evidence. But despite the cows in most herds, not all feeding stock can have been bred on the farm; many animals were plainly bought in, and farm accounts shed light on the lively traffic coming into the county, from Wales direct, or via Shropshire.[52] On the Herefordshire plain, they found lush pastures in the summer which prepared many young stock for sale as stores to graziers of the Home Counties at Michaelmas. And fodder was much enriched, certainly by the 1690s, by clover. Although Sir Richard Weston, the propagandist for clover in the 1640s, wrote of his experience in growing this crop in Herefordshire and it appears in leases from the 1660s onwards, farmers' inventories do not commonly feature clover until the 1690s. John Aubrey explained the breakthrough: farmers found the way to thresh their own seed, and no longer had to buy it from elsewhere. Thus, farmers from Archenfield, who twenty years earlier had been in the habit of sending their cows north to the river Wye around Letton in search of better grazing between May and late November, ceased to do so. They had enough good grazing at home.[53]

In comparison with the economic importance of cattle, sheep took a secondary place. Fine Leominster fleeces had once been widely celebrated, but to maintain their quality the sheep had to be cosseted by being housed at night in winter. In the early seventeenth century when Spanish Merino wool presented tough new competition against its fine English equivalent, Hereford sheep failed to hold their own. And as wool prices fell all through the seventeenth century, this probably explains why probate inventories show

[50] John Aubrey, cited in T & C, pp. 180–1.

[51] For livestock transactions on a large scale in the 1730s and 1740s, see Paul Foley's farm accounts for Newport farm in Almeley parish – Herefs. RO, E 12/F/AIII/36–9, 41–51.

[52] P. R. Edwards, 'The Cattle Trade of Shropshire in the Late Sixteenth and Seventeenth Centuries', *Midland Hist.*, vi, 1981, pp. 81–2.

[53] S. Hartlib, ed., *A Discours of Husbandrie Used in Brabant and Flanders*, 2nd edn, London, 1652, p. 20; Notts. RO, Portland MSS DD4P/63/58/16; E. L. Jones, *op. cit.*, p. 40; T & C, pp. 180–1.

relatively few sheep overall, and almost no references to wool. Some were needed to fold the ryelands of the region around Ross, and a few farmers had very large flocks, like Richard Rees of Llangarron, gentleman, with 254 sheep in 1668, Thomas Davis of Pengethly, Hentland parish, who had 380 sheep in 1690, and Thomas Hopkins of Pencoyd, who had 603 sheep in 1714; but these were unusual individuals.[54]

More important to more farmers were pigs. Indeed, it is doubtful whether any other county in the western half of England bred so many pigs as Herefordshire. They were fed on windfall apples, clover, and some of the farmers' large crops of peas, though these last produced a better flesh if they were first hardened by drying in the oven. Hence, many farmhouses had a goodly supply of bacon, which John Beale claimed to be superior to any other in the kingdom. And since salt pork is hardly mentioned at all, we may also guess that a good deal of pig meat was sold fresh. This was the farm-fed pork that was becoming something of a luxury at middle-class townsmen's tables by the early eighteenth century. It was tastier than the cheap pork, fed on the dregs and wash of distillers and brewers, which became increasingly the food of the poor. Buyers of pork in Herefordshire could thus continue to satisfy their fastidious palates. Twenty or 30 pigs were nothing unusual on the most ordinary farms in the 1660s; and by the 1690s farmers sometimes had 43, 44, 68, even 75 pigs apiece.[55]

Grain, together with the feeding of cattle and pigs, some sheep, and no more than sufficient horses for work purposes, laid the foundation of arable Herefordshire's farming economy. And the two principal improvements supporting an increasingly intensive system were the use of lime and the watering of meadows. Attempts during the Commonwealth to improve the river Wye for the benefit of Herefordshire refer to the advantages that would follow in sending down corn, fruit, and cider to Bristol and returning with coal and lime. From the 1660s onwards farmers in Herefordshire seem to have been making increasing use of lime: one letter in 1669 from a lime burner – presumably itinerant – offered his services on contract to a group of farmers. He undertook to supply lime at 4d. a bushel, and assured his clients that land so treated was improved by two parts in three. Water meadows and simpler systems of catchwork drains were constructed with increasing enthusiasm after the Restoration, and this effort gained momentum in the eighteenth century. It was encouraged, no doubt, by the expanding market for stores in south-eastern England which followed upon the passing of the Irish Cattle Act of 1667 forbidding imports from Ireland.[56]

[54] Herefs. RO, Herefordshire Wills, 36, 57, 70.

[55] T & C, p. 181; Sheffield Univ. Library, Hartlib MSS 62/15/2; Herefs. RO, Herefs. Wills, passim; pt II, ch. 16 below, pp. 336–7.

[56] Willan, 'River Navigation', pp. 74–5; Herefs. RO, E31/57. See also T. S. Willan, River Navigation in England, 1600–1760, Oxford, 1936, p. 39; E. L. Jones, op. cit., pp. 40–1; see also below, ch. 16, pp. 352ff.

Supplementing all this were other major interests, as in south Worcester-shire, in hops, and in fruit for cider and perry. A Kentish landowner had complained in the 1670s of the competition which the county's farmers were encountering from Herefordshire hops, and probate inventories support his suggestion that this was an expanding enterprise; they were ubiquitous and valuable. Thus, the hops of Humphrey Bennett of Collington in 1668 were valued at £53 8s., compared with £26 for his cattle, £15 for his corn, and £8 for his sheep. Dovetailed with hops were the orchards. Indeed, hops were often regarded as preparing the ground for fruit trees. However, many farmers had both, and the two combined yielded a substantial slice of farm income. Thomas Brace, for example, was a well-to-do farmer in Much Cowarne, whose fortune in personal goods amounted to £1,111 in January 1746. Of this, £175 represented the value of his hops at home and at the market, and £96 his cider, compared with a valuation of £86 placed on his wheat in store. In Bosbury in 1718 lived and died two farmers with substantial interests in both hops and fruit: Thomas Lylley, who in 1718 had £214 worth of hops, £18 worth of cider, perry, and verjuice, and £41 6s. worth of containers for cider; and his neighbour, Thomas Alcott, a tanner, who had £92 15s. worth of cider and apples, and £13 12s. 6d. worth of hops. Clergymen who specialized should not, of course, occasion surprise, for they could not sustain over-large agricultural enterprises: one was William King, rector of Edvin Ralph, who in 1747 had £53 worth of cider, whereas his wheat was worth only £20 and his pulses £3; he had very few livestock.[57]

Fruit growing was an ancient tradition in Herefordshire, though the trees had not originally been laid out in formal orchards, but had grown in hedgerows and along the highways – a feature of the landscape which was still noticeable around Leominster and impressed a writer in 1795: "Highways and common lanes [are] intersected with apple and pear trees, growing without the least care in cultivation", he wrote.[58] Breakfast and supper for Herefordshire people traditionally consisted of toast and cider. Hence, the county was in a position to swim with the tide when an interest in enterprises alternative to mainstream corn–livestock farming revived after 1640. Success in improving the standard of cider brewing and easier transport on the rivers enabled Herefordshire men in the course of this period to promote cider into an article of trade much further afield.[59]

Herefordshire may seem a county whose distance from London weakened commercial pressures. But it was not kept aloof from the flurry of debate on agricultural improvement, as Paul Foley's correspondence in the early

---

[57] T & C, p. 86; Herefs. RO, Herefordshire Wills, 36, 93, 72.

[58] J. Price, *An Historical and Topographical Account of Leominster and its Vicinity*, Ludlow, 1795, p. 197.

[59] See pt II, ch. 19; T. Nash, *Supplement to the Collections for the History of Worcestershire*, London, 1799, p. 55.

1730s shows. Some of its gentry, like their Welsh neighbours, had strong
links with London, and kept in close touch with current discussions on better
farming methods. Writing from London to his estate and farm manager at
Newport Farm in Almeley parish, north-west Herefordshire, Paul Foley
maintained more than just a general oversight over his land. Letters to his
steward gave precise orders about the rotations to be followed in every field,
when fields should be manured, and even which branches of the apple tree
in the kitchen garden were to be cut back.[60] In addition, he conveyed
promptly information on prices and conditions in the London food markets.
News passed about the rising price of hops in 1732, the high price of pigs
in London compared with Herefordshire, and the good opportunities for the
export of wheat in 1734. More than this, Foley's advice from London almost
certainly reflected the influence of his reading of the latest books. In 1732
his letters dwelt on the need to economize in labour employed on the land
and on the great value of vetches in feeding horses. He gave instructions on
the planting of beans, which should be spaced three feet apart, and must be
set by a line and in ridges, so that they could be hoed; thus the ground would
be prepared for the next crops of barley and clover. All these topics, and,
indeed, the exact advice on beans, were plainly, but silently, lifted from Jethro
Tull's book *Horse-Hoeing Husbandry*, which had been published the year
before, 1731. Foley's letters illustrate furthermore how the products of other
counties in southern England were regularly and easily introduced to
Herefordshire as Foley travelled back and forth to London, pursuing his
profession as a lawyer. On one journey in 1732 be bought two geldings at
Henley on Thames, and pigs and a setting bitch at Benson in Oxfordshire,
all of which were duly dispatched to his Herefordshire estate.[61] An unusual
number of references to books in farmers' probate inventories also prompt
speculation about how many treated of improved husbandry or of orchards
and gardens. One of Herefordshire's natives was Thomas, Lord Coningsby,
who presented a bill in the Lords in the 1690s to promote gardening. The
county had some dedicated pioneers in new fields of endeavour who have
not yet received full recognition.[62]

THE COTSWOLDS

The Cotswold Hills occupy the eastern third of Gloucestershire, and comprise
a sloping plateau that falls gently on the east, more sharply on the west. Based
on oolitic rocks, the soils are predominantly limestone, though here and there
they are intermixed with sand and clay. On the hills the calcareous soils are
generally thin, often only three inches deep, but these made fine grasslands,
which for many centuries had fed sheep, whose manure then sufficiently

[60] Robinson, *op. cit.*, p. 261; Herefs. RO, E12/F/AIII/60, 62.
[61] Herefs. RO, F/AIII/56-127.   [62] See pt II, ch. 16, p. 338.

enriched the soil of the valley fields – deeper liassic soils, sometimes heavy, but certainly fertile – to maintain a well-integrated sheep–corn system. This routine had a long tradition, and was the same as that prevailing in the Cotswold sector of north Wiltshire and west Oxfordshire.[63]

The neatness of the folding system undoubtedly helped to prolong the life of the common fields. But in this period other possibilities of management appeared, and so, by comparison, the old system came to be dubbed as inefficient. This is reflected in land valuations, like those on Bagendon farm c. 1740. The farm comprised 317 acres, of which 222 were arable in two common fields, worth only 1s. 6d. per acre, whereas 80 acres of pasture were valued at 7s. 6d. and 15 acres of meadow at 20s. per acre. The farm had common rights for 400 sheep. But some enclosure of part of the commons had evidently taken place recently and had robbed the tenant of commoning for 200 of his sheep flock. The old system was breaking up, and had to be replaced. A final note on this valuation gave warning of what was planned for the future: already $19\frac{1}{2}$ acres were under cinquefoil.[64]

The improvement which transformed the Cotswolds, and prompted exclamations of wonder and praise in the early eighteenth century, involved enclosure first of all, and then the sowing of clover, ryegrass, and especially sainfoin in the new rotations. The old ones sometimes consisted only of a crop and a fallow: now they gave way to longer rotations, which by the end of the eighteenth century consisted often of turnips, barley, two years of seeds, wheat, and then oats. But the essential preliminary to the improvement of worn-out arable was a period under seeds, and here the sowing of sainfoin was found extremely successful. It flourished on these calcareous soils and, when experience of its habits accumulated, was often left down for six, seven, or even ten years. Turnips won favour somewhat later.[65]

Whether sainfoin found a footing first on Salisbury Plain or on the Cotswolds is a moot, and not vital, point, for it was grown earlier still in the Thames valley. John Aubrey gave the prize to the Cotswolds, claiming that sainfoin was first grown c. 1650 at North Wraxhall by Nicholas Hall, who came from Dundry in Somerset. But Hartlib's diary mentions Oxford's Pensa Club offering in 1651 a lecture on sainfoin husbandry, as practised around Salisbury.[66] Probably both regions, so similar in their farming practices, began more or less simultaneously. What is certain is that sainfoin steadily spread in the Cotswolds in the subsequent century. A deed for land

[63] See ch. 10 below, pp. 320–3.
[64] Gwent RO, DIO 1435.
[65] W. Marshall, *The Review and Abstract of the County Reports to the Board of Agriculture...*, vol. II, *Western Department*, York, 1810, pp. 406, 413–14. For a similar account, but describing other reactions, see S. Rudder, *A New History of Gloucestershire*, Cirencester, 1779, pp. 21–2.
[66] E. Kerridge, *The Agricultural Revolution*, London, 1967, pp. 278–9; T. & C., p. 178; Sheffield Univ. Library, Hartlib MSS, Ephemerides, 1651 A–B3.

in the Cotswolds at North Cerney in 1695 names "Sainfoin Ground",[67] and by 1714 Abel Wontner of Gloucester wrote marvelling at the transformation by sainfoin, clover, and ryegrass on the southern, more gently sloping side of the Cotswolds, the part that "was formerly styled the barren part thereof". Evidently the improvement had not yet affected the northern edge.

By enclosing their open fields and sowing the same with sainfoin, clovers, ryegrass, and such like seeds [he wrote]...thousands and thousands of acres of pitiful, poor, sorry ground, not (hardly) worth the ploughing and sowing with corn alone...being enclosed and sown with some of those seeds aforesaid, amongst their corn...bring forth so great an increase that the same land which before was hardly worth ten groats an acre will not now be let or set [but] at three times ten shillings an acre.[68]

This improvement made it possible for wheat to outstrip barley. It also led to the ploughing up of some of the grazing downland, for a period of cereal growing, to be followed by reseeding with ryegrass or clover. An agreement to do this was reached at Salperton in 1712 between the manorial lord and eleven farmers. It was agreed by all that common ground, which had never been ploughed up, would benefit from cultivation, and so the lord gave permission for four to five years of corn to be taken on $18\frac{1}{4}$ acres, so long as the land was then laid down with ryegrass or other seeds, and so returned to grazing. In this state it was to be left until he again allowed cultivation. The lord himself claimed the right at the same time to sow "Farm Downs". The ploughing of this commons necessitated a reduction in sheep stints, but it was taken for granted that individual farmers would be able to keep more sheep on their enclosed land.[69] Another agreement, seemingly preparing for the cultivation of yet more downland, was drawn up at Dyrham in 1699, when a messuage situated on "Toll Down", with three acres of land, was leased, on condition that the land be enclosed as soon as possible and a farmhouse and other buildings be erected on it.[70]

The eventual result of these changes was to turn land use around in some places, so that permanent pastures and meadows lay in the valleys, with arable on the slopes. But more usually the land was treated as convertible.[71] Another result was to enable Cotswold farms to support more cattle than before, though this probably did not mean a decline in sheep numbers. The additional fodder crops in the fields could support both. Inventories show ever larger flocks in the possession of the more substantial farmers – 400 to 500 sheep in the 1660s, rising in the period 1710–20 to 800 or even 1,100.[72]

---

[67] Glos. RO, D16/T1.

[68] Bodleian Library, MS Top. Glouc. C3. See also Marshall, op. cit., p. 426, citing Thomas Tudge (1807).   [69] Glos. RO, D269C/E1.

[70] Glos. RO, D1,799 E98.   [71] Marshall, op. cit., p. 406.

[72] See, for example, Gloucester City Library, Probate Invs., 1663 (53 and 39), 1666 (20), 1712 (41 and 31).

Herds of livestock suggest that the dairy was a minor concern, for household use only on most farms, and feeding was the more substantial interest. Oxen continued to be used for draught, and were subsequently fed for beef. When better-off farmers are found with as many as ten horses and more, not all of which can have been needed for work in the fields, it is necessary to remember that the Cotswolds was gentry country, and horses were required for sport and for the carriage. Pigs were a very minor consideration.

In the arable fields wheat, barley, peas, and oats made up the principal arable crops, with the occasional appearance of vetches. Unlike other arable areas of the west Midlands, the Cotswold country was not able to introduce special crops into its farming system. Orchards, hops, dye crops, etc. are not usually noticed.[73] But in the course of the period 1640–1750 the region was supplying to the market more wheat, though less barley, than before, its fair share of sheep, and a growing number of cattle. Yet the advances that were possible in this region were still not fully attained by 1750, and, according to Samuel Rudder, writing in 1779, another prodigious improvement occurred after 1740 with the still wider use of clover and sainfoin and the addition of turnips. As a result Cotswold farmers ceased to send their sheep and cattle to winter in the vales of Gloucester, Wiltshire, and Oxfordshire, and fed them on their own farms.[74]

PASTORAL REGIONS

The pastoral regions of the south-west Midlands had economies that were intimately entwined with, and influenced by, the arable regions adjoining. But in general they underwent much more fundamental transformation than the arable areas because of the pressures of industrial growth in their midst. This was most evident in the Warwickshire Arden and in adjoining north Worcestershire, where industries, already entrenched in 1640, expanded rapidly. In the Arden, metal trades, including nail and needle making, tanning, shoemaking, and glovemaking were carried on on the western side of the county, and linked up with the industrial region of south Staffordshire and north Worcestershire. Mining and ribbon weaving prevailed in north-east Warwickshire, while linen weaving was more generally dispersed, and kept company with flax growing.[75] In north Worcestershire metalworkers were clustered in large numbers near the sources of iron ore. They included

---

[73] Hops, however, were said to grow around Stow-on-the-Wold in 1759, and so its fair was noted for this item among other products – Benjamin Martin, *The Natural History of England*, London, 1759, *I*, p. 362.

[74] Rudder, *op. cit.*, p. 21.

[75] Skipp, *Crisis and Development*, pp. 54ff; J. M. Martin, thesis, *passim*. For one parish only, see P. Styles, 'Henley-in-Arden in the Seventeenth Century', *Studies in Seventeenth-Century West Midlands History*, pp. 206–7.

nailmakers, in places like Old Swinford, Dudley, Rowley, and Halesowen, and scythemakers in Chaddesley and Belbroughton. Further west, prominent occupations in or near woodland were again tanning, for example in Bewdley, using the oak bark of the Forest of Wyre and the woods of the Malvern Hills; shoemaking using tanners' hides; and wheelmaking using forest timber. Hemp making for ropes also found a home in north Worcestershire, and, among miscellaneous textiles, capmaking at Bewdley, allegedly a migration from Monmouth. On the frontier between the Cotswolds and the Vale of Gloucester, in the Stroudwater hills, the old broadcloth industry maintained its hold, while new but related industries appeared, such as rugmaking at Painswick. Stocking knitting was important at Alcester in Arden by 1633–45 and at Tewkesbury and Winchcomb from about 1660 onwards, if not earlier. Gloucester and possibly some of the villages nearby engaged in pinmaking, while across the Severn the Forest of Dean supported a large population of iron miners and timber workers. Herefordshire in the late eighteenth century was said to have no manufactures, but it is likely that the linen weaving mentioned as a by-employment in the Golden Valley by Rowland Vaughan *c.* 1600 still survived, given the demand for linen cloth in the later seventeenth and eighteenth centuries.[76]

ARDEN WARWICKSHIRE

Industrial development was not the only factor accelerating agricultural change in the Arden. Much land was already enclosed, and so was available for new uses, and some energetic gentry lived in the Arden who were actively interested in improving run-down land, introducing new crops, and positively engaging their tenantry in these schemes. One example of enclosure in the period of the Commonwealth – at Clifton-upon-Dunsmore, near Rugby – hints at the successful collaboration of tenantry with gentry who shared the convictions and aspirations of the Hartlib circle on the subject of agricultural change. Sir Richard Lucy, a parliamentarian, was the temporary lord of the manor, holding the estate from his brother-in-law, Sir Robert Whitney, who had fallen under suspicion for his papist associations. Lucy agreed on an enclosure with the freeholders in 1648, but the allocations took nearly two years to complete and were not enrolled in Chancery until 1654. The delays sprang from the many revisions to the first plan, showing

[76] K. McP. Buchanan, 'Studies in the Localisation of Seventeenth-Century Worcestershire Industries, 1600–1650', *Worcs. Arch. Soc.*, XVII, 1940, pp. 45ff; XIX, 1943, pp. 45–7; Marshall, *op. cit.*, pp. 361–2, 429–30, 400, 306. For rugmaking at Painswick, see Gloucester City Library, Probate Invs. 1714 (9). For stocking knitting at Alcester, see *VCH War.*, III, p. 13; also in the early 1650s, *War. County Records*, III, ed. S. C. Ratcliff and H. C. Johnson, Warwick, 1937, p. 170, and in the Vale of Tewkesbury, J. Thirsk, 'The Fantastical Folly of Fashion: The English Stocking Knitting Industry, 1500–1700', in N. B. Harte and K. G. Ponting, *Textile History and Economic History*, Manchester, 1973, p. 60.

a careful concern for the small freeholders and for the rights of cottagers; the legal costs were borne entirely by the lord of the manor. Here was an enclosure that was virtually completed before the Midland controversy about the subject in general erupted again in pamphlets and was carried into parliament, between 1653 and 1656. But the provisions made at Clifton would surely have met the demands of reasonable critics. Lying behind them lay the growing conviction, confirmed in the more public debate, that enclosure was a forward-looking economic necessity, and that, in achieving such a change, the interests of all could be satisfied.[77]

Another significant enclosure took place at Allesley in this period. It was the native parish of Walter Blith, the best author to write on general agricultural improvement at this time. It was agreed in 1650 and completed in 1654. We can only speculate on the influence of Blith (who died early in 1654), lying behind the words of the enclosure decree; it described the many inconveniences of farming in the common fields, including the fact that not more than one-quarter of the land was sown with grain in any year. But enclosure, as Blith would have predicted, was only the beginning of many further improvements. Sir Orlando Bridgeman, Chief Justice and later Keeper of the Great Seal, bought the estate from the Whitney family in 1663. A system of alternate husbandry was already established in the fields by then; tenants' agreements, moreover, insisted that they plant and maintain orchards with apple and pear trees "of the best sort", plant timber trees, oaks, ashes, elms, and holly, and establish strong hedges of hawthorn and crab. They were also obliged to manure well after every three crops, put ashes on moorish land, and assist the watering of meadows on the banks of the Avon. Heavy penalties were laid for the ploughing up of pasture, suggesting that Bridgeman was resisting the tendency for more land in the Arden to be used for corn. Enclosure represented one step along the path to more intensive livestock farming, particularly for sheep and cattle, plus fruit growing.[78]

Elsewhere in the Arden the move to dairying, which was visible before 1640, was pushed further.[79] Rough land was upgraded to make better-quality pasture, some of which would then be put under alternate husbandry. An oft-quoted description of land in Hampton in Arden in 1649 succinctly described the process. The surveyor was at a loss how to describe land use accurately, and so decided to call certain land "pasture", as did the local people. But, in fact, the land was regularly put under crop for two or three

[77] A. Gooder, *Plague and Enclosure: A Worcestershire Village in the Seventeenth Century*, Coventry and N. War. History Pamphlets, no. 2, 1965, pp. 13, 8, 14–20; pt II, ch. 16 below, pp. 319ff.

[78] Gooder, *op. cit.*, pp. 27–30; War. RO, CR 299/583/1. When the enclosure of Bubbenhall was under discussion in 1717, it was expected to lead to the conversion of arable to pasture – Univ. of Manchester, John Rylands Library, Bromley-Davenport MSS, estate correspondence of William Brimley, M.P., 7 Nov. 1717.

[79] V. Skipp, 'Economic and Social Change in the Forest of Arden, 1530–1649', in *Land, Church, and People*, ed. Joan Thirsk, AHR, suppl. to vol. XVIII, 1970, *passim*.

years at a time, and then returned to grass for fifteen to twenty years. And though the writer did not say as much, this was but the beginning of a process which sometimes ended with the land being put into permanent tillage.[80]

The use of lime was one of the aids in this process, and its use from an early date, *c.* 1600, steadily increased, with consequent benefits to both arable and pasture.[81] The Arden improved its feeding capacity to the extent that five north Arden parishes close to Birmingham increased their population by about 50 per cent between 1570 and 1650. In the next hundred years grain production increased so much that the Arden ceased to make demands on the surplus of other areas, thus enabling the Felden to limit its activities in this direction and pursue other activities alongside.[82]

The extension of tillage in the Arden seems to have been accompanied by a reduction in the growing of wheat, at least in some parishes, in favour of barley, which was more useful as an all-purpose grain, and was indeed the principal bread corn of the common man. Thus barley growing and dairying came together as a farming system for feeding the local artisan population, though not all the cheese produced there stayed in the Midlands. Defoe described in the 1720s the Warwickshire (and Cheshire) cheese which was carried on the Trent via Gainsborough and Hull, to be transported by sea to anywhere in eastern and southern England.[83] The London trade is not often specified in Warwickshire documents, but Thomas Phillips of Hill, in Stoneleigh parish, was credited at his death in 1664 with cheese "that's gone to London", with some more left in the house.[84] Other Arden inventories refer to numerous cheeses in store, though they were not given a high value. One hundred, 250, 400, or even 800 cheeses in store were not unusual. Yet 80 cheeses in 1692 were worth no more than £4 5s. (12¾d. each); 800 cheeses in 1696, £8 (2½d. each); 3 cwt of cheese in 1698, only £1 5s.; 1½ cwt in 1718, £1 10s.; and 400 cheeses in 1715, £3 10s. (2d. each). Cheese was a cheap food and it was sold in many different sizes and qualities. Large bulk did not necessarily mean high value. The inventories underline how impossible it is to gauge total cheese and butter production in this area; its bulk in relation to its value called for sale by producers at frequent intervals. This deepens the explanation for the unpopularity of the merchants who kept producers waiting a long time for cash settlements.[85]

[80] T & C, p. 126.

[81] Hugh Plattes in *The Jewel House of Art and Nature* (p. 21) wrote as early as 1594 of the use of lime in country bordering on Arden. For the benefits of lime, see A. W. McPherson, *The Land of Britain: The Report of the Land Utilisation Survey of Britain*, part 62, *Warwickshire*, London, 1946, p. 697.

[82] Skipp, *Crisis and Development*, pp. 42–54, and 'Economic and Social Change', pp. 98–9.

[83] Skipp, *Crisis and Development*, p. 48; D. Defoe, *A Tour through England and Wales*, 2 vols., London, 1959, *II*, p. 141.

[84] War. RO, Stoneleigh 302.

[85] LJRO, Probate invs., *passim*; pt II, ch. 16 below, p. 362.

The expansion of grain growing in the Arden, and the infiltration of some dairying into the Felden, brought the two neighbouring, but different, farming systems into somewhat closer conformity with each other. Yet the fundamental differences in social structure ran too deep to be rapidly obliterated, and, in any case, industrial development in the Arden did not affect the Felden.[86] The Arden's woodland–pastoral characteristics also preserved it as a region of horse breeding, in contrast with the Felden: probate inventories showed many farmers possessing mares and colts. Flax and hemp growing, together with the weaving of linen and hempen cloth, also increased, rather than diminished, in the period. Both agricultural and industrial pursuits in Warwickshire plainly entailed a heavy demand for hempen sacks and rough wrapping cloths of all kinds; and occasionally a craftsman-farmer is clearly documented in the act of supplying such needs. Such was Ralph Byfield of Berkswell, near Coventry, who at his death in 1746 had a dairy herd of 11 animals, 3 mares, and 11 sheep, but was described as a weaver. He was evidently weaving linen, for he had flax seed in store, flax in the shop valued at £27 5s., and 10 loads of flax in the stalk worth £22 10s.[87]

By 1750 the fundamental transformation of the industrial and agricultural economy of the Arden had raised the standard of living higher than it had been in 1640, and by the end of the century, judging by expenditure on poor relief (1790–1804), the relative prosperity of Arden and Felden was reversed; payments to support the poor in a sample of Felden parishes varied from 18s. to 21s. per head of population, compared with only 10s. to 16s. in the Arden.[88]

NORTH WORCESTERSHIRE

The pastoral region of north Worcestershire was subject to the same pressures, caused by a rising population and expanding industries, as the Arden. A survey of population growth in parishes around Bromsgrove, for example, has shown the doubling of numbers between 1665 and 1776/7, much of which must be ascribed to the immigration of industrial workers, who were dependent on others for their foodstuffs.[89] Thus the pastoral character of north Worcestershire was modified to allow more land under the plough, a trend in no way different from that affecting Arden Warwickshire.

Normal arable farming was firmly based on the production of the staple grains, wheat and barley, rye (of which more was grown here than elsewhere

[86] See J. M. Martin, 'The Parliamentary Enclosure Movement and Rural Society in Warwickshire', AHR, xv, 1, 1967, pp. 19–31.

[87] LJRO, 1747, B.

[88] J. M. Martin, thesis, p. 153.

[89] D. E. C. Eversley, 'A Survey of Population in an Area of Worcestershire from 1660 to 1850 on the Basis of Parish Registers', in Population in History, ed. D. V. Glass and D. E. C. Eversley, London, 1965, pp. 401–2.

because of the sands and gravels), and some oats. The principal legumes were peas and beans, and sometimes vetches. But the widespread occurrence of light, sandy, gravelly soils did not allow for the easy transformation of pasture into arable – or rather, while the first ploughings might be easy, maintaining fertility was difficult. From the early seventeenth century lime had been used in some quantity to overcome these problems, and in the early days of such improvements the results were heartening. They were described with some care by Robert Plot when visiting the same sandy, gravelly soils around Swinnerton, Hatton, and Beech in Staffordshire. Without help, the land grew only rye, buckwheat, or oats, and even then crops had to be well dunged and the soil rested after three years. With the help of marl, lime, and muck, however, it would bear as many crops as arable land on more fertile soils. The rotation was wheat, then barley and oats, after which the land was laid to grass. Alternatively, a further three crops were taken, including beans and sometimes vetches. When the land was finally laid to grass, it made rich cattle feeding for some years.[90] This same procedure in north Worcestershire had raised problems by the mid seventeenth century, principally because of the excessive use of lime. Some land was so limesick it was in danger of being abandoned altogether. The manorial demesne of Crowle in 1649, for example, was credited with thirty-four acres of barren, arable closes on the side of a hill.[91] It was to this problem that Andrew Yarranton directed special attention, and gave sound, practical advice when he wrote his book in 1663 urging farmers to grow clover.[92] Yarranton lived in Astley parish in this very region and knew its problems at first hand. He strenuously argued the merits of clover for three reasons: it restored worn-out arable, afforded rich fodder to all livestock, and was superior to beans and peas because these required far more labour and were thus far more expensive in cultivation.[93] In the course of the period 1640–1750 the hopes that Yarranton placed on the spread of clover were gradually fulfilled. Wheat came to dominate the rotation, displacing barley and reducing rye and oats until, by 1700, little rye was left. Pulses steadily gave ground to clover.[94]

North Worcestershire's capacity to feed its own livestock better than before brought a change in the relationship of the north to the south of the county, succinctly described by Treadway Nash in 1781. In Elizabeth's day, he explained, sheep and cattle from north Worcestershire had been wintered in the south, but the improvement in the north by clover, sainfoin, and (by

[90] R. Plot, *The Natural History of Staffordshire*, Oxford, 1686, pp. 341–3.

[91] Cave and Wilson, *Parliamentary Survey*, p. 49.

[92] Yarranton, *The Improvement Improved*.

[93] *Ibid.*, pp. 32, 39, 11. Yarranton claimed (p. 28) that sheep put into clover in March were fat in 10 weeks.

[94] Yelling, 'The Combination and Rotation of Crops', pp. 20–1, 28–32; J. Yelling, 'Changes in Crop Production in East Worcestershire, 1540–1867', AHR, XXI, 1, 1973, pp. 21, 28–9.

that date) turnips too resulted in vale farmers from the south sending their sheep north "to keep them sound and make use of their richer fodder".[95] As north Worcestershire farmers had already shifted their attention from cattle rearing to dairying well before 1640, this tendency was reinforced when the value of clover in affording rich grass to promote milk yields and a better-quality butter and cheese was more fully recognized.[96]

Dairying, of course, suited the circumstances of north Worcestershire's population in more ways than one. Its many medium to small farms – forty acres was an average holding – favoured dairying, which produced frequent and quick returns, unlike cattle raising, which was the choice for men of substance. But the preference for dairying must also reflect the choices of consumers, who bought cheese rather than meat, and this in turn mirrors the convenience of the food to industrial workers as well as its relative cheapness. Farmers' inventories show that herds of ten to twenty dairy cows were no more than average, while the very largest dairying herds were found in the towns themselves.

Just as the dairying of north Worcestershire infected south Worcestershire, so south Worcestershire's interest in special crops as supplementary farming activities crept into north Worcestershire. We see it in the inventory of John Monnox of Great Witley, near Kidderminster, in the 1690s, who was following a traditional system but with important additions. His arable acreage amounted to 91 acres under barley, oats, pulses, and vetches. He also had a store of hay and clover, and evidently sold clover seed, for which £7 was owing to him. His livestock of all kinds were only modest, but he had 43 cheeses in store, which indicated his interest in dairying. Alongside all this he had hops lying at Worcester waiting to be sold, 3 hogsheads of cider and a perry mill at home, and £5 worth of fish in his ponds.[97] Other inventories show the same sidelines, hops, cider, and perry in particular; fish were unusual, except on gentlemen's demesnes and in the possession of more specialized fishermen. By comparison with other assets the value of these special activities increased notably from the 1660s onwards. Thus 7 bags of hops in 1711 were valued at £29 8s. compared with £24 for the same farmer's 7 cows; the hops of another farmer were worth £20 in 1715 compared with £22 for his 7 cows and 1 bull; 10 hogsheads of cider and perry were worth £9 in 1714, whereas the same owner's 4 young bullocks were worth only £10. On a mixed farm of Richard Witney of Tenbury, inspected in January 1747, grain in store was valued at £40 whereas the hops were worth £90.[98] On smaller farms, common crops in closes were hemp and flax, the acreage of which almost certainly increased in this period. They

[95] Nash, *Collections*, I, p. x.   [96] Yarranton, *op. cit.*, p. 28.

[97] Worcs. RO, invs., 008 – 7 – 339.

[98] Herefs. RO, Herefords. Wills, 68 (Edw. Ingram of Clifton on Teme), 70 (Geo. Miles of Bickley in Knighton), 70 (Edw. Hardman of Woodston in Lindridge), 94 (Rich. Witney).

were conspicuous in the neighbourhood of Kidderminster, a busy town with a perpetual need for ropes, sacks, and wrapping cloths.[99]

The interaction of industrial and agricultural change in north Worcestershire was not without tension between competing interests. The strong demand for grain from industrial workers in the immediate vicinity assisted farmers whose efforts to produce corn might otherwise have flagged in the face of falling prices. Indeed, their success in some places in their drive for a more productive agriculture resulted in zones of specialization in the eighteenth century – metalworkers being concentrated in some parishes, single-minded farmers in others. Industrial employments even disappeared from some parishes where agriculture proved the stronger competitor; scythemaking, for example, moved out of Clent and weakened in Belbroughton, moving northward to Halesowen and into Staffordshire. Farmer-artisans, who had managed to maintain their dual employment for a century or more, lost ground to those who specialized. So the struggle for land was in some places settled, but this could not but deepen the precariousness of the livelihood of industrial artisans who relied solely on wage labour. It hastened the moment in the eighteenth century when some of the metal-working industries of north Worcestershire became sweated trades.[100]

THE VALE OF GLOUCESTER

The Vale of Gloucester was another pastoral region, though without such large tracts of residual woodland as were found in Warwickshire and Worcestershire. Its soils were mostly heavy, deep Lower Lias clays and Keuper marl, intermixed with some lighter patches of loam and sand. They lent themselves, above all, to pastoral husbandry, the more so since this was, and is, a well-watered region and most of the land lies at no more than 150 to 400 feet. Difficulties of drainage, indeed, totally impeded cultivation in many places, and so a lot of land lay semi-derelict, awaiting the energies of an enthusiastic improver.

Just how much land lay under the plough is difficult to gauge. Farmers' inventories suggest that the acreage was remarkably small. For example, Margaret Francombe, who until 1698 farmed at Tockington in Olveston parish, where the soils were loamy and lighter than many others in the vale, had a mixed herd of 72 milking cows, bullocks, and young followers, but only 19 acres of land in cultivation. John Blake, farming at Henbury until 1719, specialized in dairying and fattening; grazed 25 cows, 5 heifers and calves, 16 oxen, and a bull; and yet had only 7 acres of arable crops.[101] The

---

[99] Later, when bounties were paid for the growing of hemp and flax, from 1782 onwards, the growers in Worcestershire were located in the north-east, but also in the south-east, around Evesham and Pershore – Noake, *Notes and Queries*, pp. 102–3.

[100] Large, thesis, pp. 153–72.   [101] Bristol RO, Invs. 1699/9; 1719/4.

traveller through this vale must have seen a predominantly green, and generally much enclosed, countryside. However, the proportions of arable to pasture and meadow shown in a survey of Dodington manor in 1712 gave just under one-third of the land to arable (31 per cent), the rest being in meadow (39 per cent) and pasture (26 per cent), with a smaller amount of woodland (3.5 per cent). Probably one-third of the land under crop was a maximum in the vale.[102]

We shall notice in Chapter 19, in a more general context, how much attention was given in public discussion in the seventeenth century to the possibilities of improving run-down grassland. It is not surprising, therefore, to find some energetic renovation and rehabilitation proceeding in the Vale of Gloucester. The potential for such improvement is shown in a survey of Northway and Natton in Ashchurch parish, where eight customary holdings, the largest of which were 62 acres, 34 acres, and 21 acres in extent, were rented for £5 13s. 8d. in 1666, but were deemed to have an improved value of £132 10s.[103] Renovation was usually planned to begin with consolidation and enclosure, as at Hardwick in 1735. The common grazings in their present state were considered to be worth little, being subject to rot, and being generally eaten by the livestock of outsiders. The task of enclosure was not thought difficult: it was said to be the custom there and in places roundabout, "time out of mind", for farmers to enclose, without control or question, whatever could conveniently be taken in.[104] In this case, the improvers were disappointed, for a survey of Hardwick in 1770 still referred to the common fields, and to one farm in such poor state that not a hedge, ditch, or drain had been made for the last fifty years. The pasture was covered with anthills, doubtless grown larger since 1735; most of each hillock, it was said, would fill a dungcart.[105]

Where schemes for improvement were not so thwarted, descriptions of the work involved in the general upgrading of land passed through a regular sequence: consolidation and enclosure came first, then draining, levelling, and manuring. At Oxenton in 1735 enclosure plans included a provision that each new private allotment from the common pasture be so arranged as to give each one good spring water, that the rotations in the common fields be altered from three crops and a fallow to two crops and a fallow, and that tenants should improve their land with lime and introduce clover or turnips.[106] When Stantway Farm of 193 acres, in the parish of Westbury-on-Severn, underwent major reorganization c. 1750, low-lying land was drained, hillocks levelled, thorns and bushes grubbed up, and manure liberally applied. Twenty-five acres of meadow were levelled and manured several times. The land, in consequence, was raised from a value of 16s 9d. to 25s. an acre.[107]

[102] Glos. RO, D1,610 E113.
[103] Gloucester City Library, Ashchurch 21 (18).
[104] Glos. RO, D214/E18.
[105] Westminster Abbey Muniments, no. 32,967.
[106] Glos. RO, D1,637/E7.
[107] Glos. RO, D36/E73.

Another farm at Eastington was prepared for rehabilitation in 1748, when a tenancy of fifty years' duration came to an end. The lands lay scattered, and were so intermingled with pieces which the same tenant held of other estates that he could no longer say which was which. Nor could he remember on what terms his family had entered upon the land, nor its condition half a century before. Two of the fields were overgrown with briars and studded with molehills. The first tasks for the incoming tenant were deemed to be the grubbing and ploughing of the land for three years, after which it was reseeded. The cost of renovation was expected to be high, and so the new occupier was admitted at the old rent.[108]

While evidence is plentiful of heavy physical work in restoring neglected grassland, clues to the finer points of improvement are less common. Inventories lack references to clover and fertilizers. However, estate accounts suggest that lime was often employed, and that clover spread gradually. The process seems to be mirrored at Hardwick, where an entry in the accounts of Lord Hardwick in 1728 suggests that by agreement he helped the tenant to grow clover by buying for him 120 lb of clover seed.[109]

The best opportunity for major improvement seems to have occurred only when a new tenant entered on a farm. For long periods the dead hand of routine could lie heavily on parishes where most of the land was held in small farming units. Common fields persisted for the same reason. Many were still subject to a traditional rotation, like that followed at Oxenton in 1735 – a four-course of wheat, pulses, barley, and fallow.[110] Individual farmers' inventories, however, often showed them having no more than two arable crops in any one year, wheat and beans, or, on lighter soils, barley and peas.

Since pasturage and meadow clearly predominated in the Vale of Gloucester, the main feed for stock was grass and hay, and dairying bulked largest of all in its farming specialities. Productive capacity was very high, and if the size of dairy herds and quantities of cheese described in store in farmers' inventories are a fair guide, output was steadily rising. Dairy houses, usually called 'white houses' in this region, stored more and more cheese as time passed. In the 1640s, 300 or even 500 cheeses were not uncommon. Twenty years later, in 1664, the minister of Aust had 800 cheeses, valued at £8, compared with books valued at £5. In the 1690s William Watkins of Stowick in Henbury parish had 2,400 cheeses, and Henry Rodman of Earthcott, in Alveston parish, 3,700 cheeses. Inventories made between 1710 and 1716 show Guy Pope at Almondsbury also with 3,700 cheeses, and John Francombe in the same parish with 7,100. From the 1690s onwards hardly a single farmer's property inventory fails to refer to cheese or cheesemaking equipment, sometimes in great quantity. Margaret Francombe of Tockington left behind at her death in 1698 25 cheese vats and 2 cheese presses. But the

108 Bristol RO, RC/WO14 (17) B. 109 Glos. RO, D214/E19.
110 Glos. RO, D1,637 E7.

accounts of Viscount Weymouth, who possessed an estate at Buckland, surpass all others in the period 1730–50. In August 1755 £300 was paid by bills drawn on cheesemongers in London. And since the appraisers of inventories in the vale generally valued 500 cheeses at £5, and 800 cheeses at £8, this sum of £300 may represent payment for some 30,000 cheeses.[111]

Dairying on larger farms went hand in hand with cattle rearing and fattening. Many herds included a bull and a goodly number of bullocks and fatting oxen which were sold for meat. This can be illustrated from the farm of Thomas Hodges of Redwick and Northwick in Henbury parish in 1662, who had 16 cows, 8 calves, 7 yearlings, and 6 oxen.[112] If sheep were found on farms at all they were usually few in number.

Alongside cheese ranked fruit as another conspicuous source of income. Near the Severn particularly, the climate protected the orchard trees from frost, even though it generated mists that gave rise to ague among the inhabitants. At Arlingham, for example, tithes were payable on apples, cider pears, eating pears, cherries, and plums, as well as on walnuts.[113] But appraisers of inventories do not give a fair view of the amounts involved, for not all were scrupulous in listing this item. In some parishes a convention obtained whereby valuers meticulously listed cider rooms, fruit, cider, and equipment. In other parishes they ignored these things. Appraisers at Elberton and Almondsbury always took noticeable pains: they recorded the cider mills and barrels of Thomas Cox of Almondsbury in 1699; Guy Pope's 12 barrels of cider and apples in the same parish in 1711, worth £22 10s. (compared with his cheese, worth £46 5s., and his hay, worth £50); and Mark Hollister's 300 gallons of cider waiting to be drunk or sold from his house in 1735.[114] Of the value of fruit and cider making in the vale as a whole we gain some inkling from Samuel Rudder, who singled out for notice in 1779, not one, but three, varieties of perry. Yet another clue to the value of orchards may be gained from their rents. In Oxenton 56 acres in four common fields were rented at £11 4s. in 1734, whereas the Great Orchard alone was rented at £12. Forty acres of land known as "The Old Hills" on Stantway farm was worth only £14 5s. per annum until it was planted with fruit trees and manured with ashes, when its value was raised to £20.[115]

It is not easy to pass judgment on the average size of holdings in the Vale of Gloucester, for surveys of estates are few and far between. Four surveys show over 40 per cent of holdings (not counting those of cottagers) measuring 20 acres or less; nearly another 30 per cent ranged from 21 to 40 acres.

[111] Bristol RO, Invs. 1664/12; 1699/31; 1693/28; 1711/21; 1712/20; 1699/9; Bodleian Library, MSS Top. Glouc. B4.
[112] Bristol RO, Invs. 1662/24.   [113] Glos. RO, D18/618.
[114] Bristol RO, Invs. 1699/3; 1711/21; 1735(5).
[115] Rudder, op. cit., p. 26; Glos. RO, D1,637 E7; D36/E73.

Yeomen's farms were anything between 60 acres and 160 acres in extent but not often more.[116] Here, as elsewhere in the south-west Midlands, small farms dominated the economy, and throve upon diverse sources of income. We see diversity in unusual detail in a dispute about tithe payments at Weston Subedge, involving George Clements. He was evidently an overbearing personage whose strong parliamentarian sympathies in the Interregnum persisted after the Restoration. He avoided tithe payments for thirty years until 1682, when he was presented in the Court of Exchequer. His neighbours substantially agreed in their assessment of his varied sources of income. From his dovecote he drew 8 dozen pigeons in a flight and 4 flights in a year. One hundred and twenty dozen birds – 1,500 in all – were sold in four years at Chipping Campden market, and this did not count the valuable pigeon manure that went onto his fields. He kept between 5 and 8 stocks of bees, and whenever he sold a beestock he received 5–6s. apiece. He also kept 2 cocks, 12 hens, ducks, and turkeys. He had reserves of wood and picked a quarter of apples, worth 8s. every year. All these were sidelines, supplementing his income from $2\frac{1}{2}$ yardlands, from which he harvested 20 loads of wheat, 30 loads of barley, and 30 loads of pulses. In addition, he had 10 cattle, of which 2 were yearlings and 8 dairy cows, from which he reckoned to get between 4 and 7 calves each year. He also had 100 sheep with their lambs, and generally between 1 and 3 mares which yielded him at least 1 colt in the year.[117]

THE FOREST OF DEAN

The Forest of Dean in west Gloucestershire, on the far side of the Severn, represents a dissected upland landscape of ridges and steep-sided valleys, most of it lying between 400 and 800 feet above sea level. Some of its soils on the coal measures are peaty, intermixed with clay; others on Old Red Sandstone range from coarse sand to loam and marl. Timber was a rich resource in this area, where so much land was shallow and infertile, but the woods were much despoiled during the Civil War to serve many different interests – the iron industry, the crown's grantee of the Forest, the royalist Sir John Winter, and the commoners. Dean was not one of the royal forests singled out for sale by parliament, but a bill for the Forest of Dean was debated in the Commons in 1656, ostensibly "for the mitigation of the forest laws...and for the preservation of the wood and timber", and not unnaturally the commoners' grievances and suspicions festered, since the preservation of the wood meant reafforestation, and this meant keeping the commoners out of young plantations for twelve years at a stretch. Even

[116] Glos. RO, D674a/M5; D18/564 and 565; D1,610 E113; D2559L1.
[117] PRO E 134, 34 Chas. II, Easter 9.

though they were assured that they would benefit in the end, twelve years was a long time to be deprived of grazing.[118]

After lengthy discussion at the Restoration, an act of 1668 determined on the reafforestation of Dean, and at a time when lively interest was being shown in woodland management in general, the maintenance of the Forest thereafter was not unsatisfactory, though tension between the verderers and the commoners inevitably persisted. But as happens so often after a period of energetic improvement, standards of management slowly fell, especially in the eighteenth century. When the full extent of decay was investigated and reported once more in 1788, its beginnings were traced to the years 1700 to 1730, even though we have suggested elsewhere that a tough attitude to forest management was imported into England (or at least southern England) by the Hanoverians. Order collapsed when the forest courts were discontinued; in consequence the rules of the forest were increasingly ignored, with the connivance of some junior (and poorly paid) forest officials. By 1777 one dismal reporter described the forest as going to rack and ruin.[119]

The commoners undoubtedly pressed hard on the forest, and the squatting of newcomers added to their numbers. The agricultural economy needed all the grazing it could find, for cattle and sheep rearing was the main occupation. Even though strict forest law did not allow the grazing of sheep, it was one of the rules generally ignored by the eighteenth century. A guide to the farmers' main assets is shown in a list of stock of Henry Morgan of Clearwell in Newland in June 1648. He had 32 cattle (12 kine, 9 calves, 6 oxen, a bull, and 4 young cattle) and 124 sheep, together with 2 nags and a colt and 12 pigs. Yet his arable under crop in that year was only 24 acres. The mixed cattle herd sometimes involved dairying, but it was not nearly so specialized an activity as in the Vale of Gloucester. Much more effort was put into breeding and the selling of stores. Sheep rearing was equally important to some farmers, but less so to others. It featured prominently in the accounts of a large enterprise of the Hawkins family at Minsterworth, which sent 502 sheep to London in 1748, where they sold for £342. Oxen also were fed on this farm, of which 35 were sold in 1750, 20 going to London.[120]

Another usual sideline in the Forest of Dean was cider and perry making, and the distinctive quality of the Forest cider was described by more than one Gloucestershire antiquarian. It was called 'stire', and was made around Newland on Wye. Because of its unique flavour and strength it often sold for a very high price – 15 gns. for a hogshead was quoted in 1763 – and this

---

[118] See pt II below, ch. 16, p. 376; *Diary of Thomas Burton*, ed. J. T. Rutt, I, London, 1828, pp. 37, 228–9; CJ 1651–9, p. 439; C. E. Hart, *Royal Forest: A History of Dean's Woods as Producers of Timber*, Oxford, 1966, pp. 131–51.

[119] See below, ch. 16, pp. 374ff; Hart, *op. cit.*, pp. 169ff, 193–9, 202–6.

[120] Hart, p. 170; Gloucester City Library, Invs. 1648; Glos. RO, D690/E1.

made it a luxury for the well-to-do. Its excellence was attributed to the fact that the trees only flourished on limestone or where iron ore was found.[121] Thus excellent cider making was linked with the forest's industrial potential. The need for cider barrels stimulated woodworking, and the iron ore provided work in iron mining, which in 1779 was said to earn more cash than a common labourer could expect to enjoy in any other part of the kingdom.[122]

THE HEREFORDSHIRE BORDER

The uplands along the western border of Herefordshire represent the last pastoral region of these four counties, sharing more of the characteristics of south-west Shropshire and the Welsh March country of Radnorshire. But stony loams in the north-west with some heavy intractable clays were softened somewhat along the south-eastern edge, where the upland dipped into the Golden Valley. The area is poorly documented in this period, partly because it was a region of small holdings. Crops were grown for subsistence only, and stock rearing was the main activity, though dairying played a larger role in the Golden Valley. Linen weaving was mentioned as a by-employment by Rowland Vaughan in the early seventeenth century, and this may well have persisted.[123]

In the period 1640 to 1750 the west Midlands underwent an increasing diversification of its local economies, while at the same time adjoining regions became either more interdependent or more imitative. Industry and agriculture maintained a balanced partnership in some places, but nearer the hub of industrial activity around Birmingham they were parting company, industry commanding the labour of more landless men. But the smallholding population held its own. Transport improvements were a key that opened to them many more distant market opportunities, not only for their grain and livestock, but for their cheese, hops, and cider. The whole region was more firmly integrated in this period into the larger consumer society spreading its influence from London, and in this development the pastoral districts led the way. Arable regions showed the best rewards for farm improvement on their lighter, hitherto more barren lands, which could now be improved by lime and seeds. It was not until after the end of the period covered here that farming commentators started to look to a renovation of the heavier arable soils as the next necessary step, a hope that was to be fulfilled in the nineteenth century.[124]

---

[121] B. Martin, *Natural History*, I, p. 340; Rudder, *Gloucestershire*, p. 35.
[122] Rudder, *op. cit.*, pp. 38, 63.
[123] See above, pp. 149ff.
[124] Nash, *Collections*, I, p. x.

EAST ANGLIA, THE HOME COUNTIES, AND THE SOUTH-EAST

CHAPTER 7

EAST ANGLIA AND THE FENS: NORFOLK, SUFFOLK, CAMBRIDGESHIRE, ELY, HUNTINGDONSHIRE, ESSEX, AND THE LINCOLNSHIRE FENS

THE SETTING

East Anglia is not clearly defined. The economic geography of the region has always tended to belie its relief, so much indeed that it would be possible to identify many variations upon the regional theme of land use or agricultural practice, and therefore to make a case for a proliferation of miniature zones or sub-regions. We may conclude that the regional specifications of Kerridge and Thirsk, in themselves fairly complex, are insufficient to comprehend this variety.[1] In so doing, however, our precision results in a *morcellement* too extreme to be generally useful. For the period after 1640, indeed, there is evidence that the earlier insularity of particular districts was in process of modification. A tendency towards standardization, blurring the edges between fielden and woodland, or between hard land and water land, can be seen, even against the changes wrought by improving topsoils or by altered market specialization.

The map (Fig. 7.1) is a simplified diagram of East Anglian farming zones during the later seventeenth century. It loses something in fine shading from the more accurate, but complex, delineation of regional variations which the data from probate inventories demonstrate, but it displays the essential general features of the contemporary landscape. In a countryside with so much local variety of soil types, particular townships sometimes shared the

---

[1] The historical geography of the region, and of several of its parts, is discussed in E. Kerridge, *The Agricultural Revolution*, London, 1967, pp. 56–60, 72–80, 83–113, 136–44; J. Thirsk, 'The Farming Regions of England', in J. Thirsk, ed., AHEW, *IV*, pp. 38–49, 53–5; P. Armstrong, *The Changing Landscape*, Lavenham, 1975, esp. chs 4, 5, 8; D. P. Dymond, 'The Suffolk Landscape', in L. N. Munby, ed., *East Anglian Studies*, Cambridge, 1968, pp. 17–47; J. Spratt, 'Agrarian Conditions in Norfolk and Suffolk, 1600–50', unpub. Univ. of London M.A. thesis, 1935; K. H. Burley, 'Economic Development of Essex in the Later 17th and Early 18th Centuries', unpub. Univ. of London Ph.D. thesis, 1957; R. Allison, 'The Changing Landscape of South-West Essex, 1600–1850', unpub. Univ. of London Ph.D. thesis, 1964; J. R. Ravensdale, *Liable to Floods*, Cambridge, 1974, *passim*; M. R. Postgate, 'Field Systems of East Anglia', and D. Roden, 'Field Systems of the Chiltern Hills and their Environs', in A. H. R. Baker and R. A. Butlin, eds., *Studies of Field Systems in the British Isles*, Cambridge, 1973, pp. 281–3, 338–45.

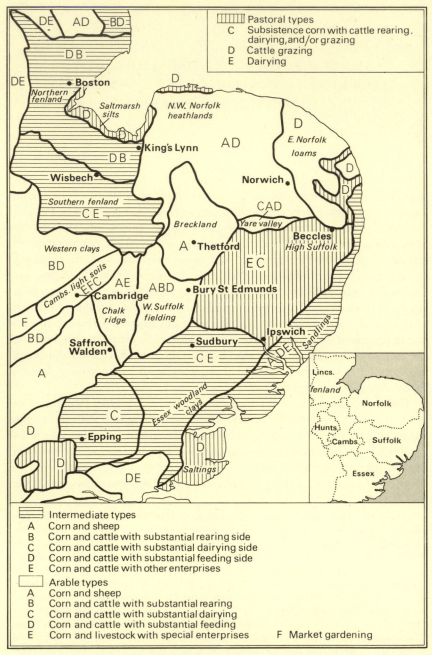

Fig. 7.1. Farming regions of East Anglia and the fens.

characteristic agricultural features of two different districts. This was especially noticeable around Norwich and in the Waveney, Wensum, and Stour valleys, but sports from the main stock could occur almost anywhere. To that extent the demarcation of each district sketched in the map is uncertain. High Suffolk, for example, despite the encroachment of the plough after 1600, remained *sui generis*, and the black fens, whatever their internal differences, were like nowhere else in England. The fielden districts, on the other hand, gradually moved in the direction of uniformity between 1600 and 1800, since what were the means to improvement in the celebrated Norfolk manner enabled and encouraged standardization of cultivation and crop selection across the whole range of light soils, from sands to tractable clays.

East Anglia was more than just a granary or a dairy. Its ancient and (in the seventeenth century) flourishing manufacturing and commercial interests not only supported an urban population as large as any in England outside London – Norwich, Colchester, Yarmouth, Lynn, Ipswich, Cambridge, and Bury were among the most substantial towns in England in 1676 – but influenced the growth and diversification of many 'industrialized' villages along the central axis of the region from East Dereham and North Walsham to Chelmsford and Harlow. In addition, the large population not dependent, or not wholly dependent, upon agriculture as an occupation encouraged food production to supply an extensive internal trade from what, as late as 1662, were marked out as surplus to deficient areas.[2] The directions of this trade were modified somewhat after 1630, and, at least in part, were overlaid by the flow of agricultural commodities to London or elsewhere outside the region, but the whole process of commercial expansion offered vastly greater opportunities for market specialization than in the sixteenth century.

Agrarian society in the region was almost as diverse as the landscape. The most obvious and fundamental distinction between areas of rural industrialization and of agricultural specialization coincided approximately with the woodland and fielden zones, but the distribution of non-agricultural occupations in the countryside was too wide to permit the simple equation of the wood–pasture economy with manufacturing and occupational dualism.[3] On the other hand, the trades which brought fame and commercial prosperity to the region, except fishing, were located in territory that had long been pastoral in character.

---

[2] See, PRO, State Papers (SP) 14/128 no. 65.

[3] See, for example, J. Thirsk, 'Industries in the Countryside', in F. J. Fisher, ed., *Essays in the Economic and Social History of Tudor and Stuart England*, Cambridge, 1961, pp. 70–88; J. Patten, 'Village and Town: An Occupational Study', AHR, xx, 1972, pp. 1–16; *id.*, 'Changing Occupational Structures in the East Anglian Countryside 1500–1700', in H. S. A. Fox and R. A. Butlin, eds., *Change in the Countryside: Essays on Rural England, 1500–1900*, London, 1979, pp. 103–21; *VCH Suffolk, II*, pp. 633–40.

The East Anglian textile trades in general, and especially the New Draperies, enjoyed a period of great prosperity between 1650 and 1700. The effects of this expansion were felt not only in the corporate towns, in Norwich or Colchester, but in dozens of small market towns and hundreds of half-agricultural, half-industrial villages. In the south, manufacturing was particularly important along the river valleys of the Blackwater, Colne, Stour, and Brett, where many specialist New Draperies were adopted and developed rapidly after 1630–50. The new centres of this trade were usually revived medieval textile towns – Lavenham, Long Melford, Sudbury, Glemsford – and each tended to specialize in a particular variety of cloth: bays, says, perpetuanas, calimancoes, etc. In Essex, the finishing processes, and even weaving, were concentrated in the towns, which were supplied with yarn from dozens of country villages right across north Essex. In Suffolk a similar pattern obtained, but rural weaving was more widespread, especially in the Brett valley.[4]

In Norfolk and the Waveney valley the domination of Norwich did not prevent the development of certain autonomous centres of worsted manufacturing. Village spinners were found in a large proportion of the parishes of east and central Norfolk and north-east Suffolk in the seventeenth century, and wool weaving was almost as broadly distributed. The organization of the woollen textile trades in the region was quite complex, but, for the goods destined as exports or for London, the commercial control over production was generally in the hands of urban drapers, who in turn were frequently answerable to Blackwell Hall factors. It was at any rate a capitalist, market-orientated industry throughout East Anglia.[5]

Some of the new draperies contained mixed fibres. The mixed fabrics for which Norwich was celebrated were made up of worsted yarn with linen or silk. As a result an East Anglian silk industry began, but on a small scale, in the later seventeenth century. The linen trade, however, was much older and much more extensive. Only a little of the linen yarn spun in Norfolk was employed in making stuffs. Most was used by peasant weavers to turn out fabrics which had their greatest vent locally. The greatest concentration

[4] K. J. Allison, 'The Norfolk Worsted Industry in the Sixteenth and Seventeenth Centuries', *Yorks. Bull. Econ. & Social Research*, XII, 1960, pp. 73–82, and XIII, 1961, pp. 61–77; J. E. Pilgrim, 'The Cloth Industry in Essex and Suffolk, 1558–1640', unpub. Univ. of London M.A. thesis, 1938; Burley, thesis, ch. 3; A. F. J. Brown, *Essex at Work, 1700–1900*, Chelmsford, 1969, ch. 1; *VCH Suffolk, II*, pp. 254–71; D. C. Coleman, 'An Innovation and its Diffusion: The "New Draperies"', *EcHR*, 2nd ser., XXII, 1969; R. Jenkins, 'Suffolk Industries: An Historical Survey', *Newcomen Soc.*, XIX, 1940, pp. 173–84.

[5] J. K. Edwards, 'The Gurneys and the Norwich Clothing Trade in the Eighteenth Century' *JFHS*, L, 1962–4, pp. 134–52; D. C. Coleman, 'Growth and Decay during the Industrial Revolution: The Case of East Anglia', *Scand. Econ. Hist. Rev.*, X, 1962, pp. 115–27; R. G. Wilson, 'The Supremacy of the Yorkshire Cloth Industry in the Eighteenth Century', in N. G. Harte and K. Ponting, eds., *Textile History and Economic History*, Manchester, 1974, pp. 240–1.

of workers and the only fully commercial production of linen goods was in the Waveney valley (Diss, Bungay, Beccles), where sailcloth was of importance in the eighteenth century.[6]

Apart from agricultural service trades a few other industries or commercial undertakings were of more than local importance in the countryside of the region: leather working, hosiery, glovemaking, shipbuilding, fishing and oyster dredging, milling and malting, each of which employed some agrarian capital and gave work to numerous labourers in various parts of East Anglia, often at slack periods of the agricultural year. In the western part of the region little manufacturing, except some spinning for Norwich or Colchester clothiers, had survived into the seventeenth century. Outside the few towns the heath, fen, chalk, and western claylands were almost entirely agricultural.

The prosperity of the rest of the region, although substantial after 1650, was always precarious because trade was so uncertain. By the 1690s several of the smaller townships which had flourished a generation earlier – Glemsford, Thaxted, Finchingfield, Haverhill – were already in decline, and the decay spread like caries eastwards into the Essex clothing districts. Suffolk also suffered from contraction of its textile industries in the first half of the eighteenth century, and further north even Norwich felt the draught as imported calicoes combined with difficult export markets to undercut the basis of the city's prosperity, at least for a time. By the 1720s the prospects for East Anglian industries looked unpromising, and for the remainder of our period stagnation rather than the buoyant expansion of 1650–80 was the most characteristic feature of economic life in most of the region's manufacturing trades. The change was bound to affect agriculture, if only because it reduced pressure upon labour at critical periods, but it also resulted in higher rates and other social burdens.[7]

The distribution of population in the region was reflected in the geography of agricultural and mixed communities. The densest village populations were to be found in the central areas, and especially in the woodland zone between Norwich and Brentwood. Moreover, the population was more markedly urban than in earlier or later times – more so, indeed, than in other English regions at the same period. Thus, according to John Patten, one-third of the people of Norfolk and Suffolk lived in towns in the 1670s, and this figure was not smaller in 1750. Essex was equally 'urbanized' after 1600, but not the counties in the west.[8] Norwich, as the second largest city in the kingdom,

---

[6] There is little directly relating to the linen trades in the region, but see Patten, 'Changing Occupational Structure'; VCH Suffolk, II, pp. 271–3; E. Pursehouse, Waveney Valley Studies, [Diss], n.d., pp. 177ff; M. Meek, 'Hempen Cloth Industry in Suffolk', Suffolk Rev., II, 1961, pp. 82–5.

[7] M. F. Lloyd Prichard, 'Treatment of Poverty in Norfolk, 1700–1850', unpub. Univ. of Cambridge Ph.D. thesis, 1949, passim; Burley, thesis, pp. 25–6, 335–64.

[8] P. Corfield, 'Urban Development in England and Wales in the Sixteenth and Seventeenth Centuries', in D. C. Coleman and A. H. John, eds., Trade, Government and Economy in Pre-Industrial

with almost 30,000 inhabitants in 1700, was alone a sufficient magnet of regional migration and an engine of Norfolk's economic development. But it was Norwich as an industrial city controlling the manufacturing activity of a large tributary countryside that gave to it its special economic importance for the region. Several of the larger towns, however, reached a peak of population in the later seventeenth century, and thereafter stagnated, or even declined, for fifty years or more.

The demographic history of the larger East Anglian towns probably reflects the general history of population in the region after 1650.[9] Insufficient research has been published in parish-register demography, but the trends revealed in the comparison of contemporary enumerations are not likely to be far wide of the mark. In 1750–1 the population of the five whole counties, together with the Parts of Holland in Lincolnshire, perhaps amounted to 700,000–750,000. Eighty or more years earlier the data from hearth-tax or religious-census returns suggest a population of about the same size. It is not inconceivable that numbers remained more or less constant in our period at about three-quarters of a million people, although it is equally likely that growth of population, which had certainly slowed down after 1630, resumed briefly after the Restoration, reached a peak early in the eighteenth century, and thereafter actually declined until the middle third of the century. Whatever internal movements may have occurred, long-run stability is of overriding importance as an element both in economic change and in the expectations of contemporaries.

RECLAMATION AND ENCLOSURE

Reclamation was a continuous and sometimes repetitive process. The drainage of a large segment of the peat fens after 1630 was the most spectacular aspect of a widespread, and usually piecemeal, exercise in 'approvement'.[10] Apart from the dry heaths, considerable patches of riverain carrs, meres, sloughs, 'hard' scrub, and woodland were brought into several

England, London, 1976; id., 'A Provincial Capital in the Late Seventeenth Century: The Case of Norwich', in P. Clarke and P. Slack, eds., Crisis and Order in English Towns, 1500–1700, London 1972, pp. 263–7; Patten, 'Village and Town'; id., 'Population Distribution in Norfolk and Suffolk during the Sixteenth and Seventeenth Centuries', Inst. Brit. Geog., LXV, 1975; id., 'Patterns of Migration and Movement of Labour to Three Pre-Industrial East Anglian Towns', J. Hist. Geog., II, 1976.

9 Patten, 'Population Distribution' and 'Patterns of Migration'; C. T. Smith, 'Population and Settlement', in J. A. Steers, ed., Cambridge and its Region, 1965, Cambridge, 1965, pp. 138ff; C. A. F. Meekings, in VCH Cambs., IV–VI; M. Spufford, 'Rural Cambridgeshire 1520–1680', unpub. Univ. of Leicester M.A. thesis, 1962, pp. 44–58; id., Contrasting Communities, Cambridge, 1974, pp. 10ff; Burley, thesis, pp. 3–26; Brown, op. cit., pp. 93–109; P. Deane and W. A. Cole, British Economic Growth, 1688–1959, 2nd edn, Cambridge, 1962, p. 103.

10 On enclosure and reclamation in general, the articles by Postgate and Roden, op. cit., are invaluable.

cultivation between 1600 and 1750. The effort was probably greatest before 1640, but the momentum acquired in years of high corn prices and pressing population endured for two generations at least after the interruption caused by the war. The problem of dating is so difficult that we can make no estimate of the extent of reclamation in East Anglia between 1640 and 1750. Modern maps still betray evidence of pre-parliamentary reclamation and enclosure of ancient woods, especially in the clays; of meres and swamps, not only in the fenland; and of small, usually isolated 'brakes' (heathland) wherever light sands occurred. In both the eastern and western clay plateaux, the woodland had been reduced before 1600 to isolated stands of ancient timber trees and dense scrub, which in the next century were stubbed up and turned into farm land. Very few old woods survived beyond 1750 in Cambridgeshire or the woodland zone unless protected within the pale of a mansion-house park, or preserved for profitable exploitation by a great estate. In the event, the loss of the woodlands was partly compensated for by the amount of new tree planting, in hedgerows or managed spinneys, which occurred after 1660 all over eastern England.

The history of carr land reclamation is rather similar. On the one hand, the clearance of alder scrub and the drying of the land increased the amount of low meadow available, but alder and withy holts continued to provide a good profit to their owners in the seventeenth and eighteenth centuries, and less marsh scrub was cleared than agriculturalists may have desired.

Important as was piecemeal reclamation, it was overshadowed by drainage work in the black fens and coastal saltings and by large-scale enclosure of the common fields which remained in Norfolk and Suffolk after 1600. Deforestation in Essex had reached some kind of peak in the early seventeenth century when pressure of population and the demand for timber had eaten away a considerable portion of Waltham Forest. The Civil War enlarged the demand for timber trees, but so alarming was depletion of forest stocks by 1660 that a policy of conservation and renewal was instigated. Apart from some new planting the result was a check upon clearance for agricultural use. From 1660 to 1750 deforestation was a distinctly minor theme in the history of agricultural improvement of Essex.[11]

Saltmarsh drainage also came to a halt after 1650. Reclamation did not cease, partly because of the need to protect and underprop the sea banks against an encroaching sea, but a good deal of sound marshland was lost by erosion after 1600, more perhaps than was gained by new reclamation. In Essex, where the saltings were very extensive, there had been much activity

---

[11] On the survival, eradication, and management of East Anglian woodlands, especially on the clay plateau, and in ancient forests, see R. Allison, thesis, pp. 85–109, 133–4; Essex RO, D/DB.11/2/16; West Suffolk RO (= WSRO), 1,754/1/21ff; East Suffolk RO (= ESRO), T/1/1/1.2.SI/13/16.1; Essex RO, D/DGh/E2; Norwich and Norfolk RO (= NNRO), MSS 10,319–22: Armstrong, op. cit., pp. 33ff. Cf. NNRO, How 572; NCC (Petre), box 17.

before 1625, and there was again in the middle and late eighteenth century. Canvey Island, exceptionally, was drained and improved by Dutch settlers after the Restoration.

Along a coast of sedimentation reclamation is quite straightforward. Flocks of sheep and an adequate supply of labour to dig embankments and drains, and to keep the outfalls open, were sufficient to bring the sea- and river-borne silt into good pasture.[12] By the early eighteenth century the Wash saltmarshes were used not only to summer-feed livestock but also to produce large crops of grain and coleseed, and even of turnips. The earliest examples of this new land use may be found in the records of Lestrange of Hunstanton, whose marsh estates were bearing coleseed and oats by 1637; but ploughing in such superb pastureland was frowned upon by most landlords before 1730, and the object of reclamation round the coast was chiefly to supply 'hard' land farmers with summer grass for grazing or mowing.[13]

Black-fen drainage is much more celebrated.[14] It is associated with the earl of Bedford, with Vermuyden and the Company of Adventurers, but what was achieved between 1630 and 1660 rested both upon earlier works and upon a long tradition of reclamation and colonization. Numerous projects were mooted, financed, and brought, at least temporarily, to fruition between 1610 and 1670, of which the Bedford–Vermuyden undertaking in the Ouse washes was the largest and most significant. Further north, Dutch engineers were engaged by projectors, the most notable of whom was the earl of Lindsey, to drain parts of the lower Witham and the Lindsey fens around Boston; and a beginning was made on what proved a prolonged scheme, the reclamation of Deeping Fen between Spalding and Stamford. Companies of adventurers, who invested in, and expected good returns from, black-fen drainage are found at work from Mildenhall to north Lincolnshire between 1625 and 1670. Apart from the crown, the projects attracted London businessmen and lawyers, but the most important part was usually played by local magnates such as Bedford, Lindsey, Hare, Cotton, and Monson. Resistance to the schemes by fen peasants and some local gentry often broke out in uproar and riot, but the factors which most seriously hindered success

---

[12] Reclamation of the saltings after 1640 is discussed in J. Thirsk, *English Peasant Farming*, London, 1957, pp. 129–34, 146; R. Blome, *Britannia*, London, 1673, pp. 144–5; C. Merret, "Observations", BL, Add. MS 34,141, f. 46ff; E. D. R. Burrell, 'Historical Geography of the Sandlings of Suffolk, 1600–1850', unpub. Univ. of London M.Sc. thesis, 1960, pp. 121–34; H. L. Gray, *English Field Systems*, Cambridge, Mass., 1915, pp. 326–7; W. Blith, *The English Improver Improved*, London, 1652, p. 208; J. A. Steers, *The Coastline of England and Wales*, Cambridge, 1946, pp. 352–3; Burley, thesis, p. 44; B. E. Cracknell, *Canvey Island*, Leicester, 1959, pp. 15–37.

[13] NNRO, Lestrange MSS KA4, KA9; see also BIR/5; NRS15,994.

[14] H. C. Darby, *The Draining of the Fens*, Cambridge, 1940; A. K. Astbury, *The Black Fens*, Cambridge, 1957, pp. 105ff; Thirsk, *English Peasant Farming*, pp. 117ff; Kerridge, *op. cit.*, pp. 227–38; W. Dugdale, *The History of Imbanking and Drayning*, London, 1662.

were the distractions caused by the Civil War and the faulty engineering of most projects.[15] Not even Vermuyden understood the problems of successful drainage in a 'saucer', with the outfalls constantly at risk of silting up. The Bedford Level, for example, was well engineered as far as realignment of the Ouse and its feeders down to Denver was concerned, but the flow proved too sluggish to prevent internal silting, and all the black-fen channels were subject to backwash from the tidal outfalls. The use of windmills assisted the flow but was inadequate to overcome the shrinkage of the peat which followed upon the drainage. Accordingly much work had to be repeated after 1630, and it was often necessary to cut new channels to relieve particular pressure points. Some drainage works were so badly damaged by riots, as at Mildenhall or Deeping Fen before 1670, that the reclamation broke down. At Deeping a running fight between drainage projectors and fenmen lasted for over a century, and the work was not completed till well after 1750. Other projects, notably that in the east Lindsey fens, were seriously underfinanced from the start.

Leaving aside any question of the return upon investment, it is fair to assume that the drainage schemes after 1630 were agriculturally quite successful. Much of the 'water land' was made dry enough to yield sound grass, and even more dry enough to produce good crops. The effects on the water table were sufficient to allow winter crops to be grown more regularly in the field land of fen villages, and several of the meres shrank and became shallow enough for piecemeal reclamation. The Bedford Level project was completed and improved in the 1650s, and for at least a generation the Ouse valley from St Ives to Denver was turned into highly productive agricultural land. By 1730 enough had been done also to the Welland, Nene, Shire Drain, Lark, and Little Ouse to lay dry thousands of acres of black fen. Moreover, despite setbacks, these efforts were sufficient to reclaim permanently somewhat more than half the acreage that had been waterlogged in the sixteenth century. The work of parliamentary commissioners in enclosing fenland waste was indubitably made easier by the activities of their predecessors in the area.

Common-field enclosure had already achieved significant changes in the East Anglian landscape before 1640, and the process continued throughout the next century.[16] In the woodland clays medieval field systems had been extinguished before 1650, by which time the once extensive common pastures and meadows were also under assault. Several 'greens' or 'tyes' (the

---

[15] For disturbances, see Thirsk, *English Peasant Farming*, pp. 123ff. Unrest was especially rife during and after the Civil War – Darby, *op. cit.*, pp. 46, 50–9; Dugdale, *op. cit.*, pp. 142, 419; *CSPD*, 1653–4, p. 366; 1655, p. 288; LJ, N.S., IV, 1699–1702, pp. 217–18; WSRO, E18/400/7, 9; NNRO, How 725/1.

[16] Gray, *op. cit.*, pp. 305–54, 401ff; Postgate and Roden, in Baker and Butlin, *op. cit.*, pp. 287–90, 365–73, and *passim*.

term used in south Suffolk and Essex) disappeared during the seventeenth century, and most of what was left in 1700 were subsequently eaten away at the edges. Common grassland, however, was still comparatively plentiful, especially along the river valleys or in the centre of the more nucleated of woodland villages.[17]

The clays of the west, by contrast, remained largely open and undivided until 1750, for even piecemeal enclosure was inhibited by the strength of manorial custom and collective action in Cambridgeshire and Huntingdonshire. A few great landowners – such as the Chicheleys and St Georges – discommoned part of their estates, but only a small number of townships appear to have been fully enclosed between 1600 and 1750. It was, however, a period of considerable strain in the social relations of landlords and peasants and of yeomen and husbandmen, which was often attributable to disputes over common rights.[18]

In the southern fens, the open fields which existed in 1640 were still more or less intact in 1750, for the increase in the area in severalty was principally confined to the newly drained 'fen grounds' which had formerly been common pasture. Further north, especially in Holland, arable assarts in the Marsh came to dominate the tillage of the region. Confusion between common fields and severalty was so widespread as to appear the normal state of affairs by the seventeenth century.[19]

The fielden districts of Norfolk, Suffolk, eastern Cambridgeshire, and north-west Essex contained not only the most distinctive but also the most complex of agrarian regimes in eastern England. Their enclosure history is

[17] Dymond, *op. cit.*, p. 30; N. Scarfe, *The Suffolk Landscape*, London, 1972, pp. 178ff; Spratt, thesis, pp. 40–1, 49–50, 63–4; N. Riches, *The Agricultural Revolution in Norfolk*, Chapel Hill, 1937, pp. 52ff; BL, Add. MS 21,054, ff. 6, 18, 21 *et seqq.*; BL, Add. MS 40,063/64 *passim*; W. R. Emerson, 'Economic Development of the Estates of the Petre Family in Essex in the 16th and 17th Centuries', unpub. Univ. of Oxford D.Phil. thesis, 1951, pp. 262ff; F. W. Steer, ed., *Farm and Cottage Inventories of Mid-Essex, 1635–1749*, Chelmsford, 1950, *passim*; Burley, thesis, pp. 38ff; G. H. Rendall, *Dedham in History*, Colchester, 1937, pp. 20–1; ESRO, 50/9/1, 51/10/11.5, 17.2; HA12/D3/1; T1/1/1; T1/1/2; HD80/1/2.20, 27, 29; WSRO, 634; 806/1/134, 176; 1,754/1/21ff; Essex RO, D/DP/E182, E34; NNRO, box 106; Clayton 17 (MS 3,226); MS 9,315; PD119/42; Meade of Earsham MSS, Windham Docs. 21; MS 17,586, Diss Tithe Book; R. C. Coles, 'Enclosures: Essex Agriculture, 1500–1900', *Essex Naturalist*, XXVI, 1937.

[18] C. C. Taylor, *The Cambridgeshire Landscape*, London, 1973, pp. 177ff; W. E. Tate, 'Cambridgeshire Field Systems', *Camb. Archaeol. Soc.*, XL, 1939–42; *VCH Cambs., V*; C. Vancouver, *General View of the Agriculture of the County of Cambridge*, London, 1794, *passim*; R. Parkinson, *General View of the Agriculture of Huntingdonshire*, London, 1813, pp. 87ff; Cambs. RO, L11/137; R72/18.

[19] For enclosure not directly connected with reclamation in the fenlands after 1600–40, see Spufford, *Contrasting Communities*, pp. 122ff; *VCH Cambs., IV, passim*; WSRO, 633/1; P. Bigmore, *The Bedfordshire and Huntingdonshire Landscape*, London, 1979, pp. 158ff; Hunts. RO, 15/219; R1/2/1. In Holland the following townships at least retained some common fields until the era of parliamentary enclosure: Bicker, Donington, Fishtoft, Frampton, Freiston, Kirton, Quadring, Wigtoft.

fittingly involuted.[20] The lack of symmetry in the field plans of the district, the emphasis upon furlongs and selions rather than fields, the uneven distribution of plots attached to particular holdings, and, above all, the dominance of the foldcourse, were not only factors peculiar to East Anglia but confined the horizons of the common-field farmers in the district. While the first three tended to promote individual occupation and enclosure, the foldcourse was for long a powerful obstacle to change. But the fielden generally contained immense tracts of rough common, furze, downland, or alder carr, which, however fundamental to foldcourse management, also contributed to satisfy the local appetite for enclosures. Enclosure even occurred within the open fields of the district in spite of the foldcourse, though it was characteristically in the form of small closes, often thrown open after harvest to allow for folding. As the foldcourses decayed, these 'half-year' lands were converted into 'whole-year' closes.

The progress of enclosure in general, within the fielden districts, sometimes caused their agrarian systems to be modified or reorganized, to accommodate a viable foldcourse, or, particularly in Breckland, to reduce the risks of soil erosion or exhaustion. In the Suffolk Sandlings the ancient system of interdependence between heath and arable was decaying by 1600, as a result of which less of the field systems remained to be enclosed by act of parliament than in the Norfolk sands.[21] Of the old champion districts only the loams of east Norfolk had gone farther towards complete enclosure by 1750. By that date very little common arable or pasture remained in this area. The transformation cannot be dated exactly, but William Marshall's surmise in 1783 that it had occurred about a century before is probably quite accurate.[22] Breckland contained many depopulated villages engrossed by a single landowner, which were technically enclosed by 1700, although soil conditions were often so difficult that agricultural practice changed more slowly. In Breckland the ecological balance between turf and tillage was often too precarious to permit any widespread change of land use before the eighteenth

[20] Gray, op. cit., pp. 308, 318ff; M. R. Postgate, op. cit., pp. 288f; VCH Cambs., VI; D. Monteith, 'Saffron Walden and Environs: A Study in Development of Landscape', unpub. Univ. of London M.A. thesis, 1957; Spratt, thesis, pp. 36–56, 254–5; Riches, op. cit., pp. 8–11; R. A. C. Parker, Coke of Norfolk, Oxford, 1975, pp. 39ff; Norfolk Archaeol., XXIV, 1932, p. 55; NNRO, D. & C. MSS, Parlt. Surveys, 1649, ff. 98 et seqq.; NCC (Petre MSS), boxes 9, 16, 17; B.L. VIb III/2, Hare 5443, KA4; How 570, 572, 573, 723/1, 5; 725/1, 6; 717; BIR31/5; LAO, Mon 7/11/66; WSRO, E7/10/26; E3/10/5, 7; BL, Harl. MS 368, f. 171; Suffolk Inst. Arch., XXV, 1951, p. 240.

[21] J. Kirby, The Suffolk Traveller, Ipswich, 1735, pp. 2ff; BL, Add. MS 32,134, ff. 24–9; E. D. R. Burrell, thesis, passim; H. M. Doughty, Chronicles of Theberton, London, 1910, pp. 94–5; D. W. Gramolt, 'Coastal Marshlands of East Essex between the 17th and the Mid-19th Centuries', unpub. Univ. of London M.A. thesis, 1960, pp. 314ff; ESRO, HA49/1/2; HA1/F 9/3; 50/22/3.5, 4.42, 12.6; Essex RO, D/DGh/M45/4, E1.

[22] W. Marshall, The Rural Economy of Norfolk, 2 vols., London, 1787, I, pp. 4, 8, 96, 116; Spratt, thesis, pp. 40–1, 51; N. Kent, General View of the Agriculture of Norfolk, London, 1796, p. 22.

century. North-west Norfolk retained the core of its open fields, and yet was able also to maintain many foldcourses and shifting cultivation in the heathland brecks until the eighteenth century. Progressive farming, however, which employed new crops and new techniques of close folding, increasingly demanded enclosures. As a result infield closes and enclosed brecks both became more numerous after 1650, but the uneasy balance between the traditional and modern was sustained at least until Arthur Young's day.[23] Finally the chalk ridge and southern fielden also saw a good deal of piecemeal enclosure which interfered with the asymmetrical field systems inherited from the Middle Ages. Most of the villages lying between Cambridge, Bury, and Harlow, however, retained their common fields until enclosed by act of parliament.[24]

By 1750 about half of East Anglia could still be classified as fielden. Only east Norfolk and the Sandlings had changed into predominantly enclosed landscapes in the previous 150 years. Elsewhere active enclosure seldom went so far, and there were few fielden parishes in 1700 with more than one-third, and less than one-tenth, of their acreage in whole-year closes. The distribution of enclosures, therefore, was about the same as in the rest of lowland England, although the proportion of enclosure involving fieldland and wasteland was different in East Anglia from that of the Midlands.

ARABLE REGIMES

Except in the western claylands, the keynote of arable management in East Anglia from 1600 to 1800 was flexibility. Right across the region farmers responded to new opportunities by adopting new crops, by adapting their rotations to take account of a new emphasis in mixed farming, and by achieving a new balance in their husbandry between foodstuffs and industrial raw materials. Product specialization propelled some of the adjustments and improvements made during the period, but the evidence of local market specialization, which is relatively abundant, must not mislead us into the belief that it exactly mirrored particular preferences in farming practice. In fact mixed husbandry remained the cornerstone of East Anglian agriculture in each of the great divisions of the region, woodland, heathland, and fenland.

New crops were introduced to modify rotations; commercial stock feeding on arable farms became more entrenched; wheat was a crop more

[23] M. R. Postgate, 'The Field Systems of Breckland', AHR, x, 1961; W. G. Clarke, *In Breckland Wilds*, London, 1926, pp. 99–100; Gray, *op. cit.*, pp. 311–12; Elveden MSS (at Elveden Hall, inspected by kind permission of Lord Iveagh), 22/H ii, 24/J.16, 29/M, 30, E.H.C. 1740; WSRO, 293/13; 399/6; E3/10/9.19; 613/758/1, 3; *Norfolk Archaeol.*, xxxii, 1970–2, pp. 343f; NNRO, PD13/38; Dun 69/16; NRS966, Michas. 1756 proposals of lease; PRA378; TL8, 9; MSS 10,687, 10,701, 18,262, 6,495.

[24] Monteith, thesis, *passim*; M. Spufford, *A Cambridgeshire Community: Chippenham*, Leicester, 1965, pp. 17ff; *VCH Cambs., VI*; Essex RO, D/DBy/E9.

widely cultivated during the period and, wherever suitable, was preferred before other grains in the winter shift. These innovations tended to diminish the ancient division between pastoral and arable in the region. More intensive production, which is the essence of improvement in East Anglia after 1600, affected every segment of the province, although in the clays of the west adherence to traditional, not to say rigid, regimes of tillage rather inhibited the reception of new practices.

Little ostensible uniformity prevailed in East Anglian arable regimes in the mid seventeenth century.[25] Tillage was seldom confined within the bounds of ancient fields. Where enclosure was almost complete by 1700, in the woodland and on the east Norfolk loams, arable farmers obviously made no distinction between former field land, reclaimed waste, and converted pasture, but for the most part East Anglian tilth masters contrived to manage open-field and other arable land somewhat differently. Convertible husbandry was common everywhere by the seventeenth century, but it probably never dominated the system of management. The field-grass system, often called 'layering' in local records, is frequently referred to, but almost always as a minor adjunct to permanent tillage rotations in field land. 'Up-and-down' courses in heath or downland intakes, in enclosed arable plots, or in fen grounds were ubiquitous, although they did not all possess the same characteristics. In the fielden, especially in the Norfolk heaths and Suffolk Sandlings, field layering was probably inhibited by the demands of the foldcourse, which even in decay could influence the pattern of agricultural land use to a significant degree. The need to feed sheep in the customary courses restricted the farmer's opportunity of cross-cropping or of extinguishing his bare fallows, since the sheepmaster needed to retain his access to the common fields.[26]

During the seventeenth century East Anglian field rotations may not have been uniform, but they contained within their organization a remarkably widespread commemoration of an ancient three-shift system. Thus the medieval distinction between tilth, breach, and fallow (masquerading at times under characteristic East Anglian names: till, broke, summerley or olland; forecrop, aftercrop, summerland or follow; etc.) survived at least nominally until the later eighteenth century. These terms, indeed, were even used in

[25] The classic statement is in Gray, *op. cit.*, pp. 298ff; cf. M. R. Postgate, 'The Open Fields of Cambridgeshire', unpub. Univ. of Cambridge Ph.D. thesis, 1964, whose findings have been questioned by Ravensdale, *Liable to Floods*, p. 85. The problem is that the apparent lack of uniformity makes possible several varying interpretations.

[26] The foldcourse is discussed below, pp. 228–31; its effects upon tenurial arrangements and cropping practice are well treated by Postgate, in Baker and Butlin, *op. cit.*, pp. 318ff. Field grass, leys, convertible husbandry in East Anglia in general loom large in Kerridge, *The Agricultural Revolution*, *passim*; cf. Postgate, in Baker and Butlin, pp. 300ff; *Gentleman's Mag.*, XXII, 1752, pp. 455f; Parker, *op. cit.*, pp. 43ff, 54ff; WSRO, E/3/10/9.19, NNRO, WKC5/152; NCC (Petre) MSS, box 17; Marshall, *op. cit.*, *passim*.

long-enclosed woodland parishes to represent some kind of rotational pattern, although surviving examples refer actually to crops rather than to shifts.[27]

At one extreme in the region, in the western clays of Cambridge and Huntingdon, and in certain villages elsewhere — at Kennett or Fowlmere in the chalk, for example — the common Midland combination of a three-field with a three-shift system had scarcely been disturbed before 1750.[28] Moreover, in this district, the convertible system, relatively so common in the Midland plain, was infrequent and small in extent, although practice differed considerably from one parish to the next. In the southern fenlands where open fields continued to be serviceable to the local economy, several villages had developed four-field systems, either to accommodate a summer corn (oats or pulses) shift or to make room for more barley. Cottenham actually worked five fields, one in winter corn, one in beans, one fallow, and two in barley.[29] Several other townships were less conventionally organized, their field systems resembling those of the northern (i.e. chiefly Lincolnshire) fenland, where the progress of reclamation had weakened field tillage by emphasizing convertible husbandry. What survived of the old fields was asymmetrical and frequently divided unequally among the farmers of the townships in a way which encouraged individual or several cultivation.[30]

Asymmetrical field systems were numerous also in the chalk and on the loam soils of the fielden, which extended from west Suffolk into north-west Essex and south-east Cambridgeshire. Here the fields were usually arranged in three-crop shifts (forecrop, aftercrop, summerland). Sometimes the shifts were set within furlongs or precincts, but there were villages like Snailwell that apparently followed no collaborative rotations, leaving the choice of crops and shifts to individual enterprise or at least to the landlord's prescription. At the same time ploughing in the upland or heathland sheepwalks, especially around Saffron Walden and Newmarket, gave farmers

[27] See, for example, Postgate, in Baker and Butlin, *op. cit.*, pp. 297–8; Spufford, *Contrasting Communities*, p. 96; Cambs. RO, P72/3/1; P9/3/4; R58/9/1/13; ESRO, T1/1/4; WSRO, 1,754/1/22 *et seq.*; Barnardiston Tithe Book, 1698–1758; NNRO, NCC (Petre), box 17; PRA358; WKC5/152. The terms are also commonplace in probate inventories. They refer, of course, to field courses rather than to territorial divisions, but could be applied both to 'campane' (whole field) and to precinctual arrangements when communal cultivation was in order.

[28] *VCH Cambs.*, V, VI; Glos. RO, H1/ST/E107/2, 4, 5; Gonville & Caius Coll., Cambridge, MSS XIV/35; Cambs. RO, R58/9/1/13; R58/5/iv, f. 70; Cambridge Univ. Library, Ely Dioc. Rec. H1/3, 4, 5; T. F. Teversham, *History of Sawston*, 2 vols., London, 1947, *passim*; PRO, C5/29/235; E 134/28, 9 Chas II, Hil. 11; Vancouver, *op. cit.*; Parkinson, *op. cit.*

[29] Ravensdale, *op. cit.*, pp. 86ff; Spufford, *Contrasting Communities*, pp. 128ff; Cambs. RO, R50/7/27; R60/24/2/42; Pembroke Coll., Cambridge, MSS A/13; C. F. Tebbutt, *History of Bluntisham & Earith*, St Neots, 1941, pp. 46ff; *VCH Cambs.*, IV; *VCH Hunts.*, III.

[30] The few open fields which survived north of Ely in the fens after 1650 (see *VCH Cambs.*, IV, pp. 201, 226, and n. 19 above) were small, dispersed, and fragmented. Cf. Thirsk, *English Peasant Farming*, p. 14.

much opportunity for up-and-down rotations, and eventually encouraged them to adopt semi-permanent ley crops like sainfoin or nonsuch.[31]

The woodland, shading also imperceptibly into the Suffolk and Essex fielden, was an enclosed landscape in which consolidation of small, scattered closes into more rational units of cultivation was going ahead very actively between 1550 and 1750. In our period the dominant arable regime of the district was convertible.[32] The different courses were divided in divers enclosed shifts, each of which was kept in tillage for three or four years, followed by about six years in a grass ley.[33] On the heaviest clays, especially in Essex, bare fallowing continued to serve farmers whose primary interest was wheat, but by 1650 the majority of woodland husbandmen were growing beans, vetches, peas, buckwheat, or the dredge known as bullimong, on the stubble of winter grains. Hemp, too, was occasionally cultivated, in riverain soils as a fallow crop before wheat, although it was most usually grown in small plots by cottagers or farmers. Nearly all the land in the woodland, except for a few common meadows, was potentially arable, but at any one time less than half of the ground was under the plough.[34]

In the southern woodland (from Stowmarket to Chelmsford) arable production was of rather greater moment than in the northern half. Thus the proportion in tillage at any time differed somewhat in the two segments, although the basic structure was the same. The south depended less upon dairying for the market than high Suffolk or high Norfolk, and the leys were regarded more for their utility in improving ploughland than as a principal source of forage for neat cattle. Even so almost all farms in the district depended upon mixed husbandry, and many of the new plants introduced into the area in the seventeenth and eighteenth centuries – turnips, cabbages, ryegrass, clover, nonsuch, buckwheat – significantly were forage crops.[35]

The classic, and distinctive, East Anglian arable regime was that of the sands in Norfolk and Suffolk. Here a sheep–corn husbandry, constructed around the requisites of the foldcourse, had for long sustained a successful

---

[31] *VCH Cambs., VI*; Spufford, *Chippenham*, p. 17; Tate, *op. cit.*; W. H. Palmer, *History of the Parish of Borough Green*, Camb. Antiq. Soc., 8ᵛᵒ vols., LIV, 1949, pp. 136–9; Pembroke Coll., Cambridge, MSS T/5; Gonville & Caius Coll., MSS. xiv/35; Glos. RO, H1/ST/E107/5; Cambs. RO, R55/7/43/10; Monteith, thesis, *passim*; C. Vancouver, *General View of the Agriculture of Essex*, London, 1795, p. 105; ESRO, V/5/23/2.1 f. 17; King's Coll., Cambridge, Mun. G82; Essex RO, D/DKw/E1/1; D/DBy/E9; BL, Add. MS 5,823. f. 20 *et seq.*; WSRO, 996/5/3.

[32] Kerridge, *op. cit.*, p. 85, 90; Kirby, *op. cit.*, p. 6; Riches, *op. cit.*, pp. 52–3; ESRO, 50/22/1.36 (1); 51/10/17.2, 17.3; HA12/D3/1; HA12/E1/1/20; S1/13/16.1; T1/1/4; WSRO, 1,754/1/22 *et seqq.*; 592/2/37, 42, 74; 592/18/25; 592/22/85; 592/34/5; NNRO, Invs. 47/87, 101, 58A/44; 58B/51; 60/43, 55; MS 17,586; microfilm 35/2.

[33] Spratt, thesis, *passim*. Most of the references in n. 32 mention the proportion of arable to pasture in area.

[34] *VCH Essex, II*, pp. 450ff; Essex RO, D/DGh/E1; ESRO, HA12/D3/1; WSRO, 634.

[35] Steer, *op. cit.*; Essex RO, D/DGh/E2; D/DKw/E1/1; D/DP/E25, E34, E182; D/DGE/506; D/DQs/58/6.

balance between grazing and tillage, which produced the largest surplus of wool and grain available in the region until the later seventeenth century. However, the townships on the best loams had generally been enclosed before 1700, and thereafter developed an essentially convertible system of husbandry that resembled the woodland arable economy.[36] East Norfolk was an important area for the production of fine malting barley and for the fattening of bullocks in the seventeenth century. William Marshall's opinion that this district pioneered the celebrated Norfolk alternate rotation about one hundred years before he wrote may well be correct. As he well knew, the regime was not four- but six-course – wheat, barley, turnips, barley, seeds (two years) – which probably evolved simply out of a once-typical up-and-down succession of tilth and leys. This rotation (or minor variations upon it) was certainly in use before 1720 on all the good loam soils of Norfolk, but whether it was their standard regime at that period remains doubtful.[37] Basically, however, some such pattern had inevitably to emerge, for the need to balance the growth of barley with fodder crops, and to maintain soil fertility in a system which tended increasingly to emphasize stallfeeding, limited the practical choice of farmers to some variety of alternating regime of tillage.

The sandy heathland villages of north-west Norfolk, of Breckland and its outliers, and of the Suffolk coast possessed a complicated system of arable management, expressed in one mode as 'infield' and 'outfield', in another as a combination of open fields, closes, temporary brecks, and outlying waste seldom if ever under the plough.[38]

The infield was regarded as permanent tillage, regularly manured and cropped, usually in a rotation which resembled the three-shift system inherited from the Middle Ages. The foldcourse served the purpose of fertilizing the arable land, and the continuing need to close-fold sheep sustained the practice of fallowing in the seventeenth-century field land. The foldcourse was not of course indispensable; and less rigid, equally efficient or more efficient means of dressing or repairing topsoil, using marl, cart dung, compost crops, or new ploughing techniques, had before 1640 begun to undermine its prevalence. The outfield was not always confined to the taking of occasional crops from soil prepared by prolonged fallowing. Outfield 'brecks' (or intakes) were often dressed by sheep, folded less often than in the infield or open-field land, but still as part of a customary fold right. Indeed, one stage in the process of reclaiming heath into permanent arable was the

[36] Kerridge, *op. cit.*, pp. 87–9; Marshall, *op. cit.*, *passim*; Riches, *op. cit.*, pp. 54, 82, 92ff; Spratt, thesis, pp. 40–1, 51, 55. The documentary material for this district is sparse.

[37] Marshall, *op. cit.*, I, p. 132; Kerridge, *op. cit.*, p. 88.

[38] K. J. Allison, 'The Sheep–Corn Husbandry of Norfolk in the Sixteenth and Seventeenth Centuries', AHR, v, 1957; Postgate, 'Field Systems of Breckland'; Parker, *op. cit.*, *passim*; NNRO, Hare 5,443; B.L. viib, ixd; NCC (Petre), boxes 9, 16, 17.

application of marl in great quantities in areas at least peripheral to the ancient fields. In the more barren sands the contrast between every-year lands supported by heavy manuring and skilful ploughing, and breck lands, intermittently in tillage, was even more marked. The plethora of half-year closes, whole-year closes, enclosed brecks, and field layers suggest not only that the heathlands were moving in the same direction as east Norfolk and the woodland after 1650, but that the methods of arable farming were themselves often diverse even on a single farm. Thus rotations were individualistic, not to say eccentric, and the only rule which seems generally to have been obeyed was not to take more than two white crops in succession. Even that sensible provision was occasionally neglected in the cultivation of temporary brecks, and by one or two small farmers whose crop selections are recorded in the Hunstanton Field Book of the early eighteenth century.[39] But before the new crops came into use farmers on the heaths, as in east Norfolk and the woodland, were employing pulses, especially vetches, lentils, and white peas, at least as occasional fallow-break crops in their rotations.

The convertible systems of the heathlands were more varied than elsewhere in the region, cheifly because the poverty of so much of the soil enjoined very brief — often one-year — tillage upon many farmers. At its best, convertible husbandry could follow a sequence of six or seven crop shifts before layering, which approximated closely to the system as it was managed in more fertile districts. Close-folding and marling both assisted in the prolongation of these arable shifts, often as a precursor of permanent enclosure. 'Brecks' still existed in the heathland landscape in 1750–1800, but the process of standardization in outfield cultivation had then gone so far that many estates practised an increasingly uniform alternative rotation, four-shift, six-shift, or, on some of the remaining weak soils, a longer course which simply allowed for a semi-permanent ley of sainfoin, nonsuch, or ryegrass after the common sequence of grains and roots. Sheep folding, increasingly freed from the foldcourse and therefore under the control of the farmers, on turnips or clover leys, and the greater supplies of yard dung available through the widespread adoption of bullock feeding underpinned the beneficial work begun in the old regime. It was the combination of new crops and new livestock management which propelled agricultural progress in north-west Norfolk and the Sandlings. In other words, what the Victorians called 'high feeding' already existed in essence, a century before Philip Pusey was born, on a considerable number of Norfolk and Suffolk farms spread over a wide area of the ancient sheep–corn country.

The diversity of East Anglian arable regimes was less marked in the pattern of crop selection. Although the list of plants grown in the region was long, the half-dozen principal ones, barley, wheat, rye, oats, beans, and peas, were not only traditional but hardly represented regional specialities. Only the new

[39] NNRO, Lestrange MSS B.H.4.

root crops and artificial grasses were sufficiently widespread by 1750 to have affected the structure of arable cultivation significantly. Particular 'industrial' crops – hemp, flax, hops, weld, teasels, saffron, madder, osiers, alders, reeds – were important, but were either grown in restricted localities or had a limited impact upon standard courses of tillage. Saffron was grown in the chalk between Saffron Walden and Newmarket, in fen soils around Burwell and Soham, in parts of the Cambridgeshire clays north of Royston, and even in a few parishes in the heath. Nevertheless, saffron, like weld, which shared an eccentric distribution, was in decline by 1670 and almost extinct in 1750.[40] Of the industrial crops, hemp was not only the most important but enjoyed the broadest distribution. It was a speciality of the reclaimed fenlands until later in the eighteenth century and was also grown as a major crop in the valley of the Waveney between Garboldisham and Bungay. Hemp there supplied an important local manufacture of canvas, sailcloth, and cheap 'linens', and its culture survived into the later nineteenth century. Hemp and, to a lesser extent, flax, however, were crops of cottage gardens, enclosed field plots, and small intakes out of common waste.[41]

Hops were largely confined to the woodland, being concentrated in land around Chelmsford, near Castle Hedingham, and between Stowmarket and Sudbury. There are several references to the crop in seventeenth-century records, but its culture apparently diminished, except in north Essex, from the early years of the eighteenth century. Like hemp, the plant was grown in severalty, in hop gardens, several of which were grubbed out in Suffolk after 1720 to permit more wheat production.[42] Of the other specialized local crops, only the culture of teasels, coriander, and caraway, usually sown

[40] For saffron, e.g. T. Cox, *Magna Britannia*, London, 1720, pp. 258, 261, 721; *VCH Cambs.*, VI; E. Carter, *A History of Cambridgeshire*, London, 1819, pp. 4, 17; *Camb. Antiq. Soc.*, XVI, p. 161; Teversham, *op. cit.*, I, pp. 11, 91, 118, 126; Monteith, thesis, pp. 164–70; C. Howard, 'The Culture of Saffron', *Philos. Trans. Roy. Soc.*, XII, 1678, pp. 945–8; J. Douglas, *ibid.*, XXXV, 1728, pp. 566–74. For weld, NNRO, PD131/38; Marshall, *Norfolk*, II, pp. 26–7; Kerridge, *op. cit.*, pp. 268, 298; Vancouver, *Essex*, p. 10.

[41] For hemp, Cambs. RO, P150/3/2.1; L92/112; R52/24/30, 46.4; Thirsk, *English Peasant Farming*, pp. 136–7; Pursehouse, *Waveney Valley Studies*, pp. 164ff; BL, Lansdowne MS 722, ff. 29–38; Kirby, *Suffolk Traveller*, p. 8; NNRO, WKC5/15 f. 198; WKC5/156; MS 17,586; B.L. VIIId(5). For flax, BL, Lansdowne MS 722, ff. 29–38; C. Merret, 'Some Observables in Lincolnshire Not Noticed by Sir William Dugdale', *Philos. Trans. Roy. Soc.*, XIX, 1696, p. 343; Blith, *English Improver Improved*, p. 254; *VCH Essex*, II, p. 422; Bodleian Library, Gough MSS Camb 103 (7); Leics. RO, DG7/2/43. For other industrial crops mentioned, WSRO, 1,754/1/237, osiers; NNRO, Lestrange KA6, osiers; J. Mortimer, *The Whole Art of Husbandry*, London, 1707, p. 202, teasels; *VCH Essex*, II, pp. 423–5, teasels; Darby, *Draining of the Fens*, p. 87, woad; Kerridge, *op. cit.*, p. 213, woad; J. Houghton, *A Collection for Improvement of Husbandry and Trade*, London, 1692–1703, VII, 18 Jan. 1699, madder; Essex RO, QSR402/131, greenweed; *VCH Hunts.*, III, p. 144, woad; NNRO, BIR/5, reed; Trafford MS 261, reed.

[42] For hops, WSRO, 1,754/1/21.237: Barnardiston Tithe Book, Sept. 1738; E19/242; 613/738; ESRO, W9/1/1.2; HA/G83/2; HD6/2/6; Essex RO, D/DP/L20/1; *VCH Essex*, II, pp. 366–7; IV, pp. 166, 266.

together in part of a regular arable shift, needs comment. The crops were very localized in a few parishes of Essex, where the farmers continued to cultivate them till late in the eighteenth century, in spite of some landlord opposition, because they were highly profitable.

Market gardening flourished in those parts of the region with access to the larger towns, and especially in suburban Essex. Near Norwich the occupation was well organized to supply the city's markets with fruit and vegetables. Both in that neighbourhood and in the part of Essex between Chelmsford and Colchester specialist nurserymen were found to supply seeds and other garden stock to horticulturists and farmers elsewhere in the country. The seed trade grew substantially in the eighteenth century, but it existed already by the third quarter of the seventeenth century.[43]

Many of the specialized industrial crops cultivated in East Anglia were consumed in local industries. The prevalence of hemp and the recurrence of dye plants among those named above illustrate the interaction between agriculture and the region's textile trades. The point cannot be laboured, however, since the acreages that were actually recorded in documents were almost all very small, and most of these crops went into decline when mainstream grain and livestock farming began to prosper once again at the end of our period. The East Anglian linen industry depended much more upon imported materials than upon native supplies in 1680 or 1750, and the textile trades in general obtained only a portion of their dyestuffs, teasels, or oil plants from East Anglian sources.

Most farmers were content to grow cereals and pulses, and to experiment with or to adopt new forage crops. In arable farming, production schedules were set according to the market and the suitability of the soil for cereals. Barley had been the major arable commodity sold off East Anglian farms in 1600, and this region's barley remained a highly marketable crop, whether at home or overseas, in 1700. The quantities of both wheat and oats that entered into trade had increased in the seventeenth century and continued to grow after 1700. But the region's leading asset was its barley. Cambridgeshire, Norfolk, and much of Suffolk were renowned nationally for their malting barleys, and so long as the demand for malt held up, the price of good barley kept it competitive with other grains. Until at least the 1790s the east-coast ports drove a good trade in malt or undressed barley to central Europe through Amsterdam.[44]

[43] Blith, op. cit., pp. 247, 262; VCH Essex, II, pp. 476–80; Philip Morant, A History of Essex, London, 1768, p. 8; A. Young, A Six Weeks' Tour through the Southern Counties, 3rd edn, London, 1772, p. 200; BL, Lansdowne MS 722, ff. 29–38; Carter, op. cit., p. 63.

[44] Opinions of East Anglian barley in the seventeenth century were golden, especially for malting – e.g. VCH Cambs., II, pp. 74f; P. Mathias, The Brewing Industry in England, 1700–1830, Cambridge, 1959, pp. 398, 428ff. Its importance is everywhere attested in the documentary records. The shipping trade in grain, especially barley, is sketched in T. S. Willan, The English Coasting Trade 1600–1750, Manchester, 1938, pp. 79–83, 123–37; A. H. John, 'English Agricultural

Table 7.1, showing the acreage devoted to each cereal crop in the various districts of the region, is based upon evidence obtained from probate inventories and tithe accounts. As such the figures are approximations only of local crop preferences, but the order of magnitude in each case is probably accurate enough. The table shows that, except in the woodland, barley occupied rather more of the sown acreage than a rotational scheme separating winter and spring shifts would justify. One of the advantages of East Anglian individualism in cultivation was that barley could be grown whenever necessary. It appeared often twice and sometimes more times in the arable courses of convertible regimes, whereas only on the strongest and most fertile soils did farmers attempt to grow wheat more than once in any cycle. Moreover, even when farmers paid attention to the traditional nomenclature of rotation, barley was often inserted as a crop in part of the winter shift (presumably spring-sown). In west Suffolk, for example, barley apparently occupied about one-third of the so-called forecrop in inventories dated between 1670 and 1730, and even in the dry ryelands barley was grown with surprising frequency where we should expect rye or perhaps wheat to have been sown. Even allowing for the fact that barley shared some part of the 'aftercrop' shift with oats or pulses, it is not unreasonable to conclude that half or three-fifths of the cereals grown on the lighter soils of East Anglia between 1650 and 1750 consisted of barley.[45]

There were natural constraints, apart from landowners' prohibitions, on the growth of the crop. Since barley was cultivated principally for malt, overcropping or cultivation in sub-marginal soils seriously affected the quality of the product, although this consideration was disguised for a time in the eighteenth century by the rapidly increasing demand for cheap grain spirits in which malting quality was relatively unimportant. Barley, moreover, could be used for other purposes. It was still the bread grain for many of the poor in parts of eastern England at least until the eighteenth century, and a new opportunity for its use was presented by the rapid expansion of stall fattening, since crushed barley, like crushed oats or wheat tailings, could be used in the diet of bullocks being overwintered after St Faith's or Hoxne fairs.

Wheat was already an important crop almost everywhere away from the barren sands. The reputation of several of Arthur Young's contemporaries for having introduced wheat into their own districts was wholly undeserved, for, except in the matter of balance between wheat and barley, little change apparently took place in crop selection on the loams and good sands after

Improvement and Grain Exports, 1660–1765', in D. C. Coleman and A. H. John, eds., *Trade, Government and Economy in Pre-Industrial England*, London, 1976, pp. 45–67. See also A. Young, ed., *Annals of Agriculture, XXII*, p. 37.

[45] At Holkham in 1641, 1,300 acres were sown to barley and 120 acres to wheat – Spratt, thesis, pp. 185–6; cf. NNRO, PD131/38 and PD228/51 for similar evidence of a preference for barley.

1750.[46] The culture of wheat on a quite extensive scale in our period is revealed in the trade statistics of several East Anglian ports, although with the probable exception of Colchester and Maldon, wheat or flour shipments were still outweighed by barley and malt shipments in the early eighteenth century. In the woodland wheat was a frequently cultivated crop, often being sown in a rotation with beans or peas and oats as often as with barley. The centre of East Anglian wheat growing in 1650 was in mid Essex and the lower Stour valley, although the crop was common everywhere on the clays even in the largely pastoral districts of high Suffolk. In east Norfolk it was extended after 1600 until in William Marshall's day wheat formed an integral and indispensable part of the fixed, recurrent rotations that he held to be characteristic of the area. In the fenlands wheat was taken up by farmers as a crop following successful reclamation. When suitably dry conditions could be obtained, wheat drove out barley as the crop of the 'hard lands', while oats still prevailed in the fen grounds. But except in the dry fens, the extension of the acreage under wheat occurred not at the expense of barley but of rye.[47]

The hot, dry ryelands of Norfolk were steadily improved by applications of marl and compost and made fit for wheat or maslin almost as a matter of course after about 1580. The worst soils remained strongholds of rye growing until the nineteenth century, and many parishes of Breckland never really grew wheat throughout their history. Most of the great farmers, including the gentry, grew token quantities of wheat before 1750, almost always in the top-dressed infield. The incidence of rye, and of its scorned companion, buckwheat (brank, buck, crap, sarasin), in about 1720–50 is almost a gauge of barrenness in East Anglia, for both crops were *pis aller* in difficult terrain.[48] Buckwheat, indeed was occasionally employed, like mustard and cammock (? comfrey), as a green compost in poor soils, although its principal purpose was for poultry feed.[49]

Buckwheat was treated as a 'summer grain', together with pulses and oats. It was occasionally sown in a dredge with other late-sown crops, though the

---

[46] See Riches, *Agricultural Revolution*, pp. 92ff; Parker, *Coke of Norfolk*, pp. 11, 57–8; NNRO, PD228/51.

[47] For the culture of wheat in the region, ESRO, HA12/E1/1/20; T1/1/4; Essex RO, D/DM/F27/7; D/DU/298/41; WSRO, E1/11; 592/18/25, 592/24/40; Spratt, thesis, pp. 185ff; NNRO, BAR22; Hare 5,365D; NRS16,023; WKC5/151, 152; MS 17,586; Cambs. RO, P72/3/1; Thirsk, *English Peasant Farming*, p. 136; Kerridge, *Agricultural Revolution*, esp. pp. 88, 89–90.

[48] For rye, Essex: see Mortimer, *op. cit.*, p. 72; Leics. RO, DG7/2/43; Cambs.: Spufford, *Contrasting Communities*, pp. 62–3; PRO, C 5/29/235; W. Sussex RO, Clough & Butler MSS 259; Cambs. RO, P42/3, P72/3/1; Norfolk: Parker, *op. cit.*, pp. 50, 52, 57–8; Riches, *op. cit.*, pp. 124–5 (citing NNRO, BAR22); NNRO, KNY575; WKC5/151, 152; MS 20,124; NRS16,023; NRS8,412; How 797; B.L. vib II; Suffolk: ESRO, HA49/1/2; S6/1/11; WSRO, E3/10/9.20; 1374/18. Rye was still grown by a majority of farmers on the East Anglian sands before 1750, according to inventory evidence.

[49] For buckwheat, ESRO, FFF/3/8; NNRO, 5/151 ff. 30, 104, 109, 156, 173, 230; WKC5/152 *passim*; WKC 5/155; Mortimer, *op. cit.*, pp. 136–7.

Table 7.1. Crop preferences by East Anglian region, 1640–1760 (sown acreages recorded in tithe collection accounts, probate inventories, etc. as percentage of total known arable sown to crops)

	Wheat	Rye	Barley	Oats	Roots/cole	Temp. grass	Hemp	Pulses
I Western claylands								
1640–80	23	3	44	4	..	..	..	25
1720–60	26	..	39	5	(2)	7	..	20
II Chalk-ridge district								
1640–80	9	20	44	..	(2)	(2)	..	23
1720–60	14	15	40	(2)	3	(8)	..	17
III Suffolk and east Cambridgeshire fielden								
1640–80	12	17	38	8	..	(1)	3	21
1720–60	18	11	40	5	(1)	8	..	16
IV Southern fenland								
1640–80	21	..	36	8	(5)	..	5	23
1720–60	20	..	34	13	(5)	2	4	21
V Northern fenland								
1640–80	28	2	12	15	(4)	..	(2)	37
1720–60	30	..	13	18	7	4	2	27
VI North-west Norfolk heathland								
1640–80	7	24	48	(2)	3	3	1	12
1720–60	16	16	38	(4)	7	6	..	8 + 4[a]
VII Breckland								
1640–80	(6)	28	46	(3)	..	3	1	8 + 4[a]
1720–60	12	18	42	5	5	7	1	8 + 2[a]

VIII	*East Norfolk*							
1640–80	25	8	42	5	..	(2)	1	16
1720–60	28	3	45	..	(4)	6	..	13
IX	*Woodland (high Suffolk)*							
1640–80	32	3	26	8	3	2	6	20
1720–60	30	(3)	16	(16)	8	8	4	15
X	*Woodland (Essex clays)*							
1640–80	36	..	20	9	..	2	2	31
1720–60	42	..	18	3	(1)	6	..	30
XI	*Sandlings*							
1640–80	8	27	38	5	8	2	2	12
1720–60	12	20	32	6	10	6	..	13
XII	*Saltings*							
1640–80	8	18	46	12	..	..	5	12
1720–60	14	18	36	14	..	(2)	(3)	12

Notes: Figures in parentheses ( ) are based on very insufficient evidence and must be regarded as doubtful.

The sign .. indicates that no data have been found for that crop in the ground for the district in question. It does not indicate that none was grown.

The proportion sown to 'Rye' includes maslin, and that of 'Pulses' the dredge called 'bullimong', which often contained oats. The figures for 1640–80 also include some buckwheat not separately indicated.

a This is the recorded acreage sown to buckwheat.

characteristic bullimong of East Anglia usually consisted of oats and pulses or of mixed pulses. Oats are the most anomalous of the traditional cereal crops. Seldom if ever grown for human consumption in the region, their chief market was as horse fodder. Oats, however, increased in acreage after 1600 almost as much as wheat, which is a reflection of the region's increasing dependence upon horses from the seventeenth century. Oats were a crop particularly suited to certain kinds of convertible management where late seeding was essential. In the fen grounds they were the only important cereal crop cultivated after reclamation, and they were favoured for the same reasons by farmers who broke up and seeded saltings and river marshes. Fen-grown oats were exported coastwise to many parts of eastern England; elsewhere in the region oats were locally consumed and may not have been in sufficient supply to satisfy the demand of East Anglian horse keepers in the late seventeenth century.[50]

Of the pulse crops little can be said. All the varieties known to English agriculture were grown in East Anglia after 1600.[51] Some specialization can be seen in the preference for beans on the heavy clays and of vetches and lentils on the lightest soils, but most species were represented to some extent in each of the districts in the region, soil and climate notwithstanding. They were essentially fodder or compost crops, and although they were often, perhaps customarily, grown in the 'aftercrop' shift before fallowing, beans and bullimong were both at times and on some farms employed instead of bare fallows in the third shift, especially in the dairy districts. As in some field systems where a pulse shift was devised, so in many convertible or individual rotations beans, peas, and vetches played their part in the sequence of cropping followed before layering.[52] What effect pulses had in improving soil fertility is doubtful, but for farmers they apparently possessed an equally important virtue, whether ploughed in or taken as a crop: that of cleansing the land of noxious weeds.

The fodder plant which attracted most *réclame* in the eighteenth century was the turnip. It certainly was not the most important of the new crops, but, because it seemed to supply a magic ingredient in the development of intensive mixed husbandry, propaganda for its virtues was perhaps inevitable. Whether the turnip culture was an East Anglian innovation is not absolutely certain, although nearly all the evidence of early cultivation relates to the region – particularly to Norfolk and Suffolk. Spratt and Kerridge have both

[50] For oats – in fen grounds and brecks – Thirsk, *English Peasant Farming*, p. 136; Merret, *op. cit.*; Darby, *op. cit.*, pp. 93, 129, 135, 164; NNRO, Lestrange KA6, KA9, KA12, 25/3; How 208; B.L. VIIIb and VIb/II. Otherwise it was a minor crop, except on the heaviest clays, where it rivalled barley – e.g. NNRO, MS 17,586; WSRO, 592/24/9.

[51] I.e. beans, grey peas, blue peas, lentils, vetches, and perhaps chick-peas.

[52] NNRO, Lestrange KA9, 25/11/XIII, BH4; How 797; MS 17,586; PD228/51; WKC5/151; KNY 575; Cambs. RO, P72/3/1; 619/M43, 44; R59/5/3/1; PRO, C 5/29/235; E 134/28–9 Chas. II, Hil. 11; Pembroke Coll., Cambridge, MSS T/5; Mortimer, *op. cit.*, pp. 138–9.

dated its introduction as a field crop to the years around 1650, and nothing so far has been found to set this date significantly further back. On the other hand, turnips were one of several new root crops grown in arable routines in the seventeenth century, and both carrots and parsnips are referred to earlier in Suffolk in similar contexts. In addition, there are two tantalizing references to "root grounds" in 1628–31 in villages in the middle Waveney valley where the turnip culture was later well established.[53]

Carrots were grown in the Sandlings of Suffolk soon after 1600 as an agricultural crop. They were used, at least in part, as forage for horses, and as such retained a measure of popularity throughout the seventeenth century. But carrots were also grown around Woodbridge as a vegetable crop for export to London in the later years of the century, and it is not evident from the records whether references to the plant relate to horticultural or fodder production.[54]

The earliest mention of turnips occurs in two separate but proximate areas. They were very early established in the Waveney valley,[55] so that between 1650 and 1680 the number of instances of the crop in cultivation runs into dozens, but they are found at the same time also in parts of south-central Norfolk between Wymondham (1651) and Norwich.[56] Here, and especially in the upper Yare valley, turnips were grown in field land as well as in the small enclosed plots common in the Waveney valley and high Suffolk, but in all early references the acreage sown with turnips was very small, and may even, as Spratt suggested, be regarded as experimental. By 1680 the plant

[53] Spratt, thesis, pp. 202ff; E. Kerridge, 'Turnip Husbandry in High Suffolk', EcHR, 2nd ser., VII, 1956. Mark Overton, 'Computer Analysis of an Inconsistent Data Source: The Case of Probate Inventories', *J. Hist. Geog.*, III, has put the date of introduction back even further, but his findings need elaboration. My references to "root grounds" are P. Millican, 'The Gawdys of Norfolk and Suffolk', *Norfolk Archaeol.*, XXVI, 1935, p. 75, and NNRO, microfilm 35/2. A very early reference to turnips and other new crops at Linton (Cambs.) in the 1630s and 1640s (Cambs. RO, R59/5/3/1 ff. 34–5) needs investigation.

[54] For carrots, J. Norden, *The Surveyor's Dialogue*, 3rd edn, London, 1618, pp. 212–13; R. Billing, *An Account of the Culture of Carrots*, London, 1765; F. de La Rochefoucauld, *A Frenchman in England, 1784*, Cambridge, 1933, pp. 180–1; Burrell, thesis, p. 56; F. Hull, 'Agriculture and Rural Society in Essex, 1560–1640', unpub. Univ. of London Ph.D. thesis, 1950, p. 84; R. Blome, *The Gentleman's Recreation*, London, 1686, pt 2, p. 220; ESRO, HD/6/2/6: Essex RO, D/DBy/E19(c); Cambs. RO, R59/5/3/1, ff. 34–5, 41; *VCH Cambs.*, VI, p. 94; Pembroke Coll., Cambridge, MSS T/5 – all references to Linton.

[55] Inventory references are numerous – e.g. Richard Hill, Toft Monks (1661); Deborah Godfrey, Weybread (1662); Thomas Wille, Wortham (1666); Aug. Castell, Raveningham (1671); Bart Roberts, Thurlton (1676); Rich. Burgoin, Belton (1677) – all in NNRO, Consistory Ct Invs. Other sources: Sir John Cullum, *History of Hawsted*, London, 1813, p. 251n; ESRO, FAA/3/9; NNRO, WKC5/156.

[56] Wymondham Tithe Accounts, 1647ff, communicated by John Wilson, Esq.; NNRO, WKC5/152 f. 146: NRS16,023; Riches, *op. cit.*, p. 85. For inventories, see John Sharpe of East Dereham (1665), John Reade of Barnham Broom (1666–7), William Bullock of Deopham (1677), and Edward Bradford of Hackford (1677).

had been taken up in the heathlands of central and north-west Norfolk, in the east Norfolk loams, and in the Sandlings. In these districts turnips were more likely to be sown in larger lots as part of a convertible routine of husbandry, and on some estates white turnips may well have been sown to be grazed by sheep in the field as early as the 1670s. One of the earliest prescriptions relating to the cultivation of turnips, that of Sir John Hobart to a tenant at Horsham St Faith in 1666, gives details of tillage, seed, and general management which imply some familiarity on his part with the crop and the existence also of tillage customs that could be invoked in setting standards.[57]

By the early eighteenth century the turnip had reached all the districts of Norfolk and Suffolk except the fen soils and the chalk, but there is little evidence of its spread into Cambridgeshire or Essex before the second quarter of the century. Within the two counties its utility as a break crop on good light soils was acknowledged by 1720, for some time during the early eighteenth century a handful of pioneering estates were beginning to specify rotations in which turnips were sown after wheat as a matter of course. Even so, cropping patterns were still far from uniform, and several farmers apparently grew turnips as a catch crop at least in part to cleanse overgrown land as much as to provide a fixed shift.[58]

Moreover, Kerridge is probably quite correct in his belief that turnips were introduced – at least into some areas – as a crop to feed cattle, even dairy cattle, and that they were grown to be drawn and stored for winter feed, and were therefore not necessarily regarded by farmers as suitable for extending or diversifying established field rotations. As such in some parts of high Suffolk they continued to be used into the eighteenth century, but

[57] Outside the two districts mentioned above early references to turnips are quite numerous: Edward Chamberlain of East Winch (1677), NNRO, INV60/85; Houghton, 1673, J. H. Plumb, *Sir Robert Walpole*, London, 1956, I, p. 85; Stoke by Nayland, 1683, ESRO, S1/13/16.2; Gresham, 1683, NNRO, WKC5/152 f. 267; Felbrigg, 1684, WKC5/156; Bury, 1690, WSRO, E14/7/2; Badmondisfield, 1674, 1,341/5/2; Yoxford, 1707, ESRO, 4A 30/312/51; Dunton-cum-Doughton (Coke estate), Spratt, thesis, p. 201; cf. Doughty, *Chronicles of Theberton*, p. 146; R. Loder, *History of Framlingham*, London, 1798, p. 302; Cullum, *op. cit.*, p. 251n. The earliest reference to prescribed management is NNRO, MSS 16,023, draft lease 15 Oct. 1666, in which a tenant is required to prepare and sow 20 acres with turnips to deliver to his landlord "at a seasonable time (i.e. about Midsomer) which are to be twice hoed" – Abbey Farm, Horsham St Faith's, Norwich.

[58] For Cambridgeshire, apart from the precocious example of Linton, small acreages are mentioned from the 1690s in several villages – Pembroke Coll., Cambridge, MSS T/5, Linton; Babraham, 1701, WSRO, MS 259; Sawston, 1719, Teversham, *Sawston, I*, p. 148. See also Cambs. RO, P9/3/3; P107/3/1; R69/61; NNRO, B.L. ixa (Soham Mere); Cambridge Univ. Library, Queens' Coll. MSS 17/40 for later references. For Essex, the earliest reference is at Saffron Walden in 1697 – Essex RO, D/DBy/E19 (c) – but Houghton, *Collection, I*, p. 213, implies an earlier innovation in the county. Manuscript data are confined to the early or mid eighteenth century, around Upminster, or on the Sandlings of the north-east – Essex RO, D/DP/L20/1; D/DE/E1; D/DTw/A2; D/DK/F2/10; D/DM/A20, F27/7; Brown, *Essex at Work*, p. 29; cf. Essex RO, D/DBy/A299 (Great Chesterford, 1748–50).

the belief, tempered by experience, quickly established itself that the crop was most apt for light soils, so that by 1750 the turnip culture on the boulder clays had declined into a minor adjunct of farming, and in the routine arable husbandry of the district had partly succumbed to a renewed interest in pulses or to the adoption of new crops, such as cabbages, which were felt to be more appropriate.[59]

Clover is first recorded growing on East Anglian farms in the years after the Restoration, that is to say, if we exclude the increasingly frequent references to indigenous clovers in the region's grasslands during the early seventeenth century. Clover, as a phenomenon of progressive agriculture, was almost certainly introduced at least as early as the turnip, and its later recorded appearance is fortuitous. At Houghton, for example, where Walpole bought 200 lb of clover for seed in 1677, his suppliers included local gentry such as Townshend and Armiger of North Creake, a freeholder, Allen of Ingoldisthorpe, and the chief tenant of the Yelvertons at Rougham, Samuel Ruding. When Roger North bought this last estate in 1679 clover was well established, and had been grown there for upwards of fifteen years.[60] As with turnips, however, a particularly important period of expansion or consolidation occurred between 1690 and 1720. The clover thus mentioned, which also featured in mid-seventeenth-century port books, was the 'broad red', much of the seed of which was then imported; but 'clover' was an elastic term referring to several different species, even to different genera (*Trifolium, Medicago, Melilotus, Lotus*). In East Anglia, too, vernacular names were diverse and often confusing – 'cow-grass', 'honeysuckle', 'suckling', and 'trefoil' were names perhaps interchangeable with 'clover'. Broad red clover, and later the 'Dutch' white clover, which were the chief forage crops of the genus *Trifolium*, were supplemented by, and gradually distinguished from, black medick ('nonsuch' or 'trefoil' commonly in East Anglia, but also 'medick fodder' and 'Ladyfinger-grass'), sainfoin ('cinquefoil', 'snail' or 'horned clover' and 'French grass'), and lucerne (also apparently 'French grass'). Non-legumes of some recognized importance between 1680 and 1760 were

[59] Kerridge, *Agricultural Revolution*, pp. 272–3 (p. 273 n. 1 for schedule of references). Most references in the present account relate to drawing or storage of turnips for cattle rather than for sheep – see ESRO, HA49/iv/5; HA30/312/51; W9/1/1.2. Grazing of turnips is inferred from evidence of large acreages sown by individuals, e.g. Robert Knopwood's 102 acres at Threxton (Norfolk) in 1732 – NNRO, BAR22; but so well established had close folding become by the 1760s that the origin of the practice must have lain far back in time.

[60] J. H. Plumb, 'The Walpoles: Father and Son', in *id.*, ed., *Studies in Social History*, London, 1955, p. 185; Riches, *Agricultural Revolution*, p. 88. The North papers are still at Rougham but were consulted by kind permission of R. North, Esq., the present owner. Other very early references to "clover" – before 1690 – include Wymondham Tithe Accounts (1660s) (consulted by kind permission of Mr John Wilson); NNRO, WKC5/152 f. 167, Felbrigg, and f. 534, East Beckham; WKC5/158 f. 41; Lestrange MSS KA12; NRS16,023; WSRO, 1,341/5/2. Kerridge, *op. cit.*, pp. 283–5, has lists of early clover growers in the region (before 1670) which is an almost complete abstract of inventory data.

ryegrass (which may not have referred solely to *Lolium perenne*), burnet, and perhaps spurrey, the last of which, if it were selected for forage was directly adopted under Dutch influence. Other less obviously nutritious plants, such as hedge-parsley, mallow, ribwort, furze, smallage, yarrow, and the green leaves of certain trees, especially oak, ash, and sycamore, were here and there employed as green fodders.[61]

The culture of temporary leys was revolutionized by the application of one or other of these 'new' plants, though it did not depend upon their being available. From 1650–80 onwards, however, the adoption of significant new plants notably improved the prospects for convertible husbandry. The knowledge that sainfoin and, in even drier conditions, lucerne were relatively durable ley plants, lasting from six to twenty years without failing, was applied throughout southern and Midland England on calcareous or dry heathland soils where long pasture breaks were essential to maintain soil structure and conserve fertility. Sainfoin in East Anglia was especially characteristic of the sandlands and the chalk-ridge country. It made its appearance, probably, in the 1670s, and had become commonplace but not ubiquitous in ploughed breckland or sheepwalks during the 1690s.[62] Lucerne was certainly being grown around Holkham, in the north-west heathlands, and possibly around Stoke Ferry in the northern Breckland during the 1720s. No earlier reference has been found, although Mortimer believed that the war of 1702–13 had interrupted supplies of seed from France. By 1770, however, lucerne was locally well established, especially on gentlemen's farms in north-west Norfolk and the Suffolk Sandlings, e.g. at Burnham and Warham on the Martin and Turner estates, but it always remained a minority interest.[63]

Ley farming was an essentially diverse system of husbandry. The treatment of long leys, of three- to four-year leys and one-or two-year leys was distinct and distinctive. The one- or two-year fallow break in permanent tillage was ideally suited to the broad red and white clovers. The Norfolk system of husbandry, so called, adapted clover to this purpose, and both the four-course and the six-course rotations used clovers in a similar way, the latter preferring a two-year ley in the corn–forage cycle, the former ploughing clover out after a single season. Both rotations, and a multitude of variants, were regularly employed east of the chalk ridge and north of the Stour by 1725, but their origins remain in doubt. On the land under a regime of convertible

[61] G. E. Fussell, *The English Dairy Farmer, 1500–1900*, London, 1966, esp. pp. 94–120.

[62] Sainfoin: *VCH Cambs.*, *VI*, pp. 65, 210; Teversham, *op. cit.*, *I*, 73, 126, 135–6; Cambs. RO, 619/M43, M45; R69/61; R72/47; WSRO, MSS 259; Cambs. RO, P 150/3/2; Spufford, *Contrasting Communities*, p. 63; WSRO, 474/3; NNRO, B.L. vıııb; Essex RO, D/DBy/E19 (c).

[63] Lucerne: Parker, *Coke of Norfolk*, p. 57n; J. E. T. Rogers, *A History of Agriculture and Prices in England*, 7 vols., Oxford, 1866–1902, *VII*, pt 2, p. 649; A. Young, *The Farmer's Tour in the East of England*, 4 vols., London, 1771, *III*, p. 148; *id.*, *Tours in England and Wales (Selected from the Annals of Agriculture)*, London, 1932, pp. 64–8.

husbandry artificial grasses, once sown, were left 'down' in two-, three- or four-year ollands. Nonsuch was especially popular in the eastern counties, especially in mixtures with clover and ryegrass, as a medium-term ley. Alone, or in combination, nonsuch (trefoil) is recorded, between about 1670 and 1770, growing on carr lands, sands, hazel loams, and middling clays.[64] Ryegrass was recommended, and around Newmarket and in some dairy districts apparently adopted, as a constituent in leys for horses and milch cows, especially in spring and early summer, when legumes were held to be costive.[65] On the heaviest clays where beans were necessarily preferred to turnips, the choice of forage plants was limited, usually to clover, as in the special alternate rotations of the eighteenth-century Essex clay country.[66] In Cambridgeshire and the fens the evidence for the introduction of artificial grasses except sainfoin (on the chalk) is fragmentary. Clover was recorded at Madingley as early as 1662, but this was unduly precocious. On the western clays clover was not fully accepted by the end of the eighteenth century, although there are many scattered references to the crop, apparently as a catch crop in the fields.[67]

"Clover-sickness" was a disorder of arable farming more characteristic of the next century, but the problem was already causing concern, at least in Norfolk, by the early years of the eighteenth century. The difficulty was that broad red clover failed from too much repetition in alternating courses. The response of farmers is obscure before the 1770s, but the adoption of nonsuch or vetches, among other plants, as a replacement for clovers in certain shifts, and the development of longer rotational patterns which were recorded by observers and farmers amid the greater publicity of the late eighteenth century, are suggestive of a protracted course of experiment and adjustment.

By 1750, many East Anglian farmers, especially those of Norfolk and Suffolk, were well versed in the use of numerous imported or introduced forage plants. Not every farmer grew any of these crops even in apt conditions during the eighteenth century, and it is probably an exaggeration to describe clover as a general crop before the last quarter of that century. The tendency of estate owners to prescribe increasingly standardized

[64] Nonsuch (trefoil): Kerridge, *Agricultural Revolution*; WSRO, MS 259; Mortimer, *Husbandry*, p. 41; Essex RO, D/DBy/A299; D/DTw/A2; NNRO, TL9; Lestrange MS BH4; How 208; WKC5/152 f. 172; WKC5/155; Rogers, *op. cit.*, *VII*, pt 2, p. 649; WSRO, 1,754/1/37.

[65] Ryegrass: Mortimer, *op. cit.*, pp. 38, 40–1; Rogers, *op. cit.*, *VII*, pt 2, p: 690; Riches, *op. cit.*, p. 90; Parker, *op. cit.*, p. 57n; Essex RO, D/DTw/A2; D/DM/A20, F27/7; NNRO, B.L. viiib; Coldham of Anmer MSS (uncat.), seed account 1741.

[66] F. W. Steer, *Inventories*, pp. 269, 271; Burley, thesis, p. 60; WSRO, Invs. 592/9/127; 592/18/135; 592/28/36; 592/22/162; 592/24/5, 25, 60; 1,754/1/139; Essex RO, D/DGh/E2; D/DM/A20; D/DTw/A2; NNRO, MS 17,586.

[67] G. Atwell, *The Faithfull Surveyor*, Cambridge, 1662, p. 101; Vancouver, *Cambridgeshire*, *passim*; *VCH Cambs.*, *V*; Cambs. RO, R51/15/45.

covenants of cropping perhaps highlighted some such need to encourage doubting tenants, particularly on estates where there was little early tradition of the crops. Nevertheless, given the lack of natural meadow throughout the East Anglian fielden, the hay crop afforded by artificial leys was so important for farmers "in a pinching season" that this in itself was a significant stimulus to change. For grazing, too, legumes were more readily accepted because the turnip crop was not entirely reliable. In most years a gap ensued between root feeding and grazing on spring grass, which had to be filled with hay or with such artificial grasses as could be managed to provide an early bite. Thus, John Mortimer recorded a practice in Essex of farmers sprinkling a pound or two of clover per acre among the seed of their etch (i.e. stubble) crops which was fed off in spring before the land was fallowed.[68] The history books, by stressing the dominance of systematic change, have failed to stress sufficiently the catch cropping of legumes, roots, and *Brassicae* for the supply of seasonal or emergency rations of livestock in the typically cereal-producing districts of eastern England during the seventeenth and eighteenth centuries. At Thorpe St Andrew, Norwich, in 1700–15 clover, like turnips, was well established as a crop, but it was grown, dispersedly, only in small parcels of one to four acres. It never occupied sufficient ground in the townfields to indicate any rational alternate system of rotation. The tithe books suggest an essentially random course of tillage consonant with a practice of catch cropping amid the cereals and pulses of routine husbandry.[69]

The only other forage crop of more than local importance in the region during this period was coleseed, which was characteristic of the fenlands, but which was also grown by some farmers on marshland silts, and in the 'upland' districts as well. But except in the fens, cole was never more than a supplementary or occasional crop to be grown in lands unfitted for turnip cultivation as a break from beans, or in ground temporarily exhausted with root vegetables. It was widely recommended by agronomes, and the extensive use of the oilcake, intended for fuel, as a fertilizer, which was well established in and around the fens and nearby uplands by 1690, suggests that some of the virtues of coleseed were practically appreciated. As green fodder cole was especially valuable as a supplement of artificial grasses in the dead of winter, especially for sheep, and outside the fens, where the means of processing the seed was not readily to hand, most was grown, like mustard, for the purpose of direct grazing. John Mortimer indicated that cole and turnips were sometimes sown together for fodder. The fenland crop was largely converted, by milling, into colza oil, and only a waste by-product, oilcake, was available for agriculturists. This cake was reputedly not

[68] Mortimer, *op. cit.*, p. 101.
[69] NNRO, Thorpe St Andrew Parish Book, 1700–15, PD/228/51. See also NNRO, Lestrange MSS, Hunstanton Field Crop Book, 1705–11, BH4, and Cambs. RO, Linton Tithe Books, 1760ff, P107/3/1, for similar evidence.

employed to feed cattle in eastern England before about 1750, when John Carr of Massingham, Norfolk, was said to have adopted the long-standing 'Dutch' practice of stall feeding with cake.[70] Oil milling remained a minor trade of towns in the fenlands before the early nineteenth century, when a new industry developed in eastern England to supply oils to commerce and oilcake to agriculture.

Coleseed was already established in the fenlands before Vermuyden had completed his work in the Bedford Level, although the great expanse of newly reclaimed land was quickly adapted to the crop, perhaps directly under Dutch influence. The destruction of much cole in the riots of 1639 is testimony to its importance by that date; moreover, Lestrange's opinions on the cole crops growing on his land in the Wash marshes in the 1630s, and his discovery of self-sown coleseed there, are similarly suggestive of a considerable experience of the plant outside the district affected by Vermuyden's drainage work. Nevertheless, coleseed was not a crop of widespread cultivation except in the black fens and the Essex saltings.[71]

PASTORAL REGIMES

The foldcourse

The foldcourse as a means of feeding immense flocks for the profit of their wool had passed its meridian before 1640. It survived remarkably until the epoch of parliamentary enclosure – its tenacity reveals much of its abiding influence upon the agrarian landscape and its management in the early modern period. Long after the great capitalist flockmasters of Tudor England had been forgotten, the foldcourse retained many of its uses and advantages. Foldcourses by name were found not only in Norfolk, but also in Essex and Cambridgeshire, while in Suffolk they were still numerous in the Sandlings as they were in the fielden and Breckland – they were rare, because inappropriate, only in the woodland and fenlands. Time had wrought some important changes, and geographical variations, perhaps always prominent, were patently obvious and certainly significant for the subsequent history of the foldcourse by the end of the seventeenth century. Local amendments, the progress of enclosure, soil conditions, and social changes in particular

[70] Arthur Young, *General View of the Agriculture of Norfolk*, London, 1804, pp. 417 *et seqq.*; H. W. Brace, *A History of Seed Crushing in Great Britain*, London, 1960, pp. 17, 21.

[71] For coleseed, in general, in the eastern counties, G. E. Fussell, 'History of Cole (*Brassica* sp.)', *Nature*, London, 9 July 1955; Fussell, *Dairy Farmer*, pp. 103–4; Kerridge, *Agricultural Revolution*, pp. 236–7; NNRO, Lestrange MSS KA4; KA9; KA6; B.L. IX (a); B.L. VIIId(2); Hare 5,44; NRS15,994; Thirsk, *English Peasant Farming*, pp. 127–9; BL, Add. MS 34,141, f. 46; WSRO, E14/7/1; Essex RO, D/DU/298/41; D/DGh/E2; Cambs. RO, P150/3/2; R52/24/46/4. One use of colza oil that has recently received attention is for lighting. The increasing demand for the oil after 1600 may well be accounted for in large measure by its use as a fuel – see M. E. Falkus, 'Lighting in the Dark Ages', in Coleman and John, eds., *op. cit.*

villages as well as the profits to be expected from sheep farming influenced foldcourse management and modified or diversified particular systems. The term 'foldcourse', therefore, may be defined only as a sheepwalk for a given number of sheep, to which the right of close folding in fallow or shack attached.[72]

The classic foldcourse, however, was uniquely East Anglian in structure and influence, but the key to its long survival was close folding, which in other forms was a practice common to most medieval and post-medieval demesne arable regimes. In Norfolk and Suffolk, however, the combination of a seignorial monopoly of sheep farming and the corn growers' enjoyment of the dung dropped by the sheep was not found elsewhere. The result was a kind of co-existence, if not collaboration, of woolmasters, typically manorial lords, and farmers, who were usually tenants of the manor, which benefited both.

In Norfolk and Suffolk, and to a less marked extent elsewhere, landlords exercised their rights of foldage by compelling tenants to receive seignorial flocks on their common-field lands. In villages of ample heathland for sheepwalks the transit between rough grazing and sheepfold was well organized. The area of the common fields to which a particular flock had access was fixed by custom, and the numbers within each foldcourse were regulated to preserve the balance between food supply and tathe. Overstocking was disapproved, and strict territorial limits were observed between one foldcourse and the next, which was especially important in the many cases in which foldcourses were not coterminous with manorial or parochial boundaries. As a rule manorial tenants were not permitted to keep sheep on commonable grassland nor to fold any flocks in the fields. Sheep were comparatively rare in 'peasant' inventories of the period before 1700 in areas where the foldcourse was still powerful.[73]

The seignorial preserve had never been accepted entirely without rancour by peasants, who resented both the restrictions upon stock keeping and arable management they were required to bear, and also the all-devouring appetite of the sheep (and of their masters), but before the late seventeenth century commercial corn production remained subservient to the fold. Close-folding, once, twice, or even repeatedly on bare fallow or shack, if well organized, was one of the soundest methods of dressing topsoil for grain. After 1650,

[72] K. J. Allison, 'Sheep–Corn Husbandry', pp. 12–30. Cf. A. Simpson, 'The East Anglian Fold-course: Some Queries', AHR, VI, 1958, pp. 87–96; Postgate, in Baker and Butlin, *Studies of Field Systems*, pp. 313–22; K. J. Allison, 'Flock Management in the Sixteenth and Seventeenth Centuries', EcHR, 2nd ser., XI, 1958, pp. 98–112. For the chalk-ridge country, see Teversham, *Sawston, I*, pp. 26–64; Monteith, thesis, *passim*; Roden, 'Field Systems of the Chiltern Hills', p. 339; Spufford, *Contrasting Communities*, p. 64.

[73] K. J. Allison, 'Sheep–Corn Husbandry', pp. 15–19; BL, Add. MS 27,403; Postgate, in Baker and Butlin, pp. 314–15; NNRO, Hare 5,443, NCC (Petre) boxes 9, 16, 17; WKC5/152; WSRO, 941/83/1; 449/4/18; 633/1; ESRO, 50/22/3.5.

however, the foldcourse was in retreat in every sense of the word. Symptomatic of many subtle changes in the village economy of fielden Norfolk were the dilution of the native Norfolk Horn sheep by introduced blood lines, the increased number of cullet or parr sheep or even of whole flocks (that is to say, of sheep owned by farmers without customary rights of folding), and the number of exceptions to the formerly invariable right of access for sheep to ploughed land, generally for the sake of industrial cash crops or fallow-break forage crops. The downfall of the foldcourse was not only a protracted affair; it was also complicated by the convergence of many different strands of cause and effect.[74]

One of these strands quite simply was the fall of wool prices after about 1620. For a generation the scales had been turning against the woolmaster. During the seventeenth century the simple geographical proximity of a buoyant clothing trade and a wool-centred pastoral economy in East Anglia was no longer sufficient for their reciprocal prosperity. The immense flocks which had made the fortunes of Townshends, Southwells, Fermors, Cokes, Bedingfelds, and many other gentry families before 1570 were not practicable by 1640. During the period 1640–1750 large flocks seldom exceeded 5,000 head[75] – Framlingham Gawdy of Harling in 1665 had 3,112 sheep in all; Lestrange of Hunstanton 2,146 in 1693 and 1,125 in 1703; the Walpoles of Houghton had 2,801 in 1665 and 3,556 in 1695, but only 1,331 in 1675 and 1,414 in 1720; Daniel Gwilt of Icklingham had 2,629 in 1733; but these were apparently exceptional graziers. Most gentry flockmasters then owned fewer than 1,000 sheep. At the same time, common farmers are recorded in possession of a few dozen or even a few hundred sheep as part of mixed arable and livestock enterprises which by 1720–50 often resembled those later so well known to Arthur Young or R. N. Bacon. A recessional wool trade cannot have been the only reason why landlords preferred to reduce the size of their flocks, since, according to Francis Blomefield in 1736, heathland mutton was superior in quality to any other he knew.[76] Yet the new emphasis upon mutton production in his day was founded upon exotic breeds, and the old Norfolk Horn sheep faded slowly into the background. The foldcourse was little adapted to this new source of profit for the sheepmaster. In addition, by 1640–80, rentier estate management was in the ascendancy

[74] Simpson, *op. cit.*, pp. 88–90; K. J. Allison, 'Sheep–Corn Husbandry', pp. 28ff; Postgate, in Baker and Butlin, pp. 319–21; BL, Add. MS 31,970, f. 91; NNRO, Lestrange MSS EH8, KA14; Elveden MSS (earl of Iveagh) F/5; NNRO, NRS16,473/32/D2; Monteith, thesis, pp. 164ff; Essex RO, D/DBy/E19(f); WSRO, E3/10/9.91.

[75] K. J. Allison, 'Flock Management', pp. 100; BL, Add. MS 36,990; NNRO, Lestrange MSS NR.

[76] F. Blomefield, *An Essay towards a Topographical History of Norfolk*, 2nd edn, 11 vols., Norwich and King's Lynn, 1805–20, *VII*, p. 234. Cf. K. J. Allison, 'Sheep–Corn Husbandry', p. 103; Young, *Annals of Agriculture*, London, 1784, *II*, p. 435; *XXII*, p. 30; Marshall, *Norfolk, I*, pp. 362–6.

over the direct commercial exploitation of the demesne, and grazing was perhaps no longer quite accepted as the vocation of a county magnate.

Yet if the mortar of profit and good business crumbled and weakened the landlords' resolve to preserve their fold rights at all costs, the edifice was also under pressure from outside. New rotations, and the crops which supported them, at first interfered with and eventually sapped the foldcourse in its role of safeguarding the fertility of the soil.

Enclosure threatened at two points. Heathland reclamation reduced the extent of the sheepwalks to which the sheep were sent in the daytime. Large-scale assarting or more extensive ploughing in the waste adversely affected the numbers of sheep which particular foldcourses could bear, sometimes to the point of no return. Moreover, the simultaneous process of dividing the common arable fields, wholly or in part, completely impaired or destroyed folding customs. Foldcourses had all but disappeared from the rich loams of east Norfolk by 1750. In the good sands districts perhaps two-thirds of those recorded before 1570 still survived in the eighteenth century, though many, possibly most, no longer supported the number of sheep that custom had decreed in their heyday. Marshland foldcourses, once common in the saltings around the coast, also diminished, largely as a consequence of inundation and coastal erosion.[77]

The foldcourse did not die in spite of its obsolescence. It retreated before enclosure and new cropping practices, but the resilience of the foldcourse in the seventeenth century is exemplified in the evolution of the 'half-year close', ground fenced off to protect particular crops in the field but thrown open after harvest to folding or common grazing.[78]

The turnip culture obviously modified foldcourses. In north-west Norfolk, for example, the new order established by the second quarter of the eighteenth century was founded upon the close folding of sheep on field-grown turnips, in which the ancient foldcourse had no place. Yet many of the great farms, leased by Coke, Walpole, Folkes, etc., retained so-called foldcourses, or 'sheep's courses'. What apparently happened was that the new foldcourses were confined to the breckland parts of the farms, that is to say, heathland flocks were employed in dressing tillage within a convertible regime at the periphery of the farms.[79] Elsewhere the culture of specialized non-cereal crops also abridged the freedom of the foldcourse. At Saffron Walden in 1697, for instance, the land devoted to saffron, as well as to new fodder crops, in the townfields was exempted from sheep grazing.

The longevity of the foldcourse need not surprise us. Its usefulness outlived the brief period of heady prosperity in the sixteenth century. Indeed, the fortunes of sheep farming, bound up with the foldcourse, were not solely

---

[77] Postgate, in Baker and Butlin, p. 303.
[78] Ibid., pp. 320–1.
[79] See e.g. Parker, *Coke of Norfolk*, ch. 7.

determined by it. In some parts of the region sheep were important as livestock when very few foldcourses existed. Many of the larger woodland farmers, for example, kept a number – a dozen, a score, or more – of sheep in the seventeenth and eighteenth centuries, though there were very few 'sheep enterprises' on the heavier soils of East Anglia. In the Essex marshlands substantial flocks were kept on the great ranges which extended out into the saltings and coastal islands. There the sheep had been used partly to reclaim saltmarsh, partly to graze land inaccessible to great cattle, but also partly to supply milk for cheesemaking. This last activity was in decay after 1650, and by the mid eighteenth century bullocks were at least as plentiful in the saltings as sheep.

Dairying

Butter and cheese were among the most important agricultural products of East Anglia from 1600 to 1800. London in 1730 apparently consumed 56,703 firkins of Suffolk and 74,918 firkins of Cambridge butter (3,029 tons), and 985 tons of Suffolk cheese. With the production of Essex and the northern fenland, East Anglia probably supplied about one-third of the capital's dairy produce in the early eighteenth century.[80]

Dairying for the market was specialized in certain districts. Cambridge, for example, was the entrepôt for the butter produced in the southern fenlands, the Norfolk marshland, the Ashwell and Granta valleys, and the upper Stour valley of Suffolk. Suffolk butter and cheese, shipped out of Yarmouth, Woodbridge, Ipswich, and Mistley, were products principally of the woodland (from Norwich to Colchester). In Essex, specialist dairy farms were located on the marshland fringe of Tendring, Dengie, and Rochford hundreds, which produced both butter and cheese; in the northern metropolitan zone, where 'Epping butter' was famous by 1700–50; and, as in Suffolk, in the woodland, where the valleys of the Chelmer, Wid, Blackwater, Colne, and Stour were especially significant: here, cheese was apparently the chief produce. Essex too had once been famous for ewe-milk cheese, produced in the marsh islands, such as Canvey, where a change in land use after 1660 brought about its decline. By 1720 ewe's cheese was apparently not made in Essex at all.[81] In addition to these specialist areas orientated towards the London market, small-scale dairying, either for subsistence or to supply the ped markets of local towns, was virtually ubiquitous in the

---

[80] Fussell, *English Dairy Farmer*, pp. 271–2, citing Henry Maitland, *History of London*, 1756, and other eighteenth-century estimates; Willan, *English Coasting Trade*, pp. 48, 84–6; CJ, XXVI, 31 May 1751, p. 273.

[81] For the geography of East Anglian dairying, see Ravensdale, *Liable to Floods*, pp. 59–61; Taylor, *Cambridgeshire Landscape*, p. 174; Brown, *Essex at Work*, p. 39; Kerridge, *Agricultural Revolution*, pp. 79, 86, 88, 90–1, 138, 144, 294; Spratt, thesis, pp. 199–201, 203–4, 235–6; Blome, *Britannia*, p. 207; Fussell, *English Dairy Farmer*, *passim*, but esp. pp. 24ff.

seventeenth century. Dairy vessels, for example, are mentioned in over three-fourths of agriculturalists' inventories from all parts of the region in 1660–1720, and cheese presses, outside the dairy districts proper, in at least one-third of the larger farmers' inventories.

Dairy herds obviously varied very much in size, and a very considerable number of farmers even in the woodland could afford to keep only a single cow in milk. Robert Reyce evidently had an exaggerated opinion, repeated by Trow Smith, Kerridge, and Fussell, of the numbers of milch cows generally kept by high Suffolk farmers.[82] Except for a few aristocratic enterprises, and a few ranch-like dairy farms in the Essex marshland, milking herds in excess of 25 head were very rare. Commercial herds commonly ranged in size from 8 to 20 beasts, with the median herd between 11 and 12. In the fenlands, dairy herds tended to be somewhat smaller, and many husbandmen producing butter for the market milked only 4–6 cows in this district. Even with all the followers (calves and heifers), herds of dairy stock seldom exceeded 40. Outside the dairy districts milking herds were obviously smaller, although substantial commercial herds were found in the heathlands and Breckland. At Great Cressingham in Breckland in 1640 the villagers possessed 113 cows in milk, the largest herd numbering 16 beasts; and at Threxton nearby a century later Robert Knopwood, Esq., admitted keeping 22 milch cows when accused by the vicar of owning 40. In the 1670s, William Wyndham of Felbrigg owned a farm at Reepham on which he and his métayer tenant kept from 13 to 18 dairy cows. In the champion districts generally many of the bigger farmers died possessed of 8 to 15 cows in 1660–1720, and the great majority of husbandmen had 2 or 3 cows in milk. Some, like Knopwood and Wyndham, certainly produced enough of a surplus to sell to butter factors or cheesemongers who collected it for wholesale distribution.[83]

Throughout the region virtually all farmers kept both dairy and beef cattle side by side. Dairy farmers as such not only bred cattle for sale as stores, but by 1700 often apparently bought in lean stock to fatten. How this was achieved without a decline in the numbers of milch cows is uncertain, but the introduction of turnips and clover was probably a major influence. The fact that several woodland farmers fed their turnips both to dairy cattle and

[82] R. Reyce, *The Breviary of Suffolk* (1618), ed. F. Hervey, London, 1902, pp. 26ff, esp. p. 28; cf. Kerridge, *Agricultural Revolution*, p. 86. See also Young, *Annals of Agriculture, II*, p. 151.

[83] It is too cumbersome to cite the inventory evidence taken from manuscript sources, but all the relevant inventories in NNRO, WSRO, and Steer, *Inventories*, were consulted for the specified period. In addition the following were also examined: ESRO, HD/330/7, 1662, Stonham (23 milch cows, 15 followers); HA/49/IV/5, 1727, Glemham, 14 cows in dairy; Essex RO, D/DU/298/41, 1724, Rochford Hall, 40 cows; NNRO, WKC/152 ff. 162–3, Reepham Dairy, 1673–8, milch cows from 13 to 18 a year, and f. 200, Felbrigg farm, 7 cows and 1 bull, 1673; BAR22; Reading Univ. Library, Norf. 14/1/1.1685, Hockwold, 24 dairy cows – all of which refer to gentlemen's estate farms – Tebbutt, *Bluntisham & Earith*, appendix pp. XXXVIII–XLII; Young, *Six Weeks' Tour*, pp. 79, 83.

to fat bullocks is significant, for it is certain that the greater variety and larger quantity of forage crops after 1660 added a new dimension to the stock management of woodland agriculture. As a rule, however, the woodland was held to be the breeding ground *par excellence* of the region. Most of the home-bred bullocks, which still made up a sizeable portion of the fatting business in East Anglia in the 1790s, were produced in the district and sold to farmers with surplus rowens, hay, or feed grain elsewhere to raise and finish.[84]

Dairying inevitably gave rise to a number of subsidiary enterprises apart from breeding. Dairy farmers as a rule kept a number of swine, breeding and fattening hogs for consumption and for sale. The swine were fed in part on skim milk and in part on the pulse crops which all dairymen seem to have grown in the region. Pig meat from the woodland found its way into London markets, where it was highly esteemed.[85] Closely related was the veal trade. In Essex and south Suffolk many calves were selected to be killed as veal and fed on milk and grain accordingly. In Essex many of the surplus calves were bought by specialist calf dealers who prepared them for the London market, often in great numbers. Finally, some Suffolk and Essex dairymen enjoyed a modest income from the sale of rancid butter as a lubricant.[86]

Milk yields are not recorded in the manuscript sources, but contemporaries believed that Suffolk cows consistently gave the highest yields in the country, averaging perhaps 300–350 gallons a year. In about 1650, however, lactation was apparently brief. Tithe milk at Cressingham (Norfolk) was taken from Crouchmas (3 May O.S.) to Lammas (1 August O.S.), which was in addition to the butter and cheese tithes due to the vicar.[87] The profitable milking season, however, was being extended. Turnips and clover hay, bullimong or pulses, and spent brewer's grains, were all used to lengthen a cow's lactation through better autumn and winter feeding. Turnips, by being drawn and fed throughout the winter to dairy stock, made it possible to prolong lactation, though the butter and cheese produced were of inferior quality.

---

[84] Defoe, *A Tour through the Whole Island of Great Britain*, Harmondsworth, 1975, pp. 82–3; Kerridge, *Agricultural Revolution*, pp. 85, 89, 298; Marshall, *Norfolk, I*, pp. 323–4. Several farm accounts mention the sale of store beasts bred at home at local fairs, e.g. ESRO, 8/2/1726–7; HD330/7; Hants. RO, 15M/50/125; WSRO, E18/455/4; 1,374/18; 1,341/5/2; NNRO, B.L. viiib.

[85] Kerridge, *Agricultural Revolution*, p. 86; Brown, *Essex at Work*, p. 39; Reyce, *op. cit.*, p. 37; Essex RO, D/DU/298/41; D/DM/A20.

[86] G. E. Fussell, 'Essex Calves Made the Best Veal', *Essex Rev.*, Oct. 1955, pp. 267ff; T. Fuller, *The Worthies of England*, ed. J. Freeman, London, 1952, p. 497; Burley, thesis, p. 273; Mortimer, *Husbandry*, p. 169; P. Kalm, *Kalm's Account of his Visit to England on his Way to America in 1748*, ed. J. Lucas, London, 1892, p. 167; Essex RO, D/DM/F2717; D/DB/A1; D/DVg/10; R. Trow-Smith, *A History of British Livestock Husbandry, 1700–1900*, London, 1959, pp. 22–4.

[87] NNRO, PD131/38, *sub anno* 1640.

Yields per annum must therefore have been greater by 1750 than in 1650, although data are lacking, but perhaps not so much greater as proponents of the forage crops claimed. At Over in Cambridgeshire, however, Houghton observed dairy cattle in 1695 still producing milk in winter when tied in stalls and fed meadow hay. Cheese and butter output may not have been fully recorded. Thus Knopwood sold 98 firkins of butter in 1734, apparently from 22 cows, but he gives no indication how much he consumed at home. The profits of cow keeping are almost equally elusive, but Wyndham's dairy farm at Reepham yielded about £33 per annum, or a little over £2 per cow, which in the gloom of the 1670s was quite encouraging.[88]

Bullock feeding

With the foldcourse in dissolution and dairying not expanding, the keynote of animal husbandry in East Anglia by 1700–50 was the beef trade. The typical mixed enterprise in the loams or good sands in 1750 consisted of beef cattle for fatting and barley and wheat production. Sheep and dairy cows were appendages to the developing regime of high feeding for which the richer fielden districts were already famous by 1780. The cornerstone of this system was the immense trade in stores from the north and west, but the feeding of home-breds retained a good deal of importance, especially on the smaller farms, throughout the period. The meat trade depended for its vitality upon the proximity to London and upon the fact that the grasslands and fold yards of the region were ideally placed between the highland zone and the metropolitan market. An additional impetus, however, was almost certainly the effect of the foldcourse in deflecting peasant farmers in the fielden district from keeping their own sheep.

The fatting business brought about several changes in farming practice in the eastern counties. The aptness of marsh grass for finishing cattle was clearly recognized by London butchers, who hired or bought parcels of Thames marshland to accommodate the droves of fatware brought down from the Midlands or East Anglia, but the marshes, freshened and divided by drains, were used all round the coast from Lincolnshire to Essex for the same purpose; and many inland farmers had acquired marsh grass, or agisted their stock, to improve the killing quality of their beeves and sheep.

The marshes, however, were insufficient to feed the immense herds of steers fattened in the period. Moreover, marsh grazing did not fulfil the essential criterion of mixed husbandry, that the cattle, like the sheep, should fertilize the arable. The half-covered fold yard, therefore, proved the best means both of fatting cattle and of mucking field land. A few farms, of yeomen as well as on the greater estates, already had quite elaborate parr yards by 1750, though yard feeding in general was still in a somewhat rudimentary state.

[88] Houghton, *Collection*, 31 May, 7–14 June 1695, vol. VII, nos. 148–50; NNRO, BAR22,23/1; WKC5/152.

The cattle, of course, still ran over the rowens and etch, on the ollands and summerleys, as well as on permanent pastures, but in-wintering was the essence of the new system as it unfolded after 1670. The muck cart was as important an adjutant of progress as the marl cart. Even in the mid seventeenth century steers and dry cows were stalled or tethered and fed on beans, crushed grain, or turnips to prime fatness. In due course new feedstuffs were added to the list – cabbages, brewer's grains, oilcake – but the practice of stall feeding was more or less established by the end of the seventeenth century. Most of the great fairs which emerged as exchanges for store beasts in the seventeenth century, St Faith or Hempton in Norfolk, Hoxne and Framsden in Suffolk, and St Ives in Huntingdonshire, occurred in the late summer or autumn. Many of the surviving farm accounts of the period referred to stock thus bought after the harvest and sold the following year between April and November.[89]

The cattle introduced into the region from the highland zone were similarly often purchased in the autumn at the same fairs, though there was also a great trade in spring-driven 'runts' fattened on East Anglian grass between April and the fall of the year. Runts therefore were put on turnips or some other forage crops. The Norths' farm at Glemham (Suffolk) had thirty Scotch steers on turnips in 1726–7, and four years earlier the agent had proposed to send six beasts to London, "though not fat, or they must go back to hay (after turnips) which will be but a poor way of grazing". Even so, it was still common to graze their Scotch cattle in Blaxhall marshes during the summer months to fatten them.[90]

Some of the beasts imported into East Anglia were 'half-fat' already. The 'finishing' trade was especially important in the Thames marshes, where both wholesale butchers and local farmers utilized part of their pasture land to prepare beasts for the metropolitan markets. Bartholomew Fair was renowned for Welsh beasts long before 1640, and it is clear from the Petre estate accounts that by 1656 many south Essex fairs, Brentwood, Romford, Ingatestone, Bush, were already well stocked with runts. At the end of the century Scotch were as numerous as Welsh in the vicinity. Some of the stock sold in south Essex almost certainly came from the Midlands and East Anglia, where they had spent some months since leaving the highland zone.[91]

[89] Manuscript evidence of fattening purchased stores, especially Welsh and Scotch runts, is immense: a significant minority of relevant inventories after 1660 (c. 12–15%) refer to imported beasts in the region, and estate and farm accounts, etc., almost without exception, mention black cattle, runts, or kyloes – e.g. Welsh: Essex RO, D/DP/A47, 1663–8; A54, 1656, A55, 1666–70 (S. Essex); D/DBy/A299, 1749 (N.W. Essex); D/DTw/A2, 1733; Cambs. RO, R74/43; WSRO, MSS 259; Essex RO, Scotch: D/DP/A47, 1676; S/SB/A1, 1749 (S. Essex), D/DTw/A (S. Essex), 1737; NNRO, NRS16,023, 1669 (S. Norfolk); B.L. VIIIb, 1741–3 (N. Norfolk); KN575, 1682–3 (Breckland); ESRO, HA49/IV/4, 5, 1724–7 (Sandlings); WSRO, E18/455/4, 1673 (Mildenhall); E18/660/2, 1717; Cambs. RO, R52/24/30.

[90] ESRO, HA49/IV/3, 4.

[91] Essex RO, D/DP/A47, A54, A55; Burley, thesis, pp. 60, 61–2; Defoe, Tour, p. 51.

Increasingly, however, East Anglia, from the Thames to the Wash, was committed to fattening stores from remote counties, rather than merely finishing them. The deficiency of home-bred lean stock had begun to be supplied from north-country stocks before 1600, but the golden age of the imported store beast was from 1660 to 1760. During this century it was the Scotch runt which predominated in East Anglia. No district of East Anglia was unfamiliar with Scotch beasts by 1720–50, though the heaviest concentration of them was on demesne farms. The custom of fatting such cattle, indeed, probably began with the gentry, and there is scarcely a gentleman's account book of the period after 1680 which does not mention Scotch or Welsh stores. By contrast comparatively few inventories, about 15 per cent between 1670 and 1720, specifically refer to runts. The custom, however, was gaining ground. By 1747–50 (during the cattle plague) districts such as the Norfolk corn country or fenlands had become dependent upon imports, and several farmers could not resist the temptation of buying uncertified Scotch beasts despite the danger. Already in the 1730s some villages, like Worlington (Suffolk) had banned the keeping of runts on their commons. By that date many thousands of Scotch cattle were being fed in East Anglia; one Lincolnshire grazier assumed that the number exceeded 30,000 in the eastern counties in the 1720s, and this was certainly no exaggeration.[92]

The profits of feeding runts are hard to determine precisely, but they were not large. Wyndham of Felbrigg apparently made £28 on 25 steers fattened in 1680; per head, and allowing for keep, he seems to have earned from 16s. to 25s., depending on the year. In a "very bad year for graziers" (1723), Nicholas Styleman in west Norfolk bought 53 bullocks for £120 and sold them, almost fat, for £154, but in 1724 he made at least £100 profit from the sale of 46. In the marshland of Norfolk in 1742–3 Scotch beasts were bought for 50s. and sold fat at £5 4s. 8d. each. Probably half the proceeds of fatstock sales in average years had been laid out in the purchase of the stores in the first place. Keep was not inconsiderable. Agistment charges for six months varied between 2s. 6d. and 8s. per beast in 1670–1740, while winter feed might cost as much as 20s. a head to procure quick results. In sum, therefore, no great fortunes were made merely by fattening imported stores. Landlords like Wyndham of Felbrigg were driven to stock farms fallen into hand in years of recession *faute de mieux*, and were grateful often to make anything. Without the muck, therefore, cattle feeding would have seemed even less attractive.[93]

[92] See n. 89 above and Cambs. RO, R52/24/46/4; Essex RO, D/DL/C22; WSRO, 1,375/2, 1730; LAO, Tyr 2/2/21. Another estimate in 1726 put the trade from Essex and Suffolk alone to London at 50,000 fat cattle, 200,000 fat sheep, 100,000 fatted calves, and 2,000,000 geese and turkeys – *Brief Deduction...of the British Woollen Manufacture*, London, 1726, p. 6.

[93] NNRO, WKC5/152 f. 166; Lestrange 25/11/XIII; B.L. VIIIb; KNY575.

Minor aspects of animal husbandry

Pig farming was very much an adjunct of dairying and has been mentioned as such already. Outside the large towns, most East Anglian farmers, tradesmen, artisans, and labourers apparently kept a pig or two for consumption in the seventeenth as in the nineteenth century. Poultry was similarly ubiquitous, but the preparation of turkeys, geese, or capons for the market was obviously more specialized. Nevertheless, large-scale poultry farms, which presumably existed, have proved very elusive. Few peasant farmers seem to have kept more than thirty head of poultry in the period, so that the trade in fowls was fragmented, and must have owed much of its coherence to the higglers who toured East Anglia in search of droves for London poulterers. My impression is that the Norfolk poultry business was centred on Norwich, Thetford, and Attleborough and again in the north-west of the county; while in Suffolk the woodland was also important in the production of capons and turkeys. Geese were found everywhere. The fens specialized in goose rearing, where the great commons fed immense flocks, but many Norfolk farmers who supplied the trade kept mixed flocks of 'pullin' – geese, turkeys, ducks, and hens. Geese were banned from common pastures in several villages, but the success of the poultry business depended less upon casual grazing than upon the supply of pulse crops, buckwheat, and other grains in the various parts of the region.[94]

Rabbits too deserve a place in this account. The London poulterers had an almost insatiable demand for conies in the period, and on thin, barren soils warrening was probably the most profitable form of animal husbandry open to landowners, despite the ecological damage caused by rabbits. They were popular not only as meat but also for their fur, much used in the making of hats. It is not surprising, therefore, that few warrens were grubbed out before 1750, in spite of the growing contempt for the rabbit which progressive farmers expressed. By 1650 warrens were found almost everywhere except on the clays. Conies burrowed in the not yet sacred turf of Newmarket Heath and in the sea walls of the coastline; warrens girdled Norwich and King's Lynn, Ipswich, and Bury; but they were concentrated chiefly in the remoter fastnesses of Breckland. The unpopularity of rabbits occasionally led to uproar and often caused friction between landlord or warrener and the rest of the village, though the warrens which were destroyed were extinguished to serve a wider public interest; some coastal warrens, for instance at Titchwell and Aldeburgh, were grubbed out because of damage to the sea defences.[95]

[94] No inventory so far examined has yielded evidence of any extensive poultry keeping, and specialists of late-nineteenth- or twentieth-century character were unknown – see Essex RO, D/DP/A55; ESRO, HA/GB3/2.

[95] NNRO, WKC5/152 f. 270; NCC (Petre), box 16; HEA589; MSS 12,090 Stafford 113: WSRO, E3/10/9–20; 613/758/3.

Warrening tended to be a specialist occupation. Landlords employed warreners as sheepmasters employed shepherds and on similar terms. Although warrens were no longer a seignorial preserve, few farmers who were not tenants specifically of manorial warrens attempted to keep conies. On the other hand good warreners were apparently difficult to find, and several of the more reputable (or ambitious) served more than one master at the same time. The duties of the conymaster were to preserve the breeding stock, to kill and perhaps flay the fatstock, and to maintain the banks and burrows in order to minimize depredation of neighbouring crops.

CHAPTER 8

METROPOLITAN COUNTIES: BEDFORDSHIRE, HERTFORDSHIRE, AND MIDDLESEX

The variety of farming practice, and the location and boundaries of the different agricultural regions within these three Home Counties, were determined by the geography of the land and by the demands of the metropolitan food market. Most of this chapter, therefore, will be devoted to examining the ways in which farmers and landlords responded to both these factors by extending the acreage under cultivation, by adopting new crops and new methods, and, in some cases, by developing rural industries to subsidize income gained from agriculture. The pattern of rural economies which emerges from such an investigation is a complex one, and by no stretch of the imagination could these three counties be described as homogeneous. Their varying experience – political, social, and religious as well as economic – from the outset in the Civil War period underlines this point very clearly.[1]

In the short term the Home Counties suffered some of the military impact of the Civil Wars. In Bedfordshire, Leighton Buzzard and Woburn were ravaged by royalist soldiers in 1644. Woburn was particularly badly hit. Houses were burnt down "besides many barns, stables, malthouses, and other outhouses". There was sporadic pillaging in Hertfordshire in 1645. But for farmers what was just as serious as these overt acts of violence was the disruption of their way of life and the means to pursue it by the movement of troops, the requisitioning of horses and waggons, conscription, and taxation. Petitioners from the Manshead hundred of Bedfordshire argued passionately in 1644 that they were quite unable to send any more men, horses, and equipment for the defence of the garrison at Newport Pagnell; so much had been taken from them already that "now being seedtime they have not horses to plough and sow their land". In 1645 Lord Bolingbroke presented a remonstrance to the Committee of Both Kingdoms complaining that in the previous two years alone the quartering of soldiers and the taking of horses had cost Bedfordshire £50,000. In such a situation taxes were bound to remain unpaid, and already some farmers had been forced to give up their farms. Landlords, too, suffered as rents remained unpaid. All in all, the Civil

---

[1] C. Holmes, *The Eastern Association in the English Civil War*, Cambridge, 1974, emphasizes the diversity of the component counties.

War must have cost the earl of Salisbury somewhere in the region of £30,000.[2]

The ferment of the Civil War period, the interaction between local and national issues, occasioned other economic developments and social changes. For one thing the sale of crown lands gave army officers the opportunity to become landowners in counties like Bedfordshire. John Crook bought Beckerings Park, Thomas Margetts acquired the manor of Biggleswade, John Okey got possession of Brogborough Park and the manors of Ampthill and Millbrook. Some royalists, like Sir Lewis Dyve of Bromham, were stripped of their estates, which accordingly came on the land market.[3] Lower down the social scale, popular discontent erupted in various ways. Levellers were at work in Hertfordshire, and a community of Diggers in Enfield. Enclosure riots took place in several places. On Hounslow Heath in Middlesex the pales surrounding enclosures made by the king were thrown down. Enclosures on Berkhamsted Common (part of a Hertfordshire manor belonging to the prince of Wales) were attacked in 1641 and again the following year. Protests such as these, Manning reminds us, demonstrate the fact that the central agrarian issue in the English Revolution was whether the landlords or the small farmers should control and develop the wastes.[4]

How deep and lasting such divisions and conflicts were within the different village communities is difficult to say. No doubt the long-term consequences can easily be exaggerated, but temporarily at least in some areas the world was indeed turned upside down in the 1640s and 1650s.[5] But before we examine in greater detail the combination of change and continuity in the rural life and organization of Bedfordshire, Hertfordshire, and Middlesex, we must first attempt to define the general characteristics and the different farming regions of these three counties.

Bedfordshire consists mainly of clays, with the exception of its southern chalklands, its central greensand ridge, and three districts of gravelly soil in the north and east. Its most northerly parts made poor arable farmland; the

---

[2] H. G. Tibbutt, *Bedfordshire and the First Civil War*, 2nd edn, Elstow, 1973, pp. 12–13; S. R. Gardiner, *History of the Great Civil War 1642–49*, London, 1905, II, p. 194; A. Kingston, *East Anglia and the Great Civil War*, London, 1897; Holmes, *op. cit.*, pp. 137, 148–9, 166; Joyce Godber, *History of Bedfordshire, 1066–1888*, Bedford, 1969, p. 282; Tibbut, *op. cit.*, p. 14; L. Stone, *Family and Fortune: Studies in Aristocratic Finance in the Sixteenth and Seventeenth Centuries*, Oxford, 1973, pp. 151–2.

[3] H. G. Tibbutt, *Bedfordshire and the Protectorate*, 2nd edn, Elstow, 1973, p. 4.

[4] H. Shaw, *The Levellers*, London, 1968, pp. 13, 68; Pauline Gregg, *Freeborn John: A Biography of John Lilburne*, London, 1961, pp. 154, 164, 269, 326, 332; J. M. Patrick, 'William Covell and the Troubles at Enfield in 1659: A Sequel to the Digger Movement', *Univ. of Toronto Qtrly*, XIV, 1944–5, pp. 45–57; B. Manning, *The English People and the English Revolution*, London, 1976, pp. 112–38, 196–215.

[5] C. Hill, *The World Turned Upside Down: Radical Ideas during the English Revolution*, London, 1972; D. G. Hey, *An English Rural Community: Myddle under the Tudors and Stuarts*, Leicester, 1974, p. 198.

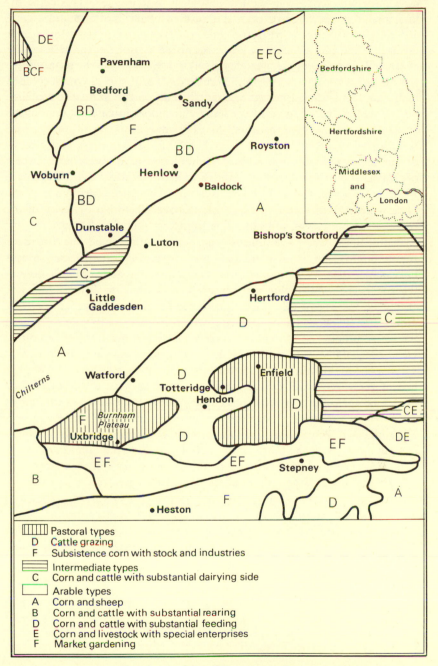

DE
BCF
Pavenham
Bedford
Sandy
BD
F
EFC
BD
Royston
Woburn
Henlow
Baldock
BD
A
C
Dunstable
Luton
Bishop's Stortford
C
Little
Gaddesden
Hertford
D
C
A
Chilterns
Watford
D
Enfield
Totteridge
Hendon
D
F
Burnham
Plateau
Uxbridge
D
CE
B
E F.
EF
EF
DE
Stepney
F
D
A
Heston

Bedfordshire

Hertfordshire

Middlesex

and

London

Pastoral types
D   Cattle grazing
F   Subsistence corn with stock and industries
      Intermediate types
C   Corn and cattle with substantial dairying side
      Arable types
A   Corn and sheep
B   Corn and cattle with substantial rearing
D   Corn and cattle with substantial feeding
E   Corn and livestock with special enterprises
F   Market gardening

Fig. 8.1. Farming regions of the metropolitan counties.

clays there were cold, thin-stapled, and easily waterlogged. This being so, local small farmers were hard pressed to survive by means of agriculture alone and were forced to rely partly on industrial by-employments. But at least the unenviable land which they possessed spared them from the enterprising efforts and hungry appetite of estate makers. Further south in the county there was the breathtaking example of the fourth duke of Bedford, who succeeded to the family inheritance in 1732 and rapidly built up a great park at Woburn, buying out other landowners large and small and eventually dominating no fewer than twenty-five parishes. Socially and economically the estate building of the Russells must have been one of the most conspicuous developments in eighteenth-century Bedfordshire as the lands of departing or extinct gentry families came to swell those of the nobility.[6] Agriculturally – as the competition for land emphasized – it was Bedfordshire south of the Ouse which was the more prosperous; the overwhelming majority of the county's market towns, reflecting this fact, were south of the river.

Bedfordshire was predominantly an arable county, and the Board of Agriculture reports of 1794 and 1808 give the impression – to some extent misleading – that farming practice in the county changed relatively little in the seventeenth and eighteenth centuries. According to Robert Morden, Bedfordshire was famed for the best barley in England. Oats were not widely grown, but Fuller and Defoe testified to the high quality of its wheat. "Indeed the whole product of this county is corn", Defoe concluded.[7] As so often, Defoe exaggerated, even though his underlying point was valid; Bedfordshire was assessed highly in the first Corn Bounty Act of 1672.[8] But by the second half of the seventeenth century market gardening was a well-established branch of agriculture in the central sandy ridge, there was a scattering of dairymen in the county, and some southern villages such as Potsgrove, Hockliffe, and Eaton Bray had their share of graziers fattening animals coming down from the north or from Wales to serve the London market.[9]

So far as Hertfordshire was concerned, contemporary commentators were mainly agreed on two paradoxical features of its agriculture: the extent of poor soils in the county, and the surprising primacy of varying systems of arable farming. According to Thomas Fuller, "this forestry ground would willingly bear nothing so well as a crop of wood. But seeing custom is another Nature it hath many years been contented to bring forth good grain, persuaded thereunto by the industrious husbandman." Other writers such as

[6] Godber, *op. cit.*, pp. 17, 303.

[7] T. Batchelor, *General View of the Agriculture of Bedfordshire*, London, 1808, p. 394; R. Morden, *The New Description and State of England*, London, 1704; T. Fuller, *The Worthies of England*, ed. J. Freeman, London, 1952, p. 14; D. Defoe, *A Tour through the Whole Island of Great Britain*, ed. G. D. H. Cole and D. C. Browning, 2 vols., London, 1962, II, p. 113.

[8] T & C, p. 163.

[9] Godber, *op. cit.*, p. 275.

Morden, Chauncy, and Salmon confirmed this general impression.[10] Wheat and oats were certainly the main crops grown in Hertfordshire in the seventeenth century, along with rye, barley, and, to a lesser extent, peas, and tithable acreages in the south-west of the county increased by as much as 80 per cent between the 1670s and the 1790s. This increase was achieved by farming both more intensively – by means of new rotations, for instance – and more extensively, by putting more pasture and woodland under the plough. George Atwell argued persuasively in *The Faithfull Surveyor* (1662) for a realistic attitude to land use, stressing that in Chiltern areas "an acre of arable is more worth than an acre of pasture".[11] Not that arable farming necessarily remained constant. There is some evidence to show that wheat and undoubtedly rye declined in importance as cash crops in this period, reflecting the general downward trend in corn prices as others, usually fodder crops, to some extent replaced them; rye had all but disappeared in some areas of Hertfordshire by the end of the eighteenth century.[12]

In the north of the county, on the chalk uplands, sheep–corn husbandry was the general practice, and barley a major crop. The malting towns of Baldock, Ashwell, Royston, and Hitchin were all concentrated in this area. Hitchin had 66 freeholders and copyholders worth £10 or more a year when a county census of men of substance was compiled in 1699.[13] One of this number was Matthew Harrold, the inventory of whose goods was drawn up in January 1705. He was worth £201 15s. 8d. and had 16 acres of wheat and rye on the ground valued at £28 and 6 acres lying fallow. Wheat was in fact his principal crop and he had a store of it in his barn from the previous year's harvest worth £50. He also had barley, oats, and peas in his barn, valued at £13 10s., £8 10s., and £6 respectively. Harrold had 3 cows, 7 pigs, and some poultry, but his first interests were obviously in arable farming, and his 3 horses, carts, ploughs, carts, waggons, and so on emphasize the point.[14] Daniel Hurst was an oatmeal maker of Hitchin who died in 1705. Oats and barley were the two crops grown by Richard Bowman, a Hitchin labourer, who died in 1667; for a labourer he was relatively prosperous, for his total

---

[10] Fuller, *op. cit.*, p. 229; Morden, *op. cit.*, p. 69; H. Chauncy, *Historical Antiquities of Hertfordshire* (1700), Bishop's Stortford, 1826; N. Salmon, *The History of Hertfordshire*, London, 1728, *passim*. Cf. Arthur Young on the small area of grassland in Hertfordshire as compared with arable – *General View of the Agriculture of Hertfordshire*, London, 1804, pp. 133–42.

[11] E. G. Longman, 'Agrarian Change in South-West Hertfordshire, 1600–1850', unpub. Univ. of London M.Sc. thesis, 1972, pp. 42–5. I am indebted to Mr Longman for giving me access to his thesis prior to its publication in revised form in 1977 under the title "*A Corner of England's Garden*": *An Agrarian History of South-West Hertfordshire, 1600–1850*, 2 vols., Bushey. G. Atwell, *The Faithfull Surveyor*, Cambridge, 1662, p. 102. Dr Joan Thirsk kindly brought this reference to my notice.

[12] Longman, thesis, p. 94.

[13] W. J. Hardy, ed., *Hertford County Records: Sessions Rolls*, Hertford, 1905, *II*, p. 18.

[14] Herts. RO, AHH.22/8.

estate was valued at £42 4s. 8d. and of his 5 acres of arable, 3 were sown with barley and 2 with oats. He also had a cow and a young bullock.[15]

In the south of the county the proximity of the London market and the presence of the Great North Road and Watling Street did much to encourage the breeding of horses; the fattening of pigs, lambs, and bullocks; and the growing of oats.[16] Barnet may be taken as an example. The town was a minor spa – visited by Celia Fiennes and Samuel Pepys among others – lying on Watling Street. James Barcock the elder, brewer, who died in 1691 worth over £1,250, was one who had grown rich in this busy place. Another who had profited – although in a less spectacular way – from Barnet's strategic position was John Carter, husbandman, whose goods were appraised at £154 6s. 4d. at his death in 1688. The main item listed in his inventory was the hay in his barn – a commodity much in demand in a place like Barnet, which must have been crowded with travellers' horses – worth £32 10s. He had a flock of about 100 sheep as well as 4 horses and colts, 5 cows, and 3 calves.[17]

The close economic links between Hertfordshire and London are clearly indicated also in the pattern of the gentry's marriage alliances and in the fact that the bulk of the county élite were newcomers. Fewer than 10 per cent of the leading gentry who took sides in the Civil War came from families settled in Hertfordshire in 1485; land was constantly changing hands as new estates were being built up.[18] Sir Harbottle Grimston, for example, consolidated his Gorhambury property by making seventy land purchases totalling £54,000 between 1651 and 1683. Just under a third of the purchases were made from local men living within a three-mile radius, while the rest were acquired from absentee landlords usually at twenty years' purchase price.[19] There is some evidence of small tenants being squeezed out through engrossing, but a great estate was essentially a unit of ownership, not of production, and no gentleman followed a policy of wholesale dispossession. Rents remained steady in the second half of the century except where they were adjusted to take account of investment in improvements. A slight

---

[15] Herts. RO, 59 HW 88; 11 HW 62.

[16] John Houghton, *A Collection of Letters for the Improvement of Husbandry and Trade*, London, 1681, includes material on the fattening of lambs at Hadley near Barnet for the London market (in T & C, p. 176).

[17] Herts. RO, 128 AW 2 and 124 AW 1.

[18] Holmes, *op. cit.*, pp. 14, 29; L. and J. C. F. Stone, 'Country Houses and their Owners in Hertfordshire, 1540–1879', in W. O. Aydelotte *et al.*, eds., *The Dimensions of Quantitative Research in History*, Oxford, 1972, p. 59; C. Clay, 'Two Families and their Estates, 1660–1815', unpub. Univ. of Cambridge Ph.D. thesis, 1966, pp. 83, 85, gives examples of London marriages contracted by the Grimstons.

[19] Clay, thesis, pp. 15, 17, 20, 49, 51, 55: Stephen Primatt, *City and Country Purchaser and Builder*, London, 1667(?), reckoned twenty years' purchase price as the norm in Hertfordshire (in T & C, p. 291).

upward movement in rents occurred in the early part of the eighteenth century, but this was halted by the agricultural depression which noticeably hit grain-producing areas in the two decades after 1730.[20] At Hertingfordbury Lord Chancellor Cowper made discriminating land purchases to build up a relatively modest estate as a social investment for his son. Since most of the land in question was acquired from absentee owners rather than from small peasant proprietors, his estate-building efforts caused very little social dislocation in the village. The small landowner had already been pushed out in the course of the seventeenth century, and it may well be that Spufford's redating of his disappearance in parts of Cambridgeshire applies to this area as well.[21]

The pattern of agriculture in Middlesex was quite different from that in Hertfordshire. Despite the fact that for half its total area the county had loamy soils well suited to arable farming, its closeness to London ensured that in this period it was predominantly a grassland region specializing in haymaking and dairy farming. (Dairy farming in Middlesex, however, meant mainly milk production; very little butter was made.)[22] Following von Thünen's theories on agricultural location, Bull has argued that around seventeenth-century London there were six concentric belts of differing land use. The innermost zone, around London and Westminster, specialized in market gardening – a very important branch of agriculture in Middlesex and one which will be closely examined later in this chapter. Next came a narrow zone of woodland around Hornsey, Highgate, and Hampstead, which provided important reserves of fuel and building material. Third was a belt – not continuous, however – of intensive grain production around villages such as Chiswick, Harrow, Heston, and the Brent valley. (According to Fuller, "the best [wheat] in England groweth in the vale lying south of Harrow on the Hill, nigh Heston". The fourth belt, which took in places like Hendon and Wembley, was one of less-intensive cultivation where pasture and meadows were as important to farmers as grain. Fifth came a belt of open-field farming as at Uxbridge, Edgware, and Enfield. (Enfield Chase remained unenclosed until 1777.) In the sixth and outermost belt cattle raising was practised, as in the Lea and Colne valleys. Few horses were bred anywhere in Middlesex; London's vast supply was almost entirely imported from such other parts of the country as Leicestershire.[23]

Of all three metropolitan counties, Middlesex – not surprisingly – was most sensitive to the demands of the London food market. It was the link

---

[20] Clay, thesis, p. 142; G. E. Mingay, 'The Agricultural Depression, 1730–1750', EcHR, 2nd ser., VIII, 1956, pp. 323–38.

[21] Clay, thesis, pp. 216–25; Margaret Spufford, *Contrasting Communities: English Villagers in the Sixteenth and Seventeenth Centuries*, Cambridge, 1974, pp. 46–92.

[22] J. Middleton, *General View of the Agriculture of Middlesex*, London, 1807, p. 427.

[23] G. B. G. Bull, 'The Changing Landscape of Rural Middlesex', unpub. Univ. of London Ph.D. thesis, 1958, p. 472; Fuller, *op. cit.*, p. 386; Bull, thesis, p. 363; Middleton, *op. cit.*, p. 460.

with London which was the most crucial economic influence at work in the county. Middlesex, said Thomas Fuller, "is in effect but the suburbs at large of London, replenished with the retiring houses of the gentry and citizens thereof besides many palaces of noblemen and three (lately) royal mansions". Daniel Defoe readily agreed. Middlesex, in his view too, was pre-eminently "a county made rich, pleasant, and populous by the neighbourhood of London".[24]

The stimulus of the London food market had far-reaching effects on agriculture in the Home Counties in the seventeenth and eighteenth centuries, and, bearing in mind the enormous increase which took place in this period in the population of the capital, this is hardly surprising. According to Wrigley's estimates, London grew in size from about 400,000 in 1650 to about 575,000 in 1700, with a further increase of the order of 100,000 taking place in the next fifty years. Proportionately London housed about 7 per cent of England's total population in 1650, and 11 per cent in 1750. Population growth on this scale, Wrigley argues, implies a corresponding increase of three-quarters in the demand for food in the London market in the course of the century, with increasing agricultural productivity occurring in the areas most involved in supplying the needs of the capital. London required three times more corn in 1700 than in 1600, according to Gras, and its annual consumption was approaching $1\frac{1}{2}$ million quarters by the later date.[25]

Contemporaries, of course, were well aware of the magnitude of these changes, but had mixed views about the economic and social consequences which they entailed for the surrounding counties. John Houghton, writing in 1681, emphasized the benefits.

The bigness and great consumption of London doth not only encourage the breeders of provisions and higglers thirty miles off, but even to four score miles; wherefore I think it will necessary follow, that if London by its bigness, or any other way, should consume as much again, the country within these four score miles would have a greater employment; or else, those that are further off will get some with them.

Similar opinions were expressed by Defoe and Richard Baxter. But all was not gain in the relationship between London and its hinterland, as John Aubrey, for one, recognized. "The gentry living in London", he wrote, "the daily concourse of servants out of the country to London makes servants'

---

[24] Fuller, op. cit., p. 386; Defoe, op. cit., II, p. 13.

[25] E. A. Wrigley, 'A Simple Model of London's Importance in Changing English Society and Economy, 1650–1750', PP, xxxvii, 1967, pp. 44, 55, 57; F. J. Fisher, 'The Development of the London Food Market, 1549–1640', repr. in E. M. Carus-Wilson, ed., Essays in Economic History, I, London, 1954, and the same author's 'The Development of London as a Centre of Conspicuous Consumption in the Sixteenth and Seventeenth Centuries', in Carus-Wilson, op. cit., II (London, 1962); N. S. B. Gras, The Evolution of the English Corn Market, Cambridge, Mass., 1915, pp. 76–7.

wages dear in the country and makes scarcity of labourers." Arthur Young elaborated the same point in the following century.[26]

Young discussed prices as well as wages and saw a clear correlation between price levels and distance from the London market. "You must certainly allow", he wrote, "that the rise and fall of these prices in proportion to the distance from the capital are too regular to be the effect of soil, or accident; they are palpably caused by the London markets." Earlier writers like Baxter and William Ellis had been hesitatingly moving towards an understanding of this key to the price mechanism, and closer investigation confirms Young's analysis. The wheat prices, for example, for 1691–1702, quoted by Gras in his study of the English corn market, show the basic distinction between the high prices of the metropolitan market area and the relatively low prices prevailing in counties which remained largely outside the London orbit. The highest wheat prices in all England were to be found in the Home Counties, London's main granary. The price of hay and straw was similarly high in these counties.

…at Barnet [wrote John Byng, the future fifth viscount Torrington in 1789] they talk of the amazing price of straw; and that in London it is dearer than hay. What's the reason? Shall I tell you? It is because London is so overgrown; and so crowded by horses that the consumption of straw is, within these few years, doubled. Consequently the adjacent counties that are much under grass cannot supply the metropolis as formerly; straw must then be fetch'd from afar. This devilish increase of London will in time cause a famine because it cannot be supply'd.[27]

London's demands for straw and hay were indeed almost insatiable, and four additional hay markets had to be set up in the course of the seventeenth century, at Whitechapel, Westminster, Chapel Street, and Haymarket (Piccadilly). The "Hay Country" serving this market extended from St Albans to Hendon and covered a large part of Hertfordshire and Middlesex. Such was the high price that hay commanded that some farmers in this area specialized exclusively in the intensive production of this commodity. William Ellis in his *Modern Husbandman* described how the farmers around Hendon "are reckoned the best in England for curing their hay by making it so as to retain a green colour for years together in order to obtain the greater price at the London market where they sell most or all their hay at times throughout the year". Much casual labour was needed in the periods of haymaking, and was recruited not only locally but from neighbouring counties like Bedfordshire and also from Ireland. Peter Kalm, the observant Swedish traveller, graphically described how

[26] T & C, p. 176; Defoe, *op. cit.*, II, p. 1; T & C, pp. 184, 180; Arthur Young, *A Six Weeks' Tour through the Southern Counties*, 3rd edn, London, 1772, pp. 337–8.

[27] Young, *Six Weeks' Tour*, p. 326; Gras, *op. cit.*, pp. 119–20; *The Torrington Diaries*, ed. C. Bruyn Andrews, London, 1954, p. 218. For comparative purposes, F. M. L. Thompson, *Victorian England: The Horse-Drawn Society*, London, 1970, is interesting.

In the beginning of May there come from Ireland over to England a very large number of Irishmen who...go and hire themselves out everywhere to the farmers. The whole of this part of England which lies immediately north and east of London carries on nearly all its haymaking and harvest work with only this people, who...remain there the whole summer leaving their own dwellings at home in Ireland to the care of their wives and children. But towards autumn after the seedtime and harvest are past they return home with the money they have been able to earn.

Itinerant labourers, however, could easily create problems of public order for the civil authorities, and in 1656, for example, parish constables in Hertfordshire were instructed to check passports and testimonials of all those travelling for "work in the hay time and harvest".[28]

But discussion of metropolitan agricultural requirements needs to take account of the fact that seventeenth- and eighteenth-century London – unlike its present-day successor – was by no means a totally urban community. Within the city itself there were farmers – dairymen and market gardeners for the most part – as well as a whole host of men employed in the different ancillary trades associated with the provisioning of the capital. Nathaniel James, who leased land in St Martin-in-the-Fields, and who died in 1677, was one of a considerable number of dairymen who maintained a high yield of milk from their cows by constantly changing and replenishing their stock. James had 33 milch cows, a young bull, 6 draught horses, and other animals, and had hay ricks in the upper field next to his house worth £65. Clearly, this farmer with a total estate worth £483 9s. 6d. was a prosperous man. He had a sideline in producing bacon and was evidently a part-time carter, since at the time of his death he was owed over £16 by the parish for the carriage of gravel used in road repairs.[29]

London's relationship with its food and fodder suppliers in the metropolitan counties, however, was far from being wholly one-sided; London was not simply a consumer. It was also – certainly by the second half of the seventeenth century – a storehouse which could be drawn upon by the surrounding counties themselves in periods of acute shortage.[30] More continuously important was London's function as a supplier of manure for the farming regions around it. Street and domestic refuse, soot, ashes, and all manner of waste from the city butchers and traders were an invaluable asset to farmers living within reach of the capital, and facilitated the intensive production of fruit, vegetables, and hay. William Ellis of Little Gaddesden

[28] P. V. McGrath, 'The Marketing of Food, Fodder, and Livestock in the London Area in the Seventeenth Century, with Special Reference to the Sources of Supply', unpub. Univ. of London M.A. thesis, 1948, p. 238; *The Diary of Benjamin Rogers, Rector of Carlton*, ed. C. D. Linnell, Beds. Rec. Soc., xxx, 1950, pp. 4, 70; W. Ellis, *The Modern Husbandman*, 8 vols., London, 1750, *VI*, p. 76; P. Kalm, *Kalm's Account of his Visit to England on his Way to America in 1748*, ed. J. Lucas, London, 1892, pp. 82–3; Hardy, *Hertford County Records*, I, p. 116.

[29] Greater London RO, (M)/DRO.AM/P1/1677/48.

[30] Gras, *op. cit.*, p. 94.

thought particularly highly of London coal soot as a fertilizer, "which as far exceeds wood soot as a shilling does sixpence and will nourish such grass ground so well for three years together that no other assistance need be given it in that time". Farmers thirty miles distant from London, Ellis went on, in a way which recalls Baxter's comments in the previous century, were regular users of this

noble manure which for many years has been used more in Hertfordshire than in any other country besides. And that it may come the cheaper home we commonly carry up chaff, corn, wood, flour, or timber, and fetch in return soot in sacks or loose in a cart or waggon, which now is sold for sixpence a bushel; when in winter and at spring it is sold in London for ninepence. And in this manner you may bring down coal ashes, ox or cows' hoofs, hogs' or oxes' hair, trotters, horn shavings, glovers' shavings, coney clippings, pidgeons' or rabbits' dung against the time of wanting them.[31]

Nevertheless, London was primarily a buyer and a consumer, and its demands, and any fluctuatons in those demands, exercised a dominant and inescapable influence over all kinds of agricultural production and related industries such as brewing in its market area in the Home Counties. As London's food and fodder imports grew in this period the marketing arrangements in the capital became increasingly complex and sophisticated. One such development was that no fewer than five new companies concerned with London's food supplies were incorporated in the course of the seventeenth century. Although the traditional method of direct selling by country folk continued into this period, London middlemen were growing in numbers and importance throughout the seventeenth century, and old prejudices against them were swept away by the realization that their services were indispensable. The normal channel through which London's food supplies were distributed remained the markets – thirteen of them in all by 1600 – and after 1666 and the Great Fire some were re-sited, the wholesale side of their trading was emphasized, and their facilities were improved. Except during the Commonwealth period, when the interference of the Council of Trade aroused Londoners' resentment, the London food market in the second half of the seventeenth century was largely unregulated.[32]

Extreme critics of the growth and influence of seventeenth- and eighteenth-century London saw the capital as a parasite. "Gentlemen drain the country

[31] Kalm, op cit., pp. 54–5; Ellis, Modern Husbandman, I, p. 82; III, pt 1, pp. 132–3; T & C, p. 184. Cartloads of animal clippings and of soot were brought from London to a farm at Pirton in north Hertfordshire in 1730 – Herts. RO, DE 4165 A.

[32] P. Mathias, The Brewing Industry in England, 1700–1830, Cambridge, 1959, pp. 454–6; McGrath, thesis, passim; R. B. Westerfield, Middlemen in English Business, Particularly between 1660 and 1760, New Haven, 1915, repr. Newton Abbot, 1968; T. F. Reddaway, The Rebuilding of London after the Great Fire, London, 1951; J. P. Cooper, 'Social and Economic Policies under the Commonwealth', in G. E. Aylmer, ed., The Interregnum: The Quest for Settlement, London, 1972, p. 137; McGrath, thesis, p. 23.

of all the money they can get, bring it to London and spend it there." So wrote one angry commentator in 1673. The agricultural improver William Ellis, in a moralizing mood, expressed his resentment of the way in which the allurements of the capital diverted the gentry's attention and resources away from their estates. Arthur Young, writing later, at the turn of the century, roundly denounced London as "the great foe to experiment".[33] In the sense that agriculture in the Home Counties was highly commercialized and provided exactly what the capital wanted, then Young up to a point was right; assured profits in catering for a known need were always likely to count for more with practising farmers than risky investment in agricultural experiments. Young, however, was a prejudiced observer, and although for agriculture in other parts of the country London's direct importance can no doubt be easily exaggerated there is no need to minimize it so far as these three metropolitan counties are concerned. The agricultural organization of Bedfordshire, Hertfordshire, and Middlesex clearly under-went changes in the seventeenth and eighteenth centuries for which London was to a large extent responsible.[34] The development of market gardening is one obvious example.

Market gardeners were well established in the immediate vicinity of London and Westminster by the middle of the seventeenth century and provided the capital with an impressively large range of fruit and vegetables. Although this branch of husbandry was not restricted to the north side of the river, in Middlesex the market-gardening regions consisted of two blocks immediately adjacent to the built-up area of the city. The first lay to the north-east and east, embracing villages like Islington, Harton, Bethnal Green, Mile End, and Stepney. But the main concentration of market gardening activity was to the west, moving out from the parishes of St Martin-in-the-Fields and St Clement Dane's through parts of Westminster (Neat Fields), Kensington, Brompton, Chelsea, and Chiswick, and thinning towards Hampton, Twickenham, Isleworth, and Sunbury. To travellers the area seemed like a continuous garden. Such at any rate was the impression of the Swedish observer Peter Kalm in 1748: "At all places between Fulham and Chelsea (2 miles) and round about Chelsea we saw little else than mere gardens." Glass frames, bell glasses, and endless rows of cauliflowers, asparagus, and radishes with banks of earth dividing them were to be seen on every side.[35]

Market gardening, as practised in the highly commercialized areas close to London and Westminster, could be a profitable undertaking. Since rents were high – possibly as much as £9 per acre even in the mid seventeenth

[33] T & C, p. 383; Ellis, *Modern Husbandman, I*, p. 117; Young, *Agriculture of Hertfordshire*, p. 233.

[34] J. G. Gazley, *The Life of Arthur Young, 1741–1820*, Philadelphia, 1973.

[35] Kalm, *op. cit.*, pp. 35, 8–9, 27.

century – holdings tended to be small and compact, but well manured with refuse from the city, and intensively cultivated. "Near great towns", John Middleton was to write at the beginning of the nineteenth century, "small farms of good land are so much better suited to the purposes of a gardener than a husbandman..." Edward Brooker, gardener, of Isleworth, for example, who died in 1681, apparently had only two acres copyhold of enclosed nursery ground near the highway to Twickenham. Yet despite high rents and high labour costs, wrote Samuel Hartlib in 1651, "I know divers which by as little as two or three acres of land maintaine themselves and family and imploy others about their ground." Richard Baxter was another who pointed to the profitability of market gardening in the London area. "Above all", he wrote, "London is a market which will take up all they bring, so that nothing vendible need to stick on their hands; and, by garden stuffs and by peas and beans and turnips, they can make more gain of their grounds than poor country tenants can do of ten times the same quantity."[36]

The London gardeners had first become incorporated in 1605, and their earliest charter referred to "the trade, craft or mystery of gardening, planting, grafting, setting, sowing, cutting, arboring, rocking, mounting, covering, fencing, and removing of plants, herbs, seeds, fruits, trees, stocks, sets, and of contriving the conveyances to the same belonging". There was considerable specialization among them, some gardeners being in effect seedsmen. A separate Fruiterers' Company was founded in 1606. By 1622, nonetheless, the Gardeners' Company itself had five hundred members who defended themselves, whenever their privileges were threatened or flouted, by reminding the authorities of the essential service they performed and of the fact that directly or indirectly they gave employment to thousands of poor people, in weeding, collecting refuse, gathering stones, and selling produce. On more than one occasion the company was forced to seek confirmation of its charter so as to prevent the intrusion of unqualified gardeners and unapprenticed labour. On the distribution as opposed to the production side of market gardening a specialized market – Woolchurch market – for the sale of fruit and vegetables was set up after 1666.[37]

A few contemporary lists survive of members of the Gardeners' Company with details of where they lived and worked, but the great majority of the company's records were lost in the Great Fire of London; to reconstruct the scale and variety of its members' enterprise, other sources, particularly

[36] Middleton, *Agriculture of Middlesex*, p. 53; Greater London RO, (M) DRO.AM/P1/1681/72; S. Hartlib, *His Legacie of Husbandrie*, London, 1651, p. 11. Hartlib was mistaken in his belief that market gardening was entirely a seventeenth-century creation – T & C, p. 184.

[37] W. T. Crossweller, *The Gardeners' Company, 1605–1907*, London, 1908, p. 9. See also C. Welch, *History of the Worshipful Company of Gardeners*, 2nd edn, London, 1900; C. S. Snow, *The London Market Gardens*, London, 1879; and R. Webber, *The Early Horticulturalists*, Newton Abbot, 1968. Kalm, *op. cit.*, pp. 24–5; Crossweller, *op. cit.*, pp. 11–12; T & C, pp. 266–7; McGrath, thesis, p. 203.

probate inventories, have to be used. Take, for example, Curtis Akers, whose market garden in Chelsea was probably typical of the smallest undertakings. When he died in 1686 he was worth only £31 3s. 8d. and had 7 acres of ground. Of these, 1½ acres were given over to herbs and asparagus, 1 acre to carrots and parsnips, and another acre to peas. In addition he had 2 acres of beans and 1½ acres under grass. The inventory refers to his 2 horses, an old harness, an old cart, and – surprisingly for such a small garden – a plough.[38] James Attwood, gardener, of Kensington, on the other hand, who died in 1729, cultivated a much larger area and was far more prosperous. Turnips were his main crop and he had 7 acres of them, worth £14, at the time of his death. On a smaller scale, he grew onions, cabbages, potatoes, peas, and beans, and had an acre of barley. John Thorne, gardener, of St Martin-in-the-Fields (d. 1670) also grew onions and cabbages, but his inventory also lists asparagus, spinach, leeks, parsnips, artichokes, and radishes. Thorne's business was evidently a modestly successful one – he died worth £98 4s. 7d. – and he grew fruit as well as vegetables. The inventory lists 5 great pear trees, 4 great apple trees, and 1 walnut tree, 50 young pear trees, 314 cherry, plum, and apple trees as well as 1,000 pears and apples ready for sale.[39]

St Martin-in-the-Fields was an important market-gardening area in London and other surviving inventories bear witness to the activity of the gardeners of this district. That of Robert Gascoine, who died in 1718, is extraordinarily full and detailed. Gascoine's personal effects and his stock (mainly the latter) were valued at £198 8s. 10d., and the inventory sets out in meticulous detail the range, quantity, and location of the different crops he grew. Vast numbers of cauliflowers were growing under glass, and in addition there were cabbages, radishes, coleworts, asparagus, lettuce, and spinach. His gardening equipment comprised hoes, dibbers, dung forks, pickaxes, watering pots, spades, rakes, garden reels with lines, dung barrows, water barrows, hatchets, hooks, shovels, water tubs, mats, and glass. Less detailed but still interesting is the inventory of another gardener from St Martin-in-the-Fields, one Richard Jupp, who died in 1694. His inventory listed effects to the value of £71 1s., of which more than two-thirds was in gardening stock and equipment. Listed were 966 "bell glasses and square ones" (worth £16 10s.) and £3 worth of radish and lettuce seed. Artichokes, carrots, savoys, parsnips, leeks, and onions were his other crops.[40]

Although the demands of the London market for fruit and vegetables were understandably felt most intensely in the Middlesex hinterland of the capital,

[38] Greater London RO, Middlesex Records M1/1686/36. The title "farming gardener" was given to those who ploughed rather than dug their ground – Bull, thesis, p. 203.

[39] Greater London RO, (M) DRO.AM/P1/1729/7 and P1/1670/1. The inventory, with great precision, lists 650 cabbage tops and 1,378 cabbages.

[40] Greater London RO, Middlesex Records, M1/1718/10; M1/1694/21.

its tentacles stretched out increasingly as the period wore on. It would be oversimplifying, of course, to see the development of market gardening in Hertfordshire and Bedfordshire as no more than a direct response to the needs of London alone; the local requirements of a growing population in the two counties themselves had also to be met. London's demands, however, were the principal factor in the extension and increasing commercialization of market gardening in the Home Counties in the seventeenth and eighteenth centuries, and with the Great North Road running through both counties and with turnpikes making an early impact access to London was easy.

The benefit of these turnpikes [wrote Defoe] appears now to be so great and the people in all places begin to be so sensible of it, that it is incredible what effect it has already had upon trade in the countries where it is more compleatly finish'd; even the carriage of goods is abated in some places, 6d. per hundred weight, in some places 12d. per hundred, which is abundantly more advantage to commerce.[41]

In Hertfordshire the area around the county town itself included market gardening among its farming specialities. The will of John Johnson, gardener, of St Andrew's parish in Hertford, was proved in 1641. Thomas Jones, gardener, died at Harpenden in 1692. John House of Berkhamsted was a small-scale gardener who died in 1714 worth only £14 18s. The brief inventory of possessions lists two bushels of turnip seed and "old glasses for cucumbers" as well as an old cow, a horse, and 2 pigs. He made known in his will that he intended his wife Sarah to enjoy his "nursery of wall fruits, trees and all other trees and stock on the ground and garden".[42]

In Bedfordshire market gardening developed in the seventeenth century in the ideal conditions of the central greensand ridge running east to west from Potton to Woburn. There are few occupational references to gardeners in the records before the 1640s, but from that date onwards they occur regularly. Sandy and Biggleswade on the eastern side of the county were the principal market-gardening parishes.

Passing through this neighbourhood [wrote John Byng somewhat later, in 1794] any observer would be astonish'd at the culture and gardening of the fields, surpassing everything I ever saw but just about London. For every field is cropp'd by peas, carrots, parsnips, French beans, cucumbers, etc. even the very open fields, and you cannot prevent your horse from smashing the cucumbers. (I once told this to a friend of mine who smiled contradiction till I led him into this garden of a country, and then he owned his surprise and conviction.)

The details of tithes listed in the glebe terrier for Sandy drawn up about 1708 include a note that "turnips, carrots, garden peas, beans, onions, parsnips etc.

[41] N. L .Tranter, 'Demographic Change in Bedfordshire from 1670 to 1800', unpub. Univ. of Nottm Ph.D. thesis, 1966, p. 15; W. A. Albert, *The Turnpike Road System in England and Wales, 1663–1840*, Cambridge, 1972, pp. 14, 33; Defoe, *op. cit.*, II, pp. 128–9.
[42] Herts. RO, 70 HW 46, 71 HW 4, 60 HW 34.

are paid for by the acre, more or less according to the several places in which they grow".

Market gardening was also carried on at Sutton, Southill, Old Warden, Steppingley, Clophill, Flitton, Silsoe, Maulden, and Woburn – all places lying in the central sandy belt of the county. At Old Warden when Walter Kating senior died in 1673 he made known that to his son "Walter I doe give a pound of carrot seed and 200 cabidge plants and a peck of good pease". The early-eighteenth-century glebe terrier for Sutton includes the information that "turnips have not been known in the field till of late years a great part of our sand land has been sown with them; the parishioners will not pay tithe for them". At Steppingley in 1683 was reported the case of a gardener digging between the asparagus beds finding the body of a dead infant. Besides the produce of the professional gardeners, however, a wide variety of vegetables and fruit was grown by the Bedfordshire gentry on their estates. Artichokes, asparagus, beans, carrots, cucumbers, cauliflowers, cabbage, mushrooms, onions, parsley, spinach, sprouts, turnips, and apples, damsons, apricots, and pears are all mentioned in the surviving records. In 1693 the earl of Kent bought over fifty varieties of pear, nectarine, plum, and cherry trees from London nurserymen at Twickenham and Knightsbridge.[43]

The development of market gardening was one of the most noticeable ways in which the agricultural organization of the metropolitan counties was changing in the seventeenth and eighteenth centuries. Another was the adoption of new crops such as clover, sainfoin, trefoil, turnips, and hemp, with associated new rotations and methods of cultivation.[44]

Writing of clover in the *General View of the Agriculture of Hertfordshire*, Arthur Young wrote that "this noble plant" had been cultivated in that county probably longer than anywhere else in England, "and it yields from its vicinity to the capital a greater profit here than is commonly experienced elsewhere". William Ellis's *Hertfordshire Husbandman* had earlier made much the same point, but Ellis had reminded his readers that there were disadvantages as well as benefits attached to the growing of this crop, that it was self-defeating to sow clover too often in the same ground, and that its introduction in some parts of the county had not gone unopposed. He recalled how in the 1690s an attempt had been made by the Aylesbury Vale men to prevent the rival growing of clover in the Chiltern or hilly parts of Hertfordshire. Ellis's book had also commented enthusiastically about the growing of sainfoin, trefoil, and lucerne – a crop which could often be mown three times in the course of a summer – and fragmentary evidence culled

[43] *Torrington Diaries*, p. 483; Beds. RO, ABE 2 and ABP/W 1673/89; Godber, *Bedfordshire*, p. 275; Beds. RO, HSA 1683 S 31; Godber, *op. cit.*, p. 287.

[44] Joan Thirsk, 'Seventeenth-Century Agriculture and Social Change', in Thirsk, ed., *Land, Church, and People: Essays Presented to Professor H. P. R. Finberg*, AHR, XVIII, 1970, suppl.).

from Hertfordshire probate and other records indicates that practising agriculturalists shared his view.[45]

Mordecai Halsey, for example, a prosperous yeoman of Great Gaddesden, had hay and clover in the barn of his house on Berkhamsted Heath worth £1 10s. when he died in 1647. John Monk of Westhide, Rickmansworth, on the other hand, was a poor man worth only £22 at his death in 1706, yet he had 2 acres of clover and grass. The inventory of Thomas Birdsey of Flamstead (dated 17 March 1732) valued the clover seed which he had sown at 15s. However, clover was evidently cultivated on a much larger scale on a farm at Harrow, Middlesex, in 1733, since the early crop of twenty loads was considered to be only an indifferent yield. The account book of Sir Thomas Rolt of Sacombe Park records that in July 1700 he disbursed £4 5s. for the mowing of his hay and sainfoin. Five acres of sainfoin – out of a total cultivated area of 156 acres – were growing on a farm at Pirton, Hertfordshire, when an inventory was compiled in 1750.[46] By the early eighteenth century Hertfordshire had acquired a reputation for its clover and trefoil seed, and a seedsman at Ware was supplying customers in Lincolnshire. In April 1748 £1 4s. was paid for 96 lb of clover seed for sowing at Beechwood Farm, Flamstead, and five years later Thomas Cox of Stanborough, Hatfield, bought 4½ cwt of clover seed for £7 7s. Clover was sold for £6 13s. at Wymondley near Hitchin in March 1746.[47]

Ellis's enthusiasm for trefoil, sainfoin, and lucerne was matched by what he had to say about turnip husbandry. "In Hertfordshire for about forty or fifty years past", he wrote in 1736, "turnips have been sown in common fields." Ellis noted, however, that turnip growing was unusual in the southern parts of the county because of the unsuitability of the soils. Some farmers, too, noticed that turnips would sometimes extract too much moisture from the soil. For example, at Hitchin in 1734 Ralph Radcliffe, a member of a prominent Hertfordshire landowning family, wrote to his elder brother in London that the barley would fall short for want of rain "especially in the land where turnips grew".[48]

The fascinating farming diary of Sir John Wittewronge (1618–93) of Rothhamsted contains several references to turnip growing. On 13 August 1687 he "sowed the ground by the hop ground with turnip seed" and the

---

[45] Young, *Agriculture of Hertfordshire*, pp. 115–18; Ellis, *Hertfordshire Husbandman*, 2nd edn, London, 1732, pp. 60–1, 65–75.

[46] Herts. RO, 56 HW 24 and 143 AW 21; Greater London RO, Middlesex Records, Acc 76/1684; Herts. RO, P/LAS 2,171C and DE 564 B.

[47] LAO, MM 4/1/8 and 4/1/14, letters dated 16 Dec. 1706 and 16 Nov. 1714; Herts. RO, 18,104, 28,972, and 61,590.

[48] Ellis, *Modern Husbandman*, II, pt 3, pp. 22–43; Ellis, *New Experiments in Husbandry*, London, 1736, pp. 12, 13; Herts. RO, DE 4,207, letter dated 12 May 1734.

following year (6 July 1688) he sowed Sheepcot field with turnip seed. The day book of an early-eighteenth-century bailiff for Westbrook Hay, Bovingdon, and Bourne End records the receipt of £2 5s 6d. for 3 bushels and 1 peck of turnip seed sold at Hemel Hempstead. The surviving accounts of Beechwood farm in Flamstead parish for the 1740s again include references to the buying and selling of turnips. In December 1747 1½ bushels of turnips were sold for 1s 6d., while in May 1748 7s. was paid for 21 lb of turnip seed. This same farmer – so another entry for July 1747 in the accounts shows – charged 3d. per week for each sheep fed with turnips. Turnips were obviously grown on a large scale on the farm of Thomas Cox of Stanborough in Hatfield, since at the end of August 1751 he paid his turnip hoers £16 10s. 6d. Glebe terriers are another source which throw light on turnip husbandry, as at Henlow in Bedfordshire in 1708 when two rates of tithe for turnips were laid down: "if sould out of the parish the tenth penny, if eat by sheep four pence by the month for every score of sheep feeding on them".[49]

Turnip cultivation was also well known in Middlesex in the seventeenth century. A Chelsea husbandman, Richard Samm, had 6 acres of turnips – his main crop apparently – worth £5 in 1673. William Smith of Kensington had ½ acre of tares and turnips in his 10-acre field in 1676. Again at Kensington, Edward Sell, husbandman, had 1½ acres of turnips two years later. John Stone of Shepperton had 14 acres of turnips valued at £10 in 1711.[50]

References to the growing of hemp and flax in the Home Counties are very infrequent, but there are indications that both crops took hold in the vicinity of Bedford. In 1648, for instance – three years before Walter Blith championed it in *The English Improver Improved* – a farmer at Biddenham near Bedford had started to cultivate hemp on a small scale, his account book specifying that he bought one bushel of seed for 3s. 4d. At Henlow the growing of hemp and flax had become sufficiently general by 1708 to necessitate the inclusion of tithing arrangements for these crops in the glebe terrier drawn up in that year. William Ellis in an eloquently mercantilist passage in his *Modern Husbandman* urged the cultivation of hemp and flax to reduce the need for imports. Growing these two crops, he argued, would

give employment to many thousands of parish poor, and lessen their tax, prevent the importation of foreign sail cloth, and enable us to supply our shipping at home and abroad with this necessary manufacture...but also by its useful oil and cakes that may be made of it for fatting of beasts...surely it ought to be attempted with all speed by every one that is a lover of his own and the nation's interest.[51]

[49] Herts. RO, D/ELW F 19, D/EB 1,622.E4 (covers 1712/14), 18,104, 28,972; Beds. RO, ABE 2 f. 109.

[50] Greater London RO, (M)/DRO.AM/P1/1673/72, DRO.AM/P1/1676/30, DRO.AM/P1/1678/81, DRO.AM/P1/1711/3.

[51] Beds. RO, TW 802/16 (account dated 12 Dec. 1648) and ABE 2 f. 109; Ellis, *Modern Husbandman*, III, pt 3, pp. 93–4.

Surviving eighteenth-century correspondence from farmers in the metropolitan counties gives glimpses of the interest they showed in agricultural experimentation taking place in other parts of England and also in foreign countries. William Lee, for example, of Totteridge Park, Hertfordshire, received a package in November 1749 from a French correspondent in The Hague who enclosed melon seeds and cantaloupes. The latter needed special attention, and Lee's foreign adviser made a number of practical suggestions. "The best method with the cantaloupes", he concluded, "is to get the seeds from Spain every year because using those that grow in a colder climate takes a great deal of the goodness out of the fruit." Another letter in 1762 from Thomas Harris in Totteridge contained an account of a phenomenally large asparagus plant which had been observed somewhere in Worcestershire, as well as a number of useful hints about the cultivation of this vegetable.[52]

Who were these agricultural innovators experimenting with new crops in the seventeenth and eighteenth centuries? How representative were they of rural society as a whole? Despite some strong economic incentives in these counties, the evidence suggests that the cost of investment necessary for most agricultural improvement, apart from gardening, was still too high for small farmers.[53] The tithe account for Watford parish in the years 1668–74, for example, refers to the growing of sainfoin by twenty-one farmers and of clover by three, and in almost every case these experimenting farmers belonged to the middling or well-to-do ranks of rural society. (Thomas Batchelor later pointed out that in Bedfordshire, similarly, the north of the county – an area of small farmers – was the most backward agriculturally.) John Alden of Watford, who grew clover and whose holding was worth only £59 in 1687, was the exception rather than the rule. The widow Elizabeth Child of Watford, who had 7 acres of turnips in 1704 and a holding worth £324, and John Gibb of Rickmansworth, who was growing sainfoin in 1689 and was worth £275, were more typical.[54] At the upper end of the range of wealth were people like Dame Sarah Bucknall of Watford, who grew sainfoin and whose estate was worth over £1,000 in 1691, and one Saunders of Abbot's Langley, a turnip grower worth £1,296 in 1707.

Agricultural improvement, however, involved new methods as well as new crops, and both writers and farmers gave much attention to this subject. Walter Blith in the dedication to *The English Improver* (1649) argued that agricultural improvement "is neither father or mother unto plenty but I may say it is the midwife that facilitates the birth"; and of the various

---

[52] Herts. RO, 68,819 (letter from A. de Rambouillet dated 7 Nov. 1749) and 68,828 (letter dated 8 Mar. 1762).

[53] See also pt II below, ch. 19, p. 542.

[54] Longman, thesis, pp. 99 table 48, 100 table 49. Widow Child was apparently an innovator in her own right, since her husband's inventory (drawn up at his death in 1685) made no reference to turnips.

improvements which he recommended and outlined most were put into practice by agriculturalists in the Home Counties. Manuring is an obvious example.

Strategically placed to receive all kinds of human and animal waste, soot, ashes, and so on from London, farmers in these counties manured their lands richly and variously. Arthur Young was to say of Hertfordshire that "there is no part of the kingdom in which this branch of husbandry, everywhere so important, is more generally attended to, or where exertions in it are more spirited". Peter Kalm, the Swedish traveller, commented on the range of manures in use. But this situation in the eighteenth century was not a recent development, as George Atwell, for instance, made clear in his *Faithfull Surveyor*. He instanced the case of Hitchin, Hertfordshire, where a spectacular improvement in the yield of the barley crop had come about in the previous fifty years

and all by buying rags and horn shavings at London, carrying up malt and bringing them down all the year long... Whereas about fifty years ago, an acre of their barley was not above £3 10s. or £4 the best, now about twenty years ago I was requested to measure two acres of barley in a field called Kings Field in Hitchin parish that the very crop of them was sold for £9 an acre by the statute pole.

Nathanael Salmon made exactly the same observations in his *History of Hertfordshire* (1728).[55]

Other methods of manuring, however, were used where appropriate. Marling was practised, lime was used, and according to one eighteenth-century writer "the way of manuring mossy ground in Hertfordshire is to burn and then plow them. They yield one or two good crops of rye and afterwards make excellent pasture lands."[56] But in many parts of Hertfordshire, even in the south of the county with easiest access to London, sheep were vitally important on account of their dung. The fact is emphasized in a mid-eighteenth-century complaint from small farmers at Totteridge near Barnet about recent encroachments which had taken place. They complained that Sir Robert Willmott's tenants had ploughed up and sown grain in part of a fallow field used for grazing sheep and driven the animals elsewhere, "where they are sure to be either famished or rotten or both... We cannot manure our land without sheep... Dung is not to be bought about us", they went on, "nor so much lime as we could dispense with. Without sheep we cannot pay our way."[57]

[55] Young, *Agriculture of Hertfordshire*, p. 157; Kalm, *op. cit.*, pp. 248, 250, 251, 265, 310; Atwell, *op. cit.*, pp. 106–7.
[56] Ellis, *Hertfordshire Husbandman*, pp. 94–5; M. Postlethwayt, *Britain's Commercial Interest Explained and Improved...*, I, London, 1757, p. 81. Cf. M. Havinden, 'Lime as a Means of Agricultural Improvement: The Devon Example', in C. W. Chalklin and M. A. Havinden, eds., *Rural Change and Urban Growth, 1500–1800*, London, 1974, pp. 104–34.
[57] Herts. RO, 68,434 (letter n.d. addressed to William Lee, Esq.).

Drainage was another improvement which had a special relevance in a county of poor soils like Hertfordshire, and Salmon was but one writer, again in 1728, who drew attention to farmers' efforts in this direction.

The cold and wet lands have been within twenty years greatly improved by draining off the rainwater which stagnated in the clay surface as in a cup and chilled the roots of the corn. This is done by an invention that first appeared upon the borders of Essex which they call dry ditching. Drains of about thirty inches deep are carried across and athwart which have communication, and carry off the water where there is a declivity. These are narrower at bottom into which were formerly thrown stones or bushes with straw scattered over them, then they are filled up again with the same earth and ploughed over, so that none of the surface of the field is lost as must be where the ditches are open. They since have contented themselves with stubble at the bottom to save stones and bushes and find their work durable enough. And some only draw a long piece of wood through the drain as they fill it up which preserves the hollowness they aim at.[58]

Improved systems of crop rotation similarly came increasingly into use in the eighteenth century; a few examples must suffice to indicate the extent and variety of the experimentation which was taking place in the metropolitan counties. The estate records of the Antonie family contain a note of one such rotation at Colworth Manor, Sharnbrook, Bedfordshire. Starting with barley, the rotation followed with wheat, oats, and clover. The clover was then ploughed in, wheat was then sown again, followed by barley, clover, or turnips. The estate papers of the Orlebar family, who held the manors of Podington and Hinwick in the clay-soil north-west corner of Bedfordshire, contain more elaborate prescriptions for crop rotations. For four-, five-, and six-field systems the rotation over a five-year period was pulses, then fallow, barley and grass, grass, and finally wheat.[59] The leases made by this and other families in the Home Counties also made stipulations about rotation and land use.

Both Arthur Young and John Middleton in their respective Board of Agriculture volumes on Hertfordshire and Middlesex were later to complain about the practice of granting short leases – even annual tenancies – which, they argued, could only lead to insecurity and thus militate against improvement. Three eighteenth-century leases in the Lyall collection at the Bedfordshire Record Office are for three, seven, and nine years respectively. Russell leases, on the other hand, varied from nine to twenty-one years, with longer ones more common. But although tenants of the duke of Bedford may not have been particularly insecure, some of them at least suffered inconveniences. In 1697, for example, John Porett of Apsley Guise was granted a twenty-one-year lease of about seventy-four acres of land in

[58] Salmon, *History of Hertfordshire*, p. 1.
[59] Beds. RO, BS 2,143/2, UN 47 (lease dated 10 Sept. 1720) and UN 48 (lease dated 22 Mar. 1730). Both leases were for three years only.

Woburn for £44 a year. So far so good, but the drawback must have been that the tenant was not allowed to kill any rabbits straying onto his land. A later lease of a farm in Maulden to Thomas Crouch gave the landlord rights of ingress, hunting, and fishing on the land.[60]

Leases offered landlords the opportunity – if they chose to take it – of implementing agricultural improvements. Manuring of land, for example, was commonly made a condition of tenure, landlords insisting that dung produced on their farms should not be sold but be used to keep the land in good heart.[61] The leases granted by Sir Harbottle Grimston of Gorhambury, at least, made a deliberate attempt to uphold soil fertility: for instance, in successive leases of Westwick Farm he laid down that tenants should sow barley only on tilth and that in the course of the last three years of the term of a lease a Lent crop of no more than twelve acres of oats should be sown and the rest be given over to peas and vetches. On the whole, however, the leasing policy of the Grimstons was negative, protective, and restrictive rather than positively directed towards agricultural improvement. Leases upheld the old three-course rotation of winter corn, spring corn, and fallow until well into the second half of the eighteenth century; virtually no mention was made of artificial grasses and turnip husbandry. And Lord Chancellor Cowper of Hertingfordbury frankly exhibited a basic lack of interest in agriculture, and ran his estate very unprogressively.[62]

So far as enclosures are concerned, the considerable unevenness both of their extent and chronology suggests that open-field farming and the commercialization of agriculture in the Home Counties were by no means incompatible. Even market gardening in Middlesex – one of the most market-oriented of all forms of agriculture – took place partly without the assistance of enclosure. The husbandmen of Chelsea, Fulham, and Kensington, so it was claimed in a report of 1635, "sowe seedes for parsnipps, turnopps, carriotts and the like *in their common feildes* whereof most of them they plough upp and others they digge up with the spade according to the nature and ritchness of their grounds...Some of them have belonging to their houses one two or three acres of ground in orchards and gardens."[63] But it was the enclosed market gardens which attracted notice, and it was the enclosed meadows and pastures around London, with their luxuriant growth of grass, which caught Peter Kalm's attention in 1748. It was in these kinds of farming

[60] Young, *Agriculture of Hertfordshire*, p. 34; Middleton, *Agriculture of Middlesex*, pp. 79, 83; Beds. RO, LL 17/3 (dated 9 May 1710), LL 1/132 (dated 10 Feb. 1714), and LL 1/133 (dated 1 Mar. 1737); Russell MSS, boxes 249–54; R box 254 (lease dated 30 Mar. 1697), R box 251 (lease dated 8 Mar. 1736).

[61] Beds. RO, RO 1/125 (lease dated 15 Dec. 1729), R box 250 (leases dated 10 Apr. 1717, 15 Mar. 1748, 8 Mar. 1736), LL 1/132 (lease dated 10 Feb. 1714), LL 1/133 (lease dated 1 Mar. 1737), UN 47 (lease dated 10 Sept. 1720), UN 48 (lease dated 22 Mar. 1730).

[62] Clay, thesis, pp. 54–5, 147, 336–40.

[63] Quoted in Fisher, 'The Development of the London Food Market', pp. 142–3 (my italics).

areas, rather than in the arable districts, that enclosures were to be found, and this was still true at the beginning of the nineteenth century when John Middleton was writing his report on Middlesex for the Board of Agriculture. "In the arable part of the county", he wrote, "where the farms are in common fields, many of them are at a very inconvenient distance from the land. But this is the necessary consequence of the land being in common and is one among many more reasons why it should be enclosed."[64]

In contrast, Hertfordshire had been largely enclosed by the sixteenth century, and in 1804 Arthur Young could note that in this "merely arable county" the difference in rent between the open and enclosed fields was as much as 5s. per acre. In places like Cheshunt in the loamy south-east area of the county enclosure was a long-established fact, and a manorial survey in 1696 showed that there was considerably more enclosed land than common arable or pastures.[65] In such districts enclosure was an accepted feature of rural organization; it was only where enclosure was new and carried through without agreement that opposition was aroused. One such case occurred at Pirton in the northern chalkland of Hertfordshire in 1692, when one Thomas Docwra of Patterbridge enclosed and reserved for his own use part of the open fields. The inhabitants of Pirton – few of whom can have been very prosperous – refused to recognize the new arrangement and made a pact among themselves to challenge Docwra's title to the enclosed land. "We and every one of us", they declared, "shall by our joint costs and charges defend any suite and do any lawful act or thing for the hindering and opposing the said Thomas Docwra from the enclosing and taking in of the same grounds."[66] No such problems, however, were experienced at Cheshunt in 1720, where it was "ordered and agreed that any person or persons who have or hold any lands within the common fields not being lammas grounds may have liberty to enclose the same paying for every acre so enclosed 5s. to the overseers of the poor as long as the lands shall remain enclosed". Nor, twenty-eight years later, was any commotion caused by Lord Morzon's enclosure of part of the common at Broxbourne. There it was agreed "that the Lord Morzon may take in a parcel of the common called Basehills containing seven acres in Broxbourne and lay it to his park". In return Morzon was to give the commoners seven acres of his own enclosed land.[67]

It was not enclosure itself which automatically produced conflict, but enclosure without the prior agreement of those whose interests were affected. "Consider in this case", wrote Leonard Meager in a pro-enclosure tract in

[64] Kalm, *op. cit.*, pp. 28–9; Middleton, *Agriculture of Middlesex*, p. 45.

[65] AHEW, *IV*, pp. 50, 52, 203; Young, *Agriculture of Hertfordshire*, pp. 44, 133–42, 182–216; Herts. RO, D/ELA M15.

[66] Herts. RO., 72,036. In 1699 there were apparently only 10 copyholders and freeholders in Pirton worth £10 or more – Hardy, *Hertford County Records*, *II*, p. 18.

[67] Herts. RO, D/E Cr 1/6, vestry order dated 5 Sept. 1720.

1697, "where the grounds are enclosed how happily people live, as in Hertfordshire." Properly arranged and carried out, argued William Ellis in the following century, enclosure could be a real benefit to all concerned so that "both the commoner and the lord of the manor, the rich and the poor man, rejoiced in the alteration." Nor was it only the dominant gentry in a given area who were the enclosers. In 1681, for example, a Hertfordshire labourer, Robert Nash of Bennington, was indicted for enclosing a piece of land in the common field.[68]

In Bedfordshire again there is evidence of enclosure by agreement in the seventeenth and early eighteenth centuries, but in this county – in direct contrast to Hertfordshire – enclosure had made relatively little headway, especially in the northern parts, even by 1780. At that date perhaps as much as three-quarters of the county remained unenclosed. The extensive enclosure of 900 acres at Melchbourne in 1679 by Lord Bolingbroke was highly unusual. The great acceleration in parliamentary enclosures came between 1780 and 1810, and prior to this enclosure, such as occurred at Hockliffe, Aspley, Chalgrave, Sutton, and Pulloxhill, was almost invariably small scale, and piecemeal. Often – as at Elstow – it was the last step in the process of agrarian reorganization, having been preceded by a concentration in the ownership of land.[69]

Interesting details survive of an enclosure agreement between the lord of the manor and some of the inhabitants of Clapham, Bedfordshire, in 1677. It was agreed that the lord could enclose Ley Field but that for the loss of their common rights the inhabitants would be compensated with new land lying on the south side of Hall Wood. Moreover, it was agreed that for the first time the lord of the manor's own common rights should be stinted in the proportion of three beasts for every twenty acres of his land. These and other details in the document suggest that the inhabitants had exacted hard terms, and a Chancery decree had to be sought – and was obtained – when it was discovered that Richard Taylor, the lord of the manor, "seemeth to decline the performance of the agreement". Similar examples of non-parliamentary enclosure can be seen in the estate-building activities of Henry Grey (1671–1740), duke of Kent, in the vicinity of Wrest Park, his family seat.[70]

This nobleman took a keen interest in agricultural improvement, and we are fortunate in having a detailed inventory of his library drawn up after his death.[71] The survival of such lists is quite exceptional, however, and one

[68] Meager, The Mystery of Husbandry: or Arable, Pasture and Woodland Improved, quoted in T & C, p. 187; Ellis, Modern Husbandman, III, pt 3, pp. 150–1; Hardy, op. cit., I, p. 311.

[69] Tranter, thesis, p. 20; Godber, op. cit., pp. 310, 244–5, 255. Cf. J. D. Chambers, Population, Economy and Society in Pre-Industrial England, Oxford, 1972, p. 124.

[70] Beds. RO, S/AM 74; L 25/10, L 25/19, L 25/1, L 25/2, L 25/6.

[71] Beds. RO, L 31/184/2 (dated Oct. 1740).

of the problems always with books on agriculture is the lack of conclusive evidence about who actually bought and read them. But the duke's library was impressively large and varied and included a considerable collection on husbandry and gardening. Besides such older works as Tusser and Markham, he had Tull's *Husbandry* (1733) and Mortimer's *Art of Husbandry* (1712). He had tracts as well, such as the undated *Proposalls for Improving Comon and Waste Lands for Securing a Supply of Wood and for Maintaining the Poor*. On gardening the duke's library was even better stocked. He had, for example, James's *Theory of Gardening* (1712), Langley's *Gardening* (1728), Meager's *English Gardener* (1688), Miller's *Gardeners' Dictionary* (1735), and many more. His library also contained works by William Ellis of Little Gaddesden in Hertfordshire.

Formerly connected with the London brewing industry, Ellis settled and remained in Hertfordshire until his death in 1758. His efforts were enthusiastically recalled by Arthur Young at the beginning of the nineteenth century, but on the whole his prolific output of books and pamphlets secured for him no more than a brief reputation as an agricultural improver which barely survived his own lifetime.[72]

The improvements which Ellis wrote about were partly, of course, his own which he had tested on his own "twenty four inclosed fields", and for publicity purposes his farm at Little Gaddesden was always open to inspection. "Any person that pleases shall be welcome to view my proceedings in farming after the several methods that are publish'd in my books." So Ellis wrote in his *Hertfordshire Husbandman*. But he was always eager to supplement his own experience with that of others. He acted not only as his own publicist, but as a clearing house through which improving farmers in all parts of the country could be put in touch and made aware of each other's experiments. Ellis's publications, however, almost invariably contained advertisements of some kind or other, not just for his books, but for farmers' supplies and equipment. In 1749, for instance, Ellis was offering for sale a variety of ploughs and other implements, rabbits, white fowls and pheasants, seeds, and cuttings. Singled out for special mention was "the excellent Lady-finger-grass seeds that produces a grass and hay, which feeds and fattens all sorts of cattle in the sweetest and quickest manner, and causes cows to give a thick, luscious milk, that makes a fine, delicate, sweet, yellow, palatable butter and cheese". Ellis also acted as a kind of agricultural labour exchange, supplying masters with servants and skilled workmen, "men that understand burning clay into ashes to great perfection, men that are masters

[72] Young, *Agriculture of Hertfordshire*, pp. xv, xvi, 55, 125. See also V. Bell, *To Meet Mr Ellis: Little Gaddesden in the Eighteenth Century*, London, 1956. Ellis's main publications were: *Chiltern and Vale Farming Explained...*, London, 1733, *The Practical Farmer, or the Hertfordshire Husbandman*, 2nd edn, 2 pts, 1732, *A Compleat System of Experienced Improvements*, London, 1749, and *The Modern Husbandman*, London, 1750.

of the art of cutting subterranean drains to carry off waters from ploughed or meadow grounds, an improvement of late much in practice, men that can burn peat into ashes for manuring of land".[73]

Ellis was a careful observer as well as an ardent publicist, and his writings abound in revealing information about the variety of agricultural practice in different parts of the country as well as on the contrasts between the different regions of a single county like Hertfordshire. But his writings are often disorganized, repetitive, and form a curious mixture of the scientific and the anecdotal, of detached observation and moralizing, and of sound judgment and sheer prejudice. He was as likely to launch into a hostile and superstitious account of gypsies as he was to take an overall view of agricultural progress and its place in the national economy. Certainly he wrote far too much; he was exploited by his publishers, and even before his death his reputation was in eclipse. To Peter Kalm, the Swedish traveller whose visit to the Hertfordshire improver ended in complete disappointment, Ellis was little more than a charlatan who conspicuously failed to practise most of what he had himself preached on agriculture. Such an opinion – and it is echoed in the *Dictionary of National Biography* – seems unduly severe, as the editor of *Ellis's Husbandry: Abridged and Methodized* (1772) tried to demonstrate: "Although his faults were very numerous, yet being a plain farmer, dependent only on his skill in common husbandry for many years, his practice could not fail of being extensive, and his observations numerous; so that all his works, as he borrowed nothing from others, were really original, and contained in numerous instances more genuine knowledge than far more shining performances abounded with." Behind all the sales talk which his books contained, all the padding made to satisfy the publisher's monthly demands for copy, there remained a store of unmistakable sound sense.[74]

Kalm's account of his visit to Ellis at Little Gaddesden in 1748, however, is as interesting for what it has to say about the village as about the famous agricultural publicist. "Around Little Gaddesden", he wrote, "and on all Chiltern land every farmer more or less had his own severalties which he afterwards divided into small inclosures by hedges. There was one inclosure sown with wheat, another with barley, turnips, pease, oats, sainfoin, clover, trifolium, tares, potatoes, or whatever he wished." Kalm was quick to point out the contrast – as he saw it – between the successful farming of Little Gaddesden, where in 1745 all but 120 acres of the parish were enclosed, and the backwardness and wretchedness of the neighbouring open-field parish

[73] Ellis, *Hertfordshire Husbandman*, pp. 43–4. Ellis's *The Complete Planter and Cyderist*, London, 1756, extended the same invitation. In the latter work Ellis acknowledged the help received from "several ingenious persons in different parts of England who have honoured me with their correspondence". Ellis, *A Compleat System of Experienced Improvements*, London, 1749, pp. 127–9.

[74] Kalm, *op. cit.*, pp. 186–93; *Ellis's Husbandry*, pp. iii–iv.

of Ivinghoe. Kalm also commented on the general practice in Little Gaddesden of relying on casual labour. "In this place it is the custom that a farmer does not keep many servants but always employs day labourers for which reason in every village there live a great many poor who hire themselves out to work for pence...I was assured that in all Little Gaddesden there were not twelve menservants who serve as such for annual wages."[75]

According to William Ellis, farmers in this and neighbouring villages had a well-established practice of raising horses. "Our farmers hereabouts", he wrote, "commonly go to Thame fair on Michaelmas day and buy the yearly colts for about two guineas apiece which they turn into their latter-math for that winter and give them some hay...and the next spring about the beginning of May put them into the vale about Aylesbury for a shilling or eighteenpence a week and so raise fine horses at a cheap rate."[76]

But discussion of agricultural improvements and improvers should not blind us to the fact that the rural economy of the Home Counties in the seventeenth and early eighteenth centuries was by no means wholly agricultural. Rural 'industrialization' is a subject too important to be overlooked. Industries were in fact an important prop to many households, except in those areas in the immediate vicinity of London where labour-intensive forms of husbandry like market gardening offered ample employment opportunities. The geography of rural industries has a complex background, and clearly no single factor will explain everything. The existence of local supplies of raw materials was important in some cases – in matmaking and basket making, for example – but not in others such as lacemaking. In all cases, however, the demands of the market (above all London) were important both initially and subsequently. Population pressure acting on a limited supply of land, as Thirsk has shown, could often be crucial. Where agriculture itself was profitable, freely expanding, and all-absorbing, then industrial development was unlikely to get very far. But where landholding had become fragmented, where the soil was too poor to yield an adequate living to those who worked it, where population was outrunning the available agricultural means of support, where poverty was on the increase – in areas like these industries had an obvious relevance and readily took root.[77]

In Middlesex, where the commercialization of agriculture had proceeded furthest, there are relatively few indications of industrial by-employments. Agriculture itself – above all market gardening and haymaking – was the

[75] Kalm, op.cit., pp. 281–2, 205–6.

[76] Ellis, Hertfordshire Husbandman, p. 115.

[77] Joan Thirsk, 'Industries in the Countryside', in F. J. Fisher, ed., Essays in the Economic and Social History of Tudor and Stuart England, Cambridge, 1961, and 'Roots of Industrial England', Geog. Mag., XLII, Aug. 1970, esp. p. 825. For comparative purposes, A. Klíma, 'The Role of Rural Domestic Industry in Bohemia in the Eighteenth Century', EcHR, 2nd ser., XXVII, 1974, esp. pp. 49–50, is extremely interesting.

predominant, and highly profitable, activity. Basket making and matmaking, however, were two rural industries known in Middlesex, and in Thames-side parishes like Sunbury and Hampton we encounter men like John Evans. Evans died at Sunbury in 1673, had a four-roomed cottage, and was worth £36 6s. 6d. He had 2 cows, a bullock, a weaning calf, and a hog, but the chief component of his modest wealth was his stock-in-trade of reeds valued at £10 10s.[78]

In Hertfordshire some clothmaking, flax spinning, and lacemaking were carried on, but above all it was straw plaiting which provided additional employment and income. In or near the wheat-growing area of the centre and west of the county, in places like Hitchin, Redbourn, Stevenage, St Albans, and Hatfield, straw plaiting was much practised, and provided vital income to the poor "having no other way to subsist". One such poor straw-hat maker was Mary Young, spinster, of Redbourn, who died in 1691. She lodged in a single room and her meagre possessions – bed, stools, and cooking utensils – were valued at only £6 12s. 4d. Within this total her stock of straw plait and thirteen straw hats came to 15s.[79]

Any threat to this important rural industry implied serious social consequences, so it is not surprising that when in the early eighteenth century imported plaited goods from Holland and Leghorn began to flood the English markets the native manufacture of such articles was vigorously defended. A 1719 petition on behalf of the poor straw-hat makers is a fascinating document with useful details about the scale and organization of the industry.[80] The petitioners pointed out that straw plaiting was a long-established local industry by means of which "many thousands have gained a comfortable subsistence and kept themselves and their families from being chargeable to the parishes". By contemporary standards the earnings gained from this part-time industrial employment could be quite considerable, and the capital expenditure was small.

The farmers' wives, children, and servants do at their spare hours earn some ten, some twenty, some thirty pounds per annum by manufacturing their own straw which is a good article towards paying their rent. That by six pennyworth of straw bought of the farmers the poor people can make by their industry and work eight, nine, and oftentimes ten shillings. That when so wrought up and manufactured they carry every week to market, for which they have ready money without any deduction, stoppage, or obligation to take part in goods, or even so much as to deal with those that buy their hatts.

[78] Greater London RO, (M)/DRO.AM/P1/1673/7.

[79] Matthew Hale, weaver, died at Little Gaddesden in 1646 (Herts. RO, 56 HW 21). The Herts. RO has the wills of three members of a clothworking family from Ickleford in the extreme north of the county (77 HW 1, dated 1708; 77 HW 34, dated 1725; and 77 HW 80, dated 1750). Herts. RO, 128 AW 19.

[80] *The Case of the Poor Straw Hat Makers in the Counties of Hertford, Bedford, Buckingham...*, London, 1719 – BL, SPR 357.b.3.(117).

At a later date Arthur Young was to endorse this view of the importance of the industry but pointed out the undesirable side effects of the profits that went with it. "The farmers complain of it", he wrote, "as doing mischief, for it makes the poor saucy and no servants can be procured, or any fieldwork done where this manufacture establishes itself...These fabricks, especially the straw, render the women averse to husbandry work." The relatively high earnings to be made from straw plaiting eventually affected agricultural wages in those areas where the craft was practised. Labourers' wages were higher in the southern straw-plaiting parts of Bedfordshire, poor rates kept at a fairly steady level, and earlier marriage was economically possible. As late as 1890 W. Ogle commented on the high marriage rate prevailing in rural Bedfordshire and linked this with lacemaking and straw plaiting, which gave employment to women and girls.[81]

The details given in the straw-hat makers' petition of 1719 make clear that the industry was by no means confined to Hertfordshire, but was equally well established in the southern, chalky parts of Bedfordshire, with Luton, Toddington, and above all Dunstable as the main market centres. The proximity of London was doubtless one factor affecting the location of the industry; favourable soil conditions producing suitable straw was another. Certainly by the second half of the seventeenth century straw plaiting was being practised in and around Luton, Dunstable, Studham, Whipsnade, Caddington, Eaton Bray, Sundon, Wingfield, and Tottenhoe. This geographical pattern remained basically the same until the end of the eighteenth century when the industry spread into the southern claylands and western half of the sandy belt of the county as far as Woburn and Ampthill. At first, since hatmaking was a seasonal trade no sharp occupational division existed between this and other branches of straw-plait manufacture, but specialization increased as the craft expanded in the eighteenth century at the expense of the woollen and lace industries.[82]

Hemp was another of Bedfordshire's rural industries, localized in the vicinity of Dunstable.

On 11 May Dunstable Fair is yearly kept [wrote William Ellis] where are sold hempen cloths for sheeting in great quantities, insomuch that many call it a cloth fair, although it is properly a horse fair and one of the greatest in England. Here their cheapest sheets are sold for about 11d an ell, but some are made of the worst sort of hemp calld sharlings, generally sold for 3d and 4d lb. This when spun is weaved 2½d an

[81] Young, *Agriculture of Hertfordshire*, pp. 222, 223; Tranter, thesis, p. 36; quoted by E. E. Lampard in H. J. Dyos, and M. Wolff, eds., *The Victorian City: Images and Reality*, London, 1973, I, p. 17.

[82] J. Dony, *A History of the Straw Hat Industry*, Luton, 1942; C. M. Law and D. J. Hooson, 'The Straw Plait and Straw Hat Industries of the South Midlands', *E. Midlands Geographer*, IV, 6, 1968; Batchelor, *Agriculture of Bedfordshire*, p. 594. The whole of Batchelor's section on manufactures is most interesting.

ell for coarse sheeting and this serves to employ farmers' children and servant-maids at their leisure time.[83]

Rush-mat making was yet another Bedfordshire industry, which because of the need to have locally accessible supplies of raw material was confined to villages such as Pavenham, Elstow, and Cranfield along the rivers Ouse and Ivell.[84]

Lacemaking, however, was far more generally practised, and by the end of the eighteenth century it was reckoned that it gave employment to three-quarters of the female population of the county. According to a protectionist petition in 1698, lacemaking was second only to woollens in national importance "and there are now above 100,000 people in England who get their living by it and earn by meer labour £500,000 a year according to the lowest computation that can be made; and the persons employed in it are for the most part women and children".[85]

Lacemaking was concentrated mainly in the northern parts of Bedfordshire, with their poorer clay soils and fragmented pattern of landholding. This was a region in which farming conditions were difficult and one noted for its agricultural backwardness in the eighteenth century, a region of open-field husbandry and small farmers with no great estate makers dominating the landscape. Lacemaking – one of the most labour-intensive of all industries – was above all a response to rural poverty and unemployment.

In the north of the county [Batchelor was to write later in his report to the Board of Agriculture] employment for the poor is represented as more deficient than in other parts: an effect which is ascribed to the poverty of the soil in the first instance which is too common a presage of the farmers who occupy it. In this district many of the boys and some of the men make lace, in the winter at least, for want of other employment.[86]

Even as late as 1851 villages like Riseley in north Bedfordshire still had a very strong commitment to this industry, 80 of the 118 separate dwellings being involved in lacemaking, and 109 individual lacemakers out of a total population of 501. Overseers' and churchwardens' accounts of several Bedfordshire parishes contain references to lace schools and payments for thread and finished work. Compared with straw plaiting and matmaking

---

[83] Ellis, *Modern Husbandman, III*, pt 3, pp. 87–8.

[84] C. D. Linnell, 'The Matmakers of Pavenham', *Beds. Mag.*, I, 1947; Godber, *op. cit.*, pp. 274–5, 362; Tranter, thesis, pp. 40–1.

[85] Victoria & Albert Museum Library, 43 A2h, *Case of the Lacemakers in Relation to the Importation of Foreign Bone Lace*. I am indebted to the Director of the Luton Museum and Art Gallery for his help in tracing this petition.

[86] Batchelor, *Agriculture of Bedfordshire*, p. 594; C. Freeman, *Pillow Lace in the East Midlands*, Luton, 1958; Tranter, thesis, pp. 16, 32. G. F. R. Spenceley, 'The Origins of the English Pillow Lace Industry', *AHR*, XXI, 1973, is an insubstantial article which misrepresents the views of Dr Thirsk on rural industries which he is supposedly challenging. Batchelor, *Agriculture of Bedfordshire*, p. 598.

lacemaking was a highly organized industry, with travelling lacemen and local lace buyers – often shopkeepers – playing an important role.[87]

But this chapter should end, as it began, by emphasizing that all was not change in the rural life of the Home Counties; there was stability and continuity as well. London's influence on farming, marketing, prices and wages, and the demand for labour was enormous but did not extend everywhere. Great estate builders such as the Russells catch the eye of the historian as they did that of contemporaries, but whole areas escaped their attention. Rural industries were spreading and diversifying in this period, and much was achieved as regards the introduction of new crops and new methods of husbandry. Agricultural improvements, however, often tended to be subject to social as well as to topographical limitations, and as a result were far from universally adopted. In this period traditional ways and the traditional framework of agriculture existed side by side with innovation and experimentation, though to a steadily diminishing extent.

[87] Kathleen T. Perfitt, 'The Pillow Lace-Making Industry in the East Midlands and Some of its Social Aspects', unpub. Univ. of London M.A. thesis, 1973, p. 9; Beds. RO, Woburn churchwardens' accounts (for 1618) P/118/5/2, and Podington overseers' accounts (for 1685) OR 975; Godber, *op. cit.*, p. 273; Beds. RO, HW 88/47, letter of 1767 from Richard How II to Silena Ramsay commenting on the relations (and trickery and double-dealing) between lacemakers and the middlemen.

CHAPTER 9

THE SOUTH-EAST: KENT, SURREY, AND SUSSEX

The farming systems of south-eastern England represented the reactions of agriculturalists to changing technologies, superimposed on differing physical and social environments, differentially located with respect to markets, in particular to London. The composite effect was an agrarian pattern which was changing far more quickly in some parts of the area than in others.

The physical skeleton of the south-east is formed of the denuded anticline of the Weald flanked by the structural depressions of the London and Hampshire basins. By the eighteenth century the main geological formations were recognized by agricultural writers, travellers, and topographers to be the Wealden central upland core; its Weald clay surround; the lower greensand escarpment; gault clay vale and Holmesdale; and the encircling chalk. Beyond the Downs were cappings of younger Eocene materials which reached down to the alluvial flats at Selsey across the flat Sussex coastal plain; to Thames-side and the north Kent coastal alluvium across the old Watling Street zone; and to the Thames across the southern part of the Vale of London. On the south coasts the marshlands of Pevensey and Romney formed important agricultural adjuncts to the inland economies.

At the centre of the Wealden anticline the High and Low Weald displayed diverse conditions of relief, soil, microclimate, and farm size, encouraging varieties of farming systems which were essentially mixed-farming wood–pasture economies, generally very reliant on animal husbandry. In 1625 Markham differentiated between "Haisell ground", "marle cope" ground, and the "wet and weeping" sandy and gravelly ground.[1] The first was a clay with a considerable sand component allowing easy working, and accounting for much of the arable area of the Weald in the seventeenth century, especially on the subsidiary sands or limestone beds in the Weald clay vale. Wheat and oats were the main crops grown, together with varying proportions of peas, tares, mixed grains, buckwheat, and flax. All could be fed to livestock, and self-sufficiency farming in severalty was the rule, although some smaller (under thirty-acre) holdings imported grain to supplement pastoral activities. In the 'Oaktree clay' parishes of West Sussex, the stiff, wet, cold clays of the "marle cope" ground, the crop mixtures were similar, but rarely accounted for as much as 20 per cent of the value of inventories. A rotation from Shipley and West Grinstead in the 1660s had

[1] G. Markham, *The Inrichment of the Weald of Kent*, London, 1625, pp. 9–19.

wheat, oats, peas, and tares continually with no intervening fallow. The poorest soils were those on the sandy and gravelly grounds, only worth cultivating with heavy applications of marl from nearby pits, producing wheat and oats, but not catch crops. Often the most profitable use of such soils, as on the podsolic soils of Ashdown Forest, or on St Leonard's Forest by the second half of the seventeenth century, was cony warren. Much of Tilgate Forest was also warren by 1666. On Ashdown 3,000–4,000 acres were so devoted, and this was one main motive behind the enclosing of much of the Forest in 1693. Considerable quantities of rabbit were sent to London by the end of the next century.[2]

With such an inauspicious basis for arable farming it is not surprising that meadow and pasture formed the predominant land uses. The breeding, and especially the fattening, of cattle was the single most important enterprise in the Weald, calves often being separated in the spring and fed in the farmhouse, while oxen, the main draught animals, were fattened at about ten years, depending on prices, preferably in stalls and on green crops and hay. Inventories recorded oxen teams of four or six, and such beasts were as numerous as all types of horses combined in the seventeenth- and eighteenth-century Low Weald, although horse numbers were possibly increasing slowly throughout the region. A small dairy containing four to six cows provided milk, butter, and cheese for the farmhouse. By 1640 a husbandman might have a herd of about fourteen in the Low Weald, with the fat cattle being sold to local butchers – only the larger Wealden fatteners such as the Pelhams or Ashburnhams sold further afield at this time. These estates made use of the droving trails from the north and Wales, or purchased lean 'scotch' cattle at St Bartholemew's Fair, since such animals fattened better than the native Sussex or 'Kentish Home Bred'. A substantial Hardham yeoman, William White, in June 1642 had 8 working oxen, 24 kine, 29 fatting beasts, a bull, and 59 young cattle. He also had a flock of 183 sheep, which was possibly six times the average flock size for Sussex, and three times that for Kent. William Baldwin of Warehorne in August 1646 had 178 sheep, amounting to 20 per cent of his wealth, and the proximity to the Romney Marsh pastures may be cited in partial explanation of the large flock size. Flockmasters and sheep fatteners lived on the higher Wealden ground at Hawkhurst, or like the Everendens at Sedlescombe or George Wightwick at Tenterden, who had a flock of nearly 6,000 sheep in 1666. In the Low Weald most farms carried some sheep, mostly from

---

[2] J. L. M. Gulley, 'The Wealden Landscape in the Early Seventeenth Century and its Antecedents', unpub. Univ. of London Ph.D. thesis, 1960, p. 136; *VCH Surrey*, IV, p. 432; PRO, E 134, 21 Chas II, Easter 7; 36 Chas II, Easter 22; P. F. Brandon, 'The Common Lands and Wastes of Sussex', unpub. Univ. of London Ph.D. thesis, 1963, p. 122, 179–80; the Rev. A. Young, *General View of the Agriculture of the County of Sussex*, London, 1813, p. 391. The term 'haisell ground' was widespread in the south-east to denote intermediate soils.

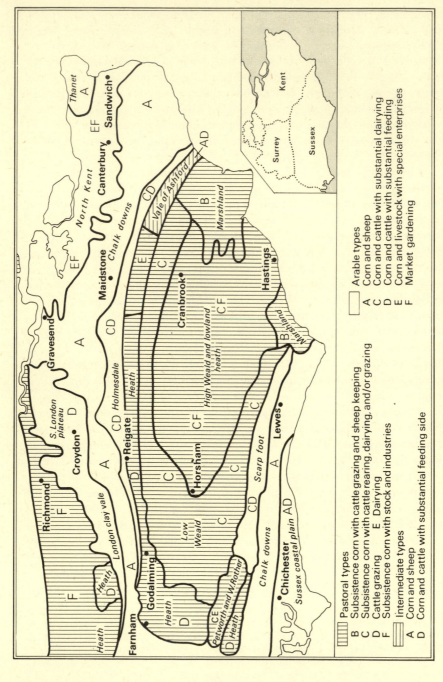

Fig. 9.1. Farming regions of the south-east.

Pastoral types

▦ B Subsistence corn with cattle grazing and sheep keeping
C Subsistence corn with cattle rearing, dairying, and/or grazing
D Cattle grazing   E Dairying
F Subsistence corn with stock and industries

Intermediate types

A Corn and sheep
D Corn and cattle with substantial feeding side

Arable types

☐ A Corn and sheep
C Corn and cattle with substantial dairying
D Corn and cattle with substantial feeding
E Corn and livestock with special enterprises
F Market gardening

'Downish' stock, and in the seventeenth century the sheep: cattle ratio in the High Weald may have been as high as 3 : 1. By 1673 a flourishing trade in fowls had been built up between Horsham and London, to be consolidated during the next century, although poultry at 6d. a bird never amounted to more than about £2 in any inventory.[3]

Both orchard production and hop gardens began to account for more Wealden investment during the later seventeenth century. Orchards were typically small, and located near to the farmhouse. If a regional concentration existed at this time, it was in the eastern High Weald, but there were apple lofts in the western Weald clay parishes of Rudgewick and Billingshurst, and much was converted into cider. Hops were becoming scattered over the eastern and central Weald with increasing consumption of beer in the later sevententh century, and by 1670 many isolated Wealden parishes had established a thriving London trade. Between 15 and 20 cwt were taken annually from West Hoathly by 1672, together with a variety of peas, apples, and walnuts, and by 1708 there were at least nineteen growers in the parish, although John Dungate, with only six acres, had the largest acreage.[4]

Enclosing the Weald clay plain was the extremely varied lower greensand formation, yielding extensive heathland between Haslemere and Leith Hill in the west, but increasing in calcareous content eastwards into Kent, where the favourable mid-Kent zone provided a strong contrast, as did the Vale of Ashford, which stretched to the coast at Sandgate. Where the Sandgate beds predominated the soil was fertile and easily worked, as near Godalming and more intensively between Petersfield and Washington in the valley of the western Rother. Where the Folkestone beds reached the surface there were light infertile soils and heathland, from Folkestone westwards to the Woolmer Forest.

Along the Rother, and around Petworth, the light sandy loams were noted by Marshall as a distinctive region, with a well-developed sheep and barley agriculture, focused on the production of early field lambs from Dorsetshire stock, purchased at Weyhill and sold in Leadenhall or Smithfield.[5] On the

[3] G. H. Kenyon, 'Kirdford Inventories, 1611 to 1776, with Particular Reference to the Weald Clay Farming', Sussex Arch. Coll., XCIII, 1955, p. 107; Gulley, thesis, pp. 115–18; A. R. H. Baker, 'The Field Systems of Kent', unpub. Univ. of London Ph.D. thesis, 1963, pp. 251–2; J. C. K. Cornwall, 'Farming in Sussex 1560–1640', Sussex Arch. Coll., XCII, 1954, pp. 77–82; Kent AO, PRC 11/13/12; 11/30/172; W. Sussex RO, Ep.1/29 Hardham n. 11; C. W. Chalklin, Seventeenth Century Kent, London, 1965, p. 102; E. Sussex RO, Dunn MSS 37/12; E. Kerridge, The Agricultural Revolution, London, 1967, p. 171; Young, op. cit., p. 392; R. Blome, Britannia, London, 1673, p. 225.

[4] Gulley, thesis, pp. 130–2; Kenyon, op. cit., p. 117; G. H. Kenyon, 'Petworth Town and Trades, 1610–1760', Sussex Arch. Coll., XCVI, 1958, pp. 84–90; PRO, E 134, 24 Chas II, Mich. 9; W. Sussex RO, Ep.1/29 Billingshurst n. 57, 170; Rudgewick n. 37, 43, 57; 379/1/1/1 f. 39. The use of oaten malt continued in the High Weald, where malt houses, malt lofts, and oasts were being erected throughout the period – Kent AO, PRC 11/20/65; D/Rb Pi 7/1.

[5] W. Marshall, Rural Economy of the Southern Counties, 2 vols., London, 1798, II, pp. 165–217.

well-watered Rother meadows some commercial dairying had developed along with hops, orchards, small fruit, and market gardens, around Sullington, Bury, and Petworth. Hops appear to have been introduced to Petworth about 1625 by Kentish planters. A wide variety of arable crops was possible here, and while wheat and barley predominated, rye was used for ewes and lambs, with winter vetches for spring feed. Sheep and milch cattle were equally important in value; Richard Ayling of Chithurst in January 1691 had 10 cows plus heifers and hay worth £30 as the most important items in his inventory.[6]

In the Vale of Ashford the arable mixture was similar, with wheat and barley a keynote, 'mended' with marl or dung at 100 loads of dung or 300–400 loads of marl per acre. Ribwort and white and 'red naturall' clover were grown, the latter certainly by 1653. Large sheep flocks were kept, but a greater proportion of young cattle and 'norden' steers were fattened for the Ashford butchery trade.[7] In the Wey valley at Peper Harow, Edward Petoe in 1720 had clover, bent, and turnip seed, wheat, rye, barley, tares, peas, hops, and buckwheat, references to the latter, probably grown on the sandy loams, being plentiful.[8]

Much of the lower greensand was sterile unenclosed heathland and commons, as at Braborne Lees in east Kent, Charing, Blackheath, and Woolmer Forest. The heaths were a source of ferns, bracken, marl, turf, peat, and sand; and near Amberley and at Durford Heath in West Sussex part of the common had been enclosed for warren, causing frequent disputes. In west Surrey the "drye and heathye grounds" at Witley and Thursley amounted to more than 5,000 acres and heath was cut from the waste for fuelling limekilns after about 1600. By an award of 1659 the lord of the manor was also entitled to cut 300,000 peats per annum at Pudmore. Richard Apew, a Wonersh yeoman, left considerable amounts of broom in 1662, which he had been selling to his neighbours. Scanty woodland provided underwood for sale at Frensham, alder being grown for iron production and later for hop poles in the Vale of Farnham. Many former hammer ponds were utilized for fish farming.[9] Agriculture was circumscribed. Thin crops of wheat and

[6] G. H. Kenyon, 'Petworth Town', pt 2, *Sussex Arch. Coll.*, XCVIII, 1960, pp. 77–8, 100, 109; Gulley, thesis, p. 118; C. R. Haines, *A Complete Memoir of Richard Haines (1633–1685)*, London, 1899, pp. 78–9; PRO, E 134, 17 Chas II, Mich. 18; 13/14 Wm III, Hil. 6; W. Sussex RO, Ep.1/29 Chithurst n. 20, and other inventories pertaining to the adjacent parishes.

[7] Kent AO, PRC 11/62/77; 11/25/66; 11/71/33; Knatchbull MSS, U951 F 18/1; Royal Soc. MSS vol. x (3), 28, p. 3; Baker, thesis, p. 252; E. C. Lodge, *The Account Book of a Kentish Estate, 1616–1704*, London, 1927, pp. XV–XLVIII.

[8] GMR, 8R/TR/Y9 (2); Middleton Papers 145, box 1. In W. Ellis, *Ellis's Husbandry Abridg'd and Methodised*, I, London, 1772, p. 115, buckwheat is specifically mentioned as not being grown on the light soils around Godalming. Ellis may have been misinformed, or the crops may have been on the Bargate loams, rather than the more sterile soils.

[9] BL, Add. MS 15,776, ff. 224–5; A. D. Hall and E. J. Russell, *Agriculture and Soils of Kent, Surrey and Sussex*, London, 1911, p. 118; Haines, *op. cit.*, pp. 93–5; E. M. Yates, *A History of the Landscapes of the Parishes of South Harting and Rogate*, Chichester, 1972, p. 27; GMR, 70/38/4; 5/2/41; 1/1/108; PRO, E 134, 4 Wm & Mary, Mich. 12; Marshall, *op. cit.*, I, p. 56.

rye were grown, together with barley, oats, buckwheat, vetches, dredge, hasties (hastings or early peas), and beans, in convertible husbandry without fixed rotations. A large flock of 'heathcropper' sheep was viewed by contemporaries as necessary for farming on these soils; but Richard Apew's flock, of 130 ewes and 20 lambs, was typical of many flocks in Linchmere or Godalming, which were intercommoned, probably with all manner of stock, with stinting at a ratio of two or three arable acres per head. Dairy cattle were kept for domestic use, rarely amounting to six in number, together with a few head of steers and oxen. Richard Apew hired out his oxen team, but probably fewer were necessary on these lighter soils, where horses might be used.[10]

In contrast, the 'red hills' of the mid Kent ragstone area between Boughton Malherbe and Mereworth possessed light, free-working loams, amongst the most favourable soils of the south-east, allowing a range of cereal and fruit cultivation, including wheat, rye (often fed green to sheep), barley, and oats, as well as a variety of podware, clover grasslands, and turnips.

A market for corn, fruit, and leather was established at Maidstone by the 1670s, and the latter, together with a specialized bullock market at Lenham, signified the importance of fattening, as in the Vale of Ashford. Young cattle were fattened for navy victualling in the 1680s and 1690s and valued for their manure, which was carted to the hop gardens, while sheep were as important for their folding on barley as for meat and wool. On the estate farm at Leeds Castle, Lady Culpeper in November 1710 had 50 Welsh ewes, 150 breeding ewes, 43 wethers, 122 lambs, and 9 rams, together with about 200 sown acres of cereals and clover. Sir Edward Filmer at East Sutton preferred Hampshire or west-country ewes for folding on turnips, but purchased Romney Marsh breeding ewes, as well as Welsh steers for winter fattening. Here the balance between arable and grassland was about equal, contrasting with the position nearer Ashford, where the Toke family had to hire arable land at considerable distances from Godinton, and where Sir Roger Twysden was forced to dispark a lately imparked area for more ploughland.[11]

Mid Kent was renowned for its hops and fruit. One of "the main springs" of Kent's wealth by 1670, the hop acreage in the Rochester collection district amounted to 17 per cent of the national total by 1724, yet few growers before

[10] GMR, 51/5/67; J. Banister, *A Synopsis of Husbandry*, London, 1799, p. 24; Kerridge, *op. cit.*, pp. 80–2. At Ulcombe in 1665 there were five areas of "fallow wheat in grass" (Kent AO, PRC 11/25/6) and at Langley Heath in 1635 there was a dispute over rights of common for "all manner of cattle" (Baker, thesis, p. 238).

[11] F. W. Jessup, *Sir Roger Twysden 1597–1672*, London, 1965, p. 129; C. Fiennes, *The Journeys of Celia Fiennes*, ed. C. Morris, London, 1947, p. 130; D. C. Coleman, *Sir John Banks – Baronet and Businessman*, Oxford, 1963, pp. 11, 50, 176; Kent AO, PRC 11/25/6; Filmer MSS U120 E11; Wykeham-Martin MSS U23 E6; Filmer MSS U120 A17; Cornwallis MSS U24 E18; Lodge, *op. cit.*, pp. XXVIII–XXIX; BL, Add. MSS 34,164 f. 86; D. W. Harvey, 'Locational Change in the Kentish Hop Industry and the Analysis of Land Use Patterns', *Inst. British Geogrs.*, XXXIII, 1963, p. 133.

1750 had as many as ten acres, and many non-specialists had part shares in gardens and poles. By 1700 several specialist holdings could be found, but acreages remained limited owing to the vagaries of yield and related prices, and with initial expenses amounting to perhaps seven times that for grain. Expert labour costs were high, and the use of London pickers alongside contracted groups of local labourers or casual rural and urban pickers can in some cases be dated to the mid seventeenth century. The gentry of the Chartlands were encouraged to dabble in this uncertain crop by the increasing accumulation of expertise by growers, labourers, and factors, the sophisticated marketing structure, the proximity of Southwark market, and the specialist provision of pole plantations in this "very uneven and much enclosed" district. Travellers between Tonbridge and Rochester "rode between hop grounds and cherry orchards most part of the way", and the latter feature also caught the attention. Heart cherries were the most valuable, with Kentish or Flemish less costly, and they were picked to be sold at nearby Tunbridge Wells and other towns. Sir John Banks planted large cherry orchards in the 1660s, and specialist growers began to appear, so that Defoe could write that around Maidstone "are the largest cherry orchards...in any part of England...and the best of them which supply the whole City of London come from hence". Apples were also sent by hoy to the Three Cranes Wharf, or were used locally for cider. Apple orchards might succeed worn-out hop gardens, often being undersown with grass for hay, but older kitchen gardens were also extended to profit from apples and pears. The $4\frac{3}{4}$ acres around Sir Edward Filmer's East Sutton farmhouse were contracted out annually for picking and sale.[12]

Between the heterogeneous lower greensand and the chalk escarpment was the narrow Holmesdale zone. Here the dark gault, less intractable than the Wealden clay owing to chalk downwash, gave "excessively stiff calcareous loam on a clay bottom".[13] The bottom itself, rather poorly drained, was suited to pastoral activities, woodland, and parkland, and some was regulated as water meadow on the Tillingbourne or at Dorking, where it was capable of "producing a plentiful burthen of excellent grass".[14] On this "cold weeping ground" around Ashford in the 1660s, oats or beans and wheat were generally followed by ten or twelve years of grassland in a landscape of enclosed severalty farms. In Holmesdale also, the ledges of upper greensand and chalk marl provided good arable soils. Here smaller farms had malt lofts but still grew poor rye, dredge (a mixture of barley and oats), or buckwheat

---

[12] T & C, pp. 85–8; P. Mathias, *The Brewing Industry in England 1700–1830*, Cambridge, 1959, pp. 486–92; Kent AO, PRC 11/16/102; D/Rb Pi 7/6; Filmer MSS U120 E5, 28; Aylesford MSS U234 A5; BL, Add. MSS 15,776 F.197; 5,842 f. 246; E. Melling, *Kentish Sources III: Aspects of Agriculture and Industry*, Maidstone, 1961, p. 85; D. Defoe, *A Tour through the Whole Island of Great Britain, 1724–6*, Harmondsworth, 1971, pp. 130–1.

[13] Young, *op. cit.*, p. 6.

[14] Surrey RO, 196/2/1.

and podware; but most of the larger farms grew wheat and barley as cash crops. Maltster Richard Francis of Amberley, West Sussex, had £100 worth of malt in his 1647 inventory; William Knowles of Birling Place and Coopers farm, Birling, in Kent, had 182 acres of Lent corn and 128 acres of wheat in the ground in August 1692. There was an intricate mix of cash cropping and livestock, taking advantage of the varied conditions. Thomas Groome at Steyning in June 1744 had 50 acres of meadow hay, 12 acres of clover hay, 82 acres of wheat, and 80 acres of barley, together with 950 sheep, 20 oxen, and 13 milch cows. Groome was a wealthy farmer, but the emphasis on sheep and the keeping of milch cows (with cheese presses very evident) was universal in this scarp-foot zone. On the chalk ledges to the east of Lewes, where springs issued from the middle chalk, giving damper conditions, and on the Arun and Adur brooklands at Amberley, Bury, and Steyning, the "feeding and depasturing of dry and working cattell", and particularly Welsh runts, assumed more importance. At Steyning specialist dairy producers flourished, for example Thomas Robins, with 18 milch cows worth £60 out of his total inventory of £111 10s. 6d. In West Sussex and in the Vale of Holmesdale proper, around Wrotham, tenanted open fields persisted into the eighteenth century, interspersed with a more visually striking enclosed and consolidated landscape of demesne farms on the 'marm' soils, where subdivision of old enclosed fields proceeded between 1640 and 1750. Into this largely enclosed landscape the innovations of the seventeenth and eighteenth centuries penetrated: clover, hops and fruit (apples being often mentioned, as at Bury in West Sussex), cinquefoil on the lower chalk at Birling and Trottscliffe in the 1690s, and trefoil at Bury by 1752 for the large sheep flocks there.[15]

A sudden change of character was perceptible as the mixed arable of the scarp foot gave way to poor grass sheepwalk on the summits of the chalk. The North Downs, with its covering of stiff, clayey loams and "stone shattery land" (superficial deposits and clay-with-flints), was more wooded, with "deep and dark valleys", leaving only Thanet, the eastern Downs, and land around Sutton and Epsom truly champion.[16] The brown-earth soils of the north downlands contrasted with the rendzinas of the open chalk on the South Downs east of the Arun and stretching to the sea at Beachy Head, where there were few trees and little surface water. West of Findon, more extensive clay-with-flints gave rise to considerable woodland areas towards the Hampshire border. Resultant differences in techniques and balances of

[15] Royal Soc. MSS, vol. x (3), 28, pp. 1–2; Brandon, thesis, pp. 266–311; W. Sussex RO, Ep.1/29 Amberley n. 43; Bury n. 95, 96; Kent AO, D/Rb Pi 7/39, 12/40; PRO, E 134, 17 Chas II, Mich. 18; 11/12 Wm III, Hil. 2; Baker, thesis, p. 131.

[16] Hall and Russell, op. cit., pp. 10–11; Royal Soc. MSS, vol. x (3), p. 1; C. Packe, Ancographia, Canterbury, 1743, p. 64. I am indebted to Mr Frank Emery for this reference. For the evolution of distinctive landscapes on the chalk, see A. Everitt, 'River and Wold', J. Hist. Geog., III, 1977, pp. 1–19.

production, and in field systems, merit a distinction between the agriculture of the North and South Downs, and within each of these a subdivision into relatively wooded and champion areas.

On the North Downs wheat and barley were produced by 1640 in a multi-field system with negligible manorial control, and with the common sheep flock of varying importance. On the Surrey hills the communal flock persisted in the eighteenth century, with tethering and folding to accommodate a remnant of intermixed strips. Hardy, thick-skinned sprat barley was the favoured cereal on the flinty soils, with more wheat being grown during the eighteenth century, possibly on new land taken in to maintain incomes in the face of falling prices. The substantial malting interests in Kent and London ensured a continuing market for barley.[17] On the "stone shattery" land, where "the blacksmith is a perpetual retainer to the farm", little profit was deemed possible without the prerequisite of a sheep flock. Manure from the herded animals was the main consideration, although William Wethersale in 1649 had a gallery in his Barham farmhouse containing lamb's wool, wool packs, and loose wool. The local Banstead Down sheep, managed along lines similar to those of South Downs flockmasters, produced mutton "long famed for its excellent quality" by heavy stocking on short grassland, and around Esher, house lambs for London. By the late seventeenth century pother (spring tares, small beans, and peas) was being supplemented by clover, although during the eighteenth century winter tares could still fill the gap when sheep had eaten off turnips but clover was not yet ready. Sainfoin, which Lewis claimed was first sown in Thanet in about 1686, was suited for horse fodder on the chalky soils, and much was sold around Northfleet for the draught horses of those renting the chalk wharves.[18]

Although the area between Guildford and Leatherhead had become by 1720 "one continued line of gentlemen's houses", and wealthy families were moving into east Kent, there were many contrasts amongst sheepwalk, commons, and heavy woodlands on the superficial clays.[19] Elham husband-

---

[17] Baker, thesis, pp. 230, 241; K. A. Bailey and I. G. Galbraith, 'Field Systems in Surrey: An Introductory Survey', *Surrey Arch. Coll.*, LXIX, 1973, pp. 76–7; *Ellis's Husbandry*, I, pp. 318–19; J. H. Andrews, 'The Thanet Seaports 1650–1750', *Arch. Cant.*, LXVI, 1953, pp. 41–2; *VCH Kent, III*, p. 45. Kerridge (*op. cit.*, p. 55) and Baker (thesis, pp. 199–203) give North Downs wheat and barley percentages in the seventeenth century as about 40–45% barley, 30% wheat, and the rest pother. The extreme rarity of the shepherd in west Kent, except on the largest farms, is noted in W. Marshall, *The Review and Abstract of the County Reports to the Board of Agriculture*, 5 vols., London and York, 1817, *V*, p. 446.

[18] Banister, *op. cit.*, pp. 20, 165, 184–5, 379; W. James and J. Malcolm, *General View of the Agriculture of the County of Surrey*, London, 1793, p. 28; Kent AO, PRC 11/16/101; D/Rb Pi 12/13; J. Aubrey, *The Natural History and Antiquities of the County of Surrey*, London, 1719, II, p. 207; LPL, UH 96/893; J. Lewis, *The History and Antiquities, as well Ecclesiastical as Civil, of the Isle of Tenet in Kent*, London, 1736, p. 17.

[19] Fiennes, *op. cit.*, p. 352; Defoe, *op. cit.*, p. 159; A. Everitt, *The Community of Kent and the Great Rebellion 1640–1660*, Leicester, 1966, pp. 26–7.

man Clement Oldfield in September 1649 had 14 acres of barley, 5 acres of wheat, and 1 acre of pother, together with 20 ewes, wethers, and lambs, 2 cows, 2 heifers, 3 horses, and 3 hogs in an inventory totalling £52 7s. In 1664 at Swingfield Minnis 29 tenants depastured 867 sheep, 31 cattle, and 37 horses, and 14 others used the common legally or illegally. At Shooter's Hill, "much overgrown with wood", Defoe commented on the faggots, small bavins, and ostrey wood sent to Woolwich, Erith, and Dartford, and noted that "this cheat of a trade" was declining with the increased use of coal in London taverns. In 1743 shopkeeper Elizabeth Lowdell of Luton, Chatham, had 29 acres of cereals, pother, and sainfoin, but also £49 10s. worth of standing wood, £8 of cord wood, 4,500 hop poles, and other wood and faggots. There were many on the clay-with-flints who profited from the woodlands, and the economy resembled that of the Weald rather than that of the champion country, even to the extent of growing quantities of fruit. A holding at Swingfield possessed an apple lathe in 1665, while at Southfleet in 1714 William Edwards was selling considerable amounts of fruit.[20]

On the western South Downs woodland served as hunting grounds for the nobility at Charleton and as "hogg commons" at nearby Singleton and East Dean. By 1640 12 of the 42 Sussex downland parishes were fully enclosed, mostly lying to the west, and here the communal sheepfold was less evident than to the east. Common for sheep was attached to copyhold yardlands in the west, amounting to 60 per yardland at Charleton and Bury. In the east, with greater pressure on commons, stints varied between 25 and 50, and were invariably reduced by 1750. The common tenantry flocks consisted of the agile and hardy polled Southdown breed on the short herbage of the dry eastern soils, rather than the taller horned Dorsets or Hampshire sheep favoured in the western damper and more wooded downland. By 1650 half of the common-field manors had demesnes being farmed in severalty. Common sheep flocks still existed, for example, at Falmer, Glynde, and Rottingdean, but a large reduction in freehold and copyhold tenants which had been occurring throughout the sixteenth century, occasioned by the expansion of the demesne and diminution of tenant holdings, rendered such undertakings increasingly less viable. Some of the formerly extensive areas of sheep downland, over 2,000 acres at Falmer and Patcham, were no longer commonable, and much was being reclaimed for cereal production, with wheat and barley of about equal importance. Westmeston Common was enclosed by 1682–3; downland was being broken up at Saddlescombe, Wilmington, and Arlington in the 1690s, Kingston in 1705, and Sompting in 1715. Stints were reduced at Telscombe from 30 sheep per yardland in 1628 to 20 or 25 in 1701, and in 1734 the vicar of Eastbourne

[20] Kent AO, PRC 11/16/97; 11/25/78; Radnor MSS U270 E1, 39; D/Rb Pi 55/6; 28/18; Defoe, *op. cit.*, p. 118; A. J. F. Dulley, 'People and Homes in the Medway Towns 1687–1783', *Arch. Cant.*, LXXVII, 1962, p. 168.

calculated a loss of £10 in tithes a year if the fold should be unavailable to tenants. At Telscombe and other highly cultivated downland parishes the remaining tenants came to place great emphasis on rights of 'cut and away' on the meadow land of the adjacent manors, while greater hay yields from clover and sainfoin helped to swell fodder supplies. At Glynde, where a formerly numerous tenantry had been eliminated by 1697, John Morley Trevor's leases stipulated the growth of both clover and sainfoin after six or seven successive straw crops. By 1700 the South Downs had become socially polarized. Large farmers such as Nathaniel Kemp of Preston, Thomas Cooper of Bishopstone, and John Scrace of Blatchington dominated wheat, barley, and sheep production with relatively low labour imputs, and at Rodmell the 17 landholders of 1622 had dropped to 7 by 1700. Economic diversity possibly still existed in the dependence of poorer husbandmen and labourers on the extensive rabbit warrens near Chichester and West Dean, and between Brighton and Eastbourne. In this latter area, near Seahouses, wheatears were also trapped and sold to Tunbridge Wells or London as a delicacy "comparable to an Ortolan or beccafica".[21]

Overlying the chalk of north Kent varied and discontinuous outcrops of Tertiary sands and gravels, London clay, alluvium, and brickearth gave rise to soils ranging from fertile retentive brickearth loams stretching from the Cray valley to Faversham and to the east of the river Stour; heavy clays of the Blean Woods; and light, pebbly commons and waste at Bromley, Bexley, and Woolwich. Large expanses of coastal marshland stretched from Thames-side through the Swale, Medway, and Wantsum. The agriculture of this north Kent zone was correspondingly varied, although intensity of production was a common characteristic in an area so accessible to London. Intensity of stock farming on the marshland, and fruit, hop, vegetable, and cereal production on the inland farms were keynotes, whether on the highly cultivated open fields of northern Gillingham or the more general enclosed severalty land, where internal boundaries were being removed, as about Boughton or Higham.[22]

The arable acreage was greater on the north Kent marshes than on other south-eastern marshlands. About Faversham the 'round tilth' method

[21] BL, Add. MSS 5,701, f. 147; 5,842, f. 246; 15,776, ff. 186, 215; 39,467; Brandon, thesis, pp. 136, 201–10, 300–16; Marshall, *Southern Counties*, II, p. 203; C. E. Brent, 'Employment, Land Tenure and Population in Eastern Sussex 1540–1640', unpub. Univ. of Sussex D.Phil. thesis, 1974, pp. 189–209; Mathias, *op. cit.*, p. 393; C. Thomas-Stanford, 'An Abstract of the Court Rolls of the Manor of Preston (Preston Episcopi)', *Sussex Rec. Soc.*, XXVII, 1921, pp. 58, 71; PRO, E 134, 6 Wm & Mary, Easter 8; 11 Wm III, Mich. 6; 2 Geo. I, Mich. 4; 33 Geo. II, Easter 2; W. Figg, 'Tenantry Customs in Sussex – The Drinker Acres', *Sussex Arch. Coll.*, IV, 1851, p. 308; E. Sussex RO, Glynde MSS 3,037; Inventories 1718/933, 1714/480, 1716/775; Cornwall, *op. cit.*, p. 49; Blome, *op. cit.*, p. 227.

[22] Baker, thesis, pp. 61–6; St John's Coll., Cambridge, MSS drawer 49 (35) 1762 terrier of Higham Abbey.

employed a continuous rotation of wheat, barley, beans, peas or seeds to give 5 quarters of wheat or 6 quarters of barley most years, and corn and malt were exported from Faversham or Sandwich, whence came the best local corn for London – the worst being reserved for local markets. Dartford was also frequented by corn chandlers and mealmen, and many here began to specialize in growing remunerative 'forward peas' for London in early June. Although prone to late frosts, overproduction, high labour charges, and transport costs, they provided fodder haulms, and an easy soil for a following turnip crop.[23] Here also, and around Faversham, madder was grown in the eighteenth century, as was flax at Tonge and weld at Canterbury.

Cattle numbers probably doubled during the seventeenth century in north Kent, partly from the supplementation of fodder from clover and sainfoin, in general use by the 1690s. Extensive sheep flocks were kept on the north Kent marshlands, and bullocks, colts, and other cattle on Sheppey. Heifers were fattened off after three years on the marshes, and hardy and compact north Welsh runts took their place, rather than the south Welsh stock favoured in Pevensey. Lean Romney Marsh sheep were purchased in the east Kent markets; and average flock size was 168. Charles Poole of Bapchild in September 1712 had a flock of 1,556 and John Randall of Harty St Thomas, 1,742, both men holding over £100 worth of fleeces in an area building a reputation for its wool. Increasingly substantial dairy herds were kept on the isolated marshland farms through to the 1740s, when many suffered the inroads of distemper, spreading from London and Blackheath.[24] The marshland was a considerable agricultural resource. It was therefore normally subdivided, and where it was commonable it was carefully regulated and stinted, as on the 'salt meades' of Higham, where Edward Hayslewood and others were presented at a court baron in July 1649 for turning in excessive numbers of horses and sheep and "treading and trampling the haye". Flooding was frequent, as in 1694 in Hoo or 1744 in Sheppey, but demand was always brisk from both Smithfield butchers and country graziers for the marshland, for regrating stock or agisting horses. On the light lands around Gravesend tracts of marshland were ideally allocated at a 1:3 ratio of marshland to upland, and the efficient utilization of this land, especially that held in severalty, was another factor in the increased cattle densities in north Kent at this time. However, saltmarsh was continuously being reclaimed, contemporaneously with assarting, as at Chatham or Keston, and woodland clearance in Chislehurst, for pasture or cereal growing. Much coarse, rush-infested ground at Hoo was being reclaimed, and at Erith and Plumstead

[23] Banister, op. cit., pp. 27, 118–30; J. H. Andrews, 'The Trade of the Port of Faversham 1650–1750', Arch. Cant., LXIX, 1955, p. 128; id., 'Thanet Seaports', p. 43; Kent AO, Knocker MSS, U55 E100/90; Blome, op. cit., p. 124.

[24] VCH Kent, III, pp. 422–3; Kent AO, PRC 11/57/24; 11/71/218, 11/71/9; D/Rb Pi 7/16; Chalklin, Seventeenth Century Kent, p. 96; St John's Coll., MSS 75/55.

large tracts were reclaimed using heavy ploughs and tackle to produce green wheat for cattle. In 1747 fresh marshland at Woodnesborough was being partly sown with hay and clover seed, ploughed and cleared, while still being grazed with sheep from downland farms. However, there were still those who depended on the woodlands and undrained marshes for their livelihoods. In 1662 Widow Susan Brooke of Teynham had "peas and 1,100 of reed etc." drawn from the Swale marshes, while college woodlands in the Blean were being let on twenty-year leases to Canterbury residents.[25]

Fruit, hops, and vegetables occupied a relatively large acreage in north Kent, stretching from London's suburbs through Crayford, where in 1694 there were 58 acres of hop garden, "some planted and some displanted", to Sandwich. All were well established by 1650, and by 1700 the modern distribution of fruit growing in north Kent was apparent, and was becoming standardized by the securing of marketing channels and the protection of orchards in leases. At either end of the north Kent lowland, around Gravesend and Sandwich, were prosperous market-gardening enterprises. The latter area had the longer history, for by 1650 there had been perhaps three generations of Flemings practising intensive seed and vegetable production, and by 1650 peas from Sandwich fetched four times the price of ordinary varieties, while onions, canary seed, and carrots were common, with the latter becoming a speciality, together with seedsmen's wares, for London. By 1650 Gravesend had acquired gardeners, perhaps from Greenwich, and by the 1740s the kitchen gardens were supplying "the towns for several miles around but also send great parcels to the London markets; particularly asparagus, which... bears a better price than any other, even that of Battersea". There was no obvious difference between gardener and husbandman. Abraham Honess, "gardner", died in Sandwich in 1692, leaving 4 cows, some pigs, 18 acres of cereals and fallow, and small areas of turnips, parsnips, beans, canary seed, flax, and other seeds and peas, amounting to at least 26 acres.[26]

The more specialized open pastures of the Romney and Pevensey marshes presented a different emphasis from the mixed farming of north Kent. By the seventeenth century the modern topography of both areas had been

---

[25] St John's Coll., MSS box 4/15, drawers 65, 49/35, 49/31; H. F. Howard, *Finances of St. John's College, Cambridge, 1511–1926*, Cambridge, 1935, p. 44; E. Sussex RO, RF 15/25; J. Malcolm, *A Compendium of Modern Husbandry*, I, London, 1805, p. 321; Banister, *op. cit.*, pp. 65, 284–8; Baker, thesis, pp. 245–6; Kent AO, Waldershare MSS U471 A3; Sondes MSS U791 E85; D/Rb Pi 12/22; PRC 11/20/46.

[26] NLW, Powis Castle Coll., 14,316; E. Hasted, *The History and Topographical Survey of the County of Kent*, I, Canterbury, 1778, p. cxxiii; Fiennes, *op. cit.*, pp. 123, 131; Defoe, *op. cit.*, p. 135; *Pehr Kalm's Account of his Visit to England*, ed. J. Lucas, London, 1892, pp. 375, 396, 448; Everitt, *Community of Kent*, p. 25; *VCH Kent*, II, p. 413; T. Read, *A New Description of...the County of Kent*, London, 1749, pp. 411, 445; Kent AO, PRC 11/57/55. Andrews ('Trade of Faversham', p. 126) points out the difficulty of reconstructing the development of fruit growing because of the eighteenth-century exemption from cocquet fees.

achieved in all essentials, apart from the rapidly silting Rother estuary near
Rye, where bitter arguments continued between town fishermen and the
graziers of the surrounding levels, whose best interests lay with reclamation.[27]
The marshlands were mostly divided into the largest enclosures in the
south-east, averaging about twelve acres, and bounded by ditches and
fencing. Ditches were easily maintained and served to contain even the
adventurous Kent sheep, but Twysden warned his son against buying land
with post-and-rail fencing, since "tymber grows skanty and will everlonge
be excessive deere". The preservation and planting of woodland was a
constant theme in Twysden's writings, while others attempted to grow
whitethorn bushes. Marshall attributed the healthier air around New Romney
to the use of fencing rather than the older "stagnant sewers", for the marshes
were long a "sicklie and contagious place", where "ague and jaundice"
carried off the majority of the population before middle age.[28]

Some resident husbandmen, though not absentee graziers, grew small areas
of crops, rarely exceeding fifteen acres, in severalty fields. Wheat was the
most common cereal, with barley, oats, beans, and finally peas, following
behind. Some alternate husbandry may have been practised, but was
discouraged on holdings of absentee graziers. Twysden advised his son: "let
him observe if he can whether it have been plowed or not for marsh land
will hardly ever recover ye auntyent goodnesse if it once have been broke
up". At Appledore Court Lodge in 1769, one thirty-acre field had been
ploughed and laid down again about twenty years previously, but was
deemed not to have recovered, this being "a president not to suffer to break
up or plow" except where the ground was rush-infested. In 1724 land at
Tenterden was leased on condition of £5 per acre payment for breaking up
Shirley Moor.[29] While some farmers had arable on the adjacent uplands, only
about two-thirds had any sown area in the seventeenth century, falling to
one-half by 1750, with population shrinking in proportion. Hasted saw
Appledore as forty-eight houses "meanly built, and mostly inhabited by
graziers, lookers and smugglers", a description equally applicable to Brenzett
or St Mary in the Marsh. By the 1670s there were seven abandoned churches

[27] L. F. Salzmann, 'The Inning of Pevensey Levels', *Sussex Arch. Coll.*, LIII, 1910, pp. 59–60;
A. J. F. Dulley, 'The Level and Port of Pevensey in the Middle Ages', *Sussex Arch. Coll.*, CIV,
1966, pp. 34–5; W. V. Lewis, 'The Formation of Dungeness Foreland', *Geog. J.*, xxx, 1932,
pp. 309–24; Chalklin, *op. cit.*, pp. 11–15; A. J. Fletcher, *A County Community in Peace and War:
Sussex, 1600–1660*, London, 1975, pp. 21, 238.

[28] Baker, thesis, p. 223; D. C. Coleman, 'The Economy of Kent under the Later Stuarts',
unpub. Univ. of London Ph.D. thesis, 1951, p. 23; BL, Add. MS 34,163, ff. 33, 146, 381; Univ.
of Cambridge Library, Add. MS 2,826, f. 28; Marshall, *Southern Counties*, I, p. 367; Banister, *op.
cit.*, p. 281; Lodge, *Account Book*, p. xviii.

[29] Marshall, *Southern Counties*, I, p. 332; BL, Add. MS 34,163 f. 33; Canterbury Cathedral,
MS 70,222; Birmingham Ref. Library, Baker Coll., 11.

on Romney Marsh, and in the eighteenth century the two market-places of Appledore were ruinous, and the fair "inconsiderable".[30]

The significance of the marshes lay in their rich perennial ryegrass. In 1644 John Everenden had paid three men for mowing forty-three acres of marshland near Winchelsea and Sedlescombe, but the grass was mostly reserved for grazing, and Daniel Jones criticized the farmers here for allowing their grass to grow too long and rank until about 1750. Pastures in the eighteenth century were 'brushed' (i.e. mowed) to leave the grass short. By 1640 distinct differences between fattening and breeding pastures were recognized. Twysden advised the purchase of land "such as will fatte cattle, not breed on younge", and Jones referred to "the breeding land which is the general quality of the Marsh...and the fatting land, which are the prime pieces and very rich". The latter were often single fields, with distributions reflecting both soil type and preferential management, since ewes and lambs were removed from breeding ground to fattening ground; and they occurred near farms and roads, which also tended to be on higher and better-drained medium-textured soils.[31] Concern over grassland quality was expressed in Twysden's note of the 1660s: "But now there is a newe devise of clover seed that spoyles all meadow land, so as we are forced to abate 5 or 6s. ye acre of good land in Romney Marsh." Seemingly ambiguous, this comment fairly certainly represents an early recognition of clover as "the vale farmer's enemy" in reducing relatively the value of natural grassland. In Surrey it was noted that the use of clover and sainfoin "hath brought down meadow hay to a much lower price than formerly". With general price falls between the 1660s and 1680s, it is not easy to isolate this problem, but certainly the worst rent arrears on Sir John Banks's estate by 1688 were from his six Romney Marsh tenants.[32]

The main emphasis on Romney Marsh was the fattening of sheep, combined in varying degrees with breeding and wool production; and in Pevensey, the production of fat cattle. Romney Marsh flock sizes were as much as five times higher than in other regions. Henry Deedes of Aldington rented 278 acres at Burmarsh, and between 1695 and 1703 his flocks remained between 3,869 and 4,004, consisting of ewes, tegs, fatting barrens, and lambs. Walter Waters of Brenzett, a grazier, had 307 barrens, 377 ewes with lambs, 413 tegs, 149 wethers, and 17 rams. Such men maintained increasingly

[30] Hasted, *op. cit., III*, Canterbury, 1790, p. 122; Chalklin, *op. cit.*, p. 75; Canterbury Cathedral, MS 70,230.

[31] E. Sussex RO, Frewen MS 520; D. Jones, "Sheep on Romney Marsh in the Eighteenth Century", a letter sent in 1786 and transcribed as *Occasional Paper of Wye College*, no. 7, 1956, pp. 5, 9; R. D. Green, *Soils of Romney Marsh*, Soil Survey of Great Britain, 4, Rothamsted, 1968, p. 136.

[32] BL, Add. MS 34,163 f. 33; *Ellis's Husbandry, I*, pp. 510–11; Kerridge, *op. cit.*, p. 288; Bodleian Library, Gough MSS, Surrey I, p. 440; Coleman, *Sir John Banks*, pp. 175–6. See also pt II, below, ch. 19, p. 554. For an alternative interpretation of Twysden's note, see Chalklin, *op. cit.*, p. 101.

intensive stocking rates, rising to eight per acre for fatting sheep and four for ewes and lambs, but varying with the time of year, being higher in early summer to eat off long winter herbage. Lookers and town craftsmen also kept flocks: carpenter Thomas Baker of Lydd in 1744 owned 100 ewes, 48 tegs, and 15 rams and barrens, worth more than all his tools and timber. Large graziers owning upland sent May lambs inland for their first winter, and those without this facility sold or agisted lambs in the Weald or overwintered them on the Marsh, as did Toke, or Edmund Swayne, whose December 1668 inventory mentions 146 ewes, 67 wethers, and 57 barrens in his marsh ground. For hardiness, early maturing, propensity to fatten, and good wool, 'Kents' had established themselves widely, and the marshland was regarded as a "kind of nursery whence the Sheepey and other graziers of this county generally supply themselves". Pevensey, used by fatteners from far into Kent and West Sussex, had no analogous 'native' cattle, and relied on Scotch, northern, Welsh, and country animals driven via the Bartholemew fair, or directly to the area. These were fattened between April and October, and dispatched to local markets and butchers or to Smithfield. Toke held annual drives of cattle and sheep from Romney Marsh to Smithfield, as well as selling locally and in north Kent, and men such as Pelham, Everenden, and Dobell sold in Kent or London, using their own drovers where possible. An increasing emphasis on meat production from wethers replaced the older concentration on wool production as the Wealden clothing industry decayed. But Kent remained one of the chief wool-producing counties with 5,500 packs annually about 1700, and between one-third and one-half of this originated in Romney Marsh, where some eighteenth-century graziers could sell over 100 packs of coarse fleeces annually. In 1671–2 Sir Norton Knatchbull made £369 from a flock of 2,000–3,000 animals, and many inventories include 'wool chambers' with stocks worth over £100. Exports through Rye customs house tripled from 1640 to the end of the eighteenth century, even allowing for the growing extent of export smuggling (owling). Sheep dominated other stock in Romney Marsh, although with poor roads the local demand for dairy produce encouraged an average number of 3.7 cows per household in the 1640s, rising to 5.5 in the 1740s.[33]

A part of the Channel coastland with a quite different agrarian basis stretched from the Adur estuary at Shoreham westwards to Hampshire: the Sussex coastal plain or seacoast. The lower coastal plain consisted of drift

[33] Univ. of Reading Library, KEN 19/1/1; Kent AO, PRC 11/71/46; 11/82/165; 11/30/41; Kerridge, op. cit., p. 136; VCH Sussex, I, p. 465; P. J. Bowden, The Wool Trade in Tudor and Stuart England, London, 1962, pp. 35–6; W. Youatt, Sheep: Their Breeds, Management and Diseases, London, 1837, p. 336; Banister, op. cit., pp. 426–8; Gulley, thesis, pp. 90–1; Fletcher, op. cit., pp. 15–17; G. O. Cowley, 'Sussex Market Towns 1550–1750', unpub. Univ. of London M.A. thesis, 1964, pp. 148–9; Chalklin, op. cit., pp. 101–3, 185; Cornwall, 'Farming in Sussex', p. 54; Young, op. cit., pp. 345–73. Average flock and dairy-herd sizes are derived from inventories.

deposits drained by rifes and a flat treeless maze of saltings and mud flats, prone to 'blasts' about Selsey. Deep, stoneless brown earths were developed on brickearth. The upper coastal plain, a narrow gravel-covered belt at the foot of the South Downs, had large amounts of flint, clay-with-flints, and silty loess, called 'shravey'. A third component was a limited area of wooded London clays and Bagshot beds with impeded drainage at Havant Thicket or Emsworth Common; and a fourth was the alluvium of the Arun and Adur valleys or coastal inlets, providing excellent fattening pasture. The coastal plain was a prosperous farming area, Marshall proclaiming that there were few districts where he had seen less to mend. Many farmers had intensified production by applying chalk and marl and reclaiming marginal land, especially coastal lagoons, for corn growing, the basis of the economy.[34] To some extent this adversely affected husbandmen who supplemented their incomes by fishing, for, especially around Selsey, shellfish were prolific, although the former speciality of mullet from the Arun seems to have declined by the 1740s. Reclamation was also being countered by severe coastal erosion affecting pasture and common land; and in particularly exposed areas, such as Bracklesham Bay, salvage money from wrecks helped to compensate farmers for losses of land and stock. The landscape consisted of closely scattered nucleated villages between Felpham and Lancing, surrounded by open, commonable fields in varying stages of decay. Around Chichester a more dispersed pattern of isolated farms and hamlets, with small hedged fields, signified older enclosure, as on the poor clay at North Mundham, but this was different again from Climping, where the demesne was enclosed but where in 1663 "divers garden plots known and called by ye name of holybreads" were "lying intermixt in larger fields and nothing to distinguish them by but a furrow, a bush or a land end and eye knowledge". The remarks of Defoe and Milles as to the enclosed country "abounding with wood" should be seen as perceptions taken from the Arundel to Chichester road, running along 'shravey' for much of its length and unrepresentative of the true nature of the agricultural landscape.[35]

Corn was produced in a sheep–corn husbandry merging with that of the downland, but unrivalled in productivity on the brickearth soils. Some combined this with, or specialized in, early lambs or fattening of sheep, bullocks, and swine, but wheat and barley were the principal marketed commodities. Wheat yields varied from a quarter per acre on the pebbly drifts of Binstead to $3\frac{1}{2}$ quarters at Ferring, although Marshall quoted 5 quarters

[34] J. M. Hodgson, *Soils of the West Sussex Coastal Plain*, Soil Survey of Great Britain, 3, Rothamsted, 1967, pp. 81, 96; Marshall, *Southern Counties, II*, pp. 223–44; F. W. Steer, *The Manor of Littlehampton with Toddington, 1633*, Littlehampton, 1961, pp. 19–25.

[35] Blome, *op. cit.*, p. 225; E. Heron-Allen, *Visitor's Map and Guide to Selsey*, Selsey, 1912, p. 41; H. Smail, *The Worthing Map Story*, Worthing, 1949, pp. 39, 57; PRO, E 134, 8 Anne, Easter 20; 9 Anne, Easter 17; Brandon, thesis, pp. 229, 376; E. M. Yates, 'The Meare Marsh of Merston', *Sussex Arch. Coll.*, CXIII, 1975, p. 120; BL, Add. MS 39,467 f. 112; Defoe, *op. cit.*, p. 147; J. Milles, 'Travels in England and Wales 1735–43', BL, Add. MS 15,776 ff. 230–8.

as an ordinary crop, and the Reverend A. Young cites yields which place the region amongst the most productive in eighteenth-century England. Fertile, retentive soils, easily drained and fallowed, and allowing a long working season, had helped a long history of corn exporting and a division of much of the region into large tenant holdings of both ecclesiastical and lay proprietors. By 1640 a flexible ley-farming system had evolved in both common field and severalty, and on 'shravey' and heavier brickearths. Longer grass leys were employed on weaker 'shravey' soils, as at Walberton, where in 1756 half the former common fields were in pasture. Inventories of the 1640s give average sown areas for wheat of 28 acres and barley 27 acres, rising to 44 and 40½ acres respectively by the 1740s, but the equipment of many implied far higher acreages. Richard Finers of Birdham in April 1710 had 100 acres of wheat and 36 fallowed for barley; 4 ploughs, probably of the one-wheeled variety, 5 harrows, 6 dungcarts, 4 waggons, an 'oat cart', and 2 rollers. 'Long carts' and waggons were very numerous to accommodate the large amounts of corn sent forty miles overland to Farnham, or by sea to London, the west, and the Continent, from Dell Quay. During the second half of the seventeenth century Chichester grain exports equalled those of all other Sussex ports combined, while only Sandwich and Margate exported more malt. By the mid eighteenth century corn exports abroad equalled all Kent and Sussex ports combined, and the erection of large granaries and the use of tide mills on the creeks of the Emsworth–Chichester area in the 1730s allowed the export of flour as well as unground wheat. Barley was grown in larger quantities in the 1640s than in any other decade before 1740, and on both brickearth and 'shravey'. John Long of Broadwater, where the favoured Coombe rock approaches the sea, had in April 1712 222 quarters of malt, 14 acres of barley, 69 acres being fallowed for barley, 30 quarters of seed barley, and another 54 quarters of barley.[36]

Crops grown for farm consumption normally included oats, peas, vetches, and tares, but rarely exceeded sixteen acres. Pother increased little, since the clover area expanded from being recorded in one inventory in fifteen in the 1660s to over two-thirds in the 1740s, although the average sown area remained about eight acres overall. Mingled (mixed) corn and dredge, hops, and fruit were also grown on some farms. Some hemp was grown in small plots before the 1670s, but no flax. Peas, both white and grey, were grown and sold at good prices at Havant for "the fatning of the hoggs which come out of the forest".[37] There was little of distinction in the grassland here. Marshall distinguished four types: relatively rich eastern upland grazings;

[36] Marshall, *Southern Counties*, II, pp. 234–9; PRO, E 134, 5 Anne, Easter 4; HO, 67/20 (1801 return for Ferring); Young, *op. cit.*, p. 92; Kerridge, *op. cit.*, p. 69; Cornwall, *op. cit.*, pp. 58–65; W. Sussex RO, Add. MS 1,802; Ep.1/29 Birdham n. 70; Broadwater n. 117; J. H. Andrews, 'The Port of Chichester and the Grain Trade, 1650–1750', *Sussex Arch. Coll.*, XCII, 1954, pp. 93–105; Defoe, *op. cit.*, p. 150; S. Farrant, 'Bishopstone Tidemills', *Sussex Arch. Coll.*, CXIII, 1975, p. 200.

[37] W. Sussex RO, Probate inventories; BL, Add. MS 39,467; PRO, E 134, 6 Anne, Easter 5; 7 Anne, Mich. 1.

poor western marsh and common; estuarine brooklands; and open saltmarshes used between tides. Water meadows gave plentiful hay for cattle along the river Lavant, and the Goodwood estate had similar facilities at Tangmere. Sheep were fattened on the alluvial grasslands and saltings, often running with local or west-country cattle and bullocks, purchased and resold at Chichester and Arundel when fat. West-country wethers or in-lamb ewes were purchased in the autumn for feeding on hay and pother, with lambs fattened quickly for spring sale. The spring sheepfold was valuable, wattles being a ubiquitous inventory feature, with flock numbers ranging between 50 and 150. With much land in arable, common pasture rights were important: a complaint against John Hale of Westhampnett in 1681 was that he put out nine score of sheep, often for the whole year, on the commons of Singleton and East and West Dean, but that he could not maintain them on his own land although he farmed over 300 acres, mostly arable, of which 60 acres lay in Westhampnett's common fields. Stints varied, so that at Eartham 40 sheep could be commoned per yardland, as well as 3 beasts, and at Merston 12 sheep in winter and 4 in summer per virgate. Some short-stapled wool was produced for the Chichester kersey trade or for fellmongers, and 21 per cent of the inventories mentioned stores of wool, although few had as much as the barley producer John Long at Broadwater, with 500 sheep, and wool worth £105. Self-sufficiency in dairy produce was obtained, and bacon was plentiful from the mottled pigs grazing on clover or tares in the fields, in the brooks, or in the beech woods of the South Downs and 'shravey'.[38]

In the London basin light sands and coarse, pebbly soils constituted the commons of the south London plateau, with coverings of gorse and heather at Dartford, Blackheath, Bexley, Bromley, and Chislehurst. To the north, heavy, stiff London clay soil capped hills at Beckenham and Bromley, but formed lowland common or poor grass at Ashtead, Epsom, and East Clandon, baking hard in summer, and cultivable only with liberal dressings of chalk and London manure. To the west was the "broad blank margin" of the Bagshot sands lowland heath. Furze-covered commons such as Wimbledon, "abandoned to pastures", or Esher and Richmond, grew in number and size west of the river Wey to Windsor and the "sandy desert" of Bagshot Heath. These poor agricultural environments contrasted with the alluvial strips, low gravels, and brickearth along the south bank of the Thames and on its tributaries, where the accessibility to London's market and manure ensured prosperity for many. Localized soil differences were reflected strongly in rents, such that at Balham in 1731 arable land on "a deep good soil" fetched 18s. per acre, while that on "a sharp, dry gravel" fetched 10s. Meadow land let at 30s. At Ashtead by 1640 the cultivated chalk loams

[38] Marshall, *Southern Counties, II*, pp. 203–6, 239–42; Young, *op. cit.*, pp. 222–3; W. Sussex RO, Goodwood MSS E 4993, E 5532; Add. MSS 524 f. 114; Ep.1/29 Broadwater n. 117; Kerridge, *op. cit.*, p. 69; PRO, E 134, 33 Chas II, Mich. 11, 12; Brandon, thesis, p. 133; Bowden, *op. cit.*, p. 51; *VCH Sussex, II*, pp. 256–7.

contrasted strongly with the marsh, pasture, and woodland on the cold and sour London clay.[39]

The commons of the London basin were jealously guarded in areas where conies, peat and gravel digging, and intercommoning were available. In 1737 about twenty-five acres of the Lower Common, Epsom, were enclosed, but rights of access to gravel pits were expressly reserved for tenants; and at Pirbright Manor on the Bagshot sands, legal action was taken in 1675 against Lord Montague by tenants who felt disadvantaged by his enclosure of a peat moor, which later became a commercial business venture. Not all enclosures were for business. Charles I's 'New Park' at Richmond took land from six parishes, leading to long disputes over rights to turf and kindling from this "bog and...harbour for deer stealers and vagabonds". There was similar unrest at Farnham, Wimbledon, and Egham, and by the 1720s the poor agricultural country of Bagshot Heath had become a centre of 'blacking'. Perhaps more than any other region in the south-east, the London basin witnessed an onslaught on the commons. However, by the 1680s large areas in Richmond Old Park were sown with rye, barley, peas, and oats or depastured with cattle and sheep, while Nonsuch was disparked and leased out by the duchess of Cleveland for "great crops of corne, hay, clover...at the first breaking up".[40] Enclosure was also proceeding among the remaining open-field areas. From Egham and Chertsey in the west to the Hoo peninsula in the east there were still open fields along the Thames by 1750. To the south the boundary between chalk and Tertiary rocks was also marked by open fields from Guildford to the Kent border, and there were remnants on the Bagshot sands to the west. The high value of the Thames-side strips, used by gardeners, farmer-fishermen, carriers, or industrial workers may have helped their survival. Wimbledon was largely enclosed by 1640, but Battersea presented a bewildering intermixture of arable, grassland, market gardening, mixed arable and vegetable production, drained marsh pastures, and severalty nurseries. In 1706 the three fields of Wandsworth totalled 633 acres, but by the mid eighteenth century perhaps one-third had been taken into a new park. To the south on the margin of the chalk, East and West Horsley common fields were shared by only four people by 1728, and the Honourable James Fox had acquired 140 of the total 179 acres.[41]

[39] Hall and Russell, *Agriculture and Soils*, pp. 14, 83–90, 153; Marshall, *Southern Counties, II*, p. 82; Kalm, *op. cit.*, p. 36; Defoe, *op. cit.*, p. 156; GLCRO, E/DCA 169; E. C. Willatts, 'Changes in Land Utilization in the South-West of the London Basin, 1840–1932', *Geog. J.*, LXXXII, 1933, p. 516.

[40] Surrey RO, Kingston Borough Archives KF1/5/3; GLCRO, E/BER/S/E/4/1; PRO, E 134, 13/14 Chas II, Hil. 7; 32 Chas II, Easter 3; 4 Anne, Trin. 7; GMR, 85/2/1(i)/1; 1,209/1/13, 26/1; RB 186; H. Walpole, *Memoirs of the Reign of King George the Second, I*, London, 1847, p. 402; E. P. Thompson, *Whigs and Hunters: The Origins of the Black Act*, London, 1975, pp. 55, 130–4, 181–2; P. Fletcher Jones, *Richmond Park*, London and Chichester, 1972, pp. 4–26.

[41] *VCH Surrey, IV*, p. 438; GMR, 97/3/21 (7), 54/1/17; Bailey and Galbraith, 'Field Systems in Surrey', p. 83; V. B. Redstone, 'The Diary of Sir Thomas Dawes, 1644', *Surrey Arch. Coll.*,

A variety of cereals and pulses were grown around London, where "all commodities come to a good market", but generally wheat and barley served as cash grains, with rye being the second crop on the western heaths. Buckwheat was also sown here, and all over the region the area of oats increased with London's horse population. Although no fixed rotation was perceptible, during the late seventeenth and early eighteenth centuries a turnip and barley system evolved on some lighter lands, such as at Putney or Byfleet, and on the Bedford estate's common fields at Streatham and Cheam. By 1700 the barley went to London maltsters, or to local concerns, such as that of the Heathfield family at Croydon.[42] Poor grasslands and meadows were relatively abundant, and hay seeds were thus easily and cheaply obtained. This fact, together with Marshall's view of the region's unenlightened approach to agriculture, has been cited to support a slow rate of adoption of improved grasses. Yet in 1705 inhabitants of Send had sown clover and blackbent seed for forty or fifty years; husbandmen in the Croydon area were certainly using clover in the 1670s, together with sainfoin in the early eighteenth century; and John Collier, a substantial Horsell yeoman, possessed both turnips and clover seed in 1689.[43] Meadows might be let under strict covenants to cowkeepers, who manured them and used a rotational grazing paddock system to maintain constant supplies of fresh grass until midwinter stall feeding. Others were Lammas lands, as at Runnymede, Mitcham Meadow, or Woking Broad Mead. Water meadows were employed on the rivers Mole and Wey. By 1640 Sir Richard Weston was improving his Sutton estate, and the resultant 100 acres of rich meadowland compared favourably with the surrounding "heathy barren fearny ground".[44] From Lee, Eltham, and Deptford, hay was carried by water to London, with return carriage of soot or ashes. Riverside breweries and the local markets at Croydon and Kingston also consumed much hay, but perhaps the largest quantities were purchased by London's cowkeepers. John Farrant of St Mary Newington in 1689 had a cowhouse with 40 cows and £92 worth of hay, but seemingly no land. Essential apparatus included carts, milk vessels, and horses, for selling the often unhygienic product. Reginald Sargant of Putney kept 9 cows and 6 asses in 1706, the latter being driven from door to door and providing cleaner, though

XXXVII, 1926, pp. 1–36; G. B. G. Bull, 'Thomas Milne's Land Utilization Map of the London Area in 1800', *Geog. J.*, CXXII, 1956, p. 26; GLCRO, E/BER/S/E/4/4; Surrey RO, Acc. 1,313.

[42] The inventory of John Hill of Barnes in 1674 contains references to wheat, rye, barley, oats, peas, beans, carrots, and tares (LPL, Inventory 1,293). Surrey RO, 212/61/7; PRO, E 134, 13/14 Chas II, Hil. 7; GMR, 1,209/29/11/2; J. Worlidge, *Systema Agriculturae*, 2nd edn, London, 1675, p. 42; LPL, Inventory 688, UH96/414; 1,240, 1,242, 1,244; Kerridge, *op. cit.*, p. 174; GLCRO, E/BER/S/E/7/4–7 and 8/2/5.

[43] Marshall, *Review and Abstract*, V, pp. 355–66; Kerridge, *op. cit.*, p. 343; PRO, E 134, 4 Anne, Mich. 7; 11 Geo. I, Mich. 23; LPL, 341, 535; Surrey RO, 212/61/7.

[44] GLCRO, E/BER/S/L/10/1; Kalm, *op. cit.*, pp. 378–9; *VCH Surrey*, IV, p. 439; Aubrey, *Natural History of Surrey*, III, p. 230; N. Nash, 'Early Seventeenth-Century Schemes to Make the Wey Navigable', *Surrey Arch. Coll.*, LXVI, 1969, pp. 33–40.

expensive, milk. Profits were badly affected by the distemper of the 1740s, and John Bennett of Rotherhithe, unable to qualify for a bounty, lost £80 during October and November 1749 through the slaughter of stricken beasts.[45] The grasslands became more intensively stocked during the period. On the lowland heaths to the west and on the lower downland dipslope small, long-horned cattle were fattened, while calves, purchased at Aylesbury, were brought south by 'calf merchants' for fattening at Esher, Cobham, Send, or Ripley. Demands for house lamb in London also ensured some large flocks. West-country ewes were purchased at Ewell or Kingston for lambs, which were fed on rye, clover, tares, and turnips around Esher or on sainfoin around Croydon. Wethers were also purchased for folding on turnips on the arable lands of the Bedford estates, and for fattening for Smithfield. In the west heathcroppers were folded on the arable and provided a sweet mutton. Birds and fish were fattened, with fish ponds frequently found in the dips and hollows of the heaths, and swine were fattened from distillery and starch factory waste.[46]

By 1640 market gardening and nursery production were well established, expanding to form a distinct zone on the flood plain terrace gravels amongst the open fields and growing suburbs. At Lambeth, Battersea, Wandsworth, Putney, and Greenwich the Gardeners' Company sought to exclude husbandmen from growing commercially within six miles of the city, and gardens became established at Deptford, Bermondsey, and Camberwell, and to the west at Kew and Mortlake. Westwards again, within easy reach of water carriage at Chertsey and Weybridge, carrots, turnips, and cabbages were grown; while Mitcham developed as a specialist herb centre. Kalm noted that "they mostly keep to something special"; such specialities were the asparagus of Battersea, the watercress of Wandsworth, the garden trees from the Vauxhall nurseries, the osier beds of the Thames aits, and the plant centre at Putney. Nurserymen could, however, hold very diverse stocks: William Blinde of Barnes in 1693 held flowers, fir and fruit trees, stocks, and seed beans and peas; while Blanche Watson in 1668 left plants at St Mary Newington ranging from cherries and gooseberries to thyme, spinach, leeks, parsnips, and cabbages. Considerable investments were made in crops and glass, and the severe south London hailstorm of 1750 brought losses totalling over £4,000 to over forty-three gardeners. Four growers from St Mary Magdalene, Bermondsey, cited losses of over £230 each.[47]

[45] Banister, *Synopsis of Husbandry*, p. 252; LPL, 900; 2,294; 2,318; P. V. McGrath, 'The Marketing of Food, Fodder and Livestock in the London Area in the Seventeenth Century, with Some Reference to the Source of Supply', unpub. Univ. of London M.A. thesis, 1948, p. 227; GLCRO, E/BER/S/E/8/1/2.

[46] E. Sussex RO, Glynde MS 2,756; Marshall, *Southern Counties, II*, pp. 85–7; E. W. Brayley, *A Topographical History of Surrey*, London, 1878, *I*, p. 236; Banister, *op. cit.*, p. 372; James and Malcolm, *General View of Surrey*, pp. 28–38; Kalm, *op. cit.*, p. 411.

[47] Bull, *op. cit.*, p. 29; R. Webber, *Market Gardening*, Newton Abbot, 1972, pp. 30–2; Kalm,

Regional variety in the farming of south-eastern England was closely related to variations in farm structure and patterns of landholding, tenure, and inheritance. Farm size, measured by acreage, seed acreage, or value, obviously varied spatially. On the Downs an average holding was 110–120 acres in size, and, as in the marshland, with its average holding of over 160 acres, the presence of a physically open landscape could be correlated with larger farming units. The north Kent average rose to over 130 acres, but on the lower greensand of Kent it was 70 to 80 acres; in Surrey, 90 acres; and in Holmesdale, 40 to 50 acres. In the generally less fertile London basin, holdings averaged 60 to 70 acres, decreasing towards London itself. The average Wealden holding was 100 to 110 acres. All these figures are probably overestimates, being based on parliamentary and private estate surveys, but omitting the multitude of cottage holdings, waste-edge reclamation, peri-urban paddock holdings, and small vegetable plots. Thus a figure of 40 acres for the central High Weald in the eighteenth century is a more realistic estimate.[48] Similarly, both seed acreages and values derived from probate data are biased towards larger holdings. A sample of 850 farm inventories gave an average overall value of £321, but regional variations were correlated with holding size in showing the wealth of the marshland at an average £457, north Kent at £427, and the chalk at £422 compared with the London basin at £157 and the West Sussex/Surrey lower greensand area at £206. Mid Kent (£254) and the Low Weald (£274) were also noticeably below average. The average acreage under crop in the south-east was 38.7 acres, but that in Kent was 42.4 acres and that of Wealden-dominated East Sussex only 26.8 acres. In the Weald holdings under 5 acres, a very large category, were rarely full-time, but reflected the wider variety of Wealden by-employments. Holdings of between 5 and 30 acres were the commonest units, many being worked by farm labourers. Holdings of between 30 and 300 acres occupied more of the land area than any other group; there were only limited numbers of units above 300 acres.[49]

No quantitative assessment of the changing size of holdings has been made for this period, but generalized impressions suggest that a concentration of landownership was accompanied by an expansion in the size of holdings by 1750. The extreme fluidity of the south-eastern land market allowed favoured

op. cit., p. 24; VCH Surrey, IV, p. 229; James and Malcolm, op. cit., p. 38; Surrey RO, 1/2/20; Clayton MSS 60/5/499; QS 6/2 Midsummer 1750/62–106; Aubrey, op. cit., III, p. 167; S. Kershaw, 'The Manor of Lambeth', Surrey Arch. Soc., 1894 report, p. 20; J. Harvey, 'The Putney Nursery: An Early Plant Centre', Surrey Arch. Coll., LXIX, 1973, pp. 134–42; LPL, 271; 2,730.

[48] D. K. Worcester, 'East Sussex Landownership: The Structure of Rural Society in an Area of Old Enclosure 1733–87', unpub. Univ. of Cambridge Ph.D. thesis, 1950, p. 190.

[49] Gulley, thesis, pp. 153–9. The estate of the earl of Thanet in Kent consisted of 47 holdings, of which 23 on the lower greensand averaged 89 acres; 10 in the Weald averaged 95 acres; 12 in north Kent averaged 123 acres; and 2 in Romney Marsh averaged 164 acres – Kent AO, Knocker MS U55 E16.

units to contract or expand as circumstances dictated, but the main processes of change, linked with tenure, landholding, and inheritance patterns, can be outlined. Piecemeal exchanges and purchase in the open fields continued, as at Puttenham where "some 20 rods gained by exchange were ditched and quickset in February 1654 and some with green hastings [hastings peas] 13/3/1654".[50] Land was purchased for addition to the farming unit, as at Preston on the South Downs, where customary yardlands were being consolidated, and among the Kentish gentry strong family connections engendered much buying, selling, borrowing, and renting. Nicholas Toke constantly rented additional Downland tenantries and pastures, as could most wealthy tenants. Much was contiguous to the original holding, but the processes of downland enclosure and assarting could also add to fragmentation while effectively enlarging farm size. In the twenty years after 1674, 500 acres in southern Ashdown Forest were granted in small parcels, although assarting in the High Weald was otherwise unimportant, no increase of farm sizes occurring in the central High Weald between 1733 and 1786.[51] The effective farm unit was also being enlarged by disparking. Depasturing in parkland was normal, and there were small tenant holdings within the pales, together with land devoted to new crops, particularly turnips, or to reclamation techniques. But in larger parks, as at Knole, Petworth, Battle, or Bletchingly, disparking in the seventeenth century, encouraged by Civil War depredations, provided new farmland. Again, this process should not be overemphasized, for there were newcomers to the south-east who saw the mansion and park as a desirable feature: Sir John Banks was making and stocking his Aylesford Park in the 1680s, and in the 1750s the duke of Bedford imparked over 200 acres of farmland and common at Wandsworth.[52] Increased farm size implied a growing social polarization; and such inequality, due in part to ingrossing, has been traced particularly on the specialized grain-producing farms of the chalk, where the numbers of freeholders and copyholders declined dramatically in the eighteenth century.[53]

Patterns of landholding also varied regionally. By 1750 fragmented and intermixed open fields were still a feature of Thames-side, much of extra-Wealden Surrey and the South Downs, and the strips at Hoo were so intermixed and poorly marked that a survey of 1762 could not locate all the

[50] GMR, 51/5/67.

[51] J. H. and S. P. Farrant, *Preston in the Seventeenth and Eighteenth Centuries*, Univ. of Sussex, Centre for Continuing Education, 1975, p. 6; BL, Add. MS 34,164 f. 86; Lodge, *Account Book*, pp. XXIII–XXXIX; Brandon, thesis, pp. 184–5, 191–5; Worcester, thesis, pp. 182–4.

[52] Gulley, thesis, pp. 68–71; Surrey RO, Clayton MSS 60/5/506, 762 (references to the sowing and hoeing of turnips in the Claytons' park at Marden in the 1730s and 1740s); Coleman, *Sir John Banks*, p. 124; GLCRO, E/BER/S/E/4/4.

[53] Baker, thesis, pp. 245–6; Chalklin, *Seventeenth Century Kent*, p. 72; J. Boys, *General View of the Agriculture of the County of Kent*, London, 1813, p. 3; Brent, thesis, pp. 192–202; U. Lambert, *Bletchingly*, Surrey Arch. Soc., 1949, p. 13.

land of some farms. At Wandsworth in 1706 a survey to stake out the common fields was undertaken to prevent further confusion, reminiscent of the situation at Littlehampton in 1640, where "there were very few or no land shares or balks left unploughed in any of the said common fields for a mere and distinguishment of one man's land from another".[54] Severalty open fields persisted at Thanet and Cliffe, and in east Kent, where at Ripple and Deal the open-field chalk by 1750 contrasted with the enclosed 'haysill moulds' in the same area. Old-enclosed farmland was also frequently highly fragmented. Of Kent, Boys remarked that there were "few extensive possessions but what are intersected by other persons' property"; and even Wealden ring-fence compact holdings were often farmed with appurtenant complementary land at some distance, forming intricate patterns of regional interdependence. In this period of active leasing and selling, Wealden severalty land became increasingly fragmented, as did that on Romney Marsh. In the latter region the land belonging to All Souls' College in 1689–93 underwent consolidation, but David Jones noted a century later that the graziers "hire their land of different owners in any parcels, and at any distance, neither the compactness of their business, nor the distance being any object with them". Twysden advised: "never let many parcells especially lying together to one man for if he dye...one is huglely [sic] troubled to let it".[55] But while fragmentation could be demonstrably increasing, the period from 1640 to 1750 was one of slow and unobtrusive transition from former open field to a more enclosed landscape in regions such as the Sussex coastal plain, South Downs, lower greensand, and Holmesdale. Much had already been enclosed by 1640, and many of the remaining fields awaited parliamentary enclosure after 1750. Enclosure also affected the inter-commoning of livestock, and as downland was enclosed and small Wealden and greensand commons were granted piecemeal, the pressure on the remaining commons intensified. Complex sets of commoning rights had evolved to govern the use of large wastes such as Ashdown Forest, but the main users were probably the small waste-edge cottagers. This pattern of commons recurred throughout the south-east, where threats to its survival met with violent protest, as at Egham in the mid seventeenth century, and with careful stinting, as along Thames-side at the 'salt meades' of Higham, Cliffe common meadow, and Shorne mead. In 1737 at Higham 26 'commonings' allowed to each commoner the depasturing of either five sheep or one horse, or one cow or two twelve-month bullocks. Fines were distributed half to the looker and half "amongst the poorest sort of people

[54] St John's Coll., MSS drawer 49 (35); GLCRO, E/BER/E/3/8/2/2; Steer, *Littlehampton*, pp. 17–18; GMR, 145, box 15.

[55] Chalklin, *op. cit.*, pp. 16–17; Baker, thesis, pp. 134, 198, 215–16, 236; Boys, *op. cit.*, p. 25; Gulley, thesis, pp. 102, 159–61; W. E. Tate, 'A Handlist of English Enclosure Acts and Awards, Part 17 – Open Fields, Commons and Enclosures in Kent', *Arch. Cant.*, LVI, 1943, p. 58; D. Jones, 'Sheep on Romney Marsh', p. 6; BL, Add. MS 34,164 f. 57.

to whom the common doth belong". Pressure here was indicated, however, by the gradual accumulation of 'commonings' by the largest farm, by the ploughing and division of marshland into arable enclosures, and by increases in the fines.[56]

One dominant influence on regional patterns of landholding and their rates of change was the steady accumulation of land into large estates. In the century after parliamentary sequestration, new families moved into rural south-east England, as it became easier to acquire and retain land. The steady accumulation of land can be seen in the mortgage transactions of the earls of Egremont, one of the wealthiest of English families, in West Sussex; or on a smaller scale by Dennis Lyddell and his successors, who built up the Wakehurst estate from 1,000 to 3,100 acres between 1694 and 1748. In Kent the families of Banks, Papillon, Furness, Best, Whatman, and Ward complemented the Surrey families of Child, Lethulier, Bateman, Clayton, and Scawen; while Sussex landowning ranks had been swelled by ironmasters such as Newnham and Jermyn. They came to join the landed aristocracy and close-knit Kentish gentry families, who often boosted their wealth by marriage settlements, as had the Derings and Sondes at various times.[57]

The accumulation of land was aided by the care taken, especially in Kent, to ensure that estates were passed down by settlements and wills, and were no longer partible according to gavelkind. But in cases of intestacy, and particularly among husbandmen and tradespeople, partible inheritance remained and accounted in large part for the fragmented nature of Kentish severalty land, implying subdivision of estates, farms, or even fields. To some extent rights of free alienation in weakly manorialized Kent compensated, and co-heirs made agreements for settlement, sale, or joint working. In Surrey and Sussex inheritance by Borough-English in copyhold tenures survived on 134 Sussex and 28 Surrey manors after 1750, although eighteenth-century custumals may have transcribed outmoded practices. Where mixtures of freehold and assart holdings, both practising primogeniture, occurred with copyhold, it proved difficult, as in the Weald, to engross land. There were large estates here, but farms were generally smaller than on the Downs, which were more prone to amalgamation.[58]

[56] Brandon, thesis, pp. 131–6, 366–81; W. Sussex RO, Goodwood MSS E 4,993; GMR, Losely MSS 603 (I am grateful to Mr More-Molyneux for permission to use this material); S. J. Madge, *The Domesday of Crown Lands*, London, 1938, p. 183; Thompson, *op. cit.*, p. 55; Chalklin, *op. cit.*, p. 19; St John's Coll., MSS box 4/15.

[57] G. E. Mingay, *English Landed Society in the Eighteenth Century*, London, 1963, pp. 61–105; Defoe, *op. cit.*, p. 177; Sir J. Dunlop, *The Pleasant Town of Sevenoaks: A History*, Sevenoaks, 1964, p. 101; Everitt, *Community of Kent*, pp. 27–35; Lord Leconfield, *Sutton and Duncton Manors*, Oxford, 1956, pp. 30–66; G. W. E. Loder, *Wakehurst Place Sussex*, London, 1907; BL, Eg. MS 1,967 522.1 a rental of the manor of Maresfield showing the extensive possessions of the Newnham family by the end of the eighteenth century); Add. MS 34,163 ff. 348, 355.

[58] Gulley, thesis, pp. 160–1; Everitt, *Community of Kent*, p. 47; Chalklin, *op. cit.*, pp. 55–7; Lodge, *op. cit.*, p. XVII; Mingay, *op. cit.*, pp. 28–39; Baker, thesis, pp. 260–1; C. I. Elton, *The

Estates usurped the power of the manorial court, diminished variety of land tenure, and established leasehold as a near-universal landholding system in the south-east by 1750. However, there were marked interregional and inter-manorial differences in the rate of decay of manorial authority. In the Weald and west Kent quit rents, reliefs, and heriots were claimed in the seventeenth century, but rarely in north-east Kent on the archbishop of Canterbury's manors. Courts still met every three weeks at Petworth, but only at Michaelmas in neighbouring Sutton. By 1640 freehold tenure was almost universal in Kent, but moving westwards and south-westwards the proportion of copyholders rose so that in some High Wealden manors the types of tenure were about equal, and included relict assart holdings, whereas on the Surrey and Sussex downland copyhold tenure was prevalent.[59] But by the middle of the seventeenth century many institutional proprietors were using beneficial leases. At Reigate in 1700 there were 20 freeholders and 46 copyholders of over 10 acres, but 22 lessees of demesne land. By 1640 two-thirds of the manor of Littlehampton was leasehold, as were all the substantial enclosed properties at Henfield.[60] The leases themselves were changing. 'Three life' or theoretical 21-year leases could still be found during the mid eighteenth century, but a great range developed, including annual agreements and tenancies-at-will. In Restoration Kent the 7-year lease was popular, reflecting the competition for land, but Surrey leases before 1680 generally ran from 9 to 21 years on the larger estates, and the duke of Bedford's Tooting Bec properties in the 1730s still favoured 21 years or longer. However, many Wealden farmers preferred to hire land from year to year, a practice which persisted, to be roundly condemned by many nineteenth-century writers.[61] Where leases were granted, covenants to safeguard good husbandry were generally included, and the Michaelmas entry and exit facilitated by complex changeover arrangements. Some landowners, such as John Fuller at Brightling, were sceptical or scathing about covenants to maintain good husbandry, "Wch I never yett knew performed by any of them – nor damages recovered when sued, all our country jury's being against landlords". In truth, many tenants were too poor to be so held, but increasingly specific covenants came to include instructions on tree planting;

Tenures of Kent, London, 1867, pp. 365, 382–407; Bailey and Galbraith, 'Field Systems in Surrey', pp. 73–85; Surrey RO, 187/1/14; R. J. Faith, 'Peasant Families and Inheritance Customs in Medieval England', AHR, XIV, 1966, pp. 82–3; G. R. Corner, 'On the Custom of Borough English, as Existing in the County of Sussex', *Sussex Arch. Coll.*, VI, 1853, pp. 164–89.

[59] Chalklin, *op. cit.*, pp. 47–8; H. de Candole, *The Story of Henfield*, Hove, 1947, p. 104; Leconfield, *op. cit.*, p. 3; BL, Eg. MS 1,967 522.1.

[60] Howard, *Finances of St. John's College*, p. 44; Surrey RO, Acc. 792/1/24; Steer, *op. cit.*, p. 2.

[61] Surrey RO, Greenwell MSS 61/5/7; GMR, LM 1,327/16; GLCRO, E/BER/S/E/11/1/2 and 14/1; B. M. Short, 'The Turnover of Tenants on the Ashburnham Estate 1830–1850', *Sussex Arch. Coll.*, CXIII, 1975, pp. 163–6.

the carrying off of produce; the ploughing of meadow land; crop rotations; soil amendments; the sowing of "woad, hemp, flax or other unusable [sic] seed"; and numbers of sheep to be folded.[62]

Improvements in the administration of estates, coupled with the steady progress of enclosure, were keys to greater agricultural output. However, the intensification of production was also being boosted by soil improvement, the use of new grasses and crops, heightened interest in stock breeding, and a keener awareness of the potential of new implements and techniques. Many gentry were well read. Giles Moore of Horsted Keynes purchased in 1667 Blith's *English Improver Improved*, Hartlib's *Legacie*, and Mascall's *Countryman's New Art of Planting*; and Sir Wyndham Knatchbull's Hatch library in 1731 included treatises by Markham, Bradley, and Mortimer.[63] Some farmers and landowners also wrote, and the work of Sir Richard Weston, through the good offices of Hartlib, became well known. Weston acquired a lease on St Leonard's Forest, and by sowing flax, turnips, and clover he hoped to see "the Russet Heath turn'd into greenest grass". Intensive folding and housing of sheep for manure was to be followed by spring denshiring (see below, p. 300) and applications of marl and lime, to give two corn crops followed by good grassland. But by the 1680s all that remained was "a parcell of plaine and arrable land...which is lett for £20", and about 100 acres was "planted...with conyes where noe woods grew". Misapplication of the intensive light land husbandry techniques of Flanders defeated Weston in an area where markets were remote, transport poor, true marl scarce, and imported lime costly, and where local industrial capital dried up. However, as an exponent of watering meadows and as an innovator with clover, Weston had a considerable influence on his neighbours, by, for example, helping to establish dairying in the Wey valley, and he remains a genuine pioneer of agricultural improvement.[64] Less well known was Kentish yeoman Robert Child, from Sutton-at-Hone, whose long tract on the deficiencies of contemporary agriculture formed the bulk of Hartlib's *Legacie* of 1651. William Child, his descendant, farming at Michelham, Sussex, was a foremost breeder of Sussex cattle in the 1760s. Richard Haines was a

[62] J. C. K. Cornwall, 'The Agrarian History of Sussex, 1560–1640', unpub. Univ. of London M.A. thesis, 1953, p. 293; E. Sussex RO, RF 15/25 (letterbooks 14 Jan. 1729 to 24 July 1735 and articles for tenants-at-will); Glynde MSS 3,031–40; Kent AO, Knole MSS U269 E167; Radnor MSS U270 E2, 10; Birmingham Ref. Library, Baker Coll., 11; GLCRO, E/BER/S/E/8/2/4 and 5.

[63] R. Bird, 'The Journal of Giles Moore 1656–1679', *Sussex Rec. Soc.*, LXVIII, 1971, p. 189; Kent AO, Knatchbull MSS U951 E14A.

[64] S. Hartlib, *A Discours of Husbandrie Used in Brabant and Flanders*, 2nd edn, London, 1652, pp. 1–27; PRO, E 134, 36 Chas II, East. 22; Brandon, thesis, pp. 176–7; A. R. Michell, 'Sir Richard Weston and the Spread of Clover Cultivation', AHR, XXII, 1974, p. 160; F. V. Emery, 'The Mechanics of Innovation: Clover Cultivation in Wales before 1750', *J. Hist. Geog.*, II, 1976, pp. 36–7.

Sullington farmer who patented in 1672 an invention for "severing and cleansing the seed called nonsuch trefoyle or hop clover from the huske...a thing never yet attained". This problem had perplexed Weston, but Haines met opposition locally from men who misunderstood his ideas or who thought them not to be new. Indeed, Aubrey cited the husbandmen of Worplesden as having "an art here, not commonly known, of cleansing the seed of sainfoine and clover". Haines's *The Prevention of Poverty* was published in 1674, and ten years later his *Aphorisms upon Making Cyder Royal* explained his new patent method for making cider and contained general advice on small-fruit and orchard management. Little wealth accrued, however, and up until his death in 1685, and afterwards until 1703, his family sold off over 500 acres of farmland on the lower greensand.[65]

A considerable variety of attitudes to improvement may be discerned. At one extreme was the innovative Weston, or William Poole of Hook farm, Chailey, whose farming diary recorded in 1749 the drilling of wheat, rather than "ye randome way", and who was growing potatoes in a close in 1748 – a very early south-eastern example of their cultivation.[66] There were, secondly, landowners who, though not innovators, were concerned to improve and care for their property. In Sussex the Newnhams, Thomas Pelham, and John Ashburnham, "a model of industry and efficiency", may be cited, while the Kentish estate diaries of Twysden, Knatchbull, and Filmer testify to similar care for detail. However, such men did not necessarily welcome innovation. Twysden looked to tradition for guidance, fearing breach with custom, and avoiding novelties.[67] In the Weald, the Fullers of Heathfield diverted little capital from their iron concerns into their estate, and many went further, being frankly uninterested in agriculture, for example the Lovelaces and Walsinghams or the younger Nicholas Toke after 1680, who eschewed stock farming and lived as a country gentleman at Godinton, leasing out his farms. Thomas Pelham-Holles, duke of Newcastle, looked on his Sussex estate as a political lever, residing at Claremont, near Hampton Court, and employing specialists such as Abraham Baley to manage his land. Newcastle admitted whimsically to Lord Kinnoull that "I can be a farmer as well as your Lordship. I have not, I own, the secret of improving my estate, as you have." Finally, there were those who basically exploited their land, such as Sir Edward Graves, leasing St Leonard's Forest after the

[65] K. Child, *Some Account of the Child Family, 1550–1861*, Chichester, 1973, pp. 7–10; Haines, *Memoir of Richard Haines*; Aubrey, *op. cit.*, III, p. 326.

[66] E. Sussex RO, Add. MS 4,461. See also Judith Brent, 'The Pooles of Chailey and Lewes: The Establishment and Influence of a Gentry Family 1732–1779', *Sussex Arch. Coll.*, CXIV, 1976, pp. 76–80.

[67] Worcester, thesis, p. 137; Fletcher, *County Community*, pp. 13–16; Mingay, *op. cit.*, p. 76; Kent AO, Kent Arch. Soc. MSS U 47/47/Z1; Knatchbull MSS U951 F18/1, 2; A15; Filmer MSS U120 E 11–28, A 19; BL, Add. MSS 34,163–7; Univ. of Cambridge Library, Add. MSS 2,825–6; Jessup, *Sir Roger Twysden*, pp. 208–10.

Restoration for warrens, and plundering the remnants of the timber there.[68] Before 1750 many south-eastern landowners, bound up with court, government, and London society, failed to display the enthusiasm which was prominently publicized during the second half of the century, and some of the clearest examples of innovative behaviour can be traced to wealthier tenant farmers, aided by complex networks of local loans and mortgages. Innovative behaviour cannot be entirely explained by wealth, nor by the existence of severalty farming – for Kent displayed no greater speed of adoption overall. Neither were proximity and access to the London market necessarily always a stimulus, for while both fruit and vegetable production undoubtedly expanded, other branches of agriculture in the vale of London were not in the van of progress.

The treatment of soils after 1640 rested on proven techniques but with refinements in the mixtures and amounts applied, and with care enforced in many lease covenants. Greater quantities and wider availability of material were exemplified by the return carriage of the "dunge and noysommes of the cittie" along Thames-side wherever boats could reach on one tide. The best east Kent practice entailed carriage of dung into the fields in summer to a 'mixon' to allow weeds to die, and about Ashford 100 cartloads per acre were spread. Thirty loads was nearer the norm – perhaps more for autumn wheat sowings – but some leases specified considerably less. John Hubble's 1650 Wrotham lease demanded "ten court loads of good well rott dunge". Child stated that ten loads of ordinary dung could be replaced by one load of pigeon's or hen's dung, being useful for wheat "that lyeth a far off, and not easy to be helped".[69] The use of marl is widely documented, although much non-calcareous clay was undoubtedly applied, since the chemical composition was not understood. On the better Wealden 'haisell moulds' deep ploughing was to be followed by 500 loads of marl per acre, or 300 loads on heavy 'marl cope' land, or 500 loads more frequently on sandy and gravelly soils. There were thus many pits serving sometimes one field, although there were large communal pits in the Ashdown Forest. Material was also extracted from the Weald clay: Paludina limestone around Bethersden; the coomb rock and brickearth of the Sussex coastal plain; and true calcareous marl from the scarp foot at Henfield, where blue marl was freely available to tenants.[70] Chalk and lime were brought from the Downs

[68] Worcester, thesis, pp. 125–6; Everitt, *Community of Kent*, pp. 27–8; Lodge, *Account Book*, pp. XXII–XXVII; R. A. Kelch, *Newcastle: A Duke without Money: Thomas Pelham-Holles 1693–1768*, London, 1974, pp. 180, 204–5; Brandon, thesis, p. 176.

[69] McGrath, thesis, p. 197; Royal Soc. MSS, vol. X (3) 28, p. 1; 29, pp. 2–3; J. C. K. Cornwall, 'Agricultural Improvement, 1560–1640', *Sussex Arch. Coll.*, XCVIII, 1960, p. 121; Baker, thesis, p. 134; S. Hartlib, *His Legacie, or An Enlargement of the Discours of Husbandrie Used in Brabant and Flanders*, London, 1651, pp. 43–6.

[70] Marshall, *Southern Counties*, I, p. 349; Gulley, thesis, pp. 135–49; Markham, *Inrichment of the Weald of Kent*; C. Pullein, *Rotherfield*, Tunbridge Wells, 1928, p. 277; de Candole, *op. cit.*, p. 105.

to the heavier acidic clays, and the Northfleet chalk quarries supplied return ballast in vessels which had carried produce to London. Lime was more effective, at a minimum one load per acre in the Weald, or nearer two loads on the cold weeping ground about Ashford, although in east Kent chalk was reckoned "more proper for cold clay than lyme". Chalk was often more economical at ten to twenty loads per acre, since lime had to be burnt and costs of fuel and wages had to be found. In 1657 older residents of Witley and Thursley on the sterile Surrey lower greensand could remember lime first being used at the beginning of the century, and for over twenty years tenants had collected heath from the waste for lime burning. In the deep clays of Capel too, the merits of lime and chalk had recently been discovered in 1649, and whereas corn was previously imported, by mid century they could market wheat, oats, and peas in plenty. By the eighteenth century leases referred to liming, and it was allowed for in tenant valuations. In the eastern High Weald were the Purbeck limestone workings of the earl of Ashburnham, referred to by Young as "the greatest lime burner in England". Grey stone was being dug, burnt, and sold before the better blue stone was discovered in Mountfield in 1779.[71]

Many husbandmen mixed their applications together, and the practice of interchanging one ingredient for another was popular. Markham advocated this for marl and lime in the Weald, and the principle was still followed in the 1760s. Many other materials were applied, including sea ooze, sleech, sand, and seaweed; woollen rags or refuse; ashes, iron slag, and malt dust, depending on the locality. Ferns and brakes were widely used, usually being first laid in winter cattle stalls.[72] By 1640 denshiring was also often combined with soil improvement. Evelyn wrote about Wootton in 1675:

The barren hills, formerly cover'd with a fine carpet of turf, have, within these forty years been excceedingly improv'd by Devonshiring, as we call it, that is, by paring off, drying, burning, and spreading the swath. Formerly they were full of sheep feeding among the wild thyme; now they are sown with corn, and maintain'd in heart with liming, and other manuring.[73]

This technique, with variations in sequence and timing, could be seen at Laughton in 1634–40 where there was reference to breast ploughing, at Lindfield in 1730, at Tudeley in 1745, and at Mayfield in the 1750s; and some

[71] Kalm, *op. cit.*, p. 416; Royal Soc. MSS, vol. x (3), 28, p. 1; 29, p. 2; 30, p. 1; GMR, 70/38/4; Surrey RO, 196/2/1; Kent AO, Knole MSS, U269 E326/1; PRO, E 134, 5 Geo. II, Easter 16; A. Young, 'A Tour in Sussex', in *Annals of Agriculture, XI*, London, 1789, p. 259; E. Sussex RO, Ashburnham MSS, 1,633–9.

[72] Kent AO, Filmer MSS U120 A 19; Gulley, thesis, p. 141; W. Sussex RO, Add. MSS 17,273; Hartlib, *His Legacie*, pp. 44–7; Marshall, *Southern Counties, I*, pp. 85, 374; *II*, pp. 14–15, 55; Banister, *Synopsis*, pp. 38–9; Cornwall, 'Agricultural Improvement', p. 124; Brandon, thesis, pp. 138–40; Surrey RO, Howard of Effingham MSS 63/1/97.

[73] Aubrey, *op. cit.*, *I*, letter of 8 Feb. 1675 (unpaginated). For his comments on this passage, see Marshall, *Review and Abstract, V*, pp. 408–9.

variant of *dencher* was common in Wealden field names, especially around the Ashdown Forest.[74]

Knowledge of grassland management grew significantly during this period, and by 1750 many knew of choices available between the familiar bents and ryegrasses; well-established clovers, sainfoin and trefoil; and perhaps the newer lucerne. Ryegrass was not generally used before 1640, although, like bent, it had long been collected and purchased in hay seed. By the eighteenth century it was being used in clover leys in north and mid Kent and the Weald, and in a 1717 Lewisham lease the tenant was to sow all arable land with "ryegrass, clover or other seeds" four years from the end of his term. On the poorer sands of western Surrey bents were first sown at Send-cum-Ripley in the 1660s, and in 1673 tithe of blackbent grass was demanded. By 1701 nineteen acres were sown, yielding about twenty loads of hay at 15s. per load. Much was sown with clover in the same fashion as ryegrass.[75] Early evidence of successful introduction of clover comes from the Wealden vales, where clovers, often imported via Maidstone, were introduced during the 1640s, to become generally accepted by 1670. On the sands of Surrey and Sussex, in the scarp-foot zone, and in mid Kent this process occurred from 1650 to 1670. At Buckland (Surrey) the accredited innovator was William Stephenson, living at Betchworth and renting land in Buckland, who first grew clover in 1663 or 1664; and a path may be outlined here from knowledge in the 1640s, trials in the 1650s, and limited adoption in the 1660s to widespread acceptance in the 1670s.[76] Thereafter clover cultivation spread to the South Downs, the Petworth district, north-west and east Kent, and the Sussex coastal plain. The Kentish Downs and the London basin were less receptive, for the former still relied on podware on its stony soils and the latter possibly had abundant hay along the Thames. Although Dutch clover was imported throughout the period, by 1690 Kentish seed was being grown for export, and during the eighteenth century many farmers were both buyers and sellers of seed, depending on the season.[77] By 1700 trefoil was also established on the Downs so that sheep

[74] Fletcher, *op. cit.*, pp. 14–15; PRO, E 134, 5 Geo. II, Easter 16; Univ. of Reading Library, KEN 13/1/1; E. Sussex RO, Glynde MS 3,116.

[75] Kerridge, *Agricultural Revolution*, p. 281; Kent AO, Knatchbull MSS U951 F 18/2, A15; Sondes MSS U791 E 91; E. Sussex RO, Ashburnham MSS 1,633; PRO, E 134, 4 Anne, Mich. 7; GMR, Weston Papers 22/1/2; 8R/TR/Y9(2).

[76] Kerridge, *op. cit.*, p. 281; R. Weston, *The Husbandrie of Brabant and Flanders*, London, 1605 (recte 1650), p. 18; Markham, *op. cit.*, p. 13; Lodge, *op. cit.*, pp. xxix–xxx; PRO, E 134, 2/3 Anne, Hil. 3.

[77] Kerridge, *op. cit.*, p. 286; Kent AO, Knatchbull MSS U951 A8; St John's Coll., MSS drawer 75 (55); Dulley, 'People and Homes', p. 168; Banister, *op. cit.*, p. 171; GLCRO, E/BER/S/E/7/4/3; GMR, LM 1,087/1/8, 24. The accounts of Sir Robert Furnesse at Waldershare reveal one difficulty on chalk: "13 March 1713/14 – Pd. 36 stone pickers for 167 days picking the clover £3 18s. 1½d." – Kent AO, U471 A17.

might "eat the grass off very clear", and was being used in Thanet instead of a fallow for a wheat season. Estate accounts from the chalk show bulk purchases of seed, and in a Stalisfield lease of 1722 Henry Wise was bound to leave at least twenty acres "twice ploughed and fit to sow with wheat and clover or trefoil". By 1750 it was ubiquitous on the chalk, although it could make little headway in the acidic claylands. Sainfoin was also a downland grass. Following early trials in the 1650s and 1660s, by Weston among others, it was being grown at Worplesden, Otterden, and East Lenham, and in parts of north Kent in the 1670s. By 1700 it was particularly established on the Kentish Downs. At Eastry in 1708 there were "about 500 acres of sainfoin...and more will be sown every year", and in north-west Kent, Kalm noted in 1748 that "30 years back they had not known so much of it used as now". Around Croydon in the 1720s sainfoin lasted fourteen or fifteen years, supporting large sheep flocks and yielding nearly a load of hay per acre for sale in London. By 1733 lucerne was sown on the Filmer estate at East Sutton, but before 1750 the care necessary in cultivation restricted it largely to the gentry's gardens to provide hay for their horses. The spread from these gardens occurred after 1750, Kalm noting that about Gravesend "some have also now begun to sow lucerne but it is still uncertain how it will succeed".[78]

While techniques in grassland management advanced steadily, the spread of newer root crops was more hesitant. Much of the Weald, London clays, clay-with-flints, and marshland was too heavy for good turnip land, and this crop appeared limited to market gardens, although by the 1670s some adoption by husbandmen in the London basin, due to the presence of gardeners, may be discerned. By 1700 scattered references point to turnip cultivation on the chalk of Kent and Surrey, mid Kent, and the Bagshot sands; and during the first quarter of the eighteenth century the root became more commonplace on these lighter soils and particularly on the larger estates, two of which, Ashtead and Mereworth, had significant East Anglian links. In the Weald a Fletching carrier, Nicholas Birchfield, had $1\frac{1}{2}$ acres of turnips in 1715, but the limited appeal of the root became manifest here after 1750, as also on the Sussex coastal plain.[79] The potato won favour only after 1750, Marshall noting that "until of very late years [it had not] been suffered to stir beyond...the garden, or hopground". Some Irish imports by Lord

[78] J. Lewis, *Isle of Tenet*, pp. 8, 12; R. Arnold, *A Yeoman of Kent*, London, 1949, p. 33; Hartlib, *His Legacie*, pp. 1–3; Kent AO, Sondes MSS U791 E81, 86; Knatchbull MSS U951 A8; account book of Sir Geo. Curtis, Otterden, U442 E4; Filmer MSS U120 A17; Aubrey, *op. cit.*, *III*, p. 326, Kalm, *op. cit.*, pp. 412–14, 439–40; PRO, E 134, 11 Geo. I, Mich. 23; Banister, *op. cit.*, p. 190; Marshall, *Southern Counties*, *I*, p. 153.
[79] Chalklin, *Seventeenth Century Kent*, pp. 86, 89; LPL, 688, and Minet Library 4,583; Lodge, *op. cit.*, pp. xxx, 427; Surrey RO, 212/61/7; GMR, Clayton MSS 84/2/2 and 22/1/2, 3; Kent AO, Fane MS. U282 A5; E. Sussex RO, 1,715/714.

Sheffield in 1765 were planted "by a man who worked on the road" – in the absence of any firmer knowledge, an Irishman, perhaps?[80]

By 1650 both hemp and flax were grown extensively. In east Kent there was "scarce a man but he will have a considerable plot of ground for hempe, and about London far greater quantities of flax is sown than formerly".[81] In Sussex in 1677,

> any indifferent good chalky land from the foot of the Downs to the seaside with double folding or dunging and twice ploughing will produce hemp in abundance, yet, though the land be rich enough and dry, it will not produce good flax; but to supply that, many thousand acres of the Wild of Sussex [i.e. the Weald] will produce crops of flax, some worth £4, some £5, some £6 an acre, and that kind for hemp worth as much.[82]

Grown in adjoining open-field strips as in the hemp plots of Broadwater (West Sussex), or more usually in small closes in the pastoral Wealden and marshland-edge parishes, these crops provided considerable supplementary income, and around Maidstone in the late seventeenth century many provided flax and tow for the thread manufacturers. In the Weald flax was as profitable as barley and oats, but during the eighteenth century leases with restrictive covenants on such exhausting crops as these began to curtail cultivation. Itinerant flaxmen continued to rent ground, often for a single crop, as at Reigate where ground was let in the late seventeenth century "unto one John Martin, a person who dealt in flax...for sowing flax". At Sompting about twenty-seven acres were cultivated in 1720 by John Rowland, who rented land or purchased standing crops to provide materials for his son Thomas, a Horsham flax dresser, and for flax dressers of Steyning and West Tarring.[83] Some other crops were grown on a restricted basis. Around Canterbury and other clothing towns weld was gathered wild or sown among beans, buckwheat, or barley, but much was imported from France by the eighteenth century. Occasional crops of woad were taken at Cobham (Kent) and at Banstead by the mid eighteenth century, and liquorice was grown near Godalming.[84]

There were no concerted improvements in livestock before 1750. Vast

---

[80] Marshall, *Southern Counties*, I, pp. 142–3; A. Young, 'A Tour through Sussex', in *Annals of Agriculture, XXII*, London, 1794, p. 27; R. W. Blencowe, 'Extracts from the Journal and Account Book of the Reverend Giles Moore', *Sussex Arch. Coll.*, I, 1848, p. 97.

[81] Hartlib, *His Legacie*, pp. 40–1.

[82] Weston, *op. cit.*, p. 18. The quotation is from Blencowe, *op. cit.*, p. 76.

[83] BL, Add. MS 39,467; Bird, 'Journal of Giles Moore', pp. 110–15; Alexander Dory died at East Sutton in 1693 leaving "9 dozen of flax and 2 dozen of tow £2 15s. 0d.; yarn £5 17s. 6d.; and a loom 10s." (Kent AO, PRC 11/57/126); Lodge, *op. cit.*, p. 428; PRO, E 134, 7/8 Wm III, Hil. 1; 2 Geo. I, Mich. 8; 7/8 Geo. I, Trin. 2; Kerridge, *op. cit.*, p. 194.

[84] Kalm, *op. cit.*, p. 377–8; Banister, *op. cit.*, pp. 197–8; J. Thirsk, 'Seventeenth-Century Agriculture and Social Change', in Thirsk, ed., *Land, Church and People*, AHR suppl., 1970, pp. 161–2; Arnold, *op. cit.*, p. 33; Brayley, *Topographical History of Surrey, I*, p. 55.

numbers of cattle were driven into the south-east, and many different breeds came to mix with the 'country' or 'rother' beasts. Newly won land was laid directly to grass, and in December 1681 998 cattle passed through the four-day fair at East Grinstead, many going to the large marshland graziers who bought Welsh runts for their supposed hardiness or their fast-fattening properties. Size and colour were major breeding criteria, but many fatteners purchased lean Cheshire, Staffordshire, and Irish cattle when possible and few people with capital interested themselves in the native 'Sussex' or 'Kentish home bred'. Child had noted in 1651 that "we are too negligent in our kine, that we advance not the best species, and better them"; and by 1737 John Fuller of Rosehill in the Sussex Weald, concerned by the neglect of country bullocks, suggested the division of marshland among poorer Wealden tenants prepared to improve native stock, rather than among graziers who imported the majority of their cattle. In 1751 it was reported that Sussex husbandmen's "greatest pride is to be thought connoisseurs in cattle", but the fast-fattening properties and prodigious weights of oxen were treated in no very scientific manner.[85] Neither were there any great strides made in dairy production. Little produce entered marketing channels in the south-east, and quality and output were low and variable. Possibly the 'Dutch' breed, commented upon by Mortimer as filtering into Kent at the beginning of the eighteenth century and being "the best sort of cows for the pail", gave better yields. A little cheese and butter were sold. Giles Moore sold inferior cheese occasionally at under 2d. a pound, but purchased Suffolk and Cheshire cheeses from London for between 2¾d. and 5d. a pound. The cheese press was a ubiquitous feature in the pastoral south-east and the Sussex Low Weald in particular produced large amounts in the eighteenth century. But in northern Surrey Aubrey noted: "they rob their cheese by taking out the butter for London, and they are miserably ignorant as to dairy".[86] Numbers of sheep increased throughout the period, and Faversham was England's leading wool exporting port before 1715, when trade declined so that Rye dominated the south-eastern trade by the 1730s. Romney Marsh wool had become longer and coarser by this time, whereas that from the South Downs was deemed little inferior to the Spanish wool by 1706, from a short-staple fleece of 1½ to 3 lb. Mutton

[85] A. H. John, 'The Course of Agricultural Change, 1660–1760', in L. S. Pressnell, ed., Studies in the Industrial Revolution, London, 1960, p. 149; Cornwall, thesis, pp. 177–8; Child, op. cit., pp. 9–10; E. Sussex RO, RF 15/25 (letter of 26 Dec. 1737); BL, Add. MS 11,571; Defoe, op. cit., pp. 146–7; E. Walford Lloyd, Sussex Cattle, Lewes, 1944, pp. 8–10; Hasted, History of Kent, III, p. 41; Kent AO, Knatchbull MSS U951 A15; E. Turner, 'On the Domestic Habits and Mode of Life of a Sussex Gent.', Sussex Arch. Coll., XXIII, 1871, p. 61. Information on the East Grinstead fair was kindly supplied by Mr M. J. Leppard.

[86] R. Trow-Smith, A History of British Livestock Husbandry, 1700–1900, London, 1959, pp. 203–4; G. E. Fussell, 'Low Countries' Influence on English Farming', EHR, LXXIV, 1959, p. 620; J. Mortimer, The Whole Art of Husbandry, London, 1707, p. 166; Bird, op. cit., pp. 100, 244; Aubrey, op. cit., III, p. 326.

was increasingly sought, such as that from the small Surrey Downs and
heathlands animals, but the Southdown remained unimproved as a mutton
producer before 1750. One hint of experimentation came from the Frewen
estate at Sedlescombe, receiving a Leicestershire ram lamb and five ewe lambs,
probably from the Sapcote branch of the family, in 1673, and presumably
hoping for a heavier animal to market in London.[87]

Increased stocking densities and amounts of grain and hay strained existing
farm buildings and carting facilities. New barns, with regional variation
marked by the late seventeenth century, separate granaries, and more efficient
rectangular brick or timber oasts were being built, together with regional
varieties of waggon and specialist carts for hops, beer, water, or chalk.[88] Some
variant of the turnwrest plough, easily fashioned and repaired, was used
unremittingly throughout the period on all soils, to the chagrin of agricultural
commentators. A heavy double-mouldboard version, with two wheels "as
large as the fore wheels of a moorland waggon", was used throughout Kent
and along the North and South Downs, since it could tackle both chalk
hillsides and heavy, flinty clays. Some older one-way ploughs also persisted,
and on the lighter soils of the Sussex coastal plain and western Surrey horses
pulled one-wheeled ploughs. On heavy Wealden soils a swing plough was
used, lighter and without wheels, and allowing cultivation close to the shaws.
In Thanet it was possible for two horses to pull a plough, whereas on the
east Kent Downs four were used, and six on the heavier clay-with-flints
between Lenham and Faversham. Oxen were used, shod on the Downs and
sometimes on the Kentish greensands, and unshod in the Weald. In the
marshlands too, farmers preferred oxen, although horses became more
popular by the 1740s for the limited amount of work to be done there.[89]
Principles of row culture and drilling were making a little progress, earlier
here perhaps than in any other part of the country. The row culture of beans
was well established by 1650 on the sandy loams of west Surrey and on the
Sussex coastal plain, but by 1750 both beans and peas were still broadcast,
and about Goudhurst "some beans were cultivated, part of which are dibbled
in rows; horse and hand-hoeing are known but by no means practised as

---

[87] Andrews, 'Trade of Faversham', p. 129; Bowden, *Wool Trade*, pp. 34–6; E. Sussex RO,
Frewen MSS 520, 525.

[88] W. Sussex RO, EP1/25/3 (Storrington glebe terrier); J. Armstrong, *A History of Sussex*,
Chichester, 1974, pp. 139–41; Royal Soc. MSS, vol. x (3) 30, p. 3; Kent AO, Waldershare MSS
U471 C5; Knocker MSS U55 T495; Kerridge, *op. cit.*, p. 243; J. G. Jenkins, *The English Farm
Waggon: Origins and Structure*, Newton Abbot, 1972, pp. 10, 157–81.

[89] Royal Soc. MSS, vol. x (3), 28, p. 1; 29, p. 1; 30, p. 1; Turner, *op. cit.*, p. 64; Marshall,
Southern Counties, *I*, p. 59; *II*, p. 405; F. Harrison, 'Sussex Ploughs', *Sussex Notes & Queries*, III,
1928, p. 48; Hall and Russell, *Agriculture and Soils*, p. 22; Young, *General View of Sussex*, p. 56;
Hartlib, *His Legacie*, p. 6; Kalm, *op. cit.*, pp. 400–1; A. E. Swanwick, 'Some Aspects of the
Economic Geography of the Sussex South Downs and Contiguous Land in the Nineteenth
Century', unpub. Univ. of Cambridge M.Sc. thesis, 1953, sheet VIII; Univ. of Cambridge Library,
Add. MS 2,825, ff. 24–39.

in the other side of the county".[90] Horse hoeing was used at Chailey during the late 1740s; was noted in Kent by Ellis prior to 1770; and was certainly in use in Thanet for wheat and barley by the 1790s. Early references exist to "sowing with barley by horse" at Puttenham in 1653; and to a "drill plough" in the inventory of Samuel Hayworth of Richmond in 1697; but most innovations awaited the enthusiasts such as Mark Duckett, the Esher inventor of ploughs, who began farming near Petersham about 1760.[91]

References to water meadows are contained in the works of Markham, Weston, and Twysden. In the Weald they were valued primarily as sources of hay and good fattening ground, where much grassland was otherwise thin and rank. Markham referred to better Wealden pastures "amended by irrigations of flouds, which there is called flowing and over-flowing". Along the western Rother near Petworth, common water meadows were carefully regulated, and they existed also along the Lavant and at Tangmere on the coastal plain. In the Medway's headwaters there were common meadows at Lingfield and Edenbridge, being annually reallocated by 1714, together with meadows at Crowhurst, Oxted, Godstone, and Tandridge. Seventeenth-century examples came from Chiddingstone and the Funk brook at Bletchingly, and it may be significant that Marshall in 1818 noted that formerly irrigation in Surrey "seems to have prevailed more".[92] Water meadows gave rise to many conflicts. On the Twysden estate in the 1630s one tenant complained of lack of water for "flowing, watring or otherwise", and in a 1636 Session of Sewers at Cranbrook, Twysden "spake with Mr. Tuck...and complayned to hym of stopping ye stream to my mylle by hys flowing hys meades wᶜʰ he excused by hys mans negligence and yᵗ he would not doe it but when it might not hynder ye mylle". John Evelyn referred to the streams about Wootton as "naturally full of trouts, but they grow to no bigness, by reason of the frequent draining of the waters to irrigate their lands, etc."[93]

The progress of these innovations was controlled by many interacting factors. Access to the London market was one such factor, and yet many contemporaries criticized husbandmen in the London basin itself for their resistance to change. London or local market prices might also induce change,

---

[90] GMR, Weston papers 22/1/2; BL, Add. MS 39,467, f. 112; G. E. Fussell, *Jethro Tull: His Influence on Mechanised Agriculture*, Reading, 1973, p. 40; Banister, *op. cit.*, p. 118; A. Young, 'A Fortnight's Tour in Kent and Essex', in *Annals of Agriculture*, II, London, 1785, pp. 94–5.

[91] E. Sussex RO, Add. MS 4,461; *Ellis's Husbandry*, II, p. 22; Marshall, *Southern Counties*, II, pp. 37–8; GMR, 51/5/67; LPL, UH96/2,945; Brayley, *op.cit.*, I, p. 55; R. R. Langham-Carter, 'The Duckitt Expedition', *Surrey Arch. Coll.*, LXV, 1968, p. 97.

[92] Markham, *op. cit.*, p. 7; Nash, 'Early Seventeenth-Century Schemes', pp. 37–9; Gulley, thesis, pp. 94–5; Lord Leconfield, *Petworth Manor in the Seventeenth Century*, Oxford, 1954, pp. 25–6, 46–7; Baker, thesis, p. 236; G. Ward, *Sevenoaks Essays*, London, 1931, p. 222; Lambert, *Bletchingly*, p. 13; Marshall, *Review and Abstract*, V, pp. 366, 376.

[93] BL, Add. MS 34,163, ff. 67, 121; Aubrey, *op. cit.*, I, letter from Evelyn, 1675 (unpaginated).

yet all over south-east England there were farmers who were ordinarily self-sufficient and who could almost ignore the market. It has also been argued that those on lighter soils, with greater flexibility of operations, could adjust quicker; yet the chalk and central sandstone uplands in the south-east shared no greater propensity to change than did the medium and heavy soil areas.[94] Interrelated with all these factors was a congerie of social and behavioural relationships which included tenure, inheritance, patterns of landholding, and farm size, together with the attitudes of, and constraints upon, individual farmers and landowners. It is to these relationships that future work might profitably turn to illuminate past work on economic, locational, and ecological determinants of farming behaviour and patterns of change.

Change was very apparent in the rural industries of the south-east. The Wealden cloth and iron industries were declining, though the woodlands continued, despite localized shortages, to furnish many with a more secure living. But generally by 1640 industries were tending to gravitate northwards towards London.

In the London basin more than anywhere else in the south-east, the husbandman could diversify his activities, take extra work, and become a part-time industrial worker or one of the many intermediaries between food production and consumption. The corn mills of the Wandle were joined by copper and dyeing works, and along Thames-side and particularly at Southwark a multitude of semi-rural processing and manufacturing industries proliferated to join older trades such as the basket making of the Thames aits. Shipbuilding, fishing, brewing, tanning, and slaughtering jostled with metal trades and formed an urban industrial scene permeating the remnants of the open fields and paddocks. In north-west Kent paper, metal, lime, brewing, and glass industries were expanding within twenty miles of London. Between the London basin and the fringes of the Low Weald were primary industries such as quarrying of building stone and fuller's earth from the lower greensand of Kent and Surrey; or the manufacture of gunpowder and paper at centres such as Dartford and Faversham, as well as in small rural mills. Around the coast was corn milling near Chichester, and the north Kent copperas industry supplying stones for dyeing, ink manufacture, and the leather industries. Fishing was also combined with farming. Off Thanet labourers fished in their boats between autumn and spring sowings and the summer harvest, and many husbandmen had boat shares. John Grant of Minster in 1665 owned 1/16 of a ketch; Nicholas Sampson of St Peter's, Thanet, in 1717 owned 1/16 of a pink and 1/3 of a fishing boat; and Nathaniel Kemp of Preston, Sussex, owned 1/32 of a galley. Along the Sussex coast shellfish and mullet were greatly reputed, while on the north Kent coast

---

[94] E. L. Jones, 'Agriculture and Economic Growth in England, 1660–1750: Agricultural Change', *J. Ec. Hist.*, xxv, 1965, pp. 1–18.

oysters were a speciality, with their starfish predators used locally for manure.[95]

The centre of Wealden cloth manufacturing had been around Cranbrook and Tenterden, with outworkers stretching into northern Sussex. Local materials had combined in a weakly manorialized pastoral area with extensive commons to attract industry and workers to the eastern Weald. But by 1640 only Tenterden was classed among England's main cloth towns. Interregional competition from centres specializing in New Draperies as well as from the urban clothiers at Sandwich, Canterbury, and Maidstone, together with disputes over timber supplies, export restrictions, and poor communications, all hastened the Wealden decline. Defoe noted that the trade "is now quite decay'd, and scarce ten clothiers left in all the county", for during the first half of the eighteenth century even urban cloth manufacturing and its linked trades fell away, thereby depriving surrounding villages of outwork. The plentiful rural population which had characterized the industry became increasingly prone to unemployment and emigration. By 1676 population density in the Wealden clothmaking area of Kent was still higher than average for the diocese of Canterbury, and there was as strong a nonconformist element as in the urban centres, but in the 1660s half the inhabitants of Cranbrook were too poor to be chargeable to the hearth tax.[96] A contemporary observed:

Tho it sets the poor on work where it finds them, yet it draws still more to the place; and their masters allow wages so mean that they are only preserved from starving whilst they can work; when age, sickness or death comes, themselves, their wives or their children are most commonly left upon the parish; which is the reason why these towns (as in the Weald of Kent) whence the clothing is departed, have fewer poor than they had before.[97]

In Surrey, only Godalming survived through to 1750 making kersies, stockings, and other cloths; and there is little evidence for a continuation of the Chichester kersey and broadcloth manufacture after 1700.[98]

[95] VCH Surrey, II, pp. 254–80, 325–7, 418–20; M. S. Giuseppi, 'The River Wandle in 1610', Surrey Arch. Coll., XXXVII, 1908, pp. 170–91; Chalklin, op. cit., pp. 146–54; VCH Kent, III, pp. 392–9; Melling, Kentish Sources, pp. 114–50; Kent AO, PRC 11/25/79; 11/73/172; E. Sussex RO, 1718/933; R. H. Goodsail, 'Oyster Fisheries on the North Kent Coast', Arch. Cant., LXXX, 1965, p. 119.

[96] Gulley, thesis, pp. 205–11; Chalklin, op. cit., pp. 118–25; Defoe, op. cit., p. 132; C. W. Chalklin, 'The Compton Census of 1676: The Dioceses of Canterbury and Rochester', in A Seventeenth Century Miscellany. Kent Records, XVII, Maidstone, 1960, pp. 172–4; A. Everitt, 'Nonconformity in Country Parishes', in Thirsk, ed., op. cit., pp. 187–9. Many Kentish Wealden families had supplies of kersey, yarn, or "new hempen and flaxen cloth" – Kent AO, PRC 11/9/8; 11/57/45; D/Rb Pi 28/35.

[97] A. Clark, Working Life of Women in the Seventeenth Century, London, 1919, p. 149.

[98] VCH Surrey, II, pp. 346–9; Bowden, op. cit., p. 51; VCH Sussex, II, pp. 256–7. The husband of Mary Toft, the notorious 'rabbit woman' of Godalming, was a journeyman clothier, and

Perhaps more important as a source of Wealden employment was the iron industry. With relatively high demands for ordnance during the mid seventeenth century, the industry was still employing by 1664 something over 1,500 people, falling to nearer 1,000 by 1717. At Heathfield, where the industry was most continuously operative, perhaps half the population was employed in some capacity during favourable periods. Few sectors of society remained untouched by the industry. The families of Dyke, Fuller, Pelham, Sackville, Goring, and Filmer had profited vastly from iron, and there were also many substantial ironmasters, such as the Infields, Paynes, and Mitchells of West Hoathly. Partnerships developed among gentry, ironmasters, and London businessmen, and mills were leased to yeomen as well as to those with capital derived from land or trade. Employees consisted of a nucleus of skilled dynasties of fillers, finers, hammermen, and founders, unskilled assistants, clerks, and twice as many miners, colliers, woodcutters, and carters, many of whom might also be poorer farmers or labourers.[99] Overall, by 1653 at least 35 furnaces and 45 forges were operating, falling to at least 14 and 13 by 1717. By 1788 just 2 Wealden furnaces were left. Here the roads were deteriorating, water power was unreliable, as in the dry season of 1743–4, and temporary local timber shortages increased competition for its use. The pressures varied from one iron works to the next, but with declining ordnance demands and eighteenth-century technical changes, decline was inevitable. The industry resisted longer in the Rother–Brede heartland area, where labour was relatively abundant, than in Wealden Surrey and the western Weald, where labour costs and water shortages destroyed manufacturing. No relationship has been traced between the decline of iron works and deforestation, since both furnace and forge were fed from carefully managed coppice woods which were expanded rather than ruthlessly exploited.[100]

The Wealden woodlands were closely linked with the fortunes of iron, and sales slumped as timber and charcoal demands lessened and as sea coal became more widely used. During the Civil War many woodlands, as in Ashdown and St Leonard's forests, had suffered from depredation and ineffectual management. Planting in the south-east before 1750 was restricted

witnesses called in 1727 to depose on her 'births' included a framework knitter and a weaver (Bodleian Library, Gough MSS, Surrey 15: 18,249).

[99] Worcester, thesis, pp. 53–4; E. R. Straker, *Wealden Iron*, London, 1931, pp. 61–8; Chalklin, *Seventeenth Century Kent*, pp. 134–7; C. E. Brent, thesis, pp. 148–57; Gulley, thesis, p. 190.

[100] C. S. Cattell, 'The Historical Geography of the Wealden Iron Industry', unpub. Univ. of London M.A. thesis, 1973, pp. 190–214; G. Hammersley, 'The Charcoal Iron Industry and its Fuel, 1540–1750', EcHR, 2nd ser., XXVI, 1973, pp. 593–613; H. C. Tomlinson, 'Wealden Gunfounding: An Analysis of its Demise in the Eighteenth Century', EcHR, 2nd ser., XXIX, 1976, pp. 383–93; G. J. Ashworth, 'A Note on the Decline of the Wealden Iron Industry', *Surrey Arch. Coll.*, LXVII, 1970, pp. 61–4; C. E. Brent, thesis, pp. 160–2; Brandon, thesis, pp. 116–29; A. Yarranton, *England's Improvement by Sea and Land*, London, 1677, p. 149; Gulley, thesis, p. 54.

mostly to coppice woodland and ornamental planting in the parklands. Encoppicing was undertaken by ironmasters, if possible within a three- or four-mile radius of their works, and at Ashburnham little change occurred after 1672 in the location of forty to fifty woodland areas – a stability aided by freedom from tithe payments and a low poor-rate assessment on woodland.[101] Elm and oak were conveyed slowly by tug along the miry roads to the Medway, and thence to the naval dockyards at Woolwich and Chatham, northwards to Rotherhithe, or southwards to Shoreham and the Sussex shipbuilding centres. Timber merchants and landowners recognized timber as a valuable crop in the Weald, and employment was guaranteed in faggoting, hedging, cutting, grubbing, cleaving, and carting. A medley of associated by-employments provided fuel and raw materials for craftsmen.[102]

The relationships between rural industry and agriculture were complex. While many were truly complementary, such as the processing of produce by tanners, clothiers, or millers, others were associated either directly, as in implement manufacture, or indirectly and incidentally. Thus much Wealden farmland was treated with marl derived from iron-ore bell pits, or with ashes and cinders from the iron works. A strongly competitive relationship may also be traced in claims for labour, raw materials, water supply, and land and capital. Perhaps the importance of Wealden iron before 1650 helped to account for the agricultural poverty of the High Weald. Certainly furnacemen commanded wages double or triple those of a farm worker, and in 1740 Fuller wrote of the "deleterious effect on the quality and value of land" at Iwood farm, Warbleton, where a succession of tenants had been "done ill or almost broke upon it" since it was "torn about so by drawing of mine".[103] Village craftsmen, tradesmen, carriers, and fishermen could still combine their pursuits with farming, however, and a typical Sussex market town might have about one-quarter of its population directly or indirectly engaged in agriculture, while even at Tunbridge Wells by 1697 farmers owned town lodging houses, and tradesmen farmed on the peripheries, while wives and

[101] Defoe, op. cit., p. 118; Kent AO, PRC 11/82/238; G. E. Mingay, 'Estate Management in Eighteenth-Century Kent', AHR, IV, 1956, p. 110; VCH Sussex, II, pp. 298–9; J. R. Daniel-Tyssen, 'The Parliamentary Surveys of the County of Sussex, AD 1649–1653', Sussex Arch. Coll., XXIII, 1871, pp. 256–68; Brandon, thesis, pp. 117–29; Ashworth, op. cit., p. 62.

[102] VCH Kent, III, pp. 374–7; Gulley, thesis, pp. 55–6; VCH Surrey, II, p. 260; Coleman, Sir John Banks, pp. 176–82; VCH Sussex, II, pp. 233–4; BL, Add. MS 15,776 f. 186; E. L. S. Horsburgh, Bromley, Kent from the Earliest Times to the Present Century, London, 1929, p. 23.

[103] Brandon, thesis, p. 198; C. E. Brent, thesis, p. 150; Cattell, op. cit., p. 157. The competitive nature of the relationship is also evidenced by Marshall, who cites the river Wandle as being calcareous and therefore suited for water meadows, but "the operations of agriculture are liable to be thwarted by those of manufacture" – Marshall, Review and Abstract, V, p. 366.

daughters brought cream, cherries, wheatears, and quails to sell in the daily market.[104]

As opportunities for supplementing agricultural wages became scarcer, many began to look to the growing market towns for employment and apprenticeship. Movements to towns such as Canterbury, Chichester, Farnham, Guildford, and Maidstone effectively entailed a redistribution of a population which grew very little during the period, and constituent regions of the south-east were affected quite differently. Depopulation was a continuous feature of the chalk downland. In east Sussex only eight downland parishes had more than twenty-five households in 1664–5, Hangleton and Sutton being effectively deserted except for the large farmhouse with living-in servants, for the downland was unattractive to migrant labourers. Costs of fuel, and probably food, were high, as wood was imported; there was little waste; few gardens were attached to cottages in this highly cultivated area; and by-employments were scarce. The downland sheep–corn husbandry demanded relatively little labour, for harvests were earlier than those of the Weald, allowing labourers to come out of the Weald after the hay harvest and before the harvest of Wealden cereals and hops. A line of houses with significantly fewer hearths than elsewhere ran in 1664 along the Surrey Downs from Addington, "aunciently...far bigger", westwards to Merrow and Compton, and population densities on the Kent Downs were also noticeably lower, migrants to Canterbury coming from Thanet and the eastern downland as well as from more enclosed parts of Kent.[105] In the coastal marshland the position was similar, with 'lookers' often being the sole employees, and with no common waste and few craft industries. The population of Romney Marsh fell by at least one-third in the century before 1670, for 'lookers' could oversee 500 acres or more and often worked for several graziers. In the 1640s the two easternmost, and smallest, of the lathes of Kent had been the most prosperous, but by 1676 west Kent certainly had the higher population density. Towards London, large villages such as Chislehurst and Eltham had assumed a dormitory aspect, while industries prospered along the lower Thames, and the Medway dockyards employed over 3,000 men by 1704.[106]

[104] Cowley, thesis, pp. 194–5; C. W. Chalklin, 'The Making of Some New Towns c. 1600–1720', in Chalklin and M. A. Havinden, eds., Rural Change and Urban Growth, 1500–1800, London, 1974, p. 234; N. B. Bagenal and B. S. Furneaux, Fruit Growing on the Hastings Beds in Kent, Wye College, 1950, p. 13.

[105] C. E. Brent, thesis, pp. 69–90, 189–209, 227–57, 291–2; Chalklin, Seventeenth Century Kent, pp. 27–35, 254; C. A. F. Meekings, 'Surrey Hearth Tax 1664', Surrey Rec. Soc., XLI, 1940, p. CXXXVIII; Bodleian Library, MSS Top. gen. e 80 f. 1; P. Clark and P. Slack, eds., Crisis and Order in English Towns, 1500–1700, London, 1972, p. 126.

[106] D. Jones, 'Sheep on Romney Marsh', p. 6; Everitt, Community of Kent, pp. 26–8; Chalklin, 'Compton Census', p. 172; D. C. Coleman, 'Naval Dockyards under the Later Stuarts', EcHR, 2nd ser., VI, 1953–4, p. 139.

The other area of higher population density was the Weald. Along the southern and eastern High Weald, into the Tenterden–Cranbrook clothing area, population remained high.[107] Here the remnants of industry lingered, and the family farmer could continue with intricate mixtures of tenures and with access to an area, albeit shrinking, of commonable waste. But to the north and west the land rose up into the forest ridges and the central Wealden heathlands, and although cottagers clung to the forest edges, there was less chance of employment in this relatively remote area. Population densities of the large inner Wealden parishes such as Rotherfield, Frant, Hartfield, or Worth were therefore low. The Weald has correctly been portrayed as a refuge for the poor migrant, but two qualifications need to be made. First, not all parts of the Weald were equally capable of receiving newcomers, for places like Ashburnham and Penhurst were as much dominated by one family as any on the Downs, and were effectively 'close' parishes. Nor could all parts offer the necessary resources; hence, population densities varied considerably over small distances. Dr Burton noted of Shermanbury on the western Weald clay, "how great...the abundance of cattle, but how strange a solitude of men; and indeed, to speak plainly, the nature of the soil seems much better adapted to cattle than to men". Secondly, from about 1600 population growth was low or static for 150 years. However, since the carrying capacity of the Weald was being cut back through industrial decline and the enclosure of waste, great strain was placed on the resources, with consequently high poverty levels and high poor rate. The "tumultuary people" of "very mean and base condition" who set upon Sir Thomas Walsingham near Tonbridge in 1643 were symptomatic of the resultant discontent, also manifest in forest riots, religious radicalism, and a reputation for lawlessness.[108] Abraham Baley wrote to the duke of Newcastle concerning Waldron in January 1763:

I have got a list of about ten poor wretches chiefly women and children that have been pilfering the woods this cold weather and intend having them all before a magistrate at the first proper opportunity and if I can prevail upon the justices to act as they ought shall get several of them whipped, the one man sent to the house of correction but I don't know that anything will be sufficient to keep them honest...they are a parcel of the most distressed and miserable objects I ever saw among the human species.[109]

Wealden poverty can be documented in the fact that 30–40 per cent of the population was exempt from hearth tax, and in the region's low income, shown by the 4s. land tax of 1693, amounting to less than £30 per square mile; this compared with £50 on the scarp foot or coastal plain. It is also

[107] J. H. Cooper, 'A Religious Census of Sussex in 1676', *Sussex Arch. Coll.*, XLV, 1902, pp. 142–8.
[108] W. H. Blaauw, 'Extracts from the *Iter Sussexiense* of Dr. John Burton', *Sussex Arch. Coll.*, VIII, 1856, p. 259; C. Hill, *Change and Continuity in Seventeenth-Century England*, London, 1974, pp. 198–9; *VCH Sussex, II*, p. 201.   [109] E. Sussex RO, HA/310.

exemplified in observations of the East Hoathly shopkeeper, Thomas Turner, in the mid eighteenth century, who noted 8–10 per cent of his parish in receipt of poor relief.[110]

In terms of rural population, few regions could have been less self-contained than the south-east. Harvesters came from East Anglia and Wales, together with drovers, and London labour might be used for hopping. Tramping among poor labourers was constant, and probably increased with regional specialization, despite attempted administrative restrictions, resulting in frequent, though short-lived, epidemics. Competition for employment was fierce. Nicholas Lutman, a Chichester timber hewer, recounted in 1710 that he had been employed as a harvestman or month man for four years at £2 per month at West Wittering, but that in 1707 the bailiff had succeeded in importing cheaper harvest labour from Emsworth. By the mid eighteenth century many larger farmers were importing 'certificate men' at cheaper rates than could be locally obtained, thereby also promoting small-scale migration. Outside the park pale, the symbol of class distinction, agricultural workers lived insecurely among other migrant workers – the iron-ore miners, fuller's earth workers, and charcoal burners.[111]

The rural south-east before 1750 was still an intensely parochial world. Movement was frequent but short-distance, as shown in the average marriage distance of just under four miles for the small parish of West Hoathly between 1674 and 1731. Migration into the larger centre of East Grinstead, with a population of about 1,500 by 1724, came predominantly from within a twenty-mile radius. External events such as those of 1640–60 were mirrored in different levels of taxation, changes of landlord, or the possibility of increased employment in the Wealden iron industry. Free quarter was felt heavily, however, and the Clubman disturbances in the 1650s showed the discontent with plunder, taxation, and indiscipline. Royalist landowners such as the earl of Thanet and Lord Lumley complained of the impoverishment of their estates during the Interregnum, and a parliamentary committee at Arundel complained in 1644 of "the deadness of the times and the malignity of the people, that much land lies waste, and none will use any but at very low rents". For many, however, the disturbances impinged little on the seasonal routine of the countryside. In August 1642 Sandys's parliamentary forces captured ships in the Medway and Upnor Castle, since the garrison men were "most or all of them forth at harvest".[112]

---

[110] Meekings, op. cit., in vols. XLI and XLII; Cowley, thesis, pp. 98–104; D. K. Worcester, The Life and Times of Thomas Turner of East Hoathly, New Haven and London, 1948, p. 47.

[111] Clark and Slack, op. cit., pp. 147–51; Kalm, op. cit., p. 83; C. E. Brent, thesis, pp. 275–9; Chalklin, Seventeenth Century Kent, pp. 38–40; PRO, E 134, 8 Anne, Easter 20; Worcester, Thomas Turner, p. 16; Gulley, thesis, pp. 184–7, 226–7.

[112] W. Sussex RO, Bishop Bower's visitation of 1724, Ep 1/26/3; A. R. Michell, 'Surrey in 1648', Surrey Arch. Coll., LXVII, 1970, pp. 67–83; Sir C. Thomas-Stanford, Sussex in the Great Civil War and the Interregnum, 1642–1660, London, 1910, pp. 124–31, 157, 228–9; Hill, op. cit., pp. 195–9; Jessup, Sir Roger Twysden, pp. 71–88; Everitt, Community of Kent, p. 113.

THE SOUTH AND SOUTH-WEST

CHAPTER 10

THE SOUTH: OXFORDSHIRE, BUCKINGHAMSHIRE, BERKSHIRE, WILTSHIRE, AND HAMPSHIRE

The five counties considered in this chapter covered an area of 5,215 square miles, roughly 10 per cent of the total land surface of England, and they embraced a wide variety of contrasting farming systems. Between the years 1640 and 1750 there was no shortage of contemporary comment on the farming of this area. William Ellis contrasted the farming system of the Vale of Aylesbury with that of the Chiltern Hills, Edward Laurence drew his conclusions on the duty of a steward to his lord largely from his experience in Buckinghamshire, and Robert Plot wrote extensively on the natural history of Oxfordshire. Jethro Tull had much to say about the farming of Berkshire and south Oxfordshire in his treatise on horse-hoeing husbandry, while Aubrey's *Natural History of Wiltshire* was full of agricultural references. John Worlidge based his best-known farming treatise on his observations in Hampshire, and Edward Lisle, also a Hampshire man, produced one of the most valuable farming commentaries of the time. In addition, the region was visited and commented upon by a number of contemporary travellers and writers, such as Celia Fiennes, Daniel Defoe, and Pehr Kalm.

But although the information is there, its interpretation presents some difficulties. It would seem that the best way of overcoming them is to approach the farming history of these counties on a regional basis, delineating and describing each region in turn, and at the same time giving an account of the main farming changes which took place within it between 1640 and 1750. The question of associated rural industries will be dealt with separately, for reasons to be explained later.

The problem of delineating farming regions is always a difficult one, and the temptation to indulge in infinite refinement and subdivision should be resisted, particularly in a study of this nature, which purports to be historical rather than geographical in approach. Therefore, only the major farming regions which may be distinguished with a minimum of controversy at this distance in time have been outlined on the map, which should be consulted in conjunction with the text.

In the northern tip of Oxfordshire we find a region described by Havinden as the "Marlstone Uplands", and also distinguished by Davis and Young

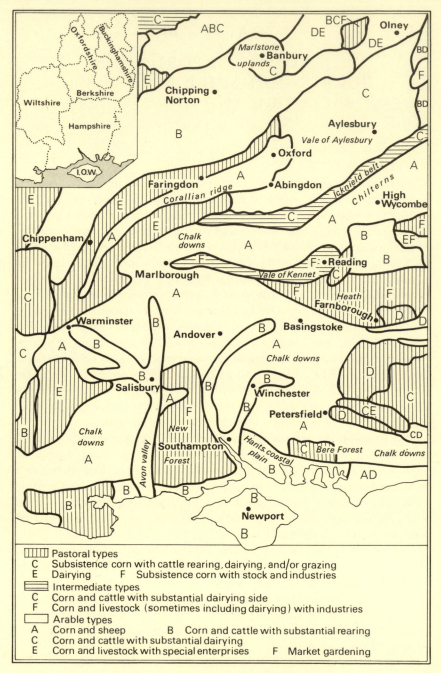

Fig. 10.1. Farming regions of the south.

as the "Northern Corner" and the "Redland District" respectively. Virtually the whole area is underlain by marlstone or ironstone rocks, and soils are chiefly of the red ironstone variety, with some clays of the lower lias in the valleys, and with upper lias outliers forming some of the hills. The red loam soils of this district were extremely fertile, and well suited for either arable or pastoral husbandry. Arthur Young wrote of them, "This red district, in respect of soil, may be considered as the glory of the county. It is deep, round, friable, yet capable of tenacity; and adapted to every plant that can be trusted to it by the industry of the cultivators."[1] In view of this, one might expect the marlstone uplands to have been a mainly arable district, but Davis described them in 1794 as "chiefly strong, deep land, partly arable and partly in a pasture state, appropriated chiefly to the dairy".[2]

Only the meadow and pasture lands of the Cherwell valley appear to have lent themselves naturally to this form of husbandry, but Havinden showed from a study of probate inventories from the area that up to 1730 there was indeed more dairying and livestock rearing in this region than one might have expected from the nature of the soils.[3] There were several reasons for this. First, the fertility of the area had made it one of early and dense settlement, and farms tended to be small, on the old medieval pattern of the virgate or half-virgate, worked in conjunction with the commons. Open-field communities were the rule, and because of the large number of small owner-occupiers in this area, enclosure by agreement was difficult to achieve and the northern corner remained to be enclosed by act of parliament, mainly in the second half of the eighteenth century. It seems likely, however, that enclosure was not the urgent necessity here that it may have been elsewhere. The small farmer was, perforce, a mixed farmer whose first consideration tended to be self-sufficiency. The open arable fields, combined with the commons and wastes for grazing, therefore suited his purposes well enough. After 1660, leys were increasingly used in the open fields to provide additional fodder for livestock, and this lessened the need to enclose land for pasture.[4] At the same time there was little need to enclose in order to extend arable cultivation, for the marketing of grain presented serious problems in this corner of Oxfordshire. The river Cherwell was not navigable by barges between Banbury and Oxford, but Oxford was the nearest marketing centre of any size, and also the nearest centre of population. When it came to marketing, therefore, it was much easier and cheaper to drive livestock on the hoof the twenty miles from Banbury to Oxford than to drag waggons laden with grain the same distance. The marketable surplus of the marlstone

---

[1] A. Young, *General View of the Agriculture of Oxfordshire*, London, 1809, p. 5.

[2] R. Davis, *General View of the Agriculture of the County of Oxford*, London, 1794, p. 7.

[3] M. A. Havinden, 'The Rural Economy of Oxfordshire, 1580–1730', unpub. Univ. of Oxford B.Litt. thesis, 1961, p. 266.

[4] M. A. Havinden, 'Agricultural Progress in Open Field Oxfordshire', AHR, IX, 1961, p. 79.

uplands therefore tended to take the form of livestock or livestock products such as wool and Banbury cheeses which, with their higher value-to-weight ratio, could bear the cost of land transport. But the main export from this area appears to have been beef cattle of the longhorn breed, with some sheep and pigs. This demonstration of how marketing considerations could exercise a stronger influence on farming systems than soil type is an interesting one, which will recur later in this chapter. The point was not lost upon Andrew Yarranton, who urged, among many other things, that the Cherwell should be made navigable from Banbury to Oxford, as part of his plan to increase the nation's cereal supplies.[5] The region was certainly capable of growing much more wheat than marketing circumstances in fact allowed, and, indeed, Havinden did detect some evidence of an increase in the wheat acreage here after 1640, at the expense chiefly of rye and maslin, with barley, peas, and beans holding a constant share of the cultivated acreage.[6] The move towards wheat was probably for the benefit of local consumers rather than for a wider market, however, for, even as late as 1730, the area remained one of classical open-field, small-farm husbandry with what was still basically a peasant economy orientated towards self-sufficiency rather than the national market. The wheat acreage was probably extended, and somewhat heavier stocking was made possible by the growth of fodder crops in some open-field leys, but beyond this there seems to have been little in the way of agricultural change. Havinden commented on the striking lack of enclosure in the area, "save of the small piecemeal variety", and remarked that in 1738 as in 1642 the region remained one of the most densely populated parts of Oxfordshire.[7]

By contrast, the region immediately to the south of the marlstone uplands was one of much more dynamic change, and it is from this area that nearly all of Havinden's examples of agricultural progress in open-field Oxfordshire are taken. It was described by Havinden as the "Limestone Uplands", by Davis as the "Cotswold District", and by Young as the "Stonebrash District". Its chief distinguishing feature from the geological viewpoint is that it is underlain by oolitic limestone, which forms an eastward extension of the Cotswold Hills. This region may be said to extend into the north-western and north-eastern tips of Buckinghamshire, but it steadily loses its distinguishing characteristics towards the east as the underlying oolitic strata dip lower and are increasingly overlain by layers of boulder clay and other heavy deposits of the type that characterise the Vale of Aylesbury. The entire limestone uplands belt is in fact a difficult region to define and describe. It contained a variety of soils, including stonebrash and cornbrash, which shaded

[5] A. Yarranton, *England's Improvement by Sea and Land*, London, 1677, pp. 180–5.

[6] Comparing the period 1584–1638 with 1666–1710, Havinden found, on the basis of a small number of inventories, that wheat's share of the cultivated acreage rose from 7% to 24%, rye and maslin fell from 14% to 2%, and barley's share moved from 49% to 43% – thesis, pp. 273–4.

[7] *Ibid.*, p. 260.

gradually into the generally heavy clay belt of central Buckinghamshire and Oxfordshire. In the west of this region, soils were of the light, reddish, cornbrash variety, similar in some respects to those of the marlstone uplands, but they became less fertile towards the north, and around Chipping Norton the brash was poor and sandy. To the east around Bicester these stonebrash and cornbrash soils became heavier due to a greater admixture of clays, and their fertility improved. Davis described the region as being "in an arable or convertible state",[8] and indeed mixed farming seems to have been the rule, with livestock increasing in importance between 1640 and 1750. It was near the end of this period that the well-known Robert Fowler of Great Rollright, building on the work of Webster of Canley (War.) and Robert Bakewell of Dishley (Leics.), began his breeding experiments in the north-west corner of this mixed farming zone, and the fame which he later achieved testified to the importance attached to livestock breeding by local farmers. Havinden found clear evidence of a marked increase in the numbers of cattle, horses, and pigs being kept on the limestone uplands between 1640 and 1730, and although the proportion of farmers who kept sheep went down, median flock size went up dramatically, so that overall the sheep population too must have increased substantially.[9] Havinden says of this development, "Of course, some of the increase must be ascribed to the effects of enclosure, and particularly piecemeal enclosure within open-field parishes; but as nearly two-thirds of this region was still unenclosed in 1730, it seems reasonable to assume that most of the increase occurred in open-field parishes."[10]

Again, it is the use of leys growing fodder crop in the open fields which appears to have made this heavier stocking possible, but here the practice appears to have been carried out on a much larger and more intensive scale than in the marlstone uplands. Ryegrasses, Dutch clover, trefoils, and lucerne were all introduced after 1660, but by far the most important of the new ley crops appears to have been sainfoin, the deep-rooting legume which is particularly suitable for the thinner, drier soils of limestone country. Some strips in the open fields were consolidated, as at Taston, and used exclusively for sainfoin growing by agreement, although common rights were not extinguished, and the land could revert to other uses. Elsewhere, as at Spelsbury and Fulwell, two or three arable fields were divided into four or six to allow for more flexible rotations and to reduce the area of fallow land.[11]

[8] R. Davis, op. cit., p. 8.

[9] As a selective breeder, Robert Fowler had by 1791 become one of the most celebrated breeders in the country, and his stock was very much in vogue, though it later lost much of its popularity. See W. Marshall, The Rural Economy of the Midland Counties, 2 vols., London, 1790, I, pp. 320–6, and R. Davis, op. cit., p. 23. Havinden found, when comparing the period 1580–1640 with 1690–1730, that the percentage of all farmers studied who kept sheep fell from 66 to 53. But the size of the median flock rose from 14 to 77 – thesis, p. 209.

[10] Havinden, 'Agricultural Progress', p. 80.

[11] Ibid., pp. 78–9, and H. L. Gray, English Field Systems, Cambridge, Mass., 1915, pp. 493–4.

But only in the limestone uplands was Havinden able to show that clover, sainfoin, or lucerne were sown on the new subdivisions. At Sherrington on the marlstone uplands, two fields had evidently been subdivided into four, but only old-established crops were being grown in 1732, with a rotation of wheat, barley, peas and vetches, and fallow. It is possible that the soils of the marlstone uplands were so good and crop yields so high that no innovations were felt to be necessary. Turnips did not figure at all as a ley crop here, and indeed they appear to have been very little grown in any part of Oxfordshire prior to 1730.

As on the marlstone uplands, there appears to have been an increase in the wheat average on the limestone uplands between 1640 and 1750. Havinden suggests a rough doubling of wheat's share of the cultivated acreage in this period, from some 14 per cent to 27 per cent of the total. Pulses too increased their share from 15 to 20 per cent at the expense of barley, down from 60 to 49 per cent, oats, down from 7 to 4 per cent, and rye, which dropped from 4 to disappear altogether.[12] Again, most of these changes must have taken place in the open fields. Yet there was a good deal of enclosure on the limestone uplands between 1640 and 1750, much more than on the marlstone uplands, and more indeed than in the clay vale to the south. This was because there were far fewer occupying owners here than further north, as Gray found from his survey of the land-tax returns from Oxfordshire for 1785.[13] Large estates were also more conspicuous here than on the marlstone uplands,[14] and the two circumstances may have been linked, for there would be a better market here for the land of any freeholder who chose to sell. Many townships had no occupying owners at all by 1785, and this would certainly have facilitated enclosure by agreement among the large landlords.[15] The whole area was less densely settled than the marlstone uplands, and farms seem to have been a good deal larger.

The limestone uplands region also extended into what has been called "Cotswold Wiltshire" in the extreme north-west of that county. Farming systems and patterns of development here were very similar to those of Cotswold Oxfordshire. The soils were again mainly stonebrash and cornbrash with some clays, but in general not deep, with sainfoin featuring again as the key crop. Large estates predominated, with few small freeholders, and the tenant farms tended to be large – from 200 to 1,000 acres in extent, according to Marshall.[16] Two-field systems were more common here than

[12] Havinden, thesis, pp. 199–200.

[13] H. L. Gray, 'Yeoman Farming in Oxfordshire from the Sixteenth Century to the Nineteenth Century', *Qtrly J. Economics*, XXIV, 1910, pp. 302–3.

[14] The evidence for this can still be found on the ground in the form of the large amount of parkland in the area, surrounding once-stately homes. See Ordnance Survey sheet 164.

[15] Gray found a close positive correlation between those townships with no occupying owners and those enclosed before 1755 – 'Yeoman Farming', *loc. cit.*

[16] W. Marshall, *The Rural Economy of Gloucestershire*, 2 vols., Gloucester, 1789, *II*, p. 28.

in limestone Oxfordshire, but enclosure was extensive and even some depopulation occurred in the late seventeenth and early eighteenth centuries.[17] In contrast to the chalk hills of Wiltshire, water meadows were almost completely absent from the Cotswolds, which were deemed "good enough already".[18]

Much larger in area than either the limestone or the marlstone uplands was the great clay vale which thrust itself through central Buckinghamshire and Oxfordshire and on into north-western Berkshire. It represented the most southerly extension of that system of farming most typical of the Midland plain, and the whole region may be conveniently referred to as the clay vale. The most important characteristics of this region are its heavy soils and its poor drainage. The vale represents an outcrop of soft clay strata between the comparatively hard and porous limestone outcrop to the north and the free-draining chalk hills to the south. It consists of clays of the Oxford, Kimmeridge, and Gault formations which in north-eastern Buckinghamshire are overlaid by deposits of glacial drift. Owing to the mixed nature of the deposits in the northern part of the vale, soil types vary widely and, as Priest and Parkinson observed, "there is scarce a single parish where the soil can be characterised by one species of earth".[19]

But James and Malcolm made a more worthwhile comment of general application:

It appears that the county [of Buckinghamshire] is principally composed of rich loam, strong clay and chalk, and loam upon gravel. As to the first, its ability to produce good crops without the assistance of much manure is evident from the uniform verdure of the herbage (as it is chiefly applied to the dairy, farming, and only occasionally mowed) and the very great supply of butter which is produced from that land.[20]

Moving to the south-west of Buckingham, the soils of the vale retain their varied character, for here isolated outcrops of Portland and Purbeck limestone form islands in the clay, as at Quainton Hill and at Brill, and the alkaline downwash from these hills has an ameliorating effect on the surrounding clays. Further to the south-west, the clay vale narrows as it is squeezed between the Berkshire downs and the Cotswolds, and just north-east of Oxford it begins to be bisected by an outcrop of corallian limestone and grit, which continues to divide the vale as it runs on through north-western

---

[17] VCH Wilts., IV, pp. 46–7.

[18] T. Davis, General View of the Agriculture of the County of Wilts., London, 1794, p. 125.

[19] St J. Priest, General View of the Agriculture of Buckinghamshire, London, 1813, p. 13. One should, however, perhaps distinguish the sandy outcrop in the Wavendon–Brickhill–Soulbury region, an intrusion into eastern Buckinghamshire of the lower greensand soils which covered a large area of adjacent Bedfordshire.

[20] W. James and J. Malcolm, General View of the Agriculture of the County of Buckingham, London, 1794, p. 8.

Berkshire to merge into the dairying area of north-eastern Wiltshire. But the limits of the great clay vale and the farming systems which typify it should probably be drawn somewhere around the middle of the Vale of Whitehorse, for the western portion of this vale can be shown to be very clearly a dairying region, in contrast to the mixed farming of its eastern half.

Dairying was, of course, an important activity throughout the vale. North of Watling Street there appears to have been a rather higher proportion of arable land, with more emphasis on dairying towards the north-west. But throughout the vale the small, open-field farms which predominated everywhere grew some wheat and barley, much of it for export to London,[21] and also raised beef cattle and sheep, the latter for mutton and lamb rather than for wool or the fold. As mentioned earlier, the small, open-field farmer was perforce a mixed farmer, and in the clay vale it appeared that substantial arable crops could be harvested from the rich, heavy soils with little expenditure on manure, although traction costs were presumably high.[22] As on the marlstone uplands of Oxfordshire, there appears to have been little enclosure in the clay vale between 1640 and 1740, and presumably for the same reasons – open-field farming worked well enough.[23] Such enclosure as there was seems to have been for the purpose of increasing the acreage under grass rather than facilitating the introduction of new crops or arable rotations.[24] With the increase in the area under grass came heavier stocking, and this feature at least the clay vale shared in common with the marlstone and limestone uplands. Sheep were the animals most affected. In the Vale of Oxford, the proportion of farmers keeping sheep fell from 50 per cent before 1640 to 45 per cent in the early eighteenth century, but the size of flocks again rose dramatically, from a median of seventeen sheep before 1640 to a median of fifty-two by 1730, according to the surviving evidence from probate inventories.[25] Cattle too seem to have become more numerous in the vale between 1640 and 1730, but there is no evidence of a corresponding rise in the numbers of pigs kept, and the spread of horses remained slow. As regards arable crops, the wheat acreage increased along with that of beans and peas, at the expense of barley, oats, and rye, although this change was

[21] Havinden, 'Agricultural Progress', pp. 73, 81.

[22] For an interesting discussion of these points, see Priest, *op. cit.*, p. 97.

[23] "The strength and stability which open-field farming was able to maintain in the Vale in this period was partly the result of economic and geographical conditions. The soils were more suited to arable farming than those on the Uplands, but this was probably a less important factor than superior communications" – Havinden, thesis, p. 217.

[24] *Ibid.*, pp. 227–8. See also M. E. Turner, 'Some Social and Economic Considerations of Parliamentary Enclosure in Buckinghamshire', unpub. Univ. of Sheffield Ph.D. thesis, 1973, p. 18. Turner noted that by 1750 only 35% of Buckinghamshire remained unenclosed, but the bulk of the open-field areas must have been concentrated in the clay vale.

[25] Havinden, thesis, p. 231.

less pronounced here than on the limestone uplands.[26] The use of such enclosure as there was to increase the area under pasture may have been associated with the spread of convertible husbandry in the vale between 1640 and 1750. William Ellis certainly believed that there had been a recent dramatic rise in the output of the vale,[27] which may have been achieved by the adoption of convertible methods, but Havinden sounded a cautionary note by pointing out that only 17 per cent of farmers' probate inventories from the vale drawn up between 1690 and 1730 showed that the deceased had owned a farm waggon. This has to be compared with a 40 per cent rate of waggon ownership in the limestone uplands. Havinden associated the spread of waggon owning with heavier cereal cropping, and if this point is valid it would suggest a lower increase in arable productivity in the vale than on the limestone uplands.[28]

A further point of interest relates to the question of enclosures and farm sizes. H. L. Gray found that in 1785 the Vale of Oxford was a curious mixture of parishes which contained no occupying owners, and which had for the most part been enclosed before 1755, and parishes with a high proportion of occupying owners, which were among the very last to be enclosed in Oxfordshire. Gray later suggested that this was because the Vale of Oxford had moved from a two-field to a three-field system in the open villages during the thirteenth and fourteenth centuries. This system was an improvement over the old two-field arrangement which lingered on the limestone and marlstone uplands, and it continued to prove satisfactory throughout the seventeenth and early eighteenth centuries when the northern villages of Oxfordshire at last began to subdivide their fields, not into three, but now into four or more. This provided an impetus to change in the north which carried through into full-scale enclosure in the later eighteenth century, while it was well into the nineteenth century before the open-field communities in the vale were persuaded to follow suit.[29] In this respect, as in others, it appears that the lighter-soiled northern uplands of Oxfordshire overtook the vale in terms of agricultural progress in the later seventeenth and early eighteenth centuries.

One drawback from which the vale may have suffered was its higher density of population, especially in the open-field parishes.[30] Many of the inhabitants of open-field villages were poor tenants or squatters who relied heavily on the commons, and this could create great difficulties when

---

[26] *Ibid.*, pp. 234–40. Wheat's share of the cultivated acreage in the vale moved from 25% prior to 1640 to average 32% between 1690 and 1732. Its gain was at the expense of rye, oats, and barley, but peas and beans also increased their share, from 21% to 29%.

[27] W. Ellis, *Chiltern and Vale Farming Explained*, London, 1733, Preface, p. 2.

[28] Havinden, thesis, p. 242.   [29] Gray, *English Field Systems*, pp. 113–31.

[30] By 1738 the median number of houses in open-field villages within the vale was 50, but in the enclosed villages it was only 15 – Havinden, thesis, p. 220.

enclosure was attempted, as in the famous case of Otmoor. Indeed, population pressure appears to have had the effect of slightly reducing the average size of farms in the Vale of Oxford after 1660. Detailed surveys of nine manors in the Vale of Oxford, taken between 1606 and 1650, showed that holdings of over 20 acres occupied 91.9 per cent of the entire surveyed acreage of 13,232 acres. The average size of farms of over 20 acres was 75 acres, and a numerical majority of holdings were in fact of more than 20 acres – 162 as against 134 of under 20 acres. Surveys of ten different manors within the vale, taken in 1728, showed that 90.6 per cent of the surveyed acreage still lay in farms of over 20 acres. But a small majority of all holdings were now in the under-20-acre range – 115 as against 112. Moreover, the average size of farms of over 20 acres had dropped from 75 acres to 69.3 acres.[31] A variety of open-field and enclosed parishes were included in the surveys, and their geographical spread was wide, but the statistical basis of the sample was small. Perhaps the only conclusion that may safely be drawn is that farms in the Vale of Oxford do not appear to have been growing larger, and may even have become slightly smaller on average between 1640 and 1750.

Before leaving the clay vale, one further distinctive feature must be noticed. This is the so-called Icknield belt, a narrow but definable line of fertile greensand loams which runs along the base of the Chiltern Hills, just north-west of the Icknield Way,[32] and on into the Vale of Whitehorse. In general, this belt is only a mile or two in width, but it broadens between Marsworth and Edlesborough in Buckinghamshire, and at the eastern end of the Vale of Whitehorse. Where the belt is broad enough to embrace whole communities, as at Edlesborough or Didcot in Berkshire, a pattern of settlement similar to that of the rich marlstone uplands of Oxfordshire was established. Settlement was early and dense, and by the eighteenth century a high proportion of small peasant freeholders working open fields could be found in these regions. Enclosure had to await parliamentary processes. Farming systems here were not conspicuously different from those in the rest of the vale, but returns were higher, owing to the exceptional fertility of the loamy soils. Medieval Cuxham, for example, consistently enjoyed higher seed–yield ratios than were normal elsewhere in fourteenth-century England.[33]

We come next to the Chiltern Hills. The hills themselves are of course a chalk outcrop, but the soils which overlie them are the result of glacial deposits, and despite the well-drained and alkaline strata on which they lie, the soils themselves tend to be acid, and may be greatly improved by

[31] Calculations based on figures provided by *ibid.*, pp. 83–4, 223–4.

[32] See W. Marshall, *Review and Abstract of the County Reports to the Board of Agriculture*, 5 vols., York, 1808–17, *IV*, p. 512.

[33] P. D. A. Harvey, *A Medieval Oxfordshire Village: Cuxham, 1240–1400*, Oxford, 1965, p. 58.

applications of lime and chalk. In the south, a clay-with-flints soil predominates, and in Buckinghamshire there is a superficial cover of red loam and clay which makes good sheep and fair barley land. Indeed, authorities are agreed in designating the Chilterns as a 'sheep–corn husbandry region', but a qualifying note, sounded a few years ago by E. L. Jones, ought to be reiterated here: "The past farming systems of light-soiled districts are often described as 'sheep and corn'. The term does not reveal the changes which took place at various times in the exact objects of sheep and grain production and in the relative importance of the two groups of products."[34]

We should, warned Jones, "stress the inadequacy of 'sheep and corn' for describing farming systems which changed in essentials over time". There were, of course, also spatial differences. Several of the areas dealt with in this chapter are officially described as 'sheep-and-corn': the limestone uplands of Buckinghamshire, Oxfordshire, and Wiltshire, the Chiltern Hills, the corallian ridge, and the downlands of Hampshire, Wiltshire, and Berkshire. Yet each region had its very distinctive features, and all were different again from the sheep–corn region of Norfolk, to give only one example.[35] One distinctive feature of the Chiltern economy was the emphasis on timber growing, particularly in the south-west, and along the thin-soiled scarp slope of the hills. The coppice-wood industry flourished here, and sizeable quantities of tanning bark, in addition to beechwood timber, were exported. Henley-on-Thames was the chief port of embarkation for these timber products, which included a good deal of firewood and were mostly bound for London.[36] In the Chilterns, moreover, the sheep–corn balance was tilted decisively in favour of corn. Over the period 1640 to 1750, this emphasis on cereals became even heavier in the south-west, but it may have eased slightly in the north-east. Between 1640 and 1729, in common with the rest of the country, cultivation of rye and maslin in the Oxfordshire Chilterns declined sharply, from about 14 per cent to about 5 per cent of the cultivated acreage. The share of oats also fell, from 21 to 11 per cent, but wheat's share rose from 19 to 34 per cent and barley too showed a slight increase, from 32 to 34 per cent. At the same time, fewer farmers kept sheep after 1660 than before, and flock sizes did not increase significantly. This was probably due in part to a falling demand for wool from the declining Berkshire cloth industry. But the lost sheep dung was more than replaced by much heavier applications of lime and chalk, often carted considerable distances, a notable

[34] E. L. Jones, 'Eighteenth-Century Changes in Hampshire Chalkland Farming', AHR, VIII, 1, 1960, p. 5.

[35] See K. J. Allison, 'The Sheep–Corn Husbandry of Norfolk in the Sixteenth and Seventeenth Centuries', AHR, V, 1, 1957, pp. 12–30.

[36] Mathew Crockford of Caversham, who died in 1723, left very specific instructions in his will for the future care of his beechwoods, which were clearly a most valuable asset – Dorothy McLaren, 'Stuart Caversham: A Thames-side Community', unpub. Univ. of Reading Ph.D. thesis, 1975, Appendix, p. 26.

feature of arable farming in south Oxfordshire after 1660.[37] Only 6 per cent of a sample of 66 farmers kept more than ten cattle, as opposed to 19 per cent of 173 farmers on the limestone uplands. Nor do south Chiltern farmers appear any longer to have shown much interest in pig rearing, despite the ready availability of beech mast.[38] Unfortunately, no detailed study of farming in the Buckinghamshire Chilterns has been made,[39] but the south-west of this range may be contrasted with the north-east. In the north-east there is some evidence to suggest that the wheat acreage may have declined between 1640 and 1750, to be replaced by fodder crops to enable heavier stocking.[40] Why this interesting contrast? The Hertfordshire Chilterns were no further from central London than those of Oxfordshire. The answer surely lies in the Thames waterway. It was always much cheaper to move arable produce by water than by land, and no better market to move it to than London. As with the marlstone uplands, marketing considerations proved more important than soil type in determining the nature of agricultural output. Even in a period of falling grain prices, it may still have paid south Chiltern farmers to increase their wheat acreage, for reasons that will be discussed later.

Certainly changes occurred in Chiltern farming over the period 1640 to 1750, but these changes ought not to be overdramatized. In 1750 we still have a recognizable sheep–corn system, with the emphasis heavily on corn, at both ends of the Chiltern Hills. Turnip husbandry was not widely adopted before 1730,[41] and little enclosure took place in old-established open-field communities such as east Caversham. The enclosure that did take place was mainly enclosure from the wastes, usually comprising intakes from beech woods which were turned to arable farming.[42] Clover and sainfoin growing also increased on erstwhile fallow, but apparently not to any great extent.[43] Average farm sizes in the Chilterns were rather larger than those in the vale, mainly because the poorer Chiltern soils required a larger area to yield a product comparable to that of a viable mixed farm on the heavier and richer soils of the Vale of Aylesbury.

[37] Ellis, *op. cit.*, pp. 24–9, 393–6. McLaren noted that surviving inventories from south Oxfordshire in the later seventeenth century showed that "more capital was invested in horses than in cattle" for the hauling of grain, malt, and lime – thesis, p. 121. See also Appendix to thesis, map 1, showing seventeenth-century chalk pits and lime kilns in south Oxfordshire.

[38] Havinden, thesis, pp. 208–9, 256–8.

[39] A vivid description of farming in the central Chilterns is, however, provided by Pehr Kalm's *Account of his Visit to England on his Way to America in 1748*, ed. J. Lucas, London, 1892, pp. 178–342. He also has some scathing and amusing remarks to make about the farming abilities of William Ellis.

[40] E. G. Longman, 'Agrarian Change in South-West Hertfordshire, 1600–1850', unpub. Univ. of London M.Sc. thesis, 1972, p. 94.   [41] Havinden, thesis, p. 254.

[42] Tithable acreages in the north-eastern Chilterns increased by as much as 80% in some parishes between 1670 and 1700 – Longman, thesis, pp. 42–5.

[43] Havinden, thesis, pp. 254–5.

The Chilterns make an interesting comparison, or rather contrast, with an adjacent system of 'sheep–corn' husbandry, that of the great chalk Downs of Wessex. By far the largest farming area under consideration in this chapter, it included the Marlborough Downs, the Berkshire Downs, the Hampshire Downs, and Salisbury Plain. Over such a wide area, soil types necessarily varied to a considerable extent, and only the most broad generalizations can be made. The most common description applied to downland soils is 'clay-with-flints' although this term is misleading, for such soils usually turn out to be loams or clay-loams, and not clay soils. Their depth varied from a few feet to a few inches, and they were usually, though not always, acid soils. They tended to be thin, and deficient in lime and potash, but if carefully manured could prove fertile enough for arable crops. These Downs are usually regarded as the sheep–corn country *par excellence*, with the fold as the sheet anchor of arable husbandry, and certainly sheep did play a much more important part in the farming economy here than on either the limestone uplands or the Chilterns. Here sheep were specially selected not for their propensity to yield mutton or wool, but for their folding qualities. Over the centuries prolonged selection had given rise to the distinctive Wiltshire and Hampshire breeds, and to a Berkshire strain known as the Berkshire Nott.[44] These animals were large, lanky, and hardy, producing a thin but fine fleece and a small quantity of sweet mutton. Their great advantage was that they were able to range the Downs all day, and had a propensity to drop their dung and urine at night, when penned in the fold. They required little water, taking most of what they needed from the grass they grazed, and this too was an important advantage on the bare, open Downs where streams and wells were few and far between.[45]

The importance of the sheepfold to arable farming in this region has been well illustrated by Kerridge, who stressed the role of water meadows in facilitating the heavier stocking of sheep after 1640.[46] There was, indeed, a great boom in the construction of water meadows on the Downs between 1640 and 1750. In many cases, enclosure by agreement would be accompanied by a simultaneous agreement among local residents to co-operate in the construction of a communal water meadow.[47] The chief advantage of the

[44] W. Mavor, *General View of the Agriculture of Berkshire*, London, 1809, p. 382 n. 1: "The Southdowns...have several advantages over the native Berkshires; but it is impossible they could walk without injury the six or seven miles every day to and from the fold to the pasture, as is necessary among the White Horse hills."

[45] H. P. Moon and F. H. W. Green, *Hampshire*, Land Utilization Survey 89, London, 1940, p. 304.

[46] E. Kerridge, 'The Sheepfold in Wiltshire and the Floating of the Water Meadows', EcHR, 2nd ser., VI, 1954, pp. 282–9. On the timing of the introduction of water meadows into this area, see T & C, p. 178.

[47] E.g. at Beenham in Berkshire in 1713 – Berks. RO, D/EAL/E4/1–3; and at Ramsbury in Wiltshire in 1727 – *ibid.*, D/EBU/E9.

water meadows was that they yielded a vital early bite of grass to the sheep and lambs in the "hungry gap" of April, after winter hay stocks were exhausted, but before the natural grass came on. Water meadows could also be mowed two or three times a year, thus yielding more heavily than dry meadows. But it should be remembered that these meadows could be constructed only where suitable streams were available: the villagers of Beenham, near the river Kennet, were lucky, but many Downs farmers found themselves in the same position as Edward Lisle at Crux Easton, far from any convenient streams. In his case, the new crops came to the rescue, and he fell back on hop clover, ryegrass, sainfoin, and turnips to overwinter his stock. Even so, he found that fodder was in short supply, and it was difficult for him to overwinter cattle as well as sheep.[48] Lisle would certainly have found a water meadow beneficial, but perhaps of only marginal benefit. Water meadows were usually comparatively small: even communal meadows very rarely exceeded 50 acres in extent. For example, in 1728 the manor of Stoke Charity in Hampshire covered 2,000 acres, of which 40 acres consisted of water meadows, some 2 per cent of the whole.[49] New Barn farm at Compton had its own water meadows, but they covered only 11 of the farm's 294 acres, less than 4 per cent of the whole.[50] The largest relative area of water meadow was found on the farm of Edward Smith at West Kennet near Marlborough. In 1743 he had 200 acres of arable land, 120 acres of down grazing, 7 acres of dry meadow, and 27 acres of water meadow, less than 8 per cent of his 354 acres, but an exceptionally high proportion.[51] Moreover, only the valleys of the larger streams were suitable for water-meadow construction.[52] The whole process was difficult and expensive, requiring ideal conditions of gradient and water flow to ensure an adequate and regular return from a very heavy investment. Thomas Davis put the cost of a properly constructed water meadow at between £12 and £20 per acre, with the watered land subsequently tripling in annual value.[53] Those farmers who could afford to build their own water meadows, as distinct from those who merely participated in a communal scheme, were the largest in Wessex, which is to say that they were among the richest arable farmers to be found in any part of the country. These qualifying factors may lead one to wonder whether water meadows were in fact such a crucial element in the faming economy

[48] E. Lisle, *Observations in Husbandry*, 2nd edn, London, 1757, pp. 229–39, 263.

[49] Hants. RO, 18M 54/coffer 4 pkt E bdle B.

[50] Hants. RO, 18M 54/coffer 6 box H.

[51] Bristol RO, AC/WO 5(57)a.

[52] T. Davis, *op. cit.*, p. 34: "Supposed Quantity of Water-Meadows in this District:– The number of acres…has been computed, and with a tolerable degree of accuracy to be between 15 and 20,000 acres." See also map following p. 268 of 1813 edn. But the total area of Wiltshire was 860,000 acres.

[53] Moon and Green, *Hampshire*, App. II, 'Water Meadows in Southern England', pp. 373–90. Also T. Davis, *op. cit.*, pp. 30–8.

even on the Downs, while their importance nationally was of course far less: outside of Wessex and the west Midlands they were very rare indeed.[54] In Wessex their importance depended to some extent on whether the accent was on arable farming, as in the river valleys, or on livestock rearing, as in the case of Edward Lisle. The water meadows were probably of more importance to the former category of farmer than the latter. They did, moreover, constitute a real and tangible improvement in farming practice, and a much heavier reliance on the water meadows was another factor which distinguished farming on the Downs from the sheep–corn systems of the Chilterns or the limestone uplands, where watered meadows were extremely unusual.

The construction of water meadows was not the only improvement adopted by downland farmers after 1640. They also took eagerly to the new crops, hop clover, broad clover, sainfoin, ryegrass, and turnips.[55] Of these, turnips were probably the least important, certainly prior to 1730, and this raises the whole question of the importance of turnip husbandry. The low nutritional value of turnips by comparison with clover or barley straw is well known, but if properly hoed they could serve as a very useful fallow crop on lighter soils. They left a clean, well–rested, and well–stirred fallow field, and provided the bonus of a fodder crop, which on dry soils need not even have been harvested, but could have been fed off. However, the scale of turnip growing prior to 1730 suggests that they were regarded mainly as a catch crop to be raised on odd pieces of fallow land, often without proper hoeing. There is no firm evidence to show that they were a regular course in established rotations in this area prior to 1730. Turnip crops of up to fifteen acres in extent were grown before this date,[56] but these acreages were exceptionally large. Most turnip patches were of under five acres. However, there appears to have been a great upsurge in the popularity of turnip growing in southern England between 1730 and 1750,[57] and by 1760 there

---

[54] In most other parts of the country expensive floating was quite unnecessary and sometimes even harmful. James and Malcolm observed: "One very respectable gentleman farmer in the Vale of Aylesbury assures us (and this was confirmed by others) that their meadows were by nature so rich that watering, as it is practised in other countries, made their crops of grass so rank and coarse that two acres of their natural meadow grass, not watered, though less in quantity, was superior in quality; and worth more than two acres and a half of similar quality of meadow in a watered state" – op. cit., p. 18.

[55] G. E. Fussell declared that Hampshire "compares very favourably with the most famous innovating county, Norfolk. All the new crops were grown in Hampshire, and they appear to have been well established by Queen Anne's reign. This is quite as early as Norfolk and distinctly a feather in the cap of North Hampshire farmers of that time" – 'Four Centuries of Farming Systems in Hampshire, 1500–1900', *Hants. Field Club & Arch. Soc.*, XVII, 3, 1949, p. 273.

[56] E.g. 15 acres of turnips grown at Duns Tew, Oxon., in 1691 – Oxon. RO, Dash. x/xiii/5; and 13 acres of turnips grown at Padworth, Berks., in 1720 – Bodleian Library, MS Oxford, Arch. Papers Berks. c 150 ff. 158–9.

[57] E.g. John Grove of Wraysbury, Bucks., clearly an arable farmer, had 31 acres of turnips

is firm evidence that turnips were an established part of some rotations, even in the open fields. Many rotation agreements made between open-field farmers specifically mention turnips as one desirable course.[58]

As regards patterns of landownership, it would appear that here on the Downs, as on the limestone uplands, between 1640 and 1750 the great estates tended to grow at the expense of the small landowners. Even small tenants found it difficult to survive, and farms tended to grow larger as, in the words of Kerridge, the "family farmer" was replaced by the "capitalist farmer", and employer of landless labourers.[59] As in other parts of the country, short leases and annual tenancies were increasingly favoured by landlords from the end of the seventeenth century onwards, giving them more opportunity to profit from favourable price movements at their tenants' expense. The large, efficient capitalist farmers could carry these rent increases, but they bore very heavily on the small farmer, more so after 1750.[60] Elsewhere, as in the clay vale or the dairying area of north-west Wiltshire, the small family farmer appears to have survived much more successfully, at least up to 1750. The small farms of north-west Wiltshire were usually enclosed, and the manorial structure here was weak. In this respect they were more 'advanced' than the downlands, but on the other hand, because of the nature of their soils, they did not adopt floating or even, to any significant extent, the new crops. This led Kerridge to conclude that it was "the manorialized, champion, sheep-and-corn countries – the Chalk, Cotswold and Corallian countries – which were the main field for the development of agrarian capitalism and for the agricultural revolution".[61]

It may appear to be something of a paradox that Kerridge should single out an open-field area as one of conspicuous agricultural progress in contrast to an adjacent area of early enclosure where there was little agricultural change, but the distinction can be justified. First, there was little point in enclosing much of the rolling, high Downs which could never be used for more than rough pasture in any case because of limitations in the supply of fertilizing agents prior to 1750. Hence the high Downs remained 'open' in the literal sense. Secondly, a good deal of the arable land in some parts of

in 1742 – Berks. RO, D/ED/E4B/2; and a farm at Stoke Charity, Hants., had 30 acres of turnips in 1744 – Hants. RO, 18M/54/coffer 4 pkt E bdle A. In 1740 the landlord William Heath wrote to his agent Robert Cropp at Stoke Charity, "I have no objection to the planting of 100 acres of turnips, since you say it will be of great service to the sheep and will encourage new tenants" – Hants. RO, 27M/54/3. See also Pehr Kalm's accounts of turnip growing in the Chilterns in 1748 – *op. cit.*, pp. 217, 230–1, 441.

[58] E.g. 1757 agreement at Ashbury, Berks. – Berks. RO, D/EC/E20/1; 1763 agreement at South Weston, Oxon. – Oxon. RO, Hedges Collection, HeII/v/8; 1765 agreement at Lewknor, Oxon. – Hedges Collection, HeVI/4.

[59] *VCH Wilts.*, IV, 1959, pp. 58–64. Kerridge says of Salisbury Plain, "By the last few decades of the eighteenth century, the liquidation of the class of family farmers was very nearly complete."

[60] *Ibid.*, pp. 60–3.

[61] *Ibid.*, p. 64.

the Downs, mainly along the river valleys, was already enclosed by 1750. Enclosure by agreement had been going on steadily since 1640,[62] although the Downs were still a long way behind the dairy regions in this respect. Finally, Kerridge showed how a process of "creeping enclosure" could operate in many nominally open-field villages by such means as the consolidation of strips and the institution of Lammas lands. He showed that open-field land could be held in severalty, and that on the other hand not all enclosed land need be free from common rights.[63] Thus many villages on the Downs which were technically open-field villages with a strong manorial structure could still enjoy many of the benefits of enclosure. But the large farmer still held the advantage. For example, when it came to folding sheep, "a private flock could hardly be less than about 400, because great numbers had to be concentrated in the fold on the arable".[64]

Between 1640 and 1750, however, an increasingly heavy emphasis was laid on corn within the downland sheep-and-corn system, while sheep diminished in importance. The sheepfold remained what it had always been, the sheet anchor of arable husbandry on the Downs.[65] But even at the time of his tours, Defoe noticed a change in progress. The Downs were still white with sheep, but, he observed, "the number of sheep fed on these Downs is lessened, rather than increased, because of the many thousand acres of the carpet ground being of late years, turned into arable land, and sowed with wheat".[66]

A similar development was taking place on the Chilterns at this time, at least on the southern tip of the range. On the Downs, we may safely assume that the land newly taken under the plough bordered the river valleys, which had always been the chief arable areas.[67] The margin of cultivation was creeping up the sides of these valleys, but there were strict limits to the feasible extent of this expansion prior to 1750. It never reached the high Downs, where Edward Lisle, for example, one of the highest of the high Down farmers and a livestock specialist, remained unaffected by the movement.[68]

[62] E.g. enclosure by agreement at Faccomb, Hants., 1711 – Hants. RO, 2M/37/18; at West Grimstead, Wilts., in 1726 – Wilts. RO, 490/100/7; and at Inkpen, Berks., in 1733 – Berks. RO, D/EC/E22/2.

[63] E. Kerridge, *The Agricultural Revolution*, London, 1967, pp. 16–24. These points are well illustrated by the field-system arrangement which obtained at Watchfield in Berkshire in 1725 – Berks. RO, D/EPb/E5.

[64] Kerridge, 'Sheepfold in Wiltshire', p. 283.

[65] Daniel Defoe observed, "'tis more remarkable still how a great part of these Downs comes by a new [sic] method of husbandry to be not only made arable, which they never were in former days, but to bear excellent wheat, and great crops too...for by only folding the sheep upon the ploughed lands, which otherwise are barren, and where the plough goes within three or four inches of the solid rock of chalk, they are made fruitful, and bear very good wheat, as well as rye and barley" – *A Tour through England and Wales*, 2 vols., London, 1927, I, p. 18.

[66] *Ibid.*, p. 282.

[67] T. Davis, *op. cit.*, map following p. 268 of 1813 edn; Defoe, *op. cit.*, I, pp. 192, 285; C. Fiennes, *The Journeys of Celia Fiennes*, ed. C. Morris, London, 1947, p. 16.

[68] Edward Lisle of Crux Easton did not acquire a reputation as a selective breeder of livestock,

It was natural that it should spread from the river valleys, for not only were they the centres of population and arable husbandry, but the rivers themselves provided, in some cases, cheap transport for arable produce. The Thames and the Kennet, made navigable to Newbury in 1723, are obvious examples, but the Hampshire Avon too had been made navigable as far as Salisbury in 1664, and the Itchen navigable to Winchester in 1710.[69]

The whole of Wessex was, in fact, very favourably placed from the marketing point of view. Along its northern boundary, barges of 50 tons' burden plied the Thames from Goring and Pangbourne, carrying malt and meal to London. By 1707, barges of well over 100 tons' carrying capacity were plying the Thames at least as far up as Reading, and from 1723 barges of comparable size carried arable produce from Newbury.[70] London was also supplied from this area by sea, through the ports of Southampton and Portsmouth,[71] and in addition Wessex had its own local markets, serving areas of dense population with low arable production levels. In the east, the greatest of these markets was Farnham, and in the west Warminster, each one described by Defoe, with a bland impartiality, as "the greatest corn market in England".[72] The elder Thomas Davis observed of Wiltshire in 1794:

Its situation is well calculated to dispose of its surplus or perhaps in other words, the energy infused into it by the advantages of that situation has enabled it to have a surplus to dispose of, and to bear the rank it has in the agricultural scale of the kingdom...The manufacturing towns within the county, and in the eastern part of Somersetshire and the cities of Bath and Bristol, furnish a constant, regular demand for these productions, and London takes no inconsiderable part of them.[73]

The spectacular growth of the London market between 1640 and 1750 meant that the malt and meal of the Downs could always find a buyer there, but such produce could be sold only at a price, the market price, and between 1650 and 1750 cereal prices in London, as elsewhere, shared a secular downward trend.[74] Great as had been the growth of London, the expansion

but in the late seventeenth and early eighteenth centuries he kept a meticulous diary of his farming activities, which showed him to be most skilful in the care and feeding of livestock. He recorded many conversations with his farming contemporaries which suggest that they were as interested in livestock rearing as Lisle himself, and just as ready to experiment. Lisle's farming diary was published by his son in 1757 under the title *Observations in Husbandry*, a work which suggests that the arts of grazing and of livestock rearing were already far advanced by 1700.

[69] C. Hadfield, *The Canals of Southern England*, London, 1955, p. 44; *VCH Hants.*, V, p. 452. Also Defoe, *op. cit.*, I, p. 188.

[70] Oxon. RO, QS/1708/Ea; Defoe, *op. cit.*, I, p. 291.

[71] N. S. B. Gras, *The Evolution of the English Corn Market*, 2nd edn, Cambridge, Mass., 1926, p. 107; R. B. Westerfield, *Middlemen in English Business, Particularly between 1660 and 1760*, New Haven, Conn., 1915, repr. Newton Abbot, 1968, p. 170.

[72] Defoe, *op. cit.*, I, pp. 142, 282.

[73] T. Davis, *op. cit.*, p. 4.

[74] See W. G. Hoskins, 'Harvest Fluctuations and English Economic History, 1620–1759', *AHR*, XVI, 1968, p. 15.

of cereal output had been even greater. There is much evidence to suggest that the 1730s and 1740s were a period of agricultural depression in southern England no less than on the Kingston estates studied by Mingay, although, as Mingay observed of the Midland counties, "the worst difficulties were over by about 1745".[75] The arable farmers of Wessex were particularly vulnerable to the depression of cereal prices, but fortunately for them they had a third outlet for their produce in addition to their own local markets and London. This was the export trade. In the two years between 1734 and 1736, Portsmouth and Southampton alone exported 21,000 quarters of wheat, 6,000 quarters of malt, and 2,500 quarters of barley. The ports received export bounties to the tune of £6,400.[76] This export trade was the vital factor, tipping the balance between solvency and bankruptcy for many Wessex farmers.[77]

Agricultural depression was of course nothing new. In the 1680s cereal prices plummeted to levels almost as low as those reached in the 1740s, although this depression has received less publicity. Complaints from farmers, agents, and landlords were bitter, not only in southern England, but also in other parts of the country.[78] This depression, if less protracted than that of 1730–50, was no less severe and was followed by a series of violent price fluctuations during the French wars which, coming hard on the heels of depression, may have been instrumental in forcing many small owners to sell up to the big estates.[79] It must also, however, have encouraged many

[75] G. E. Mingay, 'The Agricultural Depression, 1730–1750', EcHR, 2nd ser., VIII, 1956, p. 324; Wilts. RO, Longleat Papers (uncatalogued) box 26: several cases of eviction and threatened eviction because of unpaid rents on the Longleat estate between 1732 and 1745; Hants. RO, 27M/54/3 Heathcote Letter Book: Sir William Heathcote complains bitterly of too much land in hand in Hampshire in 1739, and writes on 8 Dec. 1744, "Wheat was lately sold at Reading at £7 a load, and at Gloucester from £7 to £8 a load"; Wilts. RO, Calley MSS (unsorted) Account No. 1178: 10 Oct. 1740, Edward Carpenter's goods distrained for the rent of a farm at Chisledon, Wilts.; Berks. RO, D/ED/E4B/2: goods of John Grove of Wraysbury, Bucks., distrained for rent, 9 Nov. 1742; Wilts. RO, 184/1: Peter Griffin of Avebury, Wilts., evicted for non-payment of rent, 26 June 1743; Oxon. RO, DIL xxiv/15: Thomas Mander, agent, to Robert Lytcott, landlord, 1 Mar. 1737, "The Stoke tenants are very tardy in paying their rents."

[76] Westerfield, op. cit., pp. 161–2.

[77] Clwyd RO, D/GW/534: John Paleston, a Wiltshire landowner, wrote to his brother on 22 June 1734, "By all accounts in this part of the kingdom, gentlemen's estates would have been thrown up but for ye great exportation of corn that hath lately been, for it is thought here by gentlemen and farmers that wheat would not have reached 2s. per bu. had not that been. It went last market at Devizes (which is one of ye greatest) to 4s."

[78] E.g. T & C, pp. 85–8; Hants. RO, 21M/58/F6: goods of William Wither of Marydowne, Hants., distrained for rent arrears in 1679; Wilts. RO, 413/103: tenants complain of depression in 1680; Oxon. RO, Dash. x/xiii/5: depression lowers tithe values in 1691; Staffs. RO, D593/N/10/17: rent arrears of £1,532 outstanding on Leveson-Gower estates at Lady Day 1691, and George Plaxton, chief agent, commented, "Markets are low and trading dead", 26 May 1690 (D593/P/11/4) and "rents are so ill-paid that I known not what to do", 1 Feb. 1690 (D593/L/1/8).

[79] See A. H. John, 'The Course of Agricultural Change, 1660–1760', in W. E. Minchinton, ed., Essays in Agrarian History, I, Newton Abbot, 1968, p. 248. Regional studies certainly suggest

farmers to look about for ways and means of improving the cash returns
from their lands, and may well have speeded the spread of some of the new
crops, especially in those areas where a few pioneers had already proved their
profitability.[80] Responses to falling cereal prices varied from place to place.
Farmers on the limestone uplands and in the clay vale appear to have moved
towards heavier stocking, but on the southern Chilterns and the Downs
salvation was apparently sought by an extension of the wheat acreage.[81] This
may, at first sight, appear irrational. Why increase the wheat acreage at a
time when wheat prices were falling? The answer was that given the soils
of these areas and their ease of access to the London market,[82] a higher cash
return was obtained from an acre of wheat than from any other market crop.
There were, of course, cash crops that gave a far higher return per acre than
wheat: the new commercial crops which were eagerly adopted in some areas
after 1650. They included saffron, caraway, mustard, and liquorice; the
industrial dyes such as woad, weld, madder, and safflower; flax and hemp;
and exotic crops better suited to warmer climes, such as tobacco, and
mulberry trees for feeding silkworms. If successfully cultivated, these crops
could yield spectacular profits.[83] But soil conditions had to be just right for
them, and they appear to have been very little grown on the Downs or, for
that matter, in any part of the five counties under consideration in this
chapter. There was some tobacco growing in Oxfordshire and Wiltshire in
1655, but it must have been on a very small scale, and appears to have died
out completely shortly afterwards. There was very little tobacco growing
in any part of England after 1690 in any case, owing to vigorous competition
from Virginia.[84] The only other new commercial crops which were grown
in any quantity were woad in the clay vale, and hops on the eastern Downs.[85]

a general decline of the small owner-occupier between 1640 and 1750 – e.g. A. C. Chibnall,
Sherington: The Fiefs and Fields of a Buckinghamshire Village, Cambridge, 1965, pp. 195–207.

[80] Bucks. RO, D/X/464/4/4 & 6: letters from a tenant on the Hackett estates suggest a link
between depressed cereal prices and the sowing of clover in 1674 and 1676.

[81] E.g. 120 acres of Foxcote Down were described as "lately broken up and converted to
tillage" in 1719 – Hants. RO, Hinxman MSS, 40M/73M/E/B6; while at Compton near
Winchester there was a proposal to break up and enclose 400 acres of downland in 1741 – *ibid.*,
18M/54/coffer 6 box H.

[82] It is worth noting here that in addition to its superior water-transport facilities, Wessex also
enjoyed unusually good roads, running over the comparatively hard and well-drained chalk. Many
contemporaries praised the Wessex roads, which certainly compared favourably with those of the
Midlands. See Fiennes, *op. cit.*, pp. 17, 46; Defoe, *op. cit.*, II, pp. 117–32; A. Young, *A Six Weeks'
Tour through the Southern Counties of England and Wales*, London, 1769, p. 203; T. Davis, *op. cit.*,
p. 156; C. Vancouver, *General View of the Agriculture of Hampshire*, London, 1813, pp. 391–3.

[83] See Joan Thirsk, 'Seventeenth-Century Agriculture and Social Change', AHR, XVIII, 1970,
suppl., pp. 160–3.

[84] Joan Thirsk, 'New Crops and their Diffusion: Tobacco-Growing in Seventeenth Century
England', in C. W. Chalklin and M. A. Havinden, eds., *Rural Change and Urban Growth, 1500–1800*,
London, 1974, pp. 94–5.

[85] E.g. Oxon RO, D1L/xv/e/3d on woading at Aston Abbots, Bucks., in 1730; Reading Univ.

For one reason or another, downland farmers appear to have responded to depression by seeking to grow more wheat,[86] taking advantage of their superior marketing position. In their specific circumstances, they found that an acre of wheat gave them a higher immediate cash return than an acre of any other crop in the short run. In the long run, such a policy was ultimately self-defeating, exacerbating the very problem which had forced the adoption of the policy in the first place. But a reaction of this nature was far from unusual among cereal growers of every age: in fact it was almost automatic.[87] The Downs farmers were saved only by the demographic upswing of the later eighteenth century, and by their marketing advantages.

With this shift in emphasis among the old-established crops, the introduction of new crops, the breaking up of the Downs, a certain amount of enclosure, the rise of the large capitalist farmer, and the building of the water meadows, change was more dynamic and moved at a more dramatic pace here on the Downs than in any of the other farming regions studied in this chapter. It is here, if anywhere, that the term 'agricultural revolution' might be applied to the developments of 1640 to 1750.

Curving through northern Berkshire and into north-western Wiltshire were the Vale of Whitehorse and the dairying region of Wiltshire which lay between the Cotswolds and the Downs. Bisecting both was a ridge of corallian limestone, intermixed with sandstone and grits, forming a well-drained, though narrow and barely continuous, upland belt which was better suited for arable farming and more improvable than the heavier clays which lay on either side. At the south-eastern end of the vale, however, the clays ameliorated into the fertile greensand loams of the expanded Icknield belt.

Library Farm Accounts Collection, Han. 5/1/1 on hop growing at Crondall, Hants., in 1748; GMR, 121/1/11/4 on hop growing at Exton and Meonstoke, Hants., in 1751. Traces of flax, hemp, and hops have been found elsewhere, in the Winchester and Abingdon regions, for example, but only in plots of a fraction of an acre. They were evidently garden crops, grown as a sideline by smallholders only in these areas (e.g. Boldeian Library MS, Oxford Arch. Papers, Berks. c 149 ff. 40–1; Hants. RO, G/4/7 and 21M/58/F6). The very small scale on which industrial crops of this nature were grown was commented upon by reporters to the Board of Agriculture – e.g. Vancouver, op. cit., p. 206; Mavor, op. cit., pp. 229–34; Young, General View of Oxfordshire, pp. 203–4; Priest, General View of Buckinghamshire, pp. 230–1.

[86] See E. L. Jones, 'Eighteenth-Century Changes', p. 13. In 1794 Thomas Davis observed, "The great errors in the husbandry of this district have been already noticed to be the sowing more land with corn, and particularly with *wheat*, than can be properly manured with the stock on the farm…the temptation of immediate profit is frequently too strong to allow farmers to look forward to future consequences" – op. cit., p. 108.

[87] There was another great increase in the wheat acreage in England during the agricultural depression of 1815 to 1836. See A. R. Wilkes, 'Depression and Recovery in English Agriculture, 1813 to 1850', unpub. Univ. of Reading Ph.D. thesis, 1975, App. 1. Also E. J. T. Collins, 'Dietary Change and Cereal Consumption in Britain in the Nineteenth Century', AHR, XXIII, 1975, pp. 97–115. G. R. Allen also found a backward-sloping supply curve for wheat in his study of farming in Saskatchewan during the 1930s, 'Wheat Farmers and Falling Prices', Farm Economist, VII, 1954, p. 339.

These greensands were the best soils of Berkshire, just as the redlands were the best of Oxfordshire, and in both regions small freeholders were common. Throughout the rest of the vale, the lease for three lives was the most typical form of tenure. The dairying area in the west was, indeed, one of small proprietors, as Kerridge argued, but they were small tenant proprietors. The dairy lands were owned for the most part by the absentee lords of great estates, who held scattered parcels throughout the region. At the eastern end of the Vale of Whitehorse, farming systems were essentially similar to those of the Vale of Oxford, with mixed farming in open-field communities as the general rule. A fairly representative probate inventory from this region was that of John Leaver, a substantial yeoman of Brightwell, taken on 20 June 1713. His livestock consisted of 140 sheep, 7 cart geldings and mares, a bull and 14 milk cows, 6 hogs, 6 pigs, and poultry worth £4 10s. His growing crops included 43 acres of barley, 42 acres of wheat, 23 acres of beans, and 13 acres of peas and vetches. In addition he owned 52 acres of grassland, and the fruit in his orchards was valued at £12. His stored produce included 110 quarters of malt worth £100 and 93 new cheeses worth £4. The total value of his estate was put at £1,137 19s.[88] Mrs Cottis's analysis of fifty-seven inventories from Icknield Berkshire, taken between 1660 and 1757, shows that on average barley occupied 36 per cent of the cultivated acreage, wheat 30 per cent, and fodder crops 34 per cent. The wheat acreage tended generally to grow at the expense of barley.

Progressing westwards through the Vale of Whitehorse, however, a distinct change in the emphasis of farming practice may be noted. A higher proportion of fields were enclosed, and the accent was increasingly laid on dairy farming.[89] The line between the dairying and mixed farming regions is a difficult one to draw, but this was attempted by Mavor in 1808.[90] His line has long been thought to be accurate, and Mrs Cottis's recent analysis of probate inventories from the vale confirms this assumption for the period 1640 to 1750. Taking as her criterion of a 'dairying' inventory one which included cheeses worth £20 or more, and of a 'mixed' inventory one including malt valued at £100 or over, Mrs Cottis has produced a distribution map which almost exactly confirms Mavor's line. A typical dairying inventory was that of Abraham Goulding, a yeoman of Buscot, taken on 2 July 1726. His dairy stock consisted of 57 cows, 6 heifers, and 2 bulls, while he also kept 68 sheep, 8 horses, 7 pigs, 5 hogs, and a sow. His

[88] Bodleian Library, Dept of Western MSS, MS Wills Berks. 95/43. I owe this piece of information, and a good deal more on the Vale of Whitehorse, to my research student Mrs Janie Cottis, currently working at Reading on a Ph.D. thesis dealing with agriculture in the vale between 1660 and 1760.

[89] At the boundary between the two regions, convertible husbandry was certainly being practised in the seventeenth century – Berks. RO, D/E/BpE/15 "Memoranda and Notes how the Particular Grounds of Charney and Pusey have been let for Several Years from 1634 to 1686."

[90] Mavor, op. cit., p. 23 and map facing title page.

growing crops extended to only 7½ acres of barley, 6 acres of oats, and 4 acres of wheat, while his stored hay was valued at £42. His whole estate was put at £1,027 12s., and must have included a fair area of grassland which was not mentioned in the inventory, but which probably extended to 50 or 60 acres.[91]

The dairy farming practices of north-western Wiltshire have been exhaustively described by Kerridge, who calls this region the "Cheese country" to distinguish it from another small dairying area in the south-west corner of Wiltshire, where the emphasis was on butter.[92] Small, enclosed fields were the rule in both the cheese and butter countries by 1700, and here the livestock could be left to graze with a minimum of attendance. It was here that the small family farmer continued to flourish, in contrast to the situation on the Downs. The chief products of these dairying areas were, according to Kerridge, "in order of importance, cheese or butter, beef, bacon, mutton and wool...The smaller occupiers seldom engaged extensively in tillage, and most farmers were content to supply teams for their swing ploughs from their dairy and beef herds."[93]

The corallian ridge, however, rising in places to 400 feet, presented something of a contrast to the surrounding dairy lands. Soils here were lighter and better drained, principally loams, chalky sands, and gravels. Farms were larger, common fields were much more prevalent, and sheep were more heavily stocked. This ill-defined region was primarily an arable one with barley and wheat as the chief market crops. It therefore invites once more a use of the overworked description a 'sheep–corn husbandry zone'. However, so narrow and discontinuous was the corallian ridge that many farms on it overlapped into the dairying regions, and included sizeable domestic dairies. On their lower, more ill-drained lands, sheep were raised for mutton rather than for the fold, together with some beef cattle. A typical 'corallian' inventory, which indeed is not unrepresentative of 'sheep–corn' inventories as a whole, was that of Joan Southby of Buckland, a widow, taken on 22 April 1690. Her livestock included 173 sheep, 20 milch cows, 3 heifers and a bull, 6 hogs and a sow with pigs, 11 horses and 4 colts, 7 stocks of bees worth £2 6s. 8d., and poultry worth £1. Her growing crops included 43 acres of barley, 25 acres of wheat, and 20 acres of beans. Among her stored produce were 150 quarters of malt, and the total value of her estate was put at £736 19s. 4d.[94] Mrs Cottis's analysis of 19 probate inventories taken between 1660 and 1734 in the corallian region showed that on average 42 per cent of the arable acreage was under barley, 26 per cent under wheat, 1 per cent under rye, and 31 per cent under fodder crops.

[91] Bodleian Library, Dept of Western MSS, MS Wills Berks. 74/127.
[92] VCH Wilts., IV, p. 44.
[93] Ibid., pp. 44–5.
[94] Bodleian Library, Dept of Western MSS, MS Wills Berks. 122/121.

Possibly the most difficult farming regions about which to generalize are those of eastern Berkshire and north-eastern Hampshire. The Vale of Kennet represented an intrusion of alluvial and valley gravel soils into the chalk downlands, but the soils here were fertile enough, with good grazing for the sheepfold on the nearby downs and the opportunity to construct water meadows. Wheat was the chief market crop, and the farming system basically one of sheep and corn, although again there were distinctive features, such as the large-scale growing of osiers along many parts of the valley and a flourishing coppice-wood industry.[95] From Newton to Swallowfield, however, the southern fringe of Berkshire consisted of soils of a markedly inferior quality. A wedge of soils which were on the whole sandy, peaty, stony, and generally hungry also typified north-eastern Hampshire from Newton to Farnham, and extended northwards through Aldershot and Farnborough as far as Wokingham, Bracknell, and Windsor in south-eastern Berkshire. Only in the valley of the Loddon river and the Foundry brook were better soils to be found, but even here their quality was variable.[96] For the rest, although isolated patches of better soils suitable for arable farming could be found, it was on the whole an area of heaths, woodland, and rough pasture suitable only for livestock rearing. In places, the heathy sward could bear a single crop after paring and burning, and by a system of shifting cultivation some oats, rye, and buckwheat could be grown as fodder crops. Domestic dairies were kept and plough horses reared, together with pigs where the woodlands were suitable. Sheep too were reared in some numbers, but for mutton or wool; if any folding was done, it was only through the animals being hired out to better-favoured farming regions.[97] Farming in this region could most charitably be described as the poor relation of that in the clay vale, but it was in fact more closely akin to the forest–pasture system of south-western Hampshire. Even today, much of this area is still wooded, and in 1750 one of its major industries was the regular growing and cropping of coppice wood, used in the manufacture of such items as hop poles, hedging stakes, thatching rods, and hurdles for the sheepfold. In the west, place names tell their own story: Wolverton Common, Stony Heath, Pamber Forest, and Wildmoor. In the east, Defoe's description of Bagshot Heath is worthy of quotation. It was

a mark of the just resentment shew'd by Heaven upon the Englishmen's pride: I mean the pride they shew in boasting of their country, its fruitfulness, pleasantness, richness, the fertility of the soil, etc., whereas here is a vast tract of land…which is not only poor, but even quite sterile, given up to barrenness, horried and frightful to look on, not only good for little, but good for nothing.[98]

[95] Mavor, op. cit., pp. 321–2.
[96] J. Stephenson and W. G. East, Berks., Land Utilization Survey 78, London, 1963, pp. 96–7.
[97] Kerridge, Agricultural Revolution, pp. 81–2.
[98] Defoe, op. cit., I, p. 143.

The remainder of eastern Berkshire was, however, better suited for arable farming. We may describe its last two regions as the Waltham clay vale and the eastern chalk plateau, the latter structurally a part of the Chilterns, but severed from them by the Thames. Mavor recognized the eastern chalk plateau as a distinct farming region, but always discussed it as though it were part and parcel of the Berkshire Downs, lumping the two together under the heading of the "Chalky Hills". In fact, however, farming systems on the plateau had much more in common with those of the Chilterns than of the Downs. There were extensive areas of parkland and woodland, and enclosed fields were the rule. There was also far less folding here than on the Downs: sheep were reared mainly to provide mutton and lamb for the London market. The area was surrounded on three sides by the Thames, and was ideally placed to ship malt and meal to London. Inevitably, barley and wheat were the chief market crops. The soils were generally good loams on a well-drained substratum, and, in place of the fold, farmers relied on intelligent rotations and, as on the Chilterns, the judicious application of chalk and lime where soils were suitable.

Farming in the Waltham clay vale was, in the eighteenth century, very similar to that in the clay vale of Oxfordshire and Buckinghamshire. The land was ill drained, based on impervious strata, and better suited to pastoral than to arable farming. The soils were for the most part stiff clays, with here and there some outcrops of sand and gravels, which occasionally ameliorated the clays into good loams. Drainage was the key to all improvement, but this appears to have been neglected prior to 1750.[99] Mixed farming was the rule, with an undue emphasis on cereal crops, considering the nature of the soils. A wide variety of crops was rotated, and there was some folding, although most sheep and lambs went to market. Dairying was on a domestic scale and although some beef cattle were reared, cereals were the chief marketable product of the area.[100]

That portion of Buckinghamshire which lies to the south of the Chiltern Hills has now to be considered. This area, of about 100 square miles, falls into two sharply contrasting farming regions. In the north, the Burnham plateau covers some 60 square miles and even today remains heavily wooded, mainly with the famous Burnham Beeches, but also with some silver birch and a few stunted oaks. The soils are very poor, and quite unsuited to either arable or pasture farming. At the northern end of the plateau, the chalk measures of the Chilterns dip under increasingly heavy layers of fluvio-glacial deposits, usually gravels of low fertility. Soils range from a clay-with-stones to a sandy soil devoid of pebbles with, in some areas, a high proportion of

[99] See Fiennes, op. cit., p. 274.

[100] Mavor, op. cit., pp. 177–9. There appears to be little justification for Mavor's decision to classify the Waltham clay vale as a "woodland" area, and no justification for Kerridge's classification of both the vale and the plateau as part of his extensive "Blackheaths" region.

silts that tend to set hard after rain. The area provided a little rough grazing, and some pigs were reared on the beech mast, but in general forestry was the mainstay of the local economy. The small, open-field communities of this area such as Chalfont St Peter and Hedgerley remained sparsely populated throughout our period, and typical of townships supported by a poor, forest–pasture economy.

By contrast, the southern extremity of Buckinghamshire was a rich, market-gardening plain, underlain by London clay, but well drained by the adjacent Thames. The soils were in general excellent deep loams, with a subsoil of Taplow Terrace gravels which provided free drainage. Farmers here were certainly the best in the county, taking full advantage of both the adjacent London market and the ready supplies of town manure. It was said of them in 1794:

The farmers are at great pains and expense in purchasing manure and collecting every sort of material that constitutes or assists in the increase of manure, and that is not only applied with judgment, but is aided by the most modern agricultural improvements, as well as by repeated cross-ploughings and drill husbandry, and by the cultivation of every sort of green meat.[101]

However, since market gardening was the chief economic activity of this region, its detailed description is best left to the specialized chapter on that subject.[102]

Intruding into the eastern edge of central Hampshire was the western extremity of the Wealden farming region. This too is described in more detail elsewhere,[103] but the Weald at its western extremity gave way to an extremely heterogeneous range of soil types which resulted in the most varied farming landscape to be compressed into a small area in the whole of Hampshire. The government survey of 1940 distinguished no fewer than nine separate land-utilization regions, including the Petersfield area.[104] In general, these regions spread out in a series of concentric rings, centring on Hindhead. Essentially the region was a valley, lying between the Hampshire Downs and the high chalk hills of the Weald, crossed by several small streams. These included Oakhanger stream, Deadwater brook, and the upper course of the river Wey. Vancouver, who recognized this corner of Hampshire as a distinct and separate region, noted that the lower slopes of the chalk hills consisted of "a grey, tender, sandy loam of a very good depth or staple, and lying on a soft species of sand rock...which soil and substratum is provincially termed malmy land".[105] On these better soils, wheat, barley, oats, and turnips were being successfully grown, according to the crop returns of

[101] James and Malcolm, *General View of Buckingham*, p. 19.
[102] See ch. 18 below.
[103] See ch. 9 above.
[104] Green, *Hampshire*, pp. 353–7.
[105] Vancouver, *op. cit.*, p. 21.

1801,[106] and it would appear that in these arable regions turnip husbandry had assumed a position of some importance by 1770 at the latest.[107] There was also some good pasture land, for the valley cut through several strata, and this gave rise to different soil types, including the peat and clay soils which were typical of the Alice Holt forest region in the north of the area, and the Woolmer Forest in the central zone, surrounded by a good deal of heathland. The region included some of the best, but also some of the worst, soils in Hampshire. Gilbert White's comment was, "The soils of this district are almost as various and diversified as its views and aspects."[108] The forests included stands of ash, beech, and elm trees as well as the oaks which were the chief economic asset of the forest zone. These woods, and the hop fields, provided employment for the local poor, and Gilbert White painted a rosy picture of the area:

We abound with poor, many of whom are sober and industrious, and live comfortably in good stone or brick cottages, which are glazed, and have chambers above stairs: mud buildings we have none. Besides the employment from husbandry, the men work in hop gardens of which we have many, and fell and bark timber. In the spring and summer the women weed the corn, and enjoy a second harvest in September by hop-picking...The inhabitants enjoy a good share of health and longevity, and the parish swarms with children.[109]

But the best-known forested region in Hampshire was of course the New Forest. Despite its name, almost half of this 140-square-mile area was in fact covered not by forest, but by open heathland, on soils too poor, and indeed too toxic, to bear even a forest cover. The heath-covered soils were for the most part light, hungry sands and gravels, poorer even than those of the Bagshot region. But there were also considerable areas of heavy clay soil, and it was here that the famous New Forest oaks flourished. The abundance of these "ancient oaks of many hundred years standing" greatly impressed Defoe, who wrote,

Notwithstanding the very great consumption of timber in King William's reign, by building or rebuilding almost the whole navy, and notwithstanding so many of the king's ships were built hereabouts, besides abundance of large merchant ships, which were about that time built at Southampton, at Redbridge, and at Bursledon, etc. yet I saw the gentlemen's estates within six, eight, or ten miles of Southampton so over-grown with wood...that it seemed as if they wanted sale for it, and that it was of little worth to them.[110]

[106] R. A. Pelham, 'The Agricultural Revolution in Hampshire, with Special Reference to the Acreage Returns of 1801', *Hants. Field Club & Arch. Soc.*, XVIII, 1953, pp. 140–3.

[107] G. White, *The Natural History of Selborne*, ed. G. Allen, London, 1908, pp. 6, 129, 160, 424–5.

[108] *Ibid.*, p. 4.

[109] *Ibid.*, pp. 23–4.

[110] Defoe, *op. cit.*, I, p. 140.

Naval shipbuilding went on at Bursledon and Portsmouth, and although the latter drew some of its timber supply from the Forest of Bere, New Forest timber also went to Portsmouth by sea. According to Defoe,

Southampton stands upon a point running out into the sea, between two very fine rivers (the Test and the Itchen) both navigable up some length into the country, and particularly useful for the bringing down timber out of one of the best wooded counties in Britain; for the river on the west side of the town in particular comes by the edge of the great forest called New-Forest; here we saw a prodigious quantity of timber, of an uncommon size, vastly large, lying on the shore of the river, for above two miles in length, which they told us was brought thither from the forest, and left there to be fetched by the builders at Portsmouth dock, as they had occasion for it.[111]

The New Forest was of course a royal forest, but in the early modern period the crown's interest in it moved from hunting to sylviculture mainly to supply the navy, a policy culminating in the Deer Removal Act of 1851. The region was one of smallholders who practised a forest–pasture economy, and relied very heavily on their extensive common rights in the woods themselves. These included rights of pannage, turbary, estovers, and marl, in addition to common grazing, and were vital to copyholders and freeholders alike in what was mainly a stock-rearing economy with very little arable husbandry. Sheep were traditionally exluded from the forest for the sake of the deer, and dairying was on only a domestic scale. But bee keeping was extensive, and beef cattle, horses, and ponies were reared for the market.[112] Pigs were the most numerous of the livestock kept, and Hampshire bacon was reputed to be the best in the kingdom, although Vancouver was rather scathing about the native breed of hogs, attributing the excellence of their bacon more to curing techniques.[113] In view of the often unstinted common rights available, it is surprising that more evidence of squatting and encroachments has not come to light.[114] Perhaps the native commoners defended their rights against squatters as vigorously and successfully as they had defended them against attempted encroachments by their landlords.

Along the western edge of the New Forest, the valley of the river Avon must be recognized as a separate farming region. On the other side of this valley, the Dorset heathlands extended into Hampshire, and here a forest–

---

[111] *Ibid.*, p. 139.

[112] C. R. Tubbs, 'The Development of the Smallholding and Cottage Stock-Keeping Economy of the New Forest', AHR, XIII, 1965, pp. 23–8.

[113] Vancouver, *op. cit.*, p. 378.

[114] Only one case of complaint against encroaching cottagers has been found, relating to Downton Waste at the extreme northern tip of the forest – Hants. RO, 490/909/B/7/95, John Snow to Lady Mary Aske, 14 Feb. 1694. But Abraham and William Driver mention "a considerable number of encroachments, chiefly made by poor people" just one hundred years later – *General View of the Agriculture of the County of Hampshire*, London, 1794, p. 35.

pasture economy very similar to that of the New Forest was practised. But the deep alluvial loam of the Avon valley floor, between one and two miles in width, contrasted sharply with the poor soils on either side and was well suited for both arable and pastoral husbandry. It was a region of mixed farming, but the emphasis was on cereals, with large acreages of barley and wheat grown in the south of the valley, and more oats towards the north.[115]

The Forest of Bere must also be recognized as a separate farming region because of the contrast which it presented to the rich, enclosed arable areas to the south and west, and to the characteristic downland farming systems to the north. In the eighteenth century it covered roughly 16,000 acres, of which about one-third was enclosed and the rest open forest land.[116] Soils here were a mixture of London clays and Bagshot sands, and these supported a wide variety of deciduous trees in scattered stands of over 1,000 acres each. But although the drainage was poor, there were no extensive heathlands here as in the New Forest. Instead the woods were interspersed with good pasture land which enabled stock rearing to be practised on a commercial scale, together with semi-commercial dairying. Thus, although the area was one of forests and pastures, to describe it as a 'forest–pasture region' would be to do it less than justice. As in the New Forest, natives of the area enjoyed rights of common in the woods for livestock, but the soils here were richer than those normally associated with a forest–pasture economy.[117]

The last area on the mainland of Hampshire deserving separate consideration might be described as the south seacoast country. This would include the New Forest fringe, only a mile or two in width, running along the coast from Bournemouth to Eling and then inland to Romsey, together with the whole of eastern Hampshire south of the Downs, excepting only the Forest of Bere. This area was one of very mixed soils, but on the whole their fertility was high, and the region was one of prosperous arable farms.[118] Even the New Forest fringe had a high proportion of good clay-loam soils well suited for cereals, although there were also some sandy soils which were too light to produce high yields. The Bracklesham beds of the Itchen district and the brickearths around Fareham, Portsmouth, and Havant were among the most fertile soils in the country, and great quantities of wheat were grown on the well-drained, enclosed fields of the area, which for the most part inclined towards the south. Barley, oats, and peas were also grown in quantity, but in 1801 their combined acreage was less than that sown to wheat.[119] Farms tended to be of medium size, and many included rich, enclosed pasture lands on which Sussex and Devon cattle were reared, and sheep, mainly of the

---

[115] Pelham, *op. cit.*, p. 143.   [116] Driver and Driver, *op. cit.*, p. 43.

[117] See Kerridge, *Agricultural Revolution*, p. 69.

[118] Bodleian Library, MS Top Gen. e 52 "An Account of a Tour by L.G. in 1756", f. 66: "From Porchester to Southampton the country is enclosed and well cultivated, and bears a great deal of timber."   [119] Pelham, *loc. cit.*

Dorset breed. There was some folding, but most of the livestock reared in this area were intended for the butcher.[120]

The Isle of Wight is a geological museum piece which displays in miniature the geological history and structure of the whole of south-eastern England. To do it justice, the island should be subdivided into a series of minute land-use regions, each reflecting a larger counterpart on the mainland.[121] The greatly simplified and condensed Land Utilization Survey of 1940 distinguished five separate natural divisions of the island, and so too did Charles Vancouver in 1810. Unfortunately, there is little common ground of agreement between the two authorities, although William Marshall, who in general was critical of the Hampshire reports, did congratulate Vancouver on his account of the island's soils.[122] Most of the island was enclosed, and although a few scattered common fields still remained in the eighteenth century, there was very little waste land. Farms were "of a moderate size" (from 50 to 200 acres) and concentrated heavily on arable crops, for the fertility of the soils was on the whole very high. Warner said of the island,

Its fertility is almost proverbial, having long since been said to produce more in one year than could be consumed by its inhabitants in eight; an improved husbandry introduced of late years has increased this fertility, and from what I have been able to collect, we may now estimate its annual production to be at least ten times as much as its consumption...During the last harvest, there were near seven hundred Dorsetshire and Somersetshire men employed, and as a warm press was at that time on foot, each of them was allowed a protection from government, during his passage from his own habitation to the island and back again.[123]

The main arable crop was wheat, the acreage sown to which was greater than that of oats and barley combined, and there was also a large turnip acreage in 1801.[124] Cows were mainly of the Alderney breed, and Warner estimated that some 40,000 sheep a year were shorn on the island.

If the agriculture of these five counties was varied, the industrial activity within their borders was hardly less so. Looking first at Oxfordshire, we find that the woollen industry commands attention in an age when the working of wool in one form or another was still virtually ubiquitous throughout the

[120] Driver and Driver, *op. cit.*, pp. 14–15.

[121] E. C. Willatts and L. D. Stamp, *Isle of Wight*, Land Utilization Survey 89, London, 1940, p. 393.

[122] W. Marshall, *Review and Abstract of the Reports to the Board of Agriculture from the Southern Department*, York, 1817, p. 311.

[123] J. Warner, 'General View of the Agriculture of the Isle of Wight', in Driver and Driver, *op. cit.*, pp. 48, 66. The Isle of Wight had been a granary for southern England for many years. In 1631 Sir John Oglander had written to the Privy Council, "...we have far more corn yearly grown than our island can spend or our market vent. We have also maltsters in Newport which...sendeth 500 li or 1,000 quarters of malt annually to Plymouth, Dartmouth or Falmouth" – I.O.W. RO, OG/15/27.

[124] Pelham, *loc. cit.*

country. Oxford itself was an ancient centre of weaving, and by 1750 was providing work for handloom weavers in the surrounding villages as far away as Charlbury. Banbury too was a weaving centre, also developing a small dyeing industry in the early eighteenth century, while mills for the manufacture of tilting and linsey woollens were set up at Chipping Norton in 1746. Coarser woollens were manufactured at Burford for use as duffles and rugs.[125] But the largest single consumer of wool in Oxfordshire was the Witney blanket industry. This reached its apogee around the turn of the seventeenth century when it was described in vivid detail by Robert Plot, who declared that "near 3,000 poor people, from children of eight years to decrepit old age, do work out above one hundred packs of wool per week".[126]

Other textile industries included some silk weaving at Oxford and Banbury, and domestic lacemaking in the Thame area, an extension of the Buckinghamshire lace industry.

Leather working too was a well-nigh ubiquitous craft in seventeenth-century England, and again Oxford was a great leather-working centre in 1640, although its leather crafts were in decline by 1750. Burford, however, remained famous for its saddles throughout this period, while Bampton and Witney were known for their leather dressing. Gloves were manufactured at both Oxford and Woodstock, but while the former industry declined, Woodstock had by 1750 become the major glovemaking centre in the county. There had previously been a small fine steel industry at Woodstock which had acquired some renown, but by 1720 competition from Birmingham was being keenly felt, and the industry was in decline.[127] It would seem that glovemaking took its place.

Malting and brewing were major industries in seventeenth-century Oxford, Henley, and Burford, and here we have one case of an Oxfordshire industry which did not decline in the eighteenth century. By 1800 there were sizeable malting and brewing works at Deddington, Chipping Norton, Witney, and Banbury in addition to the older-established centres.

The city of Oxford, with its university press, also provided a good deal of employment in the printing and bookbinding industries, which at that time were almost the largest in the country. Inevitably, the press called into existence a paper-making industry in the Oxford area, and paper mills were built at Wolvercote just north of the city in the early seventeenth century, and at Eynsham and Sandford in the eighteenth century, with the Wolvercote mill producing paper of a very high quality.[128]

Minor industries of the county included bell founding at Burford, Oxford,

[125] VCH Oxon., II, pp. 245–6.
[126] R. Plot, The Natural History of Oxfordshire, Oxford, 1676/7, pp. 278–9.
[127] Young, General View of Oxfordshire, p. 328.
[128] VCH Oxon., II, pp. 240–1.

and Woodstock, glassmaking at Henley, and some manufacture of chairs in the southern Chilterns. There were also brick works at Nettlebed and Caversham.[129]

As a general point it might be observed that it was the agricultural processing industries such as brewing, malting, and leather working which best survived in eighteenth-century Oxfordshire, while manufactures based on industrial raw materials, like the Woodstock steel works, the Henley glass furnaces, and even the Witney blanket industry, all suffered a severe decline, mainly owing to competition from the north.

In Buckinghamshire, by far the most important domestic industry was the making of lace. It was manufactured throughout the Vale of Aylesbury and in the Buckinghamshire Chilterns, but the main centres of the trade were Olney, Newport Pagnell, and Stony Stratford, employing among them over 4,000 lacemakers in 1698.[130] A Newport Pagnell buyer estimated the total number of Buckinghamshire lace workers at 30,000 in the year 1699, about one-quarter of the county's population.[131] The estimate may well have been too high, but the number of lace workers appears to have increased during the eighteenth century, so much so that in 1813 it was complained that no women or children were available for agricultural work in Buckinghamshire because of the industry.[132] Lesser centres were Aylesbury and North Crawley, in addition to which there were lacemaking schools at Marlow and High Wycombe in the seventeenth century, the latter town keeping "several hundred workers constantly employed" at lacemaking by 1717.[133] The industry flourished in Buckinghamshire until well into the nineteenth century, when machine-made lace, mainly from Nottingham, and foreign imports finally killed the local trade.

Miss Jamison, writing in the Buckinghamshire *VCH*, suggested that less lacemaking was carried on in the southern part of the county because here other trades, "especially chair making", offered easier and better-paid work for women. Certainly a great many wooden items were made locally from the Chiltern beeches and were shipped down the Thames to London, as Defoe observed when he passed through the area.[134] The main centre of beechwood manufacture in Defoe's day was evidently Chesham, but High Wycombe later became increasingly important in this respect.

Another important industry in Buckinghamshire was paper making, so important indeed that James and Malcolm ranked it with lacemaking in 1794.[135] As early as 1636 there were twelve paper mills in the county, the

[129] Plot, *op. cit.*, pp. 251–2.
[130] G. F. R. Spenceley, 'The Origins of the English Pillow Lace Industry', AHR, XXI, 1973, p. 86.
[131] C. Freeman, *Pillow Lace in the East Midlands*, Luton, 1958, p. 13.
[132] Priest, *General View of Buckinghamshire*, p. 346.
[133] *VCH Bucks.*, II, p. 107.
[134] Defoe, *op. cit.*, I, pp. 299–300.   [135] James and Malcolm, *op. cit.*, p. 46.

largest at Horton, producing paper of a rather low quality. By 1690 High Wycombe had become the centre of the industry, with eight mills in that town alone, employing fifty families. There were also mills at Wraysbury near Staines in the south, at Newport Pagnell in the north, and at Marsworth near Tring. Paper manufacturing in Buckinghamshire probably reached its peak in the eighteenth century, with High Wycombe eventually developing a product of superior quality which robbed the fine French paper of its English markets. By 1720 the little river Wye, which flowed from West Wycombe to join the Thames at Bourne End, boasted the densest concentration of paper mills in the country. By 1816 the ascendancy of this area was even more clearly marked, but very shortly afterwards it was overtaken by the explosive development of paper manufacture in Lancashire, Durham, and Kent.[136] The census of 1831 noted only seventy-six paper manufacturers in the county, employing a mere 220 men and boys.

The eastern spur of central Buckinghamshire, which included the paper-making centres of Horton and Marsworth, also encroached on the western fringe of the great straw-plaiting industry which centred on Luton. This industry grew from small beginnings in the later seventeenth century and had expanded greatly by Defoe's time, but petitions presented to parliament in 1689 and 1719 show that, within Buckinghamshire, only the villages of Slapton and Edlesborough were engaged in the trade at that time.[137] By the nineteenth century the industry had spread all over eastern Buckinghamshire from Bow Brickhill to Chalfont St Peter, but it seems unlikely that straw plaiting was a major employer of labour before 1750. The industry may well have originated near Luton because the soils of this district produced a wheat straw which was particularly suitable for plaiting.[138]

Tanning, cordwaining, and the manufacture of woollen cloth were industries to be found all over Buckinghamshire in the seventeenth century, but there were no major centres for these trades. Buckinghamshire was never a great woollens county, and, as Miss Jamison observed, "The cloth trade never assumed very large proportions in the county, but a certain amount of weaving and fulling was done, presumably for local use."[139]

Bell founding was carried on intermittently in Buckingham itself, and the village of Long Crendon was famous in the sixteenth and seventeenth centuries for the manufacture of needles, which in 1750 were still being produced under a putting-out system in the homes of local workers. But although it was a centre of only domestic industry, Long Crendon was to needles what Witney was to blankets, certainly the largest supplier of its own specialized product in the country. Long Crendon held its position until the

[136] D. C. Coleman, *The British Paper Industry, 1495–1860*, Oxford, 1958, pp. 57, 147, 220–1.
[137] J. G. Dony, *A History of the Straw Hat Industry*, Luton, 1942, pp. 19–20.
[138] *Ibid.*, pp. 19, 33.
[139] *VCH Bucks.*, II, p. 128.

early nineteenth century, when it finally ceded pride of place to Redditch, near Birmingham.

The last Buckinghamshire industry worthy of note was the manufacture of bricks, tiles, and pottery. This industry too was doomed eventually to go down in the face of northern competition, but for a while the clay soils of the county provided a suitable raw material for pottery manufacture. Middle Claydon was a brickmaking centre as early as 1656, and bricks and tiles were also manufactured at the nearby Brill Hills. There had been potters at Brill since at least 1254, and in 1700 there were still the makings of a promising pottery industry in the region. It declined, however, in the eighteenth century, and even the brick and tile industries migrated eastwards to centre on towns such as Fenny Stratford, the Brickhills, and Whitchurch.[140]

In Berkshire, the leather crafts and woollen working were again well-nigh ubiquitous, but here there were in addition three major centres of the woollen industry, at Reading, Newbury, and Abingdon. In the sixteenth and early seventeenth centuries, Berkshire had been one of England's major cloth-producing counties. By 1640, however, decline had already set in, and was hastened by the Civil War, in which Reading in particular suffered very badly as a result of the heavy financial demands made on it by both sides as it changed hands. By the early eighteenth century the three once-great clothing towns had gone over almost entirely to the manufacture of shalloons, sacking, and sailcloth.[141] The latter two industries consumed large quantities of hemp, but some of this appears to have been brought in from quite far afield. An abundant supply of fine-quality local wool was evidently not enough to sustain the industry on a large scale, but it did linger on in a small way where the key factor of high entrepreneurial ability was available. As late as 1811 one John Coxeter was running a water-powered woollen mill at Greenham, near Newbury, which employed 100 hands, and was instrumental in producing the famous Newbury coat in that year. Wool which had been on a sheep's back in the morning was said to have been transformed into a dyed, tailored, and fully finished coat by the evening of the same day.[142]

Another raw material in plentiful supply was barley, and malting was carried on all over the county, with concentrations of the industry at Reading, Newbury, Abingdon, Wallingford, and Maidenhead. These too were the brewing centres, providing not only local concentrations of population, but also water-borne access to wider markets.

[140] J. J. Sheahan, *The History and Topography of Buckinghamshire*, London, 1862, I, pp. 53–4.

[141] R. F. Dell, 'The Decline of the Clothing Industry in Berkshire', *Newbury & Dist. Field Club*, x, 1954, pp. 50–64. But sackmaking had been established in Reading since the early seventeenth century, when some sackcloth came from Somerset – PRO, Prob 11/134, no. 97, Will of John Ash of Stoke under Hamden, Somerset, 1619.

[142] W. Money, *The History of the Ancient Town and Borough of Newbury*, Oxford, 1887, pp. 386–9.

Indeed, another large employer of labour in the Berkshire of 1750 must have been the barging trade, with its associated industries of boat manufacture and barge maintenance. Boat building seems to have been concentrated on the Berkshire side of the river, at places such as Abingdon, Streatley, Sutton Courteney, Pangbourne, Reading, Maidenhead, Bray, and Windsor, rather than on the Oxfordshire side, where only at Oxford and Henley was there evidence of boat building on the northern bank. The yards were small, usually family businesses, building fishing punts and pleasure boats as well as the smaller type of barge. The larger craft could not work the upper reaches of the river, and it seems likely that the largest barges, of up to 200 tons' burthen, were built near London, on the Surrey shore.

It is difficult to get a clear idea of the number of men and craft used in the trade. Crews varied from four to seven men, depending on the size of the boat. According to Burton there were fifty-four boats between Pangbourne and Lechlade in 1764. Perhaps there were double that number above Windsor, all told, including some trading on the Kennet Navigation at that time. However, the river was less thriving in 1750. There were concentrations of bargemen in certain towns along the river, as at Marlow, Abingdon, and Oxford. Bow halers, who towed the boats, formed an enclave at Richmond, where there was no towpath, and presumably at other similar places.[143] After 1723 Newbury became a centre of barge manufacture, and by Mavor's time was producing a standard barge 109 feet long and 17 feet wide, drawing 3 ft 10 in of water, and carrying 128 tons. It was crewed by six men and a boy, and progressed at the stately pace of three miles per hour.[144]

Minor industries included quarrying and brickmaking, especially at Reading, where there was also some bell founding and printing. A small amount of silk was also manufactured at Reading and at Wallingford.

In Wiltshire, the leading industry by far was once again the manufacture of woollen cloth. In 1674 it employed an estimated 30,000 people,[145] and although the trade was in decline, it came through the eighteenth century more successfully than its counterpart in Berkshire. On the other hand, it survived less well than the Gloucestershire woollen industry, so it can be said that the degree of decline in the wool trade of this region between 1640 and 1750 varied in intensity from east to west. The Wiltshire trade was hard hit by the Cockayne project, the Thirty Years' War, and the Civil War, but it revived in the 1670s, assisted by an influx of Dutch immigrants into such

[143] [John Burton], *The Present State of the Navigation of the Thames Considered*, by a Commissioner, Oxford, 1764; Mary Prior, *Fisher Row: Fishermen, Bargemen, and Canal Boatmen at Oxford, 1500–1900*, Oxford, 1982, pp. 128–36, 364–7.

[144] Mavor, *op. cit.*, pp. 431–2.

[145] *VCH Wilts.*, IV, p. 155.

centres as Bradford-on-Avon and Trowbridge.[146] In 1750 Wiltshire was still a leading woollens county, although it had declined somewhat from its pre-1640 days of glory.

Tanning too was a widespread industry in Wiltshire, with some concentration on gloving. Marlborough, Warminster, and Castle Combe appear to have been the main centres of glove manufacture prior to 1750.

One of the less common English industries to provide employment in Wiltshire was the tobacco trade, both wholesale and retail, and the milling of snuff. By 1676, tobacco was no longer grown in the county, but it remained a distribution centre for the product, with snuff mills at Devizes, Poulshot, Calne, and Potterne. Distribution points for tobacco from Bristol were also concentrated in the north-west, at centres such as Trowbridge and Bradford. It was Amesbury, however, which was the capital of clay-pipe manufacturing, using clay from Chitterne, ten miles to the west. Amesbury pipes were reputed to be the best in seventeenth-century England.[147]

As in Buckinghamshire and Oxfordshire, paper making was an industry of some importance in Wiltshire, with paper mills recorded at Bemerton, West Harnham, Salisbury, Nunton, Downton, and Yatton Keynell between 1640 and 1750.

The inevitable small-scale bell founding to supply local needs was another well-documented industry, with centres at Salisbury, Aldbourne, Devizes, and Warminster.

Apart from these lesser trades, and a certain amount of quarrying, there was little other industry in Wiltshire. Even the famous Axminster and Wilton carpet industries had only just begun to get off the ground by 1750.[148] At this date, the woollen cloth industry was still the only one of real importance in Wiltshire.

By contrast, in Hampshire no one industry was of outstanding importance. Shipbuilding has already been mentioned, and was possibly the second largest employer of labour, outside agriculture, in times of heavy naval demand.[149] Malting and brewing were first in importance as employers, although some centres of these trades, such as Basingstoke, Ringwood, Andover, and Winchester, catered for a mainly local market. Others, however, such as Southampton, Portsmouth, Romsey, and Havant sent their products further afield. An allied trade was cider brewing, restricted to eastern Hampshire and the Isle of Wight by 1750, but an industry which John Worlidge of Petersfield had done all he could to encourage in the seventeenth century.[150]

---

[146] G. D. Ramsay, *The Wiltshire Woollen Industry in the Sixteenth and Seventeenth Centuries*, Oxford, 1943, pp. 71–84, 101–14.

[147] T. Fuller, *The History of the Worthies of England*, London, 1662, pp. 143–4.

[148] *VCH Wilts.*, *IV*, p. 181.

[149] D. C. Coleman, 'Naval Dockyards under the Later Stuarts', EcHR, 2nd ser., VI, 1953–4, p. 140.

[150] See his *Vinetum Britannicum*, 1676 edn.

The textile industries were, by 1750, certainly of less importance than the drink trades, for the Hampshire woollen industry had never compared in importance with that of Berkshire, and had declined even more dramatically since the sixteenth century. Even by 1700, only shalloons and druggets were being manufactured, at such towns as Alton, Andover, and Basingstoke. Romsey was probably the largest textile centre, where some 500 workers were "employed in making those shalloons which are called rattinetts" in 1768,[151] and a large silk mill was still in operation at Overton in 1808.[152]

Until 1750 iron was smelted in the Bramshott region, but on only a small scale as an offshoot of the industry in the Weald of Sussex. After 1750 the entire iron-smelting industry of eastern Hampshire appears to have migrated over the Sussex border, but the industry re-emerged at Funtley and Titchfield on the river Meon near Fareham, where tilt hammers were in operation by 1776. Free-lying ironstone was washed up on the beaches from Christchurch to Beaulieu, and for centuries this had supplied the ancient coastal iron works at Sowley near Lymington, which had almost ceased operation by 1750.[153]

The making of salt by evaporation of sea water was one of Hampshire's oldest industries, centring on Lymington, with subsidiary industries near by at Pennington, Milford, Keyhaven, and Woodside. Portsea provided the only other major salting centre, and both sources of supply were heavily drawn on by the Navy Victualling Department at Portsmouth.

Paper making was an industry which arrived in Hampshire only after 1640, greatly assisted by an influx into the county of Huguenot refugees. There was probably a paper mill at South Stoneham, near Southampton, in 1688 when James II granted a patent to "The Governour and Company of White Papermakers in England". Later, however, the industry migrated north to concentrate in the Whitchurch–Laverstoke–Overton district in the upper valley of the Test. Here the industry flourished so successfully that in 1724 the Portal family, of Huguenot descent, acquired the privilege of manufacturing the paper for Bank of England notes.[154]

Finally, mention should be made of the old-established brickmaking industry of Hampshire. This was concentrated mainly in the south, especially around Southampton, as at Bitterne, Sholing, West End, Chilworth, and Chandler's Ford, where the Bracklesham and Lower Bagshot clays were utilized. Fareham was another important centre of the industry, producing fine red bricks from the upper weathered London clay brickearth which occurred locally.

Brickmaking was also extensively practised on the Isle of Wight, using

[151] Young, *Six Weeks' Tour*, p. 207.
[152] Vancouver, *op. cit.*, p. 403.
[153] See H. W. Trinder, 'The Meon Valley', *Hants. Field Club & Arch. Soc.*, VI, 1907–10, p. 83.
[154] *VCH Hants.*, V, p. 490.

a variety of local earths at such centres as Sandown, Ryde, Newport, Niton, and the Atherfield district. But the industry could also be found as far west as Fordingbridge and as far north as Whitway and Burghclear, with other centres on the Reading beds, as at East Stratton and Bishop's Waltham.

The industries to be found in these five counties between 1640 and 1750 were so many and varied that wholly valid generalizations about their siting and the reasons for their growth, or more often decline, are very difficult to make. When it comes to the location of metalworking and heavy manufacturing industries based on factory production and employing steam power, the close proximity of coalfields is clearly an important factor. But there were very few factories, and no steam engines, save of the Newcomen variety, in the England of 1750. Industry was still for the most part rural domestic industry, and the reasons for the siting of industry of this type are many and varied. In terms of numbers employed, the largest single industry in the counties considered here appears to be the Wiltshire cloth industry, and the second largest the Buckinghamshire lace industry. Both were found in stock-rearing areas with an emphasis on dairying, and there are good reasons why this should have been so.[155] But the two regions were not entirely similar. The former was one of small, enclosed farms centring on the dairy, the latter an area where there were still many open fields and commons with the accent rather on mixed farming. In north-eastern Buckinghamshire the balance tilted more heavily in favour of grain, but here too a lively domestic industry was found in the form of straw plaiting, for which the local wheat straw was particularly well suited. But the third largest employer of labour must have been the malting and brewing industries of Hampshire, Berkshire, and Oxfordshire. The reason for their location on or near the Downs was the obvious one of a plentiful barley supply. As food-processing industries, they were among the very few southern industries of 1750 which could look forward to a reasonably secure future.

The woollen, lace, and drink industries were in a league of their own. Not even the Witney blanket trade with its worldwide export markets could rival them in terms of numbers employed. But there was no shortage of smaller-scale industries, liberally scattered all over the southern counties. Explaining the location of industry really resolves itself into a question of why so many of these industries declined in the long term, while northern industries flourished after 1750. If the English coalfields had been concentrated in lowland Britain, as they were in lowland France, Belgium, and Germany, there can be no doubt that this factor alone would have made a great difference to the eventual siting of major industrial enterprises. But the industrial decline of the south had begun well before the advent of the steam engine, and before even the widespread adoption of coal in many industrial processes. The Industrial Revolution was begun with water power, and the presence of

[155] See Joan Thirsk, 'Industries in the Countryside', in F. J. Fisher, ed., *Essays in the Economic and Social History of Tudor and Stuart England*, Cambridge, 1961, pp. 70–88.

fast-flowing streams giving an ample supply of preferably soft water was a great asset in many industrial processes. In this respect, highland Britain held an advantage, but not a decisive one. Concentration of population is another factor which must be considered. As population grew in areas which were ill equipped to absorb an additional agricultural labour supply, such as enclosed dairying regions or poor-soil farming zones, there may well have been a strong incentive to turn to rural industries. Manufactured goods such as woollens or furniture could then be traded for cereals with arable regions which produced a surplus. On the thinner, poorer soils of the Chilterns, for example, settlement was much less dense than in the clay vale, and a wide range of by-employments sprang up, such as lacemaking, plaiting, wood turning, paper mills, and a whole range of forest-based trades in firewood, timber, barks, and coppice wood. In general terms, the arguments put forward by Thirsk and later amplified by Jones[156] undoubtedly hold good. Pasture–farming areas and poor-soil zones, especially where a system of partible inheritance obtained, were more likely to develop handicraft industries when population pressures began to build up. But the location of industries in the south shows that this rule does not always apply: we would hardly expect it to. Pasture regions and poor-soil regions did not always necessarily develop handicraft industries, and neither were richer arable areas always devoid of industrial by-employments. The dairying region of Wiltshire did indeed have a woollen industry, but it did not occupy the whole dairying region. Woollen manufacture was not found much further east than Malmesbury,[157] and rather more than half of the dairying region, including the western end of the Vale of Whitehorse, boasted no appreciable industry of any kind. The thin-soiled and well-wooded Chilterns did indeed produce a wide range of industries, but this did not apply to all the forested areas. Those of south-eastern Berkshire and north-eastern Hampshire were concerned mainly with the supply of coppice wood and firewood to London prior to 1750, although woodcraft industries did emerge here after this date. The Burnham Beeches and the forests of Savernake and Bere were also devoid of handicraft industries, and so too was the New Forest, except for the manufacture of a very small amount of pottery along its western fringe.[158] The pasture and poor-soil regions did have an alternative to the development of handicraft industries as their population increased. This alternative was emigration, and it appears that many of the people took it. However, it may well be that the surplus labour force simply migrated to the nearest area of available industrial employment, which was probably to be found in another poor-soil or pasture area.

But industrial employment could be found in richer farming regions as

---

[156] E. L. Jones, 'Agricultural Origins of Industry', *PP*, no. 40, 1968, pp. 58–71.

[157] Ramsay, *op. cit.*, map facing contents page.

[158] I owe much of my information on woodland areas to Dr E. J. T. Collins, who intends to publish his findings in due course.

well. The Wiltshire textile industry stretched right across the Downs, from Warminster to Wilton and Salisbury, following the fertile valley of the river Wiley. The Vale of Aylesbury, with its lace and plaiting industries, was hardly a poor-soil zone, or even one where pasture farming was overwhelmingly predominant: it is best described as a mixed farming region. In the barley lands, malting and brewing were major industrial employers.

The question of why some pasture and poor-soil areas should have developed industries while others did not is a difficult one, but it must have depended to a large extent on fortuitous regional factors. One of these may well have been the timely intervention of enterprising capitalists with a reasonable level of entrepreneurial skill, as in the case of the straw-hat industry,[159] while in other places landlords positively resisted the introduction of industries.

It could well be argued that in 1640 the bulk of England's industrial manufacturing capacity lay to the south-east of a line from the Severn to the Wash. But slowly, inexorably, northern competition wore down southern industry until at last we might almost speak of a collapse of the industrial economy of the south. Why was this? The south had certain advantages in its closer proximity to the London market, its longer coastline, and its good river system. In the early eighteenth century, many industries were firmly established in the south, more than enough to provide that training for future factory employment which Jones thought so important.[160] Even if we allow the dubious argument that self-employment in domestic industry provided a vital training for the later discipline of the factory, it would not be difficult to prove that the "roots of industrialization" were at least as long in the south as in the north. Nor was there a crippling dearth of key raw materials. Even coal could be supplied at economic prices via the coasting trade, and later by canals.[161] In addition to the famous Wealden deposits, iron ore was available in north Oxfordshire, south Hampshire, and west Wiltshire, at the last location in rich concentrations.[162] The whole issue is surely a question of degree. The south had its poor-soil and pasture–farming regions, but the north had them in much greater abundance. Over large areas, the rugged northern hills offered little prospect of absorbing a rising population into agricultural pursuits, but good prospects for the discovery of minerals among the convoluted rock strata, and good opportunities for developing water-powered or handicraft industries to employ the cheap surplus labour which such regions were likely to generate. The south was much better able to

[159] Dony, *op. cit.*, p. 25.

[160] Jones, 'Agricultural Origins', p. 71.

[161] The Somerset coalfield was near at hand, and from 1810 was served by the Kennet and Avon canal. By 1815 the more remote Yorkshire steam mills were paying more for their coal than the best-situated Wiltshire mills – *VCH Wilts.*, IV, p. 170.

[162] J. Aubrey, *The Natural History of Wiltshire*, ed. J. Britton, London, 1847, p. 41.

supply both itself and the north with arable produce, and to absorb the agricultural labour force necessary to achieve this. The south had its water-power resources, but highland England was much better equipped in this respect. The south had its coal and iron, but these vital commodities were cheaper and more readily available in the north. The south offered opportunities for investment in industry, but here the opportunities to invest on the agricultural side were usually more tempting. Neither was the performance of those southern entrepreneurs who did invest in industry very impressive. The blanket makers of Witney, the clothiers of Reading, the fine-steel workers of Woodstock, and the glassmakers of Henley all failed to adopt improved production techniques which were readily available to them, and failed also to adapt their products to meet changing market demands.[163] Some entrepreneurs of ability were to be found in the south, such as John Coxeter, the Newbury clothier, and Joseph Portal, the Laverstoke paper maker. These men proved that well-utilized water power was a very economical substitute for steam. But such figures were the exception, and they swam against the tide. As transport facilities improved, the advantages of the north came increasingly to tell, bearing down on southern industry, and it became evident that exceptionally high entre-preneurial talent was necessary merely to sustain industry in the south, as in the case of nineteenth-century Reading. In the north, even mediocre entrepreneurs were under nothing like the same pressures. One by one, the southern industrialists gave up the unequal struggle. Woollen mills were turned over to corn grinding, or tumbled into decay, and Sowley's famous hammer fell silent. Capitalists withdrew investments, and craftsmen migrated to the north. Woollen workers from Wiltshire and Dorset moved to the West Riding,[164] the fine-steel makers of Woodstock moved to Birmingham,[165] and the needle makers of Long Crendon moved to Redditch.[166] An explanation of this migration of industry from lowland to highland Britain must be sought primarily in the fundamental differences between the farming systems of the two regions, which in turn both reflected, and derived from, their basic geographical differences.

[163] For the ineptitude of the Long Crendon needle makers, see *VCH Bucks.*, *II*, p. 127. For the complacency of the Witney blanket makers, see A. Plummer, *The Witney Blanket Industry*, London, 1934, pp. 84–109.

[164] E. Lipson, *The History of the Woollen and Worsted Industries*, London, 1921, pp. 251–4; J. Aikin, *England Delineated*, 6th edn, London, 1809, p. 273.

[165] *VCH War.*, *II*, p. 207.

[166] *VCH Bucks.*, *II*, pp. 127–8.

CHAPTER 11

THE SOUTH-WEST: DORSET, SOMERSET, DEVON, AND CORNWALL

Its westerly situation and the uplands of granite, hard sandstone, chalk, and limestone that adorn much of its area give south-west-country farming its predominantly pastoral emphasis. The river valleys and the narrow coastal strip of southern Cornwall, the South Hams in Devon, and the more extensive vales of Somerset and Dorset supported systems of a more mixed agriculture, but in general the south-west was still in 1750 less notable for intra-regional variations than for its basic uniformity as an upland pastoral region.[1] As in earlier decades west-country farming maintained its close links with the cloth, tin-mining, fishing, and tanning industries, and many farmers had by-employments in these industries.

The century following 1640 saw a progressive regional specialization in livestock within the south-west. The region embraced a nationally famed sheep husbandry in Dorset, an expanding cattle-fattening industry in the Somerset Levels, a dairy industry in south-east Devon and parts of south Somerset, and a livestock-rearing business in north Devon and Cornwall, having well-established droving links by 1750 with London and other markets in south-east England. In many areas the arable acreage contracted and became subordinate to livestock husbandry. The period also saw growing regional specialization in another direction – the rise of the west-country cider industry. Orchard growth, too, was almost entirely at the expense of the arable. Hops, teasels, flax, potatoes, and market-garden crops also witnessed an expansion of production in more localized areas.

Over most of the south-west, this period saw substantial changes in farming – changes in land organization and tenure, in crop and technical innovations, and in an increasing commercialism and regional specialization of production. Only Cornwall lagged visibly behind. Enclosure and the improvement of land, brought about by greater attention to fertility and the application of manures, were dominant features of the age. The first forty years of the seventeenth century had seen in Dorset and Somerset the disafforestation and enclosure of several 'forest' and moorland areas. These had included Gillingham Forest in Dorset and Neroche Forest, Frome–Selwood Forest, and parts of Alder Moor in Somerset. The 1640s and 1650s saw extensive improvements on these recently disafforested areas in Somerset.

[1] M. A. Havinden, 'Agricultural History in the South-West', *Exeter Papers in Econ. Hist.*, II, 1969, p. 7.

Neroche Forest, immediately to the west of the Levels, and disafforested seven years before the Civil War, was said in 1658 to have seen "a great increase of tillage and improvement of pasture" consequent upon the disafforestation. An area of between 6,000 and 7,000 acres, it was claimed to have been worth £2,000 per annum before disafforestation, but by 1658 it was "one-third parte in value by the year more" than before disafforestation, and the same had been "neere a third parte marld over" by the latter date. One estimate put the total gain from the disafforestation as high as £1,500 per annum up to 1658.[2]

To the east of the Levels the disafforestation of Frome–Selwood, and its partition, gave an allotment of one-third part to the tenants of the manor of Marston Biggot, which was described in 1661 as being "the third parte more valuable [to the tenants and commoners of the manor] than their former common of pasture" in the forest. This was partly due to the removal of the deer, but also because, before the enclosure, many persons did "over-presse . . . by putting in of cattle into the said forest who had noe commonable right there" and who did "eat it out soe that it was little worth to the tenants".[3]

The 1630s also saw the first enclosure of part of Alder Moor in the Glastonbury area, comprising 450–500 acres out of the 1,100-acre moor.[4] The further enclosure of the New Cutts, a part of Alder Moor of about 100 acres, was implemented about 1649.[5] The late 1670s saw other enclosures from the moor including 100 acres enclosed by William Strode, and the enclosure of the 115–140-acre Coaksmoor. In 1692 it was stated that only 300 acres of Alder Moor remained open and in common.[6] The remaining area, together with Common Moor and Black-acre, was enclosed in the early 1720s under the first parliamentary Enclosure Act for Somerset.[7] The 300-acre Common Moor and the 20 acres of Black-acre were divided up into five hundred shares or allotments of 16s. to 18s. per annum each.[8]

As Williams has observed, enclosures in Somerset did not proceed without disruptions, and in all the above-mentioned areas the enclosures were thrown down for eight or nine years during the Civil War. Enclosure was particularly vigorously opposed by the commoners on Alder Moor. This was for a variety

[2] PRO, E 134, 1658, Easter 37.

[3] PRO, E 134, 13 Chas II, Mich. 45.

[4] PRO, E 134, 1654, Easter 8; M. Williams, *The Draining of the Somerset Levels*, Cambridge, 1970, pp. 102–4, 110–12. There appears to be some discrepancy between the dates of enclosure and acreages of parts of the moor as given here from the manuscript records and those given by Williams, who implies that a much larger part of the moor was already enclosed by 1640 than was the case.

[5] PRO, E 134, 21 Chas II, Mich. 10.

[6] PRO, E 134, 4 Wm & M., Mich. 15; E 134, 1 Geo. II, Mich. 9.

[7] Williams, *op. cit.*, p. 112; PRO, E 134, 1 Geo. II, Mich. 9.

[8] PRO, E 134, 1 Geo. II, Mich. 9.

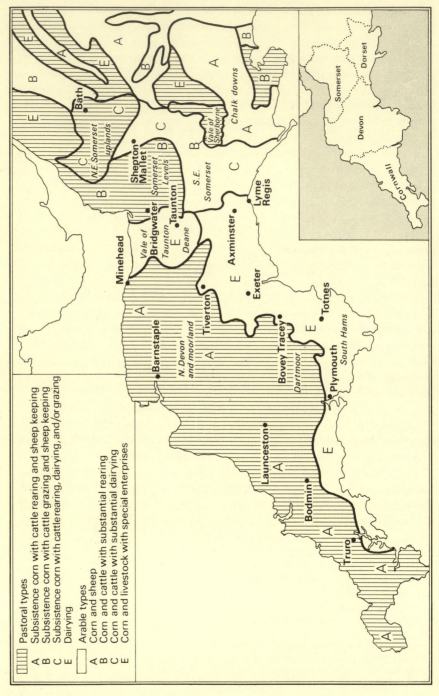

Fig. 11.1. Farming regions of the south-west.

of reasons including the blunt manner in which the enclosures were often implemented, the small size and poor land of the tenants' allotments, poor access, and the loss of much-valued herbage through grubbing up.[9] The major result was a fall in the numbers of cattle and sheep that tenants were able to keep, for want of pasture: a $12\frac{1}{2}$ per cent drop in numbers was common, and in many cases the fall was nearer 25 per cent. Prior to the enclosure, sheep and cattle had been customarily folded on the upland arable, which had been "a great improvement and mannurance to the uplands". Over 500 acres of arable were affected in the Glastonbury area, and some of this was converted to pasture to compensate for the loss of common pasture.[10]

More typical of the post-1640 period than the enclosure of large territories of disafforested lands were the small, piecemeal enclosures. It was stated in 1662 that some part of the common fields of West Pennard in the Somerset Levels, "time out of mind used as arable lands", had been enclosed and converted to meadow six to eight years previously.[11] Similar enclosures and changes in land use were particularly common in the area to the north-east of the Levels in the second half of the seventeenth century. At Kilmersdon, in the period 1640–1705, there were "several inclosures made out of the common arable fields...amounting to fifty acres or thereabouts, some parte whereof have been sowne with French grass seed [sainfoin] and hath been mowed and some other parte hath been improved with marle and hath been made and used as meadow".[12] This reference to sainfoin is echoed in 1705 in nearby Shoscombe where sainfoin was growing on land enclosed out of the common arable fields, some of which enclosures had taken place forty to fifty years before, and others in the last twenty years.[13]

In Dorset enclosures of downland for pasture were being made throughout the period, and constituted the most usual form of enclosure in this kind of country.[14] The progress of enclosure in Devon is more difficult to establish. That open fields existed in sixteenth- and early-seventeenth-century Devon is no longer disputed.[15] However, estimation of their total extent at any given time is not possible, and the problem is further accentuated by difficulties of assessment arising from the widespread use of convertible husbandry in the county, and the confusion between this and the system of outfield

[9] PRO, E 134, 1654, Easter 8; Williams, *op. cit.*, pp. 103–4.
[10] PRO, E 134, 1 Geo. II, Mich. 9; Williams, *op. cit.*, p. 104.
[11] PRO, E 134, 14 Chas II, Mich. 25.
[12] PRO, E 134, 5 Anne, Mich. 15.
[13] PRO, E 134, 4 Anne, Mich. 16; E 134, 5 Geo. I, Easter 2.
[14] J. H. Bettey, *Dorset*, Newton Abbot, 1974, p. 49; C. Taylor, *Dorset*, London, 1970, pp. 127–9.
[15] H. P. R. Finberg, 'The Open Field in Devon', in *Devonshire Studies*, ed., W. G. Hoskins and H. P. R. Finberg, London, 1952, pp. 265–88; M. Havinden and F. Wilkinson, 'Farming', in *Dartmoor: A New Study*, ed. C. Gill, Newton Abbot, 1970, pp. 148–50; Havinden, *op. cit.*, p. 14.

cultivation common in many areas of upland Devon at this period.[16] Nevertheless, it appears probable that a high proportion of cultivated land in Devon was already enclosed by the mid seventeenth century in comparison with the other counties of the south-west. The incomplete county survey in the 1750s disclosed open arable only at Braunton.[17] The same survey showed, however, that common grazing was still practised in a surprising number of fertile down-country parishes.[18]

Enclosure took place in the Devon uplands in this period, but it lagged far behind the progress made on the downlands of Dorset. On Dartmoor eight-acre newtakes continued to be enclosed out of the moor, the cost of enclosing each newtake being about £30 in the late seventeenth century.[19] In Cornwall, enclosures proceeded slowly in this period. An early enclosure was carried out in 1653 by James Lance on Keggan Downs near Truro, which, prior to this date, were described as coarse, barren lands bearing only scrubbed furze, heath, and thorns. Lance enclosed thirty acres of the Downs at a cost of at least £20 for the hedging and enclosing thereof, at 16d. per yard, and a charge of between 50s. and 56s. 8d. per acre for burning, beating, sanding, and manuring, besides 10s. per acre for the cost of carrying the sand. For his outlay, Lance was able to sow the land to wheat and barley in 1654.[20]

The south-west was a progressive farming region in its use of manures in this period.[21] In particular, burn beating, marling, and liming were extensively practised. Burn beating or devonshiring was commonly implemented upon moors and wastes in the west country to reclaim and prepare land for tillage, and was similarly employed to break up land rested under long leys in readiness for cultivation again. On the farms of Tyneham and Eggleston in Dorset in the period 1675–87, a close of fifteen to sixteen acres "all incumbered with furzes and bryers" was "clensed and burnt beate" at a cost of about £30.[22] After heavy liming this reclaimed ground was sown to clover and French grass (sainfoin) by 1687.[23] Burn beating was often a specific preparation for a crop of turnips in south-western counties. At Liskeard in Cornwall "the season...for burning and preparing ground for

---

[16] Havinden and Wilkinson, *op. cit.*, pp. 150–4; R. G. F. Stanes, 'Devon Agriculture in the Mid-Eighteenth Century: The Evidence of the Milles Enquiries', *Exeter Papers in Econ. Hist.*, II, 1969, p. 45; H. S. A. Fox, 'Outfield Cultivation in Devon and Cornwall: A Reinterpretation', *Exeter Papers in Econ. Hist.*, VIII, 1973, pp. 19–38. The essential differences between convertible husbandry and outfield cultivation are concisely presented by Fox in his article, p. 22.

[17] Stanes, *op. cit.*, p. 45.

[18] *Ibid.*, pp. 45–6.

[19] PRO, E 134, 3 Anne, Mich. 11.

[20] PRO, E 134, 14 & 15 Chas II, Hil. 9.

[21] R. G. F. Stanes, ed., 'A Georgicall Account of Devonshire and Cornwall in Answer to Some Queries concerning Agriculture, by Samuel Colepresse, 1667', *Devonshire Assoc.*, XCVI, 1964, pp. 272–4.

[22] PRO, E 134, 3 & 4 Jas II, Hil. 14.   [23] *Ibid.*

turnips" is mentioned in 1725, and on the Weld estate at East Lulworth, Dorset, a close on Park farm was burn-baked and sown in turnips in 1742.[24] Burn beating appears to have been most widespread in Dorset and in Devon, but in the latter, at least, may already have been of diminishing importance by 1750.[25]

Marling was particularly important in Dorset, east Somerset, and south-east Devon. Marl was applied by Sir Philip Sydenham to improve a large area of Brimpton farm in West Coker, Somerset, towards the end of the seventeenth century.[26] In 1703 it was stated that "Marle is a common, lasting and a great improvement" in and about the parish of Gillingham in Dorset.[27] Lime was a well-established manure in the west country by 1640, and it retained its popularity in the succeeding decades.[28]

Notwithstanding the widespread use of a few key manures and manuring techniques, the real strength of the south-west as a well-manured and improved region lay in the extremely wide variety of manures used and adapted to local conditions. These ranged from dung to ashes, sea sand, and seaweed.[29] In the parish of Bridestowe on the north-western fringes of Dartmoor, sixty bushels of lime of sixteen gallons each were stated in the 1690s to be "the usuall dressing in that countrey" per acre; this would last for three crops.[30] In the same parish, a dressing of eighteen score horse seams of good stall and stable dung per acre, applied on the tenement of Way in the 1690s, was described as a "better dressing than is commonly used in that country".[31] These application rates of the 1690s, taking into account the geographical position of Bridestowe within Devon and the poor soils of the district, correspond closely with those shown in the mid-eighteenth-century survey of the county, which records a significant difference in application rates for both dung and lime between north and south Devon, the southern parishes applying less dung than but almost double the amount of lime per acre as parishes in north Devon.[32]

The pace of agrarian change was substantially reflected in the spread of the new root crops and artificial grasses in the south-west, and in this respect the years between 1670 and 1690 witnessed the greatest transformation. In a few progressive districts the new crops and grasses were grown in a limited or experimental way in the 1660s, but generally it was the following two decades that constituted the era of the new crops in the west country, although in Cornwall these changes did not come until the eighteenth

[24] PRO, E 134, 4 Geo. II, Mich. 5; Dorset RO, D10/E81.
[25] Stanes, 'Devon Agriculture', p. 53.
[26] PRO, E 134, 8 Geo. II, Mich. 8.
[27] PRO, E 134, 3 Anne, Easter 28.
[28] Havinden, op. cit., pp. 15–16.
[29] Stanes, 'Devon Agriculture', pp. 50–3.
[30] PRO, E 134, 12 Wm III, Trin. 8.   [31] Ibid.
[32] Stanes, 'Devon Agriculture', pp. 50–1.

century. Frequently the new crops brought with them new rotations, and changes in landholding and land use, but, particularly in Dorset and east Somerset, these changes were often accommodated within the structure of the old common fields until well into the eighteenth century.

Somerset was in the forefront in the introduction of the new crops. In the productive Vale of Taunton Deane, clover grass was sown in Lydeard St Lawrence and the surrounding parishes of Combe Florey, Kingston St Mary, Cheddon Fitzpaine, West Bagborough, and Bishop's Lydeard from about 1665, and for six or seven years before that, experimentally.[33] In 1679 it was stated that 440–500 acres were planted with clover grass in the parish of Lydeard St Lawrence alone, and the view was expressed that it had occasioned great improvement, the parish being able to support a greater number of sheep and cattle than previously. Moreover, the arable lands "now usually sowen with clover and corne, which, before clover was sowen in these p[ar]ts, would not without dressing after three cropps taken therein be in a condition for corne againe within six or seven yeares, will now after three cropps by the meanes of the clover sowen therein, if eaten and depastured with sheep and cattle and not mowen, be in a condition for corne againe in about three yeares".[34] At Norton Fitzwarren just outside Taunton, it was stated in 1700 that turnips had been grown in the fields there for "the space of thirty years and upwards".[35]

The north-eastern corner of Somerset, north of the Mendips, also experienced the early introduction of the new crops. Artificial grasses were being sown in the Wellow area by 1670 and probably had been grown there since the early 1660s.[36] In the Levels their introduction came less swiftly, undoubtedly owing, in part, to the relative abundance of natural pasture. Clover was being grown at Middlezoy by the early 1680s, and at Compton Bishop the first artificial grasses appear not to have been sown until the late 1680s.[37] The introduction of artificial grasses in the Levels generally appears to date from this decade, but in some localities the new root crops were adopted very much earlier in the Levels, and in the late 1660s an acre of turnips was grown on land enclosed out of Alder Moor near Glastonbury.[38]

In the south of Somerset these changes appear to have come after 1680 rather than before. At Misterton in 1693 it was said that there had been a great improvement "of late yeares" by the sowing of artificial grasses on lands "soe impovereshed and worne out that they would not well beare Corne", and that, as a further result, cattle numbers had increased by a third,

---

[33] PRO, E 134, 31 Chas II, Easter 4; E. Kerridge, *The Agricultural Revolution*, London, 1967, pp. 283, 309.

[34] PRO, E 134, 31 Chas II, Easter 4.

[35] PRO, E 134, 12 Wm III, Trin. 7.

[36] PRO, E 134, 4 Anne, Mich. 16; E 134, 5 & 6 Geo. I, Trin. 4.

[37] PRO, E 134, 8 & 9 Wm III, Hil. 21; E 134, 5 Geo. I, Mich. 17.

[38] PRO, E 134, 24 Chas II, Mich. 4.

whilst more sheep were also being kept.[39] In Dorset the new grasses made their impact from the late 1670s. Clover grass was grown in the parish of Hampreston, Dorset, from 1677–8, and in the 1680s clover and French grass (sainfoin) overcame a fodder shortage for the livestock on the farms of Tyneham and Eggleston.[40]

Payhembury in east Devon records one of the earliest introductions of clover in Devon, dating from about 1666, whilst at Buckleigh in the Exe valley clover/ever/trefoil husbandry was introduced about 1670, there being nearly 200 acres under artificial grasses in the parish of Buckleigh by 1700.[41] Further west, at Morchard Bishop, clover was stated to have been "very little used" in the early 1670s, and not generally sown there until 1677. By 1683 about 100 acres were under clover in the parish, and it was stated to be "a very great improvement".[42] Turnips were being grown at Bovey Tracey in 1686, but generally they were still a very minor crop in Devon in 1750, by which time they appear to have been grown predominantly in the northern half of the county.[43]

In Cornwall the agrarian revolution came only in the eighteenth century, partly owing to the lesser significance of many of the new grasses and crops for the county's farming systems, partly to the county's greater geographical isolation and the lesser importance of agriculture within the Cornish economy, and partly to greater farming poverty and resistance to agrarian change.[44] Significantly, on a tour through the county in 1670 Mr Pips observed "how they who do work in the mines were more intelligent than ye tillers of ye soil".[45] The earliest advances came in the more progressive south-east of the county, with turnips being grown in St Germans by 1715 and at Liskeard by 1725.[46] Sheep were being folded upon a substantial acreage of turnips on the Rashleigh estate at St Ive near Liskeard in 1740–1, and sixty acres were being prepared for the next crop of turnips there in spring 1741.[47] An acre of turnips was growing at St Mewan near St Austell in central Cornwall in 1746, indicating that turnip husbandry had spread at least this far west by this date.[48] These facts undermine the argument, derived

[39] PRO, E 134, 5 Wm & M., Easter 3.

[40] PRO, E 134, 5 Wm & M., Mich. 20; E 134, 3 & 4 Jas II, Hil. 14.

[41] PRO, E 134, 28 Chas II, Trin. 1; E 134, 1 Anne, Easter 5.

[42] PRO, E 134, 34 Chas II, Mich. 14.

[43] Inv. no. 247: of Thomas Wills of Bovey Tracey, yeoman (12 Nov. 1686), in M. Cash, ed., 'Devon Inventories of the Sixteenth and Seventeenth Centuries', Devon & Cornwall Rec. Soc., NS XI, 1966, p. 157; Stanes, 'Devon Agriculture', pp. 54–5.

[44] M. Overton, 'The 1801 Crop Returns for Cornwall', Exeter Papers in Econ. Hist., VIII, 1973, pp. 49–53, touches on some of the factors limiting the impact of the 'new husbandry' in Cornwall.

[45] 'Fragments of Mr. Pips, his Diary during a Tour in the Western Provinces (September 1670)', Roy. Cornwall Gazette, 27 Sept. 1850, p. 7.

[46] PRO, E 134, 5 Geo. I, Hil. 1; E 134, 5 Geo. I, Mich, 10 (St Germans); E 134, 4 Geo. II, Mich. 5; E 134, 1 Geo. II, Easter 3; E 134, 2 Geo. II, Trin. 2 (Liskeard).

[47] Cornwall RO, DDR 5299.   [48] PRO, E 134, 22 Geo. II, Hil. 1.

from the 1801 crop returns, that turnips spread to Cornwall from Devon only in the late eighteenth century.[49]

Clover grass too was growing at St Germans by 1714, and the most common of the artificial grasses were to be found in several places in east and central Cornwall by 1750, although acreages generally were extremely small.[50] Thomas Pitt, owner of a large estate in east Cornwall at Boconnoc and of property in Devon, wrote to a merchant company in Bordeaux in December 1722 that he had been informed that "your country produces a sort of grass seed called lucern that affords four or five crops a year...I desire you to send me five or six bushells of ye newest and freshest seed of it." Pitt received the seed in the following March, but there is, unfortunately, no record of whether it was sown on his Cornish or on his Devon estates, or of what success attended his venture.[51]

Agrarian improvement was assisted in many areas by better drainage and watering techniques. Drainage work continued at a very slow pace in the Levels of Somerset during this period, whilst increased attention was paid to coastal protection in north Somerset.[52] More significant was the spread of water meadows, particularly in Dorset and Devon. A network of these was established in Dorset in the Frome and Piddle valleys, and they have been described as "the vital link" in the closer integration of the sheep and corn husbandries on the Dorset Downs in the first half of the eighteenth century.[53] In the parish of West Knighton, Dorset, Lewell farm was stated in 1675 to have more than doubled in value since being improved by "watering".[54] In Devon, watering of meadows is recorded at Kenn in 1683, and at Northleigh, also in 1683, a field formerly tilled to crops was converted to a meadow by water "brought upon ye said field".[55]

Agricultural change manifested itself boldly in changes in land use over the period. In general the arable gradually but continually contracted in many areas of the south-west as more land was put to meadow and pasture. The increasing importance of pasture farming represented a positive shift towards specialization in that branch of agriculture to which the south-west was best suited, and which the dawning of a national economy increasingly allowed it to pursue. In some areas, particularly in north-east Somerset, it was the artificial grasses that replaced the traditional arable husbandry.[56] In others,

[49] Overton, op. cit., p. 53.　　　[50] PRO, E 134, 5 Geo. I, Hil. 1.

[51] PRO, C 108/424, pt I, no. 14, letter book: 11 Oct. 1714 – 11 Dec. 1724.

[52] Williams, op. cit., pp. 110–22; PRO, E 134, 25 & 26 Chas II, Hil. 18; E 134, 26 Chas II, Easter 23.

[53] Taylor, op. cit., pp. 130–1; Bettey, op. cit., pp. 50–1; B. J. Whitehead, 'The Management and Land – Use of Water Meadows in the Frome Valley, Dorset', Dorset Nat. Hist. & Arch. Soc., LXXXIX, 1967, pp. 258–67, 277.　　　[54] PRO, E 134, 27 Chas II, Mich. 2.

[55] PRO, E 134, 36 & 37 Chas II, Hil. 7; E 134, 5 Wm & M., Mich. 19.

[56] PRO, E 134, 4 Anne, Mich. 16; E 134, 5 Geo. I, Easter 2 (Wellow); E 134, 5 Anne, Mich. 15 (Kilmersdon).

orchard expansion eroded the arable.[57] In two areas only did no decline in the arable acreage occur: on the downlands of Dorset, particularly after 1700, pasture was broken up for tillage to support a more integrated and economically viable sheep–corn husbandry; in Cornwall, an overextended arable acreage in many areas remained little touched in this period.

In Cornwall, Whetter has detected a substantial shift from wheat to barley growing in the first half of the seventeenth century, and, on the basis of his statistical sample, it appears that by 1680–1700 barley occupied a slightly greater acreage than wheat (7 to 6) in Cornwall as a whole.[58] Available evidence suggests that the period 1700–50 saw little change in the relative importance of these two grains except possibly for further increases in barley acreage in the far west of the county. Oats were considerably less important than wheat in Cornwall as a whole by 1750, and rye was already an insignificant crop by 1700 in the county. The acreage under peas and beans – always small – appears to have declined over the period, and beans were virtually unknown over large areas of the county.[59]

In Devon, wheat was the most important grain by acreage.[60] Peas and beans, and, in many parts of the county, oats too, were relatively more important crops in Devon than they were in Cornwall. Rye also was still an important crop in north and moorland Devon in 1700, although by 1750 it was little cultivated in the county.[61] Dartmoor, despite the poorness of its soils, supported sizeable acreages of oats and, in the seventeenth century, also of rye.[62]

In these two westernmost counties, crop rotations remained simple and traditional almost without exception. Convertible husbandry with its temporary leys was a satisfactory system which served to ensure that the new crops and artificial grasses had not established themselves in regular rotations in either county by 1750. Colepresse in 1667 stated that in both counties a six-course rotation was usual. In Cornwall two crops of wheat were followed by three of barley and one of oats or peas. In Devon one wheat crop was followed by two of barley, one of oats, one of peas, and another of oats,

[57] PRO, E 134, 22 Chas II, Easter 37 (Poughill, Cornwall); E 134, 10 Geo. I, Hil. 3; E 134, 10 Geo. I, Hil. 24 (Broadclyst, Devon); E 134, 11 Geo. I, Easter 4 (West Lydford, Somerset).

[58] J. Whetter, Cornwall in the Seventeenth Century: An Economic Survey of Kernow, Padstow, 1974, pp. 46–8.

[59] C. Fiennes, The Journeys of Celia Fiennes, ed. C. Morris, London, 1947, p. 267, records the dearth of beans in part of west Cornwall; PRO, C 108/424, pt I, no. 14, letter book: letter dated 24 Sept. 1724 states that there are no horse beans in at least a part of east Cornwall.

[60] Stanes, 'Devon Agriculture', p. 54.

[61] PRO, E 134, 3 Anne, Easter 1 (Lydford, 1704); E 134, 13 Wm III, Trin. 7 (Lapford, 1701); E 134, 4 & 5 Wm & M., Hil. 12 (Wembworthy, 1692); E 134, 12 Wm III, Trin. 8. (Bridestowe, 1700). These indicate the importance of rye in north Devon c. 1700. Stanes, 'Devon Agriculture', p. 54, underlines its decline by 1750.

[62] PRO, E 134, 3 Anne, Easter 1; E 134, 1658/9, Hil. 14. See also Havinden and Wilkinson, op. cit., pp. 160, 165.

whilst a slightly modified rotation, sometimes extending over seven years, was practised in the "marl country" of south-east Devon.[63] The temporary ley that followed such rotations was commonly of seven to eight years.[64] In Cornwall, at least, other evidence suggests that for many areas the full six-course rotation was too exhausting, and not in fact commonly practised, a three- or four-course rotation instead being the norm. These shorter rotations were clearly normal in the parish of St Tudy in the 1660s and in the parish of Lezant in the 1680s: in both parishes wheat was the first crop of the rotation, and occasionally the second too, being generally followed by one or two years of barley and/or oats and a fourth-year crop of oats.[65] Similarly, Fussell implies that a four-course rotation was usual in Devon, and on Way farm at Bridestowe, on the poor soils of the western fringes of Dartmoor, a three-course rotation of rye and oats was considered to be the only profitable rotation in the 1690s.[66]

Colepresse in the 1660s gave wheat yields as being 10–20 bu per acre in Cornwall, and slightly higher in Devon; for barley 10–16 bu in Cornwall as against 10–25 or 30 in Devon, and for oats 10–16 bu in Cornwall and 10–20 in Devon; in respect of the "marl country" of south-east Devon he specifically drew attention to the fact that wheat and barley yields were considerably below, and oats yields above, those in the rest of Devon.[67] George King's observation in 1657 that in that year he had the best barley growing in the parish of St Columb Major, Cornwall, and that he believed he had 20 bu to an acre would appear to accord well with Colepresse's statement of yields at that date.[68] In the 1690s, however, Roger Maddaford was complaining bitterly of a poor crop of barley yielding 9 bu of 16 gallons (equivalent to 18 Winchester bushels) per acre, after sowing 2 such Devon bushels per acre, which he regarded as overgenerous, on well-dressed but basically poor soils at Bridestowe, Devon.[69] Comparing Colepresse's best yield figures with those given in the Milles survey for Devon in the 1750s, Stanes has concluded that, with the exception of oats, there was little advance over the century.[70] Such a conclusion is perhaps better regarded as tentative, since it depends heavily upon there having been little change in sowing rates between 1660 and 1750, the Milles survey unfortunately including no

[63] Stanes, 'A Georgicall Account', p. 289.

[64] G. E. Fussell, 'Four Centuries of Farming Systems in Devon, 1500–1900', *Devonshire Assoc.*, LXXXIII, 1951, p. 187. See also PRO, E 134, 31 Chas II, Easter 4, for a statement of a similar length of 'ley' after cropping in west Somerset in the 1670s.

[65] PRO, E 134, 22 Chas II, Mich. 17; E 134, 4 Jas II, Mich. 6.

[66] Fussell, *op. cit.*, p. 187; PRO, E 134, 12 Wm III, Trin. 8.

[67] Stanes, 'A Georgicall Account', p. 292; R. V. Lennard, 'English Agriculture under Charles II', EcHR, IV, 1932, p. 40.

[68] PRO, E 134, 1660, Easter 18.

[69] PRO, E 134, 12 Wm III, Trin. 8.

[70] Stanes, 'Devon Agriculture', p. 58.

information on sowing rates.[71] On this crucial issue there was almost certainly more local variation than Colepresse concedes, and therefore also in the upward movement of yields in the century after 1650.

Change on the arable in Dorset during this period was of a distinctive nature. Adoption of the new crops and grasses, and their integration in new rotation systems, was carried much further than in Devon or Cornwall, yet alongside this in other parts of Dorset the common fields and fallowing continued, and it was these latter features that signalled the conclusion in late-eighteenth-century surveys that Dorsetshire farming was backward.[72] If the quality of agrarian change was particularly uneven in Dorset, it should be remembered that over large areas of the county arable farming was secondary to livestock — sheep on the chalk downs and cattle in the clay vales — and it was livestock husbandry that better reflected the advances in the county's farming during this period. However, some of the best arable practices were to be found on the many downland farms where a closer integration of arable and livestock farming was forged in the first half of the eighteenth century.

On the chalk downs of Dorset barley acreage exceeded that of wheat, in some areas greatly so. Vetches were an important downland crop and the area devoted to them appears to have increased over the period. On the heathlands wheat and barley acreages were more or less equal in the seventeenth century, but one effect of the low-price decades of the early eighteenth century was a gain in barley acreage against that of wheat. Rye was still an important crop on the heathlands in the 1690s, but thereafter showed a sharp decline. The eighteenth century also saw an increase in the popularity of vetches on the heathlands. Beans were unimportant in Dorset except in the clay vales.[73]

The sole surviving Royal Society report for Dorset, covering the hilly borderlands with Wiltshire and the vale between Shaftesbury and Blandford, indicates that seed was sown in the 1660s there at the rate of $2-2\frac{1}{2}$ bu per acre for wheat, 3–4 bu for both barley and oats, and 2 bu for peas.[74] In the same area, at Gussage All Saints in 1735, wheat was being sown at the rate of $2\frac{1}{3}$ bu per acre, thus indicating no change over seventy-five years.[75] Less is known of crop yields, but in fertile west Dorset in the Beaminster area a farmer's notebook records in 1738 that 30 bu of wheat per acre was "a great crop", 20 bu, middling, and 15 bu, small.[76]

[71] *Ibid.*, pp. 57–8.

[72] See, for example, Bettey, *op. cit.*, p. 53.

[73] The information in this paragraph is based upon a study of the Dorset inventories for the period.

[74] G. E. Fussell, 'Four Centuries of Farming Systems in Dorset', *Dorset Nat. Hist. & Arch. Soc.*, LXXIII, 1951, p. 122; Lennard, *op. cit.*, p. 39.

[75] Dorset RO, DA/I 1730–60/8.

[76] Dorset RO, D279/E4.

Convertible husbandry was very much less important in Dorset than in the more westerly counties and is not mentioned at all in the only extant Royal Society report for the county. However, a primitive type of this husbandry was practised in parts of Dorset. On the Weld estate at East Lulworth in the period 1655–1714 several parcels of pasture land were broken up for a few crops of grain, and then allowed to revert to pasture: the crop rotations on this estate in the 1670s included three crops of wheat and barley, four crops of oats and rye, five crops of oats, wheat, barley, and peas, and six successive crops of wheat and barley.[77] Such rotations had been changed beyond recognition by the 1730s and 1740s on the same estate, mainly by the bold incorporation of clover and French grass in the rotations, but also through the introduction of turnips and the increased cultivation of vetches. In Peers Close on the estate, crops of peas, wheat, barley, and of barley and oats in the years 1738–41 were followed by two years under clover. In 1744 the close was put to a further four-year rotation of grains – oats, wheat, barley, and oats – followed by two more years under clover.[78]

In respect of its arable farming, Somerset was the wheat county *par excellence* of the south-west, with wheat assuming a dominance among the grains unequalled elsewhere in the west country. Only on a small minority of Somerset farms did barley occupy a superior acreage, and in 1750 barley as a second-ranking crop was still considerably less important relative to wheat than was the case in 1801, as revealed in the crop returns for the latter date. The other distinctive feature of the arable in Somerset was the importance of peas and beans relative to the major grains: these two crops had always been important in open-field rotations in Somerset, and enclosures did not diminish this importance.[79] Only in the hills of north and west Somerset were peas and beans absent. Elsewhere they occupied significant acreages: in many areas of south Somerset both crops were important, but on the heavy soils of the Levels beans predominated, whilst in the Vale of Taunton Deane peas were the more favoured crop. Wheat was only an insignificant crop on the poor upland soils of the hills of west Somerset and the Mendips: in these areas oats were the dominant grain crop.[80] Rye was being grown at Clatworthy in the Brendon Hills in 1690 but generally was very little grown in Somerset by this date.[81]

Despite the early adoption of artificial grasses in parts of Somerset, their spread throughout the county was slow, and open-field farming with

[77] PRO, E 134, 1 Geo. I, Hil. 10.

[78] Dorset RO, D10/E81.

[79] M. Williams, 'The 1801 Crop Returns for Somerset', *Somerset Arch. & Nat. Hist. Soc.*, CXIII, 1968–9, pp. 78–9.

[80] The statements in this paragraph concerning the relative importance of different crops are based on the evidence from inventories and farm account books.

[81] PRO, E 134, 4 Wm & M., Trin. 2.

traditional rotations and fallowing remained typical features of arable farming in the south of Somerset generally in the early eighteenth century. On an estate at Yeovilton in 1695 there were "seventy-five acres of arrable land, whereof one year, thirty-three, another year, twenty-four, and a third year, eighteen acres, according as the course of the fields comes round, doe lye for fallow", whilst in 1702 it was stated that "about a third part of the said arrable land [of the parsonage of Stoke-under-Hambdon] commonly lyes fallow...according to the method and usual management of arable grounde within the parishes of Stoke-under-Hambdon and Norton-under-Hambdon and other places neere thereto adjoining".[82] Convertible husbandry was not widely pursued in Somerset, but at Carhampton on the west Somerset coast it was said in 1698 that several parcels of land had "beene sometime in tillage and sometime in pasture" in an irregular alternation over the previous thirty years.[83] The narrow coastal plain in this part of Somerset was a very prosperous and productive area of mixed and arable farming: Richard Withers, a yeoman who died in 1677 leaving an estate, crops, and livestock worth about £850 at West Quantoxhead, was said to be "a lender of moneyes" in the area.[84]

At Yeovilton in 1695 it was stated that "the usuall way of husbandry" in preparing the ground for seed was to plough it four times for wheat, twice for barley, and once for oats, beans, or peas.[85] In the Cannington area, the arable was usually ploughed thrice for barley c. 1708.[86] Records of crop yields in Somerset for this period are scanty, but the progress of the better farms in Somerset is probably fairly indicated by an 18 bu per acre yield for wheat obtained at Wembdon, near Bridgwater, in 1710, and by yields of 20 bu for wheat and 25 bu for barley, beans, and peas per acre, obtained at Bleadon in the 1740s.[87]

Some areas of the south-west, and in particular Somerset and the South Hams in Devon, were districts with a grain surplus in most years, and there were regular coastwise shipments to London from the south Devon ports, and also shipments from Somerset to south Wales.[88] In some years Cornwall too exported grain coastwise.[89] However, the margin between surplus and shortage remained slender in an age so heavily dependent on the harvest, and when the harvest failed, as in 1727 and 1728, corn had to be imported from

---

[82] PRO, E 134, 8 Wm III, Easter 15; E 134, 1 Anne, Trin. 5.

[83] PRO, E 134, 10 Wm III, Easter 7.

[84] PRO, E 134, 34 Chas II, Trin. 8.

[85] PRO, E 134, 8 Wm III, Easter 15.

[86] PRO, E 134, 7 Anne, Trin. 1.

[87] PRO, E 134, 10 & 11 Anne, Hil. 4 (Wembdon); Somerset RO, D/D/C 1747 (Bleadon).

[88] PRO, E 134, 6 Geo. II, Mich. 10, provides an example of shipments of grain from Kingsbridge, Devon, to London in the 1720s; E 134, 8 Chas I, Mich. 48, provides information about the grain trade between the Somerset ports and south Wales at the beginning of the period.

[89] Whetter, op. cit., p. 54.

abroad.[90] In Cornwall particular marketing difficulties existed: the poor arrangements for the distribution and marketing of grain in the county provoked disturbances among Cornwall's large population of tinners and served to accentuate the effects of a poor harvest.[91]

Market gardening was well established in the neighbourhood of all the region's concentrations of population by the mid eighteenth century. It flourished in south-east Devon, where as early as the 1650s several small plots of cabbages, carrots, beans, and turnips are recorded growing in the parish of Ottery St Mary, some of the produce of which was sold at Axminster, Lyme Regis, and other towns in the area.[92] Exeter had an extensive market-gardening hinterland. Several growers in the parish of Shobrooke, seven miles north-west of Exeter, were said in 1719 to carry great quantities of their best fruit and vegetables to market in Exeter and Crediton.[93] South of Exeter, at Lympstone, carrots, leeks, and cabbages were being raised in the 1680s.[94] The parish of Egg Buckland had developed by 1750 as a market-gardening area supplying Plymouth with cabbages, carrots, turnips, and beans.[95] At Bovey Tracey on the fringes of the prosperous and populous area east of Dartmoor carrots and turnips were being raised in 1686.[96] Market gardens were also extensive in the neighbourhood of Paignton by 1750, and a speciality of this area was the cultivation of cabbages. Between 150 and 200 acres were devoted to large cabbages there in 1755, and these were marketed throughout Devon and adjacent counties, and also shipped coastwise to south-coast ports and London.[97] In many places along the South Hams seaboard, market gardens, supplying the many fishing settlements, were well established by the last quarter of the seventeenth century: in the years 1670–3 Mr Buddaford had twenty acres of arable in the parish of Dittisham, the produce of which included carrots, cabbages, and turnips, much of which was sold at markets out of the parish.[98]

In Somerset, Taunton was a natural focus of population, with the Vale of Taunton Deane its fertile food-providing hinterland. The vale emerged as a carrot-growing area of the first importance between 1670 and 1690.[99] The parish of Bishop's Lydeard, just outside Taunton, was described as being

[90] *Kentish Post*, 1,007 (17 Jan. 1728), p. 1; 1,035 (24 Apr. 1728), p. 1; 1,048 (8 June 1728), p. 1; 1,086 (19 Oct. 1728), p. 1.

[91] *Ibid.*, 1,040 (11 May 1728), p. 4; 1,042 (18 May 1728), p. 1; 1,044 (25 May 1728), p. 1; 1,047 (5 June 1728), p. 1; 1,048 (8 June 1728), p. 1; 3,229 (19 Oct. 1748), p. 1.

[92] PRO, E 134, 1659, Easter 22; E 134, 1659, Mich. 11; E 134, 1659/60, Hil. 11.

[93] PRO, E 134, 6 Geo. I, Mich. 12.

[94] PRO, E 134, 1 Wm & M., Mich. 8.

[95] Stanes, 'Devon Agriculture', p. 54.

[96] Inv. no. 247 in Cash, 'Devon Inventories', p. 157.

[97] Stanes, 'Devon Agriculture', pp. 50, 55–6.

[98] Devon RO, CC27/103.

[99] Kerridge, *op. cit.*, pp. 269, 309.

"a great gardening country" in 1718.[100] Stephen Dringe rented an acre of pasture in the parish of Norton Fitzwarren on the outskirts of Taunton which he converted to a garden and in which he grew beans, turnips, carrots, and cabbages in 1698 and 1699.[101] Shepton Mallet market in east Somerset handled considerable quantities of vegetables and fruit from a surrounding area of market gardens as early as the 1640s.[102] In north Somerset several persons living in the parish of Axbridge were renting small parcels of land in the common fields of Cheddar, the next adjacent parish, in the 1690s and raising onions, leeks, lettuce, and carrots.[103]

Bristol was a major market, supplied with produce from Gloucestershire and the Vale of Evesham to the north as well as from Somerset. The development from the 1690s of a significant potato-growing area in Bristol's Somerset hinterland was an important characteristic of the Bristol market. In the parish of Portbury, one of several growers, George Collett, had an average four or five acres (with as many as nine acres in one year), annually planted to potatoes in the years 1707–12, and he claimed that if an acre of potatoes "hit right, it was worth as much as three acres of wheat". The total cost of planting and of raising and delivering the potatoes to market in this area was £20 or £21 per acre in the first year, but perhaps only half of this in the second year, the potatoes usually being grown in the same ground for two or three years together. An acre of good potatoes in the Portbury area generally yielded forty bushels in the early eighteenth century.[104] An instance of the regional spread of agricultural seeds and practices is recorded for the parish of Yatton, eight miles south of Portbury, where in about 1699 two Lancastrians settled, bringing potatoes from Lancashire with them and planting "that kind of potatoes" in Yatton. It was claimed that in one favourable year they made as much as £50 out of one acre of their potatoes.[105]

The spread of potato husbandry in the south-west is unfortunately poorly documented. In the mid eighteenth century potatoes were positively recorded as being grown in only three parishes in Devon as a crop – at Dolton-Dowland in the heart of north Devon, and at Collompton and Holcombe Rogus in the east of the county.[106] In the parish of Beaford, adjacent to Dolton-Dowland, several persons were growing small quantities of potatoes for sale in neighbouring markets in 1732 and 1733.[107] The spread of potatoes in Cornwall appears to have been at least as early as and far more

[100] PRO, E 134, 4 & 5 Geo. I, Trin. 3.
[101] PRO, E 134, 12 Wm III, Trin. 7.
[102] PRO, E 134, 7 Wm III, Trin. 16.
[103] PRO, E 134, 13 Wm III, Trin. 19.
[104] PRO, E 134, 11 Anne, Mich. 3.
[105] Ibid.
[106] Stanes, 'Devon Agriculture', p. 54.
[107] PRO, E 134, 9 Geo. II, Hil. 6.

extensive in the first half of the eighteenth century than in Devon: there is abundant evidence from parishes in all parts of Cornwall to give substance to Borlase's observation in 1758 that the potato was "everywhere cultivated" in the county.[108]

The important fishing industry of the south-west ensured that hemp and flax were locally significant crops in several areas of the region. All four counties contributed to hemp production, and in Devon and Cornwall hemp growing was clearly concentrated in the fishing districts. In the east of the region, many of the growing districts were well inland, the crop being grown in small quantities in most districts of west Dorset in the seventeenth century. Somerset also had an important hemp area in the extreme south of the county which broadly represented a northward continuation of the west Dorset growing area.[109] Generally, individual hemp plots rarely exceeded 1½ acres, particularly in the west of the region, but in the period 1640–90 several plots of 3–4 acres were recorded in the south Somerset area.[110] The late seventeenth century, however, saw a marked decline in hemp growing throughout the south-west, foreign imports of ropes and nets becoming increasingly significant, and by 1750 hemp production tended to be found mainly in the immediate vicinity of the smaller fishing ports, Combe Martin in north Devon being a typical example.[111]

Cornwall's flax production followed the pattern of that of hemp, declining through the second half of the seventeenth century to become inconsiderable by 1700.[112] In the other south-western counties, however, a quite different pattern was apparent, the crop experiencing expansion, particularly after about 1690. In Devon the major flax area lay in the south-east of the county and merged with the west Dorset growing districts.[113] The west Dorset area was important throughout this period, but continued to grow to its maximum extent after 1750. A small flax-growing area in south Somerset, centred in the East and West Coker district, was augmented in the 1690s by the development of a major flax-growing area in the Bridgwater, Taunton, and east Quantocks districts. The cultivation of flax dates from 1690–1 in the parish of Creech St Michael, and in the 1730s large crops of flax are known to have been cultivated at Wembdon and at West Bagborough.[114]

[108] W. Borlase, *The Natural History of Cornwall*, Oxford, 1758, p. 89.

[109] The information on hemp-growing areas is drawn from the surviving inventories (housed in the county record offices) and from exchequer depositions (PRO) for each county.

[110] Somerset RO, DD/SP 1644/66 (S. Petherton, 1644: 3½ acres of hemp); PRO, E 134, 1654, Mich. 3; E 134, 1655, Easter 13 (Chiselborough, 1647–53: various parcels of hemp of 3–4 acres); PRO, E 134, 3 Jas II, Easter 3 (E. Coker, 1685; 3 acres, 1 yard of hemp).

[111] Stanes, 'Devon Agriculture', p. 55. The decline in hemp growing is clearly revealed in the inventories over the period 1640–1750.

[112] Whetter, *op. cit.*, p. 49.   [113] Stanes, 'Devon Agriculture', p. 55.

[114] PRO, E 134, 3 Jas II, Easter 3; C 107/126; E 134, 7 Wm III, Mich. 6; E 134, 7 & 8 Wm III, Hil. 13; Somerset RO, D/D/C 1741.

Teasels were a speciality of a few areas in the north of Somerset and were grown to supply both the local and the Gloucestershire and Wiltshire woollen-cloth industries. The centre of the growing area lay around Cheddar, Winscombe, and Congresbury, but in the 1650s, at least, teasels were being grown in the Bath area, and a few teasels were recorded as far south as Meare in the Levels in the 1680s.[115] In the main area of production around Cheddar teasels were being cultivated before 1640, and the remainder of the seventeenth century saw both an expansion of the teasel acreage in the old growing areas and an extension into adjacent parishes. In the parish of Winscombe in 1640 the teasel crop was only one-third of the value of the parish's teasel crop in 1700, when it occupied 155 acres, mainly land which would formerly have been sown to wheat and barley.[116] In the parish of Congresbury teasels were first grown about 1654 by John Eve, who brought teasel seed from Cheddar. Total teasel acreage in Congresbury never reached much above twenty acres until the 1690s, but then rose sharply to eighty acres in the years 1696–9.[117] The teasels were set from seed about March, and between July and Michaelmas of the same year transplanted, remaining then until the following July when the cutting season commenced.[118] In the Bath area in the 1650s it was not uncommon for the teasels to be raised on a partnership basis, with two or more persons holding shares of varying sizes in the land sown.[119] Woad was also cultivated in some areas of the Mendips and in the Keynsham area in this period.[120]

Climate, soils, and topography combined, however, to ensure the dominance of livestock over crops in the south-west as a whole. Cattle breeding was of primary importance in the interior of Cornwall and north Devon. In the east of the region, in the vales of Dorset, and in the Somerset Levels, cattle fattening assumed the highest importance. The Dorset downlands supported a thriving sheep husbandry, whilst south-east Devon, west Dorset, and some southern districts of Somerset were important dairying areas. The Levels, additionally, were famed for the rearing of horses.

The moorlands and hills of Devon and Cornwall supported a significant stock-rearing industry. Of the agriculture of Molland in north Devon it was said in the 1750s that "this parish breeds fine cattle, poor wheat, poor cider". It was in the markets of east Cornwall and north Devon that graziers and others bought their stock for fattening: most were bought for fattening further east, particularly by the Somerset graziers. The Levels of Somerset and the Blackmoor Vale in Dorset were the two prime fattening areas of

[115] PRO, E 134, 11 Wm III, Easter 4; E 134, 13 Wm III, Trin. 19; E 134, 1656, Easter 12; E 134, 1656, Trin. 8; E 134, 4 Jas II, Mich. 16.
[116] PRO, E 134, 13 Wm III, Trin. 19.
[117] PRO, E 134, 11 Wm III, Easter 4.
[118] Ibid.; E 134, 13 Wm III, Trin. 19.
[119] PRO, E 134, 1656, Easter 12.
[120] A. W. Coysh, E. J. Mason, and V. Waite, The Mendips, 3rd edn, London, 1971, pp. 180–1; Letters & Papers on Agriculture of the Bath & West of Eng. Soc., IV, 1788, pp. 273–4.

the south-west. Some of the poorest pastoral areas in the west of the region were so dependent on cattle rearing that a crisis such as the cattle plague in the mid eighteenth century brought severe financial hardship and even ruin. In early 1748 it was bemoaned from the Barnstaple area of north Devon that

You would be surprised to hear how prodigiously the estates are fallen in this country. Most of them are reduced to half value, and some of them not able to discharge the taxes. The orders about the cattle gaul'd the farmers and tenants in this large breeding country so much that they were disabled from paying any rent; the consequence of which was, the landlords were forced to enter and distrain and obliged to take their estates into their hands and make nothing of them.[121]

Cattle fattening became an increasingly large-scale and organized business in east Somerset and Dorset during this period. A farmer at Pilton in the Levels was estimated to have made £1 per head profit on stock fattened on his lands for a year from 1683 to 1684 and afterwards sold at Bruton, Frome, and Priddy fairs.[122] In the parish of Hammoon on the edge of the Blackmore Vale in Dorset, John Haine fattened 300 oxen, steers, and heifers and about 180 sheep on his estate there in 1739. Markets in Devon (Exeter, Tiverton, Crediton, and South Molton) and west Somerset (Taunton, Bridgwater, Wellington, and Wiveliscombe) predominated amongst the places where the stock were purchased, whereas, after fattening, sales were effected primarily in Hampshire (Lymington, Romsey, and Winchester) and in London. Despite the fact that 1739 was alleged to have been "a very bad year to graziers", it was estimated that £193 profit was made by the feeding of this stock of cattle and sheep on Haine's farm in that year.[123]

It is clear that by the mid eighteenth century several areas in the south-west had organized droving links with markets in the London area for the sale of fatstock. Salcombe in south Devon participated in such a trade, and at Lamerton in west Devon, near the Cornish border, cattle "were reared, grazed, fattened, and drove up easterly to London".[124] From Hasellgrove farm at Queen Camel in the south of Somerset, where Humphrey Mildmay kept between 80 and 100 fatting oxen yearly, he was regularly sending droves of them to London for sale in the 1680s.[125] Welsh cattle occupied an important place in many west-country fattening enterprises.[126] In the early part of the seventeenth century a sizeable trade in Welsh cattle was conducted

[121] 'Extract of a Letter Dated 29 March 1748 from Near Barnstaple, Devon', Kentish Post, 3,178 (23 Apr. 1748), p. 2.

[122] PRO, E 134, 2 Jas II, Easter 12.

[123] PRO, E 134, 16 Geo. II, Mich. 2.

[124] Stanes, 'Devon Agriculture', p. 48.

[125] PRO, E 134, 4 Jas II, Easter 1.

[126] Various farm/estate account books confirm the importance of Welsh cattle in the south-west in this period. See, for example, Devon RO, L1,258M/F27 and W1,258/LP/1/1 (duke of Bedford's Devon estates). See also J. H. Hamer, 'Trading at St. White Down Fair, 1637–1649', Somerset Arch. & Nat. Hist. Soc., CXII, 1967–8, p. 65.

across the Bristol Channel to supply such markets as Dunster in west Somerset and the fair at St White Down in the extreme south of Somerset. In summer during the early 1630s, 300–320 head of cattle, besides horses, sheep, and pigs, were said to have been shipped weekly from the port of Aberthaw in Glamorgan to the Somerset ports. At this date there were also "divers droves of cattle and sheep...landed out of Ireland at Millfourd in Pembrokeshire" which were driven to Aberthaw and ferried across to Minehead and other Somerset ports.[127]

The substantial growth in the number of cattle kept on west-country farms in this period was in many areas faster than the increase in the provision of additional fodder, both in summer and in winter, but particularly the latter. The slow spread of clover in the pastoral areas of the south-west contributed to the deficiency. It was stated in 1718 that Southcott Luttrell generally lost some cattle on his Saunton Court barton at Braunton in north Devon each winter for lack of fodder, and about two years earlier had lost "a great many" in this way.[128] Milles's survey of Devon shows that almost everywhere in the county in the 1750s meadow land was nearly twice as valuable as arable. At Colyton in south-east Devon considerable acreages of both meadow and pasture lands were let at annual rack rents, again illustrative of the overall shortage.[129]

In Somerset the same shortage of pasture and meadow was partly reflected in the complex network of intercommoning rights and agisting practices that existed across the county. Mary Strode summered some of her fatting cattle in the 1680s on Stoke, Wedmore, and Cheddar moors where she had a right of common, at ten to fifteen miles' distance from her estate at Pilton.[130] An Ilchester yeoman who "used to grasse and fatt greate numbers of oxen" leased grazing for them "at several places in the marsh places of the county of Somerset" in the early 1690s.[131] A notable feature of the parishes of the western Levels in this period was the substantial proportion of their meadow and pasture lands rented by "outdwellers" or "foreigners", residing out of the parish in other parts of Somerset.[132] In the two westernmost counties the extensive moorlands provided valuable summer pasturage, and Dartmoor especially assumed the nature of a vast common for Devon farmers in the summer. John Clement, a yeoman of Lydford, had the oversight of about 550 bullocks and 2,000 sheep annually brought to him to be summered on

[127] PRO, E 134, 8 Chas I, Mich. 48.
[128] PRO, E 134, 5 Geo. I, Mich. 15.
[129] Stanes, 'Devon Agriculture', p. 50.
[130] PRO, E 134, 2 Jas II, Trin. 6.
[131] PRO, E 134, 8 Wm III, Easter 15.
[132] See, for example, PRO, E 134, 16 & 17 Chas II, Hil. 10 (Aller, 1665); E 134, 1657, Easter 15 (E. Brent); E 134, 15 Chas II, Easter 15 (Huntspill, 1663); E 134, 5 Wm & M., Easter 10 (Burnham, 1693).

Dartmoor in the early eighteenth century.[133] Similarly, in Cornwall in the 1710s it was the common practice of farmers in the St Germans area to summer their bullocks on common moors at St Cleer and St Neot, on the edges of Bodmin Moor and ten to twelve miles distant from St Germans.[134]

The heart of the west-country dairy industry lay in the east of the region and particularly in Dorset and south-east Devon. The Dorset industry was characterized by the practice of renting out dairy cows on an annual basis, but this system was not restricted to Dorset, as has sometimes been stated, and was also found in both south-east Devon and in east Somerset in the earlier part of the period.[135] The normal custom in the Mappowder area of Dorset was to rent an animal out on the third day in May in each year for twelve months.[136] Daniel Holland had a dairy of twenty-four cows in Mappowder which he rented out at £3 per cow per annum in 1712–13.[137] In the rich Devon dairy district at Colyton it was stated in 1679 that the "usuall rate" for the rent of "the milke of a cowe with her calve lett for a year" was £3 10s., the owner of the cow finding grass and fodder for her.[138] Further west, in a less favourable area, the milk of each of five dairy cows on the tenement of Hole at Lapford, Devon, was valued at 24s. or 25s. per annum in 1697, but at Liskeard in Cornwall the profit arising from a dairy cow was put as high as £3 10s. to £4 in 1728.[139] The latter figure is comparable with the good profits obtained from dairying on the rich pastures of the western Levels in Somerset: the milk from Samuel Hipsley's dairy of twenty cows at Bleadon in 1745–7 was valued at £4 per animal.[140] Elsewhere in Somerset profits were lower. At Henstridge, near the Dorset border, the profit of milk of a cow was estimated at £2 10s. to £2 15s. in 1715.[141] As in the Levels, dairying was an expanding industry in parts of south Somerset in this period: at Kingstone near Ilminster, as the number of dairies increased in the period 1640–70, pasture land was extended at the expense of meadow.[142]

Very little evidence of milk yields exists. At Henstridge in Somerset,

[133] PRO, E 134, 3 Anne, Mich. 11.

[134] PRO, E 134, 5 Geo. I, Hil. 1.

[135] C. A. Horn, 'Two Centuries of Incentive Payments in Agriculture', *Accountants Rev.*, XXVI, 1975, p. 223, is incorrect in stating that the annual renting out of dairy cows was known only in Dorset. PRO, E 134, 24 Chas II, Mich. 4, records the renting of dairy cattle in the Glastonbury area of Somerset *c.* 1640, and E 134, 31 Chas II, Easter 3, records the existence of the system at Colyton, Devon, in the second half of the seventeenth century.

[136] PRO, E 134, 13 Anne, Easter 10.

[137] *Ibid.* See also Dorset RO, P11/IN5 for a dairy agreement at Corfe Castle, Dorset, dated 27 Feb. 1756, in which the rental concluded is similarly £3.

[138] PRO, E 134, 31 Chas II, Easter 3.

[139] PRO, E 134, 13 Wm III, Trin. 7; E 134, 1 Geo. II, Easter 3.

[140] Somerset RO, D/D/C 1747.

[141] PRO, E 134, 5 Geo. I, Mich. 2.

[142] PRO, E 134, 23 Chas II, Mich. 15.

assuming a milking season restricted to twenty-four or twenty-five weeks in the year, some dairy cows appear to have had yields of the order of 170–185 gallons per annum in 1715.[143] Whetter has calculated a yield of nearly 600 gallons per annum in the parish of Towednack in west Cornwall in the late 1670s, but this is a large overestimate. If a lower figure for butter made per week of $2\frac{1}{2}$ to 3 lb per cow (instead of the 6 lb taken by Whetter) is taken, as the evidence would seem to favour, and Whetter's eight-month milking season is reduced to six months, a yield similar to those obtained at Henstridge would be given. Since the dairy cows at Towednack were rented at £2 per annum, this would appear to indicate that they were by no means exceptional milkers, and so the lower yield would seem much more probable.[144]

Before about 1760 cheese and butter making remained very largely a highly localized occupation, supply being determined by the demand in a particular locality. In the south-west the day of the butter and cheese jobbers operating from London lay in the future, and cheese was invariably sold at local markets and fairs.[145] Only in a few districts in the east of the region did cheesemaking represent a specialized industry, reaching far beyond the confines of the district itself. Cheddar in Somerset was nationally known for its cheese in this period, and Defoe considered it to be the best cheese in England.[146] Apart from a few areas like Cheddar, however, Lisle held that Somerset cheeses generally in the first half of the eighteenth century were inferior to those made in north Wiltshire owing to the wetter and damper nature of the pastures in most Somerset cheese districts.[147] On the other hand, Somerset cheese bore a higher price than the average Dorset product because Somerset cheeses were commonly rich and creamy, whereas skimmed cheeses were much more usual in Dorset.[148] In the parish of Buckland Newton, Dorset, several types of cheese were made, but it was stated that the making of "skim cheese" was the most profitable in that part of Dorset.[149] Quality apart, cheesemaking was a sizeable farm industry in Dorset. Thomas Jenkins died in March 1732 with a half "tun" of cheeses worth £10 on his farm at Marston, and John Green of Hazelbury Bryan died in January 1718 with cheese valued at £14 in store, both farms lying on the edges of the Vale

[143] PRO, E 134, 5 Geo. I, Mich. 2.

[144] Whetter, *op. cit.*, pp. 27–8; PRO, E 134, 31 Chas II, Mich. 6; E 134, 32 Chas II, Easter 29.

[145] J. Wimpey, 'Of the Necessity of Adapting or Suiting the Crop to the Nature, Condition, and the Circumstances of the Land to be Planted', *Letters & Papers on Agriculture of the Bath & West of Eng. Soc.*, IV, 1788, pp. 155–8. Note: great changes took place in cheese and butter marketing in the latter third of the eighteenth century.

[146] D. Defoe, *A Tour through England and Wales*, 2 vols., London, 1928, I, pp. 277–8.

[147] E. Lisle, *Observations in Husbandry*, 2nd edn, London, 1757, pp. 302–3.

[148] T. Davis, 'On the Superior Advantage of Dairy to Arable Farms', *Letters & Papers on Agriculture of the Bath & West of Eng. Soc.*, III, 1786, p. 75.

[149] PRO, E 134, 2 Anne, Trin. 4. See also E 134, 2 Anne, Easter 16.

of Blackmoor.[150] In Devon, Up Ottery was known for its butter and cheese.[151] According to Lisle, Devonshire butter was made at this period in a different manner from that in other counties. By the Devon process, a very rich butter was produced, but a poor cheese, observations which match those made by Risdon of Devon dairying in the early seventeenth century.[152] On many of the region's dairy farms pigs, fed on the whey and skimmed milk, were moderately important, although less so than in Wiltshire.

Sheep occupied a prominent position in west-country farming, and their importance was reinforced in this period through the emergence of Devon as the second most important maker of woollen cloth in England, 1660–1700. Devon made the New Draperies, while traditional broadcloth manufacture held sway in east Somerset, this being an extension of the region centred in Wiltshire and Gloucestershire. Over most of the south-west sheep were farmed for wool, but in some eastern districts fattening was also of great importance.

Dorset sheep enjoyed a national reputation in this period and were sold to farmers in the south-eastern counties in large numbers for finishing. Sales of Dorset sheep were very important at both the large Burford and Weyhill fairs.[153] The early and prolific lambing quality of the Dorset breed was highly regarded at this time. Sheep husbandry was highly organized on the Dorset downlands, and large flocks were the rule. In the Winterborne Came and Herringston area south of Dorchester, one Gillett kept a flock of up to 2,200 sheep in the 1670s.[154] Defoe states that 600,000 sheep fed on the Downs within a six-mile radius of Dorchester.[155] Frequently large flocks were kept by men farming very small arable acreages, who nevertheless had extensive grazing rights elsewhere. Gillett of Winterborne Came put some of his sheep to pasture in Sedgemoor, over thirty miles distant in Somerset, in the 1670s.[156] Similarly, in Devon, Dartmoor provided essential summer pasturage for sheep. Flocks as large as 1,800 or 2,000 were summered by shepherds on Dartmoor for distant owners.[157]

Wool sales were sizeable for the owners of the larger flocks. Twenty-two packs of wool were sold from the Courtenay family estates in the Powerham and Kenton area of Devon in 1739, for the princely sum of £104 10s.[158] George Strode of Beaminster, Dorset, estimated in March 1744 that his flock

---

[150] Dorset RO, DA/A 1733/21; DA/I 1718/11.

[151] Stanes, 'Devon Agriculture', p. 48.

[152] Lisle, op. cit., p. 301; Fussell, 'Four Centuries of Farming Systems in Devon', p. 183.

[153] Defoe, op. cit., I, p. 210; Dorset RO, D279/E4, entries for 29 Sept. 1748 and 29 Sept. 1749; D406/1, entry for 29 Sept. 1758.

[154] PRO, E 134, 31 Chas II, Easter 6.

[155] Defoe, op. cit., I, pp. 187–8, 210.

[156] PRO, E 134, 31 Chas II, Easter 6.

[157] PRO, E 134, 3 Anne, Mich. 11; E 134, 13 Wm III, Mich. 14.

[158] Devon RO, 1,508M/V36.

of 632 sheep and lambs would, when shorn, provide wool worth about £41 4s.[159] The wool was sold in several yarn markets in towns and at fairs, it being commonly bought from individual farmers by yarn jobbers or buyers for 'bulk' delivery to market. In the 1720s Sampson Pett, a yarn jobber who also farmed a sizeable estate near Liskeard, bought up yarn in the east Cornwall area, and on Monday of each week carried it to Tavistock market.[160] Tavistock was one of the most important yarn markets in the south-west, serving large areas of Devon and Cornwall, and acting as a distribution centre for yarn for the clothiers east of Dartmoor. Tavistock's enhanced importance went hand in hand with the decline of many smaller, local markets like Ashburton in the early eighteenth century.[161] Dunster served as a similar regional yarn market for the west Somerset and Exmoor areas and also received wool from south Wales.[162] In south-east Devon, Honiton, Ottery St Mary, and Colyton were the more important yarn markets.[163]

The folding of sheep was almost universally practised in the west country in this period, and in Dorset particular attention was paid to the provision of adequate grass for the lambing ewes over the winter. At Henstridge in the extreme south of Somerset near the Dorset border, ewes were agisted from the end of November to the beginning of May at the rate of £8 per score, that being "the usual price" in this area in the 1710s.[164] In the Winterborne St Martin area of Dorset, the usual rate for depasturing "hogg sheep in this country all the yeare att grass and hay" was stated in 1689 to be £15–16 per hundred.[165] In some areas clover eased the winter fodder problem, and, in Cornwall particularly, the turnip became a valuable winter food for sheep, and partly explains the considerable increase in the size of flocks in that county between 1700 and 1750.[166] The turnip also heralded an increasing emphasis on mutton rather than wool in Cornwall in the second quarter of the eighteenth century.[167]

In the hills of west Somerset turnip husbandry also spread quickly in the early eighteenth century, again in conjunction with expanding sheep-farming systems. Fattening was of prime importance, and in 1722 John Hill had forty

[159] Dorset RO, D279/E4.

[160] PRO, E 134, 1 Geo. II, Easter 3; E 134, 4 Geo. II, Mich. 5.

[161] PRO, E 134, 1 Geo. I, Easter 16.   [162] PRO, E 134, 8 Chas I, Mich. 48.

[163] PRO, E 134, 4 Jas II, Mich. 38.

[164] PRO, E 134, 4 Geo. I, Mich. 5; E 134, 5 Geo. I, Mich. 2.

[165] PRO, E 134, 1 Wm & M., Mich. 32.

[166] Whetter, op. cit., p. 33, draws attention to the small size of Cornish flocks in the seventeenth century. The increase in 1700–50 is clearly indicated in the inventories for this period. For the importance of turnips to sheep husbandry in Cornwall, see Cornwall RO, DDR 5,299 (St Ive area, 1740s). For their similar importance in Devon, see Devon RO, W1,258/LP 5/2 (Tavistock area, 1740s).

[167] See, for example, Cornwall RO, DDR 5,299.

very good fattening sheep on his farm in Skilgate worth £16 per score, Hill having, so it was stated, "the best of sheep in that countrey". Such fat sheep were sold at the autumn fairs, Hill selling some at Wiveliscombe fair held in September, and at Bampton fair in mid October.[168] On the Dorset Downs too, mutton became increasingly important in place of wool after 1700.

Fruit gave to west-country farming much of its distinctive character. Devon and Somerset were cider-apple regions *par excellence*, and in these counties the orchard area expanded, sometimes slowly and sometimes briskly, throughout the entire period 1640–1750. In Somerset, orchards were widely distributed throughout the county, but large concentrations were conspicuous in an extensive area around Taunton, and also in favourable locations in east Somerset and the Levels. In the parish of Buckland St Mary, south of Taunton, it was estimated that by 1670 "there have bin planted above three tymes as many orchards" in the parish as there were *c.* 1600. Moreover, most of these new orchards were planted in the years 1640–70.[169] West Pennard and West Lydford were typical of parishes in the Levels where the extension of orchards occurred in the years 1640–1725.[170]

In Devon, the South Hams and the broad region around Exeter including the south-east, were the main cider regions. Traditionally, the South Hams was the more important production area, but it is probable that in this period the greatest expansion of orchard acreage occurred in the "Exeter region". In the parish of Bickleigh estimates of orchard extensions ranged from an increase of one-third between 1650 and 1700 to an increase of 50 per cent between 1660 and 1700.[171] Shobrooke, Broadclyst, and Northleigh were other parishes in this region which saw large increases in orchard acreage over the period.[172] In the parish of Shobrooke orchard acreage was stated to have doubled in the years 1703–19, and the number of cider pounds in the parish, static at four in the period 1660–99, increased to twelve with another under construction in the years 1700–19.[173] The engine pounds, which Stanes has drawn attention to at Paignton in the 1750s, as distinct from the traditional stone pounds, were in fact already in use at Shobrooke in 1719.[174] Defoe claimed in the 1720s that that part of the Exeter region between Topsham and Axminster sent between 10,000 and 20,000 hogsheads of cider annually to London.[175] In 1750 Pococke expressed the view that "by the introduction

---

[168] PRO, E 134, 12 Geo. I, Mich. 9.

[169] PRO, E 134, 23 Chas II, Easter 23. See also E 134, 25 Chas II, Mich. 11.

[170] PRO, E 134, 14 Chas II, Mich. 25; E 134, 11 Geo. I, Easter 4.

[171] PRO, E 134, 1 Anne, Easter 5.

[172] PRO, E 134, 6 Geo. I, Mich. 12; E 134, 6 Geo. I, Mich. 3 (Shobrooke); E 134, 10 Geo. I, Hil. 3; E 134, 10 Geo. I, Hil. 24 (Broadclyst); E 134, 5 Wm & M., Mich. 19 (Northleigh).

[173] PRO, E 134, 6 Geo. I, Mich. 12.

[174] Stanes, 'Devon Agriculture', p. 59; PRO, E 134, 6 Geo. I, Mich. 12.

[175] Defoe, *op. cit.*, I, pp. 222, 266. Fussell, 'Four Centuries of Farming Systems in Devon', p. 187, incorrectly attributes Defoe's figure for the cider export to London to the quite distinct South Hams region.

of the Herefordshire redstreak of late years they make far better cyder near Exeter" than in the South Hams, where the White Sour variety was particularly prominent.[176]

In the northern half of Devon orchards were also important in favourable locations, but yields per acre were generally substantially below those in south Devon, whilst production was almost solely for local consumption, in contrast to the commercial production in the south. In the north Devon parish of Chittlehampton orchards were stated to have been "very much increased" in the period 1645–85, and by the 1750s there were 400 acres of orchards in the parish, a much larger acreage than in most parishes in south Devon.[177] However, Chittlehampton's 400 acres produced on average only 800 hogsheads of cider annually, a yield of only 2 hogsheads per acre compared with 10 hogsheads commonly achieved in many south Devon parishes in bearing years.[178] The parish of Paignton produced in "some years at least four thousand hogsheads", some of which were sold "by watercarriage both east and west from London to ye Lands End".[179] Several other parishes in south Devon produced 1,000 hogsheads or more of cider per annum in the 1750s, and total Devon cider production at this time has been estimated by Stanes at about 170,000 hogsheads.[180]

In Dorset and Cornwall cider apples were less important, but in the latter county, proportionate to other categories of farm output, cider was significant and, in south-east Cornwall, particularly so. In Cornwall, too, orchard expansion was a feature of the period. In the parish of St Merryn it was stated that the number of orchards had increased from five to thirty-three between 1635 and 1685.[181]

The apple harvest varied considerably from year to year and this was clearly reflected in the price of cider. In 1713 cider was scarce and dear in Devon, and one seller in the Tavistock area made 40s. per hogshead compared with a price of 25s. for some of the previous year's cider.[182] By contrast, at Elworthy in west Somerset "the year 1724 was exceedingly remarkable for cyder apples...[there being] never such a year in ye memory of man. Cisterns, great vates and other contrivances besides all sorts of vessels [were]

[176] R. Pococke, *The Travels through England of Dr. Richard Pococke*, ed. J. J. Cartwright, Camden Soc., NS XLII, 1888, p. 142.

[177] PRO, E 134, 36 Chas II, Mich. 9; Stanes, 'Devon Agriculture', p. 59.

[178] Stanes, 'Devon Agriculture', p. 60; Sir Roger Lethbridge, 'Apple Culture and Cider-Making in Devonshire', *Devonshire Assoc.*, XXXII, 1900, pp. 142–94. The latter includes a full return of all the parish answers to the questions relating to cider production in the Milles survey, including orchard acreage and cider production by parish. It should be noted that Lethbridge wrongly transcribes the figure for orchard acreage for Chittlehampton as 700 acres instead of the correct total of 400 acres.

[179] Stanes, 'Devon Agriculture', p. 59; Lethbridge, *op. cit.*, p. 187.

[180] Stanes, 'Devon Agriculture', pp. 59, 60.

[181] PRO, E 134, 35 Chas II, Easter 4. E 134, 22 Chas II, Easter 37, similarly records orchard expansion in the mid seventeenth century at Poughill, Cornwall.

[182] PRO, E 134, 4 Geo. I, Easter 8.

made use of in order to keep it, it being almost as plenty as water and ye common drink instead of small beer.''[183]

The orchard expansion of these decades appears to have been almost entirely at the expense of the arable in the west country, the good and the more marginal arable disappearing alike.[184] The extension of orchards created a considerable demand for young apple-tree stocks. In part this was met through consignments from London and other parts of the country, but increasingly it was satisfied by the establishment of nurseries in the south-west. Small nurseries for raising apple trees existed at Payhembury, Devon, in the 1760s and at St Germans, Cornwall, in the 1720s. At Payhembury it is specifically stated that some of the young trees were sold out of the parish from the nursery.[185]

Although quantitatively much less important than apples, other fruits, particularly pears, were grown in many parts of the west country. In the Bath district in the early 1650s, Robert Fisher and others were growing pears, plums, cherries, gooseberries, and strawberries, some of which were sold.[186] In the early eighteenth century, besides pears and plums, quantities of crabs or wildings, which were converted to vinegar, some of which was sold, were being grown in the parish of Beercrocombe in Somerset.[187]

Amongst small farmers, particularly those with diversified farming operations, as well as fruit farmers and part-time farmers, bees were a popular source of additional income in this period. Hive ownership was widely distributed throughout the south-west, although numbers of hives declined in the eighteenth century with the increasing import of sugar, which replaced honey as the main sweetener in the common diet. However, in 1745–7 a farmer at Bleadon in north Somerset kept twenty hives, producing 200 lb of honey and 100 lb of beeswax annually.[188]

Hops were of some importance in the west country. In Dorset and Somerset hops were grown in tiny lots of ground, covering a small total acreage, but in Devon and Cornwall hop cultivation was much more extensive. In Devon cultivation was widely dispersed throughout the county, but three growing areas may be distinguished – the fruit and dairy district of south-east Devon, the rich soil area of the southern South Hams, and a much less-favoured north Devon area. In the former two areas production tended to be concentrated among a few individuals who grew hops on a semi-specialized basis, but in north Devon the pattern was one

[183] 'Somerset Cider, 1724', *Somerset & Dorset N. & Q.*, XVII, 1921–3, p. 173.

[184] Evidence of land-use changes from arable to orchard is found in PRO, E 134, 10 Geo. I, Hil. 24 and 10 Geo. I, Hil. 3 (Broadclyst, Devon); E 134, 1 Anne, Easter 5 (Bickleigh, Devon); 11 Geo. I, Easter 4 (W. Lydford, Somerset); and E 134, 22 Chas II, Easter 37 (Poughill, Cornwall).

[185] PRO, E 134, 28 Chas II, Trin. 1 (Payhembury); E 134, 11 Geo. I, Hil. 4 (St Germans).

[186] PRO, E 134, 1656, Easter 12.

[187] PRO, E 134, 3 Anne, Easter 3.

[188] Somerset RO, D/D/C 1747.

of a multitude of tiny hop hays scattered across the area, each yielding minute quantities of hops.[189]

Cornwall had the largest acreage of hops of all the south-western counties, and it was in the south-eastern area of the county and in the lands bordering the southern coast as far west as Truro that the bulk of these hops were concentrated. The parishes of Gorran, Mevagissey, and St Michael Caerhays formed one of the more noteworthy growing districts, and one in which hop acreage increased considerably in the period 1640–1713, and particularly rapidly after 1700. In the mid seventeenth century there were stated to be "very few hopp gardens" in the parish of Gorran, yet in the period 1703–13 twenty hop yards were newly erected in the parish. By 1713, amongst a sizeable number of hop growers in these parishes, there were at least two or three at Gorran possessing four or more hop yards apiece.[190] At an earlier period in Devon there is similar evidence of expanding hop acreage: in the northern parish of Buckland Brewer it was stated that there were three times as many hop grounds in the parish in 1660 as there had been in 1640.[191]

Unfortunately, hop-production figures for the south-western counties are extant for only the few years 1722–32. These show that, whilst in Dorset hop acreage reached a maximum extent of $18\frac{3}{4}$ in these years, in Cornwall up to $141\frac{1}{4}$ acres were recorded. Acreages varied sizeably from year to year, with yields showing an even more dramatic variation. In Dorset 10,263 lb of hops were collected from the 9 acres of hop ground in the county in the year ending midsummer 1725, compared with only $1,165\frac{1}{2}$ lb from the same acreage in the following year. The production figures show that yields in Cornwall tended to vary less than elsewhere in the west country in this period, but were of a fairly modest order generally.[192]

West-country hops were much inferior to Kentish and Worcester hops, a fact reflected in their relative market prices. The west country did not therefore emerge as a significant hop area, and the evidence suggests that, with the exception of Cornwall, where hop growing was still important in 1750, the seventeenth-century expansion in hop acreage was followed by an

---

[189] Among the places where hops were recorded are: in the South Hams, at Salcombe, 1660s (PRO, E 134, 21 & 22 Chas II, Hil. 5), Ermington and Kingston, 1680s (E 134, 3 & 4 Wm & M., Hil. 11), Blackawton, 1710s (E 134, 7 Geo. I, Mich. 12), and Modbury, 1710s (E 134, 7 Geo. I, Easter 8); in south-east Devon, at Northleigh, 1670s (E 134, 5 Wm & M., Mich. 19, and 5 & 6 Wm & M., Hil. 9), Payhembury, c. 1640–75 (E 134, 26 Chas II, Trin. 4, and 28 Chas II, Trin. 1; also Somerset RO, DD/WO box 53), Ottery St Mary, 1680/90s, (PRO, C 107/112), and Musbury, 1670s (Devon RO, CC 27/71); in north Devon, at Buckland Brewer, c. 1640–70 (PRO, E 134, 12 Chas II, Mich. 15, and 2 Geo. II, Trin. 1), Hartland, c. 1640–73 (E 134, 25 Chas II, Mich. 3), and Alverdiscott area, 1710s (C 108/416).

[190] PRO, E 134, 12 & 13 Anne, Hil. 2; E 134, 13 Anne, Easter 3; Whetter, op. cit., p. 50.

[191] PRO, E 134, 12 Chas II, Mich. 15.

[192] Customs & Excise Dept Archives, 48/12/221–2 and 48/12/369; PRO, TI 271/23 and TI 278/41. It should be noted that these figures underestimate hop acreage in Devon, since hedge hops, numerous in this county, were usually omitted from the returns.

overall contraction in the period 1700–50. In few areas outside Cornwall were hops grown in any quantities by 1750, and many former hop hays had been converted to orchards, the south-west possessing much superior competitive advantages in fruit production.[193]

Timber and coppice woodland was an important asset on estates in many parts of the west country, but nonetheless this period saw a heavy depletion of the region's timber reserves. Large areas of woodland were completely swept away. At the disafforestation of Neroche Forest in Somerset seven years prior to the Civil War, timber to the value of between £3,000 and £4,000 was felled and sold.[194]

North Devon was particularly well endowed with timber woodland and coppice in this period. On large estates plots of coppice were sold at public surveys by the manorial steward or reeve and, after purchase, were cut down by their buyers.[195] Timber was an expensive investment and often sales were to partnerships rather than to individuals, as was the case with the sale of West Stonyfield wood in the parish of Chawleigh, which was felled in 1696–7. When previously felled, twenty-eight to thirty years earlier, this wood of 15–16 acres had fetched between £400 and £500. Upon its felling in 1697 much was sold for building purposes, some to a Crediton builder. The parish of Chawleigh alone possessed between 100 and 130 acres of such coppice or salewoods at the end of the seventeenth century.[196]

Coppices were also extensively cultivated in the south-east of Devon. Coppice of twenty-three to twenty-four years' growth, and worth £8–12 per acre, was cut in the parish of Woodbury in 1699 and mainly converted to charcoal.[197] On his estate in the parishes of Northleigh and Offwell, James Marwood had ten coppices managed in regular rotation, as well as an extensive hedgerow wood supply. The seven coppices lying in Northleigh were each felled once and one was cut twice in the fifteen years up to Michaelmas 1691, yielding altogether 40,000 sale faggots and 3,000 poles. Large quantities of the faggots were carried to the nearby towns of Honiton and Colyton and sold at the rate of 7s. 6d. to 8s. per hundred.[198]

The primary use for wood was for charcoal and faggots on most estates. Much was consumed by the farmers themselves, but for others wood represented an important market cash crop. In the Devon parish of Broadclyst several farmers were supplying furze and salewood from their lands to people

[193] PRO, E 134, 32 Geo. II, Mich. 2, records a hop garden converted to an orchard in the 1730s in the Devon parish of Bampton. E 134, 12 Chas II, Mich. 15, records in 1660 a long-standing hop hay in the north Devon parish of Buckland Brewer having "of late years" been converted to an orchard.

[194] PRO, E 134, 1658, Easter 37.

[195] PRO, E 134, 24 Geo. II, Hil. 2.

[196] PRO, E 134, 10 Wm III, Mich. 11; E 134, 10 & 11 Wm III, Hil. 9.

[197] PRO, E 134, 12 Wm III, Trin. 2.

[198] PRO, E 134, 5 Wm & M., Mich. 19. See also E 134, 5 & 6 Wm & M., Hil. 9.

in the town of Broadclyst and in Exeter in the early eighteenth century, the salewood or faggots selling at 1s. 10d., 2s., or 2s. 2d. per dozen faggots or one horse seam. William Moor, who farmed in the parish, supplied several people in Broadclyst with furze at 1s. per seam all the year round from his lands, bakers and brewers being prominent amongst his customers.[199] Despite the bleaker landscape, Andrew Rosewall was able to find "furze and fuell" to sell in St Ives from his tenement in the parish of Towednack in the west of Cornwall in the 1670s.[200]

Over the south-west as a whole, oak and ash appear to have been the dominant types of tree, the former providing large building timber and the latter being used especially for farming implements and fencing. Locally, birch, halse, hazel, alder, and willow were also of importance.[201] These were commonly employed, together with ash, in making hurdles, gates, and hop poles on the farm.[202] Certain areas also experienced a sizeable demand for wood for herring casks.[203]

The Somerset Levels supported a flourishing willow, osier, and reed industry, thriving on the marshy, dyke-cut landscape of the area.[204] At Compton Pauncefoot on the southern fringes of the Levels, a one-acre withy bed, which was enclosed out of a meadow and planted about 1722, was being cut annually from 1726 to furnish the raw material for making baskets and bonds for bundles of faggots and reeds.[205] The demand for willow was widespread because its high resistance to water and its flexibility made it eminently suitable for a wide range of outdoor uses. Whilst the Levels were the traditional centre of this industry in the south-west, it was also to be found in other parts of the region. At Blackawton in the South Hams willow beds on a farm were cut annually in the years 1712–18, and part of the 'harvest' was sold to a local basket maker for baskets and panniers. Withy sticks were also cut and used on the farm itself to furnish hoops for cider barrels.[206]

The juxtaposition of large herds of cattle and oak woodland in many parts of the south-west formed the basis of a sizeable leather industry. To the farmer this meant an important market for hides and tree bark. Tavistock and

---

[199] PRO, E 134, 10 Geo. I, Hil. 3.

[200] PRO, E 134, 32 Chas II, Easter 29.

[201] Information on the composition of woodland and coppice in the south-west counties in this period is found in PRO, E 134, 12 Wm III, Trin. 2 (Woodbury, Devon); E 134, 5 Wm & M., Mich. 19 (Northleigh, Devon); E 134, 25 Geo. II, Mich. 2 (Linkinhorne, Cornwall); E 134, 1656, Mich. 5 (Moor Crichel, Dorset); E 134, 16 Chas I, Mich. 2; E 134, 4 Wm & M., Mich. 15 (Glastonbury area, Somerset).

[202] PRO, E 134, 31 Chas II, Easter 5, and E 134, 31 Chas II, Mich. 26, indicate that coppice wood was employed to make hurdles at Swell, Somerset, in the 1670s; E 134, 1656, Mich. 5, records coppice being cut for hop poles at Moor Crichel, Dorset.

[203] See, for example, PRO, C 108/424, pt 1: letter dated 17 Mar. 1720.

[204] Fiennes, *Journeys*, p. 243; Williams, *Draining of the Somerset Levels*, p. 170.

[205] PRO, E 134, 2 Geo. II, Easter 2; E 134, 2 Geo. II, Mich. 1.

[206] PRO, E 134, 7 Geo. I, Mich. 12.

Liskeard, both in the west of the region, were two of the more important tanning towns in this period.[207] The purchaser of several acres of oak coppice in the parish of Linkinhorne, Cornwall, in 1748 sold the 'rinds' or bark of five acres to Mr Avery, a tanner, of Liskeard, seven miles distant. It was usual in this part of the country for the bark to be contracted for sale whilst the wood was standing, and for the tanner to undertake responsibility for 'rinding' the trees.[208] Sales of bark on the larger, wooded estates provided a respectable source of income, but labour costs for stripping the bark were high and commonly approached 50 per cent of the market value of the bark. On the Dunster Castle estate of the Luttrells in Somerset, £28 19s. 3d. was received for bark sold in 1749 and £12 16s. 11d. paid for the 'ripping' of it; in 1750 sales amounted to £35 18s. and the labour costs to £16 8s. 11d.[209]

The evidence suggests that there is a sound basis for Cromwell's much-cited verdict on the agriculture of Devon that it was the best in England, and, albeit within systems that retained many of the features of traditional open-field farming, striking agrarian advances were apparent over much of Somerset and in parts of Dorset at the same date. In these three counties the period 1640–1750 saw the spread and consolidation of earlier improvements on the arable land, alongside a yet stronger movement towards regional specialization in animal husbandry and, in Devon and Somerset, the growth of a flourishing cider-apple industry. The essence of agrarian advance in the south-west in these decades lay in the growing weight of livestock farming and the realignment of arable farming subordinated to this. General evidence in respect of the growth in livestock numbers on west-country farms and the increased numbers and status of the region's cattle and sheep at important markets throughout southern England is fairly plentiful, but, compared with arable farming, the economics and progress of animal husbandry are very poorly documented for this period. A similar paucity of detailed material exists for the cider industry. Unfortunately, therefore, the full truth of the most important developments in west-country farming in this period remains inaccessible and untold.

In making this assessment of the region's agrarian development two further points need to be underlined. First, the dominant trend towards specialization in livestock farming was relative rather than absolute. Somerset in 1750 had one of the most diversified farming systems of any English county, and it was a diversification which was much more pronounced then than it had been in 1640. Secondly, in terms of agrarian progress, Cornwall was very much a unit standing apart from the other three counties in this period. With its mineral wealth and large fishing interests Cornwall was less absolutely

---

[207] D. M. Trethowan, 'The Leather Trade of Tavistock', *Devon & Cornwall N. & Q.*, xxx, 1965–7, pp. 220–1; Defoe, *op. cit.*, I, p. 233.

[208] PRO, E 134, 25 Geo. II, Mich. 2.

[209] Somerset RO, DD/L 1/5/16.

dependent on its agriculture, and farming was frequently a part-time occupation and of second rank in the county. In discussing the profitability of his Cornish estates and the possibility of further purchases of land in the county, Thomas Pitt ordered his agents in 1721 to "remember to inquire into all ye other estates where there are mines working for I fear I am ill dealt with on that acco.ᵗ for I hear of a great many Cornish people that have increased their estates very much by mines yᵗ have been discovered upon them, and never more need of looking out sharp than now".[210] This statement can be seen as a realistic verdict upon the status, progress, and relative profitability of Cornish agriculture at this time, and must cast strong doubts upon the validity of several recent writings which have attempted to portray Cornish farming in this period in a more favourable light than the long tide of history has traditionally accorded it.

[210] PRO, C 108/424, pt 1: letter dated 8 July 1721.

WALES

CHAPTER 12

WALES

"The advance of change from east to west was slow, and its speed rarely exceeded a mile a year." So says a recent author about Welsh agriculture in this period.[1] As we are not given much indication of the nature of change, it is hard to see how its snail-like advance could be measured, or indeed if it had any final goal other than the cliffs of Cardigan Bay. The point was made to show the folly of looking for revolutionary changes in Welsh farming, and as such has much to commend it. Nevertheless, there is the presumption that "a frontal attack on tradition and reaction" was going on, and, quite apart from the specific claims of Kerridge and E. L. Jones for their respective 'agricultural revolutions' running partly or wholly within this period, one is justified in viewing the Welsh agrarian scene from an improving standpoint. There must be alternatives to the dialectic search for agricultural revolutions, and one will be suggested here: the identification of a sequence of interrelated changes in agriculture, which (for particular periods of time and areas) produced a measure of improvement. This could be manifested in various ways, from a simple gain in nutritional levels for more people, to increases in productivity and profitability for most of the farming community.

THE NATURE OF CHANGE

We may begin with the contemporary testimony of informed men who state that there was in fact a momentum of improving change at work in Wales before about 1700. Even if this was not maintained afterwards, their words should be taken seriously. John Aubrey knew parts of Wales at first hand; when he attempts to explain falling rents in Wiltshire *c.* 1680 by imports of foreign corn, he adds another cause – "besides the improvement in Wales". He can only mean that Wales had become a competitive supplier of agricultural produce, beyond its traditional strengths in cattle and wool. He thought that Pembrokeshire corn came in after the Civil War, and cites evidence that the Monmouthshire dealers began to take corn to Bristol *c.* 1660. The bakers found that Welsh wheat yielded more flour than English grain bought at Warminster, and was no dearer, thanks to water transport.

[1] E. D. Evans, *A History of Wales, 1660–1815*, Cardiff, 1976, p. 124. Ch. 8 is entitled 'Agriculture and the Land'.

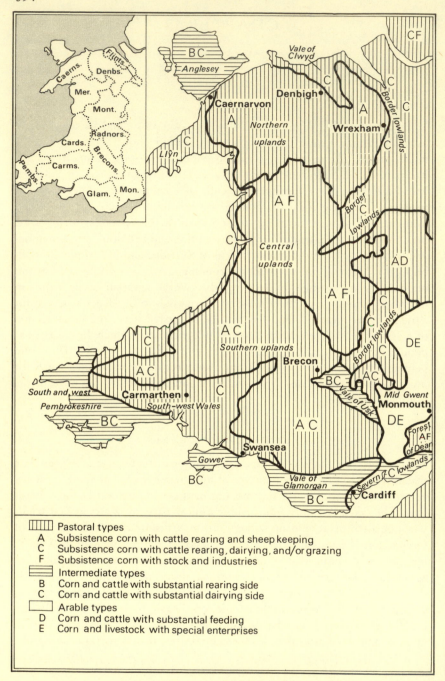

Fig. 12.1. Farming regions of Wales.

When the Bristolians opted for this supply, "the Welsh markets that before were glutted with twenty bushels of wheat, will carry off now two or three hundred". Aubrey's further comments on the early adoption of clover will be discussed later.[2]

Similar testimony comes from north Wales. In the 1690s John Lloyd, one of Lhuyd's scholarly correspondents, described the Vale of Edyrnion on the upper Dee, near Corwen: "I am sure we live plentifully in it, God make us thankfull. Tho I can't deny but most of our neighbourhood has been improv'd since Camden's days, by liming, ridding and good husbandry as much as any countrey I believe in England or Wales beside." Lloyd adds evidence of what had been in progress on farms during the previous century. Finally, there are the words of Henry Rowlands, describing "ye three late mediums of improvement" used in Anglesey, namely marl, lime, and sand. He states that "no certain testimonies appear of the usage of any of them above forty or fifty years (now 1693)". The full impact of those improvements are assessed later, but taken together with Aubrey and Lloyd they surely furnish a clear perception of beneficial change.[3]

As for those who did not leave behind any formal expression of their opinions, we may bring forward an Usk farmer whose goods were valued in December 1763. William David's wheat and other corn in store, with 21 acres of wheat "at fallow", his waggon, cart, and implements all amounted to 38 per cent of his total farmstock (£197) – not surprising in the good arable country of Gwent. His cattle, horses, sheep, and pigs came to 37 per cent, and his 22 tons of meadow hay, 5 tons of clover hay, and 10 bushels of clover seed to no less than 25 per cent. Over three years of his tenancy, he had spent £98 on repairing and building his farmhouse, dairy, barn, gates, and ring hedge; he had also spent £16 on liming his fields.[4] One can only speculate as to how much more William David could expect to gain from any 'agricultural revolution' after 1750, or indeed if it is necessary to accept him as the representative of a majority group of improving farmers.

Nor is there much doubt as to the satisfactory levels of productivity that could be achieved on home farms, such as the demesne at Picton Castle (Pembs.). The results in 1703 were well up to the standards expected under good management in 1815. Wheat ground was first broken in November 1702, then ploughed again, dragged, and limed from May to August 1703.

---

[2] Bodleian Library, MS Aubrey 2 ("Naturall Historie of Wiltshire. Part IId."), ff. 123, 149–51.

[3] Bodleian Library, MS Ashmole 1,816, f. 232; Bryn Roberts, 'Llythyrau John Lloyd at Edward Lhuyd', *Nat. Lib. Wales J.*, XVII, 1971, pp. 184–6; Henry Rowlands, *Idea Agriculturae. The Principles of Vegetation Asserted and Defended. Being an Essay on the Theory and Practice of Husbandry: Proceeding on the Three Noted Mediums of Improvement, viz. Marle, Lime, and Shells, Principally relating to the Isle of Anglesey*, Dublin, 1764, p. 183. Rowlands wrote the book during the 1690s, completing the manuscript by 1704.

[4] NLW, Aberystwyth, Milborne MS 2,354.

The liming was heavy, at 200 bushels per acre; agricultural writers of the time, for instance Mortimer, recommended 160 bushels, and 160–200 bushels were still common practice in 1815. Wheat was sown at the end of September, and the yield was 1:3.5, compared with 1:5 on the best arable in south Wales in 1815. Barley was not limed, sown early in March, and yielded 1:4 (1:5 in 1815); oats were sown in late February, yielding 1:5, and peas gave a return of 1:3. The total area under crops at Picton was 78 acres; allowing for the lower volume of seed sown in 1815, the returns were still surprisingly good more than a century earlier.[5] If the ordinary farmer was able to lime and (although it is not mentioned at Picton, it was probably done) manure his smaller acreage of arable to the same extent, he was not backward by the standards of 1815. Is there evidence to the contrary?

One thing is certain, however: because Wales was as diverse in its way as England in its physical and social resources, the interrelated changes making for improvement were hardly likely to be synchronous or uniform in their geographical incidence. What was the nature of this environmental diversity? The first and most obvious characteristic, imposed on the land by inherent contrasts between mountain and plain, upland or valley, has been stressed for the Welsh farming regions as they stood before 1640. They may be illustrated again by comparing the differing proportions of qualities of land on certain estates scattered over the country.[6]

The Monmouthshire properties of the Mackworths show by far the highest amount of land fit for the plough, and at St Mellons the extensive meadows had been reclaimed from the Severnside saltmarshes. In Pembrokeshire, the Phillips demesne at Picton also had a high proportion of arable; its share of woodland is higher than would be the case on most farms. On the Mostyn estate near Llanidloes, in an upland setting, the distinction of arable from pasture has become blurred, while one-fifth of the land was barely agricultural in quality. The two estates in north-east Wales were more heavily slanted towards pasture and meadow for their high densities of cattle and other livestock. So ran the basic spectrum of Welsh resources, conditioned by slope, altitude, climate, soils, and accessibility, within which changes might occur. How different were the extremes of farming potential? Two regions may be cited by way of answer.

Snowdonia in the 1690s was bleak and taxing. A visitor to Llanberis found

[5] NLW, Picton Castle MS 1,709; Walter Davies, *General View of the Agriculture and Domestic Economy of South Wales*, 2 vols., London, 1815, I, pp. 332, 378, 413, 456, 461, 500.

[6] Gwent RO, Medlycott MS D760 and D43.4,168, dated 1723; NLW, Picton Castle MS 1,694, survey dated 1729; UCNWL, Mostyn MS 6,051, dated 1750; Clwyd RO, D/G 3,334, Trevor estate, dated 1712, and Galltfaenan MS D/GA 782, dated 1735. The Mackworth surveys in Gwent are given in land units of 'covers', the regional Welsh unit of *cyfar*; a conversion ratio is taken from the survey of Raglan Castle, 1674, where 1.5 'covers' equal 1 acre: NLW, Badminton MS 14,170. See also Brian Howells, 'The Distribution of Customary Acres in South Wales', *Nat. Lib. Wales J.*, xv, 1968, pp. 226–37.

	Percentage of total acreage			
	Arable	Pasture	Meadow	Woodland
Mid Gwent (Mon.)	64	18	12	6
St Mellons (Mon.)	23	24	50	3
Picton Castle (Pembs.)	55	—	13	32
Llanidloes (Mont.)		59	21	12[a]
Holt-Ruabon (Denbs.)	24	56	17	3
St Asaph (Flints.)	29	62	9	—

[a] Also 8% "marshy and mossy".

"their best bread being black, tough and thick oat-bread, [they have] neither miller, fuller, and any other tradesman but one tayler; there's not a cock, hen, or goose, nay ne're an oven in ye parish". Sheep, goats, and store cattle could be reared, and extra flocks grazed in summer, while a few rough fields of oats and rye could be cultivated, but that was all. Cattle had to be stall-fed on hay in winter, whereas the flocks continued "mostly on grass as in the summer season. Those who own many sheep sometimes suffer a heavy loss: for in places 10, 15, 20 or even 30 and 40 sheep may be found buried in a single mound of snow." It snowed off and on between late September and May. Life in Snowdonia was exceptionally bleak during the 1690s, one of the severest decades during the 'Little Ice Age'. A record of the weather kept at Llanberis shows how the winter of 1697–8 began early in December, and harsh conditions with storms, snow, and frost persisted until early March. It followed an unsettled, cool summer, and it is not surprising that the parish registers reveal more burials than average between 1695 and 1698. Wild animals such as the pine marten, polecat, and wild cat were still numerous in that rough terrain, finding good cover in the woodlands that clothed many of the valleys. On the Gwydir estate, timber was a profitable source of income, where the tree trunks, logs, and planks could be floated down the river Conwy. Quantities of oak and ash, as well as bark for tanneries, were sold locally and increasingly to the Liverpool shipwrights.[7]

By contrast, a survey of Gower in the 1690s reveals a totally different mode of life in that region of south Wales. The low-lying coastal plateau of west Gower was almost wholly corn ground. On its level tracts of tillage there grew all the field crops – wheat, barley, oats, rye, peas, vetches, and even clover. It had "stores of limestone", some of which (together with corn and

[7] F. V. Emery, 'A New Account of Snowdonia, 1693, Written for Edward Lhuyd', *Nat. Lib. Wales J.*, XVIII, 1974, pp. 405–16; W. Linnard, 'A Glimpse of Gwydyr Forest and the Timber Trade in North Wales in the Late 17th Century', *ibid.*, pp. 397–404; F. V. Emery and C. G. Smith, 'A Weather Record from Snowdonia, 1697–98', *Weather*, XXXI, 1976, pp. 142–50.

livestock) were shipped to the west country. The well-drained loams were "plain, all corn ground, very good and profitable", with saltings, common pastures, and some meadow besides. Gower was anglicized, as "in former times all people both high and low did talk the old English". Such wealth of farming resources stood out sharply against the neighbouring "mountain country" of Blaen Gŵyr, a more difficult terrain where the land was better suited to feed sheep than cattle, or to support cattle than to bear corn; its main crops were oats and barley.[8] In this respect Gower, with its two faces of rich lowland and poor hills and the degrees by which one landscape gave way to the other, stands as a microcosm of all Wales.

POPULATION AND LANGUAGE

Some knowledge of levels and fluctuations in rural (and urban) population is indispensable in assessing the demand for holdings, the market for farm produce, and the supply of labour. Unfortunately the historical demography of Wales in this period is still an unopened book, despite such specific sources as the Notitiae for St Asaph diocese in the early 1680s, which would reinforce any findings from the Compton census (1676). All we can do, therefore, is to presume that the pattern of population already reconstructed for the period down to 1640 (see AHEW, *IV*, map on p. 144) served as a continuing base for the shifts in numbers known to have occurred in England: a steady but slower growth, slackening off even further by 1700. There followed a static situation until well into the eighteenth century, with slight falls in the 1720s and 1730s. Hints of the high mortality that caused these decreases come from Carmarthenshire in September 1731: "it is a very sickly time in this neighbourhood, where many die, and many more are sick of a nervous kind of feavour". Conversely, there is evidence for successful self-inoculation against smallpox by the common people in Pembrokeshire. 'Buying the smallpox' had been practised for over a century before 1723, when it was claimed "that hundreds in this country have had the smallpox this way is certain; and it cannot produce one single instance of their ever having it a second time".[9]

As to regional variations in population, the hearth-tax returns of 1670 (not a particularly reliable source) have been mapped for Glamorgan. They show clear contrasts between the hill country of Blaenau Morgannwg, with fewer than ten households per thousand acres near Aberdare or Merthyr Tudful, and

---

[8] F. V. Emery, 'Edward Lhuyd and Some of his Glamorgan Correspondents: A View of Gower in the 1690s', *Hon. Soc. Cymmrodorion*, 1965, pp. 59–114.

[9] Mary Clement, ed., *Correspondence and Minutes of the S.P.C.K. relating to Wales, 1699–1740*, Cardiff, 1952, p. 163; Dr Perrot Williams, 'A Method of Procuring the Smallpox in South Wales', *Philosophical Trans.*, CCCLXXV, Jan. 1723, pp. 262–8; Brian Howells, 'Social and Agrarian Change in Early Modern Cardiganshire', *Ceredigion*, VII, 1974–5, pp. 256–72.

the populous Vale of Glamorgan, whose parishes had more than thirty households per thousand acres. It is less easy to understand why the highest densities of +40 or even +50 in the Vale are not also found in peninsular Gower, further west along the coastal lowland and practically an identical region. Little is known, again, about the internal or external migration of people, nor about the hierarchy of Welsh towns. Wales did not possess a metropolis of its own comparable with Dublin or Edinburgh, and its social and commercial leanings were therefore all the stronger on non-Welsh centres, notably London, Bristol, and Liverpool. It is unlikely, therefore, that there was any great change in the relative size of towns as depicted before 1640.[10]

The seaport of Carmarthen remained one of the largest towns, as were Wrexham, near the English border, and Brecon. The latter was a typical town of the uplands, enjoying good access by road along the Usk valley to the west Midlands. The occupational structure of Brecon in 1664 resembled that of many pre-industrial market towns. It also reflected the pastoral slant of farming within its region. Far and away the predominant trades were those concerned with leather and woollen cloth. Tanners, curriers, and their allies accounted for 37 per cent of the business community, followed by tuckers, weavers, and dyers (27 per cent). Next to them came the omnipresent and versatile mercers (13 per cent), with builders (10), foodstuffs (8), and personal trades such as barbers (in all, 5 per cent) completing the urban picture. Brecon's service and residential attractions gave it the appearance of a thriving town with quality houses: "As good inns as any on [the] London road. Sixteen families in this town that keep chaises or coaches. The town but small, yet elegant." Little wonder that Brecon sponsored a successful agricultural society before 1755.[11]

The people of Wales were still predominantly Welsh-speaking, a situation that makes a special case of the spread of new information and farming innovations from sources outside the country. "We have whole parishes in the mountainous parts", wrote Lewis Morris in 1761, "where there is not a word of English spoken", and even at New Radnor "there is nothing but Welsh". Along the March, however, and throughout the southern littoral bilingualism was on the increase and more children were learning English beyond the strict limits of old 'Englishries' like Gower and south Pembrokeshire. Linguistic divides were part of people's lives in most of the peripheral counties. The higher hinterland of Carmarthenshire had parishes like Trelech, Llanllwni, and Llanwrda where the church services were

[10] Glanmor Williams, ed., *Glamorgan County History*, *IV*, Cardiff, 1976, pp. 311–16, pl. III. Ch. VII is a study called 'The Economic and Social History of Glamorgan, 1660–1760', by Moelwyn I. Williams.

[11] *The Letters of Lewis, Richard, William and John Morris of Anglesey*, (*Morrisiaid Môn*), *1728–1765*, ed. J. H. Davies, London, 1909, *II*, p. 393; Henry Edmunds, 'History of the Brecknockshire Agricultural Society, 1755–1955', *Brycheiniog*, III, 1957, pp. 67–125.

"entirely Welsh". In more accessible districts, such as the small market town of Llandeilo, the weekly sermons were "alternately Welsh and English", or again "sometimes in English, sometimes in Welsh". On the coast at Llanstephan and Laugharne, the bilingual bias was such that prayers were read half in Welsh, half in English, but sermons were always in English.[12]

For the bulk of the population, if they had the ability to read anything on improved methods of farming (as increasing numbers did), the text would have to be in Welsh. A good standard of education also became synonymous with a facility in English. Some of the Carmarthenshire clergy were "schollers brought up to the English tongue", whereas "the rest who have the Welsh tongue pretty perfectly are generally ignorant, not having had the advantage of education". The premium was thus squarely on popular education if new ideas were to spread by the written word, and it is revealing that one of the first ventures of the charity schools of the Society for Promoting Christian Knowledge was to translate into Welsh "an agreeable treatise upon agriculture fitted to the capacities of youth". This would help to keep young men's interest in farming. *The Husbandman's Manual* had appeared in 1704, the work of Edward Welchman, archdeacon of Cardigan, and the Welsh translation came out in 1711 as *Llawlyfr y Llafurwr*. It was being read in upland Breconshire by 1714 and was distributed to every county within the next ten years.[13] Unfortunately, the pamphlet was not concerned with the technicalities of farming, being instead a series of prayers and meditations each fitted to a particular activity in the husbandman's year. But it does indicate a general concern with vocational reading on agriculture, the prevalence of Welsh, and the growing strength of nonconformity in religion, which may have had some bearing on farmers' attitudes.

[12] Hugh Owen, ed., *Additional Letters of the Morrises of Anglesey*, London, 1947, I, pp. 108–14; G. Milwyn Griffiths, 'A Visitation of the Archdeaconry of Carmarthen, 1710', *Nat. Lib. Wales J.*, XIX, 1976, pp. 311–26. Francis Jones, 'Pontfaen', *Nat. Lib. Wales J.*, XX, 1977, pp. 177–203, provides some inferences about Welsh and English in north Pembrokeshire in this period.

[13] Bodleian Library, MS Rawlinson c. 743, f. 25, letter from John Dalton, Carmarthen, 25 Feb. 1714; Mary Clement, *The S.P.C.K. and Wales, 1699–1740*, London, 1954, p. 4. Sir John Phillips of Picton Castle (Pembs.) hoped the book might "in some measure prevent the inconvenience of the children being too much dispos'd of the meckanick's trades". This was a real danger, as a Monmouthshire vicar expressed it in 1719: he had some promising pupils at school, but "the parents are very averse to husbandry, tho' nothing is more wanted through the nation" (Clement, *The S.P.C.K. and Wales*, p. 106). See also Clement, *Correspondence and Minutes*, p. 29. The full title of the booklet in question was *The Husbandman's Manual: Directing him How to Improve the Several Actions of his Calling, and the Most Usual Occurrences of his Life, to the Glory of God, and the Benefit of his Soul. Written by a Minister in the Country, for the Use of his Parishioners.*

THE LITERATURE OF IMPROVEMENT AND AGRICULTURAL SOCIETIES

It is clear that a proliferation of English books on agricultural improvement after 1650 had a direct, reciprocal link with practising farmers. So far as Wales is concerned, its distinctive culture was bound to affect the spread of information by means of the printed page, at two levels. Wales lacked a metropolitan focus of its own with civic tradition and national institutions to foster its native culture (and perhaps to make it less of a rural heritage). Consequently, the magnetism of London was unchallenged: it continued to attract Welsh talents and men of substance, as it had done since the sixteenth century. Somewhat paradoxically, therefore, many Welshmen were well placed at the centre to keep abreast of new developments. Secondly, the odds were heavily against the appearance of a Welsh book on improved agriculture, so the English authors held the field. The first volume published in Wales dates only from 1719, and the thin stream that followed it relied on subscription, for instance David Thomas's *Arddwriaeth Ymarferol* (*Practical Husbandman*, 1816). But Wales was not unproductive of such books before 1750: in pride of place is the masterly essay by Henry Rowlands, *Idea Agriculturae* (see pp. 417–18 below). Overlooked by Fussell, this was completed by 1704, and several manuscript versions are known from Anglesey, but it is symptomatic of the Welsh condition that the book was not published until 1764, and then in Dublin. It is also rash to assume that Rowlands was alone in this branch of authorship. According to the *Chester Chronicle* (there were no Welsh newspapers before 1802), a Mr Bulkeley of Llangelynen planned to publish in 1726 "an entire system of Agriculture entitled *Cae'r Gorlan improv'd*".[14]

Anglesey furnishes our best proof of the efficacy of the farming literature, in the person of Edward Wynne at Bodewryd. His land management has been analysed elsewhere and is discussed briefly again on p. 418, but mention should be made here of his devotion to the authors from whom he copied long passages into his work books. The prolific Richard Bradley was clearly a respected source, perhaps because he was strong on costing, and Wynne copied section after section from *A Compleat Body of Husbandry* (1727). Another standard work he used was Edward Laurence's *Duty of a Steward to his Lord* (2nd edn, 1731), good on enclosure, consolidation, and the sown grasses; Fussell calls him "a very prominent character in the progress of agriculture". Giles Jacob's *Country Gentleman's Vade Mecum* (1717), an influential and original book, was also studied by Wynne, who discriminatingly chose the best authors. It is also significant that he did not own copies

[14] Peter R. Roberts, 'The Act of Union in Welsh History', *Hon. Soc. Cymmrodorion*, 1972–3, pp. 49–73; Eiluned Rees, 'Pre-1820 Welsh Subscription Lists', *J. Welsh Bibliog. Soc.*, XI, 1973–4, pp. 85–119.

himself, but was able to borrow them from others for copying out what he wanted. Again in north Wales, the steward of the Gwydyr estate wrote his notes about the cultivation of ryegrass and clover as addenda to his copy of the best-known book on farming published in the later seventeenth century – *Systema Agriculturae: The Mystery of Husbandry Discovered*, by John Worlidge (1669). Watkin Owen had a copy of the reissue of the fourth edition, 1698, bought in that year, and he had bound in (after Worlidge's text) forty blank pages for his own addenda. The book contained, of course, a section "Of several new species of hay or grass", in which Worlidge wrote mainly about clover, sainfoin, and lucerne.[15]

It is also instructive to see which titles had been bought for the libraries of great country houses. Worlidge appears again in the collection of Sir Erasmus Phillips at Picton Castle (Pembs.), in the third edition of 1681. The same author reappears at Margam Abbey in Glamorgan, where the Mansels had a first edition (1669) among a set of some thirty volumes on agriculture and gardening. They had John Mortimer's *Whole Art of Husbandry, or the Way of Managing and Improving of Land*, in the fourth edition with additions (1716). Not far away from Margam, the Jones family of Fonmon Castle also had Mortimer (3rd edn, 1712) in their good-sized selection, including Richard Bradley's *Gentleman and Farmer's Guide for the Increase and Improvement of Cattle* (1729). The Baldwyn library at Gregynog (Mont.) again had the books by Mortimer (1716) and Bradley. Farther north, the Yorkes of Erddig (Denbs.) had titles by Bradley, Laurence's *Duty of a Steward* (1731), and John Lawrence's *New System of Agriculture* (1726), as well as others dating variously back to 1616. These bibliographical patterns are surely not random or without influence in the diffusion of knowledge about new methods and objectives.[16]

By 1704 Henry Rowlands had suggested, far ahead of his time, the formation of agricultural societies as one of his "Practical Experiments", not confined to the upper crust of rural society. Gentleman improvers should form themselves, he wrote, "in little societies, in several parts of the country they live in, admitting among themselves such of their neighbouring farmers as are known to be men of sense and veracity". They would meet regularly in summer to make trials and experiments, recording the results in a book that was revised from year to year. It is not known if anything came of Rowlands's suggestion, but by the time his book appeared in print a fully

[15] NLW, Bodewryd MSS 61E, 63E, 64F, 66D, 68B; MS 5.977D. On Worlidge, see G. E. Fussell, *The Old English Farming Books from Fitzherbert to Tull, 1523 to 1730*, London, 1947, pp. 56, 68–72, 95–6; the publishing history of Worlidge's book is even more complicated than Fussell suggests.

[16] NLW, Picton Castle MSS 1,740, 1,743 (catalogues dated 1744); Penrice and Margam MS 2,208; Glam. RO, D/DP 885 (catalogues dated 1747 and c. 1750); Margaret Evans, *A Catalogue of the Library at Fonmon Castle, Glamorgan*, Cardiff, 1969: NLW, MS 9,030; information kindly supplied by Mrs Rosalind Powell-Jones, librarian at Erddig, Wrexham.

fledged agricultural society had in fact been created in Wales. The oldest body of its kind still extant in Britain, the Brecknockshire Agricultural Society was formed in 1755, springing from an older "County Club for Gentlemen" at Brecon. Among its activities, the society paid premiums to enterprising farmers who sowed red clover (the crop had been grown in the Vale of Usk for three-quarters of a century before then), subsidized local clover seed and machines for dressing and cleaning it, gave free turnip seed to small farmers. It may also be suggested (as an example of new religious influences) that the Calvinistic Methodist 'commune' at Trefeca was an ideal seedbed for the society's innovations. On their farms by 1771 the corn acreage was exceeded by clover, turnips, hay, and fallow; the Trefeca settlement was even advising English improvers at Leominster and Bristol – a reversal, from west to east, of the usual flow of new practices.[17]

ESTATES, FARMS, AND MARKETS

In the size and structure of landed estates and of their constituent farms, the diversities within Wales are again striking. It is as difficult to generalize about 'a Welsh estate' or 'a Welsh farm' as it is to assume common ground in these matters between Northumberland and East Anglia. What is certain is that the selective building up of larger estates, already clear by 1640, went on with the extinction of many of the lesser gentry in the late seventeenth century. This piecemeal, relentless expansion of such big properties as Crosswood and Gogerddan in Cardiganshire, for example, also meant that they spread over a variety of farming environments. Eventually the 28,000 acres of Gogerddan extended from saltmarsh to the mountain sheepwalks on Pumlumon, while Nanteos (much the same size) had its farms scattered in blocks and parcels from Aberystwyth through the deserted abbey of Strata Florida to the Teifi valley. Crosswood was even larger and covered half a dozen sprawling parishes, but there were also more modest demesnes such as Cilgwyn, with its 2,000 acres surveyed in 1773; these tended to be more compact and restricted to the lower valleys and coastal lowlands.[18]

On balance, the size of farms showed a positive relationship with the size of the estates to which they belonged. On properties like Cilgwyn, some 60 per cent of farms were of under 100 acres, compared with 37 per cent on Gogerddan and the other great estates. But the calculation of farm size (which may also conceal the problem of fragmentation) demands some refinement, owing to two complications at the extremes. On the lower side, there was always the likelihood of very small units of under 10 acres. Only

[17] Rowlands, *Idea Agriculturae*, pp. lv–lvi; Edmunds, *op. cit.*, Gomer M. Roberts, *Portread o Ddiwygiwr*, Cardiff, 1972.

[18] R. J. Colyer, 'The Size of Farms in Late Eighteenth and Early Nineteenth Century Cardiganshire', *Bull. BCS*, XXVII, 1976, pp. 119–26.

a few would be full-time farms; others were associated with inns or smithies, or their occupants were in a dual economy with woollen manufacture or mining in combination with farming. Increasingly, upon expiry of their leases some were relet as part of a larger farm — the first step towards consolidation, although only to a limited extent by 1750. Over 50 per cent of farms on the Hengwrt estate in Merioneth were still under 10 acres in area by the 1790s. When calculating the mean area of farms in Cardiganshire, therefore, a case can be made for excluding these tiny holdings, which merged with those of cottagers, who themselves were a substantial group in the rural community: two Carmarthenshire parishes had thirty-one landholding families as against sixty-nine cottagers.

Equally, at the other extreme it was quite usual to find the surveyors listing as farms the vast, often unenclosed sheepwalks on the mountains. About half the Pryse estate of Gogerddan was in this category, thirty-seven 'farms' in all, amounting to over 15,000 acres. While they are indicative of the growing primacy of sheep farming in this region, a case can again be made for omitting them from any calculation of mean farm size. If this is done, the average unit emerges as 117 acres at Gogerddan, 131 acres at Nanteos, and 140 acres at Crosswood. Even so, the prevailing image of the modest size of farms in Wales can be upheld. By the late eighteenth century on ten Cardiganshire estates, large and small, half the farms were of under 100 acres. Even in neighbouring Carmarthenshire, with its fatter lands for dairying along the Tywi, the general run of farms was no more than 50–60 acres. On the Mostyn estate near Llanidloes there were thirty holdings with a mean acreage of 65, and the biggest farm was only 275 acres.[19] Such a scale of operations must depress the threshold of potential productivity and, perhaps, the number of farmers who could adopt and implement expensive improvements in 'Welsh Wales'.

Opportunities and means of marketing their produce, too, varied for farmers at all levels, whether simply to find their rents or in the steady business of selling their surpluses. A determining factor was whether or not a farm was land-locked and remote, or near the coast and accessible. Being in easy reach of one of the numerous ports and shipping places was the salvation of many producers. The co-ordinating influence of Liverpool merchants was undisputed round north Wales as far as Cardigan Bay; in the south, Bristol's hegemony of trade continued. There was brisk traffic both outwards and inwards from all regions bordering the Bristol Channel, and it was a similar picture in Anglesey, where barley and malt were shipped direct to Liverpool, Dublin, Warrington, and Chester.[20]

[19] Colin Thomas, 'Estate Surveys as Sources in Historical Geography', *Nat. Lib. Wales J.*, XIV, 1966, p. 453; Charles Hassall, *A General View of the Agriculture of Carmarthenshire*, repr. London, 1974, p. 11; Griffiths, *op. cit.*, p. 318; UCNWL, Mostyn MS 6,051.

[20] UCNWL, Penrhos MS i 1,387B (dated 1723–8); General Collection 7,137.

Inland, the pastoral interest was well served by many seasonal fairs, some held at market towns, others virtually in wide-open spaces to which sellers and dealers drove their beasts. Wrexham fairs were thriving: that held on 12 March lasted eight or nine days; another fell on 5 June; the two fairs in early September each lasted two days. At the much smaller town of Llandeilo (Carms.) there were also four fairs through the year, but of such a size that (as the archdeacon complained) "horses, sheep and lambs and casks of ale are brought in to the churchyard and sold there". August saw the gathering in Cardiganshire at "a great fair kept on the hills of Rhos, and most schools in those parts keep a sort of a carnival during the week this fair falls upon". Camden had noted the magnitude of Rhos fair. From them went the droves of cattle on the long walk to distant buyers, and their timing was all-important. Anglesey people were worried because the English drovers "do not come as they would if the fairs were more timely kept", finding it difficult to take Anglesey beasts to the London marts, especially Bartholomew fair on 24 August, "many of their cattle being much damnified on the road by overdriving".[21] To this end a petition to the crown (1703) asked that Newborough fairs be advanced to new dates (8 August, 10 September).

Spasmodic collection of rents in pastoral regions was in tune with sales at fairs, especially when farmers were troubled by seasons that were too cold, wet, or dry. Early in 1723 came "a great drought in Monmouthshire, insomuch that cattle, by reason of the shortness of grass and the poor prospect of fodder, yield no price...Your tenants are very much behind with their rents. They promise to clear part after Usk Fair a week after Whitsun." Business at weekly markets was also affected by extremes of climate, and the environmental dangers of cold spells were acute in the Welsh uplands where the growing season was short at the best of times. Nowhere is this better seen than in the notorious winter of 1739–40. Hardship struck even in the relatively prosperous Vale of Clwyd. The diarist Owen Thomas noted "the great frost" as beginning on the 23rd of December 1739 and lasting until the 10th of February 1740; it was still freezing at night throughout April and there was snow on the mountains until the 11th of May. By then high prices for corn in the markets (due to exports by sea) were bringing out the colliers, lead miners, and Denbigh craftsmen in open rioting with loss of life, and soldiers marched in to keep the peace. Prices went on rising until wheat was 43s. a quarter in August. Lack of rain had also caused a shortage of fodder for livestock, and another dry spring in 1741 was disastrous: by April "no one can recall such expense for the simple necessities to keep man and beast

[21] Clwyd RO, MS D/E 541 (dated 1718); Owen, *Additional Letters of the Morrises*, II, p. 481 (dated 1760); UCNWL, Baron Hill MSS 1704–5, 1708, 1715; Colin Thomas, 'Bodidris yn Iâl', *Bull. BCS*, xxv, 1973, pp. 337–45, which discusses the accounts of the Mostyn estate of Bodidris, on the borders of Denbighshire and Flintshire, between 1701 and 1716, including the use of fairs and markets.

alive". Wheat was then 45s. a quarter, even with imported corn reaching the markets; fortunately, the harvest of 1741 was of average quality, but still not so fruitful as in England.[22]

RURAL INDUSTRIES

"The people of Montgomeryshire", Lewis Morris observed in 1743, "talk purer Welsh than Cardiganshire, which last is full of miners of all nations." The presence of a mining population in west Wales fitted an industrial pattern that was less concentrated and more rural than it became after 1750. Lead ore was the attraction in Cardiganshire, rich in silver and accordingly more sought after by the monopoly companies and their successors. A rich find at Esgair-hir in 1690 brought a rush of enterprise that lasted until the Mine Adventurers of Sir Humphrey Mackworth fell away in 1710. Speculation was triggered off afresh in the 1730s, much of it on crown lands among the bleak hills. Working costs and transport access were lower and better in Flintshire, the other focus of lead working. Mines were in profitable operation around Halkyn Mountain by the Quaker Company from 1702, and by individuals like Sir George Wynne of Leeswood, who made a lucky strike in 1728. Low wages were earned by miners and labourers because they rarely worked full time underground and still tended their small holdings.[23]

Iron mining and smelting were carried on in every county; furnaces, forges, chaferies, fineries, and water wheels were to be seen along many of the Welsh streams. The southern landowners became more involved with iron, for example the Mansels of Margam, whose estates provided plenty of timber for 'coaling' the furnaces, at least initially. But the incoming English ironmasters began to supersede them, as with Thomas Pratt who acquired the Tredegar and Machen works in 1732. By then tinplates were being rolled by the Hanburys at Pontypool, and in coastal Carmarthenshire. As each year went by, it was increasingly clear that 'the coal districts' were in possession of a new order of resources. Coal production expanded both to service the metal trades and as a prime export. Pits proliferated along the southern littoral from Llanelli to Margam, in Pembrokeshire, and in Flintshire. Deeper pits with steam engines to drain them became the rule; tramroads carried the coal to ships waiting at the water's edge.[24]

[22] Gwent RO, Medlycott MS D760, 135; E. D. Jones, ed., 'Llyfrau cofion a chyfrifon Owen Thomas, 1729–1775', *Nat. Lib. Wales J.*, xvi, 1969–70, pp. 43–60, 148–62, 381–93; K. Lloyd Gruffydd, 'The Vale of Clwyd Corn Riots of 1740', *Flints. Hist. Soc.*, xxviii, 1975–6, pp. 36–42; *The Mold Riots*, Clwyd RO, Hawarden, 1976.

[23] Owen, *op. cit.*, I, p. 115; W. J. Lewis, *Lead Mining in Wales*, Cardiff, 1967.

[24] William Rees, *Industry before the Industrial Revolution*, 2 vols., Cardiff, 1968; Michael C. S. Evans, 'Coedmore Forge, Llechryd', in Tudor Barnes and Nigel Yates, eds., *Carmarthenshire Studies*, Carmarthen, 1974, pp. 186–95; W. E. Minchinton, ed., *Industrial South Wales*, London, 1969. Donald Moore, ed., *Wales in the Eighteenth Century*, Swansea, 1976, does not have a chapter

Such developments had consequences for the farmers. Five "coal horses" were part of the stock belonging to Leyson Rees at Cadoxton-juxta-Neath (1739), as were "two small coal-carrying horses" of Thomas John David at Llanfrechfa (Mon.) in 1719. William Edward of Pontypool was more deeply involved (1721); although described as a yeoman, a third of all his goods (valued at £17) consisted of "five old horses for carriage, picks for digging coal, the winding rope, with his tools and implements of husbandry, boards, six sacks". A good sum of money was owing Morgan Howell, a farmer at Whitchurch (Glam.) "for lime and carrying coals and stones to the furnace" (1722).[25]

For every Welsh county, the inventories of men and women working in woollen manufacture, the spinners, weavers, tuckers, and knitters, are by far the most numerous of the rural craftsmen. Cloth, notably flannel, ranked next to the cattle trade in the Welsh economy, and throughout the clothing districts of Merioneth, Montgomery, and Denbigh the Shrewsbury Drapers maintained their influence. Welshpool grew as a subsidiary depot by 1700, as did Barmouth, from which Liverpool merchants shipped the Merioneth webs. Men were also setting themselves up as drapers, supplying wool for spinning or cash for buying yarn to the clothiers, supervising and paying for the weaving and finishing of the cloth. Spinning-wheels and hand cards were within the reach of most families, but weaving was craftsman's work, so sheds and looms were investments for the more affluent farmer. The *pandy* or fulling mill was a common feature in the countryside, concentrated here and there as at Dolgellau. Knitted stockings were sold through small market towns like Bala. Rather than process their raw wool into cloth, the southern counties preferred more and more to export it, but for many country people the yarn, cloth, and stockings remained sources of by-employment.[26]

At the summit we find a successful farmer–draper, William Jones of Tal-y-llyn beneath Cadair Idris. He died in February 1700, and as much as 60 per cent of his goods, worth in all £252, was somehow connected with clothmaking. He had six webs (£42), 200 lb of wool and warp (£34), and 338 sheep (£75). Lower down the scale at the same time and in the same county, Griffith ap Rees was a yeoman cattle farmer who had two white webs worth £10 among his goods (£59 in all). A man might be described as a weaver, but the bulk of his goods could be in cattle and crops; such was Thomas Edwards of Mathrafal (Mont., 1699) with only £6 out of £37 in his sheep, wool, yarn, a great and a little spinning-wheel, and two looms. At a much humbler level, a pair of looms also figured among the possessions of William Prichard, weaver of Llanstephan (Radnors., 1690, £4); all he had

on agriculture, but see ch. 6 on the woollen industry, by J. Geraint Jenkins, and ch. 7 on the early industrial expansion in south Wales, by R. O. Roberts.

[25] NLW, Probate MSS for the diocese of Llandaf, 1720–2, 1739.
[26] J. Gareth Jenkins, *The Welsh Woollen Industry*, Cardiff, 1969.

besides was a cow and calf, an old horse, a couple of pigs and hens, and corn worth £1. Typical of those who eked out a living by handcraft was Mary Miles of Bonvilston (Glam., 1725, £3); she had fifteen pairs of stockings worth 6s., probably destined to go with a cargo of such goods to Minehead or some other port in Bristol's pocket.[27]

Fisheries should also be credited as an adjunct to farming in coastal districts. In 1674 an ambitious scheme for commercial fishing was devised by Edward Lloyd of Llanforda. About forty boats were regularly engaged in the herring fishery of Cardigan Bay, employing some 240 hands. The catch was divided into ten shares, five going to the owners and one to each fisherman. A boat could clear £50 profit per annum, but if they copied the Dutch rate of selling at five herrings a penny, "their gains [said Lloyd] would have been doubled, but indeed they rather murder than promote a real trade". Lloyd planned greatly to widen the distribution of fish to buyers, and to diversify to other fish besides the red and pickled herring, as well as to the north Wales beds "of oysters as green and fat as any be in Colchester". He was dealing in fish in some quantity by 1676 and had built a 'conservatory' or curing shed. Such commercial expertise was a far cry from the small-scale fishing carried on as a sideline by most seaside communities, especially in Pembrokeshire, Gower, and the Vale of Glamorgan.[28]

Finally, the growing demands of industry could lead to the drastic clearance of woodlands, sometimes opening the way for agricultural uses. The Vaughans of Gelliaur (Golden Grove, Carms.) had great expanses of timber on their estate, for instance, and followed a policy of controlled felling. Richard Vaughan sold parcels of woodland near Llanelli in 1705, "fit for making of charcoal" with the buyer having a year for "falling, cutting down, cording, coaling, and carrying away all the said trees". Then some total destruction followed in 1713 when the Vaughan heiress married Lord Winchester, who paid his debts by selling off the dense stands of oak and ash on his share of the estate. His wife opposed him over this, and although she sold cordwood in quantity in the 1730s, most of it going as charcoal to local iron furnaces and forges, she also replanted and coppice-managed the timber. By the 1750s John Vaughan was once more selling on a big scale, including to the admiralty dockyards, and creating new farmland in the process.[29]

[27] NLW, Probate MSS for the dioceses of Bangor, 1700; St Asaph, 1700; St David's, 1690; and Llandaf, 1725.

[28] NLW, Sweeney MS 3 (= I); 5 (= III), "A Short Narrative of Designes in the Fishing Trade".

[29] Francis Jones, 'The Vaughans of Golden Grove. II. Anne, Duchess of Bolton, 1690–1751' and 'The Vaughans of Golden Grove. III: Torycoed, Shenfield, Golden Grove', Hon. Soc. Cymmrodorion, 1963, pp. 223–50; 1964, pp. 167–221.

FARMING REGIONS

A beginning will be made with the more diversified regions of the Welsh lowlands because they would most probably experience change. If new modes of farming became available they would be taken up more readily where the land was productive and even small producers made a fair living under the old regime. On grounds of proximity to England and the known quality of its agriculture before 1640, furthermore, it is reasonable to start in Monmouthshire, most of which was thoroughly Welsh at this time. The language was still spoken, as indeed it was in neighbouring parts of Herefordshire; many of its manors had been 'Welshries' in the marcher lordships; farmers, farms, and fields carried un-English names; in the inventories their crops were often listed by the 'cover' (the Welsh land measurement, *cyfar*) rather than by the acre; it was a Monmouthshire farmer who "did make and ordaine his last will in ye Welsh tongue" – the only one encountered in sifting through many thousands of probate papers.[30]

Of all the Welsh regions, the coastal belt between Chepstow and Newport (continuing as far as Cardiff) was the most uniformly prosperous. Good arable soils were blended with excellent grazing and meadows on the reclaimed saltmarshes of the levels and moors along the Severn. The farmers concentrated their efforts on their corn fields and dairy herds; some bullocks and heifers were "for fattening"; they bred horses and kept good numbers of pigs; sheep did not interest them. The density of livestock was impressive. At Magor in 1680 Rowland Jones, yeoman, had 7 milch kine and their calves, and 7 young cattle; with a plough team of 4 oxen he had cultivated a crop worth £20; he had 5 horses and 16 pigs, but no sheep; cheese and butter valued at £5 and hay at a similar amount completed his goods. Temperence Blethin had 2 cwt of cow's milk, half cow's milk, and skim cheeses; a well-to-do farmer had 12 firkins of butter and 123 cheeses, worth £24. A labourer at Marshfield kept 10 cows and heifers, 4 oxen, 3 working horses and 3 colts, 9 pigs, and 8 sheep; as he had very little land, his corn came to only £1, but the numbers of his livestock show how even a labourer could benefit from the rights to abundant common grazing in this region. The order of field crops was wheat and muncorn, oats (sometimes mixed with peas), barley, horse beans, and a little rye. Farmers were well equipped with implements of husbandry, "tackle for horse and oxen", carts and waggons.[31]

It it one thing to delineate the characteristics of this kind of farming, and

---

[30] William Rees, 'The Union of England and Wales', *ibid.*, 1937, pp. 27–100, the constitutional position of Monmouthshire being discussed on pp. 74–8; NLW, Probate MSS, Llandaf, 1680: John Christopher of Ystradowen made his will on 28 Sept. 1680, his inventory is dated 21 Oct. 1680, and his farmstuff was valued at £32.

[31] NLW, Probate MSS, Llandaf, 1680, 1690 (Mordecai Leyson, labourer, Marshfield, will dated 19 Jan. 1691), 1710 (Temperence Blethin, widow, inv. dated 4 Oct. 1709).

another to establish how much change took place by 1750. The best way to tackle the problem is to compare individual farmers of similar standing from the same parish, one at an earlier date, say 1675, the other in 1750. Thanks to the availability of some Welsh inventories down to 1750, later on average than in England, this can be done, and has been followed as far as possible for the more advanced regions of south Wales (see Annexe 1, p. 422 below). So far as the Severn lowlands are concerned, there seems to have been a minimum of change through time. Apart from slight increases in the numbers of cattle and horses, it is as if the traditional modes were persistent. More farmers had better equipment in the form of corn wains, waggons, and dung cribs with wheels; some were sowing ryegrass and clover, as at Mathern in the 1720s, when labourers were paid "to mow down all ye hay grass and clover and barley and oats".[32] But compared with other regions the impact of innovation was slight.

The mixed farming of central Monmouthshire or mid Gwent (most of the county, in terms of area) was based on red soils that favoured both crops and grass. By contrast with the coastal belt, the dairying interest was less pronounced, allowing more scope for stores and fat cattle; more corn and pulses were grown; sheep were a little more numerous, and pigs remained so; the range of ancillary crops such as flax, apples and pears, hops, and hemp was wider than elsewhere in Wales. The average yeoman (see Annexe 1) had a couple of oxen, 5 cows, and 8 young beasts; 3 working horses, a score of sheep, and a dozen pigs; his wheat, oats, and barley accounted for a quarter of his goods, which included several hogsheads of cider, bacon, cheese, butter, and hops. It is quite usual to find 20 or 30 acres of growing corn and pulses listed in the inventories, together with hay worth up to £10, unmown in the meadow or stored in ricks, mows, cocks, and barns. With the big farmer, corn and pulses could be worth half of all his goods; for instance, 45 acres of peas, 40 acres of wheat and maslin, 28 acres of oats, 12 acres of barley. Seven working bullocks made all this cultivation possible, and several horses; 3 ploughs, half a dozen yokes and chains, a drag and harrows were used in the fields, as were corn wains, waggons, carts, and dung cribs. Eight cows, 16 steers and young beasts, a flock of 60 sheep and lambs, and 10 pigs completed this versatile system.

The cultivation of flax is evidenced by a dealer, William Best, who had a wealth of farm stock at Raglan, Abergavenny, and Monmouth (£1,648; 1722). He had flax seed, flax in the rough, watered flax unswinged, flax ready dressed, linen yarn, linen cloth including "200 ells of cloth at Bristol whitening", all worth £435, with some wool and hemp. Apple orchards were common in this landscape, and cider mills, screws, and cogs were in use on farms, often on a considerable scale; for example, Morgan Williams, a yeoman at Llanbadog (£181; 1724) had 18 hogsheads of cider worth £18.

[32] Gwent RO, D501/955.

Perry was also made. In terms of buildings, the farmers were well provided
with barn, stable, dairy, oxhouse, bakehouse, cider house; the Dutch barn
makes an early appearance when Elizabeth Morgan of Bryngwyn bequeathed
in her will (1725) "my two ffrench barnes", and when the tithe corn at
Llanwenarth (1732) "was put up into two Dutch barnes".[33]

With some farmers, the distinction is made between wheat "sowed upon
ye lay" and "fallow wheat", the latter carrying a higher valuation. This
suggests a full commitment to convertible husbandry: some fields alternated
between crops and grass leys on a regular, short-term basis, while others lay
fallow for a couple of years before being broken, limed, and manured for
wheat. To get some idea of the proportions of the various field crops, all
the 31 farmers whose inventories give their cropping for 1675, 1680, and
1690 were studied; with a total of 565 acres, the mean crop was 18 acres
per farmer. The picture emerging is a distinctly symmetrical threefold split
among winter corn, spring corn, and pulses; it might even seem as if the
medieval open fields of this region had never been enclosed and hedged:

Wheat and winter corn	39 per cent
Barley and oats	27 per cent
Oats and peas	14 per cent
Peas and beans	20 per cent

This could mean there was more scope to replace the animal feed grown
under the old order (pulses and oats) with better, cheaper grass, using clover
leys in rotation. Hence by the end of this period big acreages owned by the
duke of Beaufort are reported as "lately laid down to grass grounds, used
to be plowd and pay tythes".[34]

As to the total numbers of livestock, calculated in the same way, the
pattern is as follows: distributed among 83 farmers, there were 1,443 cattle
of all sorts (half of them cows and followers), and 2,241 sheep and lambs,
giving mean herds per farmer of 17 and flocks of 27. By 1750, when the
inventories of only 15 farmers can be used, they had 280 cattle and 405 sheep;
multiplying by 5.5 to produce figures proportional to the earlier data, the
result is uncannily identical (1,540 cattle; 2,227 sheep). But the nature of the
1750 sample is such that it would be wrong to minimize, on these figures,
the increase in stock numbers and the decrease in corn. For a number of
changes took place in this region, the chief being a drop in the amount of
corn cultivated at all levels; more cattle, sheep, and horses were being kept,
especially by the bigger farmers. Clover had made great headway among
rich and poor alike; as early as 1672 the special value of this new crop was
signalled by an estate steward – "as for the profitts of this yeare I have not

[33] NLW, Probate MSS, Llandaf, 1723, 1725, 1727, 1732 (inv. of Thomas Williams, dated 29
Oct. 1732).

[34] NLW, Badminton MS 9,849, "Lands Grazed in the Parish of Monmouth, 1755".

recd. anie except what hath beene made of clover grasse wth. wch. money I am now repairing the mills".[35] It is thus imperative to trace the adoption of clover in this region.

A varied range of evidence shows that the "adventitious grasses", clover, sainfoin, and ryegrass, were being grown in several parts of Wales from the 1650s. That was as early as in England: knowledge and experimentation went ahead simultaneously in both countries, so much so that it would be unwise to assume that Herefordshire (known from Yarranton's efforts to have been a 'threshold region' for clover) was the source of expertise, example, and seed for adjoining parts of Wales. The relationship could have been the other way round, or there could have been a separate, dual process of innovation. However, the fact is that a reporter from mid Gwent in the 1690s could say that "by sowing clover, greater numbers of cattle are of late bred and fed than was formerly". His words echo those of John Aubrey at the same time in Herefordshire: "they are fallen into the vein of clover, and those which kept no kine before now keep some 12, some 20".[36] The earliest clover growers so far met with in the inventories all farmed in mid Gwent; eight farmers thus form a group for examination, all coming from selected years between 1675 and 1695 (see Annexe 2(1) below). It is not an exclusive group by any means, as the most rapid count of their status will show: three were described as yeomen, two as gentlemen, one as husbandman, and another as bachelor.

They were also heterogeneous in other ways, as in their wealth so far as it was reflected in the value of their movable goods, farmstock, and various moneys and credits: £138 (twice), £78 (twice), £76, £64, £53, and £38 – modest enough, and certainly not confined to the most affluent section of rural society. A key factor in whether or not they adopted clover might be the kind of farming they practised, perhaps sharing some special emphasis within the regional system. This notion is undermined by three of them whose goods (all listed in winter) amounted to virtually the same value: with one, cattle came to £29 and corn to £17; with another, £9 and £8, with the last, £36 and £29. The sole recurrent feature among them is a good proportion of arable farming with plenty of spring corn and pulses; all kept cattle, but some were more interested in the dairy and others in rearing or fattening; sheep were not kept by two of them, and the other flocks varied between 77 and 22 without any correlation to wealth. Four of these clover growers lived in adjoining parishes, and specific family ties and other links may be traced between them. Catchmayd Tyler, a small squire at Mitchel Troy, was related to Charles Morgan of Bryngwyn, gentleman, who also

---

[35] NLW, MS 11,019E, Clayton Letters, 4, George Scudamore to John Morris, Esq., London, 28 Sept. 1672.

[36] F. V. Emery, 'The Mechanics of Innovation: Clover Cultivation in Wales before 1750', *J. Hist. Geog.*, II, 1976, pp. 1–14.

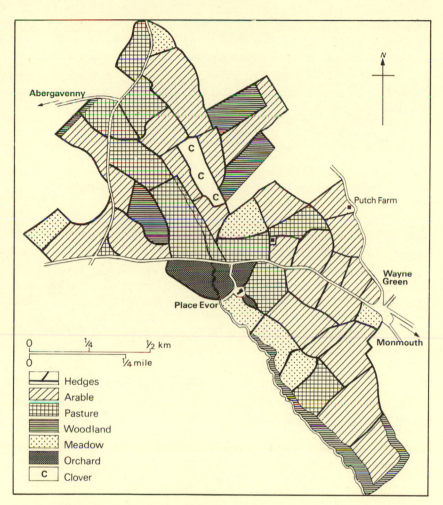

Fig. 12.2. Land use on a large mixed farm in mid Gwent, 1704. The map is drawn from the original plan entitled "An Estate of William Prichard: Senr Knowne By the name of Place Evor Lands & The Putch Ffarme Lands. Described in Anno:Domi: 1704. By Herbert Croft" (NLW, Badminton MS 6,059). The enclosed estate lay in the middle region of Monmouthshire (Gwent), an amalgamation of farms that originally would have carried the Welsh names of Plâs Ifor and Pwll. It ran to 294 acres; the fields were predominantly arable (60 per cent of the total area); the pastures (20 per cent) were on the lower, damper slopes, and arranged contiguously to ease the movement of cattle and sheep from one to the other; meadow (7 per cent) lay chiefly by the stream. Woodlands ran to 8 per cent of the area, and there was a substantial acreage of apple orchards (3 per cent). One of the fields was under clover (2 per cent), the earliest known cartographic record of this new crop in Wales.

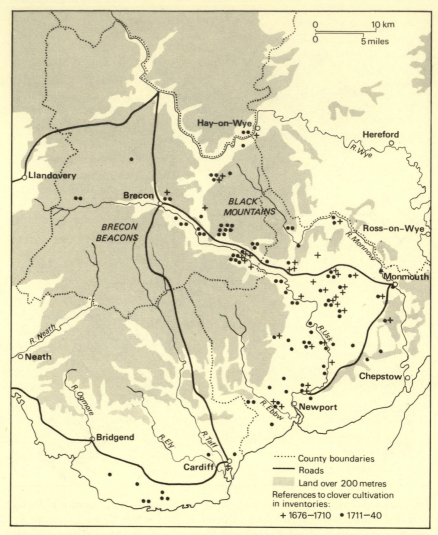

Fig. 12.3. Early adopters of clover in south-eastern Wales, 1676–1740. The map covers the counties of Brecon and Monmouth and most of Glamorgan (omitting the deanery of Gower in west Glamorgan). It locates each farmer (139 in all) whose inventory contains some reference to clover (data from NLW, Probate MSS Llandaf and St David's, archdeaconry of Brecon, 1675, 1680, 1685, 1690, 1695, 1700–40). The choice of 1710 as a break point is simply to give two equal phases in the period studied. Roads are taken from Morden's maps in the 1695 edition of Camden's *Britannia*.

had hay and clover worth £20. William Prichard left cattle to his son of the same name, whose large farm (typical of this region: Fig. 12.2) when mapped in 1704 also had a field of clover; one of the appraisers of his goods, William Knight, in turn had clover in his inventory twenty years later. As an alternative way of looking at them, the characteristics of another nine clover cultivators from Monmouthshire, Breconshire, and Glamorgan, all dating from the same twelve-month period between October 1704 and October 1705, are summarized in Annexe 2(2). The improving image they present is far different from anything that may be derived from the Board of Agriculture reporters a century later.

The Vale of Glamorgan was also a corn-growing region. A set of 129 farmers whose inventories give details of growing crops had 1,223 acres in all at a mean acreage of 9.5 per farmer. Nearly all the arable was devoted to grain, half of it under wheat and the rest split pretty equally between barley and oats; very little pulse was grown, most of it peas. Sheep were fairly important with everyone, generally with flocks of about 30; scarcely one farmer in three had 100 or more sheep. Cattle were decidedly important, mainly dairy cows and followers for the butter and cheese produced in quantity for the markets, but also with appreciable numbers of steers and 'staggs' (see Annexe 1). The marketing of animals was in the hands of men like Thomas Charles, a drover living at Llandaf; he had some farm stock of his own, but had done well enough in the trade to buy two farms (1702). The arable fields were well tended, the lias limestone underlying them supplying a cheap means of improvement: it was worth £5 "for lime and dung and plowing three acres of ground twice" (1740). Maritime enterprise was common: Freelove Scacy included with her farm stock "one quarter of a boat at Sully", worth £5 (1732). By the end of this period, there was a tendency for farmers to have more livestock, notably store cattle and sheep, and a lower corn acreage. The latter change was manifesting itself by 1720 on the manors of St Bride's and Pitcott: in 1670 the 26 farms had 121 acres of crops divided 37 per cent wheat and 63 per cent oats and barley; in 1720 the 19 farms had 103 acres of crops divided 45 per cent wheat and 55 per cent oats and barley. If there was also a shift to wheat at the expense of spring corn, it could have been because more land was put under grass leys. Clover does not appear in the vale inventories until after 1715, and (although this was the most anglicized region) it does not seem to have been adopted on the same scale as in mid Gwent and Gower. The minimal cultivation of peas and beans in the past would have obviated their replacement with clover.[37]

[37] NLW, Probate MSS, Llandaf, 1702, 1733, 1740 (Thomas Morgan, yeoman of Wick, inv. dated 8 Oct. 1740); NLW, Penrice and Margam MSS 2,620, 5,838 (3,183 and 5,698 have comparable data for Dunraven, Southerndown, and Wick); M. Griffiths, *Penmark and Porthkerry Families and Farms in the Seventeenth-Century Vale of Glamorgan*, Dept of Extra-Mural Studies, University Coll., Cardiff, 1979; P. Riden, *Farming in Llanblethian, 1660–1750*, Dept of Extra-Mural Studies, University Coll., Cardiff, 1980.

The summation of vale farming as practised on two demesnes in 1686 and 1742 is given in Annexe 3.

Mixed agriculture in the regions of Gower and south Pembrokeshire – both 'Little Englands' – was broadly similar: dairying was carried on but was subservient to the rearing of steers and bullocks; good-sized flocks of sheep were kept; cropping was heavy with a bias towards barley. Clover was being grown in Gower by 1700, probably introduced by Henry Lucas of Stout Hall, following a practice advocated in the books of improved farming: a fallow of lime and manure was prepared in summer and sown with clover in September; this gave excellent feeding in spring and cut twice for hay, lasting for two or three years. The arctic winter of 1739–40 destroyed such crops, so farmers switched to sowing it in the spring with barley and oats. It was grazed the first year, two hay crops were taken in the second, and then the ley was sown with wheat. By 1742 clover clauses were being written into Gower leases, but equally the duke of Beaufort's tenants-at-will explained why clover was not for them. As they could not plough old pastures, they had no corn ground to spare for clover, and without their corn money they would have to sell cattle at a time of low prices – "so clover would deprive them of a quarter of their corn land, already by far too little". Sainfoin was being grown in Pembrokeshire as a means of upgrading land that had lain idle, and "hurdles for the fould" are so common in the inventories that sheepfolding on fallows must have been widespread. Maritime enterprise is also typical: Mary Elliott, a rich widow of Herbrandston, had corn worth £115 and 40 strikes of barley with the master of the *Rebecca* bound for Dublin; her quarter share in the *Friends' Adventure* was valued at £50, and she also owned "One limestone boate with her materialls, quarrie implements and share of stones" (1703).[38]

With a reduced acreage under crops, throughout south-west Wales there was a high level of stocking on farms, particularly cattle, with dairying on the best lands such as the Vale of Tywi above Carmarthen. Longbody carts, "hurdles and dung about the house", "hay and thatch in ye haggard" are common items, and many small farmers had a couple of cows and followers, a dozen sheep, and a little corn. At the other end of the scale were men like Rowland Gwynne of Taliaris, with 88 head of black cattle worth £183, carefully itemized by their ages "next May", the traditional start of the Welsh pastoral year. Clover was being grown by a carpenter at Llangunnor in 1719, and a prosperous farmer who had adopted it was William Penry of Llanedy,

[38] F. V. Emery, 'Early Cultivation of Clover in Gower', *J. Gower Soc.*, XXVI, 1975, pp. 45–9; NLW, Probate MSS, St David's, 1703 (Mary Elliott's inventory is dated 30 June 1703, showing goods worth in all £463); NLW, Picton Castle MS 1,694 (stock and crops on the demesne in 1729); F. V. Emery, 'Open Fields in Gower', *J. Gower Soc.*, XXV, 1974, pp. 7–12; Joanna Martin, 'Estate Stewards and their Work in Glamorgan, 1660–1760', *Morgannwg*, XXIII, 1979, pp. 9–28.

who had 42 cattle, chiefly a dairy herd; 41 sheep, 11 horses, 9 pigs; dairy produce worth £10; wheat, barley, and oats at £34 (1744). This mode of farming was recurrent throughout the narrow margin of better land that fringed the western coast of Wales as far as the Llŷn peninsula. The house of Gogerddan, for example, stood "in a pleasant valley through which ye brook gently glides makeing severall small meanders and thereby expanding ye vale, known by ye name of Dyffryn Clarach, famous for its fertilyty in bearing barley". This region was also more open to external influences than is often supposed. Thus the archdeacon of Cardigan, John Parry (who left bequests to his four hedgers), wrote to Oxford for seed in 1697 "for trial of sanfoin and direction how to use the land it is to be sown in and what manner of soil it requires"; evidently he could get clover seed elsewhere if need be.[39]

Anglesey's mixed farming is brought into sharper focus than that of any other Welsh region because of the contemporary evidence of Henry Rowlands and Edward Wynne. The island's variations in soil texture were well understood by Rowlands, who even drew a map showing eight "tracts of ground" – possibly only the second sketch map to show soils in Britain. Some parishes were heathy, barren, by nature "of a coarser make", but could be made to yield rye and oats by pinfolding the cattle, spreading manure on the fallows, and denshiring. Others were producing barley and wheat "through the industry of the farmers" who applied "the late practices" of sanding, marling, and liming, adopted in the 1640s, 1650s, and 1660s respectively. Still others were naturally fertile, like Llanfihangel Ysceifiog, one of the richest soils in Anglesey for corn, meadow, and grass for fattening cattle. Rowlands's own parish of Llanidan was in this category, but he reported in 1698 that recently "it is strangely slackened in its vegetative vigours, as other parts of this country". Was this due to overcropping during forty years of more intensive cultivation and excessive manuring? In his book Rowlands hit out at prolonged cultivation – "plowing and harrassing the ground out of heart" – and advocated the restoration of such farms by sowing clover, sainfoin, and ryegrass. He writes about these as if they were a familiar element of local practice; unlike the Gower way of management (p. 416), clover was sown with spring corn without previous manuring, and double-cut for hay for two or three years. It was the best feed for store cattle before leaving the farm (Rowlands urged the Anglesey breeders to sell more

[39] NLW, Probate MSS, St David's, 1703 (Rowland Gwynne, gentleman, left goods worth £183 in his inventory, 16 Mar. 1702), and see Francis Jones, 'Taliaris', *Arch. Camb.*, CXVII, 1968, pp. 157–71; NLW, Probate MSS, St David's, 1719, inv. of Henry Kendrick, 13 Aug. 1719; *ibid.*, 1744; Francis Jones, 'Abermarlais', *Arch. Camb.*, CXVI, 1967, pp. 165–91, giving other data for the Vale of Tywi; NLW, Probate MSS, St David's 1726, John Parry's will dated 10 Oct. 1726; Bodleian Library, Ashmole MS 1,817a, f. 74, letter dated 16 Feb. 1697; Carte MS 108, f. 107.

fat cattle on their own account, to reduce their dependency on the drovers and English graziers); dairy cows thrived on it in springtime; and it rapidly built up the working stock.[40]

Wynne of Bodewryd on the northern side of Anglesey is the best-documented improver in Wales at this time. He initiated new methods as an agent of diffusion from Hereford, where he was chancellor of the diocese. His farming regime was modelled on that of a tenant farmer of 300 acres near Ross-on-Wye, the only modification being that Wynne had to sand, lime, and dung his land more frequently. The six-year rotation was wheat; barley; peas and beans; barley and clover (with seed first brought from Ross in 1717); mowing clover; grazing clover; "and so begins again with wheat". By 1720 he could buy clover seed at Wrexham market when selling cattle, and later he bought some at Chester, reflecting the spreading interest in "adventitious grasses"; he sowed a mixture of clover and ryegrass on his wet, sour ground. The structure of Anglesey mixed farming may be deduced from the stock on one of Wynne's demesnes (November 1734); the total value was £445 and the components are ranked by their percentage of this sum.

24 oxen (four years old and upwards), 6 bullocks of three years, 6 of two years, 8 yearling bullocks	31 per cent
Barley worth £90, wheat, oats, peas, and beans worth £20	25 per cent
34 cows, 2 bulls, 8 heifers of two years and one year, 9 calves, mainly of the black breed	22 per cent
5 stacks of hay	11 per cent
19 horses, mares, colts	8 per cent
53 sheep and lambs, 42 goats and kids	3 per cent

Nor was such a structure peculiar to Wynne's enterprise, because William Bulkeley, the diarist of Brynddu, paints a similar picture – barley and oats sold as far afield as London, sanding his fields and watering his meadows, clearing "wild ground" for crops, sowing clover and "our country hay seed" in the 1730s.[41] The inventory of a modest farmer, Richard ap William Pugh of Llanbadrig (1700), provides further confirmation (see Annexe 1).

A basically similar system was followed in the Vale of Clwyd and

[40] NLW, Church of Wales MS B/Misc. Vols./16; 'Antiquitates Parochiales', from unpublished papers by Henry Rowlands, *Arch. Camb.*, I, 1846, pp. 127, 130, 310, 317, 393; II, 1847, pp. 9, 139; IV, 1849, pp. 109–10, 178–9, 184, 187, 193, 264, 271, 278, 281, 284; NLW, MS 13,215E, pp. 569–95.

[41] Emery, 'Mechanics of Innovation', pp. 7–8; NLW, Bodewryd MS 1,089, account of the stock at Penrhos demesne and at Bronheulog, 13 Nov. 1734; J. Oliver, 'The Weather and Farming in the Mid-Eighteenth century in Anglesey', *Nat. Lib. Wales J.*, x, 1958, pp. 301–11. Bulkeley's diary covers the periods 1734–43 and 1747–60.

throughout the lowlands of the border counties of Flint, Denbigh, Montgomery, and Radnor, distinguished for instance by the early (pre-1668) experiments with sainfoin by Sir John Trevor on his estates near Wrexham. There is also the appearance of Jethro Tull's father on an estate near New Radnor in 1674, insisting on the construction of a watercourse to irrigate the fields; this was a condition to a marriage settlement and the channel (over two miles long) was dug at a cost of £400. Typical farmers' inventories from all these regions are given in Annexe 1, but a closer view will be taken of one of them, the Vale of Usk in Breconshire. As to its environment and potentialities, the vale had much in common with mid Gwent: good red soils, a relatively low rainfall, and easy access to markets. Early in this period, the small farmers (with up to about £35 in goods) concentrated on dairying, corn, and tiny flocks of a dozen or so sheep. Bigger men kept more sheep, pigs, and in addition a herd of store cattle; one of them, Thomas Lewis of Llangorse, had adopted clover by 1680; his books, incidentally, were worth £15. The cultivation of clover spread early within this region, and permeated to all levels of farming, including a widow whose goods were worth only £7. Nowhere is this more clearly shown than in the will of Walter Watkins, a butcher of Brecon town who died in the summer of 1729 (£67); his only farmstuff was some growing corn and clover which may have been for seed, because he left to his wife "the clover and all the profitt to be made thereof". The preferred order of field crops is represented by a well-to-do farmer (1737) who had harvested of wheat 41 acres, barley 36, oats 29, peas 18; he was also credited £15 for 41 acres of "fallow ploughing & mucking", presumably on his wheat ground.[42] By 1750 the smaller farmers in the Vale of Usk were still dairymen and corn growers, but a new feature is their increased numbers of sheep. The bigger men had also turned to keeping many more sheep, at the expense of cattle, and they were growing less corn (see Annexe 1).

Such trends are also discernible in the upland farming regions of Wales. Most of the country, in terms of area, fell into the category of stock-rearing uplands of differing intensities of use. Even in the various plains, vales, and lowlands, when reading through inventories of the mixed farmers who were so strongly entrenched there, one has the feeling that the 'mountain' environment is never far away. To a large extent this is because of functional links with the summer grazings used in common, often some distance away, and with out-pasturing in winter on hills closer at hand. We read of "dry mountainy cattle", "100 sheep upon the hills" (in February), or "six wild horses and seven wild mares on the hills". Upland farming was distinguished

[42] UCNWL, Kinmel MSS 1,475, 1,675; Mostyn MSS 5,508, 6,051, 6,431–2; Clwyd RO, D/HE 169, D/E 556; Thomas, 'Bodidris'; J. P. Ferris and R. C. B. Oliver, 'An Agricultural Improvement of 1674 at Trewern, Llanfihangel-Nant-Melan', *Radnors. Soc.*, XLII, 1972, pp. 23–9; NLW, Probate MSS, St David's, 1680, 1729, 1737.

by a greater emphasis on sheep and cattle, and on store cattle rather than dairy herds; the keeping of more horses than in lowland regions; a more limited range of field crops, and the cultivation of rye; the wealthier farmers were not able to diversify their practices, being wealthy simply because they had more (not better) land or access to more pasture than the poor majority; consequently, there may have been less scope for innovative change during this period, and rather a shift to specialization in sheep farming on a growing scale. As before 1640, there was some difference of degree within upland Wales between the extremes of Snowdonia (see p. 397 above) and the more genial slopes of Dyfed, or between the *blaenau* of Glamorgan and the Black Mountain. But as the differences diminished with time, it is enough to illustrate the main characteristics, in a progressive contraction of farming opportunity from south to north.

Massive flocks and herds could be kept by some on the high pastures of Carmarthenshire and Cardiganshire. A classic example is William Williams of Dôl-goch in the upper Tywi, who climbed the social ladder sufficiently to become high sheriff of his county in 1725. Three years later his inventory shows that he had well over 1,000 sheep and lambs, accounting for 53 per cent of his goods. He had 57 cattle and 45 horses, and left 7 farms to his son. This second William Williams of Pantseiry, who died in 1773, built so successfully and ruthlessly on the pastoral foundations of his father's farming that he was called 'King of the Mountains' and 'Job of the West' on account of the legendary size of his flocks of sheep and herds of wild horses. Behind such wealth was the more intensive use of summer grazings, with the decay of traditional transhumance. Turning to the hill farmers of Glamorgan, it was usual for the ordinary man to have a herd of 30 cattle of various kinds and ages; bigger herds of over 80 head were not rare. Sheep were becoming more numerous than they were before 1640; one farmer in two had more than 100 in his flock, some had over 500, their meat of better quality than the wool. Upland stock were worth less than elsewhere, reflecting less attention to breeding; this is emphasized in such items as "a yoke of small mountany bullocks", "a small number of mountany sheep on ye mountain", "ten mountany cows and ten small oxen". There is a distinctive flavour to the hill farmers' inventories — "a he goat if found", "an old despairing cow"; where local conditions were against wheels, "ten sleye full of hay", and sleds among the implements, turf and turf irons, hedging gloves, and time and again the "dungle", dung hill, or *miskin*.[43]

In the uplands of mid Wales the environmental uncertainties of a region of difficulty always threatened the farmer. On a Montgomeryshire estate shortages of winter fodder in the 1670s were a constant refrain; as late as

---

[43] NLW, Castle Hill MS 717; the will of the 'King of the Mountains' is to be found *ibid.*, 232, but there is no inventory with it; Probate MSS, Llandaf; Brian S. Osborne, 'Glamorgan Agriculture in the Seventeenth and Eighteenth Centuries', *Nat. Lib. Wales J.*, xx, 1979, pp. 387–407.

June "their cattle are as yett scarce markettable". Endemic shortages were cruelly exaggerated by the severe winter of 1739–40 and the destructive floods that followed in the summer. "Having spent [i.e. used] all that the floods left uncarried away", and after spending their rent money on fodder, the tenants had still lost half their livestock. "In fine, no part of England [*sic*] has suffered so much by flood and famine."[44] Among the stock, horses were still reared in numbers, sometimes modestly as with the Beguildy (Radnors.) farmer who had "his horses, little wild ones rear'd on the hill". Other small farmers were coming to specialize in sheep. With David Morris of Llangurig (£49; 1700), for example, two-thirds of his goods consisted of a flock of 160 sheep, lambs, and their wool. A similar trend was taking place in the hill country of north Wales: the characteristics of Snowdonia have already been outlined, and the peak of its farming as attainable by most men is represented by a yeoman of Drwsycoed (Caerns.) with stock worth £107 (January 1701). William Griffith had a flock of 87 milking sheep, 70 wethers, and 63 yearlings, 220 in all; 18 cows with calves and 18 bullocks; corn is not mentioned in his inventory, but he had 3 horses, a mare, and 21 goats.[45]

Many of the northern hill farms were comparatively new creations. Of one in Denbighshire it was said in 1693 "tho not so steep and woodie on ye eastern side, yet it appears yt it has been as woodie before they rid ye ground for plowing... The owners have carried away most of ye stones to make their walls and indeed to clear ye ground. It was but a wild place, they say, and this is but ye eighth heir of yt house, since it was built or any of yt land cultivated."[46] This places the beginning of the farm somewhere in the middle of the sixteenth century, and the basic business of reclaiming new farms was still going on, notably on the lower margins of common grazings as enclosure gained momentum. Even in the hill country, by such agricultural advances an increasing degree of similarity emerged between Wales and the rest of the kingdom. The suspicions of outsiders were engendered by cultural differences to do with people rather than by any special, inherent hostility of the Welsh farming environment. It is not easy to understand why, when a Kentish landowner went to Wales to inspect his property there, his brother should wish him "a good deliverance and a safe return to a Christian country".[47]

[44] Herts. RO, D/ELW E60; NLW, Powis Castle Correspondence, 9,211, dated 26 Apr. 1741.

[45] NLW, Probate MSS, St David's (1695), Bangor (1700); Elwyn Davies, 'Hendre and Hafod in Caenarvonshire', *Caernarvon Hist. Soc.*, XL, 1979, pp. 17–46.

[46] Bodleian Library, MS Ashmole 1,829, f. 171; Bryn Roberts, 'Llythyrau John Lloyd at Edward Lhuyd', pp. 108–9; the farm, Clegir Mawr, still stands on this site near Melin-y-wig, in broken country to the south of Clocaenog Forest.

[47] Kent AO, U951 C82/36.

ANNEXE I

FARM STOCK IN SOUTH WALES, 1675–1750

Comparison of individual farmers of similar standing from the same locality, wherever possible using inventories compiled in the same season of the farming years. They depict farming systems in south Wales, drawn from NLW, Probate MSS for the dioceses of Llandaf and St David's (archdeaconry of Brecon), at dates *c.* 1675–1750. (Values are rounded to the nearest £.)

COASTAL BELT BETWEEN CHEPSTOW AND CARDIFF: THE SEVERN LOWLANDS

David Lawrence, Marshfield, July 1680, £114 (total value of goods): 33 cattle (dairy herd of 27), 3 horses, 17 sheep, 6 pigs, corn and implements worth £23 (wheat, barley, oats, rye, beans).

David William, Bassaleg, May 1749, £120: 24 cattle (dairy herd of 12), 7 horses, 20 sheep, 10 pigs, corn and implements worth £27 (wheat, barley, oats), hay worth £6.

Rowland Jones, Magor, January 1680, £120: 25 cattle (dairy herd of 14), 5 horses, no sheep, 16 pigs, corn and implements £21, hay £5.

Edward Stephens, St Bride's Netherwent, March 1750, £123: 43 cattle (dairy herd of 29), 6 horses, 9 sheep, 18 pigs, corn and implements £16 (wheat, barley, peas, beans), hay £7.

MID GWENT

James Prichard, Bryngwyn, January 1680, £40: 14 cattle (dairy herd of 5), 3 horses, 21 sheep, 12 pigs, corn and implements £10.

Thomas Timothy, Llangattwg, December 1749, £48: 15 cattle (dairy herd of 5), 4 horses, 16 sheep, 10 pigs, corn and implements £6; clover seed.

William Baker, Treleck Grange, April 1690, £270: 31 cattle (dairy herd of 21), 5 horses, 60 sheep, 10 pigs, corn and implements £127 (wheat, maslin, barley, oats, peas).

Abel Jenkin, Shirenewton, July 1750, £312: 55 cattle (dairy herd of 35), 22 horses, 98 sheep, 26 pigs, corn and implements £57 (wheat, barley, oats).

VALE OF GLAMORGAN

Evan Yorath, Coychurch, January 1675, £26: 6 cattle (3 dairy), 1 horse, 35 sheep, no pigs, corn £2 (barley, oats).

Howell Edward, Coychurch, March 1750, £31: 15 cattle (9 dairy), 3 horses, 50 sheep, no corn.

Jenet Robert, St George, December 1675, £79: 16 cattle (13 dairy), 1 horse, 16 sheep, 4 pigs, corn and implements £16.

Jenkin John, Colwinston, September 1750, £83: 19 cattle (15 dairy), 3 horses, 40 sheep, 6 pigs, corn and implements £4, hay £7.

Lewis Jones, Sully, March 1675, £98: 27 cattle (24 dairy), 5 horses, 35 sheep, 4 pigs, corn and implements £12.

Edward Howell, Cogan, May 1750, £107: 48 cattle (20 dairy), 3 horses, 39 sheep, 5 pigs, corn and implements £8 (wheat, barley, beans).

VALE OF USK

Thomas Powell, Llangynidr, August 1675, £19: 7 cattle (6 dairy), 5 horses, 10 sheep, no pigs, corn and implements £3 (barley, oats), hay £2.

Roger Watkins, Llanfihangel Cwmdu, March 1735, £21: 7 cattle (5 dairy), 2 horses, 100 sheep, 2 pigs, corn and implements £2, hay £1 (including clover).

John William Lewis, Llandyfaelog tre'r graig, May 1675, £35: 18 cattle (16 dairy), 3 horses, 16 sheep, 1 pig, corn and implements £6.

Thomas Phillip, Llanbedr, September 1738, £38: 12 cattle (5 dairy), 2 horses, 55 sheep, 5 pigs, corn and implements £11, hay £2 (clover).

Thomas Lewis, Llangors, November 1680, £492: 69 cattle (21 dairy), 11 horses, 141 sheep, 39 pigs, corn and implements £99, hay £22 (clover).

Walter Watkins, Llanfihangel Cwmdu, August 1739, £574: 25 cattle (13 dairy), 2 horses, 377 sheep, 14 pigs, corn and implements £62 (wheat, barley, oats, peas, maslin), hay £4 (clover).

UPLAND FARMING

Glamorgan

Richard Lewis, Llangynyr, November 1675, £45: 24 cattle (16 dairy), 3 horses, 60 sheep, no pigs, corn and implements £3.

William Morgan, Eglwys Ilan, June 1750, £53: 20 cattle (8 dairy), 2 horses, 80 sheep, no pigs, no corn.

William Lewis, Geligaer, April 1680, £208: 108 cattle (70 dairy), 18 horses, 512 sheep, 4 pigs, corn and implements £10.

William David, Llandyfodwg, January 1750, £215: 43 cattle (18 dairy), 5 horses, 670 sheep, 4 pigs, corn and implements £5.

Monmouthshire

Ieuan John Rosser, Trevethin, August 1680, £17: 6 dairy cattle, 19 sheep, 1 pig, no corn, hay £1, no horses.

William Charles, Trevethin, September 1750, £29: 9 dairy cattle, 1 horse, 80 sheep, 1 pig, corn and implements £3.

Breconshire

Jenkin Griffith, Ystradgynlais, September 1675, £127: 62 cattle (40 dairy), 6 horses, 149 sheep (and 26 goats), no pigs, corn and implements £12.

Rees Williams, Merthyr Cynog, October 1737, £175: 37 cattle (16 dairy), 4 horses, 65 sheep, 5 pigs, corn and implements £65, hay £10 (clover).

To complete the annexe, a selection of single farmers' inventories from various regions is given in summary (NLW, Probate MSS., Bangor and St David's):

Anglesey

Richard ap William Pugh, Llanbadrig, 4 October 1700, £45: 10 cattle (6 dairy), 4 horses, 34 sheep and lambs, no pigs, corn and implements of husbandry £11, share of a boat and nets £2.

Vale of Clwyd

Simon Roberts, Llandyrnog, 17 April 1699, £100: 22 black cattle (16 dairy), 4 horses, 40 sheep, 2 pigs, corn and implements £20.

Upper Severn valley

John Arthur, Carno (Mont.), 27 September 1700, £70: 19 cattle (14 dairy), no horses, 59 sheep, 4 pigs, corn and implements £3, hay and fodder £4.

Border lowlands

Meredith Phillip, Llandeilo Graban (Radnors.), 7 February 1675, £91: 11 cattle (6 dairy), 1 horse, 6 sheep, 3 pigs, corn and implements £18.

Rowland Vaughan, Nantmel (Radnors.), 1 June 1675, £72: 26 cattle (13 dairy), 5 horses, 89 sheep, 4 pigs, corn and implements £5.

Mary Morris, Ceri (Mont.), 20 May 1675, £73: 15 cattle (7 dairy), 2 horses, 70 sheep, no pigs, corn and implements £10.

ANNEXE 2

FARM STOCK OF CLOVER GROWERS, 1676–1705

(1) Summaries of the farm stock of eight farmers from the region of mid Gwent, 1676–95, who had adopted the cultivation of clover. They are ranked according to the total value of their goods as listed in their inventories; the percentage values relate to this figure (except for Waters,

Gowens, and Phillip, for whom moneys, credits, etc. have been deducted to leave a total that more accurately reflects their working stock-in-trade). Because of overlap between the items, of course, the percentage values cannot add up to 100. See Table, p. 427.

(2) Summaries of the farm stock of ten farmers from the counties of Monmouth, Glamorgan, and Brecon whose inventories were compiled between October 1704 and October 1705, all of whom had adopted the cultivation of clover. They are ranked in order of the total value of their goods, as given in the inventories; but in five cases (Evans, Parry, Roberts, Charles, Edmond John) the percentages relate to a total calculated by deducting the moneys, credits, etc. from the overall inventory total. See Table, p. 428.

ANNEXE 3

FARM STOCK ON TWO DEMESNES IN THE COASTAL VALE OF GLAMORGAN, 1686 AND 1742

Summaries of farm stock held on two major demesnes in the coastal Vale of Glamorgan, made from probate inventories at the National Library of Wales, diocese of Llandaf. Because Stradling's list was compiled in September, he has a stock of hay and corn already harvested; Jones, whose inventory dates from early July, does not have hay (not yet mown) and most of his corn is still growing in the fields. The various components of each farming system are ranked according to their percentage shares of the total value of farmstock.

Sir Edward Stradling, Bart, of St Donat's Castle, Glamorgan; 17 September 1686; total farm stock £250

Sheep, 25 per cent, 227 head (50 wethers, 31 ewes, 31 feeding sheep, 110 lambs, 5 rams)

Cattle, 23 per cent, 26 head (8 cows, 1 heifer, 11 calves, 2 bulls, butter and cheese worth £10, 4 steers and gales)

Corn and implements of husbandry, 18 per cent (wheat, barley, oats, peas)

Working oxen, horses, mares, colts, 15 per cent (4 oxen, others unspecified)

"Hay well harvested and ill harvested", 15 per cent

Pigs and poultry, 4 per cent

Robert Jones, Esq., of Fonmon Castle, Glamorgan; 2–3 July 1742; total farm stock £748

Cattle, 31 per cent, 82 head (18 cows and heifers, 5 calves, 8 splayed heifers, 8 steers of 3 years, 30 cattle of 1 and 2 years, 6 bull staggs, 7 fat oxen)

Sheep, 29 per cent, 646 head (161 sheep of 1 year, 151 breeding ewes, 165 lambs, 20 suckling lambs, 80 ewes and small sheep, 58 fat sheep, 5 breeding rams, wool)

Corn and implements of husbandry, 27 per cent (wheat and oats in store, 27 acres of growing wheat, 29 acres of barley, 5 acres of oats)

Working oxen (16), *horses, mares, colts* (9), *12 per cent*

Pigs, bacon, and poultry, 1 per cent

ANNEXE 2 (1)

	All livestock (%)	All cattle (%)	No. of sheep	Oxen, horses, corn, implements (%)	All corn (%)	Hay and clover (%)
Evan John Evan, bachelor, Llangattwg-juxta-Caerleon, 25 Mar. 1695, £138	64	48	22	44	19	1
Herbert Lewis (no designation), Llanfihangel-juxta-Usk, 4 Sept. 1685, £138	40	23	60	64	45	4
William Price, yeoman, Grosmont, 18 Feb. 1676, £79	51	36	63	45	21	2
Thomas Waters, yeoman, Usk, 25 Nov. 1690, £78	35	20	24	34	23	7
William Prichard, gent., Llantillio Crossenny, 5 Jan. 1685, £76	49	47	—	59	38	1
Catchmayd Tyler, gent., Mitchel Troy, 6 Dec. 1689, £64	71	17	77	43	28	1
John Gowens, yeoman, Llanarth, 26 June 1695, £53	44	36	—	19	12	1
George Phillip, husbandsman, Penrose, 9 Aug. 1680, £39	44	30	4	41	38	1

	All livestock (%)	All cattle (%)	No. of sheep	Oxen, horses, corn, implements (%)	All corn (%)	Hay and clover (%)
Thomas Evans, gent., Llanfihangel Ystum Llywern (Mon.), 11 Oct. 1705, £564	41	30	—	45	26	1
William Knight, yeoman, Llanwytherin (Mon.), 25 Apr. 1705, £139	44	34	41	57	30	1
Phillip Parry, yeoman, Talgarth (Brecons.), 15 Jan. 1705, £126	54	38	30	19	Corn and hay 11%	a
David Morgan, gent., Tregare (Mon.), 1 Nov. 1705, £120	38	a	—	53	30	a
Thomas Roberts, butcher, Grosmont (Mon.), 6 Apr. 1705, £86	31	—	—	a	25	a
William Hugh, husbandman, Llantillio Crossenny (Mon.), 30 March. 1705, £84	43	32	42	46	31	3
John Burch, yeoman, Llanrhidian (Gower, Glam.), 11 Oct. 1704, £81	32	16	37	57	50	4
John Charles, yeoman, Llangattwg-juxta-Usk (Mon.), 29 Nov. 1704, £70	40	29	—	41	14	1
Edmond John (no desig.), Llanelli (Brecons.), 20 Oct. 1704, £64	53	10	51	30	11	11
Jenkin John (no desig.), St Mary's, Cardiff (Glam.), 5 Mar. 1705, £9	33	—	24	8	4	6

SELECT BIBLIOGRAPHY

Addison, W. *English Fairs and Markets*. London, 1953.

Airs, M. *The Making of the English Country House, 1500–1640*. London, 1975.

Albert, W. A. *The Turnpike Road System in England and Wales, 1663–1840*. Cambridge, 1972.

Alcock, N. W. *Stoneleigh Houses*. Birmingham, 1973.

Allison, K. J. *The East Riding of Yorkshire Landscape*. London, 1976.
   'Flock Management in the Sixteenth and Seventeenth Centuries', EcHR, 2nd ser., XI, 1958.
   'The Norfolk Worsted Industry in the Sixteenth and Seventeenth Centuries', *Yorks. Bull. Ec. & Soc. Research*, XII–XIII, 1960–1.
   'The Sheep–Corn Husbandry of Norfolk in the Sixteenth and Seventeenth Centuries', AHR, V, 1, 1957.

Ambler, L. *Old Halls and Manor Houses of Yorkshire*. London, 1913.

Amery, C. *Period Houses and their Details*. London, 1974.

Andrews, J. H. 'The Port of Chichester and the Grain Trade, 1650–1750', *Sussex Arch. Coll.*, XCII, 1954.

Andrews, L. S. 'Vaynor Lands during the Eighteenth Century', *Mont. Coll.*, XLVI, 1940.

Appleby, A. B. 'Disease or Famine? Mortality in Cumberland and Westmorland, 1580–1640', EcHR, 2nd ser., XXVI, 1973.

Ashton, T. S. *Economic Fluctuations in England, 1700–1800*. Oxford, 1959.
   An Economic History of England: The Eighteenth Century. London, 1955.

Ashworth, G. J. 'A Note on the Decline of the Wealden Iron Industry', *Surrey Arch. Coll.*, LXVII, 1970.

Astbury, A. K. *The Black Fens*. Cambridge, 1957.

Atwell, G. *The Faithfull Surveyor*. Cambridge, 1662.

Aubrey, J. *The Natural History of Wiltshire*, ed. J. Britton. London, 1847.

Austen, R. *The Spiritual Use of an Orchard; or Garden of Fruit Trees*. Oxford, 1653.

Bailey, J. *A General View of the Agriculture of Durham*. London, 1810.

Bailey, J. and Culley, G. *General View of the Agriculture of Cumberland*. London, 1794.
   General View of the Agriculture of the County of Northumberland. 3rd edn. London, 1805.

Baker, A. H. R. and Butlin, R. A. (eds.). *Studies of Field Systems in the British Isles*. Cambridge, 1973.

Banister, J. *A Synopsis of Husbandry*. London, 1799.

Bankes, J. and Kerridge, E. *The Early Records of the Bankes Family at Winstanley*. Manchester, 1973.

Barley, M. W. 'The Double-Pile House', *Arch. J.*, CXXXVI, 1979.
   The English Farmhouse and Cottage. London, 1961.

'A Glossary of Names for Rooms in Houses of the Sixteenth and Seventeenth Centuries', in *Culture and Environment*, ed. I. Ll. Foster and L. Alcock. London, 1963.

The House and Home. London, 1963.

Barley, M. W. and Summers, N. 'Averham Park Lodge and its Paintings', *Thoroton Soc.*, LXV, 1961.

Barnes, D. G. *A History of the English Corn Laws from 1660–1846.* London, 1930. Repr. New York, 1965.

Barratt, D. M. (ed.). *Ecclesiastical Terriers of Warwickshire Parishes, II.* Dugdale Soc., 1971.

Batchelor, T. *General View of the Agriculture of the County of Bedford.* London, 1808.

Batey, Mavis. 'Oliver Goldsmith: An Indictment of Landscape Gardening', in P. Willis (ed.), *Furor Hortensis.* Edinburgh, 1974.

Baxter, R. *The Reverend Richard Baxter's Last Treatise*, ed. F. J. Powicke. Manchester, 1926.

Beale, J. *Herefordshire Orchards.* London, 1657.

Beale, J. and Lawrence, A. *Nurseries, Orchards, Profitable Gardens and Vineyards Encouraged...* London, 1677.

Beastall, T. W. *A North Country Estate.* London and Chichester, 1975.

Beavington, F. 'Early Market Gardening in Bedfordshire', *Inst. Brit. Geographers*, XXXVII, 1965.

Beckett, J. V. *Coal and Tobacco: The Lowthers and the Economic Development of West Cumberland, 1660–1760.* Cambridge, 1981.

'English Landownership in the Later Seventeenth and Eighteenth Centuries: The Debate and the Problems', *EcHR*, 2nd ser., XXX, 4, 1977.

'Regional Variation and the Agricultural Depression, 1730–50', *EcHR*, 2nd ser., XXXV, 1982.

Bell, V. *To Meet Mr. Ellis: Little Gaddesden in the Eighteenth Century.* London, 1956.

Bennett, M. K. 'British Wheat Yield per Acre for Seven Centuries', *Ec. Hist.*, III, 1935.

Beresford, M. W. 'The Common Informer, the Penal Statutes, and Economic Regulation', *EcHR*, 2nd ser., X, 1957.

'Glebe Terriers and Open Field Leicestershire', in *Studies in Leicestershire Agrarian History*, ed. W. G. Hoskins. Leicester, 1949.

'Glebe Terriers and Open-Field Yorkshire', *Yorks. Arch. J.*, XXXVII, 1951.

'Habitation versus Improvement', in *Essays in the Economic and Social History of Tudor and Stuart England*, ed. F. J. Fisher. Cambridge, 1961.

Best, Henry. *Rural Economy in Yorkshire in 1641, being the Farming and Account Books of Henry Best of Elmswell, East Riding of Yorkshire.* Surtees Soc., XXXIII. 1851.

Bettey, J. 'The Cultivation of Woad in the Salisbury Area during the Late Sixteenth and Early Seventeenth Centuries', *Textile Hist.*, IX, 1978.

Bigmore, P. *The Bedfordshire and Huntingdonshire Landscape.* London, 1979.

Billing, R. *An Account of the Culture of Carrots.* London, 1765.

Blake, S. *The Compleat Gardener's Practice.* London, 1664.

Blith, W. *The English Improver.* London, 1649. 2nd edn. 1649.

The English Improver Improved. 3rd edn. London, 1652. 4th edn. 1653.

Blome, R. *Britannia.* London, 1673.

Blomefield, F. *An Essay towards a Topographical History of Norfolk*. 5 vols. Norwich and King's Lynn, 1739–75. 2nd edn. 11 vols. 1805–20.

Blundell, N. *The Great Diurnall of Nicholas Blundell of Little Crosby*, ed. J. S. Bagley. 3 vols. Lancs. & Cheshire Rec. Soc. Manchester, 1968–72.

Bonfield, L. 'Marriage Settlements and the "Rise of Great Estates": The Demographic Aspect', EcHR, 2nd ser., XXXII, 1979.

Bonser, K. J. *The Drovers*. London, 1970.

Bouch, C. M. L. and Jones, G. P. *The Lake Counties, 1500–1830*. Manchester, 1961.

Bowden, P. J. *The Wool Trade in Tudor and Stuart England*. London, 1962.

Boys, J. *General View of the Agriculture of the County of Kent*. London, 1813.

Brace, H. W. *A History of Seed Crushing in Great Britain*. London, 1960.

[Braddon, L.]. *To Pay Old Debts without New Taxes by Charitably Relieving, Politically Reforming, and Judiciously Employing the Poor*. London, 1723.

Bradley, R. *A General Treatise of Husbandry and Gardening, II*. London, 1726.

Brigg, M. 'The Forest of Pendle in the Seventeenth Century', *Hist. Soc. Lancs. & Cheshire*, CXIII, 1961.

Broad, J. 'Alternative Husbandry and Permanent Pasture in the Midlands, 1650–1800', AHR, XXVIII, 2, 1980.

Brodrick, G. C. *English Land and English Landlords*. London, 1881.

Brooks, C. E. P. *Climate through the Ages*. 2nd edn. London, 1949.

Brown, E. H. Phelps and Hopkins, S. V. 'Builders' Wage-Rates, Prices and Population: Some Further Evidence', *Economica*, NS, XXVI, 1959.
    'Seven Centuries of the Prices of Consumables, compared with Builders' Wage-Rates', *Economica*, NS, XXIII, 1956.

Brown, J. *General View of the Agriculture of the County of Derby*. London, 1794.

Brunskill, R. W. *Illustrated Handbook of Vernacular Architecture*. London, 1970.

Buchanan, K. M. 'Studies in the Localisation of Seventeenth-Century Worcestershire Industries, 1600–1650', *Worcs. Arch. Soc.*, XVII, 1940; XIX, 1943.

Bulkeley, W. 'The Diary of William Bulkeley of Brynddu, Anglesey', ed. H. Owen, *Anglesey Antiq. Soc.*, 1931.

Campbell, Colin. *Vitruvius Britannicus, or the British Architect*. 3 vols. London, 1715–25.

Campbell, M. *The English Yeoman*. New Haven, 1942.

Carter, E. *A History of Cambridgeshire*. London, 1819.

Carter, W. *The Proverb Crossed*. London, 1677.

Cartwright, J. J. (ed.). *The Travels through England of Dr. Richard Pococke*. 2 vols. Camden Soc., NS, XLII, XLIV, 1888–9.

Cathcart, Earl. 'Jethro Tull, his Life, Times and Teaching', *J. RASE*, 3rd ser., II, I, 1891.

Chalklin, C. W. 'The Rural Economy of a Kentish Wealden Parish, 1650–1750', AHR, X, 1962.
    Seventeenth Century Kent: A Social and Economic History. London, 1965.

Chalklin, C. W. and Havinden, M. A. (eds.). *Rural Change and Urban Growth, 1500–1800: Essays in English Regional History in Honour of W. G. Hoskins*. London, 1974.

Chambers, J. D. *Nottinghamshire in the Eighteenth Century*. London, 1932.

Chambers, J. D. and Mingay, G. E. *The Agricultural Revolution, 1750–1880*. London, 1966.

Chapman, S. D. 'The Genesis of the British Hosiery Industry, 1600–1750', *Textile Hist.*, III, 1972.

Chartres, J. A. *Internal Trade in England, 1500–1700*. London, 1977.
  'Road Carrying in England in the Seventeenth Century: Myths and Reality',
    EcHR, 2nd ser., xxx, 1977.
Chauncy, H. *Historical Antiquities of Hertfordshire* (1700). Bishop's Stortford, 1826.
Chesney, H. E. 'The Transference of Lands in England, 1640–60', *Trans. RHS*, 4th
    ser., xv, 1932.
Chibnall, A. C. *Sherington: The Fiefs and Fields of a Buckinghamshire Village*.
    Cambridge, 1965.
Child, Sir J. *Discourse about Trade*. London, 1690.
  New Discourse of Trade. London, 1694.
Clapham, Sir John. *A Concise Economic History of Britain from the Earliest Times to
    1750*. Cambridge, 1949.
Clarke, P. and Slack, P. (eds.). *Crisis and Order in English Towns, 1500–1700*. London,
    1972.
Clarkson, L. A. 'The Leather Crafts in Tudor and Stuart England', AHR, xiv, 1,
    1966.
  The Pre-Industrial Economy in England, 1500–1750. London, 1971.
Clay, C. '"The Greed of Whig Bishops"? Church Landlords and their Lessees,
    1660–1760', PP, no. 87. 1980.
  'Marriage, Inheritance, and the Rise of Large Estates in England, 1660–1815',
    EcHR, 2nd ser., xxi, 3, 1968.
  'The Misfortunes of William, Fourth Lord Petre', *Recusant Hist.*, xi, 2, 1971.
  'The Price of Freehold Land in the Later Seventeenth and Eighteenth Centuries',
    EcHR, 2nd ser., xxvii, 2, 1974.
  Public Finance and Private Wealth. Oxford, 1978.
Cliffe, J. T. *The Yorkshire Gentry from the Reformation to the Civil War*. London,
    1969.
Clifton-Taylor, A. *The Pattern of English Building*. London, 1972.
Coate, M. *Cornwall in the Great Civil War and Interregnum*. 2nd edn. Truro, 1963.
Coleman, D. C. *The Economy of England, 1450–1750*. Oxford, 1977.
  'Growth and Decay during the Industrial Revolution: The Case of East Anglia',
    Scand. Ec. Hist. Rev., x, 1962.
  'An Innovation and its Diffusion: The "New Draperies"', EcHR, 2nd ser., xxii,
    1969.
  'Labour in the English Economy of the Seventeenth Century', EcHR, 2nd ser.,
    viii, 1956.
  'Naval Dockyards under the Later Stuarts', EcHR, 2nd ser., vi, 1953.
  Sir John Banks – Baronet and Businessman. Oxford, 1963.
Coleman, D. C. and John, A. H. (eds.). *Trade, Government and Economy in Pre-Industrial
    England*. London, 1976.
Colville, James (ed.). *Letters of John Cockburn of Ormistoun to his Gardener, 1727–1744*.
    Scottish Hist. Soc., xlv. 1904.
Colvin, H. M. *Biographical Dictionary of British Architects*. London, 1978.
  History of the King's Works, V. London, 1976.
Colvin, H. M. and Harris, J. (eds.). *The Country Seat*. London, 1970.
Colvin, H. M. and Newman, J. (eds.). *Of Building – Roger North's Writings on
    Architecture*. Oxford, 1981.

Colyer, R. J. 'Cattle Drovers in the Nineteenth Century', *Nat. Lib. Wales J.*, XVIII, 1973–4.

The Welsh Cattle Drovers. Cardiff, 1976.

Cooper, J. P. 'Patterns of Inheritance and Settlement by Great Landowners', in J. Goody *et al.* (eds.), *Family and Inheritance*. Cambridge, 1976.

'The Social Distribution of Land and Men in England, 1436–1700', EcHR, 2nd ser., XX, 1967.

Cordingley, R. A. 'British Historical Roof-Types and their Members', *Ancient Monuments Soc.*, NS, IX, 1961.

Cornwall, J. C. K. 'Agricultural Improvement, 1560–1640', *Sussex Arch. Coll.*, XCVIII, 1960.

Court, W. H. B. *The Rise of the Midland Industries, 1600–1838*. Rev. edn. Oxford, 1953.

Cox, T. *Magna Britannia*. London, 1720.

Cracknell, B. E. *Canvey Island*. Leicester, 1959.

Cranfield, G. A. *The Development of the Provincial Newspaper, 1700–1760*. Oxford, 1962.

Crosweller, W. T. *The Gardeners' Company: A Short Chronological History, 1605–1907*. London, 1908.

Darby, H. C. *The Draining of the Fens*. Cambridge, 1940. 2nd edn. 1956.

Davies, Margaret G. 'Country Gentry and Falling Rents in the 1660s and 1670s', *Midland Hist.*, IV, 2, 1977.

Davies, Walter. *A General View of the Agriculture and Domestic Economy of South Wales*. 2 vols. London, 1815.

Davis, O. R. F. 'The Wealth and Influence of John Holles, Duke of Newcastle, 1694–1711', *Renaissance & Mod. Stud.*, IX, 1965.

Davis, R. *General View of the Agriculture of the County of Oxford*. London, 1794.

Davis, T. *General View of the Agriculture of the County of Wiltshire*. London, 1794.

Deane, P. and Cole, W. A. *British Economic Growth, 1688–1959*. Cambridge, 1962. 2nd edn. 1969.

Defoe, Daniel. *The Complete English Tradesman*. 2 vols. London, 1745.

A Tour through the Whole Island of Great Britain, ed. G. D. H. Cole and D. C. Browning. 2 vols. London, 1962.

Dell, R. F. 'The Decline of the Clothing Industry in Berkshire', *Newbury & Dist. Field Club*, X, 1954.

Dexter, K. and Barber, D. *Farming for Profits*. London, 1961.

Dodd, A. H. 'Caernarvonshire in the Civil War', *Caerns. Hist. Soc.*, XIV, 1953.

'The Civil War in East Denbighshire', *Denbs. Hist. Soc.*, III, 1954.

'Flintshire Politics in the Seventeenth Century', *Flints. Hist. Soc.*, 1953–4.

The Industrial Revolution in North Wales. Cardiff, 1933.

Life in Wales. London, 1972.

'The North Wales Coal Industry during the Industrial Revolution', *Arch. Cambrensis*, LXXXIV, 1929.

'The Pattern of Politics in Stuart Wales', *Hon. Soc. Cymmrodorion*, 1948.

Studies in Stuart Wales. 2nd edn. Cardiff, 1971.

Doddington, George Bubb. *The Political Journal of George Bubb Doddington*, ed. J. Carswell and L. A. Dralle. London, 1965.

Donnelly, T. 'Arthur Clephane, Edinburgh Merchant and Seedsman', AHR, XVIII, 2, 1970.

Dony, J. G. *A History of the Straw Hat Industry*. Luton, 1942.

Doughty, H. M. *Chronicles of Theberton*. London, 1910.

Douglas, J. 'The Culture of Saffron', *Philos. Trans. Roy. Soc.*, XXXV, 1728.

Downes, K. *English Baroque Architecture*. London, 1966.

Driver, A. and Driver, W. *General View of the Agriculture of the County of Hampshire*. London, 1794.

Drummond, J. C. and Wilbraham, A. *The Englishman's Food*, rev. D. Hollingsworth. London, 1957.

Dugdale, W. *The History of Imbanking and Drayning*. London, 1662.

Dyer, Alan. 'Growth and Decay in English Towns, 1500–1700', *Urban Hist. Yearbook*, 1979.

Eaton, Daniel. *The Letters of Daniel Eaton to the Third Earl of Cardigan, 1725–32*, ed. Joan Wake and Deborah Champion Webster. Northants. Rec. Soc., XXIV. 1971.

Edie, C. A. *The Irish Cattle Bills: A Study in Restoration Politics*. Amer. Philos. Soc., NS LX. 1970.

Edmunds, Henry. 'History of the Brecknockshire Agricultural Society, 1755–1955', *Brycheiniog*, III, 1957.

Edwards, J. K. 'The Gurneys and the Norwich Clothing Trade in the Eighteenth Century', *JFHS*, L, 1962–4.

Edwards, P. R. 'The Cattle Trade of Shropshire in the Late Sixteenth and Seventeenth Centuries', *Midland Hist.*, VI, 1981.

'The Development of Dairy Farming on the North Shropshire Plain in the Seventeenth Century', *Midland Hist.*, IV, 3–4, 1978.

'The Horse Trade of the Midlands in the Seventeenth Century', AHR, XXVII, 2, 1979.

Ellis, W. *Chiltern and Vale Farming Explained*. London, 1733.

A Compleat System of Experienced Improvements. London, 1749.

The Compleat Planter and Cyderist. London, 1756.

The Practical Farmer, or The Hertfordshire Husbandman. London, 1732. 2nd edn., 2 pts. 1732.

The Modern Husbandman. 8 vols. London, 1750.

Emery, Frank V. 'Early Cultivation of Clover in Gower', *J. Gower Soc.*, XXVI, 1975.

'The Mechanics of Innovation: Clover Cultivation in Wales before 1750', *J. Hist. Geog.*, II, 1, 1976.

'A New Account of Snowdonia, 1693, Written for Edward Lhuyd', *Nat. Lib. Wales J.*, XVIII, 1974.

Emery, Frank V. and Smith, C. G. 'A Weather Record from Snowdonia, 1697–98', *Weather*, XXXI, 1976.

Evans, E. J. *The Contentious Tithe*. London, 1976.

'Tithing Customs and Disputes: The Evidence of Glebe Terriers, 1698–1850', AHR, XVIII, 1, 1970.

Evans, G. N. 'The Artisan and Small Farmer in Mid-Eighteenth Century Anglesey', *Anglesey Antiq. Soc.*, 1933.

Evelyn, John. *Acetaria: A Discourse of Sallets*. London, 1699.

Diary, ed. E. S. de Beer. 6 vols. Oxford, 1955.

Sylva...to which is annexed Pomona. London, 1664.

Everitt, Alan M. 'The English Urban Inn, 1560–1760', in *Perspectives in English Urban History*, ed. Alan Everitt. London, 1973.

'Social Mobility in Early Modern England', *PP*, no. 33, 1966.

Eversley, D. E. C. 'A Survey of Population in an Area of Worcestershire from 1660 to 1850 on the Basis of Parish Registers', in *Population in History*, ed. D. V. Glass and D. E. C. Eversley. London, 1965.

Ferris, J. P. and Oliver, R. C. B. 'An Agricultural Improvement of 1674 at Trewern, Llanfihangel-Nant-Melan', *Radnors. Soc.*, XLII, 1972.

Fieldhouse, R. T. 'Agriculture in Wensleydale from 1600 to the Present Day', *Northern Hist.*, XVI, 1980.

Fieldhouse, R. T. and Jennings, B. *A History of Richmond and Swaledale*. Chichester, 1978.

Fiennes, Celia. *The Journeys of Celia Fiennes*, ed. C. Morris. London, 1947.

Firth, C. H. and Rait, R. S. (eds.). *Acts and Ordinances of the Interregnum, 1642–60*. 3 vols. London, 1911.

Fisher, F. J. 'The Development of London as a Centre of Conspicuous Consumption in the Sixteenth and Seventeenth Centuries', in *Essays in Economic History, II*, ed. E. M. Carus-Wilson. London, 1962. (Repr. from RHS, 4th ser., XXX, 1948.)

'The Development of the London Food Market, 1540–1640', in *Essays in Economic History, I*, ed. E. M. Carus-Wilson. London, 1954. (Repr. from EcHR, V, 1935.)

Fisher, F. J. (ed.). *Essays in the Economic and Social History of Tudor and Stuart England*. Cambridge, 1961.

Fisher, H. E. S. 'Anglo-Portuguese Trade, 1700–1770', EcHR, 2nd ser., XVI, 1963.

Fletcher, A. J. *A County Community in Peace and War: Sussex, 1600–1660*. London, 1975.

Flinn, M. W. 'The Growth of the English Iron Industry, 1660–1760', EcHR, 2nd ser., XI, 1958.

Fowler, J. and Cornforth, J. *English Decoration in the Eighteenth Century*. London, 1974.

Fox, Sir Cyril and Raglan, Lord. *Monmouthshire Houses*. 3 vols. Nat. Museum of Wales, 1953–4.

Fox, H. S. A. and Butlin, R. A. (eds.). *Change in the Countryside: Essays on Rural England, 1500–1900*. Inst. Brit. Geographers, Special Publ., no. 10. London, 1979.

Freeman, C. *Pillow Lace in the East Midlands*. Luton, 1958.

Fuller, T. *The Worthies of England*, ed. J. Freeman. London, 1952.

Fussell, G. E. *The English Dairy Farmer, 1500–1900*. London, 1966.

'Four Centuries of Farming Systems in Hampshire, 1500–1900', *Hants. Field Club & Arch. Soc.*, XVII, 3, 1949.

'Four Centuries of Leicestershire Farming', in *Studies in Leicestershire Agrarian History*, ed. W. G. Hoskins. Leicester, 1949.

'History of Cole (*Brassica* sp.)', *Nature, London*, 9 July 1955.

The Old English Farming Books from Fitzherbert to Tull, 1523 to 1730. London, 1947.

Fussell, G. E. and Goodman, Constance. 'Eighteenth-Century Traffic in Livestock', *Ec. Hist.*, III, 1936.

Garret[t], Daniel. *Designs and Estimates for Farm Houses...*3rd edn. London, 1772.

Gazley, J. G. *The Life of Arthur Young, 1741–1820*. Philadelphia, 1973.

Gentles, I. 'The Sales of Bishops' Lands in the English Revolution, 1646–1660', EHR, xcv, 1980.

'The Sales of Crown Lands during the English Revolution', EcHR, 2nd ser., xxvi, 4, 1973.

Gerarde, John. *The Herbal, or General Historie of Plantes*. London, 1636.

Gill, H. and Guilford, E. L. (eds.). *The Rector's Book of Clayworth, Notts*. Nottingham, 1910.

Girouard, M. *Robert Smythson*. London, 1966.

Girouard, Mark. *Life in the English Country House: A Social and Architectural History*. New Haven and London, 1978.

Godber, Joyce. *History of Bedfordshire, 1066–1888*. Bedford, 1969.

Godfrey, W. H. *The English Almshouse*. London, 1955.

Gooder, A. *Plague and Enclosure: A Worcestershire Village in the Seventeenth Century*. Coventry & N. War., Hist. Pamphlets, no. 2. 1965.

'The Population Crisis of 1727–30 in Warwickshire', *Midland Hist.*, i, 4, 1972.

Gough, R. *Antiquityes and Memoyres of the Parish of Myddle*. London, 1875.

Grainger, J. *General View of the Agriculture of Co. Durham*. London, 1794.

Granger, C. W. J. and Elliott, C. M. 'A Fresh Look at Wheat Prices and Markets in the Eighteenth Century', EcHR, 2nd ser., xx, 1967.

Gras, N. S. B. *The Evolution of the English Corn Market from the Twelfth to the Eighteenth Century*. Harvard Ec. Stud., xiii. Cambridge, Mass., 1915.

Gray, H. L. *English Field Systems*. Cambridge, Mass., 1915.

'Yeoman Farming in Oxfordshire from the Sixteenth Century to the Nineteenth Century', *Qtly J. Ec.*, xxiv, 1910.

Green, D. *Gardener to Queen Anne: Henry Wise and the Formal Garden*. Oxford, 1956.

Green, F. 'The Stepneys of Prendergast', *W. Wales Hist. Rec.*, vii, 1917–18.

Green, I. M. 'The Persecution of Parish Clergy during the English Civil War', EHR, xciv, 1979.

Gunther, R. T. *The Architecture of Sir Roger Pratt*. Oxford, 1928.

Habakkuk, H. J. 'Daniel Finch, 2nd Earl of Nottingham: His House and Estate', in *Studies in Social History*, ed. J. H. Plumb. London, 1955.

'The English Land Market in the Eighteenth Century', in *Britain and the Netherlands*, ed. J. S. Bromley and E. H. Kossmann. London, 1960.

'English Landownership, 1680–1740', EcHR, x, 1940.

'The Land Settlement and the Restoration of Charles II', RHS, 5th ser., xxviii, 1978.

'Landowners and the Civil War', EcHR, 2nd ser., xviii, 1965.

'Marriage Settlements in the Eighteenth Century', RHS, 4th ser., xxxii, 1950.

'Public Finance and the Sale of Confiscated Property during the Interregnum', EcHR, 2nd ser., xv, 1962–3.

'The Rise and Fall of English Landed Families, 1600–1800', RHS, 5th ser., xxix–xxx, 1979–80.

Hadfield, Miles. *A History of British Gardening*. London, 1969.

Halfpenny, William. *Twelve Beautiful Designs for Farmhouses*. London, 1750.

Hammersley, G. 'The Charcoal Iron Industry and its Fuel, 1540–1750', EcHR, 2nd ser., xxvi, 1973.

'The Crown Woods and their Exploitation in the Sixteenth and Seventeenth Centuries', *Bull. IHR*, xxx, 1957.

Harris, A. 'The Agriculture of the East Riding before the Parliamentary Enclosures', *Yorks. Arch. J.*, XL, 1962.

The Open Fields of East Yorkshire. York, 1959.

Hartley, M. and Ingilby, J. *The Old Hand-Knitters of the Dales*. Clapham, 1951.

Hartlib, S. *His Legacie, or An Enlargement of the Discours of Husbandrie Used in Brabant and Flanders*. London, 1651. 2nd edn. 1652.

[C. Dymock]. *A Discovery for Division or Setting Out of Land*. London, 1653.

Harvey, John H. *Early Gardening Catalogues*. London, 1972.

Early Nurserymen. London, 1974.

'The Family of Telford, Nurserymen of York', *Yorks. Arch. J.*, XLII, 167, 1969.

'Leonard Gurle's Nurseries and Some Others', *Garden Hist.*, III, 3, 1975.

'The Nurseries on Milne's Land-Use Map', *London & Middx Arch. Soc.*, XXIV, 1973.

'The Stocks Held by Early Nurseries', AHR, XXII, 1, 1974.

Havinden, M. A. 'Agricultural Progress in Open Field Oxfordshire', AHR, IX, 2, 1961.

Henrey, Blanche. *British Botanical and Horticultural Literature before 1800*. 3 vols. Oxford, 1975.

Henstock, A. 'Cheese Manufacture and Marketing in Derbyshire and North Staffordshire, 1670–1870', *Derbs. Arch. J.*, LXXXIX, 1969.

Hervey, Lord Francis (ed.). *Suffolk in the Seventeenth Century: A Breviary of Suffolk by Robert Reyce, 1618*. London, 1902.

Hey, D. *An English Rural Community: Myddle under the Tudors and Stuarts*. Leicester, 1974.

Packmen, Carriers and Packhorse Roads. Leicester, 1980.

The Rural Metalworkers of the Sheffield Region. Leicester, 1972.

Hill, M. C. 'The Wealdmoors, 1560–1660', *Shrops. Arch. J.*, LIV, 1951–3.

Hill, O. and Cornforth, J. *English Country Houses: Caroline*. London, 1966.

Holderness, B. A. 'The Agricultural Activities of the Massingberds of South Ormsby, Lincolnshire, 1638 – *c.* 1750', *Midland Hist.*, I, 3, 1972.

'Capital Formation in Agriculture', in *Aspects of Capital Investment in Great Britain, 1750–1850*, ed. J. P. P. Higgins and S. Pollard. London, 1971.

'Credit in English Rural Society before the Nineteenth Century', AHR, XXIV, 1976.

'The English Land Market in the Eighteenth Century: The Case of Lincolnshire', EcHR, 2nd ser., XXVII, 4, 1974.

Holiday, P. G. 'Land Sales and Repurchases in Yorkshire after the Civil Wars, 1650–1670', *Northern Hist.*, V, 1970.

Holland, H. *General View of the Agriculture of Cheshire*. London, 1808.

Hollingsworth, T. H. 'The Demography of the British Peerage', suppl. to *Pop. Stud.*, XVIII, 1964.

Holmes, G. S. 'Gregory King and the Social Structure of Pre-Industrial England', RHS, 5th ser., XXVII, 1977.

Holt, J. *General View of the Agriculture of the County of Lancaster*. London, 1795.

Hopkins, E. 'The Bridgewater Estates in North Shropshire during the Civil War', *Shrops. Arch. Soc.*, LVI, 2, 1960.

'The Re-Leasing of the Ellesmere Estates, 1637–42', AHR, X, 1, 1962.

Hoskins, W. G. 'Harvest Fluctuations and English Economic History, 1620–1759', AHR, XVI, 1, 1968.

Houghton, John. *A Collection for Improvement of Husbandry and Trade.* 9 vols. London, 1692–1703. Ed. R. Bradley. 4 vols. London, 1727–8.

A Collection of Letters for the Improvement of Husbandry and Trade. 2 vols. London, 1681–3.

Howard, C. 'The Culture of Saffron', *Philos. Trans. Roy. Soc.*, XII, 1678.

Howells, B. E. (ed.). *A Calendar of Letters relating to North Wales.* Cardiff, 1967.

Hughes, E. *North Country Life in the Eighteenth Century: The North-East, 1700–1750.* Oxford, 1952.

North Country Life in the Eighteenth Century, II, Cumberland & Westmorland, 1700–1830. Oxford, 1965.

Hull, F. 'The Tufton Sequestration Papers', *Kent Rec.*, XVII, 1960.

Hussey, C. *English Country Houses: Early Georgian.* London, 1965.

Innocent, C. F. *The Development of English Building Construction.* Cambridge, 1916. Newton Abbot, 1971.

Jacob, G. *The Country Gentleman's Vade Mecum.* London, 1717.

James, M. 'The Political Importance of the Tithes Controversy in the English Revolution, 1640–60', *Hist.*, XXVI, 1941.

James, W. and Malcolm, J. *General View of the Agriculture of the County of Buckingham.* London, 1794.

General View of the Agriculture of the County of Surrey. London, 1793.

Jancey, E. M. 'An Eighteenth-Century Steward and his Work', *Shrops. Arch. Soc.*, LVI, 1, 1957–8.

'The Hon. and Rev. Richard Hill of Hawkstone, 1655–1727', *ibid.*, LV, 1954–6.

Jenkins, J. G. *The Welsh Woollen Industry.* Cardiff, 1969.

The English Farm Waggon: Origins and Structure. Newton Abbot, 1972.

Jenkins, R. 'Suffolk Industries: An Historical Survey', *Newcomen Soc.*, XIX, 1940.

Jennings, B. (ed.). *A History of Harrogate and Knaresborough.* Huddersfield, 1970.

A History of Nidderdale. Huddersfield, 1976.

John, A. H. 'Agricultural Productivity and Economic Growth in England, 1700–1760', *J. Ec. Hist.*, XXV, 1965.

'The Course of Agricultural Change, 1660–1760', in *Studies in the Industrial Revolution*, ed. L. S. Pressnell. London, 1960. Repr. in W. E. Minchinton (ed.), *Essays in Agrarian History*, I. Newton Abbot, 1968.

'English Agricultural Improvement and Grain Exports, 1660–1765', in D. C. Coleman and A. H. John (eds.), *Trade, Government and Economy in Pre-Industrial England.* London, 1976.

The Industrial Development of South Wales, 1750–1850. Cardiff, 1950.

'Iron and Coal on a Glamorgan Estate, 1700–40', EcHR, XIII, 1943.

Johnson, George W. *A History of English Gardening.* London, 1829.

Jones, E. L. 'Agricultural Conditions and Changes in Herefordshire, 1600–1815', *Woolhope Naturalists' Field Club*, XXXVII, 1962.

'Agricultural Origins of Industry', PP, no. 40, 1968.

'Agricultural Productivity and Economic Growth, 1700–1760', in E. L. Jones (ed.), *Agriculture and Economic Growth in England, 1650–1815.* London, 1967.

'Agriculture and Economic Growth in England, 1660–1750: Agricultural Change', *J. Ec. Hist.*, XXV, 1965.

'Eighteenth-Century Changes in Hampshire Chalkland Farming', AHR, VIII, 1, 1960.

Seasons and Prices: The Role of Weather in English Agricultural History. London, 1964.

Jones, F. 'The Old Families of Wales', in *Wales in the Eighteenth Century*, ed. D. Moore. Swansea, 1976.

'A Squire of Anglesey', *Anglesey Antiq. Soc.*, 1940.

'The Vaughans of Golden Grove. I, The Earls of Carbery', *Hon. Soc. Cymmrodorion*, 1963, pt 1.

'The Vaughans of Golden Grove. II, Anne, Duchess of Bolton, 1690–1715', *ibid.*, 1963, pt 2.

'The Vaughans of Golden Grove. III, Torycoed, Shenfield, Golden Grove', *ibid.*, 1964, pt 2.

Jones, G. P. 'Sources of Loans and Credits in Cumbria before the Rise of Banks', *CW2*, LXXV, 1975.

Jones, Stanley and Smith, J. T. 'Breconshire Houses', *Brycheiniog*, IX, 1963.

Kalm, Pehr. *Kalm's Account of his Visit to England on his Way to America in 1748*, ed. J. Lucas. London, 1892.

Kelch, R. A. *Newcastle: A Duke without Money: Thomas Pelham-Holles 1693–1768.* London, 1974.

Kent, N. *General View of the Agriculture of Norfolk.* London, 1796.

Hints to Gentlemen of Landed Property. London, 1775.

Kenyon, G. H. 'Kirdford Inventories, 1611 to 1776, with Particular Reference to the Weald Clay Farming', *Sussex Arch. Coll.*, XCIII, 1955.

'Petworth Town and Trades, 1610–1760', *ibid.*, XCVI, 1958.

Kerridge, E. *The Agricultural Revolution.* London, 1967.

Agrarian Problems in the Sixteenth Century and After. London, 1969.

'The Sheepfold in Wiltshire and the Floating of the Water Meadows', EcHR, 2nd ser., VI, 1954.

'Turnip Husbandry in High Suffolk', EcHR, 2nd ser., VII, 1956.

Lambton, L. *Temples of Convenience.* London, 1978.

Lane, Carolina. 'The Development of Pastures and Meadows during the Sixteenth and Seventeenth Centuries', AHR, XXVIII, 1980.

Langley, Batty. *The City and Country Builder's and Workman's Treasury of Designs.* London, 1745. Repr. 1969.

La Quintinye, M. de. *The Complete Gard'ner*, tr. G. London and H. Wise. London, 1701.

Laurence, Edward. *The Duty of a Steward to his Lord.* London, 1727.

Laurence, John. *A New System of Agriculture.* London, 1726.

Law, C. M. and Hooson, D. J. M. 'The Straw Plait and Straw Hat Industries of the South Midlands', *E. Midlands Geographer*, IV, 6, 1968.

[Lee, J.]. *Considerations concerning Common Fields.* London, 1654.

Lees–Milne, J. *English Country Houses: Baroque, 1685–1715.* London, 1970.

Leigh, C. *The Natural History of Lancashire, Cheshire and the Peak of Derbyshire.* Oxford, 1700.

Lennard, R. V. 'English Agriculture under Charles II: The Evidence of the Royal Society's "Enquiries"', EcHR, IV, 1932.

L'Estrange, R. *A Treatise of Wool and Cattel.* London, 1677.

Lewis, W. J. 'The Cwmsymlog Lead Mine', *Ceredigion*, II, 1, 1952.

Lightoler, Thomas. *Gentleman and Farmer's Architect*. London, 1762.

Linnard, W. 'A Glimpse of Gwydyr Forest and the Timber Trade in North Wales in the Late 17th Century', *Nat. Lib. Wales J.*, XVIII, 1974.

Linnell, C. D. 'The Matmakers of Pavenham', *Beds. Mag.*, 1, 1947.

Lisle, Edward. *Observations in Husbandry*. London, 1757. 2nd edn. 2 vols. London, 1757.

Lloyd, T. H. *The Movement of Wool Prices in Medieval England*. EcHR suppl., no. 6. Cambridge, 1973.

Lodge, E. C. (ed.). *The Account Book of a Kentish Estate, 1616–1704*. Oxford, 1927.

Long, W. H. 'Regional Farming in Seventeenth-Century Yorkshire', AHR, VIII, 2, 1960.

Loudon, J. C. *An Encyclopaedia of Gardening*. London, 1822.

Lowe, N. *The Lancashire Textile Industry in the Sixteenth Century*. Manchester, 1972.

Lowe, R. *General View of the Agriculture of Nottinghamshire*. London, 1798.

McCutcheon, K. L. *Yorkshire Fairs and Markets*, Thoresby Soc., XXXIX. 1940.

Machin, R. 'The Great Rebuilding: A Reassessment', *PP*, no. 77, 1977.

Machin, R. (ed.). *Probate Inventories and Memorial Excepts of Chetnole, Leigh and Yetminster*. Bristol, 1976.

Madge, S. J. *The Domesday of Crown Lands*. London, 1938.

Manley, G. *Climate and the British Scene*. London, 1952.

Manning, B. *The English People and the English Revolution*. London, 1976.

Markham, G. *The Inrichment of the Weald of Kent*. London, 1625.

Marshall, G. 'The "Rotherham" Plough', *Tools & Tillage*, III, 3, 1978.

Marshall, J. D. *Furness and the Industrial Revolution*. Barrow in Furness, 1958.

Kendal, 1661–1801: The Growth of a Modern Town. Kendal, 1975.

Old Lakeland. Newton Abbot, 1971.

Marshall, W. *Review and Abstract of the County Reports to the Board of Agriculture*. 5 vols. London and York, 1808–17. 5 vols. in 1. 1818.

The Rural Economy of Gloucestershire. 2 vols. Gloucester, 1789.

The Rural Economy of the Midland Counties. 2 vols. London, 1790. 2nd edn. 1796.

The Rural Economy of Norfolk. 2 vols. London, 1787.

Rural Economy of the Southern Counties. 2 vols. London, 1798.

The Rural Economy of Yorkshire. 2 vols. London, 1788.

Mathias, P. *The Brewing Industry in England, 1700–1830*. Cambridge, 1959.

Mavor, W. *General View of the Agriculture of Berkshire*. London, 1809.

Meager, Leonard. *The English Gardener*. London, 1670.

Meek, M. 'Hempen Cloth Industry in Suffolk', *Suffolk Rev.*, II, 1961.

Mercer, Eric. *English Vernacular Houses: A Study of Traditional Farmhouses and Cottages*. RCHM (England). London, 1975.

Meredith, R. 'A Derbyshire Family in the Seventeenth Century: The Eyres of Hassop and their Forfeited Estates', *Recusant Hist.*, VIII, 1965.

Michell, A. R. 'Sir Richard Weston and the Spread of Clover Cultivation', AHR, XXII, 2, 1974.

Middleton, J. *General View of the Agriculture of Middlesex*. 2nd edn. London, 1807.

Millward, R. 'The Cumbrian Town between 1600 and 1800', in *Rural Change and Urban Growth, 1500–1800*, ed. C. W. Chalklin and M. A. Havinden. London, 1974.

Mingay, G. E. 'The Agricultural Depression, 1730–1750', EcHR, 2nd ser., VIII, 1956.
    'The Eighteenth Century Land Steward', in *Land, Labour and Population in the Industrial Revolution*, ed. E. L. Jones and G. E. Mingay. London, 1967.
    English Landed Society in the Eighteenth Century. London, 1963.
    'Estate Management in Eighteenth-Century Kent', AHR, IV, 1, 1956.
    'The Size of Farms in the Eighteenth Century', EcHR, 2nd ser., XIV, 3, 1962.
Mitchell, B. R. with Deane, P. *Abstract of British Historical Statistics*. Cambridge, 1962.
Moore, B. J. S. *Goods and Chattels of our Forefathers: Frampton Cotterell and District Probate Inventories, 1539–1790*. Chichester, 1976.
Morant, P. *A History of Essex*. London, 1768.
Mordant, J. *The Complete Steward*. 2 vols. London, 1761.
Mortimer, J. *The Whole Art of Husbandry*. London, 1707.
Mullett, C. F. 'The Cattle Distemper in Mid-Eighteenth Century England', *Agric. Hist.*, XX, 3, 1946.
Munby, L. N. (ed.). *East Anglian Studies*. Cambridge, 1968.
Myddelton, W. M. (ed.). *Chirk Castle Accounts, 1666–1753*. Manchester, 1931.
Neve, Richard. *City and Country Purchaser and Builder's Dictionary*. 3rd edn. London, 1736. Repr. Newton Abbot, 1969.
Nichols, J. *The History and Antiquities of the County of Leicester...* 4 vols. London, 1795–1811.
Norden, J. *The Surveyor's Dialogue*. London, 1607.
North, Roger. *The Lives of the Norths*, ed. A. Jessopp. 3 vols. London, 1890.
Oliver, J. 'The Weather and Farming in the Mid-Eighteenth Century in Anglesey', *Nat. Lib. Wales J.*, X, 1958.
Ormrod, D. J. 'Dutch Commercial and Industrial Decline and British Growth in the Late Seventeenth and Early Eighteenth Centuries', in *Failed Transitions to Modern Industrial Society: Renaissance Italy and Seventeenth-Century Holland*, ed. F. Krantz and P. M. Hohenberg. Montreal, 1975.
Osborne, B. S. 'Glamorgan Agriculture in the Seventeenth and Eighteenth Centuries', *Nat. Lib. Wales J.*, XX, 1979.
Outhwaite, R. B. 'Dearth and Government Intervention in English Grain Markets, 1590–1700', EcHR, 2nd ser., XXXIII, 3, 1981.
Overton, M. 'Computer Analysis of an Inconsistent Data Source: The Case of Probate Inventories', *J. Hist. Geog.*, III, 4, 1977.
Owen, L. 'Letters of an Anglesey Parson', *Hon. Soc. Cymmrodorion*, 1961, pt 1.
Owen, W. *Owen's Book of Fairs*. London, 1756.
Parker, R. A. C. *Coke of Norfolk: A Financial and Agricultural Study 1707–1842*. Oxford, 1975.
Parkinson, John. *Paradisi in Sole*. London, 1629.
Parkinson, R. *General View of the Agriculture of Huntingdonshire*. London, 1813.
Patten, J. 'Patterns of Migration and Movement of Labour to Three Pre-Industrial East Anglian Towns', *J. Hist. Geog.*, II, 1976.
    'Population Distribution in Norfolk and Suffolk during the Sixteenth and Seventeenth Centuries', *Inst. Brit. Geographers*, LXV, 1975.
    'Village and Town: An Occupational Study', AHR, XX, 1972.
Peate, I. C. 'A Flintshire Barn at St. Fagan's', *Country Life*, July–Dec. 1952.
    The Welsh House. Liverpool, 1944.

Pelham, R. A. 'The Agricultural Revolution in Hampshire, with Special Reference to the Acreage Returns of 1801', *Hants. Field Club & Arch. Soc.*, XVIII, 1953.

Penney, N. (ed.). *The Household Account Book of Sarah Fell.* Cambridge, 1920.

Perkins, J. A. *Sheep Farming in Eighteenth- and Nineteenth-Century Lincolnshire.* Occ. Papers in Lincs. Hist. & Arch., no. 4, Soc. Lincs. Hist. & Arch. Sleaford, 1977.

Peters, J. E. C. *The Development of Farm Buildings in... Staffordshire.* Manchester, 1969.

Pettit, P. A. J. *The Royal Forests of Northamptonshire: A Study in their Economy, 1558–1714.* Northants. Rec. Soc., XXIII. 1968.

Petty, W. *Economic Writings...* ed. C. H. Hull, Vol. I. Cambridge, 1899.

Pilkington, J. *A View of the Present State of Derbyshire.* Derby, 1789.

Plot, Robert. *The Natural History of Oxfordshire.* Oxford, 1676/7. 2nd edn. 1705.
   The Natural History of Staffordshire. Oxford, 1686.

Plumb, J. H. *Sir Robert Walpole.* 3 vols. London, 1956.
   'Sir Robert Walpole and Norfolk Husbandry', *EcHR*, 2nd ser., V, 1952.

Plumb, J. H. (ed.). *Studies in Social History.* London, 1955.

Plymley, J. *General View of the Agriculture of Shropshire.* London, 1803.

Postgate, M. R. 'The Field Systems of Breckland', *AHR*, X, 1961.

Postlethwayt, Malachy. *Britain's Commercial Interest Explained and Improved...I.* London, 1757.

Poynter, F. N. L. *A Bibliography of Gervase Markham, 1568?–1637.* Oxford, 1962.

Prichard, M. F. Lloyd. 'The Decline of Norwich', *EcHR*, 2nd ser., III, 1951.

Priest, St John. *General View of the Agriculture of Buckinghamshire.* London, 1813.

Prince, H. *Parks in England.* Shalfleet Manor, I.O.W. 1967.

Pringle, A. *General View of the Agriculture of Westmorland.* Edinburgh, 1794.

Radley, J. 'Holly as a Winter Feed', *AHR*, IX, 2, 1961.

Raistrick, A. and Jennings, B. *A History of Lead Mining in the Pennines.* London, 1965.

Ramsay, G. D. *The Wiltshire Woollen Industry in the Sixteenth and Seventeenth Centuries.* Oxford, 1943.

Ravensdale, J. R. *Liable to Floods.* Cambridge, 1974.

Rawson, H. Rees. 'The Coal Mining Industry of the Hawarden District on the Eve of the Industrial Revolution', *Arch. Cambrensis*, XCVI, 1941.

Rees, Alwyn. *Life in a Welsh Countryside.* Cardiff, 1950.

Rennie, G. B., Brown, R., and Shirreff, S. *General View of the Agriculture of the West Riding.* London, 1794.

Reyce, R. *See* Hervey (ed.).

Riches, N. *The Agricultural Revolution in Norfolk.* Chapel Hill, 1937.

Roberts, P. 'The Decline of the Welsh Squires in the Eighteenth Century', *Nat. Lib. Wales J.*, XIII, 1963–4.

Roebuck, P. 'Absentee Landownership in the Late Seventeenth and Early Eighteenth Centuries: A Neglected Factor in English Agrarian History', *AHR*, XXI, 1, 1973.
   'The Constables of Everingham: The Fortunes of a Catholic Royalist Family during the Civil War and Interregnum', *Recusant Hist.*, IX, 1967.

Roebuck, P. (ed.). *Constables of Everingham Estate Correspondence, 1726–43.* Yorks. Arch. Soc. Rec. Ser., CXXXVI. 1974.

Rogers, Benjamin. *The Diary of Benjamin Rogers, Rector of Carlton*, ed. C. D. Linnell. Beds. Rec. Soc., XXX. 1950.

Rogers, J. E. T. *A History of Agriculture and Prices in England from 1259 to 1793*. 7 vols. Oxford, 1866–1902.

Rogers, Nathan. *Memoirs of Monmouthshire*. London, 1708.

Rowlands, Henry. *Idea Agriculturae*. Dublin, 1764.

Rowlands, M. B. *Masters and Men in the West Midland Metalware Trades before the Industrial Revolution*. Manchester, 1975.

Salaman, R. N. *The History and Social Influence of the Potato*. Cambridge, 1949.

Salmon, N. *The History of Hertfordshire*. London, 1728.

Scarfe, N. *The Suffolk Landscape*. London, 1972.

Schumpeter, E. B. *English Overseas Trade Statistics, 1697–1808*. Oxford, 1960.

Seaborne, M. *The English School*. London, 1971.

Sharp, Lindsay. 'Timber, Science and Economic Reform in the Seventeenth Century', *Forestry*, XLVIII, 1, 1975.

Sharrock, Robert. *The History of the Propagation and Improvement of Vegetables*. Oxford, 1660.

    An Improvement to the Art of Gardening. London, 1694.

Sheail, J. 'Rabbits and Agriculture in Post-Medieval England', *J. Hist. Geog.*, IV, 4, 1978.

Sheppard, J. A. *The Draining of the Hull Valley*. York, 1958.

Sidwell, R. W. 'A Short History of Commercial Horticulture in the Vale of Evesham', *Vale of Evesham Hist. Soc., Research Papers*, II, 1969.

Simpson, A. 'The East Anglian Fold-Course: Some Queries', AHR, VI, 1958.

Skipp, V. *Crisis and Development: An Ecological Case Study of the Forest of Arden, 1570–1674*. Cambridge, 1978.

    'Economic and Social Change in the Forest of Arden, 1530–1649', in *Land, Church and People: Essays Presented to Professor H. P. R. Finberg*, ed. Joan Thirsk. Suppl. to AHR, XVIII, 1970.

Slicher van Bath, B. H. 'Yield Ratios, 810–1820', *A.A.G. Bijdragen*, X, 1963.

Smith, J. T. 'The Evolution of the English Peasant House in the Late Seventeenth Century: The Evidence of Buildings', *J. Brit. Arch. Assoc.*, XXXIII, 1970.

    'The Long-House in Monmouthshire, a Reappraisal', in *Culture and Environment*, ed. I. Ll. Foster and L. Alcock. London, 1963.

    'Medieval Roofs: A Classification', *Arch. J.*, CXII, 1958.

Smith, Peter. *Houses of the Welsh Countryside*. London, 1975.

Smith, W. J. (ed.). *Calendar of Salusbury Correspondence*. Cardiff, 1954.

    Herbert Correspondence. Cardiff, 1963.

Smout, T. C. *Scottish Trade on the Eve of Union, 1660–1707*. Edinburgh, 1963.

Speed, Adolphus [Adam]. *Adam Out of Eden*. London, 1659.

Spenceley, G. F. R. 'The Origins of the English Pillow Lace Industry', AHR, XXI, 1973.

Spufford, Margaret. *A Cambridgeshire Community: Chippenham*. Leicester, 1965.

    Contrasting Communities: English Villagers in the Sixteenth and Seventeenth Centuries. Cambridge, 1974.

Stanes, R. G. F. (ed.). 'A Georgicall Account of Devonshire and Cornwalle in Answer to Some Queries concerning Agriculture, by Samuel Colepresse, 1667', *Devonshire Assoc.*, XCVI, 1964.

Steer, F. W. (ed.). *Farm and Cottage Inventories of Mid-Essex, 1635–1749*. Chelmsford, 1950.

Steers, J. A. *The Coastline of England and Wales*. Cambridge, 1946.

Steers, J. A. (ed.). *Cambridge and its Region*. Cambridge, 1965.

Stern, W. M. 'Cheese Shipped Coastwise to London towards the Middle of the Eighteenth Century', *Guildhall Misc.*, IV, 1973.

Stone, L. *Crisis of the Aristocracy, 1538–1641*. Oxford, 1965.

   Family and Fortune: Studies in Aristocratic Finance in the Sixteenth and Seventeenth Centuries. Oxford, 1973.

   The Family, Sex and Marriage in England, 1500–1800. London, 1977.

Stone, Lawrence and Stone, Jeanne C. F. 'Country Houses and their Owners in Hertfordshire, 1540–1879', in *The Dimensions of Quantitative Research in History*, ed. W. O. Aydelotte *et al.* Princeton and Oxford, 1972.

Stout, William. *The Autobiography of William Stout of Lancaster, 1665–1752*, ed. J. D. Marshall. Manchester, 1967.

Straker, E. *Wealden Iron*. London, 1931.

Strickland, H. E. *General View of the Agriculture of the East Riding of Yorkshire*. London, 1812.

Summerson, J. *Architecture in Britain 1530 to 1830*. London, 1953.

   'The Classical Country House in 18th-Century England', *J. Roy. Soc. Arts*, CVII, 1959.

Switzer, Stephen. *A Compendious Method for the Raising of Italian Brocoli*. London, 1729.

Tate, W. E. 'Cambridgeshire Field Systems', *Proc. Cambridge Arch. Soc.*, XL, 1939–42.

   A Domesday of English Enclosure Acts and Awards, ed. M. Turner. Reading, 1978.

   'Inclosure Movements in Northamptonshire', *Northants. Past & Present*, I, 2, 1949.

Taylor, C. C. *The Cambridgeshire Landscape*. London, 1973.

Thirsk, Joan, 'Agrarian History, 1540–1950', in *VCH Leics.*, II. London, 1954.

   Economic Policy and Projects: The Development of a Consumer Society in Early Modern England. Oxford, 1978.

   English Peasant Farming: The Agrarian History of Lincolnshire from Tudor to Recent Times. London, 1957. Repr. London, 1981.

   'The Fantastical Folly of Fashion: The English Stocking Knitting Industry, 1500–1700', in *Textile History and Economic History*, ed. N. B. Harte and K. G. Ponting. Manchester, 1973.

   'Horn and Thorn in Staffordshire: The Economy of a Pastoral County', *N. Staffs. J. Field Stud.*, IX, 1969.

   Horses in Early Modern England: For Service, for Pleasure, for Power. Stenton Lecture, 1977. Reading, 1978.

   'Industries in the Countryside', in *Essays in the Economic and Social History of Tudor and Stuart England*, ed. F. J. Fisher. Cambridge, 1961.

   'New Crops and their Diffusion: Tobacco-Growing in Seventeenth Century England', in *Rural Change and Urban Growth, 1500–1800*, ed. C. W. Chalklin and M. A. Havinden. London, 1974.

   'Plough and Pen: Agricultural Writers in the Seventeenth Century', in T. H. Aston *et al.*, *Social Relations and Ideas*. Cambridge, 1983.

   'Projects for Gentlemen, Jobs for the Poor: Mutual Aid in the Vale of Tewkesbury, 1600–1630', in *Essays in Bristol and Gloucestershire History*, ed. P. McGrath and J. Cannon. Bristol. 1976.

'The Restoration Land Settlement', *JMH*, xxvi, 4, 1954.

'The Sales of Royalist Land during the Interregnum', EcHR, 2nd ser., v, 1952–3.

'Seventeenth-Century Agriculture and Social Change', in *Land, Church and People: Essays Presented to Professor H. P. R. Finberg*, ed. Joan Thirsk. Suppl. to AHR, xviii, 1970.

Thirsk, Joan (ed.). *The Agrarian History of England and Wales, IV, 1500–1640.* Cambridge, 1967.

Thirsk, Joan and Cooper, J. P. (eds.). *Seventeenth-Century Economic Documents.* Oxford, 1972.

Thomas, D. 'The Social Origins of the Marriage Partners of the British Peerage', *Pop. Stud.*, xxvi, 1972.

Thomas, H. *A History of Wales, 1485–1660.* Cardiff, 1972.

Thomas, K. R. 'The Enclosure of Open Fields and Commons in Staffordshire', *Staffs. Hist. Coll.*, 1931.

Thompson, E. P. 'The Moral Economy of the English Crowd in the Eighteenth Century', *PP*, no. 50, 1971.

Whigs and Hunters: The Origins of the Black Act. London, 1975.

Thompson, F. M. L. 'The Social Distribution of Landed Property in England since the Sixteenth Century', EcHR, 2nd ser., xix, 1966.

'Landownership and Economic Growth in England in the Eighteenth Century', in *Agrarian Change and Economic Development*, ed. E. L. Jones and S. J. Woolf. London, 1969.

Thomson, G. Scott. *Family Background.* London, 1949.

Life in a Noble Household, 1641–1700. London, 1937.

Tibbutt, H. G. *Bedfordshire and the First Civil War.* 2nd edn. Elstow, 1973.

Torrington Diaries, ed. C. Brayn Andrews. London, 1954.

Trinder, B. S. *The Industrial Revolution in Shropshire.* Chichester, 1973.

Trinder, B. S. and Cox, J. *Yeomen and Colliers in Telford.* Chichester, 1980.

Trow-Smith, R. *A History of British Livestock Husbandry to 1700.* London, 1957.

A History of British Livestock Husbandry, 1700–1900. London, 1959.

Tubbs, C. R. 'The Development of the Smallholding and Cottage Stock-Keeping Economy of the New Forest', AHR, xiii, 1965.

Tucker, G. S. L. 'Population in History', EcHR, 2nd ser., xx, 1967.

Tuke, J. *General View of the Agriculture of the North Riding of Yorkshire.* London, 1800.

Tull, J. *A Supplement to the Essay on Horse-hoing Husbandry…* London, 1736.

Tupling, G. H. 'The Early Metal Trades and the Beginnings of Engineering in Lancashire', *Lancs. & Cheshire Arch. Soc.*, lxi, 1951.

Turner, J. 'Ralph Austen, an Oxford Horticulturist of the Seventeenth Century', *Garden Hist.*, vi, 2, 1978.

Turner, M. *English Parliamentary Enclosure: Its Historical Geography and Economic History.* Folkestone, 1980.

Underdown, D. 'A Case concerning Bishops' Lands', EHR, lxxviii, 1963.

Unwin, R. W. 'The Aire and Calder Navigation, Part II: The Navigation in the Pre-Canal Age', *Bradford Antiq.*, ns xliii, 1967.

Utterström, G. 'Climatic Fluctuations and Population Problems in Early Modern History', *Scand. Ec. Hist. Rev.*, iii, 1955.

Vanbrugh, Sir John. *The Complete Works, IV, Letters.* London, 1928.

Vancouver, C. *General View of the Agriculture in the County of Cambridge*. London, 1794.

    General View of the Agriculture of Essex. London, 1795.

    General View of the Agriculture of Hampshire. London, 1813.

Verney, F. P. *Memoirs of the Verney Family during the Civil War*. 2 vols. London, 1892.

Verney, F. P. and Verney, M. M. *Memoirs of the Verney Family during the Seventeenth Century*. 2nd edn. 2 vols. London, 1904.

Veysey, A. G. 'Col. Philip Jones, 1618–74', *Hon. Soc. Cymmrodorion*. 1966, pt 2.

Warner, J. 'General View of the Agriculture of the Isle of Wight', in A. and W. Driver, *General View of the Agriculture of the County of Hampshire*. London, 1794.

Watts, S. J. 'Tenant-Right in Early Seventeenth-Century Northumberland', *Northern Hist.*, VI, 1971.

Weatherill, L. *The Pottery Trade and North Staffordshire, 1660–1760*. Manchester, 1971.

Webber, Ronald. *Covent Garden, Mud-Salad Market*. London, 1969.

    Market Gardening. Newton Abbot, 1972.

Webster, C. *The Great Instauration*. London, 1975.

Westerfield, R. B. *Middlemen in English Business, Particularly between 1660 and 1760*. Conn. Acad. Arts & Sci., XIX. New Haven, 1915. Repr. Newton Abbot, 1968.

Weston, R. *A Discours of Husbandrie Used in Brabant and Flanders*. London, 1605 [recte 1650].

Weston, Richard. *Tracts on Practical Agriculture and Gardening*. London, 1773.

Whetter, J. *Cornwall in the Seventeenth Century: An Economic Survey of Kernow*. Padstow, 1974.

Whistler, L. *The Imagination of Vanbrugh*. London, 1954.

White, Gilbert. *The Natural History of Selborne*, ed. G. Allen, London, 1908.

Wiliam, Eurwyn. 'Adeiladau Fferm Traddodiadol yng Nghymru' (with English summary), *Amgueddfa*, XV, 1973.

Willan, T. S. *The English Coasting Trade 1600–1750*. Manchester, 1938.

    The Inland Trade. Manchester, 1976.

    'The River Navigation and Trade of the Severn Valley, 1600–1750', *EcHR*, VIII, 1937–8.

    River Navigation in England, 1600–1760. Oxford, 1936. New impr. London, 1964.

[William, Richard]. *Wallography, or the Britton Described*. London, 1673.

Williams, Glanmor (ed.). *The Glamorgan County History, IV*. Cardiff, 1976.

Williams, J. E. 'Whitehaven in the Eighteenth Century', *EcHR*, 2nd ser., VIII, 1956.

Williams, L. A. *Road Transport in Cumbria in the Nineteenth Century*. London, 1975.

Williams, Michael. *The Draining of the Somerset Levels*. Cambridge, 1970.

Wilson, C. H. *England's Apprenticeship, 1603–1763*. London, 1965.

Wood-Jones, R. B. *Traditional Domestic Architecture of the Banbury Region*. Manchester, 1963.

Woodward, D. M. 'The Anglo-Irish Livestock Trade in the Seventeenth Century', *Irish Hist. Stud.*, XVIII, 72, 1973.

    'Cattle Droving in the Seventeenth Century: A Yorkshire Example', in *Trade and Transport: Essays in Economic History in Honour of T. S. Willan*, ed. W. H. Chaloner and B. M. Ratcliffe. Manchester, 1977.

'A Comparative Study of the Irish and Scottish Livestock Trades in the Seventeenth Century', in *Comparative Aspects of Scottish and Irish Economic and Social History, 1600–1900*, ed. L. M. Cullen and T. C. Smout. Edinburgh, 1977.

Wordie, J. R. 'Social Change on the Leveson-Gower Estates, 1714–1832', EcHR, 2nd ser., XXVII, 4, 1974.

Worlidge, J. *Systema Agriculturae*. London, 1669.

Systema Horti-Culturae, or the Art of Gardening. London, 1677.

Wrigley, E. A. 'A Simple Model of London's Importance in Changing English Society and Economy, 1650–1750', *PP*, no. 37, 1967.

Yarranton, Andrew. *England's Improvement by Sea and Land*. London, 1677.

The Improvement Improved, by a Second Edition of the Great Improvement of Lands by Clover. London, 1663.

Yates, E. M. 'Aspects of Staffordshire Farming in the Seventeenth and Eighteenth Centuries', *N. Staffs. J. Field Stud.*, xv, 1975.

'Enclosure and the Rise of Grassland Farming in Staffordshire', *ibid.*, XIV, 1974.

Yelling, J. A. 'Changes in Crop Production in East Worcestershire, 1540–1867', AHR, XXI, 1, 1973.

'The Combination and Rotation of Crops in East Worcestershire, 1540–1660', AHR, XVII, 1, 1969.

Common Field and Enclosure in England, 1450–1850. London, 1977.

Youd, G. 'The Common Fields of Lancashire', *Hist. Soc. Lancs. & Cheshire*, CXIII, 1961.

Young, A. *The Farmer's Tour in the East of England*. 4 vols. London, 1771.

General View of the Agriculture of Hertfordshire. London, 1804.

General View of the Agriculture of the County of Lincoln. London, 1799.

General View of the Agriculture of the County of Norfolk. London, 1804.

General View of the Agriculture of Oxfordshire. London, 1809.

A Six Months Tour through the North of England. 4 vols. London, 1770.

A Six Weeks' Tour through the Southern Counties. 3rd edn. London, 1772.

Tours in England and Wales (Selected from 'The Annals of Agriculture'). London, 1932.

Young, A. (ed.). *The Annals of Agriculture*. 46 vols. London, 1784–1815.

Young, the Rev. A. *General View of the Agriculture of the County of Sussex*. London, 1813.

INDEX

BEARDMORE

The Viking Hoax That Rewrote History

DOUGLAS HUNTER

Carleton Library Series 246

McGill-Queen's University Press
Montreal & Kingston · London · Chicago

ISBN 978-0-7735-5466-5 (cloth)
ISBN 978-0-7735-5534-1 (ePDF)
ISBN 978-0-7735-5535-8 (ePUB)

Legal deposit third quarter 2018
Bibliothèque nationale du Québec

Printed in Canada on acid-free paper that is 100% ancient forest free (100% post-consumer recycled), processed chlorine free.

This book has been published with the help of a grant from the Canadian Federation for the Humanities and Social Sciences, through the Awards to Scholarly Publications Program, using funds provided by the Social Sciences and Humanities Research Council of Canada.

Funded by the Financé par le
Government   gouvernement
of Canada   du Canada

Canada Council Conseil des arts
for the Arts   du Canada

We acknowledge the support of the Canada Council for the Arts, which last year invested $153 million to bring the arts to Canadians throughout the country. Nous remercions le Conseil des arts du Canada de son soutien. L'an dernier, le Conseil a investi 153 millions de dollars pour mettre de l'art dans la vie des Canadiennes et des Canadiens de tout le pays.

Library and Archives Canada Cataloguing in Publication

Hunter, Douglas, 1959–, author
    Beardmore : the Viking hoax that rewrote history / Douglas Hunter.

(Carleton library series ; 246)
Includes bibliographical references and index.
Issued in print and electronic formats.
ISBN 978-0-7735-5466-5 (cloth). – ISBN 978-0-7735-5534-1 (ePDF). –
ISBN 978-0-7735-5535-8 (ePUB)

    1. America – Discovery and exploration – Norse. 2. Ontario – Antiquities.
3. Vikings – Ontario. 4. Hoaxes – Ontario. 5. Royal Ontario Museum –
Archaeological collections. 6. Museums – Acquisitions – Ontario – Toronto.
I. Title. II. Series: Carleton library ; 246

E105.H86 2018   971.3'01   C2018-901855-0
                                                 C2018-901856-9

This book was typeset by True to Type in 10.5/14 Sabon